ENCYCLOPEDIA
OF CONTEMPORARY
CHRISTIAN FICTION

ENCYCLOPEDIA OF CONTEMPORARY CHRISTIAN FICTION

From C.S. Lewis to *Left Behind*

Nancy M. Tischler

GREENWOOD PRESS
An Imprint of ABC-CLIO

A B C ✤ C L I O

Santa Barbara, California • Denver, Colorado • Oxford, England

Library of Congress Cataloging-in-Publication Data

Tischler, Nancy M.
  Encyclopedia of contemporary Christian fiction : from C.S. Lewis to left behind / Nancy M. Tischler.
      p. cm.
  Includes bibliographical references and index.
  ISBN 978-0-313-34568-5 (hardcover : alk. paper) — ISBN 978-0-313-34569-2 (ebook)
1. Christian fiction, American—Bio-bibliography—Dictionaries. 2. Christian fiction, English—Bio-bibliography—Dictionaries. 3. Novelists, American—20th century—Biography—Dictionaries. 4. Novelists, American—21st century—Biography—Dictionaries. 5. Novelists, English—20th century—Biography—Dictionaries. 6. Novelists, English—21st century—Biography—Dictionaries. I. Title.
PS374.C48T57 2009
810.9'3823—dc22
[B]   2009018291

13 12 11 10 09   1 2 3 4 5

This book is also available on the World Wide Web as an eBook.
Visit www.abc-clio.com for details.

ABC-CLIO, LLC
130 Cremona Drive, P.O. Box 1911
Santa Barbara, California 93116-1911

This book is printed on acid-free paper ∞

Manufactured in the United States of America

CONTENTS

PREFACE

Scope and Purpose of Encyclopedia

This work is designed for the novel reader who wants a quick way to find information on a contemporary Christian writer's life, faith, works, and influence. Readers should also find the encyclopedia valuable as a guide to further reading in a favorite author or to discovering other writers whose works are also worth exploring.

"Contemporary" refers to works written in the past 60 years, when the postwar culture was also becoming post-Christian on the one hand and increasingly evangelical on the other. "Christian" does not designate any particular denomination or style of writing, but rather a worldview, a set of assumptions, often left unexpressed, but nonetheless apparent in the work of the writer. These would include:

1. The fatherhood of God, the creator and sustainer of life.
2. The brotherhood of man, and the value of each human person.
3. The saving substitutionary sacrifice of Jesus Christ, his resurrection, and his promise of a second coming.
4. The power of the Holy Spirit to comfort, to answer prayers, and to inspire believers.
5. The existence of an afterlife, a time of judgment, in which Justice will finally be accomplished, and a Heaven and a Hell in which humans will live beyond this time on Earth.
6. The temporary nature of time, sandwiched between the Creation and the Last Days.

A number of the writers in this study reject one or more than one of these principles or they edit them selectively, emphasizing the brotherhood of mankind over the fatherhood of God, preferring to believe in Heaven and not Hell, and debating both the Creation and the idea of the Last Days. Many readers will also agree or disagree with elements of this overly simple listing, which is intended only for classifying those who hold membership in certain churches, assume a certain worldview, or have had certain spiritual experiences that they have made public—and are therefore appropriate for inclusion in this encyclopedia. This inclusion or exclusion is not intended as a judgment of a writer's faith or life. While many of the writers in this study are forthright about their beliefs, memberships, and experience, others are silent on the subject of their own faith, which they consider a private matter. They nonetheless reflect in their work a set of beliefs. The novel, after all, is a mirror of its creator as well as its society.

For some professing Christians, certain art forms are appropriate, some not. From earliest times through our own day, the church has puzzled and sometimes battled over the proper role of art in the life and worship of the Christian. The Iconoclastic Controversy resulted in the great schism between the Eastern and Western churches; some of the Reformers whitewashed the images on the walls of the cathedrals, and the contemporary evangelicals fret about the limits of fiction. All are part of the ongoing philosophical debate about the role of beauty in the worship of God. The various novelists have made their individual choices about the nature and value of fiction and the limits that might appropriately be imposed. These choices become obvious in the study of the various writers, some of whom accept stringent guidelines, fencing in their imaginations and protecting the purity of their readers. Others reject all theological and editorial restrictions, choosing to celebrate the absolute freedom of the artist, whom they consider to be a creator in God's own image.

It is amazing what a rich array of art can spring from the deceptively simple message of the Old and New Testaments, which has dominated so much of Western thought for the past two millennia. Many modern writers continue to find their faith central to their creativity. In their poetry, plays, and novels, they sing unto the Lord "a new song."

Selection Process

In a field as rich as contemporary Christian literature, no encyclopedia can be definitive. New writers are appearing daily, and established writers pour out new novels at a great rate. This particular collection describes over ninety novelists who have written their books in English since World War II. Unfortunately, this time limit excludes some of the liveliest modern Christian writers such as Dorothy L. Sayers, J.R.R. Tolkien, and Charles Williams. The language limit excludes such remarkable writers as Sholem Asch, who wrote in Yiddish, and Aleksandr Solzhenitsyn, who wrote in Russian. And it stops short of the innumerable young writers who are just beginning to receive recognition. Though much modern writing by Christians or about Christianity is in the form of essays, plays, poems, or short stories, this study focuses exclusively on those writers who have produced novels.

Those selected are from a variety of backgrounds and persuasions. Most of them are self-identified Christians, though not always members of a church, whose novels have been popular with the reading public and are readily available in book stores and in libraries, sometimes labeled as "inspirational fiction." The majority have won acclaim, not only from critics, but from distinguished judges who have awarded them the Nobel Prize, the Pulitzer, the Christy, or any number of prizes granted by regional writers' societies, publishers, and other groups. They are trendsetter writers frequently mentioned by other writers as significant influences. And finally, they are worth reading, as tested by the compiler of this encyclopedia, who read over four hundred of their novels to test the quality of their work and judge their books against the great masterpieces of Western literature.

Of course, there is no such thing as a "Christian" novel. Christians are people, not books. A book may be important to the Christian community even if it is not written by a self-proclaimed Christian. Among the novelists included in this encyclopedia are several types:

1. Traditional, practicing Christians who write from a Christian worldview and make frequent reference to church services, prayer, and Scripture. Among this group are writers who continue in their beliefs, but call into question certain matters of doctrine or practice. They may seem quite traditional at one point and then take an unorthodox or secular by-path at another. (More often among this collection, the seeker moves from doubt to commitment in the course of life. Like **Francine Rivers,** they begin with success as writers of secular romances and end by writing evangelical ones.)

2. A number of the authors have uneasy relationships with the churches to which they belong. While they may, at some point, reinforce traditional Christian doctrines and behavior, at others they embrace Gnostic views or a vague, undefined spirituality. This explains the inclusion of radical feminists, like **Sue Monk Kidd,** who have studied many religions and selected elements for celebration—such as reverence for the Mother Goddess.

3. Some make no pretence to be a part of any faith community, choosing to be confrontational, arguing vigorously against either Christian institutions or theology. In cases such as **Dan Brown's** *The Da Vinci Code,* the furore over the novel within the Christian community makes the book significant to thoughtful readers. The same argument would seem to justify including **William Young's** *The Shack* in the listing, even though this author is neither so prolific nor so talented as most of the others included.

Time and space limited the selection process, forcing the exclusion of significant novels and novelists: those from other English-speaking countries like Australia, South Africa, and India. This explains the omission of writers like Alexander McCall Smith, whose charming studies of life in Botswana are enormously popular among Christian readers. It also omits Morris West, an Australian writer whose Catholic novels became best-sellers all over the English-speaking world.

Other moderns might well have been included, though they are less explicit about their ties to Christianity. A number of the more popular contemporary favorites, such as John Irving or Cormac McCarthy, have an implied faith background that critics have spent considerable time studying. Christianity is so pervasive an influence on the mind of modern and postmodern writers that rarely does the astute reader find a major novel with no spiritual insights.

Design of Entries

The entries are arranged in alphabetical order. At the end of the collection is a General Bibliography. Within the individual entries, cross-references to other writers included in the study are indicated in bold type.

Each entry includes:

1. **Background material on the individual writer,** including details of birth (and death), place of residence, education, marriage(s), and the career path that has led to the novels for which he or she is best known. The author's religious background and experience as well as literary influences appear in this section.

2. **A discussion of the major works and ideas of the writer,** including religious ideas, a summary of the major works, ideas, and themes. In this section, individual works may be used to explore a pattern of thought and reveal some development of style and ideas.

3. **The critical response.** This section brings together some quotations from the better-known critics and summarizes the flavor of the reviews, the extent and enthusiasm of the reviewers regarding individual novels. It also indicates the level of popular success the novelist has enjoyed. This section also draws on interviews and other sources to provide a sense of the author's stature in the literary world—whether among mainstream critics or evangelicals or others.

4. **The major awards won by the writer**, which may be regional, national, literary, or other. In some cases, these are honorary awards presented by a university or government.

5. **Bibliography of the novels by the author.** At the conclusion of this section is included a notation of other kinds of writing the author has done and any novels or other works that have been used for films or radio presentation—sometimes even plays or operas.

6. **Bibliography of works about the author.** These may be autobiographical books and articles, websites, reviews of books, interviews, full-length scholarly studies, collections of letters, bibliographies, and biographies.

Patterns among the Writers and Their Reception

These colorful people from America, Canada, and Britain come from a number of different faith backgrounds. Most of the earlier writers are college educated, though many of the more recent ones are not. A large number are women, not surprising since most novel readers, throughout the history of the genre, have been female. Many of them know one another, either from college or from writing workshops. The Writers' Workshop at the University of Iowa appears in the biographies of several talented mainstream writers. A number are clustered in the same regions, primarily the South or the West. Some grew up a few miles from one another or attend the same church or Bible study.

Probably the most dramatic difference among the writers is whether they have been classified by the critics as *mainstream* or *evangelical*. Roman Catholic, Anglican, Lutheran, Methodist, or Presbyterian writers, are considered "mainstream." Those who fall into the evangelical category, regardless of their sales numbers, who are considered a part of the "Christian ghetto," are rarely reviewed by major newspapers. In some cases, however, the writers who have chosen to write about Quaker or Amish culture (such as **Jessamyn West** and **Beverly Lewis**) are more welcome, perceived as students of peculiar cultures rather than proselytizers for a religion.

A few "cross-over" writers have moved from evangelical presses to larger publishing houses and have won the attention of the major critics. Some are recognized as important talents, but denigrated for their religious views. Other writers included in the study, like **Frederick Buechner, Marilynne Robinson,** or **Wendell Berry,** have been considered significant talents from their first publication. A constant lament among the writers for evangelical presses, like Bethany or Thomas Nelson, is that even their run-away best-sellers seldom appear on the *New York Times* Best Seller List or merit reviews in the *Wall Street Journal*. If they mention these literary misfits, like the "Left Behind" series, the major papers' critics regularly emphasize the astonishing market for such books, dismissing both their ideas and artistic quality.

In the larger world, hundreds of Christian writers are producing novels that are being bought and read by millions of fans. This modest study is only a small selection out of this ever-expanding literary movement.

INTRODUCTION

Stories are intrinsic to the Judeo-Christian tradition. From the beginning, when God created the physical world and placed it in space and time, he has revealed great truths and rules of behavior through narratives. The Creation, the Temptation, the Fall, and the expulsion of humankind from the Garden of Eden, found in the opening chapters of Genesis, present the complicated story of humans, their place in the world, their "domination" of nature, their concept of sin and punishment, and a foreshadowing of the lives they will live until the end of time The rest of the Bible, including the New Testament, tells the stories of the Incarnation, the life, teachings, crucifixion, and resurrection of Christ in a great drama of reconciliation.

Rather than presenting believers with nothing more than an abstract philosophical discourse or some tablets of laws brought down from the mountain, God chose to point believers toward the path they should walk, reveal where they might stray or stumble, and warn them about the Valley of the Shadow of Death. The Bible is the grand narrative of the pilgrim searching for the path of blessedness, of joy, and of eternal life. It also tells of the rebel, the scoffer who chooses a crooked path, filled with perversion and nastiness, pointed toward damnation. Yet in spite of human transgressions, this prodigal is always offered God's grace and the chance for redemption, a path toward home. The Bible is the "greatest story ever told," a drama of creativity and destruction, violence and solace, brutality and love, selfishness and self-sacrifice, damnation and salvation.

Jesus himself, during his brief life on earth, taught through his parables as well as his actions, opening the door for centuries of artists to use their creative imaginations in the service of their God. Dorothy L. Sayers famously proclaimed that the Incarnation redeemed the Image, allowing artists to carve or paint the world around them and writers to tell new stories based on old truths. They are, in a small and limited way, themselves imitating the Creator, making something out of nothing. She believed that creativity is included in the image of God shared by all humankind. Francis Schaeffer, who has inspired many of the moderns, also believed that Christians may glorify God through the arts, noting that the image of God in us includes our ability to create and enjoy things of beauty.

The rich heritage of Christian fiction reaches back to earlier times, to the medieval romances, the early English epics, Chaucer's Canterbury pilgrims, Milton's epics of Paradise lost and found, and John Bunyan's Pilgrim on his way to the Celestial City. *Pilgrim's Progress* is often cited as the first novel in English. Eighteenth-century English novelists, like Daniel Defoe, justified their fiction by proclaiming their religious purpose (even as they exploited their pagan practices), and pretended they were telling truth. Nineteenth-century novelists often heaped scorn on the church and clerics, following the famous example of Chaucer's pilgrims—his pardoner and prioress as opposed to his simple parson. By the 20th century, British literature had developed a lively and mature tradition of fiction, which the Americans had absorbed as a part of their own flourishing culture. The Victorian novelists were read by avid fans and invited to tour this country, leaving their indelible stamp on American writing that continues into the modern—and postmodern novels.

The Christian Novel in America

Americans have their own heritage of Christian writing, drawn in the Colonial times from the first books brought to America—the King James translation of the Bible and well-worn copies of *Pilgrim's Progress*. Americans imported their copies of Defoe, Richardson, Goldsmith, Austen, Dickens, and Trollope. Nathaniel Hawthorne, in *The Scarlet Letter*, found a way to turn the 18th-century clerical novel on its head, making the pastor both the villain and the lover, and characterizing the "fallen woman" as the heroine. The justifiably famous abolitionist novel by Harriet Beecher Stowe, *Uncle Tom's Cabin*, is filled with Christian messages and faithful heroes. Stowe's powerful judgment on the institution of slavery is based on the author's deep faith, which she makes manifest in her heartrending tales of suffering and sacrifice. Later, less artistic and less dramatic Christian stories captured a wide readership in America. Charles Sheldon's *In His Steps* (1896) encouraged several generations of young people to ask themselves, "What would Jesus do?" For its impact on modern novelists, Lew Wallace's *Ben Hur* (1880) was even more significant. This melodramatic recreation of life in Jesus's day led a host of others to design their own fiction reflecting Biblical characters and times.

John Mort, in his detailed study of Christian fiction, lists a number of early 20th-century American writers who have influenced the moderns, including Harold Bell Wright, who wrote *The Shepherd of the Hills* (1904), a "hybrid of the social gospel novel and the western." A bestseller in the 1920s and 1930s, the prodigious Grace Livingston Hill is credited with inventing the Christian romance. These Christianized versions of the Cinderella tale are stories of simple, sweet, pretty Christian girls finding mates, usually wealthy and handsome, as well as Christian, without compromising their virtue. The predestined pairing required that both of the lovers become believing Christians before the marriage would be blessed. This became the model that inspired the far superior works of **Catherine Marshall** and her host of followers.

At the same time these writers were establishing a climate for Christian fiction in America, other writers used their novels to attack certain practices of the churches and church members who disgraced their heritage. Sinclair Lewis went far beyond Hawthorne in his creation of Elmer Gantry, a crude descendent of the Reverend Arthur Dimmesdale. Gantry, the hypocritical, womanizing evangelist, sets the stage for later attacks on ministers who have little appetite for poverty, celibacy, or obedience. Somerset Maugham had explored the sexual problems of a missionary in "Rain" and others were to laugh at the failures of those who purport to do God's will. Even the far more gentle Pearl Buck, in *The Good Earth*, indicates that Christianity is not an easy faith to transplant in alien soil. Barbara Kingsolver's very popular novel, *The Poison-wood Bible*, pictures the evangelical missionary as a fool, laughed at by the natives of the Congo for whom he gives his daughter's life and his own.

America saw a powerful surge of Christian fiction in the 20th century. Most of the major modern American novelists included the Christian faith in their stories, either to promote it, exploit it, or attack it. Faulkner sneered at the Baptists, but showed deep respect for religious ideas among the African American community. His concept of covenants, of humans' obligations to nature, come right out of the Old Testament. And John Steinbeck wrote feelingly of the sacrifice of the poor and disenfranchised, using the image of Christ to emphasize their suffering. All through the modern era, Christianity was the underlying worldview of most American writers, even when they mocked their heritage. That set of assumptions has changed with the postmodern, post-Christian era—bringing into play a whole new set of writers.

The Growth of Christian Literature in Great Britain

In England, during the middle years of the 20th century, the Inklings, who had begun as a band of friends in the Oxford community, sharing sherry and good conversation, began crafting stories in various genres that combined lively scholarship and imaginative writing. **C. S. Lewis,** who had previously been known for his sober literary studies, wrote multi-layered fables for both children and adults. His most famous were his stories of Narnia, his imaginary world entered through the upstairs wardrobe, opening the Christian community to the lavish use of fantasy, full of talking animals and rich symbolism. He also explored the curious academic world, an "Inner Circle" that mirrors Oxford. He combined these apparently realistic satires with narratives of interplanetary travel, thereby opening the way for faith-based science fiction writing. In such flights of creativity, Lewis encouraged his fellow Christians to indulge in the free play of imagination. Lewis attributed much of his love of myth and magic to George MacDonald and G. K. Chesterton. Chesterton had insisted, despite the Puritans' rejection of fairy tales, that he believed in magic: "I had always believed that the world involved magic: now I thought that perhaps it involved a magician." He saw magic as a path to faith—as did Lewis, who came to believe in "the deeper magic" of the Great Magician.

A fellow Inkling, J.R.R. Tolkien, a philology professor at Oxford who had studied the great epics of the medieval world, used his vast knowledge to create his own modern-day epic. *Lord of the Rings* is a multi-volume tale of good and evil grounded on Tolkien's Catholic faith, his rich understanding of medieval epic and romance, and the rumblings of the war beginning in Europe. Since the publication of *The Hobbit* in 1937, this amazing epic of Middle Earth has delighted fans of all ages, many of whom have not understood Tolkien's Christian intent. A number of moderns have tried to follow his lead, sometimes even using medieval settings for their narratives.

Another Inkling, Charles Williams, an editor at Oxford University Press and a devout Anglican, died just as World War II ended. Although he is not as famous as his fellows, he became a highly influential writer of fantasies, for whom (according to T.S. Eliot), "the supernatural was perfectly natural, and the natural was also the supernatural." Williams's path into occult studies made him more obscure and difficult than his fellows, but nonetheless influenced writers who followed. The reality of his spirit world, in works like *The Greater Trumps*, encouraged later writers like **Frank Peretti** to portray a set of vivid demonic presences that live side by side with a warring angelic army, both rarely acknowledged by the "real" world which serves as their battlefield. Each of Williams's novels assumes active spirits on Earth, pressing humans to choose good or evil, Heaven or Hell.

Although not a member of the all-male Inklings, Dorothy L. Sayers was a close friend of Williams, corresponded regularly with Lewis, and shared their faith and their love of the medieval world and of G.K. Chesterton. A scholar by nature, Sayers turned her attention to stories of detection, providing Lord Peter Wimsey, her favorite sleuth, with a strong moral and religious background. By the time the war ended, Sayers was deeply engaged in her studies of Dante and her occasional essays, but her earlier fiction set a pattern that influenced **P. D. James** and other religiously-grounded lovers of detective fiction.

Since World War II, the English-speaking world has seen a remarkable growth in faith-based fiction on both sides of the Atlantic. The hunger for a new understanding of Christianity opened the market for novels about religion and the made translations of Sholem Asch's books about Jesus, Mary, and Paul Book-of-the-Month Club selections in the years after World War II. Historical reconstructions of Biblical times, such as Irving Wallace's *The Word* (1972), which followed in the romantic tradition of *Quo Vadis*, were enormously popular, allowing readers to feel they were learning about history in a pleasant and entertaining way.

The Emerging Market for Christian Novels

In the meantime, the literary marketplace was changing with the culture: it was becoming more experimental; the authors frequently turned away from the Victorian restrictions on language and subject matter dictated by censors and by the reading public. Especially in novels about the violence and lawlessness of warfare, the writers broke all the rules. Sex scenes grew steamier, language more crude, and brutal behavior was not inevitably punished. The form of the new novels was also changing: the postmodern novelists rejected the more rational structure of storytelling; insisting that the old logic of the narrative line did not mirror the confusion of modern life—which is full of sound and fury and signifies nothing. Rather than heroes, the writers placed anti-heroes in the center of their stories. Nor did the women long for men to save them from spinsterhood or danger. The new feminists preached the empowerment of women and described traditional marriage as servitude. Freshly out of the closet, the gay writers celebrated an alternate lifestyle rather than disguising their preferences. The Christian church was seen increasingly as irrelevant. The hero might sit on the steps of the cathedral, but choose not to enter. The pastor was portrayed as benevolent and befuddled or judgmental and hopelessly anachronistic.

Middle-class Christian readers, especially women, found themselves shocked by the new license, but still hungry for novels of romance and inspiration. The audience was eager for a fresh kind of Christian novel. Two important new writers explored the possibility of crafting their novels for this audience that was largely female, white, and Protestant. Catherine Marshall, the wife of Dr. Peter Marshall, discovered her voice in *Christy*, the story of a young woman who finds her faith and her assumptions about life challenged at a mission station in the Great Smoky Mountains. The beautiful descriptions of the countryside, the sympathetic treatment of the people, and the thoughtful consideration of the faith that each of the characters reveals when faced with the challenges of this rugged life made this a classic of the new type of novel. The novel uses the old-fashioned narrative techniques, avoids explicit sexuality, and is never obscene. Eventually, the awards for the best evangelical novels each year were to be named the "Christy Awards."

Another writer who targeted this same audience was **Janette Oke.** Her romantic story of a young woman heading West, who loses her husband just as the winter arrives, her struggle to accept the love of another man, to win the heart of his young motherless daughter, and to understand the hardships and wonders of this country make *Love Comes Softly* a grand opening for a long line of sequels. Oke was also a pioneer in her use of the prairie romance, which has produced a host of followers among writers. Readers found that they could follow this family of Christian pilgrims from novel to novel as they searched for the best path through the challenges of life on the frontier. Later novelists adopted Oke's focus on the family, the traditional roles of mother and father, the attention to details of food, clothing, work, and worship, easily shifting the setting, the period, and the cast of characters. Her constant refrain throughout the series is God's abiding love. Oke was not the first to utilize sequels, but the modern evangelical novelists have turned the device into a standard practice.

The appetite for romances found a great supply of writers who gave the stories of fair maidens and handsome heroes a distinctly Christian spin, creating the excitement by moving them to another century or another country. Writers of "chick lit" stories have made a fortune by writing safe stories of young women who take foolish risks and learn life's hard lessons. Realistic writing also abounds, telling more forthright stories of failed love affairs and disappointing adventures. **Francine Rivers** tells much of her own colorful life in her descriptions of the anguish of promiscuity and abortion. In her famous re-write of the astonishing story of the prophet Hosea, *Redeeming Love*, she turns the classic romance on its head, awarding forgiveness and grace to the fallen woman.

A masculine audience, especially among young readers, has also flourished, often overlapping with the feminine one. Frank Peretti, for example, tells exciting stories of modern Christians fighting the dark forces of New Age occultism. Small towns are suddenly filled with demonic warriors who seek to attack the schools, churches, and the lives of the decent people. **Tim LaHaye** and **Jerry Jenkins** have used the same flat characterization of the romances and the wild visions of Armageddon to spell out their vision of the end-times. **James BeauSeigneur** takes his readers on a space odyssey.

The appetite for reality is alive and well among male readers as well as female. An interesting young talent is **W. Dale Cramer,** who tells of working-class men, often confused about their relationships with their fathers, and determined to make a success of their marriages. A number of the new writers draw from their own lives to tell of the film business, the music industry, or the building trade. The realism of their stories, as **Leif Enger** demonstrates in his beautifully crafted *Peace Like a River*, does not exclude miracles or mysticism. **Dean Koontz** has a great deal of fun with Brother Odd and his mysterious dog, in the midst of some grand adventures.

The New Publishers for Evangelical Novels

The talent and taste that match the new audience of readers soon attracted new publishers. The group known as the Evangelical Christian Publishers Association, along with publishers of Catholic, Mormon, and Amish/Mennonite materials, were to fill a void created by the prejudices of many of the mainstream publishing houses who were blind to the opportunities presented by these rising stars. Many of these presses had previously limited their output to church materials, for Christian education or evangelism. Since the move to publishing novels was a break with their traditions, they realized that they needed to establish clear guidelines before transforming themselves into different kinds of presses.

Lynn Neal, in *Romancing God*, cites the limitations imposed by evangelical publishers: Bethany House asks its authors to deliver "one main scriptural teaching, skillfully incorporated into the story without being either 'preachy' or too obscure." Multnomah admits that "people express their faith in unique ways," but even so indicates that both the man and the woman must be believers to avoid the peril of being "unequally yoked." The author may include love scenes, but avoid anything too sexy or prurient. Even the length and nature of kisses is stipulated. Barbour Books' writers should avoid the dangerous topics of divorce, drinking, dancing, and "sticky topics" such as the details of baptism (water and spirit), speaking in tongues, end-times, and women's ordination. Authors may not present a woman character who is either a pastor or a youth pastor. They do, however, approve of women ministering through fiction.

John Mort lists a number of these publishers of Christian fiction, including Bethany House, Barbour, Harlequin/Steeple Hill, Multnomah, Tyndale, Zondervan, Waterbrook, Crossway, Broadman and Holman, Thomas Nelson, Word, Harvest House, Baker, Moody, Eerdman's, and others. Often the writer will establish a relationship for one of these presses and find a favorite editor, and remain with the publisher throughout his or her career.

Mainstream Novelists—Christian and Anti-Christian

At the same time that explicitly Christian fiction was pouring out of these presses, mainstream American, English, and Canadian writers found large publishers eager to accept their work. Generally more liberal in theology, more radical in their political, sexual, and religious ideas than the evangelical writers, they still reveal a core of faith in their worldview. A writer like **Graham Greene,** for instance, was clearly a Roman Catholic, but felt free to portray his priest as an alcoholic and a fornicator who punishes himself for his sins.

The unspoken guidelines of these publishers mirror the cultural elite of the era. The mainstream press and the prestigious critics, the university awards and the grants available usually go to those who try to keep their art uppermost in their writing, and who accept no limits on language, violence, or sexuality. A few forthright Christians have won praise among this group, but with difficulty. **Frederick Buechner,** for example, has found that the very admission of his role as a Presbyterian minister has diminished the critics' estimate of his artistry. He and others who are openly Christian consider the term "Christian novel" a stigma, usually reserved for those who have an agenda—to convert, reinforce the faith of the reader, or provide succor for those who suffer.

The large number and excellent quality of these non-aligned writers who hold a strong Christian world-view is testimony to the continuing tradition of Christianity that lingers in our "post-Christian" world. Often alienated from regular worship, these writers nonetheless cherish much of Christian tradition. Some of these, like **Gail Goodwin,** continue to use the symbols, the language, the mind-set of Anglicanism. Some, like **Sue Monk Kidd,** blend the old Baptist traditions with ancient views of mysticism and modern theories of feminism to create their own sacred space. Few feel obliged to conform to rigid orthodoxy or to bow to the authority of any particular church. In modern England, where a small minority still attend regular worship, and in America, where each individual feels free to worship according to his or her individual vision of eternal verities, discipline and order have virtually disappeared in matters of the spirit. The prevailing religion among modern writers is one Emerson would have called "ego-theism." Every man (or woman) has his own religion, his own God.

Many of the more popular modern writers are not sympathetic to Christianity or to the church. Some have developed a large following of fans by selectively twisting the materials of church history to develop conspiracy theories. The most famous of these is **Dan Brown,** whose *The Da Vinci Code,* a wildly popular story that purports to be based on fact, is actually derived from a combination of myth and Gnostic Gospels, shaped by a long tradition of anti-Catholicism.

The novel is by nature rooted in reality, usually reflecting the society that produced it. If the audience is excited about the environment, writers deplore the deforestation of the land; if feminism is in the ascendancy, the central character is a woman battling a patriarchal society; if America is horrified by terrorist threats, the first responders become heroes. Gradually, as they have felt more self-assured and free to express themselves forthrightly, African American novelists began exploring their faith tradition, using their very different American experience and the echoes of African religions in yet another kind of Christian writing. With the modern interest in diverse cultures, Quaker, Amish, and other groups have found voice for their lifestyles and beliefs. Sometimes, the writers choose to write about the simple life of a people who are set apart because of the frustrations of the urban, hurried world of their own experience. The range of writers and their novels is astonishing.

The real wonder of contemporary Christian writing is the sheer mass of it. Clearly, the world is hungry for conversations about ultimate reality—even if the stories are encumbered by mundane descriptions of food and clothing. An enormous reading public watches for the next thoughtful book to be published, and a host of talented and some dazzling writers are publishing at a rapid rate to satisfy that hunger. The real test, the test of time, will determine which of the post-World War II novels will stand as masterpieces like *The Scarlet Letter* or *Moby Dick* or *Uncle Tom's Cabin,* revered by readers into the next century.

ALCORN, RANDY

Personal, Professional, and Religious Background

Randy Craig Alcorn (1954–) was born in Portland, Oregon, to Arthur and Lucille Alcorn. His father owned a tavern. While still in high school, Randy gave his life to Christ. Two years later, while reading Dietrich Bonhoeffer's *The Cost of Discipleship*, he became convinced that there is no "cheap grace." It is free but costly.

> I saw fiction as the opposite of truth. Finally I saw that it could be true and effective. . . . Often it can cut to the truth more effectively than nonfiction. In Luke 15, the story of the prodigal son most clearly captures the imagination regarding God's grace.
>
> —Randy Alcorn, quoted by Janice DeLong and Rachel Schwedt in *Contemporary Christian Authors: Lives and Works*

After attending Western Seminary from 1966–67, he went to Multnomah Bible College, where he received his Th.B. and M.A. and then became the founding pastor of Good Shepherd Community Church in Boring, Oregon. He served the lively, growing church there from 1977–90. Having become involved with Randall Terry's Operation Rescue, he found himself the target of a court case that stripped him of his salary. He resigned from his pastorate fearing that the church would become responsible for claims made against him.

Alcorn then formed Eternal Perspective Ministries (EPM), where he has served as director since 1991. To earn a living, he began an extensive writing, speaking, and consulting ministry. He has also served as a conference speaker, and part-time faculty member at Western Baptist Seminary and Multnomah Bible College.

Alcorn was married in 1975 to Nanci. Their two daughters, Karina and Angela, have written novels with their father, and a number of Alcorn's nonfiction books are coauthored by his wife. The Alcorns now live in Gresham, Oregon on a modest salary from the EPM, in the same small home that they have had since their early married days. He has found writing to be his vocation, a means to reach a much wider audience about such topics as the sexual revolution,

Christian stewardship, abortion, birth control, and numerous others. He is a dynamic speaker in great demand all over the world, often appearing on radio and television shows.

Randy Alcorn is deeply involved in current issues, in both his words and his deeds. His activities on behalf of unborn children have cost him his pastorate and inspired some of his strongest writing. Periodically, he takes his laptop computer, gathers a large number of books that may prove useful to him, and goes for a "two-to-five day writing retreat at a beach cabin on the Oregon coast." Because it is secluded and he goes there alone, he can get vast amounts of work done without interruption.

Major Works and Themes

Randy Alcorn sees his audience as Christians who are "hungry, serious" and open to challenges. Unlike much evangelical fiction, his stories extend far beyond the range of entertainment, and may not have happy endings—at least not on Earth. His characters undergo horrible temptations and terrors, reaping their rewards only in the afterlife.

In his first novel, *Deadline*, Alcorn introduced the strategy of picturing two worlds simultaneously—the temporal and the eternal. The story opens with a tragic accident and leaves the protagonist, Jake Woods, to unravel the mystery behind the accident.

Dominion, Alcorn's second novel, introduces racial issues, again with the perspective of eternal salvation or damnation. Life is seen once again as the refining fire by which God tests the true metal of his people. In the story, he compares life to a tapestry: most people see only the underside of the cloth. Only when seen from above is God's beautiful design and workmanship apparent. Alcorn wants his readers to live beyond the present, "not sacrificing the eternal on the altar of the immediate."

Alcorn is deeply concerned about the plight of Christians in China, where they are faced with daily experiences of repression and persecution. His novel *Safely Home*, which draws on his own experience in China as well as extensive research, is a powerful and dramatic study of house churches in Communist China, the forced abortions of women failing to conform to the one-child policy, slave labor, organ harvesting, and total government control over the life of the citizens. It tells of two Harvard roommates, one an American, Ben Fielding, who has become a successful executive in a company that has targeted the Chinese market for its microchips. His old roommate, Li Quan, a brilliant scholar and a professed Christian, has been denied any position at Chinese universities. Reduced to work as an assistant locksmith in a small, rural Chinese village, living in a run-down hut without indoor plumbing, Quan maintains his faith and his courage. After spending several weeks as a house guest, Fielding realizes the shallowness of his own faith, the incredible suffering demanded of Chinese believers, and comes to a new birth of Christianity in his own life.

The book, which includes scenes of Heaven as well as Earth, some of them sounding like **C. S. Lewis,** who also saw the here-and-now as a Shadowland, echoing Charles Williams's and **Frank Peretti's** world of demons and angels. Alcorn also employs the influence of Bonhoeffer, one of his heroes for his stand against Fascism. Some of his scenes could have been taken straight out of Foxe's *Book of Martyrs*.

Randy Alcorn openly acknowledges his great debt to C. S. Lewis—his *Space Trilogy, Chronicles of Narnia, The Screwtape Letters*, and *Mere Christianity*. Alcorn's *Lord Foulgrin's Letters* and the sequel, *The Ishbane Conspiracy*, which he wrote in collaboration with his daughters, are both clones of *The Screwtape Letters*.

Randy Alcorn makes no pretence that he is writing art for art's sake. He wants to communicate truth: "I have no illusions that I can accomplish anything of value apart from Christ. My desire is to be used of God to help people learn to see the invisible, to gain an eternal perspective, and to live each day with heaven in mind." He sees each of his novels as potentially subversive, a well-intended Trojan horse, "reflecting truth in a disarming way."

Critical Reception

Because critics see Randy Alcorn as a moralist rather than an artist, presenting a specific message, they tend to summarize his plot, note his thesis, and ignore his skill as a storyteller. In his review of *Deadline,* for example, John Mort ties the story to the new abortion pill, and notes that Alcorn shows interest in abortion, gay rights, and school vouchers in the story. He reviews the sequel, *Dominion,* in much the same manner, noting that it too is didactic. This time the protagonist is a black columnist and former football player who allies himself with a conservative white detective to find the truth behind a ghetto murder, discovering a great deal about gang violence and drug addiction, as well as racial issues. Mort notes that the presentation is "passionate and ably presented but may be alienating to some black readers," especially those who will resent his attack on Louis Farrakhan.

John Bunyan is the influence that Mort notes in *Edge of Eternity,* where "the journey of his sinful hero, Nick Seagrave, is a bit confusing." He allows that Alcorn "manages some extraordinary scenes in which Nick must look down on his own infidelity, but otherwise, Alcorn is so intent on his allegory that he neglects to develop a story, and the result makes the reader's head swim."

The Lord Foulgrin books, imitations of *The Screwtape Letters,* are not on a par with Lewis. The temptations in *The Ishbane Conspiracy*—alcohol, drugs, sex, the occult—are nowhere near so complex and interesting as those that Lewis confronted with his minor demons.

By and large, Alcorn's compulsion to preach interferes with his ability to tell a story simply and well. He is a compelling writer, but one flawed by his hunger to be a preacher rather than an artist.

Awards

Safely Home was named a Gold Medallion winner by the Evangelical Christian Book Publishers Association in 2002.

Bibliography of Novels by Author

Deadline. Sisters, OR: Multnomah, 1994.
Dominion. Sisters, OR: Multnomah, 1996.
Edge of Eternity. Colorado Springs, CO: WaterBrook, 1998.
The Ishbane Conspiracy. Sisters, OR: Multnomah, 2001. (Coauthored with daughters Angela Alcorn and Karina Alcorn.)
Lord Foulgrin's Letters: How to Strike Back at the Tyrant by Deceiving and Destroying His Human Vermin. Sisters, OR: Multnomah, 2001.
Safely Home. Wheaton, IL: Tyndale House, 2001.
Deception. Colorado Springs, CO: Multnomah, 2007.

Bibliography of Works about Author

DeLong, Janice, and Rachel Schwedt. *Contemporary Christian Authors: Lives and Works*. Lanham, MD: Scarecrow Press, 2000.

Mapes, Creston. "Author Randy Alcorn: Passion in His Pen." Eternal Perspective Ministries, http://www.epm.org/articles/passion_In_Pen.html.

Mort, John. Review of *Deadline*. *Booklist* (December 15, 1994): 737.

Mort, John. *Christian Fiction: A Guide to the Genre*. Greenwood Village, CO: Libraries Unlimited, 2002.

"Randy Alcorn." *Contemporary Authors Online*. Detroit: Thomson Gale, 2007.

Stafford, Tim. "The Pastor without a Paycheck." *Christianity Today*, April, 2003.

ALEXANDER, HANNAH

Personal, Professional, and Religious Background

"Hannah Alexander" is the pen name for Cheryl and Melvin Hodde. Cheryl Hodde was born in Southern California in the mid-1950s. Her father was a farmer and a carpenter, her mother a machinist during World War II and a quality control person at Tyson Foods for 20 years. She had an eclectic education beyond high school. Cheryl Hodde acknowledges that she was a rebellious teenager, much like her character Fawn. Although she too was a teenage runaway, she was not "a prostitute, con artist or thief, and I had no wicked stepfather." Even her writing is self-taught: she learned through college courses, conferences, and on-the-job training. Cheryl Hodde is now a full-time novelist. She has been writing novels for over twenty years.

Mel Hodde was born in the state of Washington in the early 1960s. His father was a dairy farmer, his mother a housewife. He was educated at Kirksville School of Osteopathy in Missouri and is an emergency medicine physician.

The Hoddes told the interviewer for Christianbook.com that they were "set up on a blind date" by their pastor. Cheryl Hodde explains that she had a "broken past, a very difficult, painful past and was determined that I would never have anything to do with men again. My pastor had a different idea." Her pastor arranged for them to meet at a pizza place with a group from church one Sunday night, arranging that they sit together. Her first question to Mel Hodde was how she could paralyze someone—information she needed for a novel she was writing. As it turned out, he had also been writing since he was a child, and was eager to read her manuscript. "He had some wonderful ideas for it and it just clicked. Our plotting worked together, we sparked ideas off of each other, and it was so much fun that we just kept doing it."

From that point on, they used medical situations in their novels, with Cheryl taking the lead in plotting and character development, Mel providing medical details. Mel says, "I love to share my world. I find it fascinating and I like to think that it is for everybody else, too." After they were married in 1995, they chose the name "Hannah Alexander" to emphasize that they worked together as a team. As they told Tricia Goyer in a 2006 interview, they chose names with which they identified: "I chose Hannah because I could identify with Hannah in the Bible, pre-Samuel, as I have no children. Hannah means 'her hope is in the Lord.' Mel chose Alexander because it means 'servant of mankind.' Since he is a physician, he likes the thought of being in service to mankind."

> Influences? Life. Struggle. Disappointment. Rejection. Pain. All is grist for the mill, and all is necessary for imagination to emerge.
>
> —Cheryl Hodde, in e-mail to Nancy Tischler, March 5, 2008

In order to protect their professional privacy, the Hoddes release few precise details of their own lives, only acknowledging that they live in the Missouri Ozarks, in a place much like Hideaway.

> Preachiness is boring to the reader.
>
> —Hannah Alexander in an "All about Romance" roundtable on romantic suspense

Major Works and Themes

Hannah Alexander has chosen to set most of her stories in Hideaway, a tiny town in the Branson, Ozark region of Missouri. Readers gradually get to know the lake, the peninsula on which the town is located, the camp for young boys, the cottages around the lake, the old farms with goats and walnut trees, the town with its general store, and later a pharmacy, a clinic that is growing into a hospital, and a bed-and-breakfast that fills up with summer visitors eager to visit the interesting shops with their brick fronts and awnings. The annual pig race attracts great crowds who enjoy black walnut pies and goat cheese.

Hideaway, Missouri is a place of peace and healing, with neighbors who know one another's histories, attend church together, comfort the afflicted, and mourn together beside the fresh graves at the local cemetery. They are near to parks, a sawmill, and the grand entertainment industry at Branson. Characters do drift off to Columbia, Springfield, Jefferson City, and even to an Indian reservation or Hawaii, but usually return at some point to Hideaway.

Each of the novels focuses on a different cluster of characters, using other members of the community for background. In *Hideway*, for example, a young physician in the college town of Columbia, Missouri, finds herself traumatized by her sister's death, her own struggle with long hours in the emergency room serving others, and a lawsuit brought by her supposedly "Christian" brother-in-law, holding her responsible for her own sister's death. Offered a cabin on the lake near Hideaway, Cheyenne retreats to a refreshingly primitive pattern of living, soon finding friendships, intrigue, love, and healing. She is clearly destined to find a new home here, a fresh and more rewarding kind of service to the community, a new family, and a renewed faith in God's love and guidance.

In addition to medical details—broken bones, accidental and intentional deaths, heart attacks, and other events that drive characters to the emergency room—the novels have some common characteristics. They often use an attractive professional woman in her thirties, damaged by a bad marriage and an ugly divorce, who comes to a new place hoping for healing. The women have often confronted two-timing husbands, men who use drugs, cheat with finances, or exact brutal control in their relationship. The handsome young men they meet, who help them to heal, have often had their own share of disappointments: wives who cheated on them, deserted them, or habitually lied to them. The world-weary pair come together tentatively, talk about their problems, and find a genuine attraction. The faith of one is usually stronger than the other, but they eventually share much the same view of God.

This writing pair is currently considering a new series at Knolls or in a nearby area, acknowledging that they "like the small town atmosphere and we enjoy writing this particular type of novel."

Critical Reception

The husband and wife team who call themselves "Hannah Alexander" began work with *The Healing Promises* in 1998. Their first works were classified as suspense romances. Diane

Johnson, writing for Romantictimes.com, noted that the novel provided "just the right touch for an uplifting read." The first cluster of novels, published by Bethany House and Heartsong, revealed what Roberta Blair called a "Christian spin on medicine." She did complain that the author included "too many characters stuffed into too little space" (in *Sacred Trust*), but also acknowledged that the book is "satisfying." Roberta Blair also found *Solemn Oath*, the sequel to *Sacred Trust*, to be a "fast-paced read that medical romance fans should enjoy."

The critics have noted that the novels have "interesting twists and an easy writing style, well-blended with romance." Bev Huston thought that *Ozark Sunrise* provided the reader with a "likeable story." The critics cited the derivative nature of these medical dramas, including the "Healing Touch" series, apparently based on the emergency room series on television, starring Dr. Mercy Richmond and Dr. Lukas Bower. Hannah Alexander argues that the situations she provides are more authentic than television dramas, based on actual emergency room experience.

It has been the "Hideaway" books that have won over the most enthusiastic readers. Starting with the Christy Award–winning *Hideaway*, the books have included the same cluster of characters, drawing on one family history, one mystery, and one romance after another. New figures are introduced to bring new adventures, fresh romance, and new spiritual struggles. Hideaway itself proves a refuge for those who have been betrayed, threatened, abused, or filled with regret for their sinful ways. The characters invariably find the solution to the central puzzle of their lives, satisfaction of their hunger for human relationships, and for a living faith in God.

The books are character-driven with strong and elaborate plots, using the spiritual problems as one facet of human hunger and healing. The authors note that "Actions speak louder than words. Preachiness is boring to the reader."

Awards

Hideaway won the Christy Award for the best romance in 2004. In 2006, the Virginia Romance Writers awarded the Holt Medallion Award to Hannah Alexander for *Last Resort*.

Bibliography of Novels by Author

The Healing Promise. Uhrichsville, OH: Heartsong, 1998.
Ozark Sunrise. Uhrichsville, OH: Heartsong, 1999.
Missouri: A Living Soul. Uhrichsville, OH: Barbour Publishing, 2005.
A Crystal Cavern. Uhrichsville, OH: Barbour Publishing, 2006.

"Sacred Trust" Series (Minneapolis, MN: Bethany House)

Sacred Trust. 2000.
Solemn Oath. 2000.
Silent Pledge. 2001.

"Healing Touch" Series (Minneapolis, MN: Bethany House)

Necessary Measures. 2002.
Second Opinion. 2002.
Urgent Care. 2003.

"Hideaway, Missouri" Series (New York: Steeple Hill)

Hideaway. 2003.
Last Resort. 2005.
Note of Peril. 2005.
Fair Warning. 2006.
Under Suspicion. 2006.
Death Benefits. 2007.
Grave Risk. 2007.
Double Blind. 2008.
Hidden Motive. 2008. (Reprint of *The Crystal Cavern*)
Hideaway Home. 2008.

In addition, Cheryl Hodde wrote novels for a number of years before she became known as part of "Hannah Alexander." She acknowledges that none of her books sold until after she married Dr. Mel Hodde.

Bibliography of Works about Author

"All About Romance." http://www.likesbooks.com/inpproundtable.html.
Cheryl Hodde Web site, http://www.hannahalexander.com.
Christian Books, http://www.christianbook.com/html/DPEP/Interviews/hodde_interview.html/event=SP.
Goyer, Tricia. "An Interview." August 24, 2006. www.triciagoyer.com.
"Hannah Alexander." *Faithful Reader.* http://www.faithfulreader.com/authors/au-alesander-hannah.asp.
Romantic Times. http://www.romantictimes.com/authors_profile.php?author=1228.

ARVIN, REED

Personal, Professional, and Religious Background

Reed Arvin was born on a cattle ranch in Kansas and grew up in a "world of fence-building, working cattle, and praying for rain." He sees the farm country of Kansas as "a great place for a young imagination to take hold." His mother, who influenced his work substantially, earned a law degree, became a successful lawyer, and finally a judge.

Reed Arvin has two degrees in music. This study of music and his experiences as a professional musician provided him the skills and materials for his later writing. "For me, studying music was actually better preparation for writing than studying writing. Some things you have to learn by coming at them sideways."

Reed Arvin had a successful career in Christian contemporary music, making his living as a studio musician and record producer for nearly 20 years. He acknowledges that his "musical voyages" have taken him to some strange places: "I was once in a reggae band in which the drummer's name . . . was Turnip Greens. . . . I've been in salsa bands, and I once played in a Latin band in the garage of a Ford dealership in Guadalajara." He accompanied Amy

> A sentence that sings is just as beautiful as a good melodic line. And, yes, my travels as a musician showed me many sides of this world, experiences which I draw from for my novels.
>
> —Reed Arvin in an interview with Book Browse

Reed Arvin accompanied Amy Grant for several years, touring the world with her and with other artists.

Grant for some years, touring the world with her; he also played for drug dealers in Colombia, only realizing their identity when they tried to pay him with cocaine. He finally became a producer, a change in roles that allowed him to stay home.

Two of his works are a result of this experience in the Christian music industry. The *Wind in the Wheat*, his first novel, which chronicles some of his discoveries, and *The Inside Track—to Getting Started in Christian Music*. The second book is a group of essays by thirteen writers, most of them well-known in Christian music. Arvin edited the collection and provided insights in his essay on Christian music as a business.

When interviewed after the publication of *The Last Goodbye* (2004), Reed Arvin listed five big things that could happen in a life: "divorce, moving from a long-held residence, change of career, a life-threatening illness, and the death of a family member." He said "In a 90 day period, I experienced 4 of the 5. I got cancer, got divorced, put my house on the market, and decided to become a full time writer." In addition, his father had a heart attack just before this happened, but he did recover. Arvin noted that he survived through his faith, "the prayers of many, and the sheer catharsis of writing." He believes that one source of his strength is his mother, who is blind, but has accomplished an astonishing amount in her life. She was named one of the Outstanding Lawyers in America, becoming the first blind woman judge in American history. "She taught me that life is for living, not whining. You get up. You go to work."

Major Works and Themes

Reed Arvin's small-town background shaped his first two novels, *Wind in the Wheat* and *The Will*. *Wind in the Wheat* follows a talented musician from a cattle ranch to Nashville, where he makes it big—only to discover that this is not the direction God wants him to take his life. His second mainstream novel, *The Will*, is set in a small town, the world he knows well. As he grew more interested in writing for a larger audience, he turned his next book, *The Last Goodbye*, into an urban thriller, starring a detective/lawyer hero with roots in a small Southern town.

Arvin likes to contrast the slow pace of the rural life with the sounds and sights of the big cities—Nashville, Chicago, or Atlanta. His country folk live in farm houses with lots of land, go to small churches, and hold on to traditional family values. His multicultural city people live in anonymous apartments, strive for success, cheat on spouses and business associates. They are ultimate egoists, ignoring the poor and needy. Reed Arvin clearly prefers the small town yet his characters respond to the siren call of city life.

The Wind in the Wheat, Arvin's most clearly Christian statement, is a semiautobiographical account of a talented farm boy's ascent to success in Gospel music. He betrays his talent, recognizes the true source of his miraculous gift, and finally retreats to the country to do penance. The very real call of sin in human experience is a common thread in all of Arvin's novels. Sometimes the sin that lures his characters becomes a crime; more often it is a betrayal of others, of self, or of God. At the heart of his stories is the acknowledgement that man is conceived in sin and born in iniquity and there is no health in him. The best he can hope for is the revelation of the truth and the sincere and public repentance that follows.

Although Reed Arvin is not always explicitly Christian in his narratives, he is deeply serious about the Christian worldview. His characters drift through a meaningless universe until they recognize the mystery of God and his plan for his world. Nature reminds the characters that they are merely bit players on a much larger stage. Music, in his stories, represents the expression of human longing for God and for connection with other people. Sexuality serves much the same purpose, drawing people together and testing their faithfulness. Lawyers and policemen become the interpreters and enforcers of human law. Only in his first novel does a minister perform the function of God's spokesman. In *The Will*, it is the Birdman, a mad prophet crying in the town park, who calls the town to repentance. And it is an old seminary professor who provides the personal counseling for the confused protagonist.

The Wind in the Wheat, Reed Arvin's meditation on his own career in music, has something of the same qualities we find in **Davis Bunn's** *The Maestro*. Both chronicle the coming-of-age of brilliant young musicians. While Bunn tells of the European music scene, the cabarets and the touring Gospel musicians, Arvin limits himself to the local churches and the Nashville music industry. Both authors are insiders who know about marketing strategies, the cultivation of the hero image, and the problems with using one's message to evangelize.

Reed Arvin sees his novels, like his music, as "crossover" works, efforts to appeal to an audience beyond self-identified Christians. He portrays the language of his characters and their activities with taste and care, but nonetheless is more explicit than is typical of most Evangelical press publications. His later novels have the same popular appeal as John Grisham's, with fast-paced action and quick turns of the plot, weaving a love story through a mystery, using his lawyer-hero to bring the truth to light. *The Last Goodbye* sounds a good bit like the classic American hard-boiled detective story, but with Tom Wolfe's details of clothing and character. Arvin says that he has chosen law, big business, genetic research, drug therapies, and computer hacking because these arenas are the ones where ethics are currently "being played out in our society. There's nothing as interesting to me as the great debate going on right now about how people decide right and wrong." Our great religious tradition is being undermined as we experiment with "little gods." Like the people of Israel in the time of the Judges, "everyone gets to decide what's right and wrong for themselves." They are "making up their morals as they go." Arvin is particularly concerned with those who get taken along for the ride.

Blood of Angels returns the scene to Nashville, a city Reed Arvin knows intimately. Once again, this is a thriller, full of crime and suspense. The story is also about retribution, revenge, truth, and decency. At the center is a district attorney with a conscience and a task he must perform. He must prosecute Moses Bol, a Sudanese refugee who has been charged with murdering a white woman from a slum area, called The Nations. In the midst of this complex case, the protagonist is accused of having sent the wrong man to Death Row in a previous case. Suddenly, his whole career is called into question.

Reed Arvin has a great sense of humor, which shows in his blend of characters, situations, and dialogue. The romance at the center of his stories reminds the reader that man was not meant to be alone. And always, there is music that drifts through the story, sometimes country Western, sometimes classic opera, one of the many tools this talented writer uses to characterize his people.

Critical Reception

Arvin's first novel, published by Thomas Nelson, was largely ignored by the mainstream critics. John Mort, who reviewed two of his books for *Booklist*, saw him as an interesting new talent. In his collection of essays and summaries of Christian fiction, Mort notes that Arvin is a good example of the kind of writer who cannot conform to the restrictions of the Christian Book Association Code, especially the way that writers are expected to express their faith. He notes that *The Wind in the Wheat* "is one of the most lyrical and affecting evangelical novels ever written, this coming-of-age story about a Kansas farm boy with a gift for music who won't let his Christian principles be corrupted by the recording industry." Both it and *The Will*, a story of "a lawyer and former seminary student in the midst of a profound spiritual search," are "nuanced" expressions of faith rarely found in products of ECPA publishers.

Joe Hartlaub says of Reed Arvin that he is "a marvel, pure and simple." He packs enough intrigue and suspense in each of his novels to fill three stories, and does this with "perhaps the fairest, most balanced discourse on capital punishment" that the critic has seen. He manages this while drawing an array of characters whom "the reader will honestly care about, and wonder about when the tale is told." Hartlaub compares *Blood of Angels* and *The Will* to masterpieces like *To Kill a Mockingbird* and *Presumed Innocent*.

The more recent novels have been reviewed favorably in the *New York Times*, by Knight Ridder/Tribune News Service, and many others. These critics are pleased with Arvin's characterization, plotting, and style. Janet Maslin, reviewing *The Last Goodbye*, suggests that "Anyone with a taste for sultry, devious, adrenaline-boasting suspense stories may want to cancel a few appointments before opening this one." She compares Arvin to Raymond Chandler.

The intricate plotting and details of legal maneuvering are interesting to all readers, but Christian readers will find a conscience at the heart of all of Reed Arvin's stories. He sees the need for a coherent vision of human life and a respect for all of God's creatures.

Bibliography of Novels by Author

The Wind in the Wheat. Nashville, TN: Thomas Nelson, 1994.
The Will. New York: Scribner, 2000. (Paramount Pictures has purchased the film rights for *The Will*.)
The Last Goodbye. New York: HarperCollins, 2004.
Blood of Angels. New York: HarperCollins, 2005.

Bibliography of Works about Author

Hartlaub, Joe. Review of *Blood of Angels*. *BookReporter*, http://www.bookreporter.com/reviews2/0060.
Maslin, Janet. Review of *The Last Goodbye*. *New York Times*, February 16, 2004, E8.
Mort, John. *Christian Fiction: A Guide to the Genre*. Greenwood Village, CO: Libraries Unlimited, 2002.
Mort, John. Review of *The Wind in the Wheat*. *Booklist* (December 15, 1994): 737.
Mort, John. Review of *The Will*. *Booklist* (October 1, 2001): 282.
"Reed Arvin," *Contemporary Authors Online*. Detroit: Thomson Gale, 2005.
"Reed Arvin: An Interview with Author." http://www.bookbrowse.com/author_ interviews/full/index_ number=969.

ATWOOD, MARGARET

Personal, Professional, and Religious Background

Margaret Eleanor Atwood (1939–) was born in Ottawa, Ontario, Canada. Her father, Carl Edmund Atwood, was an entomologist. Her mother was Margaret Dorothy Killam Atwood, a nutritionist. *Cat's Eye*, Atwood's strongly autobiographical tale, describes the family's early days of camping in the wilds of the north while the father searched for interesting "infestations" of woodlands. Seven-year-old Margaret and her family moved to Toronto, and by this age, she was already trying her hand at writing.

> Writing was a way of sending your voice to someone you might never meet.
>
> —Margaret Atwood in an interview in *The Washington Post*, 2006

At age 11, she entered public schools for the first time, having previously been homeschooled. She always felt slightly different from the other children, an outsider because of her early life, which they found quite peculiar.

Her parents taught her little about religion or the stories in the Bible, but did introduce her to fairy tales and mythology—which she loved. She was a voracious reader, especially fond of recent history and of fiction. After high school, Margaret Atwood entered Victoria University, where Northrop Frye and Jay Macpherson were her professors. She credits them with much of her early success. In 1961, she took honors in English with minors in philosophy and French, and then won a Woodrow Wilson scholarship to Radcliffe, completing a master's degree in 1962. She continued her graduate study at Harvard University from 1962–63 and 1965–67, but never wrote the dissertation on "The English Metaphysical Romance," leaving her without her doctorate.

In 1968, Margaret Atwood married Jim Polk, whom she divorced in 1973, and has rarely referred to him in her interviews. Shortly after the divorce, she joined forces with Graeme Gibson, who is also a writer. They have one daughter, Jess, in addition to two sons from Gibson's previous marriage.

Atwood and Gibson are active members of the Green Party of Canada. She calls herself a "William Morrisite" and an "Immanent Transcendentalist." At other times, she has labeled herself a "pessimistic Pantheist." She thinks God, if he (or she) exists, is everywhere, in everything both organic and inorganic. Atwood notes that, if she were God, she would be annoyed at what humans have done to the "good" earth that she created.

In addition to her writing, Atwood has lectured at Sir George Williams University in Montreal, York University in Toronto, and has been editor and member of directors of the House of Anansi Press in Toronto, writer-in-residence at the University of Toronto, the University of Alabama in Tuscaloosa, and visiting professor at New York University and Macquarie University, Australia.

Major Works and Themes

Margaret Atwood appeared at the perfect time for a woman of her talents and ideas. Her early poetry, collected in *Double Persephone*, first established her as an impressive voice for natural flux in contrast to human artificiality. Such human constructs as marriage and religion, houses and art, are in constant tension with natural change and growth. In many of her novels, Atwood continues this theme of duality, portraying our futile efforts to fix relationships and experiences while the world changes. The largely autobiographical *Cat's Eye* is a witty commentary on how critics strive to turn human experience into pat ideology. The painter at the center of the story, who uses her own life as a source of her art,

> The human race is decimating species at an alarming rate. It is thereby diminishing God, or the expressions of God.
>
> —Margaret Atwood in an interview with Random House

does not conform to the theories of the doctrinaire feminists who seek to explain and exploit her and her work.

Atwood's feminist concerns are clearest in *The Edible Woman, Surfacing, Life before Man,* and *Bodily Harm.* All of these have strong, independent female protagonists, successful career women who are also competent at home. *The Edible Woman* is the story of Marian McAlpine, a young woman whose body revolts against her impending marriage. As in several of Atwood's novels, food reflects the female experience. When Marian bakes a sponge cake shaped like a woman and feeds it to her fiancé, a man who has been trying to "assimilate" her, she finds the strength to break off the marriage and eat the cake herself. *Lady Oracle* also uses food as the symbol for identity, with Joan Foster first devouring everything in sight to become an enormous, ballooning child. Then, to win freedom, she loses a hundred pounds, becomes desirable to men, and needs to discover freedom yet again by escaping to Italy. Atwood's women are both attracted to relationships and frightened by them, too timid to announce their dissatisfaction and too tormented to accept their entrapment. They make abrupt and confusing moves to escape situations that they have thoughtlessly invited and allowed. They then tend to live double lives, artistic or romantic in a secret life, modest and conformist in the public one. They worry about their choices of clothes, their appearance, their weight, and their wrinkles. They seem to live in the mirrors of other people's eyes.

A feminist and an "immanent transcendentalist," Margaret Atwood finds more comfort in Mother Nature than any church or synagogue. She muses that she is really an agnostic, since being an atheist would suggest too firm a position. She simply does not know the truth about God, but if she had to choose a religion, she would be a Roman Catholic—because she likes the image of the Virgin Mary and all of the female saints. She also loves the stained glass windows and the liturgy, but puts no faith in the creeds. When she portrays religious people in her stories, they tend to be rigid, judgmental, and cruel.

The Handmaid's Tale shows clearly that she fears the political power of the Christian Right, which appears to her to be threatening the United States and would rip away from women most of their hard-earned rights. This dystopia, the United States of Gilead, projects a fearsome future in which radical Christians have gained control of the country and reestablished the old patriarchal powers of Abraham's time, with women stripped of their credit cards, right to work, and sexual freedom.

Critical Reception

Critics and scholars have applauded Margaret Atwood's work from the beginning, finding her witty, powerful, sensitive, and thought-provoking. She has been widely reviewed, her works the subject of seminars and frequently listed in feminist college courses.

The mainstream press praise her vigorously as a rule: Anatole Broyard, writing for the *New York Times*, in a review of *Bodily Harm*, insists that the book "knocked me out." Anne Tyler reviewed the book for the *Detroit News*, noting that Atwood is a "cataloguer of current fads and fancies," in this case the response to a partial mastectomy.

Stephen McCabe, writing about *The Handmaid's Tale* for the *Humanist*, said the book is "a chilling vision of the future extrapolated from the present." On the other hand, Mary McCarthy, who reviewed the book for the *New York Times*, thought Atwood's fears excessive. "I just can't see the intolerance of the far right . . . as leading to a super-biblical puritanism." She insisted that the projections of the book "are too neatly penciled in." Richard Grenier did not think the fundamentalists who run Gilead, the imaginary future country replacing the United States, even seem to be Christian. "There seems to be no Father, no Son, no Holy Ghost, no apparent belief in redemption, resurrection, eternal life." As is typical of her presentation of Christians and Christian churches, she portrays the behavior rather than the beliefs. On the other hand, Janet Lawson, reviewing the book for *Christian Century*, notes that Atwood reveals a deep familiarity with scriptural tradition. She then wonders why this "nonreligious writer" should bother to do this close study, especially of the Old Testament. Her answer to her own question is: "Of course, to expose Gilead's backward-looking fundamentalism, Atwood needs to use material from the patriarchal narratives and distorted quotations from Jesus and St. Paul." She notes that some readers will be "amused and appalled by its grotesque cartoon of theocracy" and impressed by her "considerable subtlety, which challenges us to look deeper into her satire." Christopher Lehmann-Haupt, less offended by the anti-Christian tone, considered the book far more than an attack on environmental waste, anti-feminist attitudes, or nuclear terror; he thought the book "ultimately succeeds on multiple levels: as a page-turning thriller, as a powerful political statement, and as an exquisite piece of writing."

Although Atwood's later books have been reviewed enthusiastically, none of the others have stirred up the warfare that *The Handmaid's Tale* precipitated. In Margaret Atwood's universe, the cardinal sins are the pollution of the Earth and the abuse of women. Her characters are far more concerned with self-discovery than with the search for God or the condition of their soul. They love the good Earth, without much need for a Heaven hereafter.

Awards

Margaret Atwood is among the most honored fiction writers in recent history. She has been the runner-up for the Booker Prize twice, and won it once, for *Blind Assassin* in 2000. She has also been named a fellow of the Royal Society of Canada. She has won numerous awards for her many books of poetry, novels, story collections, and essays. The majority of these were for *The Handmaid's Tale*. She also won many awards for *Cat's Eye*, including the Torgi Talking Book Award, Periodical Marketers of Canada Award, the Foundation for Advancement of Canadian Letters citation, and the Canadian Booksellers' Association Author of the Year and Book of the Year Award. She has also been on the shortlist for a number of prizes and has won international citations from several countries.

She has won honorary degrees from Trent University, Concordia University, Smith College, the University of Toronto, Mount Holyoke College, the University of Waterloo, the University of Guelph, Victoria College, the University of Montreal, the University of Leeds, Queen's University, Oxford University, and Cambridge University.

In addition, Margaret Atwood has been named Woman of the Year by *Ms. Magazine* and *Chatelaine* magazine, and won the Enlightenment Award at the Edinburgh International Book Festival in 2005.

Bibliography of Novels by Author

The Edible Woman. Toronto: McClelland & Stewart, 1969.
Surfacing. Toronto: McClelland & Stewart, 1972.
Lady Oracle. New York: Simon & Schuster, 1976.
Life before Man. New York: Simon & Schuster, 1979.

Bodily Harm. Toronto: McClelland & Stewart, 1981.
Encounters with Element Man. Concord, NH: William B. Ewert, 1983.
Unearthing Suite. Toronto: Grand Union Press, 1983.
The Handmaid's Tale. Toronto: McClelland & Stewart, 1985.
Cat's Eye. Toronto: McClelland & Stewart, 1989.
The Robber Bride. New York: Doubleday, 1993.
Alias Grace. New York: Doubleday, 1996.
The Blind Assassin. New York: Random House, 2000.
Oryx and Crake. New York: Nan A. Talese, 2003.
The Tent. New York: Doubleday, 2006.

Bibliography of Works about Author

Atwood, Margaret. Author Interview. Random House, http://www.randomhouse.com/features/at wood/interview.html.
Atwood, Margaret. "The Writing Life: A Canadian Novelist Learns to Rephrase a Basic Question in the Far North." Washingtonpost.com, http://www.washingtonpost.com/wp-dyn/content/article/2006/02/09/AR2006209017.
Beran, Carol L. *Living over the Abyss: Margaret Atwood's Life before Man.* Toronto: ECW Press, 1993.
Bloom, Harold, ed. *Margaret Atwood.* Philadelphia, PA: Chelsea House, 2000.
British Council. *Contemporary Writers,* http://www.contemporarywriters.com/authors/?p=atwood margaret.
Broyard, Anatole. Review of *Bodily Harm. New York Times,* March 6, 1982, 13.
Cooke, Nathalie. *Margaret Atwood: A Biography.* Toronto: ECW Press, 1998.
Davidson, Arnold E., and Cathy N. Davidson, eds. *The Art of Margaret Atwood: Essays in Criticism.* Toronto: House of Anansi Press, 1981.
Grace, Sherrill. *Violent Duality: A Study of Margaret Atwood.* Montreal: Véhicule Press, 1980.
Greiner, Richard. Review of *The Handmaid's Tale. Insight,* March 24, 1986.
Lawson, Janet Karsten. "Margaret Atwood's Testaments: Resisting the Gilead Within." Religion-online, http://www.religion-online.org/showarticle.asp?title=1021.
Lecker, Robert, and Jack David, eds. *The Annotated Bibliography of Canada's Major Authors.* Toronto: ECW Press, 1980.
Lehmann-Haupt, Christopher. Review of *The Handmaid's Tale. New York Times,* January 27, 1986, C24.
"Margaret Atwood." *Contemporary Authors Online.* Detroit: Thomson Gale, 2006.
McCabe, Stephen. Review of *The Handmaid's Tale. Humanist* (September-October, 1986): 31.
McCarthy, Mary. Review of *The Handmaid's Tale. New York Times Book Review,* February 9, 1986, 1.
Rao, Eleanora. *Strategies for Identity: The Fiction of Margaret Atwood.* New York: P. Lang, 1993.
Sandler, Linda, ed. *Margaret Atwood: A Symposium.* Vancouver: University of British Columbia, 1977.
Stein, Karen F. *Margaret Atwood Revisited.* New York: Twayne, 1999.
Tyler, Anne. Review of *Bodily Harm. Detroit News,* April 4, 1982.

AUSTIN, LYNN

Personal, Professional, and Religious Background

Lynn N. Austin (1949–) was born in Florida, the daughter of a librarian and a sales manager. She considers herself "one of those blessed people who grew up in a Christian family with parents and grandparents who loved the Lord and attended church faithfully." Her father's family was Methodist, her mother's Lutheran. They took their children, Lynn and her sisters, to the only Protestant church in town—a Reformed church with "an excellent Sunday school and a year-long catechism class."

She chose to go to Hope, a church-related college. After three years, she finished her undergraduate work for a B.A. at Southern Connecticut State University. She did some graduate work at Southwestern Baptist Theological Seminary.

It was during her college years that she was convinced of her sinful nature and realized that she had

> As I strive to bring the Old Testament to life, I'd like readers to see its characters not as plastic saints but as struggling human beings, just like us, and recognize that the Bible has relevance today.
>
> —Lynn Austin in an interview with Janice DeLong and Rachel Schwedt

the need of God's grace. She notes that she was sitting in chapel one day, singing the words of the old hymn "Be Thou My Vision," when she began her prayer for forgiveness and committed herself to God's service. The hymn, she says, is still her favorite.

She is married to Ken, who is a Christian musician. He performs with two orchestras, so classical music has a major role in the life of the family. Frequent travel has also been a part of their life, forcing Lynn Austin to postpone her career for years. For two years, the family lived in Bagota, Columbia, then returned to the United States, moving to Anderson, Indiana, Thunder Bay, Ontario, and later to Winnipeg, Manitoba, and finally to Chicago, Illinois. They have three children, all now grown.

Lynn Austin's interest in stories goes back to her childhood, when she read everything she could find. Primarily interested in history, especially Bible history, she cherished the dream that she might one day become a writer, but could never find the time. When her family moved to Canada, she discovered that the long winters allowed her some leisure during her children's nap time, which she began to use for her writing. She had written several of her historical novels without finding a publisher, but with great support from her husband, who eagerly agreed to fix meals and help with the children so that she could continue her work. Up until this time, she had worked as a teacher, resigning in 1992 to devote herself to full-time writing as a free-lance author.

At present, she and her husband live in Chicago. She belongs to a medium-sized Presbyterian church, where she serves on committees, teaches Sunday school, and acts as a lay reader for worship services. She says that the church's two pastors, who "have a deep love for Christ and for Scripture," preach sermons filled with "rich, poetic use of language." Their words serve as an inspiration to her. She jots down notes during their sermons for use in her writing.

Lynn Austin has been on the editorial board of *Profile*, the journal of the Chicago Women's Conference, and has served as a contributing editor for *The Christian Reader*. She is a popular speaker at churches, schools, conferences, and retreats.

Major Works and Themes

In 1989, Austin and her son traveled to Israel for the summer to take part in an archaeological dig at the ancient city of Timnah, an experience that inspired her novel *Wings*

> Lynn Austin and her son spent the summer of 1989 at an archaeological dig at the ancient city of Timnah, stoking her already intense love of history.

of Refuge. This novel tells of Abigail MacLeod, an amateur archaeologist who travels to participate in a dig and escape her family problems, only to find herself enmeshed in a murder investigation.

In this seminal experience and through her reading of history and archaeology, Lynn Austin has found that she has a talent for bringing ancient stories to life. Lynn Austin's major successes have been her historical novels. The "Chronicles of the King" series of five novels reveals both her ability to make Bible stories come to life and her own application of those stories to contemporary situations. Her theme of God's strength and mercy and her awareness of human greed, pride, lust, and other sins undergird all of these stories.

In *The Strength of His Hand*, Austin uses her vivid sense of place effectively to tell the story of Hezekiah and the threat of Assyria. She blends segments from Isaiah, Chronicles, and Psalms in a rich tapestry to portray Jerusalem at a crucial time in its history, involving a vast array of characters who represent the rising Babylonian power, the Egyptians, the Assyrians, and the Judeans. Taking the same experience that inspired Byron's great poem "The Destruction of Sennacherib," Lynn Austin tells about the miracles surrounding the defeat of the enormous Assyrian forces, proving God's strength and his everlasting love for his holy city, Jerusalem.

Lynn Austin is also interested in American history, undertaking in her "Refiner's Fire" series to describe the events of the Civil War. *Candle in the Darkness* features a young woman, Caroline Fletcher, who is born on a plantation in Virginia, comes to love the slaves she knows there, and is transplanted to Philadelphia when her mother dies. Growing up in this abolitionist milieu, she finds herself torn on her return to Virginia, loving both her family and the slaves she now supports. *Fire by Night*, the sequel to this story, takes up the Civil War and its effect on two young women from the North.

Lynn Austin has also written other novels set in more recent times, including *Hidden Places*, a story of the Great Depression. This gentle story traces a family struggling to care for an orange grove after all the men have died, leaving only a grandmother, a mother, and two young children to cultivate and harvest the crop. A greedy San Francisco bank is threatening them when a handsome stranger appears. Gabriel turns out to be no regular hobo but a troubled young writer, a hard worker, a competent foreman, and finally a loving husband and father—an angel in disguise.

Other novels include *Fly Away*, the account of a cancer victim seeking solace with a retired professor of music, and *Eve's Daughters*, the chronicle of four women who whose lives span more than 100 years, from Germany to New York.

She has read widely in a variety of genres—revealing an interest in Christian authors, Jewish ones, and contemporary favorites. She says that she brings a Christian worldview to all of her novels, trying to show the importance of making the right choices and the consequences of making the wrong ones. She notes that her recurring theme is "the greatness of God and His infinite love."

Critical Reception

Three of Lynn Austin's historical novels, *Hidden Places*, *Candle in the Darkness*, and *Fire by Night*, have won Christy Awards for excellence in Christian Fiction. *Fire by Night* was also one of only five inspirational fiction books that *Library Journal* picked as their favorites for 2003.

All She Ever Wanted was one of their five inspirational picks in 2005. Hallmark Channel chose *Hidden Places* for a film that starred Shirley Jones, winning Ms. Jones a 2005 Emmy Award nomination.

John Mort has reviewed a number of her books for *Booklist* and for his collection *Christian Fiction: A Guide to the Genre*, noting that she tells a good story, filled with good characterization and strong research. Her books have been used as supplemental texts in some Christian schools, a testimony to her care and accuracy in working with both Scripture and historical detail.

Awards

Lynn Austin was named New Writer of the Year by the Moody Bible Institute Write-to-Publish Conference in 1993. She was also named Writer of the Year by the Wheaton Write-to-Publish Conference in 1996. She received the Silver Angel Award for *Eve's Daughters* (1999) and the Christy Award for historical novels: *Hidden Places* (2002), *Candle in the Darkness* (2003) and *Fire by Night* (2004).

Bibliography of Novels by Author

"Chronicles of the King" series (Kansas City, MO: Beacon Hill Press)

The Lord Is My Strength. 1995.
The Lord Is My Salvation. 1996.
The Lord Is My Song. 1996.
My Father's God. 1997.
Among the Gods. 1998.
Songs of Redemption. 2005.

"Refiner's Fire" series (Minneapolis, MN: Bethany House)

Candle in the Darkness. 2002.
Fire By Night. 2003.

Other Novels for Adults

Fly Away. Kansas City, MO: Beacon Hill Press, 1996.
Eve's Daughters. Minneapolis, MN: Bethany House, 1999.
Wings of Refuge. Minneapolis, MN: Bethany House, 2000.
All She Ever Wanted. Minneapolis, MN: Bethany House, 2005.
The Strength of His Hand. Minneapolis, MN: Bethany House, 2005.
A Woman's Place. Minneapolis, MN: Bethany House, 2006.
A Proper Pursuit. Minneapolis, MN: Bethany House, 2007.

Bibliography of Works about Author

DeLong, Janice, and Rachel Schwedt. *Contemporary Christian Authors: Lives and Works.* Lanham, MD: The Scarecrow Press, 2000
Hudak, Melissa. Review of *My Father's God. Library Journal* (September 1, 1997): 166.

Lynn Austin Web site, http://www.lynnaustin.org.

"Lynn Austin, Faithful Fifteen." http://www.faithfulreader.com.

"Lynn N. Austin." *Contemporary Authors Online.* Detroit: Thomson Gale, 2004.

Mort, John. *Christian Fiction: A Guide to the Genre.* Greenwood Village, CO: Libraries Unlimited, 2002.

Mort, John. Review of *Eve's Daughters. Booklist* (October 1, 1999): 326.

Mort, John. Review of *The Lord Is My Strength. Booklist* (March 15, 1995): 1309.

B

BALDWIN, JAMES

Personal, Professional, and Religious Background

James Arthur Baldwin (1924–1987), born to Bernice Emma Jones, an unwed mother, never knew who his birth father was. In 1927, his mother, who had moved to New York from Deal Island in Maryland around the turn of the century, married David Baldwin, a clergyman and worker in a bottling factory. Baldwin's stepfather had moved to New York in the early 1920s, with his mother, who was a former slave, and a 12-year-old son. The Baldwins had eight other children while living in various crowded apartments in Harlem. The last of these babies was born the year that David Baldwin died.

The Harlem of Baldwin's youth was primarily African American. At the time, it was largely a Southern community, filled with black refugees from beyond the "cotton curtain," as was the case of Baldwin's parents. The family was poor. Baldwin's mother made a few dollars cleaning white people's apartments and his stepfather never earned more than $27.50 a week working at the bottling plant. Ironically, Harlem was also rich in culture, the flourishing of the renowned Harlem Renaissance, and a lively enthusiasm for the arts, with opportunities opening up for African American artists.

James Baldwin pictures his family in great detail in his powerful novels and short stories, especially *Go Tell It on the Mountain* and *Going to Meet the Man*. James Baldwin was a bright child, sensitive to the moods and pressures of the growing family. He pictures the perennial battle of black families to protect their young men from the corrupting culture of the Harlem streets, seductive with easy sexuality, drink, and drugs. The Baldwins escaped as a family

> If the concept of God has any validity or any use, it can only be to make us larger, freer, and more loving. If God cannot do this, then it is time we got rid of Him.
>
> —James Baldwin

While still in high school, James Baldwin served as youth minister for his church.

through dedicated worship at the Fireside Pentecostal Assembly.

The family lost Baldwin's grandmother to death and his older step-brother to hostility that erupted between the boy and his father. The burden of helping with the family increasingly fell on James, the oldest of the remaining children. In the meantime, financial constraints forced the large family to move several times, always within Harlem. Occasionally, they were forced to accept relief.

James Baldwin meantime was proving himself an exceptional student, first at the Frederick Douglass Junior High School, where he was influenced by Countee Cullen, a leading poet of the Harlem Renaissance who was teaching there at the time. One of his teachers, Orilla Miller at PS 24, took Baldwin to plays and films. She helped him to stage and direct his first play. She was involved with the WPA, a federal works project designed to discover new talents. His math teacher, Herman W. Porter, a Harvard graduate, befriended him as well. He came to the Baldwin apartment, where he was confronted by the hostility of David Baldwin, took the young James on a subway to the public library on 42nd Street for the first time, and showed him how to begin a research project there. He also handed him carfare for his return home. The young boy was so disturbed at leaving Harlem to enter the white world that he vomited all over Porter's shoes on the subway. This adventure was the beginning of Baldwin's discovery of literary classics and of a world outside the African American community.

Shortly after his 14th birthday, James Baldwin had a profound conversion experience at the store-front Pentecostal church he and his family attended. While he was still a student at the renowned De Witt Clinton High School in New York, he became youth minister for the church. At the same time, he was making friends with artists who revealed to him the vibrant, bohemian culture of Greenwich Village. Emil Caponya introduced him to music—especially blues and jazz—which was not welcome in the Baldwin home. By this time, Baldwin's stepfather, always an explosive personality and a deeply disappointed man, was becoming unstable. As Baldwin felt himself drawn more away from the family and the church to the artistic life, he gradually moved away from his faith, preaching his last sermon at the end of his senior year and leaving the church after three years in the ministry.

In 1942, having completed high school, he took a laboring job in the defense industry in Belle Meade, New Jersey, where his friend Caponya was also employed. His father's increasing mental instability and his mother's need for help with support of the family kept him from any consideration of higher education. In New Jersey, he confronted racism and the effects of segregation in ways he had never seen when growing up in Harlem. He was fired from his job and returned home to find work in a meatpacking plant. When his stepfather died, in 1943, James Baldwin moved to Greenwich Village, determined to become a writer. He worked as a waiter in a village restaurant and enjoyed the artists who gathered around the area, finally acknowledging that he was a homosexual.

He began to meet people who were already or were soon to become famous—Marlon Brando, who was taking a theatre course nearby and who was to become a longtime friend, and Richard Wright, who encouraged him and recommended his manuscript "In My Father's House" to Harper & Brothers publishers. The contact with Wright, who was already the most famous black author of the time, led him to a $500 grant in order to work on a novel, the draft of which was finally rejected by Harpers. At about this time, his good friend Eugene Worth committed suicide, an act that had a great effect on Baldwin, who later used the event in *Another Country*.

Baldwin's writing career gradually took shape, with reviews in *The Nation*, *The New Leader*, and *Commentary*. As he gained prominence as a commentator on racism, he continued to read, immersing himself in French, Russian, and American literature. When he won the Rosenwald Fellowship to write a book on Harlem, he moved to Paris, where he joined forces with a number of Wright's friends, and other artists from all over the world.

From this point on, his life was rootless. Occasionally he stayed with friends, sometimes in small hotels, usually in Europe, but sometimes returning to America. He used his escapades, his love affairs, and his discoveries for a number of his books and essays. He became friends with most of the black writers of his day and many of the prominent white ones: he knew Maya Angelou, Chester Himes, Frank Yerby, Norman Mailer, William Styron, and many others. He became a follower of Martin Luther King, and planned to write his biography.

Baldwin also became increasingly outspoken about racial injustice, teaching at colleges and universities, appearing on symposia, writing and producing plays on the subject. Some critics accused him of being permanently angry and shrill. The deaths of President Kennedy, Martin Luther King, and Robert Kennedy alienated him still further from American culture. His anger is clear in *The Fire Next Time*, his play *Blues for Mr. Charlie* (dedicated to Medgar Evers, who was assassinated in Jackson, Mississippi in 1963), and in his interviews and talks. Though he was welcomed all over the country, many of the meetings held in churches, he increasingly felt that the American dream had been achieved at the expense of the American "negro." He blamed the Christian community for reinforcing bigotry and excusing slavery.

He also had public arguments over the years with members of the black community, first with Richard Wright, of whom he became increasingly critical, and then Eldridge Cleaver who, in *Soul on Ice*, criticized him for taking the point of view of the white man. He did preach primarily to whites, convinced that they held the key to transforming the world and to helping the African American community to find hope.

His health began deteriorating in the early 1970s, though he continued his frenetic pattern of speaking and writing. By 1974, when he was awarded a medal from the Episcopal Cathedral of St. John the Divine in New York as the "artist as prophet," he was already being called passé by Henry Louis Gates, Jr. in a piece written for *Time* magazine. The honors continued to flow his way, teaching opportunities at colleges and universities, fresh publications, and continual travel.

He completed his last year of teaching in 1986, returned to France to be made an officer of the Legion of Honor by President François Mitterand, and began a series of tests that revealed cancer of the esophagus. His brother David and other relatives and friends tended to his needs as he grew too weak to walk. He died in 1987. The funeral service at the Cathedral of St. John the Divine including eulogies from **Toni Morrison,** Maya Angelou, and Amiri Baraka. He was buried on December 8 in Ferncliff Cemetery, Hartsdale, New York.

Major Works and Themes

Race is the predominant theme in most of James Baldwin's writing, but his earliest work shows a deep and powerful concern with religion. *Go Tell It on the Mountain*, which he published in 1953, is the rich study of his own family and their community of faith. It tells of his own powerful conversion experience, full of pressures and intense emotions. The songs, the falling down, the shouts, the dancing are all part of the spontaneous life of this store-front Pentecostal church, where the tiny congregation calls for "the anointing of the Holy Spirit."

In *Going to Meet the Man*, Baldwin pictures this same congregation on an outing. They take a picnic lunch along for a boat trip up the Hudson, concluding with a passionate worship service. Again in this shorter story, Baldwin portrays the "good" and the "bad" boys, some choosing the path of holiness, some the path of nature and the temptations of the streets. The congregation uses the power of faith to give joy to their dreary lives, hope to their sad poverty, and morality to their children. They rail against drink, drugs, and the "filth" of the Harlem streets. Baldwin pictures the church as waging a war for middle-class morality—family, respectability, and purity. He also sees his own stepfather using his faith as a club to control his sons. His seems embarrassed by his earlier life as a preacher and his being nothing more than an assistant at the Harlem church. The women are the central figures in the church, a culture of faith that gives their lives a significance they would never otherwise know.

In his essays about life in Europe, Baldwin describes the isolation he feels as a black man and a Christian in such an alien culture. He feels disassociated from the white European faith symbolized by the cathedrals, but also from the black African tribal religions, which provide him no solace. Though he has given up on the church, Baldwin never forgets the language and the themes of the Bible. Many of his titles are taken from Scripture, and many of his phrases and rhythms remind the reader of the prophets. His Christian heritage is deep in his writings, even though he complains that he has no home, nobody knows his name, and he is the permanent outsider.

James Baldwin eventually replaced Christianity with his private cult of love—sexual and other relationships that cross lines of race, nationality, and gender. As a homosexual, he believed that gay sexuality is the purest form of love; as a black man, he believed that the white lover is the ideal; and as an American, he preferred a European partner. He upset the black writers of his time, who were concerned with a separatist black culture, by his efforts to write for a white audience, feeling his mission was to bridge the gap over the racial divide.

Critical Reception

Critics have discussed James Baldwin at great length, generally preferring his short works to his long ones, his novels and essays over his plays, and his early works rather than his later ones. Several of his books became best-sellers: both *Nobody Knows My Name: More Notes of a Native Son* and *The Fire Next Time* had very wide readership. They reveal the depth of black bitterness at a time when the white community was trying to understand African Americans. As Juan Williams noted: "Black people reading Baldwin knew he wrote the truth. White people reading Baldwin sensed his truth about the lives of black people and the sins of a racist nation."

Carolyn Wedin Sylvander believes that *Go Tell It on the Mountain*, Baldwin's family chronicle, deals "comprehensively and emotionally with the hot issue of race relations in the United States at a time" when white ignorance and black powerlessness were not "conducive to holistic depictions of black experience." At least one critic, David Littlejohn, saw the book as "autobiography-as-exorcism."

The very volume of the criticism available on this remarkable American original testifies to his significance. His anger at the Christian church for its role in racism and its failure to bridge the great divide between the races is a stark indictment by a man who once wanted deeply to be a believer, even a minister.

Awards

James Baldwin was showered with fellowships, awards, and medals: Among these were the Eugene F. Saxton Fellowship in 1945; the Rosenwald Fellowship in 1948; a Guggenheim Fellowship in 1954; Partisan Review Fellowship; National Institute of Arts and Letters grant for literature; the National Institute of Arts and Letters Award; the National Conference of Christians and Jews Brotherhood award in 1956, for *Nobody Knows My Name: More Notes of a Native Son*; the George Polk Memorial Award, 1963; a Doctorate of Literature from the University of British Columbia, Vancouver, in 1964; and he was named Commander of the Legion of Honor in France in 1986.

Bibliography of Novels by Author

Go Tell It on the Mountain. New York: Knopf, 1953.
Giovanni's Room. New York: Dial, 1956.
Another Country. New York: Dial, 1962.
Tell Me How Long the Train's Been Gone. New York: Dial, 1968.
If Beale Street Could Talk. New York: Dial, 1974.
Just Above My Head. New York: Dial, 1979.

James Baldwin also wrote a story for children about childhood, numerous short stories that appeared in magazines and were reprinted in collections, many essays, speeches, and articles. He wrote six plays, one of which was a dramatic version of his novel *Giovanni's Room*.

Bibliography of Works about Author

Bigsby, C.W.E., ed. *The Black American Writer, Vol. 1: Fiction*. New York: Everett/Edwards, 1969.
Bone, Robert. *The Negro Novel in America*. New Haven, CT: Yale University Press, 1965.
Cleaver, Eldridge. *Soul on Ice*. New York: McGraw-Hill, 1968.
Hardy, Clarence E., III. *James Baldwin's God: Sex, Hope, and Crisis in Black Holiness Culture*. Chattanooga: The University of Tennessee Press, 2003.
Harris, Trudier. *New Essays on "Go Tell It on the Mountain."* New York: Cambridge University Press, 1995.
Hughes, Langston. Review of *Notes of a Native Son*. *New York Times*, February 26, 1958.
"James Baldwin," *Contemporary Authors Online*. Detroit: Thomson Gale, 2002.
Kenan, Randall. *James Baldwin*. New York: Chelsea House, 1994.
Kinnamon, Kenneth, ed. *James Baldwin: A Collection of Critical Essays*. New York: Prentice-Hall, 1974.
Leeming, David Adams. *James Baldwin: A Biography*. New York: H. Holt and Col, 1995.
Littlejohn, David. *Black on White: A Critical Survey of Writing by American Negroes*. New York: Viking, 1966.
Lynch, Michael F. *"Just Above My Head: James Baldwin's Quest for Belief." Literature and Theology* 11, no. 3 (1997): 284–298.
Pratt, Louis Hill. *James Baldwin*. New York: Twayne, 1978.
Stadley, Fred and Nancy. *James Baldwin: A Reference Guide*. New York: G.K. Hall, 1980.
Sylvander, Carolyn Wedin. *James Baldwin*. New York: Frederick Ungar, 1980.
Williams, Juan. "Baldwin: The Witness' Testament: Passion, Insight and Accuracy: Hallmarks of a Writer's Life. *Washington Post*, December 2, 1987.

BATEMAN, TRACEY

Personal, Professional, and Religious Background

Tracey Victoria Bateman (1970–) was the youngest of seven children. She dropped out of high school at 15, earned her GED at 18 and married Rusty at 19. The Batemans have four children, the first three of whom were born in the first five years of their marriage. At that point, Tracey decided she needed to find a career to help with family finances. She enrolled in college, took about half of the courses she needed for a degree, earned good grades, and then found she was pregnant with her fourth child. Compelled to drop out of college, she felt called to write. Since 2000, she has published more than 18 books. She says that she learned to write by writing.

Major Works and Themes

Tracey Bateman's books fall into the "Chic Lit" or "Mom Lit" categories of religious fiction. She is a great favorite among young readers, who love her action-filled plots, her lovely and feisty heroines, and her strong heroes. The lovers, clearly destined for one another, face barriers and complications before God's will for their lives becomes apparent. The couples are reconciled and the plot is brought to a proper conclusion. She is not afraid of dealing with political corruption, murder, or rape.

Tracey Bateman produces at a rapid pace, often in series with three or four in a sequence. In one case, *Oregon Brides*, she takes a single idea—brides for Western men in the 19th century—and weaves three separate but intertwined tales, using characters and places from one novella in the ones that follow. Each of the stories presents a young woman (Star, Hope, and Eva) who has a pioneer spirit and the need to build a new life in a distant place. The plots often begin with a shock or a tragedy that motivates this dramatic move. One of the women is an orphan, one a widow, and one a farm girl threatened by a lustful neighbor. They have very different adventures along the way, one becoming briefly a saloon girl, one leaving a loveless marriage. The young widow must buy a husband to accompany her West and fight Indians. One of Bateman's heroines, having been raped, thinks she is no longer fit to marry a decent man. All are determined to escape immorality and find a life that conforms to God's plan.

Tracey Bateman is full of interesting ideas, has a real flair for adventure, and writes with amazing speed.

Critical Reception

Romantic Times regularly recommends Tracey Bateman's books to faithful readers, finding such works as *Defiant Heart* to be "filled with action, drama and endearing characters." Readers are assured that "These four lives show how God's grace and love is upon those who deserve it least. Reading this book feels like snuggling up in a warm blanket on a cold day." *Catch a Rising Star,* the first of a new series, which appeared in 2007, is applauded by the *Romantic Times* reviewer as being "full of humor and lighthearted fun." The reviewer warns the readers that some may find the "doormat tendencies" of the heroine to be a bit grating, but "the unique plot points appeal."

> I think the most important thing for any writer, published or otherwise, is let the Word dwell inside of you. . . . I don't want to write my words, but His.
>
> —Tracey Bateman to Lisa Tuttle in interview

Awards

Tracey Bateman has served as president of the American Christian Fiction Writers and vice-president of American Christian Romance Writers.

Bibliography of Novels by Author (Published by Heartsong Presents, Uhrichsville, OH, Unless Otherwise Indicated.)

Darling Cassidy. 2000.
Tarah's Lessons. 2001.
But for Grace. 2003.
Emily's Place. 2003.
Laney's Kiss. 2003.
A Christmas Sleigh Ride. (With Jill Stengl.) Uhrichsville, OH: Barbour. 2004.
Everlasting Hope. 2004.
Timing Is Everything. 2004.
Torey's Prayer. 2004.
Beside Still Waters. 2005.
Betrayal of Trust. 2005.
A Love So Tender. 2005.
Reasonable Doubt. New York: Steeple Hill, 2005.
Second Chance. 2005.
Suspicion of Guilt. New York: Steeple Hill, 2005.
Oregon Brides. Uhrichsville, OH: Barbour, 2006.
365 Secrets of Beauty. Uhrichsville, OH: Barbour, 2006.
"The Penbrook Diaries" series (2005)
"Claire" series (published in New York by Warner Faith, 2006)
"Westward Hearts" series (2007)
"Drama Queens" series (2008)

Tracey Bateman has also written a number of articles, short stories and novellas. Some of her stories have been re-issued under new titles. "The Mahoney Sisters," for example, includes *Reasonable Doubt, Suspicion of Guilt,* and *Betrayal of Trust. Kansas Home* is a collection of four Heartsong Novels.

Bibliography of Works about Author

Bateman, Tracey. Homepage. http://www.traceybateman.com.
Romantic Times Web site. http://www.com/authors_profile.php.
"Tracey B. Bateman," *Contemporary Authors Online.* Detroit: Thomson Gale, 2006.
Tuttle, Lisa. Interview with Tracey Bateman on homepage. http://www.lisatuttle.com.

BEAUSEIGNEUR, JAMES

Personal, Professional, and Religious Background

James BeauSeigneur (1953–) was born in Waltham, Maine. His father was in the Army, requiring the family to move

> If God chooses to use my writing or anything else I have or am, He knows where to find me.
>
> —Interview with James BeauSeigneur

Descended from Auguste BeauSeigneur of Thaincourt, France, James BeauSeigneur explains that his name in French means "beautiful lord." In French translations of the Bible, "Seigneur" is used for "Lord." Probably for this reason, he was mistaken for an angel once by a woman in Washington whom he helped in the D.C. metro.

In 1980 James BeauSeigneur ran unsuccessfully against Al Gore for a Senate seat in Tennessee.

frequently. Consequently, James BeauSeigneur went to school in Edgewood, Maryland; Memphis, Tennessee; three schools in Oahu, Hawaii, and Shelbyville, Tennessee. BeauSeigneur has commented that he was raised in a "pretty dysfunctional home but the existence of God was accepted as fact and we did go to church occasionally." Sometimes his family would attend the Catholic church, sometimes the Baptist. His mother was a Christian, but his father had his own views of God, which had little relationship to the Bible. By the age of ten, James BeauSeigneur began to worry about Hell, recognizing his own inability to obey the ten commandments. His older brother, Fred, who was away at college at the time and active in college ministry, took time to explain the Gospel to the child. Later, in the 1970s, James was hitchhiking across the country when he ran into a group of Christians in Kansas City. He notes that the city was "crawlin' with Jesus freaks and Bible studies and Christian houses in those days." It was then and there that he discovered the full meaning of Christianity and committed his life to Christ.

BeauSeigneur attended 10 different colleges while earning his B.A., did his post graduate work at Middle Tennessee State University in Murfreesboro, Tennessee, at Tennessee State in Nashville, and at the University of Tennessee in Knoxville. For a time, he worked on a doctorate in political science, planning, he said, "to change the world." He served in the United States Army from 1976–1981, assigned as an intelligence analyst for the National Security Agency.

His early writing was primarily political—letters to the editor and articles. He stood for election in Tennessee, as a Republican against Al Gore in 1980. BeauSeigneur notes dryly: "As you might have guessed, Al won. Later I wrote a slightly syndicated op-ed column called 'Conservatively Speaking.'" Along the way, he also served as a political science instructor, a technical writer, a political campaign manager, a lobbyist, and a newspaper publisher.

BeauSeigneur has done considerable work for the United States Government, writing proposals, providing technical writing, and suggesting new strategies. He wrote two "very technical and very expensive books" on defense technology that sold for $1200–$1500 each. In his work for industry and government, he became excited about science fiction, especially the use of new and evolving technologies for political purposes.

He tells interviewers that he is *very* happily married to Geri, and that they have two children. At the time of his interview (March, 2000), one of his daughters, Faith, was a missionary in Romania and the other, Abigail, was a college student working for Young Life. James BeauSeigneur and his wife joined the Montgomery Evangelical Free Church in Derwood when they settled in Derwood, Maryland—the home of Decker Hawthorne, the center-of-consciousness for the *Christ Clone Trilogy*.

Major Works and Themes

James BeauSeigneur's political and scientific background led him naturally to a taste for sci-fi writing. He has been particularly influenced by C. S. Lewis, especially his space trilogy. He also found works such as *Hunt for Red October* and *1984* gripping. He has reread Orwell's book five times over the years. He enjoys many popular works, including Pierre Boulle's *Monkey Planet* or *Planet of the Apes*.

He has also read a number of time-travel books, such as Mark Twain's *A Connecticut Yankee in King Arthur's Court*—which is not science fiction, but is interesting literature. He acknowledges his eclectic reading habits, which range from *Star Trek* to New Age mystics—many of which he cites in his writing and seeks to demystify for the common reader.

His own images of Lucifer and the Antichrist in the *Christ Clone* Trilogy pay tribute to Milton's epics, particularly *Paradise Lost*. His strongest influence is Scripture. The clear teachings of Scripture serve as the guide in his writing, allowing the reader to determine the truth or falsehood spoken by the characters.

James BeauSeigneur considers the "Christ Clone" trilogy a single novel. This massive work of imagination took 10 years to complete. It opens with the idea of cloning some cells from the Shroud of Turin. This section is heavily documented to provide an aura of realism to the events that follow. The writer wants the DNA science, the attempts at cloning humans, and the implications for medical research to serve through all three volumes of the book. He also bases his story on the history of the Ark of the Covenant, a central image in the scenes revolving around the restoration of the Temple in Jerusalem. Using the apocalyptic prophesies in Daniel, Ezekiel, Matthew, and Revelation, BeauSeigneur builds on current reality—the growing power of the United Nations, the concept of One World government, the increasing desire for a New Age mysticism that allows worship without morality or judgment.

The ruler over this futuristic world is Christopher Goodman, the clone of Christ, who may be perceived as either the Messiah or the Antichrist. His early life has close parallels to the Gospel stories of Christ; he seems a loving and intelligent young man, eager to do good in the world. His rise to power is without violence, managed through avenues to talented young people. Only as he reaches his maturity do we become increasingly aware of his miraculous powers, his ability to travel through space and to heal. He limits his use of such abilities, much as Christ himself proved reluctant to use his powers until his time had come.

The divergence from Christ's path becomes increasingly explicit—but in such a way as to disturb and confuse the conservative Christian reader. Since Christopher has been presented as the Christ of the Second Coming in *In His Image*, his explanations of the story of Eden or the Crucifixion seem perverse. He insists, for instance, that he remembers his life on earth as Jesus, and that the Crucifixion was planned to end with his being saved by a host of angels, not death, That explains his words, "My God, why has Thou forsaken me?" He also insists that Decker, who is his guardian and friend, is the reincarnation of Judas, who was led to betray him by John. Such twists of Scripture blend in with scenes such as the 40 days of fasting in the Wilderness, confusing the reader and leading to increasing suspicion of this new "savior."

By the end of *Birth of an Age*, the reader knows that this New Age is the pop culture concept of peace on earth—not Isaiah's. The rising antagonism to Jehovah, the acknowledgement that Christopher's father is Lucifer, not God, and the pernicious influence of the Lucius Trust, a twisted group of mystics, clarifies the truth about Christopher.

With the coming of the various tribulations in *Acts of God*, we grow increasingly sure that the great catastrophe of the opening scenes was the Rapture. By the end of this segment of the trilogy, more and more things become clear. At the very end, finally in the Millennium Kingdom with Christ, Decker has the comfort of knowing that all things will finally be explained, that he is with his family again, and that he is free from the wrath he had so feared.

Critical Reception

Because the trilogy was self-published at first, it received few reviews, but gradually developed an enthusiastic following. Readers are delighted by the remarkable blending of science, government machinations, and apocalyptic speculation. The manner in which BeauSeigneur creates suspense over the three volumes pleases readers, who compare him with Tom Clancy. John Mort of *Booklist*, who has judged this trilogy superior to the much more popular "Left Behind" series, praises his writing: "a tough, driving style in perfect cadence." When the trilogy was republished by Warner in 2003, he noted that BeauSeigneur's paranoia "is a perfect fit for these times of religious hatred and political terror." Jackie Alnor of the *Christian Sentinel* liked his use of an agnostic news reporter as the protagonist, considered it "compelling" and appreciated the fact that the trilogy is not "preachy with gospel messages." "A non-believer can enjoy *The Christ Clone Trilogy* without getting the impression that it's a ruse to sneak in the Gospel. Yet at the same time the reader will be left with the impression that Bible prophesies of the latter days are credible and today's world events testify to the Bible's prophecy's truthfulness."

Jay Carper, who found the book less than perfect in its writing, still appreciated the creativity and the details, calling it the classic of the apocalyptic books. "Surprise! Apocalypse fans, here is your Hobbit. Every turn was unexpected. The characters were real. The plot was real. And never have I seen the Seven Seals broken with such clarity and imagination. If you think you know darkness, think again."

Bibliography of Novels by Author

"Christ Alone" series (New York: Warner Books)

In His Image. New York: Warner Books, 2003.
Birth of an Age. New York: Warner Books, 2003.
Acts of God. New York: Warner Books, 2003.

Bibliography of Works about Author

Alnor, Jackie. "'Christ Clone' trilogy," *Christian Sentinel* (May 2003). http://cultlink.com/sentinel/ChristClone.htm.
BeauSeigneur, James, Interview. http://www.secp.com/christian-fandom-jbs.html.
Doyle, Tom. "Strange Horizons: Christian Apocalyptic Fiction." http://www.strangehorizons.com/2002/20020408/apocalyptic.html.
Carper, Jay. "A Review of James BeauSeigneur's *The Christ Clone Trilogy*." http://www.historycarper.com/articles/christclone.html.
"James BeauSeigneur." *Contemporary Authors Online.* Detroit: Thomson Gale, 2004.
Mort, John. *Christian Fiction: A Guide to the Genre.* Greenwood Village, CO: Libraries Unlimited, 2002.
Mort, John. Review of *In His Image. Kirkus Reviews* (December 1, 2002): 38.
Mort, John. Review of *Birth of an Age. Kirkus Reviews,* (May 15, 2003): 694.

BELL, JAMES SCOTT

Personal, Professional, and Religious Background

James Scott Bell (1954–) was born in Los Angeles, California, a city he loves and considers home. As he describes Los Angeles, "The sunset over the ocean, silhouette of palm trees against the burnt orange sky, the mountains, the Hollywood Bowl on a warm summer evening.

I guess I am one of the few people who lives here who admits liking it." After finishing high school, Bell attended the University of California at Santa Barbara, where he played basketball and studied for a degree in film. In his senior year, he worked with Raymond Carver and was awarded a prize for a screenplay he wrote.

> We (Christians) live in a world that is sometimes very dark indeed, yet we are not to be tarnished by it, nor afraid. We are to take our stand and show the redemption that is real and near.
>
> —James Scott Bell, Interview with "Faith in Fiction," May 5, 2006

Bell's interest in theatre and in writing took him to New York where he hoped to write for the theatre and to act. He did land some small roles in off-Broadway, and off-off-Broadway. On one trip back to Los Angeles, he met the woman who was to become his wife—an actress herself. On his return to New York, Bell worked on television commercials—making good money for holding up a tray of McDonald's hamburgers. When Bell and Cindy married, they decided that one thespian in the family was enough. Jim enrolled in law school at the University of Southern California, from which he graduated with a J.D. (cum laude) in 1984. He won an award for top student in trial practice.

After graduation, Bell worked for a large law firm, moved to his own practice, and finally decided—after seeing the film *Moonstruck* with his wife—that he really wanted to write. He wrote a number of manuals for lawyers on legal practices while he developed his writing skills, became a columnist for *Christian Communicator* and editor of the monthly newspapers *Trial Excellence* and *DUI Report* as well as *Writer's Digest*.

His great challenge was to learn to write Christian fiction. He studied the genre of Christian fiction and decided that the whole field of Christian thrillers appealed to his tastes and talents. He landed a five-book contract, coauthored a series with **Tracie Peterson,** and discovered the methods for turning adventures and legal knowledge into exciting and inspiring stories.

Major Works and Themes

James Scott Bell has been quite open about his influences, themes, and techniques. He published a book on the craft of writing fiction, displaying his workmanlike approach to the subject. When he needed deeper and more subtle characterization in his stories, he found some of the books he most admired and studied them carefully for the means the authors used to enrich the character portrayal. Just as he approached the law in a logical and careful manner, so he has approached writing. His first novels made heavy use of his legal background and experience. Then, as he began his collaboration with Tracie Peterson in the "Shannon Saga," Bell learned more about the techniques of writing for a Christian audience. These were so successful and the main character so engaging that he continued these stories of an early 20th-century female lawyer in three more books that he wrote without a collaborator.

The Kit Shannon books are about an orphan who goes to live in California with her rich aunt, determined to study the law, a remarkable decision at the time. She subsequently becomes involved in a number of investigations—along with her fellow male students. One of the second series, *A Greater Glory*, includes the real life magician Harry Houdini in the cast of characters and a sequel, *A Higher Justice*, uses Carrie Nation, the famous Prohibitionist activist.

> Early in his acting career, James Scott Bell worked on television commercials—making good money for holding up a tray of McDonald's hamburgers for the camera.

Bell's old favorites, whom he considers the "classics" of the genre, are Dashiell Hammett, Raymond Chandler, Jim Thompson, James Ellroy, Michael Connelly, and John D. MacDonald. He once said that he thought of Raymond Chandler's description of the modern detective: 'Down these mean streets a man must go who is not himself mean, who is neither tarnished nor afraid.'" He then added, "Isn't that exactly what Christians must be? We live in a world that is sometimes very dark indeed, yet we are not to be tarnished by it, nor afraid. We are to take our stand and show the redemption that is real and near."

Bell is willing to take on tough issues—incest, rape, abortion, violence, alcoholism, or drug addiction—but without excessive detail or prurience. He begins with the idea that he has a story to tell, that his characters have to struggle honestly with their conflicts, and that this struggle involves their faith.

Critical Reception

John Mort includes a number of Bell's books in his massive study of Christian fiction, noting that Bell is didactic and sometimes overly simplistic in his characterization of saints and sinners, but finding his plots and his legal expertise entertaining.

Other critics, such as the writer for *Publishers Weekly*, consider his books "techno-thrillers." All of the reviewers admit to being delighted with the pace of his actions, which are cinematic and suspenseful. Tamara Butler calls him "a master of legal suspense" who will appeal to fans of John Grisham. Writing for *Library Journal*, Shawna Saavedra Thorup called *Deadlock*, Bell's book about a Supreme Court justice caught up in the abortion controversy, "a thought-provoking fantasy."

James Scott Bell is still eager to learn more about his craft, is willing to undertake any controversy, knows how to present edgy issues in a manner that appeals to a conservative audience of both men and women, and is likely to remain a strong writer for years to come. He does his homework, builds a compelling plot with believable characters, and presents a balanced and thoughtful case for Christianity.

Awards

Christy Award for Excellence in Christian Fiction for *Final Witness*, 2001.

Bibliography of Novels by Author

The Darwin Conspiracy: The Confessions of Sir Max Busby. Nashville, TN: Broadman & Holmes, 1995.
Circumstantial Evidence. Nashville, TN: Broadman & Holmes, 1997.
Final Witness. Nashville, TN: Broadman & Holmes, 1999.
Blind Justice. Nashville, TN: Broadman & Holmes, 2000.
The Nephilim Seed. Nashville, TN: Broadman & Holmes, 2001.
Deadlock. Grand Rapids, MI: Zondervan, 2002.
Breach of Promise. Grand Rapids, MI: Zondervan, 2004.
Glimpses of Paradise. Minneapolis, MN: Bethany House, 2005.
Sins of the Fathers. Grand Rapids, MI: Zondervan, 2005.
Presumed Guilty. Grand Rapids, MI: Zondervan, 2006.
No Legal Grounds. Grand Rapids, MI: Zondervan, 2007.
The Whole Truth. Grand Rapids, MI: Zondervan, 2008.

"Shannon Saga" series (with Tracie Peterson). All published by Broadman & Holmes
Angels Flight, 2001.
City of Angels, 2001.
Angels of Mercy, 2002.
"The Trials of Kit Shannon" series. All published by Bethany House.
A Greater Glory, 2003.
A Higher Justice, 2003.
A Certain Truth, 2004.

James Scott Bell has also written books on writing (*Plot and Structure: Techniques and Exercises for Crafting a Plot That Grips Readers from Start to Finish*—published by Writers Digest Books of Cincinnati, 2004) and on legal procedures and is the editor of the monthly newspapers *Trial Excellence* and *California DUI Report*, a contributing editor to *Writers Digest*, and a contributing writer for *Teachers in Focus* and *Writers Digest* magazines and for *Multnomah Quarterly*.

Bibliography of Works about Author

Bell, James Scott. Interview with "Faith in Fiction." http://www.faithinfiction.blogspot.com/2006/05/interview-with-james-scott-bel.html.

Bell, James Scott, Interview with C.J. Darlington. http://www.titletrakk.com/James_Scott_Bell_Interview.html.

Bell, James Scott. Web site for author. http://www.jamesscottbell.com.

"James Scott Bell." *Contemporary Authors Online*. Detroit: Thomson Gale, 2007.

Butler, Tamara. Review of *A Certain Truth*. *Library Journal* (June 1, 2004): 54.

Mort, John. *Christian Fiction: A Guide to the Genre*. Greenwood Village, CO: Libraries Unlimited, 2002.

Lott, Jeremy. Review of *The Nephilim Seed*. *Christianity Today* (February 4, 2002): 87.

Thorup, Shawna Saavedra. Review of *A Greater Glory*. *Library Journal* (February 1, 2003): 68

BERRY, WENDELL

Personal, Professional, and Religious Background

Wendell Erdman Berry (1934–) was born in Henry County, Kentucky, during the Great Depression. His father and grandfather taught him to farm the land that his family had lived on and worked since before the Civil War. He grew up watching the agricultural transition from the deliberate pace of mules and horses to the reckless speed of tractors and combines, a change he deplores. As he told Kimberly Smith, "I began my life as the old times and the last of the old-time people were dying out."

As a boy, he went with his grandfather to the local Baptist Church. Although he was baptized at the New Castle Baptist Church and is still technically a Baptist, over the years his relationship with the church has become difficult. In his Sabbath poems, he describes Sundays when he walks in fields or woods rather than worshipping in the Port Royal Baptist Church, which he sometimes attends with his family. Like his character Jaber Crow, he tends to sit near the door. Kyle Childress says of him that he is "a farmer and not a pastor." Nonetheless, Berry's work is permeated with a

> An essayist is, literally, a writer who attempts to tell the truth. Preachers must resign themselves to being either right or wrong; an essayist, when proved wrong, may claim to have been "just practicing."

> I confess that I have not invariably been comfortable in front of a pulpit; I have never been comfortable behind one.
>
> —Wendell Berry in "Christianity and the Survival of Creation," *Cross Currents*

sense of the holy, insightful meditations on Scripture, and stern disagreements with some of his fellow Christians.

Berry graduated from the University of Kentucky (A.B., 1956; M.A., 1957). He married Tanya Amys in 1957, a marriage he celebrates frequently in his novels as a major blessing in his life. After his marriage, he studied creative writing at Stanford University with Wallace Stenger and then traveled for a year in Europe, returning to write and teach in New York. At this point, the Berrys decided to move back to Kentucky, where he bought a small, marginal farm. His friends thought him insane, but he was committed to a settled existence, reclaiming the land, working it with horses and mules, living a self-sustaining existence on just enough land for one family to manage without machinery.

The 125-acre homestead, Lane's Landing, is near Port Royal, Kentucky, in north-western Kentucky, on the banks of the Kentucky River, close to where it joins the Ohio River. In the early years on the farm, in the 1970s and 1980s, Berry edited and wrote for the Rodale Press, especially its publication *Organic Gardening and Farming* and *The New Farm*. From time to time, he has left briefly to teach or lecture, returning to the English Department at the University of Kentucky in 1987. He insists though that he is not hungry for intellectual companionship; he hears better stories and more colorful language in the tobacco barn than on a college campus.

Tanya Berry, his wife, is active in the church, serving as a church deacon and a board member of the Kentucky Baptist Seminary in Lexington, apparently not so uncomfortable with the theology as her husband. She types up the manuscripts that he writes laboriously by hand, and tells him what she thinks about them. As Wendell Berry noted in his essay in *Harpers*, and explained in a later essay in *Crosscurrents* ("Feminism, the Body, and the Machine"), neither he nor Tanya sees this relationship as exploitation. He insists that there are still some married couples "who understand themselves as belonging to their marriage, to each other, and to their children. What they have they have in common, and so, to them, helping each other does not seem to damage their ability to compete with each other. To them, 'mine' is not so powerful or necessary a pronoun as 'ours.'"

Wendell Berry describes writing, for him, as a "walker's art." "Going off to the woods, I take a pencil and some paper (*any* paper—a small notebook, and old envelope, a piece of a feed sack), and I am as well equipped for my work as the president of IBM." As he expresses it, "My mind is free to go with my feet."

Berry and his family continue to live on and work the family farm in Port Royal, Kentucky. They have a son and a daughter, Pryor Clifford and Mary Dee, and now enjoy showing their grandchildren how to clean a barn. Berry still identifies himself as a farmer, but he has also held a number of academic appointments at universities, including Stanford University, where he was the Wallace Stenger writing fellow (1958–59) and lecturer (1959–60), and visiting professor (1968–69); New York University, where he was lecturer (1962–64); the University of Kentucky, faculty member (1964–70) and distinguished professor of English (1971–72), professor of English (1973–77, 1987–93). Since 1973 he has called himself simply "farmer."

He writes about the Kentucky towns in which he has lived, touching only tangentially on the colleges that have been such a large part of his life. He is a curious blend of agrarian and Christian, finding his calling in his writing.

Major Works and Themes

Over the years, Wendell Berry has been very clear about his ideas. He has expressed them in fiction, nonfiction, in novels, short stories, poems, essays, speeches, and interviews. He has written over 40 books of fiction, biography, and poetry. Although he often writes of Port William, his mythical version of Port Royal, his ideas engage the modern world and its discontents.

Early on, Wendell Berry decided it was important to belong somewhere. "To feel at home in a place, you have to have some prospect of staying there," says Jaber Crow. He admires the Amish for their strong commitment to a place, a community, and a simple way of life.

Berry's own commitment to rural Kentucky parallels his commitment to his wife. He sees the "sacred bonds between man and the land, of the marriage of husband to his literal and mystic wife." To know the land thoroughly, to reclaim what has been damaged and to serve as a steward to what it provides, a person must limit himself to a few acres and resolve to dedicate himself to them.

Work is essential for happiness, and that work must be useful to provide dignity. It must provide opportunities for independence, creativity, and a sense of worth. For Berry, the real horror of modern industrial society is the trivialization of work. People employed by large corporations are often subservient, their work repetitive and tedious. By contrast, farming the land engages the whole being, ties the worker to the history of the place, allows him to make his own decisions, to see progress, to enjoy the fruits of his labor.

Out of this conversation with the land grows the community that Berry cherishes, a settled community of people who know one another, remember events, have a history together. Like a family, they tease one another, share sorrows, understand one another's pain and joy. Suffering is a very real part of life, as is the ceremony by which the community deals with loss. Love is also a rich component in Berry's world, a love of men for women, of parents for children, of friends for one another, and of all for the land that sustains them.

Jaber Crow is one of Berry's most powerful expressions of his ideas. Jaber attends seminary, but rejects the ministry, in part because of what Norman Wirzba calls a "discarnate form of Christianity." Jaber's objections to orthodox Christianity, include selective literal interpretation of Scripture, public prayers, and belief in the resurrection of the flesh while denying the beauty of the physical, natural life. Both Berry and Crow love the Gospels, but have real problems with some of Paul's epistles. This kind of fundamentalism, which they see in much of American Christianity, is a kind of Gnosticism. Berry cannot understand how Christians can love this earth and God's good creation while denying the flesh.

Wendell Berry's pacifism grows out of his hatred of mechanization. He sees much of warfare as an extension of dehumanization. In his manifesto *Blessed Are the Peacemakers: Christ's Teachings about Love, Compassion & Forgiveness* (2005), he makes this explicit. He also makes explicit his love of Christ and his dislike for the Christian Church in America. Fellowship built on natural relations seems more in keeping with Berry's sense of communion than the kind he sees in most churches.

Berry's Jeffersonian commitment to agrarianism—his hatred of machines, mass production, the despoliation of the earth, of cities, warfare, and big business, his individualism and outspoken defense of his views—these intrinsic qualities of his life and thought have made him the darling of some critics and an adversary of others. His meditations on these themes force even his fiercest critics to consider his gentle and rational point of view—that God made the earth and called it "good," that humankind was created out of both dust and the breath of God, that man was given stewardship over the earth, not a permit to exploit it.

Critical Reception

Nathan Coulter (1960), which was Wendell Berry's first novel in the Port William Membership series, won praise from numerous critics. Some compared his intensely felt setting to Faulkner's Yoknapatawpha County, Mississippi, and Sherwood Anderson's Winesburg, Ohio. *The Los Angeles Times* described the Coulter family, who "like the rest of the people who dwell in this tiny farming community . . . are caught on the wheel of nature, which is at once blindingly beautiful and unwittingly cruel." The reviewer also noted that "the narrative is stunning, the natural scene is beautifully evoked." This novel, which Berry had written during his graduate studies, introduces the community of Port William through the eyes of Nathan Coulter, a farmer who remembers his own boyhood, his family, and his beginnings. Later, Berry continued this rich narrative by giving his full attention to Nathan's wife, Hannah, a young war widow with a small child.

A Place on Earth tells of the losses and gains that came to Port William with the Second World War. In this story, some of Berry's favorite characters, the Feltners, Burley Coulter, Jayber Crow, and Jack Beechum, respond to the pain of Vergil Feltner's fate in World War II; this beloved son and husband is "missing in action" in Europe. His young widow, Hannah, who later becomes Hannah Coulter, completes the story in the later narrative of her life.

The Memory of Old Jack takes place in Jack Beechum's ageing mind. At ninety-two, this old farmer, who has respected his land, his neighbors, and his family, sits on the porch of the town's ancient hotel, which now serves as a kind of old folks' home, and remembers his life. His slow progress through the town reveals the loving concern of the entire community as they watch for him, care for him, feed him, and love him for who he is and what he represents. The novel embodies Berry's theory of the accidental community, not the family, which forms around settled people, providing them comfort and sustenance through all of their lives.

The great favorite of these novels, with many readers, is *Jayber Crow: The Life Story of Jayber Crow, Barber, of the Port William Membership, as Written by Himself.* This bachelor barber, who becomes the center of much of the community activity, is a thoughtful critic of the town and its people. His very ordinary life is full of extraordinary insights and events. He makes few claims on the people, is content to love a woman he can never marry, share friendships he never fully articulates, and live out his last days in a cabin he does not own. This novel appeared several times in a listing of the favorite fiction of a number of modern religious leaders that appeared in *WORLD Magazine* (June 2006). Its gentle criticism and wry humor stimulate and engage readers who follow this unlikely hero through his idiosyncratic life.

In *That Distant Land*, Berry arranges a number of his stories in chronological order, helping those readers who originally read them as they emerged from his pen. In this collection, he provides a map of the region and family trees, revealing his intricate and rich conception of his few square miles of Kentucky with its blend of farmers, bankers, tradespeople, lawyers, barbers, and housewives. He knows their history, the streams and forests on their land, the mules that pull their plows, and the kinds of cars they keep in their barns.

From the beginning of his career, Wendell Berry has been recognized by critics as a major talent, full of ideas and insights, blessed with a sensitivity to people, to the land, and to words.

His prose has been hailed as beautiful, redolent of Scripture and traditional literature, yet spare and elegant. He circles around his narrative, picturing his characters from various perspectives, entering their minds and recounting their histories, characterizing them by their gestures, choices, words, and the totality of their lives.

Awards

Wendell Berry has been recognized for his remarkable creativity and productivity over the years. He has won both the Guggenheim Fellowship and Rockefeller Fellowships, the Jean Stein Award, the T.S. Eliot Award, the 2000 Poets' Prize, the Thomas Merton Award, 1999, the Aiken Taylor Award for poetry, the John Hay Award, the Art of Fact Award, 2006 for nonfiction, and the Kentuckian of the Year 2006 Award from *Kentucky Monthly*, for his writing and his efforts to bring attention to environmental issues in eastern Kentucky.

Bibliography of Novels by Author

Nathan Coulter: A Novel. Boston: Houghton Mifflin, 1960.

A Place on Earth: A Novel. New York: Harcourt, 1967, revised 1983.

The Memory of Old Jack. New York: Harcourt, 1974.

The Wild Birds: Six Stories of the Port William Membership. Berkeley, CA: North Point Press, 1986.

Remembering: A Novel. Berkeley, CA: North Point Press, 1988.

Fidelity: Five Stories. New York: Pantheon, 1992.

Watch with Me: And Six Other Stories of the Yet-Remembered Ptolemy Proudfoot and His Wife, Miss Minnie, Née Quinch. New York: Pantheon, 1994.

A World Lost. Washington, D.C.: Counterpoint, 1996.

Two More Stories Of The Port William Membership. Frankfort, KY: Gnomon Press, 1997.

Jayber Crow: The Life Story of Jayber Crow, Barber of the Port William Membership as Written by Himself. Washington, D.C.: Counterpoint Press, 2000.

Three Short Novels: Nathan Coulter; Remembering; A World Lost. Washington, D.C.: Counterpoint Press, 2002.

Hannah Coulter: A Novel. Washington, D.C.: Shoemaker & Hoard, 2004.

That Distant Land: The Collected Stories of Wendell Berry. Washington, D.C.: Counterpoint Press, 2004.

Andy Catlett: Early Travels. Emeryville, CA: Shoemaker & Hoard, 2006.

Bibliography of Works about Author

Angyal, Andrew. *Wendell Berry*. New York: Twayne, 1995.

Berry, Wendell. "Christianity and the Survival of Creation," *Crosscurrents*. http://www.crosscurrents.org/berry.htm.

Berry, Wendell. "Feminism, the Body, and the Machine." excerpted from *The Art of the Commonplace*, Norman Wirzba, ed. *Crosscurrents*. http://www.crosscurrents.org/berryspring2003.htm.

Berry, Wendell. "Life Is a Miracle: An Essay Against Modern Superstition." Review in *Eco Books*. http://ecobooks.com/books/fifemiracle.htm.

Brockman, Holly M. "How Can a Family 'live at the center of its own attention'?": Wendell Berry's Thoughts on the Good Life. *New Southerner*. January/February 2006. http://www.newsoutherner.com/Wendell_Berry_interview.htm.

Childress, Kyle. "Good Work: Learning about Ministry from Wendell Berry." *Look Smart*. http://www.findarticles.com/p.articles/mi_m1058/is_5_ai_n13493345/.

Goodrich, Janet. *The Unforeseen Self in the Works of Wendell Berry.* Columbia: University of Missouri Press, 2001.

McEntyre, John E. "Practicing Resurrection: Community and Continuity in Wendell Berry's *A Place on Earth.*" *Look Smart.* http://findarticles.comp/articles/mi_qa3664/aii_n87329/.

Merchant, Paul, ed. *Wendell Berry (American Authors Series).* Lewiston, Idaho: Confluence, 1991.

Peters, Jason. *Wendell Berry: Life and Work.* Lexington: University of Kentucky Press, 2007.

Smith, Kimberly. *Wendell Berry and the Agrarian Tradition: A Common Grace.* Lawrence: University Press of Kansas, 2003.

"Wendell (Erdman) Berry," *Contemporary Authors Online.* Detroit: Thompson Gale, 2005.

"Wendell Berry." *Wikipedia.* http://en.wikipedia.org/wiki/Wendelll_Berry.

BETTS, DORIS

Personal, Professional, and Religious Background

Doris Waugh (1932–) was born in Statesville, North Carolina. Her father, William Elmore Waugh, and her mother, Mary Ellen Freeze Waugh, were born on farms in Iredell County. Her father was an adopted child who did not meet his own "real mother" until he was an adult. Doris Waugh's parents had married young and worked for a time in the Statesville cotton mill. Although he was not a bookish person, William Waugh could transform the mundane events of his day in his storytelling. These "yeomen" and their plain, hard lives in the mill and on the land gave their daughter, the budding writer, a sensitivity to ordinary people who find delight and tragedy in their circumscribed existence.

Both of Doris Waugh's parents encouraged her interest in books, eagerly supplying her with novels and encyclopedias. Mary Ellen Baugh, a member of the Associate Reformed Presbyterian Church (ARP), was a strict believer in Calvinist theology, and a stern critic of the gaudy covers of Western best-sellers. William Waugh followed his wife into this church, becoming a Sunday school teacher, an elder, and the church treasurer. A small, conservative denomination, the ARP is noted for its well educated male clergy and its profound love of scripture, especially the Psalms. Although Doris Betts was to abandon this denomination, for a time becoming an "unaffiliated Theist," then an agnostic, and finally a recovering Calvinist, she remembers it as "not as fundamentalist as I perceived it when I was a rebellious adolescent." She notes the leavening of her church's stern theology by kindness and by the songs, "good songs." Eventually she joined the "mainstream" Presbyterian Church U.S.A., where she serves as an elder. She notes that she teaches Sunday school and is an organist, "but I play poorly. In a small church everybody has to pitch in."

The growing child discovered the Statesville public library, which her mother used for free babysitting from time to time. Although she was not permitted to check out adult novels, she could read them undisturbed by the hour in the quiet study rooms. The most influential of Doris Betts's early books was the classic by Hurlbut, *Story of the Bible for Young and Old*, a lively retelling of the story of God's people and his plan for them. This, in combination with the King James translation of the Bible and her regular attendance at the Associate Reformed Presbyterian Church meeting infused her life and thought with imagery, stories, and a worldview

> The Bible, from the creation story onwards, is a cornucopia of language.
>
> —Doris Betts, "Everything I Know about Writing I Learned in Sunday School"

that informs all of her work. She often responds to the questions about her ideas for fiction by noting, "Bible stories, beyond question" (Elizabeth Evans 1997, 4). One of her fullest explanations of this impact on her work appeared in *The Christian Century* when Betts was named the winner of the Presbyterian Writer Award for 1998. It is entitled "Everything I know about Writing I Learned in Sunday School." Even today, she sees herself as a pilgrim, insisting that faith is not synonymous with certainty.

> When Doris Betts was being promoted to full professor at Chapel Hill, in spite of being a woman without a college degree, one of her colleagues inquired hopefully if she had at least graduated from high school.

Doris Waugh attended the Women's College of the University of North Carolina (now the University of North Carolina at Greensboro) for three years, from 1950–55, before dropping out to marry a law student—Lowry Matthews Betts. They had two of their three children while he was still in college. Lowry Betts completed his degree at the University of South Carolina (in art and philosophy) before moving to Chapel Hill for law school. After graduation, he joined the firm of Pittman and Staton as an attorney and later was elected a district judge, serving as a judge until his retirement.

During these years as a new wife and mother, Doris Betts tried to keep her talent for writing alive. The year that they moved to Chapel Hill, she won the *Mademoiselle* College Fiction Contest with her story "Mr. Shawn and Father Scott." Doris Betts believes that the experience she has shared with other women has made her a better writer. In her essay "Daughters, Southerners, and Daisy," she notes the weariness that comes to the writer-mother: "Listen, kid, you're going to be tired, and as soon as you've gotten the best sentence you've ever written, the baby will cry or vomit."

Even when her children were young, Betts worked part-time as a journalist, on the staff of the *Statesville Daily Record* (1950–51), the *Chapel Hill Weekly and News-Leader* (1953–54) and as a member of the editorial staff of the *Sanford Daily Herald* (1956–57), and the *North Carolina Democrat* (1966–74). By then, Betts was recognized for her abilities and, in spite of her lack of a college degree was invited to join the faculty of the University of North Carolina at Chapel Hill. She served there for the rest of her career, rising from lecturer to full professor, heading the freshman composition program, teaching creative writing, serving as assistant dean of the honors program, and becoming the chairperson of the faculty. In 1983, she was named the Alumni Distinguished Professor. Her outstanding abilities as a teacher and a writer have led her to speak and teach all over the country at seminars and conferences.

Now that their children are grown and have their own children, the Bettses have moved to an 80-acre farm in Chatham County, where they raise Arabian horses. Both are now retired, she from her university professorship and he from his role as district judge of Chatham and Orange Counties. As for her faith, she acknowledges that "for me faith was always going to be a pilgrimage."

Major Works and Themes

Doris Betts describes herself not as a Christian writer or a feminist writer but as a regional writer. She has rejected both the "superficial fictions" of modern evangelical writers and the prevailing mode of deconstructionism preferred by many academic writers. The Christian romance novels she classifies as "piously moral for all of the soft pornography in them." She

believes that the writers are pandering to audiences who want everyone to get their just deserts. She prefers those authors who ask hard questions and learn to live with ambiguity, liking
"content wedded to an excellent style."

She is fond of many of the moderns, including **Gail Godwin, Graham Greene,** and John
Irving; but she considers her own writing most closely akin to that of **Flannery O'Connor** and
Walker Percy. Like Flannery O'Connor and Carson McCullers, she loves the peculiar, the
eccentric, the frustrated, or the mad—what Gerard Manley Hopkins called "speckled things."
She firmly believes that God loves the sparrows, the people with limited lives who experience
prosaic grace. Though she often portrays the disfigured misfits of the community, she is not
really gothic in tone. Sam, the horribly abused child in *The Sharp Teeth of Love,* is handled
realistically, his future left ambivalent. While presenting a 12-year-old who has little memory
of his parents or siblings, and who has been sold to a sexual predator and mutilated for profit,
she also refuses to accept the judgment that he is "ruint." With love, he may survive.

Betts has great faith in the power of love. Although she is suspicious of the devouring love of
a mother or the selfish love of a wife, she does believe that the kind of long-suffering love that
Paul describes in 1 Corinthians can redeem people. The soldiers who accidentally join up with
the "Ugliest Pilgrim" make her shout with delight, "Praise God!"

Betts portrays human sexuality here and in other stories—such as *The River to Pickle
Beach*—as a kind of sacrament, the human potential for communion and communication. She
appears to lament the loss of the sacramental aspect of marriage with the Reformation. For
her characters, words often fail, but their bodies can express the love and need their tongues
cannot pronounce.

Like Walker Percy, she shows her inarticulate characters discovering language and imagery
in movies, allowing her characters to see themselves and one another as images in various films.
Without any rich heritage of nurture or education, Betts' characters adjust their imagination to
the familiar landscape of Hollywood. Percy's people tend to be more affluent, more educated,
choosing film as an escape from life or as an alternative means of living, not out of the frustration that Betts's simpler folk suffer.

Doris Betts has also discovered the techniques of Eudora Welty, who loved the traditions
and materials of folk culture. In her tales, she sometimes uses the old-time song fests and pic-
nics, the family gatherings to clean up the cemetery, the rituals of birth and burial. Her family
reunions, with all the crazy-quilt quality of the amazing diversity in ages, background and taste
make these scenes her very best.

She sets her stories firmly in time, relating the micro-events to the macro-world—the assassination of Robert Kennedy or the massacre at Waco. Her own narratives play out against the
flickering television snippets of a larger, more chaotic and frightening world. This technique
provides *The River to Pickle Beach* or *The Sharp Teeth of Love* with more universal meaning—
the darkness of the human heart, the violation of children whom we should nurture and
protect.

At the same time, Betts often includes an other-worldly aspect to her tales, the haunting
by the dead or even ghosts of historical figures. The spirit of Tansen Donner or of a mother-
in-law or a neighbor appears in dreams, in apparitions, in visions at the final moments of life.
Her strange story of the death of Benson Watts suggests that the spirits of the dead wander the
earth for some time before they disappear. Betts attributes this interest in "double-exposure"
to a curious experience she once had of re-living a moment at 24 1/2 that she had previously
known at 17, being both ages at once.

BETTS, DORIS   39

Betts writes from a religious background, but without a religious agenda. Biblical allusions pepper her pages, inform her plots and symbols, give resonance to her names and references, but she resists any explicit pronouncements about her beliefs. As she tells those who inquire about her faith, she is of the "Tribe of Thomas." She wants to see, to touch the resurrected Christ to confirm her faltering hope in the truth of Christianity. When, after the modest success of her first two novels, her editor at Putnam encouraged her to write Christian novels, she firmly refused even though she knew that her sales would skyrocket.

Her rejection of the stern Calvinism of her early years in the Associate Presbyterian Church is apparent in her stories. She is also clearly suspicious of the evangelists whose televised healing ministries give false hope to thousands of poor, ignorant country people. In "The Ugliest Pilgrim," she pictures a young woman who has been brutally disfigured by an accident in which an axe blade flew directly into her face, destroying an eye and leaving a deep scar. Strangers stare at her for a moment and then turn away in disgust. She hopes for a miraculous transformation by a preacher she has watched on television. In preparation for her trip to his headquarters, she has researched all of the biblical examples of healing ministries, clearly lining them up with her own request. The "healer's" staff turn the poor pilgrim away, not even allowing her to meet her anticipated savior. She finds her "salvation" in a pair of soldiers who love her for her spirit, her delight in poker, and her openness to all experience.

Doris Betts's plots are never simple. Her ideas are informed by a massive background of reading, her characters are idiosyncratic and funny, and her books are compelling. The theme of love and human happiness permeates her work. Selfish love becomes the sin that eats away at families and destroys the children. Her uneducated people understand that the abundant life comes with the willingness to love without conditions.

Doris Betts sees the job of literature not as preaching but as exploring the fundamental questions everybody faces. The good writer redeems the time, giving transcendence to the mundane. Although many Christian readers argue that her treatment of sexuality is excessive, she responds that "God made the pleasures." She sees it as her obligation to explore all of the delights of nature, children, animals, and sex. Readers will find her stories challenging and rewarding.

Critical Reception

Doris Betts is better known for her short stories than her novels. Her first prize, from *Mademoiselle* magazine, was for a short story. Her only Academy Award was for a version of "The Ugliest Pilgrim," revised and scripted by Brian Crawley as *Violet*. Critics often note that her novels seem more like a collection of short stories than as integrated narratives.

Critics have also noted her talent for describing isolation and the hunger for love. Whether it is the poor "pinheads," as the retarded mother and child in *Pickle Beach* are called, or the brutal ex-G.I. who shoots them, Betts tries to understand her characters and enter into their motivation.

The River to Pickle Beach won some praise for her "fascinating characters" that "come to life with a few vivid, beautifully selective strokes" according to William Peden. A later novel, *Souls Raised from the Dead*, struck Stephen P. Miss as a "modern parable." Other writers, like Jill Pelaez Baumgaertner, consider it a powerful presentation of a parent's worst nightmare, pushing the "reader beyond catharsis to reconciliation."

Her story of an artist heading west with her fiancé, *The Sharp Teeth of Love*, has won a number of rave reviews. Barbara Bennett sees it is as a modern-day version of Franz Kafka's

"A Hunger Artist," and others have noted her amazing use and abuse of food and humor in this modern survival tale. She has been criticized for her sharp divisions of narrative—a technique she enjoys and uses frequently.

Jonathan Yardley has been one of her most faithful reviewers, finding from the beginning that she transcends geographic labeling. Michael Mewshaw, in the *New York Times Book Review*, however, thinks she echoes the Southern gothics—"the grotesque, black humor, surrealism and fantasy." Yardley and Betts herself reject this label. This writer is far too realistic in her details and characterization to fit the Southern gothic category. Her work does deal with dreams and fantasies, but she also has a "great deal to say about human relations, the gulf between young and old, and about love and understanding or the lack of it," according to H.T. Kane in the *Chicago Sunday Tribune*.

Awards

Doris Betts won the short-story prize for *Mademoiselle's* College Fiction Contest, in 1953, for "Mr. Shawn and Father Scott." Her collection of short stories, *Beasts of the Southern Wild and Other Stories*, was a National Book Award finalist in 1974. She also won the Medal of Merit from the Academy of Arts and Letters in 1989 for short stories. In addition, she has won the G.P. Putman-University of North Carolina Fiction Award for *The Gentle Insurrection* (1954), the Sir Walter Raleigh Award for Fiction, the Historical Book Club of North Carolina Award for *Tall Houses in Winter* (1967) and *The Scarlet Thread* (1965). She won a Guggenheim fellowship in fiction (1958–59), and numerous other awards for her writing and her community service. *Violet*, the musical version of "The Ugliest Pilgrim," won the 1998 New York Drama Critics Circle Award.

Although she has won numerous North Carolina and national awards for her work, many of her former students and fans who love her lament she is not as well known or received as she deserves.

Bibliography of Novels by Author

Tall Houses in Winter. New York: Putnam, 1957.
The Scarlet Thread. New York: New York: Harper, 1964.
The Astronomer and Other Stories. New York: Harper, 1966.
The River to Pickle Beach. New York: Harper, 1972.
Beasts of the Southern Wild and Other Stories. New York: Harper, 1973.
Heading West. New York: Knopf, 1994.
The Gentle Insurrection and Other Stories, 2nd ed. Baton Rouge: Louisiana State University Press, 1997.
The Sharp Teeth of Love. New York: Knopf, 1997.

Bibliography of Works about Author

Baumgaertner, Jill Pelaez. Review of *Souls Raised from the dead*. "Suffer the Little Children." *Christian Century* (October 12, 1993): 927.
Bennett, Barbara. Review of *The Sharp Teeth of Love. The Review of Contemporary Fiction* (Summer, 2007).
Betts, Doris. "Everything I Know about Writing I Learned in Sunday School." http://www.religion-online.org.

Betts, Doris. "Flannery O'Connor's Sacramental Art." *Church History* (June 21, 2006).

"Betts, Doris." *Contemporary Authors Online.* Detroit: Thomson Gale, 2005.

Brown, W. Dale. *Of Fiction and Faith: Twelve American Writers Talk about Their Vision and Work.* Grand Rapids, MI: William B. Eerdmans Publishing Company, 1997.

Bush, Trudy. Review of *Sharp Teeth of Love. Christian Century* (October 8, 1997).

Ends, Martha Greene. "Sex, Money, and Food as Spiritual Signposts in Doris Betts' *Sharp Teeth of Love.*" *Christianity and Literature* (July 14, 2006).

Evans, Elizabeth. *The Home Truth of Doris Betts.* Twayne's United States Authors Series No 689. New York: Twayne Publishers, 1997.

Howard, Jennifer. "Doris Betts." *Publishers Weekly* (April 25, 1994): 42–43.

Ketchin, Susan. "Doris Betts: Resting on the Bedrock of Original Sin." In *The Christ-Haunted Landscape: Faith and Doubt in Southern Literature.* Jackson: University of Mississippi Press, 1994.

Mewshaw, Michael. "Surrealism and Fantasy." Review of *Beasts of the Southern Wild. New York Times Book Review*, October 28, 1973.

Miss, Stephen P. Review of *Souls Raised from the Dead. America*, October 15, 1994.

Peden, William. "Myth, Magic, and a Touch of Madness." Review of *The Scarlet Thread. Saturday Review* (February 6, 1965): 32.

Yardley, Jonathan. "Best Betts Yet." Review of *Beasts of the Southern Wild. Washington Post Book World,* October 7, 1973.

Yardley, Jonathan. Review of *The River to Pickled Beach. New York Times Book Review,* May 21, 1972: 12.

Yardley, Jonathan. "The Librarian and the Highwayman." Review of *Heading West. Washington Post Book World*, November 21, 1981: 3.

BLACKSTOCK, TERRI

Personal, Professional, and Religious Background

Terri Blackstock (1957–) was born in Belleville, Illinois, where she lived only a few months. Her father, O.L. Ward, Jr., an Air Force colonel and airline pilot, and his wife, Jo Ann Weathersby, a secretary, moved from one military base to another through her early years. Terri attended high school in Jackson, Mississippi, where she was an average student.

Blackstock was an English major in college, starting at Hinds Junior College. She earned a B.A. from Northeast Louisiana University in 1981, proving herself a straight A student in college. Her first marriage and her first children came soon afterwards. An untold part of her life is hinted at in her postscript to *Emerald Windows* (2001). She notes that she joined her current church "10 years ago," when she was a "broken, grieving, divorced mother of two." She notes that her pastor, Frank Pollard, and his flock embraced her and drew her into a "healing place." Since that time, she has become active in the Baptist church, remarried, and has another daughter. She often mentions her second husband, Ken Blackstock, in her credits. Terri Blackstock began writing by the time she was 12 years old, publishing her first poem, which was about Vietnam, in her local newspaper. Twelve years later, she wrote her first novel, but could not find a publisher until 1983, when she sold a novel to Silhouette Books, later turning

> Over the next few years we will see Christian fiction catching up with secular fiction, and the Christian best-seller list will look more like the secular best-seller list. The difference will be that readers—Christian and non-Christian alike—will know that they can buy our books and not be offended by gratuitous sex and violence or profanity.
>
> —Terri Blackstock in interview with Janice DeLong and Rachel Schwedt

Terri Blackstock began her writing career as a romance writer in 1983, going on to write 32 novels in this genre in the next decade, before turning to Christian fiction. Her work for Harlequin won her a wide readership—three and a half million of her books are in print world-wide.

to Dell Publishers and Harlequin, printing these romances under pseudonyms: Terri Herrington, Tracy Hughes.

The year 1994 signaled a major change in Blackstock's writing career. She turned from romances to suspense novels, saying: "I found that those were the books I most liked to read. I loved the idea of a ticking bomb and ordinary people in jeopardy. I decided I wanted to write those types of stories instead." She wanted to speak forthrightly about her faith, the roots of the problems that people face, and the ultimate solutions. "I also wanted to speak to Christians about forsaking their first love, being lukewarm, making wrong choices, God's provision for their mistakes. . . . These are all things I've had to learn the hard way, and I'd like to pass them on to my readers now." As it turned out, she joined the Christian book market at the perfect time and has been a great success with over thirty Christian books to her credit—and millions of readers.

Terri Blackstock's children, "a blended family," Lindsey, Michelle, and Marie, are now grown. She can give her time to church activities and to her writing. In recent years, she and Beverly LaHaye became the founders of Concerned Christian Women for America. Blackstock, like LaHaye, is in great demand as a public speaker and has appeared frequently on television.

She and her husband, Ken Blackstock, now make their home in Clinton, Mississippi, near Jackson. As she told a student from the local high school who interviewed her: "I moved to Mississippi when I was eleven, and though I did move away for a time, I came back because I love it. The people are warm and kind, the days are sunny and usually warm, and it has been a great place to raise children. The southern culture is very rich and offers lots to write about, which is why so many writers come from the South."

She continues to write about "flawed Christians in crisis and God's provisions for their mistakes and wrong choices." She looks back at her own life and claims to be "extremely qualified to write such books."

Major Works and Themes

Terri Blackstock began her writing career as a romance writer in 1983, going on to write 32 novels in this genre. Her works for Harlequin won her a wide readership—3 1/2 million of her books in print world-wide. They also won her numerous prizes, beginning in 1986, and continuing until she closed that chapter in her life. In 1994 she undertook the writing of Christian suspense novels. She determined to "tell the truth in my stories." She now wants to "change the lives of my readers for the better."

In addition to a number of individual stories, such as *Sweet Delights: For Love of Money* and *Seaside: A Novella*, she has written three series: "Suncoast Chronicles" (1995–1999); "Second Chances" (1996–1998), and "Newpointe 911" (1998–present). In 2005, she published the first in her "Restoration" series, *Last Light*. The "Seasons" series, with Beverly LaHaye, began in 1999 with *Seasons under Heaven* and have continued, with the most recent being *Season of Blessing* (2002). John Mort notes that the "Second Chances" series reveals Blackstock's "crossover" to Christian fiction; it is a series of novels that rework her old romance themes and plots into Christian romances. In these, the characters are disappointed men and women who decide to give love another chance.

Terri Blackstock most often selects a group of Southern middleclass, educated, prosperous, suburban people who are nominal Christians. She then tests them with some catastrophe or shock. *Last Light*, for example, begins with an electromagnetic pulse in the atmosphere that shuts down all the electricity and electronics over the globe. The people then have to learn how to cope without all their normal lavish provisions—telephones, watches, washing machines, running water, refrigerators, and stoves. Eventually, they have to rediscover the older ways of doing things and the older values of faith and community. The Scripture message at the heart of the novel—which explains the larger message of the events—is that we should not take thought for what we eat or drink or wear, but allow the Lord to handle all of these things.

Her novels have fairly simple plots, often opening with a decision or catastrophe that forces the characters to respond and reconsider their lives. In the course of sorting out responses to the problem, solving the mystery, or choosing their proper path, they discover deep truths about themselves, their faith, and their relationships. The novels are fast-paced, involving the standard scenes of violence, intrigue, hidden motives, dangerous encounters, romance, misunderstanding, and reconciliation.

Terri Blackstock's God is a very personal one, who responds to earnest prayer, blesses relationships, and elicits rich feelings of love and joy. Blackstock does challenge the reader in stories like *Word of Honor* to consider the complex nature of covenants, relying heavily on a variety of biblical accounts of covenants and the obligations they place on the participants.

Her characters, like her settings, are contemporary and easily understood. Her slim, lovely heroines have names like Brooke, Blaire, or Tiffany. Her heroes are tall and athletic, sensitive to women's concerns. They all sound like the generation of which she is a part—and match the tastes of her avid readers.

Blackstock does much of her research on the Internet, reading biographies of famous people to try to understand the nature of their challenges and dreams. Often she places a young woman as the center of consciousness, providing most of the intrigue and suspense. A talented artist with a scent of disgrace must come to terms with her family, her town, and her attractive art teacher. The redemption is clearly in marching ahead, performing with perfection, and prevailing over petty suspicion—the plot of *Emerald Windows*. Blackstock loves dealing with mysteries, mistaken identities, hidden pasts, using her final scenes as revelations of the truth of her characters' background. She ties this revelation to their conversion and regeneration as children of God.

Blackstock cares deeply about relationships between men and women, parents and children. She includes small-town lawyers, doctors, firemen, and ministers in her stories. They tend to know one another, go to the same church, teach one another's children in Sunday school, and share the same values. In some of her thrillers, like the "Newpointe 911" series, the shocker is the interruption of this pleasant Southern life by an act of violence, raising the question of God's love that he allows such anguish among his people.

In an interview regarding *Last Light*, the fifth in the "Newpointe 911" series, Blackstock explained that suspense novels are a "great backdrop for showing common, ordinary people in great mortal danger because of evil coming against them. In such stories, God becomes the hero, not sweeping out of the sky to rescue them," but protecting, comforting, and redeeming them, sometimes in the quiet, surprising ways we are all familiar with. She believes that such cataclysms help people to identify with her characters and become challenged to walk closer with the Lord themselves.

Terri Blackstock and Beverly LaHaye, cofounders of Concerned Christian Women for America, have also written a series of novels that illustrate some of the issues faced by contemporary Christian women, such as marriage to non-Christians, divorce, single motherhood, homeschooling, sex education in the schools, and discipline. Toward the conclusion of one novel, the authors provide a wrap-up, listing the blessings that the community derives from a child's near death experience. They make it quite clear that they consider most large churches too fixated on property and activities, while the small, more evangelical congregations, with their praise songs and prayer sessions, are more flexible and more attuned to the workings of the Holy Spirit. The churches involved in the narrative are Protestant, but only the large Baptist church responds quickly and enthusiastically to the needs of the hurting community. This fellowship of believers seem less concerned with the creeds and the doctrines of the churches than with their ability to minister to people and to reach out to the unchurched with love. Her stories often deal with mission churches, without educated clergy, but filled with the Holy Spirit.

Critical Reception

Gradually winning over the critics to her new writing of Christian romances, Blackstock began with the "Second Chances" series, which are rewrites of some of her earlier successful romance novels published with Silhouette, Harlequin, and Dell. Even with their new Christian messages, they met with some favorable reviews by critics. *Never Again Goodbye*, her first of her new Christian novels, the story of a woman who put her baby up for adoption, only to have a second chance to be that child's mother, received little notice. The second in the series, *When Dreams Cross*, the story of a woman who opens a Christian-themed amusement park, received the lukewarm comment by Melissa Hudak: "While not essential reading, this is still an entertaining romance that should please most readers." John Mort also liked the idea of second chances. *Blind Trust*, more of a love story with a trail of betrayal and mystery, was called "a fun, undemanding thriller." *Broken Wings*, the final novel in the "Second Chances" series, opens with a plane crash. The subsequent investigation results in revelations and romance. Again Hudak liked the novel, noting that it is a "solid if unspectacular romance from the prolific Blackstock."

The "Suncoast Chronicles" are more forthrightly suspense dramas with romantic twists. Published between 1995 and 1997, these four novels are mysteries, sometimes involving her detective Larry Millsap. Christian motives do figure in these largely popular romantic mysteries involving false accusation, sabotage, and abuse.

The "Newpointe 911" series, a set of melodramatic thrillers and mysteries, have overlapping casts of characters and setting. In the first of the series, Mark Branning is a firefighter who is trying to solve the murders of two firemen's wives. Mort noted that, "Blackstock is always workmanlike, but she has a better-than-average opener here, perhaps because it's based on actual murders in her hometown, and perhaps, too, because Mark and Allie's marital difficulties seem real." The next of the series, *Shadow of Doubt*, also deals with murder and scandal. This time, Celia Shepherd is accused of murdering her first husband and attempting to poison her second. The fast-paced action and the surprise ending delighted Hudak, who reviewed the novel for *Library Journal*. *Word of Honor*, which opens with a bombing at the local post office. Jill Clark, an attorney, becomes involved (against her better judgment) in sorting out the crime and the rationale for the cover-up. This time, the theological issue is the actual concept of covenant in Scripture and in practice. Melanie Duncan judged the plot reasonable, but improbable.

In her novel *Seaside*, Blackstock broke her usual pattern, focusing in closely on the tortured relationship between a mother and her estranged daughters. In the course of the story, the young women learn that their mother is dying. She encourages them to search for the meaning in their lives and relationships and to renew their faith in God. Reviewers thought it "predictable" but liked the fully developed women characters and the natural dialogue.

The collaborative efforts of Terri Blackstock and Beverly LaHaye have Blackstock's standard characters and setting, but are rooted in LaHaye's concerns for Christian marriages. (**Tim** and Beverly **LaHaye** had earlier coauthored *The Act of Marriage* [1978], a best-selling self-help book for Christians, which spells out many of their views on women and the family.) These abstract ideas take the form of fictional characters living around a cul-de-sac in a small Southern town, where a group of neighbors struggle with their marriages and share their troubles. *Seasons under Heaven* is the story of four middle class families who are suddenly united in love and concern when a little boy needs a heart transplant. John Mort called the novel a popular tear-jerker. *Sweet Delights: For Love of Money* shows the perils that accompany unexpected wealth, including the tests of faith. Again, the formulaic plot seems too contrived.

Blackstock's recent work, the "Restoration" series, deals with the apocalyptic vision of a world changed forever. Those who survive the opening catastrophe must learn to survive under circumstances they had never contemplated. This science fiction series mirrors the current concern with the Last Days and the role of the believer in the midst of troubled times. Rather than following the pattern of the famous "Left Behind" series by Tim LaHaye, Blackstock portrays a natural catastrophe that catapults humanity back into the days before electricity, transforming the lives of the affluent Alabama characters. Personal, selfish dreams disappear as people are forced to pull together, forming a community of mutual support. Recent world events undoubtedly gave inspiration to Terri Blackstock and others to consider the prospects of a global catastrophe that would reveal the darkness of the human heart and light the way to the restoration of a more loving world.

No critic can keep up with Terri Blackstock's prodigious productivity. At the same time she was at work on two other series of novels, she returned to her old favorite, the mystery novel. Her "Cape Refuge" series disturbs the settled community where everyone expects rest and relaxation with the shock of murder. Critics note that, although the first in the series starts slowly, it quickly picks up its pace and is an example of good writing. Once again she finds pleasure in searching beneath the surface of human relationships to discover the nature of evil and the need for God.

Awards

Terri Blackstock won numerous awards as a writer of romances, culminating in 1987 with the Gold Medallion Award from Romance Writers of America and 1989 with the Lifetime Achievement Award, awarded by *Romance Times* magazine.

Bibliography of Christian Novels by Author

The Heart Reader. Nashville, TN: W Publishing Group, 2000.
The Heart Reader of Franklin High. Nashville, TN: W Publishing Group, 2000.
The Gifted. Nashville. TN: W Publishing Group, 2000.
The Gifted Sophomores. Nashville, TN: W Publishing Group, 2000.

Sweet Delights: For Love of Money. Wheaton, IL: Tyndale House, 2000.
Emerald Windows. Grand Rapids, MI: Zondervan, 2001.
Seaside: A Novella. Grand Rapids, MI: Zondervan, 2001.
Cape Refuge. Grand Rapids, MI: Zondervan, 2002.
Covenant Child. Nashville, TN: W Publishing Group, 2002.

"Suncoast Chronicles" series (1995–1999)

"Second Chances" series (Grand Rapids, MI: Zondervan, 1996–1998)

"Newpointe 911" series (Grand Rapids, MI: Zondervan, 1998–2005)

"Seasons" series, with Beverly LaHaye (Grand Rapids, MI: Zondervan, 1999–2002)

"Restoration" series (Grand Rapids, MI: Zondervan, 2005–2007)

"Cape Refuge" series (Grand Rapids, MI: Zondervan, 2002–2004)

Bibliography of Works about Author

Cuevas, Laci. Interview with Terri Blackstock, Mississippi Writers and Musicians Project of Starkville High School, http://shs.starkville.k12.ms.us/mswm/MSWritersAndMusicians/writers/Black stockTerri/TerriBlackstock.html.

DeLong, Janice and Rachel Schwedt. *Contemporary Christian Authors: Lives and Works.* Lanham, MD: The Scarecrow Press, 2000.

Duncan, Melanie C. Review of *Seaside: A Novella. Library Journal* (September 1, 1999): 172.

Duncan, Melanie C. Review of *Emerald Windows. Library Journal* (February 1, 2001): 75.

Hudak, Melissa. Review of *Blind Trust. Library Journal* (February 1, 1997): 66

Hudak, Melissa. Reviews of *Broken Wings* and *Private Justice. Library Journal* (September 1, 1997): 166.

Hudak, Melissa. Review of *Shadow of Doubt. Library Journal* (February 1, 1998): 70.

Mort, John. *Christian Fiction: A Guide to the Genre.* Greenwood Village, CO: Libraries Unlimited, 2002.

Mort, John. Review of *When Dreams Cross. Booklist* (January 1, 1997): 819.

Mort, John. Review of *Private Justice. Booklist* (June 1, 1998): 1728.

Mort, John. Review of *Seasons Under Heaven. Booklist* (May 1, 1999): 1579.

Mort, John. Review of *Emerald Windows. Booklist* (January 1, 2002): 804.

Murphree, Randall. "Author Gives Insight on Disaster Novel Last Light," an interview with author Terri Blackstock on Blackstock's Web page.

Publishers Weekly. Review of *Seaside.* (January 29, 2001): 67; Review of *Emerald Windows.* (September 17, 2001): 55.

"Terri Blackstock." *Contemporary Authors Online.* Detroit: Thomson Gale, 2003.

Terri Blackstock Web site, http://www.terriblackstock.com/ "Terri Blackstock."

Today's Christian Woman. Review of *Sweet Delights: For Love of Money* (March, 2001): S6.

BLY, STEPHEN

Personal, Professional, and Religious Background

Stephen Arthur Bly (1944–) was born in Visalia, California. His father was Arthur Worthington Bly and his mother Alice Wilson Bly. He grew up on his father's ranch, the perfect background for a man destined to love the American West and become a writer of westerns.

In 1963, he married Janet Chester, a freelance writer who encouraged his writing and who has frequently served as his coauthor. They have three children, Russell, Michael, and Aaron.

He attended Fresno State University, earning a B.A. (summa cum laude) in 1971

> A fiction book can be aimed at a much wider audience than a nonfiction book.
>
> —Stephen Bly, in interview with Janice DeLong

and then earned an M.Div. from Fuller Theological Seminary in 1974. For a time after his marriage, he was a ranch foreman in central California. While studying for his degree, he became a youth pastor in Orosi, California, then in Los Angeles, Woodlake, California, and Filmore, California. In 1974, he was ordained to the Presbyterian ministry. At the time that he was preparing for the ministry, he was also scribbling away at his western tales that revealed both his love of the region and his deep faith in Christ.

In 1976, when Stephen Bly was 32 years old and an established pastor, his wife began to submit his writings to various publications. Bly was delighted to find that publishers and readers were interested in his stories, noting that "Christian fiction gives me an avenue to be creative and to encourage people to seek after and hold on to a Christian worldview." He has found he can reach a wider, more diverse audience with fiction than with sermons. Eventually, he became a full-time writer.

He and his family now live in Winchester, Idaho (elevation 4,000, population 340), where he was earlier the pastor of the Winchester Community Church and mayor of the city. He loves Western activities—riding, roping and rodeo. *Contemporary Authors* notes that he is at work constructing a false-front Western village, Broken Arrow Crossing, at his home in Idaho. It is named after the setting in the first of the Stuart Brannon novels.

He is a popular speaker at colleges, churches, camps, and conferences. Bly has been on television and radio (including Dr. James Dobson's "Focus on the Family"), and has lectured at Moody Bible Institute and Mount Hermon Christian Writers' Conference.

Major Works and Themes

While Stephen Bly continues to conduct seminars and radio programs, he also writes several articles and western novels each year. The novels are frequently set in the 19th century, when the West was full of challenges for pioneers or mountain men struggling against the elements, the native Americans, and the outlaws. Steven Bly (and often his wife) love to feature a hero who prefers to be a man of peace, but when forced by circumstances can be good with his gun or his fists. In preparation for his writing, Bly does extensive research on the history of the period, the manners and artifacts, the language, and even the weather of the region he is describing. He believes this provides an air of authenticity to his dramatic tales of a mythic era.

Stuart Brannon, one of his favorite heroes, is a kind of western Job. He has lost his wife and child, his cattle, and now risks losing his ranch in Arizona. Along the way, he has also lost his faith, but reclaims it as he sees God's hand in miracles and in a design much larger than he can understand.

> Stephen Bly is constructing a Western village on his land in Idaho that will eventually resemble his mythic Broken Arrow Crossing—the setting for his Stuart Bronson novels.

He tries to treat others with courtesy, but finds that some people are too brutal to respond to reason or accept defeat gracefully. When necessary, he does kill his adversaries, but accords even his enemies the dignity of burial before moving on.

In both the "Stuart Brannon" series and "The Goldfield Skinners," Bly uses the California Gold Rush as background for his story. In the later series written with his wife, a naive easterner who is new to the West stumbles into God's will for himself and his family.

The westerns are written in the style of Zane Grey and Louis L'Amour, full of wild action, stock characters, fast twists in plot, chance meetings, violent climaxes, and satisfying conclusions. They are short, lively, simple, and fun to read. He writes them with a strong sense of place: he knows his history and the quarrels of Western history. His stories are also clean, full of true love, minimal sex, and drinking.

By contrast, the "Austin-Stoner Files" are contemporary stories featuring a heroine, Lynda Austin, who is a New York editor. She is now 30 years old and has never been able to find the right man. An apparent lunatic, raving about a lost manuscript, breaks into her office. His death and the evidence he shares with her before dying convince her that that he is telling the truth. Lynda lights out for the West, to Arizona, where her guide, Brady Stoner, a rodeo rider, gradually turns out to be her soul mate. Their adventures in search of the manuscript take them through three volumes and several territories. Only after a chase through Montana with ruthless men in pursuit do the quest and the love story come to a satisfactory conclusion. The series is witty and packed with adventure.

A number of stories written either by Stephen Bly alone or in collaboration with his wife feature women as "heroes." One such strong lady is Grace Denison, who runs away from the stifling life her father, a United States senator, would have her live. She prefers to be on her own, as a telegraph operator. When Grace eventually chooses a mate, he is not one her father would have chosen for her. She and the other "Belles of Lordsborg" represent women of culture from the East bringing civilization to the rough and tumble man's world out West. The heroine of *Sweet Carolina*, Carolina Cantrell, is another heroic woman—a tough businesswoman who is lively and clever. Several of the novels in "Heroines of the Golden West" and "Old California" as well as the coauthored "Carson City Chronicles" have women at the center, and are filled with adventure. These romances are good entertainment for young adults or their parents.

Steven Bly sometimes pictures characters with a tarnished past who have headed to the West to start afresh. His "Code of the West" series uses Tap Andrews and Pepper Paige, taking them from their earlier lives as a gunfighter and a dance-hall girl through a romance, a wedding, and finally to life on a ranch in Colorado. Tap becomes a deputy at one time, fights off Indians and outlaws, and eventually clears his name. The dialogue is lively, the characters colorful, and the plot moves swiftly.

In yet another series, this talented husband-and-wife team laugh at their own experiences. The "Hidden West" is a three-book series about a husband and wife who solve mysteries while writing westerns. Even though he has a good sense of humor, Bly takes his work seriously. He has told Janice DeLong that he begins his research on his books with reading contemporary historical accounts of the era that is background for his stories. He insists on on-site research of the places and "serious lexicographical studies to ensure the vocabularies and dialects are authentic." He also checks the details of the characters' lives—the type of guns they would have used, the clothes they would have worn. He stories are "heavy on dialogue and action," aimed at touching the emotions of the readers through character-driven plots.

Steven Bly's early reading included Ernest Hemingway, John Steinbeck, William Faulkner, William Saroyan, Louis L'Amour, Zane Grey, Luke Short, and others. His protagonists are versions of himself or people he has met or read about. His recurring theme is, "God wants to rule in every area of my protagonist's life and . . . he/she must come to a decision to allow Him to be Lord." His dream is to demonstrate that "a committed Christian can write quality fiction equal to that of any other writer in the country and still hold on to biblical standards." He also wants his readers to "have fun and enjoy the work . . . and in the process be encouraged and/or challenged in their life of faith."

Critical Reception

John Mort considers Stephen Bly's Christian westerns, though sometimes didactic and overplotted, witty and full of "deep lore of the West that readers expect from Louis L'Amour." He considers his "Code of the West" series his most successful. The later series, "Skinners of Gold Field," Mort considers a good follow-up, recapturing the wit of his "Code of the West series in this disarming tale of the God-fearing, seemingly foolhardy family of Orion Tower ('O.T.') Skinner." Having been wiped out by a tornado, they mean to pass through Goldfield, Nevada, but end up stumbling their way into a great find. Mort thinks that O.T. sounds a bit like Jeeter Lester in *Tobacco Road*.

Melanie Hudak has reviewed a number of Bly's novels for *Library Journal*, generally finding him a good read. She calls *My Foot's in the Stirrup—My Pony Won't Stand* a "fast-moving Western adventure with touches of romance and humor." Melanie Duncan, writing for *Library Journal*, says *Fool's Gold* "is filled with humorous characters and an abiding appreciation for the Lord's mysterious ways."

Awards

Stephen Bly was named Writer of the Year at the Mount Hermon Writers' Conference in 1982 and won the Christy Award for *The Long Trail Home* in 2002.

Bibliography of Novels by Author

Stephen Bly has written several children's books and two series for young adults—the "Nathan T. Riggins" series and the "Lewis and Clark Squad" series.

"Stuart Brannon" series (Wheaton, IL: Crossway Books, 1991–1993)

"Austin Stoner Files" series (Wheaton, IL: Crossway Books, 1995–1997)

"Old California" series (Wheaton, IL: Crossway Books, 1998–2000)

"Heroines of the Golden West" series (Wheaton, IL: Crossway Books, 1998–1999)

"Fortunes of the Black Hills" series (Nashville, TN: Broadman & Holman, 1999–2003)

"Crystal" series with Janet Bly (Bel Air, CA: Chariot Books, 1986)

"Hidden West" series, written with Janet Bly (League City, TX: Servant Publications, 1996–1998)

"The Goldfield Skinners" series (Wheaton IL: Crossway Books, 2000–2001)

"The Carson City Chronicles" series with Janet Bly (Ann Arbor, MI: Vine Books & Servant Publications, 2000)

"The Belles of Lordsburg" series (Wheaton, IL: Crossway Books, 2001)

"Retta Barre's Oregon Trail" series (Wheaton, IL: Crossway Books, 2002)

"Homestead" series (Wheaton, IL: Crossway Books, 2002–2003)

"Adventure on the American Frontier" series (Wheaton, IL: Crossway Books, 2003)

Stephen and Janet Bly have also written a number of books on parenting (and grand parenting) as well as advice on discipleship, grace, and death.

Bibliography of Works about Author

Bly Books: http://www.blybooks.com.

DeLong, Janice and Rachel Schwedt. *Contemporary Christian Authors: Lives and Works.* Lanham, MD: The Scarecrow Press., 2000.

Duncan, Melanie C. Review of *Fool's Gold. Library Journal* (June 1, 2000): 104.

Hudak, Melissa. Review of *My Foot's in the Saddle—My Pony Won't Stand. Library Journal* (November 1, 1996): 52.

Mort, John. *Christian Fiction: A Guide to the Genre.* Greenwood Village, Colorado: Libraries Unlimited, 2002.

"Stephen A(rthur) Bly. *Contemporary Authors Online.* Detroit: Thomson Gale, 2003.

BROWN, DAN

Personal, Professional, and Religious Background

Dan Brown (1964–) was born in Exeter, New Hampshire, the son of a professional sacred musician and a math professor. He attended the very selective Phillips Exeter Academy during his final years of high school. Living in an Episcopalian school community in his early years, he sang in the choir and attended the church camp in summers—along with his younger siblings, Valerie and Gregory.

After high school, Brown studied at Amherst College, enrolling for a double major in Spanish and English. He was a writing student of Alan Lelchuk while at Amherst and played squash and sang in the glee club. He toyed with the possibility of a musical career before becoming an English teacher at Phillips for a time. His interest in music led to the production of a children's cassette entitled "SynthAnimals." Although this product sold only a few copies, Brown formed his own record company called Dalliance, and self-published a CD entitled "Perspective" in 1990, which was aimed at an adult audience.

> For me, the spiritual quest will be a life-long work in progress.
>
> —Dan Brown, quoted on his Web site www.danbrown.com/novels/davinci-code/faqs.html

While he was working on his musical projects in Los Angeles, he joined the National Academy of Songwriters and met Blythe Newlon, the Academy's Director of Artistic Development, a woman 12 years his senior. She took an

> *The Da Vinci Code* became the best seller of all time, earning Dan Brown an estimated income of $250 million, with an estimated annual income of $76.5 million.

unusual interest in Brown's projects, writing press releases, setting up promotional events, and even putting him in contact with people who could help advance his career. In the meantime, they developed a personal relationship, which led to their marriage in 1997—at Pea Porridge Pond, a spot near North Conway, New Hampshire. His wife has been a major influence on Brown's career, both in singing and in writing. She continues to assist in the promotion of his books, and coauthored one of his early "humor" books, *Men to Avoid: A Guide for the Romantically Frustrated Woman*, written under the pseudonym "Danielle Brown" (http://en.wikipedia.org/wiki/Dan-Brown).

By 1994, Brown had begun to show an interest in cryptology, symbolism, religious codes, and conspiracies. He released a CD entitled *Angels and Demons*, with artwork designed by John Langdon, which included an ambigram that was later used as a central symbol in the novel by the same name. That same year, while he was on holiday in Tahiti, he read *The Doomsday Conspiracy*, a novel by Sidney Sheldon, which he thought inferior to his own efforts. By 1996, he had become so interested in code-breaking and covert government operations that he devoted himself full-time to studying and writing about this topic. He published *Digital Fortress* in 1998.

This was followed by his novel about a conspiracy to destroy the Vatican, the conclave of cardinals, the major contenders for the papacy, and even to murder the Pope himself. Like his next novel, *Deception Point* (2001), the book sold fewer than 10,000 copies. In 2003, with his block-buster *The Da Vinci Code*, he changed all this. This book became the best seller of all time, earning him an estimated income of $250 million, with an estimated annual income of $76.5 million. The enormous popularity of this book and the film that followed revived interest in his earlier novels, leading Hollywood to bid for the film-rights to *Angels and Demons*, for which Akiva Goldsman was commissioned to write a film adaptation.

Dan Brown is now a celebrity, listed by *Time* in 2005 as one of the 100 most influential men of the year, celebrated by *Forbes* magazine as #12 on their 2005 "Celebrity 100" list, and able to give generously to his alma mater, in his father's honor, for high-tech equipment and computers for "students in need."

Major Works and Themes

In his first three novels, Dan Brown provided glimpses of some of the themes and techniques that shaped his masterpiece, *The Da Vinci Code*. The first of his thrillers, *Digital Fortress* (1998), reveals his suspicion of large, powerful organizations and his delight in codes and code-breaking. In an interview with Claire E. White, Brown noted that one of his students at Phillips Exeter Academy was interviewed by the U.S. Secret Service because of his on-line political debate with other students. Brown was puzzled by the methods used to mine vast amounts of e-mail. He began to study government organizations and their access to computers. The resultant techno-thriller involves the attack on a government super-computer named TRNSLTR, designed to intercept and decode terrorist threats. It features Susan Fletcher, a cryptographer employed by the government, who is asked to help with a code that appears unbreakable.

The secret society in this case is the government's own manager, whose sinister designs are finally uncovered by the beautiful young woman and her handsome companion, a brilliant college professor. Hired assassins and evil forces are at work in a network that challenges the survival of the whole intelligence system of the United States. Happily, these bright young people, through quick action, shrewd judgment, and skilful puzzle-solving, save the day. The characters are as flat and silly as those in any action film, but Brown does tease the audience with his knowledge of computer technology. The reviewer for *Publishers Weekly* noted that the novel is "fast-paced" and "plausible." It does reveal Brown's strong tendency toward paranoia and his clear lines between good and evil. These moral positions seem to derive from Natural Law, not from any religious code.

Brown's second novel, *Angels and Demons*, introduces another young professor, Robert Langdon, who is a famous Harvard symbologist. He also links up with a brilliant and beautiful young woman, Vittoria, a scientist at CERN, which is a scientific think tank in Switzerland. This time, the threat by nefarious villains is destined to change the world. Although technology is important in solving the problems involved, the basic conflict is between science and religion, especially the story of creation. Leonardo, a priest-scientist, seeks a private meeting with the Pope because of the breath-taking discovery he has made that demonstrates Genesis is physically possible. His discovery has "profound religious implications" that enemies of the reconciliation between science and religion find threatening. In a tumultuous plot, involving airplanes, helicopters, secret codes, the Illuminati, the Vatican, various statues and churches around Rome, and many clues and surprises, the talented pair of detectives find one murdered cardinal after another, uncover the murder of the Pope himself, and finally expose the malefactors.

This time, Brown was obliged to do thorough research on the Vatican (which is threatened with destruction), the workings of the conclave of cardinals, the political structure of the Catholic Church, and the environs of Rome. The story is full of details from art history, religious ceremony, and science. Brown's own attitude toward religion becomes more apparent in the telling of the story: a condescending awareness of the value of faith for some people, a distrust of the political workings of the Roman Catholic Church, and a preference for clerics who have "progressive" tendencies.

This time *Publishers Weekly* commented that the premises of the tale "strain credulity" though the story is "laced with twists and shocks that keep the reader wired right up to the last revelation." *The Library Journal* cited it as "one of the best international thrillers of recent years."

Brown's third novel, *Deception Point* (2001), again involves science, is again a techno-thriller, and again travels at breakneck speed. It involves NASA's discovery of a meteor in the Arctic circle. Again the writer begins with the mysterious death of a scientist in the context of important national concerns—an important presidential election. The meteor apparently may provide proof of extraterrestrial life. The reviewers for *Library Journal*, *Kirkus Reviews*, *Publishers Weekly*, and *Booklist* all saw it as a good example of the thriller genre. The wooden characters and clever use of suspense in this, the least popular of his novels, were to reappear as characteristics in the far more popular *The Da Vinci Code* (2003).

Returning to his suspicion of religious intrigue, Brown investigates a number of topics in *The Da Vinci Code*. He uses the Louvre as the site for the murder and the chief curator as the victim. He also relies on hidden messages in the famous picture, *The Last Supper*, by Leonardo da Vinci. The renowned Harvard symbologist, Robert Langdon, once again serves as his sleuth, and once again is paired with a brilliant and beautiful young woman intimately involved in the case. The villains this time are the Roman Catholic Church and its secret society of Opus

Dei, whom he considers to be responsible for hiding the true story of the Holy Grail and Mary Magdalene's marriage to Jesus.

Brown's research has provoked a number of critics to insist that he is mistaken on a number of points. His blending of fact and fiction has led many readers to accept his assertions about Christian theology, Mary Magdalene, and Opus Dei without reservation. He also draws heavily on other sources, including Lewis Perdue's 2000 novel *Daughter of God* and Michael Baigent and Richard Leight's 1982 novel *Holy Blood and Holy Grail*. Perdue brought action against Brown for copyright infringement, but the court refused to hear the case, accepting Brown's assertion that he was not familiar with Perdue's book. The Supreme Court refused to hear the case. In 2006, Baigent and Leigh brought suit against Brown in Britain's High Court, alleging similar infringement. Again the High Court judge rejected their claim and their appeal.

In his most successful novels, Brown has turned the Christian thriller, introduced by writers of the 1980s like **Frank Peretti**, on its head, making his novels anti-Christian thrillers. He uses the same devices of fast action, suspense, sudden changes in direction, supernatural powers, but sees Christians and right-wing politicians as the conspirators at the heart of the mystery. Brown insists that he is a Christian, though "perhaps not in the most traditional sense of the word." He believes that "Faith is a continuum, and we each fall on that line where we may. By attempting to rigidly classify ethereal concepts like faith, we end up debating semantics to the point where we entirely miss the obvious—that is, that we are all trying to decipher life's big mysteries, and we're each following our own paths of enlightenment. I consider myself a student of many religions. The more I learn, the more questions I have."

Critical Reception

The books, articles, Web sites, and blogs that take issue with various assertions of Dan Brown's *The Da Vinci Code* could fill a small library. The book includes so many assertions, factoids, references to Gnostic gospels and secret societies, and casts so much suspicion on the Roman Catholic Church that it has stirred up furor in numerous religious communities. Several Christian denominations have issued detailed critiques of the novel, even publishing inserts to be used in church bulletins to refute Brown's claims. Among those most disturbing to orthodox Christians include these: that Jesus is not God, only a man, who was not deified until the fourth century; that he married Mary Magdalene, who was worshipped as a goddess and was designated as the person to establish the church; that they had a child together, that this daughter is the progenetrix of a famous European family still living today.

Brown's attacks on the Bible as the Word of God also alarm many of the orthodox. He asserts that the Bible was assembled by a pagan Roman emperor, who deliberately excised the materials on Mary Magdalene. The Catholic Church was especially incensed by the presumption that all of these "facts" that Brown details were known by the Church, which had been fighting for centuries to keep this information from coming out. He asserts that the Church has assassinated the descendants of Christ to keep his bloodline from surviving.

Needless to say, the critics are divided on religious grounds in their reviews of this novel. Some readers continue to see the riddles in the story as playful, some complain that the book has too much religious history, some insist he has overloaded the plot. The reviewer for *Publishers Weekly* believes it will "please both conspiracy buffs and thriller addicts." The brain-teasers and claims to historical accuracy delight critics for the *New York Times* and others.

Janet Maslin calls the book "a gleefully erudite suspense novel." It remained on the *New York Times* best-seller list for months and has been translated into over 30 languages.

Anita Gandolfo traces the long tradition of anti-Catholicism in modern fiction, showing that "*The Da Vinci Code*'s demonizing of the Catholic Church resonates with most American readers," especially since the novel's publication coincided with the worst scandal in American Catholic history—the multitude of cases of priests accused of molesting children. Thus "the reader of *The Da Vinci Code* would be inclined to believe (and relish) any villainy attributed to Catholicism. Moreover, the novel's premise that the Church was guilty of suppressing the worship of the Goddess to promote its patriarchal culture would resonate as the prequel to contemporary misogyny in its intransigent attitude toward ordaining women priests." She insists that the book proved a perfect match for the prejudices of the period.

Awards

Book of the Year, British Book Awards, 2005, for *The Da Vinci Code*.

Bibliography of Novels by Author

Digital Fortress. New York: St. Martin's Press, 1998.
Angels and Demons. New York: Pocket Books, 2000.
Deception Point. New York: Pocket Books, 2001.
The Da Vinci Code. New York: Doubleday, 2003.

Both *The DaVinci Code* and *Angels and Demons* have been produced as films starring Tom Hanks as the hero.

Bibliography of Works about Author

Allen, John L. *Opus Dei*. New York: Doubleday, 2005.
Ayers, Jeff. Review of *Angels and Demons*. *Library Journal* (November 15, 2000): 124.
Burstein, Dan. *Secrets of the Code*. New York: CDS Books, 2004.
Bock, Darrell L. *Breaking the da Vinci Code*. Nashville: Thomas Nelson, 2004.
Brown, Dan. Webpage. www.danbrown.com/novels/davinci_code/faqs.html.
"Cracking the Da Vinci Code." in Catholic Answers, Inc., 2004. http://www.catholic.com/library/cracking-da-vinci-code.asp.
"Dan Brown." *Contemporary Authors Online*. Detroit: Thomson Gale, 2007.
"Dan Brown." http://en.wikipedia.org/wiki/Dan-Brown.
"Da Vinci Code, by Dan Brown: Relevant Readings, Resources and Responses." http://www.ratzinger fanclub.com/da-vinci-code/ (includes substantial bibliography).
Gandolfo, Anita. *Faith and Fiction: Christian Literature in America Today*. Westport, CT: Praeger, 2007.
Kirkus Reviews. Review of *Deception Point* (September 1, 2001): 1232.
Maslin, Janet. Review of *The Da Vinci Code*. *The New York Times*, March 17, 2003.
Olson, Carl and Sandra Miesel. *The Da Vinci Hoax*. San Francisco: Ignatius, 2004.
Pitt, David. Review of *The Scarlet Thread*. Review of *Deception Point*. *Booklist* (September 15, 2001).
Publishers Weekly. Review of *Digital Fortress* (December 22, 1997): 39.
Publishers Weekly. Review of *Angels and Demons* (May 1, 2000): 51.
Publishers Weekly. Review of *Deception Point* (September 10, 2001): 56.
Publishers Weekly. Review of *The Da Vinci Code* (February 3, 2003): 53.
White, Claire E. Interview with Dan Brown for *Writers Write*. http://www.writerswrite.com/May, 1998.

BRUNSTETTER, WANDA

Personal, Professional, and Religious Background

Wanda Landess Brunstetter was born into a German family. The Landess family, who came to America in 1750, were Dutch Quakers, connected with the Dunkerd Church, a part of the Anabaptist movement. Wanda Brunstetter grew up in the Mennonite Church in Pennsylvania. Many of her family members continue to live in this area, which has had a powerful influence on her creative work.

Wanda married Richard Brunstetter, a Nazarene pastor, in the 1960s. Her husband also grew up in a Mennonite church in Pennsylvania. Both of them have had a lifelong attachment to Lancaster County and to the Amish and Mennonite families in that region. Although he is a Nazarene pastor, Richard Brunstetter continues—along with Wanda—to visit and study the Amish families in various parts of the country.

Wanda Brunstetter wanted to be a writer since she was a child. She wrote her first poem in the second grade and continued to write regularly, producing skits for her church teenagers for special occasions when she was a bit older. In 1980, still interested in writing, but concerned she was unschooled in the skills of this trade, she took a writing course. She then undertook her first book, which was published by Heartsong Presents, a Barbour subsidiary, in 1997. The remainder of her works, which have appeared in rapid succession, have been published by the same press.

In addition, she is a recognized puppeteer and ventriloquist. She has written books on these subjects, as well as cookbooks with Amish recipes. Some of her books are designed for children.

The Brunstetters have two grown children, Richard Jr. and Lonne, and six grandchildren. The Brunstetters currently live in Washington state, but make frequent trips to Amish communities.

Major Works and Themes

Wanda Brunstetter's love of the Amish culture led her into creating a series of books that deal with this separate people. Although they view her as "English," they have praised her sympathetic view of their ways. She writes in a simple, romantic style, focusing on the young Amish, in either Pennsylvania or Iowa. Although she has written some stand-alone novels, cookbooks, and nonfiction, her reputation is based primarily on her sequences of stories about these communities.

An interesting example of her work, in the "Sisters of Holmes County" series, is the story Grace Hostettler. This pretty Amish girl has her *rumschpringe* (running around year) and then goes to Holmes County, Ohio, where she joins the Amish church. She has secrets regarding her escapades during this year of freedom that Gary Walker, an "Englisher," knows about. She had "gone English" for a time, but has repented privately and has hoped to put this episode behind her. The Amishman, Cleon Schrock, whom she plans to marry, does not know her secret. This is the central concern of *A Sister's Secret*. Any reader

> I enjoy writing about the Amish because they live a peaceful, simple life—something I feel everyone needs in this day and age.
>
> —Wanda Brunstetter on her homepage (www.wandabrunstetter.com)

of romances knows that there will eventually be a revelation, a time of forgiveness, and a happy ending.

Brunstetter's plots are simple, revolving around some complication in the simple life—paralysis, love of a sister's boyfriend, disappointments of various sorts. The problem is to reconcile with the community while overcoming the barrier to the good life.

Her major themes are healing, the need for the help of friends, family; the importance of studying Scripture and prayer. Always, her focus is on the Amish way of life. Her love of good food, good fellowship, and simple pleasures serve as a constant delight to her many readers.

Critical Reception

Fans love her works, while most of the critics ignore her, believing her to be less edgy than **Beverly Lewis** or **W. Dale Cramer.** Writing in the romance tradition, she is more sympathetic to the Amish lifestyle and less critical of the theology and habits of the culture that frustrate more independent spirits. Reviewers tend to see her books as dealing skillfully with her stories, blending the loving family with a faith-filled community. Words like "sensitive," and "inspiring," apply to her work. They note that she can show the community's serenity in the face of calamity.

Awards

In 1992, Wanda Brunstetter won the Grand Prize Award as a Children's Writer for her book on ventriloquism. In 2002, Heartsong Press's readers' poll named her the #4 favorite.

Bibliography of Novels by Author (Published by Heartsong, Barbour, Uhrichsville, Ohio)

Most of these have been reprinted in omnibus volumes as well.

"Brides of Lancaster County" series (1997–2002)

"Sisters of Holmes County" series (2007–2008)

"Brides of Webster County" series (2005–2008)

"Daughters of Lancaster County" series (2005–2006)

Other Novels

Talking for Two. 2001.
The Neighborly Thing. 2002.
Clowning Around. 2003.
Kelly's Chance. 2004.
Patchwork Holiday. 2005.
Betsy's Return. 2007.
White Christmas Pie. 2008.

Bibliography of Works about Author

Barbour Books: www.barbourbooks.com/author/detail/wanda-e-brunstetter. Christian Books: www.christianbook.com Library reviews: www.intellibraryreviews.net/BrunstetterWanda.

Novel Journey Blogspot: www.noveljourney.blogspot.com/2008/07/Wanda.
Wanda Brunstetter's homepage. www.wandabrunstetter.com.

BUECHNER, FREDERICK

Personal, Professional, and Religious Background

Carl Frederick Buechner (1926–) was born in New York City to Carl Frederick and Katherine Kuhn Buechner—both members of respected and affluent families. The Depression forced the father of the family to move from one job to another, until he finally committed suicide, leaving behind a message that he loved his wife, but was himself no good. This trauma shocked the 10-year-old Frederick and his younger brother, uprooted the family, and led the new widow to move her family to Bermuda, a place they came to love. Supported by their grandmother, the fatherless family eventually moved back to New York. Buechner, in the first of his lyrical autobiographical meditations, *The Sacred Journey*, says little of his mother and father, and only vaguely describes the suicide, but makes his devotion to his two grandmothers abundantly clear.

Frederick's grandmother sent him to Lawrenceville School, a prestigious private academy, where he made friends with another nonathletic aspiring poet, James Merrill. From there Frederick Buechner won a scholarship to Princeton, where he watched one after another of his friends leave to fight in World War II. Buechner studied German, hoping to avoid fighting in the front lines. He ran into debt, waited on tables to eke out his scholarship, and finally went to see his father's brother, his favorite uncle, to ask for the $100 he needed to complete the year. Shortly after generously handing the lad the money he needed, this benefactor committed suicide. For a while, Frederick Buechner feared some fatal family flaw took these two handsome, talented men in the prime of life.

This "dangerous downward pull" was interrupted by a call to join the Army, where Buechner did not distinguish himself. Failing the simulated battle preparing the recruits for warfare, he was declared "disqualified for combat duty." He spent the rest of his time on clerical duties, compiling AWOL and VD reports, and was discharged a week short of his 20th birthday.

Buechner returned to Princeton, honed his literary skills, and fell under the spell of such eloquent and fervent 17th-century writers as Sir Thomas Browne and John Donne. R. P. Blackmur, one of his teachers, said of him that he had a way with words—either speaking or writing. Buechner had a way of making people listen. In college, he also had considerable help from grants, scholarships, and family, causing a friend to comment of him, "Freddy is like royalty. He never pays."

Buechner finished his first novel shortly after his graduation, signing a contract with Alfred Knopf himself. This novel, *A Long Day's Dying*, was greeted with profuse praise. The title was taken from *Paradise Lost*, and was a story of people dying of "loneliness, emptiness, sterility, and such preoccupation with themselves and their own problems that they are unable to communicate with each other about anything that really matters very much."

> I am trying to explore what I believe life is all about, to get people to stop and listen a little to the mystery of their own lives. The process of telling a story is something like religion if only in the sense of suggesting that life itself has a plot and leads to a conclusion that makes a lot of sense.
>
> —Frederick Buechner in interview with *Publishers Weekly*

> Even Buechner's saints have feet of clay. He says this is the only kind of human he knows—whether saint or sinner.

Frederick Buechner had chosen to dwell on the theme of melancholy—much as his seventeenth century precursors had done. He was almost immediately hailed as a bright light in the literary world who had produced "a remarkable piece of work."

In spite of this adulation, the young writer felt a deep sadness: Because he had been very lucky, he "wanted to say something or do something." Buechner came to recognize his talent and his opportunities to write were gifts and that his life was on the verge of becoming trivial and meaningless. St. Paul was right: he needed to work out his salvation with fear and trembling. His own family was not religious, yet he came to believe that he needed God in his life.

He returned to Lawrenceville as an English teacher for the next five years (1948–53), an experience he remarked was full of "terror and delight." Because he realized he was not much older or brighter than his students, Buechner found the teaching a challenge. He spent a weekend in a monastery on the Hudson River considering the path of his life, his need to be cleansed of the "too-muchness and too-littleness." After five years, and a second novel, *The Seasons' Differences*, which was generally greeted as a disappointment, he gave up his Lawrenceville job and went to live in New York. He planned to become a full-time writer. He found instead he could not write a word.

Frederick Buechner began a search for his vocation, considering that he might try advertising or work for the CIA as a spy. As it turned out, he discovered his true path when he began attending the Madison Avenue Presbyterian Church and listening carefully to the sermons of the scholarly pastor George Buttrick. In 1952, the year of the coronation of Queen Elizabeth, he heard a sermon that Buttrick preached on the coronation of Christ the King. Buechner tells the story of his conversion experience in several of his memoirs, most notably in *The Alphabet of Grace:* "the coronation of Jesus took place among confession and tears and then, as God was and is my witness, great laughter." The phrase "great laughter" transformed his life. He suddenly decided to study theology and returned to discuss this abrupt decision with Buttrick, who insisted that he needed to go to seminary. Buechner rejoiced that the pastor immediately took him to Union Theological Seminary, where he enrolled with the help of a Rockefeller scholarship.

Although he was not committed to a vocation as a minister, Buechner completed seminary, serving for some time in East Harlem at a center designed to help the unemployed find work. In Harlem he discovered a part of society previously unknown to him. He felt that this work, though useful, "smacked more of social service than anything else." He wanted, instead, "to try to bring the Christian faith to life in all its richness and depth for others the way people like Buttrick," Tillich, and other teachers and mentors had brought it to life for him.

On graduation in 1958, he met and married Judith Frederick Merk. The same year, he was offered the chaplaincy at Phillips Exeter Academy in New Hampshire, where he also served as the religion professor. Instead of being ordained a traditional pastor, he became a "minister without pastoral charge, or evangelist." During his years at Exeter, he did preach at chapel at least once a month and taught religion courses to the students. He saw himself as the apologist for Christianity against the "cultured despisers" of the faith. He used literary examples to make his points, challenging the students to look at the deeper meanings of their own faith or lack of faith. Under his leadership, the department grew to include the study of comparative theology.

While at Exeter, he and his wife had a child—the first of three girls. In 1963, he took an extended leave to go to Vermont, where he worked on a novel informed by his Christian faith, *The Final Beast*. In 1960, the growing family decided to leave Exeter to live and write permanently in what had been their vacation home in Vermont. They remain in the same spot today. The Buechner family love their life in Vermont. When the two oldest girls went away to boarding school, their parents were deeply saddened. Later, Buechner's daughter struggled with anorexia, which brought her to the verge of death. Her recovery from this horrible disorder and her subsequent decision to become a minister taught her father a great deal about resilience.

Buechner calls himself an "accidental Presbyterian," having chosen that denomination because of George Buttrick. He currently attends an Episcopal church, which he loves because of the pastor. For the most part, he considers churches the enemy of religion. As he travels about the country, speaking to church groups or college chapels, he shocks his audiences by proclaiming that ". . . the best thing that could happen to your church is for it to burn down and for all your fax and e-mail machines to be burned up, and for the minister to be run over by a truck so that you have nothing left except each other and God." He has lectured at Harvard, Tufts, Yale, Columbia Seminary, Virginia Theological Seminary, and elsewhere. The lectures he prepares grow into books he subsequently publishes. He spent a year at Wheaton College as a guest professor, an experience he found delightful—very different from the nonevangelical New England community of which he is a part. Although he is a liberal in most of his thinking, he is much admired by the evangelical community for his lively and personal expressions of faith.

Major Works and Themes

Frederick Buechner has the brains, the contacts, the drive, and the opportunity to write novels that dazzle the literary world. His first novel, *A Long Day's Dying*, encouraged him and his critics to believe he would be a latter-day Henry James. Like James, he was less concerned with plot than character and tone. Harold Watts commented that, in his early novels, Buechner was able to cast a ironic eye on modern relationships, noting the "rather delicate and tenuously resolved relations among cultivated and privileged Americans." They reveal a talent for comedy, but a curious sort of comedy, based on living in a world that is bereft of generally shared values. Each individual creates his own system of values, which do not seem to have any wider relevance. Buechner completed the third of these early novels, *The Return of Ansel Gibbs*, just as he entered seminary. He had found his subject.

Buechner says, in *Now and Then*, "since my ordination I have written consciously as a Christian, as an evangelist, or apologist even." Though he does not preach, he chooses to portray people with feet of clay. In an effort to be true to his faith, he writes of his Christian experience—just as a woman will write of her experience or a black person of his. In *The Final Beast*, which Buechner wrote while he was teaching at Exeter, he included a portion of the Christian life he found conspicuously absent in most of the books he was teaching to his students. The book contains horrible things happening to good and innocent people in Nazi concentration camps. The young minister who hopes for a religious vision has nothing more than a curious experience of apple branches clacking together in the wind. But something fine happens as well: a young woman who thought herself sterile conceives a child; a young minister who has fled God determines to return to his calling—however vaguely he understands it.

Buechner also incorporated in the novel his own experience of prayer, his fresh understanding of the Holy Spirit. This, the first of his post-conversion novels, reveals a new, more inclusive vision. Now the psyche is also a soul, "a focus of energy that achieves fulfillment by coming into relations with patterns that religion and mythology testify to." This shared story of Scripture has led him to adopt a somewhat simpler style.

The Buechners' move to Vermont, a place that seemed in winter to have something of the spirit of Narnia, led the artist to write a book about dreams and fantasy—*The Entrance to Porlock*. The idea derived from Coleridge's visitor from Porlock who woke the poet out of his trance, according to the poet's introductory note to "Kubla Khan." Buechner saw this shocking awakening as the tension between everyday reality and the reality of dreams, the imagination. He based the plot of the book on *The Wizard of Oz*, telling the story of an old man running a secondhand bookstore on a mountain in Vermont. He sees ghosts of dead writers, of the reality behind the books, and loses touch with his family. Buechner notes that "He is the Tin Woodsman in search of a heart. One son, a pathetic failure and compulsive joker, is the Scarecrow in search of a brain." Another son, "the bullying and hypochondriachal ideal of a school like Exeter . . . is the Cowardly Lion in search of courage." The grandson takes the role of Dorothy, searching for a home—just has Buechner himself had done as a child. The Wizard is an Austrian who runs a community for mentally disturbed patients. Buechner acknowledges that the novel "is symbolic autobiography, a strange, dense, slow-paced book, the labor of writing which was so painful that I find it hard, even now, to see beyond the memory of the pain to whatever merit it may have." He felt he had written himself into a wall and needed a new direction.

Reading a magazine while waiting his turn at a barbershop, Buechner began to think of a character who was to dominate his life for the next six years: Leo Bebb was a "plump, bald, ebullient southerner who had once served five years in a prison on the charge of exposing himself before a group of children and was now head of a religious diploma mill in Florida and of a seedy, flat-roofed stucco church called the Church of Holy Love, Incorporated. He wore a hat that looked too small for him. He had a trick eyelid that every once in a while fluttered shut on him." Leo became the hero of Buechner's next four novels, later combined to constitute "The Book of Bebb."

Buechner's writing path changed dramatically in the 1980s. He grew increasingly interested in medieval saints' legends, even studying accounts of their lives and travels. Out of this interest came *Godric*, the tale of an English saint born in the year before the Norman Conquest, who died in 1170, at the age of 105. Godric had a colorful life: peddler, master of a merchant ship, pirate, and finally hermit. He spent his last 60 years by the river Wear, near Durham. Although Godric considered himself a great sinner, his followers revered him as a saint. A contemporary monk, Reginald of Durham, wrote an "excessively reverent biography" of Godric, which Buechner drew from liberally in his extraordinary book.

The book begins with an astonishing announcement that Tune and Fairweather, snakes in his cave, are Godric's last "friends." The old saint's mind wanders back over the century of his adventures and the people he has loved and outlived. Through it all, his faith has survived. As Buechner describes the story in *Now and Then*, "He prays. He sins. He dreams." Then, one day when he is bathing in the icy waters of the river, as he has done daily for many years to chasten his flesh, he feels his arms and legs go numb. His response echoes the poetry of Gerard Manley Hopkins, "Praise, praise!" Buechner comments that he, like Godric, must learn to praise God for "all we lose . . . for the stillness in the wake of pain." Even, finally, "Praise him for dying and the peace of death."

Frederick Buechner has followed *Godric* with more books about saints and figures from the Bible. His novel *Brendan* carries an Irish saint, born in 484, after the conversion of Ireland by St. Patrick, through his many adventures to his death at the age of ninety. Again,

Buechner draws on medieval documents that chronicle his voyages in search of the terrestrial Paradise or Tir-na-nóg. A fanciful 10th-century account of this remarkable saint's adventures was to become "the most popular of all medieval legends." He sailed as far as Newfoundland in a leather-covered curragh at one time and visited with King Arthur at another. Along the way, he established many monasteries, settled claims to royal thrones, and converted a multitude. Buechner tells the story in the spirit of Old English poetry—"The Wanderer" and "The Seafarer." The comic scenes in the New World echo Buechner's old delight in Shakespeare's *Tempest*. He brings a vast historical knowledge to the story to create the amazing scenes of the Celtic middle ages.

Other of his later novels also draw on his faith: *Sons of Laughter* tells of the family of Isaac, whose name means "laughter." Jacob is the main character, a man of faith faced with considerable moral challenges. Much of the story is told in flashbacks. Buechner uses the biblical characters, events, time frame, and even much of the tone of biblical prose, exaggerating the scenes, and reminding the reader of physical reality such as the oil poured over the head, dripping down the beard, or the sense of dread suggested in calling Jehovah "Fear."

On the Road with the Archangel, a retelling of the Book of Tobit, a book considered apocryphal by most Protestants, is a lighter-hearted version of Job. In *The Storm*, Buechner returns once more to his beloved *Tempest*, which he places in a modern setting.

Frederick Buechner has never been a writer who discusses the current social situation, even though he clearly cares deeply about the environment and the condition of his fellow man. He is no lover of warfare, but has avoided becoming an antiwar spokesman. His subject is the relationship between humans and God. Since his conversion experience, Buechner has written more of himself and his faith than ever before. He still loves the classics of Western literature and quotes from a wide range of writers, but he also peppers his essays and tales with bits of Scripture. He is inclined to see life as a sacred journey, in which the footprint of God becomes increasingly visible to the alert pilgrim or saint. His love of language has led him to capture the ancient tone of Anglo-Saxon speech, much as it did his old favorite Gerard Manley Hopkins. In a sentence, Buechner can reveal the essence of a person, the comic as well as the tragic nature of each individual. Always surprising, sensitive to nuances, accepting few limits to his imagination, full of astonishing insights, Frederick Buechner is a remarkable writer.

Critical Reception

Frederick Buechner's critics have greeted his many publications with mixed reviews. Of his three early novels, *A Long Day's Dying*, *The Seasons' Difference*, and *The Return of Ansel Gibbs*, only the first received critical praise. The reviewer for the *San Francisco Chronicle* applauded *A Long Day's Dying* by noting that "Mr. Buechner" is not just a "novelist of great promise" but one who has "already arrived in superlative fashion." *The Seasons' Difference* was generally considered a disappointment. H. L. Roth lamented that Buechner was emphasizing atmosphere rather than plot, "but even that emphasis seems to get lost in an arty attempt at developing a feeling of mysticism." The third of these early books, *The Return of Ansel Gibbs*, which was written at the time of his conversion, marked a change that puzzled the secular critics. Some of the critics found it "disconcerting" for a minister to be writing novels with "vivid sex scenes and a four-letter word or two." In all three of these novels, the characters seem to be preoccupied with their own difficulties. After his ordination, Buechner came to see writing as a kind of ministry. "As a preacher I am trying to do many of the same things I do as a writer. In both I am trying to explore what I believe life is all about, to get people to stop and listen a little to the mystery of their own lives." He saw the Bible, and religion itself, as a story-telling process, leading to a "conclusion that makes some kind of sense."

The Final Beast, the first of his novels to be written after his ordination, revealed the full shift in his interest to religious novels. The critics acknowledged it as a deeply religious book "without the slightest hint of" either piety or sentimentalism, but were less enthusiastic than earlier. In 1971, Buechner published the first book in the Bebb tetralogy—*Lion Country*. This and *Open Heart*, *Love Feast*, and *Treasure Hunt* came to be collected finally in a single volume entitled *The Book of Bebb*. Christopher Lehmann-Haupt, writing his critique in *the New York Times*, notes that "Frederick Buechner keeps getting better with each new novel, for when he was gently amusing in *Lion Country*, he is funny and profound in *Open Heart*." Others praised his prose and his ability to blend theology and entertaining fiction. Jonathan Yardley praised him in the *Washington Post*, for his "celebration of life and the interrelation of lives." And Thomas Howard notes that he has the vision of a Christian poet.

Reviewers have also lauded *Godric* for its effective characterization. Noel Perrin commented in the *Washington Post Book World* that "the old saint is so real that it's hard to remember this is a novel." He compared it to Thomas Mann's *The Holy Sinner*. Some Christian critics have grumbled that Buechner's saints all have feet of clay. He insists that he knows of no other kind of humans, saint or sinner.

Sons of Laughter, the story of Jacob and his family, again emphasizes the moral issues faced even by the passionate man of God. Brooke Horvath, writing for the *Review of Contemporary Fiction*, found the story both moving and disturbing. Others worried whether his blend of comedy and spiritual truth could be truly effective.

Frederick Buechner defends his choices, especially his choice of comedy, in his nonfiction books and essays. He has been compared to C. S. Lewis in his effective blend of narrative, anecdote, and meditation. Edmund Fuller, writing in the *New York Times*, sees him at work in "the vineyard of theology." Almost without exception, the critics note his remarkable gift for words, for comedy, for discovering the sublime in the ridiculous. Even when they disagree with his theology, they admire his presentation.

Awards

Frederick Buechner's career has been filled with awards, scholarships, and honors. He won the Irene Glascock Memorial Intercollegiate Poetry Award in 1947, the O. Henry Memorial Award in 1955 for the short story "The Tiger," the Richard and Hinda Rosenthal Award in 1959 for *The Return of Ansel Gibbs*, and the American Academy Award in 1982 for *Godric*. He had scholarships through most of his college career, including a Rockefeller grant for the first year of his theological studies at Union Seminary. He has received honorary doctorates from Virginia Theological Seminary (1983), Lafayette College (1984), Cornell College (1988), and Yale University (1990). Sewanee University and Lehigh University both awarded him Doctor of Literature degrees. He has been invited to give named lecture series at Yale, Harvard, Tufts, Bangor Seminary, Columbia Seminary, Virginia Theological Seminary, Trinity Institute and Barlow School.

Bibliography of Novels by Author

A Long Day's Dying. New York: Knopf, 1950.
The Return of Ansel Gibbs. New York: Knopf, 1958.

The Final Beast. New York: Athenaeum, 1965.
The Entrance to Porlock. New York: Athenaeum, 1970.
The Seasons' Difference. New York: Knopf, 1992.

The Book of Bebb

Lion Country. New York: Athenaeum, 1972.
Open Heart. New York: Athenaeum, 1972.
Love Feast. New York: Athenaeum, 1974.
Treasure Hunt: New York: Athenaeum, 1977.
Godric. New York: Athenaeum, 1980.
Brendon. New York: Athenaeum, 1987.
Wizard's Tide: A Story. New York: Harper, 1990.
The Sons of Laughter. San Francisco: HarperSanFrancisco, 1993.
On the Road with the Archangel. San Francisco: HarperSanFrancisco, 1997.
The Storm. San Francisco: HarperSanFrancisco, 1998.

Bibliography of Works about Author

Brown, W. Dale. *Of Fiction and Faith.* Grand Rapids, MI: William B. Eerdmans Publishing Company, 1997.
Buechner, Frederick. *The Hungering Dark.* New York: Seabury, 1969.
Buechner, Frederick. *The Alphabet of Grace.* New York: Seabury, 1970.
Buechner, Frederick. "The Bible as Literature," in *A Complete Literary Guide to the Bible,* ed., Leland Ryken and Tremper Longman III. Grand Rapids, MI: Zondervan Publishing House, 1993.
Buechner, Frederick. *The Sacred Journey: A Memoir of Early Days.* New York: Athenaeum, 1982.
Buechner, Frederick. *Now and Then: A Memoir of Vocation.* New York: Athenaeum, 1983.
Davies, Marie-Helene. *Laughter in a Genevan Gown: The Works of Frederick Buechner, 1970–1980.* Grand Rapids, MI: Eerdmans, 1983.
"Frederick Buechner," *Contemporary Authors Online.* Detroit: Thompson Gale, 2005.
Hassan, Ihab. *Radical Innocence: Studies in the Contemporary American Novel.* Princeton, NJ: Princeton University Press, 1961.
Howard, Thomas. Review of *The Book of Bebb. New York Times Book Review,* November 23, 1980.
Kauffman, Richard A. "Ordained to Write: an Interview with Frederick Buechner." *Christian Century.* http://findarticles.com/p/articles/mi_m1058/19_119ai_92083562.
Mort, John. Review of *On the Road with the Archangel. Booklist* (October 1, 1998): 290.
Publishers Weekly. Review of *Speak What We Feel (Not What We Ought to Say).* (July 30, 2001): 80.
Roth, H. L. Review of *The Seasons' Difference. Library Journal,* January 1, 1952.
Watts, Harold H. "(Carl) Frederick Buechner," Brief Biographies, Contemporary Novelists, Vol. 3. http://biography.jrank.org/pages/4189/Buechner_Carll_Frederick.
Frederick Buechner's papers have been donated to Wheaton College, Wheaton, Illinois.

BUNN, T. DAVIS (AND ISABELLA BUNN)

Personal, Professional, and Religious Background

T. Davis Bunn, also known as Thomas Locke (1952–), was born in North Carolina. He says that he was an avid reader as a child: "There were weeks when I read a book a day." He attended Wake Forest University, earning a B.A. in 1974, and then took a M.S. in international finance and economics at Gresham Institute, London.

T. Davis Bunn became a Christian when he was 24 years old. Up until that time, he felt he was unable to see his natural calling. He likes to compare his own experience to that of Moses,

> Authors (of Christian fiction) have an opportunity to give more than just a good read. They can challenge, comfort, make a plea for forgiveness, call the reader to love or understanding. There must something that ties to God's message. The reader should be able to find some small facet of God's call or God's heart in the heart of the story.
>
> —T. Davis Bunn interview in Janice DeLong and Rachel Schwedt's collection

who was chosen in spite of his speech impediment, forcing him to rely on God for his voice and strength. This particular insight is one he often uses with his characters, flawed people who, with the grace of God, become useful members of his family of believers.

By the time he completed graduate school, Bunn was fluent in three languages and prepared to begin a career that took him all over the world. He used his degree in psychology and economics in international management, serving as a consultant and lecturer on international finance. He has worked at many jobs: as a teacher at the American College of Switzerland, marketing director of a pharmaceutical and hospital equipment company in Switzerland, and managing director of a trade office in Dusseldorf, Germany. In 1991, he decided to leave consulting and work full-time as a writer. By this time, he had written nine novels, with only one of them published.

At the time, Bunn's wife, Isabella, was pursuing a degree in theology at Oxford University, leading them to settle in England, where in 1992, he became novelist-in-residence at Regent's Park College, Oxford. Isabella Bunn has been her husband's collaborator for many years. She contributes creative plot ideas, in-depth research, and authentic details in almost all of his stories. She shares a byline as coauthor of the "Heirs of Acadia" series, a sequel to the series that T. Davis Bunn coauthored with **Janette Oke**, "Song of Acadia." Isabella Bunn is an international lawyer, affiliated with the Centre for Christianity and Culture at Regent's Park College, Oxford University. She frequently lectures and writes on subjects related to justice and ethics.

T. Davis and Isabella Bunn now make their home in Oxford, but they travel extensively to do research for novels they are writing. They like to stay in a place long enough to feel "the place lives in me."

Major Works and Themes

The Presence was Bunn's first book accepted for publication, but his seventh attempt at novel-writing. In this story, he uses his understanding of finance and politics to portray the machinations of American government, taking good men and chewing them up. He was to use his love of music in another novel, *The Maestro*, which includes his intimate knowledge of Switzerland and Germany. In *Elixir*, he draws on his observations of the pharmaceutical industry to build a thriller in the mode of Tom Clancy.

T. Davis Bunn is a remarkable writer. He has worked with an established writer of prairie romances, Janette Oke, to produce a series of twentieth century tales and with his talented wife to write historical romances set in the days of William Wilberforce. He writes of political intrigue, sounding like a *Mr. Smith Goes to Washington* in the post-Watergate world. He tracks the genius of a fine musician who eventually turns from secular music to Christian concerts.

> By the time T. Davis Bunn completed graduate school, he was fluent in three languages.

He writes thrillers, full of fast movement and violence, love and greed. And he writes stories for young people, far simpler than the elaborate tales he spins for adults. He insists that he tailors his stories for his readers, aware whether they are young or old, picturing individuals as he develops his story. *Tidings of Comfort and Joy*, a historical romance about Christmas, for example, was written for his sister, "who loves women's stories where everything works out in the end." *To the Ends of the Earth* is a fantasy series designed for young adults, published under the pseudonym Thomas Locke.

He says that he "always had a lot of ideas for stories, and I love the search, the structuring. I enjoy putting together people, places, and plot . . . watching in my mind how it all comes together." He uses his own personal experience in character development, showing how T.J. Case, the black lawyer and politician in *The Presence*, has the same sense of inadequacy that Bunn himself felt when undertaking his writing career. Each of his stories includes a "point of illumination," a moment when God and his will become real to the central character. The conclusion may not be happy in the standard sense, but the protagonist does find peace, sometimes in the realization that the afterlife will be the locus of the "happy ending." He likes to deal with flawed characters, shaped by a hard life, full of questions, but courageous enough to continue the exploration of their predestined path.

In his stories, Bunn draws on his own fascinating career and his travels all over the world. He digs deeply into the spirit of his various locales, making us see and feel the monastic world on the Isle of Iona, or the cabaret scene in Switzerland, or the grim educational structure of Germany. We can go from St. Augustine's historic district to the Basque coast of Spain in a single story, with all of the buildings, people, and historical background richly described. In his coauthored historical romances, Bunn brings a level of detail about the squalor on the streets in Soho, the architecture of the Houses of Parliament, or the furnishings of homes, along with thousands of other bits of trivia that help to produce a realistic tone. He clearly does his homework and has an eye for detail, an ear for the speech of the people, and a deep sense of the emotional background in each area. He can make his audience feel the cold protocol of the subordinate entering the Oval Office or the excitement of a rock concert. He can even differentiate the kinds of waves that surfers catch on the coast of Spain or the coast of Scotland.

His stories are as varied as his settings. For the most part, he prefers to use a handsome man for his central figure, but does not require that he be white or young. When he has a female coauthor, he seems more comfortable exploring the psychology of women—young and old. Although love is a major component of his plots, most of his stories are not standard romances. The protagonist is more often intent on discovering who he or she is, what his or her relationship with God must be, what purpose God has intended for the time being, and how best to serve him. The Bunn protagonist may start as a nonbeliever, but he becomes a believer by the end of the story, often in a series of steps. In a romance like *The Innocent Libertine*, the hero sounds rather like John Newton—a former slaver and murderer who has been brought to his knees, and is ever mindful of God's saving grace. This conversion often requires a reversal of the path the character's life had previously taken, a rejection of the people who seemed attractive or the fame that appeared so important, and a commitment to a work for which the Lord has created either him or her.

Bunn's plots are complex, often becoming clear only in retrospect. His casts of characters are enormous, including a smattering of real historical personalities in the midst of a fictional story line. He assumes that God has a hand in human activity, but reveals this guidance slowly, often by means of everyday miracles. He also believes that God answers prayers, though not always as we would desire.

Critical Reception

John Mott believes that Bunn is a better writer without a collaborator. Though his coauthored books sell well and receive mild praise as being "good reads" or "thoughtful, moral," they are often clichéd romances. Even so, they are among the best of the genre, with strong research. Paulette Kozick wrote of *Florian's Gate*, a novel about London antique dealers in search of treasures plundered by the Nazis, that this is a "carefully researched, slice-of-life insider's view."

Unfortunately, most of the early novels, written by Bunn alone, rarely received critical notice. Mort did praise one later novel, *Elixir*. He noted that Bunn has "comfortably made the transition from evangelical to mainstream readers." This novel, which draws on Bunn's international travel and his business experience, particularly in the pharmaceutical field, is lively and complex. A more recent novel, *Heartland*, uses Bunn's experience in Hollywood to delve into the complexities of the television business and the problems of moving from TV to the large screen. The story, which combines the corn-fed character of a modern day Saul, the Old Testament shepherd turned hero, with Faust, Pygmalion, and Pinocchio in a story that reveals the miracle of an alternative universe, is imaginative and touching. The hero of Bible-belt country takes on the reptilian connivers of the Hollywood jungle to win out through decency, prayer, bravery, and love. W. Terry Whalen, writing for *Faithful Reader* said of the book that he highly recommended it "because of Bunn's engaging style and the fact that the unexpected twists and turns keep coming." He does know how to build suspense and keep several plot lines going at once.

Awards

T. Davis Bunn's first novel in the "Song of Acadia" series, coauthored with Janette Oke, *The Meeting Place*, won the Christy Award for Excellence in Christian Fiction in 1999. He has won two other Christy Awards for suspense novels: a 2001 award for *The Great Divide*, and 2002 for *Drummer in the Dark*.

Bibliography of Novels for Adults by Author

The Presence. Minneapolis: Bethany House Publishers, 1990.
The Maestro. Minneapolis: Bethany House Publishers, 1991.
Promises to Keep. Minneapolis: Bethany House Publishers, 1991.
The Quilt. Minneapolis: Bethany House Publishers, 1993.
The Gift. Minneapolis: Bethany House Publishers, 1994.
Riders of the Pale Horse. Minneapolis: Bethany House Publishers, 1994.
Light and Shadow. Elgin, IL: Chariot Family Publishing, 1995.
The Messenger. Minneapolis: Bethany House Publishing, 1995.
The Music Box. Minneapolis: Bethany House Publishers, 1996.
Return to Harmony (with Janette Oke). Minneapolis: Bethany House, 1996.
To the Ends of the Earth. Nashville, TN: Thomas Nelson Publishers, 1996.
One False Move. Nashville, TN: Thomas Nelson Publishers, 1997.
Tidings of Comfort and Joy. Nashville, TN: Thomas Nelson Publishers, 1997.
The Dream Voyagers. Minneapolis: Bethany House Publishers, 1998.
One Shenandoah Winter. Nashville, TN: Thomas Nelson Publishers, 1998.
Tomorrow's Dream (with Janette Oke, sequel to *Another Homecoming*). Minneapolis: Bethany House, 1998.
The Book of Hours. Nashville, TN: Thomas Nelson Publishers, 2000.
The Great Divide. New York: Doubleday, 2000.

Kingdom Come (with Larry Burkett). New York: Doubleday, 2000.
Drummer in the Dark. New York: Doubleday, 2001.
Winner Take All (sequel to *The Great Divide*) New York: Doubleday, 2003.
The Delta Factor (as Thomas Locke). Minneapolis: Bethany House Publishers, 2004.
Elixir. Nashville, TN: WestBow Press, 2004.
Impostor. Nashville, TN: WestBow Press, 2004.
The Lazarus Trap. Nashville, TN: WestBow Press, 2005.

"Jeffrey Sinclair" series (Minneapolis, MI: Bethany House Publishers, unless otherwise indicated)

The Amber Room. 1992.
Florian's Gate. 1992.
Winter Palace. 1993.
Heartland. Nashville, TN: WestBow Press, 2006.

"Song of Acadia" series with Janette Oke (Minneapolis, MI: Bethany House Publishers, 1999–2002)

"Rendezvous with Destiny" series (Minneapolis, MI: Bethany House Publishers, 1993–1995)

"Reluctant Prophet" series (Nashville, TN: Thomas Nelson Publishers, 1998–1999)

"Heirs of Acadia" series, with Isabella Bunn (Minneapolis, MI: Bethany House Publishers, 2004–2006)

A number of these have been collected in new editions or published as audiocassettes.

Bibliography of Works about Author

Bunn, T. Davis. *Home Page*. http://www.davisbunn.com.
DeLong, Janice and Rachel Schwedt. *Contemporary Christian Authors: Lives and Works*. Lanham, Maryland: Scarecrow Press, 2000.
FaithfulReader.com, Interview with T. David Bunn. http://www.faithfulreader.com.
Hudak, Melissa. Review of *The Meeting Place*. *Library Journal* (April 1, 1999): 80.
Kozick, Paulette. Review of *Florian's Gate*. *Rapport* (1993): 24.
Mort, John. Review of *Another Homecoming, Booklist* (May 1, 1998): 1662.
Mort, John. Review of *Tomorrow's Dream*. *Booklist* (May 1, 1998):1478.
Mort, John, Review of *Elixir. Booklist* (March 1, 2004): 1100
"T. Davis Bunn" *Contemporary Authors Online*. Detroit: Thomson Gale, 2007.
Whalin, W. Terry. Review of *Heartland*. http://www.Faithful Readercom/reviews

BUTLER, ROBERT OLEN, JR.

Personal, Professional and Religious Background

Robert Olen Butler Jr. (1945–) was born in Granite City, Illinois. His father, Robert Olen Butler, was a college professor and his mother, Lucille Frances Hall Butler, was an executive secretary. Robert Butler went to Northwestern University, earning a B.S. summa cum laude in oral interpretation in 1967. In 1968, he married his first wife, Carol Supplee. The following

> I do believe the artist and the preacher are basically in the same business. We respond to the moment-by-moment sensual flow of existence on planet earth, and we are subject to that deeply embedded personal fear that we are utterly alone here in spite of the surface appearance of other preachers of similar sorts floating around us.
>
> —Robert Olen Butler Jr., as told to W. Dale Brown in an interview in Louisville, 1996

year, he served as a member of the U.S. Army Military Intelligence in Vietnam, becoming a sergeant. This experience proved life-changing for him, introducing him to a very different culture, which he loved, and which became the subject of his most successful fiction.

On his return in 1972, he divorced his first wife and married Marilyn Geller, a poet, by whom he had his only child, Joshua Robert. They were later divorced. Butler enrolled at the University of Iowa to study play writing, earning an M.A. He then worked as an editor and reporter for *Electronic News* in New York City, returned briefly to teach high school in Granite City, Illinois, from 1973 to 1974. He then became a reporter in Chicago from 1974–1975. In 1975, Butler became editor-in-chief for *Energy User News*. While living in New York, he did postgraduate studies at the New School for Social Research from 1979–1981.

It was when he was working at the *Energy Users News* in New York that Butler began writing his first novel, *The Alleys of Eden*. He drafted the novel on legal pads during his morning subway commutes and sent the manuscript to two different publishers before Horizon Press accepted it in 1981. This sensitive portrayal of Vietnamese people, which was markedly different from most of the other novels emerging from the Vietnam War, brought him critical attention.

With a new enthusiasm for fiction, Butler accepted a position teaching at McNeese State University, Lake Charles, Louisiana, where he came into contact with the Vietnam refugees who had settled in the region. His short stories about the Vietnamese in America, *A Good Scent from Strange Mountain*, won him the Pulitzer Prize for Fiction in 1993. Butler married Maureen Donlan in August of 1987, when he moved to Louisiana. During the next few years, Butler rose in the ranks, from assistant professor to professor of fiction writing, and then to a named chair, the Francis Eppes Professorship. In 1988, he accepted a position at Florida State University in Tallahassee—the Michael Shaara Chair in creative writing. Since then he has served as a speaker at many regional conferences on creative writing.

In 1995, Butler divorced his third wife. Within twenty-four hours of meeting her, he married the poet **Elizabeth Dewberry** in a ceremony at the Tavern on the Green in New York City. Although he continues to teach and to write novels, he now spends more of his time on screenwriting. Until 2007, he and his wife served as editors of one another's works, and considered themselves "best friends." At that time, Butler sent an e-mail to the English department at Florida State University, telling his students and colleagues that Elizabeth was leaving him to become Ted Turner's "girlfriend," not his only one apparently. Butler attributed this sudden shift in affection to two causes: she had never been able to "step out of the shadow" of Butler's Pulitzer Prize, and Ted Turner reminded her of her grandfather, who had molested her as a child. He told the department that he would keep the house, his dogs and cats. "I wish her the best." And he asks that no one "think ill of her in any way."

Major Works and Themes

Robert Olen Butler refuses to be categorized as a Southern author, or one whose primary subject is the Vietnamese people. Nonetheless he has clearly found his voice in describing the challenges facing people of different cultural backgrounds who fall in love, the displacement of Vietnamese people in this country, and the alienation of Americans abroad.

For his wartime romances, he often uses the old Vietnamese legend of the dragon from the sea and the princess from the forest who fall in love and produce 100 offspring, before they find they must part. His lovers are fiercely attracted to one another, overpowered by their physical desire, but unable to establish a stable relationship. Sometimes the ending is death, sometimes desertion.

He loves to tell his stories of star-crossed lovers through gentle flashbacks, dwelling with excruciating detail on the women's bodies, their reactions, and the hero's feelings for them. (In *They Whisper*, he spends two pages on his admiration of his lover's navel). His prose and tone have the intimate, dreamy poetic quality, full of sounds and smells, that Proust uses—as well as some of that writer's flashbacks and emotional evocations. In Butler's case, the evocations are primarily sexual. He notes that sex and death are the "only things that interest a serious mind." He is also inclined to see one woman as all women, one experience as all experience, thus making this obsession with sexual detail somehow universal.

Butler, who identifies himself as a Catholic, was converted by his second wife, the mother of his son. Like Fiona, in *They Whisper*, Marilyn Geller was "intensely Catholic," bringing into their household a "particular kind of fanaticism" that Butler felt to be out of tune with what he saw in the universe. In this novel, he pictures his wife's exaggerated awareness of sin, particularly sexual sin, and her compulsion to confess every transgression to her priest, even in the middle of the night. She fills the house with Catholic art and tries to lead their son into the priesthood.

Although Butler rejected his wife's type of Catholicism, he does use the sacramental sense of this faith—except for seeing sex as a kind of secular sacrament, a way of "knowing" and a kind of grace. In *They Whisper*, the most controversial, and the most frequently reviewed of his novels, Butler insists that Ira is not simply a womanizer, but is a man of particular sensitivity to women, who finds all women beautiful for the "absolutely individual personal shape of their bodies" and "the deeper mystery of personality." At the end, yet another woman becomes for the hero, "his holy grail." Butler transforms the language and symbolism of faith—a pill becomes the wafer, rain becomes baptism, the woman becomes the "Grail." In this, he draws on the tradition of **Graham Greene, John Updike,** and **Walker Percy,** all of whom mingle religious language and secular life with great skill and power.

Butler notes that rigid adherence to orthodoxy repels him, but he finds delight in reading in and meditating on the Bible. He believes that the King James Bible, which he considers a "wonderful document of storytelling and voice" has had a profound influence on him. He especially admires the prophets Daniel, Jeremiah, and Isaiah. He sees in the inspiration and proclamations of the writer a strong kinship with the Old Testament prophets.

He is also interested in Buddhism, which he discovered during his time in Vietnam. The references to Eastern thought and Vietnamese folk mythology give his work a particular flavor. The fanciful stories of these people, like the final path to "Strange Mountain" in death, the ghosts that return to visit the living, make their way into his stories. By use of interior monologues, judiciously interspersed with dialogue and narrative, he inserts himself into his characters, sensing their alienation from their new culture.

Butler's sensitivity first won notice in his trilogy of stories about American soldiers who married Vietnamese women. His talent really flowered in his volume of short stories about Vietnamese refugees living along the Gulf coast near New Orleans—*A Good Scent from a*

Strange Mountain. This remarkable book, full of humor and charming insights into this transplanted culture of the "children of dust," won him the Pulitzer Prize. A later novel, *The Deep Green Sea*, describes an ex-GI who returns to Vietnam, discovers a beautiful young woman, whom he loves obsessively, only to discover that she is his own daughter.

The third of his early Vietnam novels, *Sun Dogs*, is the one he considers his "most openly Christian book" in the sense that Wilson Hand "enacts the central Christian ritual." His joy finally comes, after a long search, through sacrifice, a version of the Eucharist. Although some readers understood the novel, it was generally "wildly misunderstood by critics" who wanted to read it as a badly written detective story.

Butler considers his deeper concern "human connection and identity." Love of men and women, parents and children are his continuing themes.

Critical Reception

Robert Olen Butler has been widely reviewed. The *New York Times* has taken each of his novels seriously, assigning the reviews to such impressive writers as Jane Smiley. The reviewers have found *They Whisper* particularly interesting, calling it a portrait of the "dance of sex and dance of death" and "purification of death." Dwight Garner says of Butler that he is "America's most olfactory minded novelist; he samples the world through a pair of inquisitive nostrils." Christopher Lehmann-Haupt finds his portrait of the fanatical Fiona "masterly"

Earlier novels also won him critical acclaim, especially the trilogy of stories about star-crossed lovers in Vietnam. John Grant, writing for the *Philadelphia Inquirer*, considered *The Alleys of Eden* comparable to Graham Greene's *The Quiet American*. Butler had written six "well-received but small-selling novels" before finding his voice in the short stories about Vietnamese refugees that won him the Pulitzer Prize for fiction in 1993—*A Good Scent from a Strange Mountain*. Richard Eder called it a "collection so delicate and so strong, the title story stands out as close to magical." Almost all of the critics tend to praise his beautiful language and delightful style, but rarely his characterization or plotting.

Awards

Robert Olen Butler has won a number of awards; the TuDo Chinh Kien Award for Outstanding Contributions to American Culture by a Vietnam Vet from the Vietnam Veterans of America in 1987; the Emily Clark Balch Award for Best Work of Fiction, *Virginia Quarterly Review* in 1991; the Pulitzer Prize for Fiction, the Richard and Hilda Rosenthal Foundation Award, American Academy of Arts and Letters, and the Notable Book Award, American Library Association in 1993 for *A Good Scent from a Strange Mountain*; he was a Guggenheim fellow in 1993; and won the National Magazine Award for Fiction in 2001.

Bibliography of Novels by Author

The Alleys of Eden. New York: Horizon Press, 1981.
Countrymen of Bones. New York: Horizon Press, 1983.
On Distant Ground. New York: Knopf, 1983.
Sun Dogs. New York: Horizon Press, 1983.
Wabash. New York: Holt, 1987.
The Deuce. New York: Holt, 1989.

They Whisper. New York: Holt, 1994.
The Deep Green Sea. New York: St. Martin's Press, 1998.
Mr. Spaceman. New York: Grove Press, 2000.
Fair Warning. Boston, MA: Atlantic Monthly Press, 2002.

Robert Olen Butler has also written three volumes of short stories: *A Good Scent from a Strange Mountain* (1992), *Tabloid Dreams* (1996), and *Had a Good Time* (2004).

He has also written a number of feature-length scripts for screen and television for Disney, New Regency, Paramount, Twentieth Century Fox, Universal Pictures Warner Brothers, and Home Box Office.

Bibliography of Works about Author

Barbash, Tom. "Dead Heads," *New York Times*, September 3, 2006.
Brown, W. Dale. *Of Fiction and Faith: Twelve American Writers Talk about Their Vision and Work.* Grand Rapids, MI: William B. Eerdmans Publishing Company, 1997.
Brown, W. Dale, "Writers in the Same Residence: An Interview with Robert Olen Butler and Elizabeth Dewberry. Southern Writers. http://www.southernledger.com/southernlife/southernwriters/DAle_Brown/Interview.
"Butler, Robert Olen." http://www.enotes.com/contemporary-literary-criticism/butler-robert-olen.
"Butler, Robert Olen," Wikipedia. http://www.en.wikipedia.org/wiki/Robert_Olen_Butler.
Elder, Richard. *Los Angeles Times Book Review*, March 29, 1992: 3.
Garner, Dwight. "Return of the American," *New York Times Book Review*, January 11, 1998.
Grant, John. *Philadelphia Inquirer*, January 24, 1982.
Lehmann-Haupt, Christopher. Review of *They Whisper. New York Times*, January 27, 1994.
Nicholson, Geoff. "Beam Me Up, Desi." Review of *Mr. Spaceman. New York Times*, February 20, 2000.
"Robert Olen Butler," *Contemporary Authors Online.* Detroit: Thomson Gale, 2006.
Smiley, Jane. "Something Is Wrong with This Life," *New York Times*, February 13, 1994.

CARLSON, MELODY

Personal, Professional, and Religious Background

Melody Hickman Carlson (1956–) was born in San Francisco. Her father, William Hickman, was a musician, her mother, Nancy Haga Hickman, a teacher. From the time she was a child, Melody loved to make up stories and to write. She went to a community college, where she earned an associate of science degree in early childhood education and child development. In 1978, she married Christopher Carlson, a contractor

After ten years as a preschool teacher in Eugene Oregon, Melody Carson left her teaching to become an executive assistant for Holt International Children's Services. She then became senior editor for Multnomah Publishers. When Melody Carlson reached her 30s, in the 1990s, her husband encouraged her to write about her own ideas. Her first effort, a "how-to" book, was published in 1995. She soon found that she could make a career as a full-time freelance author. Since that time, she has written, illustrated, and published over a hundred books, gaining over two million readers.

Melody Carlson describes her life in Sisters, Oregon, in the "beautiful Cascades," in idyllic terms: "My husband and I live in a comfortable cabin next to the national forest, where deer, rabbits, squirrels, and all kinds of birds keep us entertained. It is a perfect place to write." The Carlsons have two grown sons, who live nearby.

> I've found that writing is a wonderful way to 'take a break.' I've also found that a lot of the tough stuff of life creates great fodder for stories. It's my firm belief that God doesn't waste anything and I shouldn't either.
>
> —Melody Carlson on her Web site (www. melodycarlson.com)

Major Works and Themes

Melody Carlson is best known for her books for children and young adults, but she has also written fiction and nonfiction for adults, primarily for Christian women. Her stories are usually set in Oregon or

Seattle, her central characters young and female. She does have the capacity to draw believable portraits of old ladies and middle-aged women as well. The problems they face are contemporary yet universal: dysfunctional families, brutality, alcohol abuse, infidelity, drug addiction; isolation, loneliness, bad career choices, and unfulfilling lives. She is known for her "issues-driven" novels.

One of her most famous is *Crystal Lies*, the harrowing story of a woman dealing with her son's drug addiction and her husband's infidelity. Carlson is not content with a simple explanation or a happy bromide for a solution. She insists that addiction is a lifelong problem, that addicts lie, and that mothers struggle to keep from being enablers in their loving concern for their children. She also acknowledges that adultery can destroy a marriage, and is not a sin that is easily forgiven. She has a realistic streak and a toughness in her approach that mark her novels as more interesting than many contemporary Christian romances.

Homeward, Melody Carlson's first and most successful novel, features a heroine (Meg) who has just given up the good life in San Francisco, where she has a great job. She is a sleek and stylish executive, loves a wealthy (if untrustworthy) fiancé and is inordinately proud of her shiny new Jaguar. Confronted with evidence of her fiancé's infidelity, she returns home for the first time in 20 years to the cranberry bogs of Oregon. Meg finds her family has changed as much as she has: her mother (Sunny) is now more settled and is very ill; her sister (Erin) is happily married and eager to welcome her home; her grandmother has aged and is now living back in the family home, ill and tormented by those "care givers" who are seeking to control her property. Much of the story is about twisted family relationships, bitterness caused by sin and the refusal to forgive. As Meg (formerly "fat little Meggie") wanders about town, she discovers the decline of the family cranberry business, the plans of her corrupt cousin Abner, and her own dissatisfaction with her life in the fast lane. The slower, simpler life, the return to faith and family, the discovery of real love—these open her up to a different, more natural way to live her life with greater fulfillment.

Carlson is careful to conform to Multnomah standards: The only violence in the story is the shooting of a dog (though Abner does seem to berate his wife and son when he is drunk). The language and sexuality are under the author's gentle control. The new suitor apologizes for tarnishing the heroine's reputation by going to her apartment at night, never tries to kiss her good night, and proposes without any steamy sex scenes.

In *Looking for Cassandra Jane*, a tougher example of Carlson's writing, she follows a young girl from her early days living with her widowed father, who in drunken rages beats her hideously. He lands in jail, and she in the hospital. From there, we track her painful adolescence, bounced from relatives to foster homes to a cult and finally to caring counselors. Through God's grace, she survives with her mind and courage intact in spite of the adult delinquents who inhabit her world, finding love and fulfillment through her one true friend—who finally becomes her husband.

An especially interesting book for people interested in schizophrenia is *Finding Alice*, a first-person narrative of a college senior who suddenly begins to believe she is Alice in Wonderland, living with the Mad Hatter and the Red Queen. Her tenuous hold on reality grows increasingly fragile as she tries dealing with her paranoia on her own, then with the help of her hovering mother, then her overbearing pastor, then an over-prescribing doctor who wants to institutionalize her. She finally escapes, has a wild set of adventures among hippies and outcasts, ending as a street person, taken in by the "cat lady" who nourishes her, helps her to find more appropriate and faith-based treatment, and offers her security and understanding. The book reveals two types of religious approaches to mental illness—one blaming it on sin, the other seeking to understand and help with love and care, allowing the patient to make free choices for herself and take control of her own cure.

Melody Carlson also writes historical romances, always with the same guidelines used by evangelical publishers: careful attention to details, action illustrative of God's will and his grace, little violence or sex, and no obscene language. She builds suspense, introduces characters, and moves to a satisfactory conclusion in a careful pattern that works for the reconciliation of family members, the forgiveness of sins, the discovery of God's path for the individual's life, and the union of Christian couples for happy families.

Critical Reception

Melody Carlson sees her role as a modern version of the old biblical one—teaching through parables. It is often possible in her novels to discover the underlying parable—the need to separate the tares from the corn, the ministry of the Good Samaritan, or the desirability of building one's house on stone. She prefers to use her fiction to instruct: "Jesus taught through stories."

Tamara Butler has noted that Carlson writes on "Female-centered topics—such as post-partum depression and marital relationships." She tells a good story, full of action, suspense, and good practical advice. Her stories are aimed largely at younger readers, those seeking to find their vocation, to establish their families, to avoid the dangers that lurk like lions along the path of life. Carlson believes that the Bible is the best guide in life, but must be reinforced by a Christian community—preferably a church—where the believer can have fellowship and support. DeLong notes that Carlson's focus, in writing *Wise Man's House*, is on "issues of faith, self-perception, and the rewards of achieving a goal through hard work."

Awards

Melody Carson has won the RITA Award for the best inspirational romance in 1998, from the Romance Writers of America in 1998 for *Homeward*, the RITA Gold Medallion in the children's book category the same year for *Benjamin's Box*, and the RITA Gold Medallion the following year in the children's book category for *King of the Stable*.

Bibliography of Novels by Author

Homeward. Sisters, OR: Multnomah Publishers, 1997.
The Wise Man's House. Sisters, OR: Multnomah Publishers, 1997.
Awakening Heart. Minneapolis, MN: Bethany House, 1998.
Heartland Skies. Sisters, OR: Multnomah Publishers, 1998.
Shades of Light. Sisters, OR: Multnomah Publishers, 1998.
Isaac's Angel. Carmel, NY: Guidepost Books, 1998.
Blood Sisters. Eugene, OR: Harvest House, 2001.
Angels in the Snow. Grand Rapids, MI: Fleming H. Revell, 2002.
Looking for Cassandra Jane. Wheaton, IL: Tyndale House Publishers, 2002.
Armando's Treasure. Wheaton, IL: Tyndale House Publishers, 2003.
Crystal Lies. Colorado Springs, Co: WaterBrook Press, 2004.
A Gift of Christmas Present. Grand Rapids, MI: Fleming H. Revell, 2004.
Three Days: A Mother's Story. Grand Rapids, MI: Fleming H. Revell, 2005.
The Christmas Bus. Grand Rapids, MI: Fleming H. Revell, 2006.

My Son, The Savior: A Mother's Story. Grand Rapids, MI: Fleming H. Revell, 2007.
These Boots Weren't Made for Walking. Colorado Springs, CO: WaterBrook Press, 2007.

"Whispering Pines" series (Eugene, OR: Harvest House, 1999–2001)

"Tales from Grace Chapel Inn" series (Carmel, NY: Guideposts, 2003–2004)

Bibliography of Works about Author

Butler, Tamara. Review of *On This Day. Library Journal* (February 1, 2006): 62.
DeLong, Janice and Rachel Schwedt. *Contemporary Christian Authors: Lives and Works.* Lanham, MD: The Scarecrow Press, 2000.
Faithful Reader Interview: http://www.faithfulreader.com/wuthors/au-carlson-melody.asp.
"Melody Carlson," *Contemporary Authors Online.* Detroit: Thomson Gale, 2007.
Melody Carlson Web site: http://www.melodycarlson.com.

CAVANAUGH, JACK

Personal, Professional, and Religious Background

Jack Cavanaugh (1952–) was born in Youngstown, Ohio, the son of William and Marjorie Cavanaugh. He attended Granite Hills High School in El Cajon, California, before going to Grand Canyon College, where he earned a B.A., and then Southwestern Baptist Theological Seminary, where he earned an M.Div. After seminary, he became the pastor of the First Baptist Church, Imperial Beach, San Diego, California for two years, then the managing editor for Christian Education Publishers in San Diego. Since 1992, he has been a full-time writer. He says that a seminary professor inspired him to write, telling the class: "Men, if you want to expand your ministry, even beyond your own lifetime, write."

He is married to Marlene, or "Marni," whom he met at Azusa Pacific College. They have three grown children—Elizabeth Ann, Keri Marie, and Samuel Brand, all of whom are artistically talented: Elizabeth, who lives in Iowa, is a "gifted writer;" Keri is a singer, who does musical theatre in San Diego, where she is also a police-dispatcher; and Sam works at Disneyland as the Mad Hatter by day and performs in musical theatre productions at night. Jack and Marni Cavanaugh now live in Southern California.

Major Works and Themes

Jack Cavanaugh is most famous for his historical fiction, a "weaving together of two colorful strands—historical fact and imaginative fiction." He cites as his mentors the classic authors of Christian epics—Dante and Milton. He also praises recent Christian writers, like **Brock and Bodie Thoene** as well as **Frank Peretti**, for "expanding the market" with *This Present Darkness.*

> Stories have the ability to reach people on several levels: intellectual, visual, and emotional. This triple punch is a powerful method of teaching spiritual truth.
>
> —Jack Cavanaugh in interview with Randall Murphree, June 22, 2006—quoted on the Jack Cavanaugh Web site under "Author Bio" (www.jackcavanaugh.com)

Jack Cavanaugh and Marni were engaged for two years before they married and then waited five more years before having children.

In Cavanaugh's best known work, *The Puritans* (which includes an afterword describing his technique), he brings together several of the religious and political groups of 17th-century England with fictional characters who form the nucleus of the American colonial family he traces through subsequent volumes into the Vietnam era. In this series, he includes real people, like Bishop Laud, John Winthrop, and King Charles I; real places, such as the Star Chamber, the Tower of London, and Boston colony; with fictional characters like his hero and his arch villain. Cavanaugh weaves a lively tale, full of fights, murders, intrigue, double-crosses, sea voyages, trials, and temptations. He highlights the conflict between the established Church of England and the growing Puritan community whose members finally become the nucleus of the new colonies. He says, "*The Puritans* will always have a special place in my heart" because this was his first novel

Another of his historical series tracks the rise of Nazi Germany. "Songs in the Night" features a German pastor, the Reverend Josef Schumacher, who is momentarily tempted to succumb to the stirring nationalism and pride of Hitler's massive propaganda program, but refuses to demean himself and his church by praising everything, even nature, as the work of the Nazis. SS troops beat and terrify him. They also enroll the youth of his church in Nazi programs, to spy on their own families, brutalize a helpless old Jewish-Christian scholar, and turn their back on their Christian heritage. The first of the series, *While Mortals Sleep*, reveals the slow but steady increase of Nazi tyranny directly confronting the Christian church. The subsequent volumes trace Schumacher's family and the church youth as the oppression grows. The pastor builds a community for those seeking refuge, keeping watch over his beloved youth, at least one of whom, a rabid follower of Nazi doctrine, gradually becomes a doubter and finally a rebel. The series ends with the tearing down of the Berlin Wall and the reconciliation of family and friends after years of pain and separation.

Yet another of Cavanaugh's historical explorations is dedicated to the early translations of Scripture, with all the problems and intrigue involved in this forbidden work. The "Book of Books" series deals with the English Bible, beginning with *Glimpses of Truth*, which features Thomas Torr, a peasant who assists John Wycliffe in his great work. The Catholic Church is the grand adversary, seeking to stop or destroy any efforts to provide a vernacular translation. *Beyond the Sacred Page*, the second volume, picks up the story of translations two centuries later, this time focusing on the forbidden William Tyndale translation, which was widely distributed through England.

Cavanaugh's collaborative efforts are also interesting and lively books. He worked with Jerry Kuiper on *Death Watch*, a contemporary story set in Los Angeles, quite different from his usual historical narratives. The heroine of this mystery story is Sydney St. James, a reporter for the local television station who sets out to discover the key to a series of e-mails, telephone messages, and telegrams correctly predicting the deaths of various recipients within 48 hours. Sydney teams up with a German reporter, only to discover that her interest in the case threatens friends and coworkers. This was Cavanaugh's first try at contemporary suspense—and unlike his earlier novels, not part of a series.

Jack Cavanaugh was particularly delighted to learn that the well known revivalist Bill Bright was seeking to collaborate with a novelist on the topic of historical revivals in America. Since Cavanaugh had written the "American Family Portrait" series in the mid-1990s, he seemed the perfect partner. The two men prayed side by side for two days, talked about history and story ideas, realizing that Dr. Bright would not live long enough to see the release of even the first book in their projected four-novel series they called "The Great Awakenings." In one of the series, *Proof*, a New York attorney takes the Holy Spirit to trial in an attempt to win back his daughter who has had a life-changing experience. This is a courtroom thriller with amazing twists to the plot. In the second volume, *Fire*, Josiah Rush, pastor of First Church in Havenhill, Connecticut, meets with the historical Great Awakening preachers Jonathan Edwards and George Whitefield, who correctly diagnose the sin-sick nation's need for spiritual revival. *Storm*, the third volume, follows the declining spiritual fervor after the Great Awakening as a young Yale student finds himself the target of attacks for his faith. The fourth volume, *Fury*, tells the story of a young man, witness to a murder, who travels to upstate New York, where he finds Charles Finney preaching the Holy Spirit. As in the others, an ordinary citizen, situated in a particular historical context, discovers the power of the great preachers of the time and finds his life transformed by the experience.

The influence of Frank Peretti is clear in Cavanaugh's latest series, "Kingdom Wars," which opens with *Hideous Beauty*. Unlike his earlier stories, this time Cavanaugh undertakes to explore the realm of angels and demons as these creatures are inserted into human life. Grant Austin, the protagonist, who has won fame with a prizewinning biography of the president of the United States, discovers that his success has been orchestrated by rebel angels who now plot the President's assassination.

Critical Reception

Jack Cavanaugh is a prolific writer, a talented teller of suspenseful thrillers, and a committed Christian whose dramatic novels have won numerous, well deserved awards. His first series, based on the history of the Puritans in America, was well received, leading him to expect that he could carry on this same level of enthusiastic response in his second series. In 1996 and 1997, Cavanaugh traced the beginnings of the European colonization of South Africa, hoping that this "African Covenant" series would win much the same acclaim as his "American Family Portrait" series had done. He was disappointed. It was probably the wrong time in history to use his style of sympathetic narrative when talking about white Europeans in Africa.

His had great success with the series on Nazi Germany, "Songs in the Night," which did include some strong criticism of the fanatical Nazis and their willing tools in the Christian community, but again revealed his sympathy for the spirit of the times. His villains are not completely vile, nor his heroes without flaw. This careful analysis of time, place, and people helps to explain why the reviews are generally enthusiastic in the *Library Journal*, *Publishers Weekly*, and *Booklist*. John Mort, Philip Tomasso III, and Melissa Hudak have all praised his work, commenting primarily on the content of the books rather than Cavanaugh's style. Tomasso does note the author's strong story-telling ability with good suspense.

By taking ordinary people and placing them in dramatic scenes with historical figures, Cavanaugh brings to life the great conflicts and challenges that Christians have faced in various times and places. He tells a good story, based on solid research.

Awards

Jack Cavanaugh has won the Silver Medallion Award from the Christian Publishers Association for *The Puritans* and Christy Awards for excellence in Christian fiction for *While Mortals Sleep* and for *His Watchful Eye*. He has also won a number of California awards: Best

Historical Fiction, San Diego Book Awards (for *The Puritans*) in 1994; Writer of the Year, San Diego Christian Writers Guild, 1994; Book of the Year, San Diego Christian Writers Guild, 1994, and Book of the Year, San Diego Christian Writers Guild, 1995, for *The Patriots*. In 2001, he won the Gold Medal for Best Historical Fiction by ForeWord Magazine and in 2005 he once again won the San Diego Christian Writers Guild Award.

Bibliography of Novels by Author

"American Family Portrait" series (Wheaton, IL: VictorBooks; later Colorado Springs, CO: Chariot Victor Publishing, 1994–1999)

"African Covenant" series (Chicago, IL: Moody Press, 1996–1997)

"Songs in the Night" series (Minneapolis, MN: Bethany House Publishers, 2001–2004)

"Book of Books" series (Grand Rapids, MI: Zondervan Publishing, 1999–2003)

Other Fiction

Dear Enemy. Minneapolis, MN: Bethany House Publishers, 2005.
Postmarked Heaven. Grand Rapids, MI: F.H. Revell, 2002.

"Great Awakening" series. Coauthored by Bill Bright. (West Monroe, LA: Howard Publishing, 2005–2006)

"Kingdom Wars" series (West Monroe, LA: Howard Publishing, 2007)

Bibliography of Works about Author

DeLong, Janice and Rachel Schwedt. *Contemporary Christian Authors: Lives and Works.* Lanham, MD: The Scarecrow Press, Inc., 2000.
Duncan, Melanie C. Review of *While Mortals Sleep. Library Journal* (November 1, 2001): 74.
Hudak, Melissa. Review of *The Peacemakers* and *Glimpses of Truth. Library Journal* (June 1, 1999): 94.
"Jack Cavanaugh," *Contemporary Authors Online.* Detroit: Thomson Gale, 2007.
"Jack Cavanaugh," http://www.stevelaube.com/authors/jackcavanaugh.htm.
Jack Cavanaugh Web site: http://www.jackcavanaugh.com.html.
Mort, John. *Christian Fiction: A Guide to the Genre.* Greenwood Village, CO: Libraries Unlimited, 2002.
Mort, John. Review of *The Puritans. Booklist* (October 15, 1994): 401.
Mort, John. Review of *Glimpses of Truth. Booklist* (May 1, 1999): 1579.
Mort, John. Review of *While Mortals Sleep. Booklist* (October 1, 2001): 281.
Tomasso, Philip III. Review of *While Mortals Sleep.* In the Library Review. http://www.inthelibrary review.com/.

COLLINS, BRANDILYN

Personal, Professional, and Religious Background

Brandilyn Seamands Collins (1956–) was born in India to missionary parents, J.T. and Ruth Seamands. She was the last of four daughters. Although her parents were in India for

20 years, the family came back to the United States on furlough when Brandilyn was about three, and ended up staying in the States because one of the daughters had a long-term illness—from which she later recovered. The Seamands family were readers and writers. Her sister had taught Brandilyn to read before she started kindergarten. Brandilyn remembers her mother sharing the proofs from a nonfiction work with the entire family, seeking their advice. Although Brandilyn was only 10 at the time, she spotted a misspelling that the rest of the family overlooked.

> My task in life, after all, is to keep you off balance, not quite sure of what new trials you must endure in my hands.
>
> —Brandilyn Collins's address to the reader in *Coral Moon*

She attended San Francisco State University, earning a B.A. in journalism before beginning work in theatre and in marketing. All through high school and much of college, she had planned on having an acting career, but changed her major in the middle of her college work. Her time as an actress, studying Stanislavsky's method acting, has proven a great help to her in her writing. Brandilyn Collins used many of these insights in her book on the writing of fiction and in her seminars for writers. Her work in marketing taught her some of the means to connect with an audience, which have served her well in her writing career.

In 1981, Brandilyn married Mark Collins. Ryan, Mark's son, from an earlier marriage, is now grown. They also have a daughter, Amberly. The Collins family lives in the California Bay area, spending much of their time in Coeur d'Alene, Idaho.

Major Works and Themes

Brandilyn Collins's first efforts at writing came with her interest in a true crime story. She followed a famous trial, which led her to research and then to the drafting of her first book, *A Question of Innocence*, published by Avon in 1995, and later by Zondervan as *Eyes of Elisha*. Because she received national coverage of this nonfiction event, she expected that her next fiction works would also find a publisher, but was disappointed until one agent suggested that she consider bringing her Christian values into her writing. This agent, who also represented **Francine Rivers**, inspired her to take a very different approach: instead of aiming her books at the "general market," she re-wrote her first three secular novels interweaving her faith into the characterization and plot. Within 5 years, she had written and published 14 books, 12 of them novels.

Her "Hidden Faces" series feature a forensic artist, Annie Kingston. Collins acknowledges that she began her research on the Internet, then the study of a textbook on forensics by Karen Taylor, then consultation with this authority as she worked on her novels. Like the C.S.I. stories on television, most of her stories open with a violent, often gory, murder scene, which then generate the narrative along with the investigation. She has visited the local forensics laboratories and talked with the directors, using their firsthand experiences in her descriptions. An unusual element in the "Web of Lies" series is that Chelsea Adams has visions from God. She sees the crimes in her mind and tries to communicate these visions to dubious friends and neighbors. In *Dread Champion*, Chelsea is chosen to be on the jury, creating a particularly odd situation.

The "Kanner Lake" series, which follow something of the same path, are what Collins calls "seatbelt suspense." She uses the classic detective story device of introducing a shocking crime in a bucolic lake community, disturbing the apparently placid citizens, and uncovering hidden angers and intrigues. The same characters and places reappear in the stories, with everyone hanging out at the Java Joint and watching the budding romance between the police chief's deputy and the heroine. The novels use not only the attractive young professional women Paige and Leslie, but also Ali, a bright new kid at the high school, who has been home-schooled previously and feels like an alien in this context. She falls in with a group who are under the spell of demonic forces, engaging in séances and dabbling in the dark arts. The story is designed to appeal to young readers as well as the standard audience for Christian romances.

Brandilyn Collins is good at suspense. She tells a compelling story, includes a strong sense of the battle between satanic forces and the people of God and she involves prayer and the power of a sovereign God in her outcomes. She is talented, lively, and fully aware of current tastes as well as enduring values.

Critical Reception

The critics have praised Brandilyn Collins for her skill in handling multiple points of view and time shifts, for the interesting details of police procedure and crime investigation which she includes in her "Kanner Lake" series, and for her sympathetic heroines. They generally acknowledge she is accomplished at the craft of writing: "Collins knows how to weave faith into a rich tale," according to *Library Journal*.

Awards

Brandilyn Collins is a three-time winner of the ACFT award. *Eyes of Elisha* was named the American Christian Romance Writers Book of the Year in 2001, and *Color the Sidewalk for Me* in 2002, this book also winning the Romantic Times Reviewers Choice Award in 2003.

Bibliography of Novels by Author

"Bradleyville" series (Grand Rapids, MI: Zondervan, 2001–2003)

"Chelsea Adams" series (Grand Rapids, MI: Zondervan, 2001–2002)

"Hidden Faces" series (Grand Rapids, MI: Zondervan, 2004)

"Kanner Lake" series (Grand Rapids, MI: Zondervan, 2007–2009)

Bibliography of Works about Author

Brandilyn Collins blogspot: www.forensicsand faith.blogspot.com.
Brandilyn Collins Interview with *Focus on Fiction*: www.focusonfiction.net/brandilyncollins.html.
Brandilyn Collins Web site: www.brandilyncollins.com.
Darlington, C.J. Interview: www.titletrakk.com/Brandilyn_Collins_Interview.html.
Duncan, Melanie C. Review of *Eyes of Elisha*. *Library Journal* (September 1, 2002): 154.
Publishers Weekly, Review of *Eyes of Elisha* (August 27, 2002): 49; Review of *Color the Sidewalk for Me*. (February 25, 2002): 44.
Zondervan Web site: www.Zondervan.com.

CRAMER, W. DALE

Personal, Professional, and Religious Background

> When God wants to accomplish something he uses the last person you'd expect.
>
> —W. Dale Cramer, interview about *Sutter's Cross* with Narelle Mollet

W. Dale Cramer reveals little of his background, acknowledging only that he draws his stories and characters from his own experience and that of his family. His father was raised Amish but left the community. It took him 50 years to get back into the graces of his father—a theme of alienation and sorrow that Cramer uses several times. A terrible fire in a mine where he worked also appears as a scene in one of his novels. Entries about him begin with his marriage to Pam Crowe in 1975 and cite his two children, Ty and Dusty. Cramer has worked as an electrician, a part-time construction worker, and a homemaker. Almost all of his work, including his time as homemaker, has served as fodder for his imagination.

In 1996, during his time as caretaker for his children, Cramer first began his writing career. He had already become an avid reader and private writer when an argument with a friend led him to submit an article to a magazine. "In the process, my friend taught me how to edit myself and convinced me that I was actually capable of writing publishable material." As he notes, "Writing doesn't take that long; learning to write does." While taking care of his children, 4 and 6 years old at the time, he got in contact with a Compuserve writers forum and began to write short stories for an online critique group. Because of reassurances, he decided to take his writing seriously, bought a book on the market for fiction, and started submitting pieces to magazines.

He and his family live in northern Georgia.

Major Works and Themes

W. Dale Cramer loves to write about working people, children, and families. Unlike many writers, he makes his children clearly and distinctly drawn individuals. He can capture the dynamics of the family—the resentments, the lingering love, the pain, the reticence, the hunger for understanding—in the same way that Eudora Welty does. His backgrounds have the reality of **Wendell Berry**'s, with the same sense of delight in nature and in ecology. He sets most of his tales in Georgia, where he portrays both cities and small towns. He helps his reader to know the history of Sutter's Cross, the town itself, the Appalachian mountains nearby, and the view of the river from Jacob's Knee. He also reveals an array of the people who live there: an old woman whose family has lived for generations in the mountains can tell a visitor about each field and tree, the developers with grand visions, who plan to flatten much of her property and pave it over for an airport. Cramer's preference is as clear as Berry's would be under the same circumstances.

W. Dale Cramer is particularly sensitive to issues between the male members of the family. All four of his novels deal with an estrangement between the father and the son. Sometimes the father has left the family, or died, sometimes the son has left. In his first novel, *Sutter's Cross*, for

> Most of the time I make an effort to restrain my sense of humor in my writing because it can interfere with the real story. But life is funny.
>
> —W. Dale Cramer in Narelle Mollet interview, TitleTrack.com

example, he reveals the deep division between Web Holcombe and his father. Web thought he would prove that he could make money on real estate faster than his father and in greater amounts by trading on some inside knowledge. His father rebuked him, explaining that it was legal, but it was not right. A chastened Web never seemed to understand the difference, never was reconciled with his father. The old man died while the bitter and rebellious son was fighting in Vietnam. It is only when Web grows older and has a son of his own that he comes to understand the importance of doing what is right, not just staying within the letter of the law.

In another of Cramer's stories, *Levi's Will*, the tyrannical Amish father pressures his son into a stifling conformity. Forced to rebel, both physically by running away and psychologically by remaining angry and resentful for years, Will also comes to a period of understanding and need for reconciliation. In this hunt for repentance, for understanding, for a return to one's roots, paying one's debts to the previous generation becomes imperative. It is also coupled with the need for grace, the grace of God in forgiving human sins, and the grace of other people in showing love and compassion even where it is not deserved. The Amish funeral service that concludes the book is a powerful summary of this community's values.

Cramer's young men are usually not formally educated. If they begin college, they soon drop out to take blue-collar jobs. They are bright, serious, but alienated and rootless. In *Bad Ground*, the young man turns to hard work, finding some gratification in learning how to do things well—tasks required for mining the hard ground. In *Levi's Will*, the son learns to build steel bridges. In *Summer of Light*, the young father is a steelworker, who loves laboring atop high buildings. When reduced because of an accident to the role of baby-sitter, he still finds pleasure in fixing his truck and building his neighbor's home.

The loss of mother and father and the separation from other kin cannot be entirely compensated for by marriage and establishing a new family. Instead, the solitary heroes carry the burden of their separation into the next generation, hurting their own sons by their inability to show love, sadly replicating their fathers' failures. Grudges continue for decades, finally resolved only by amazing grace—moments in which they forgive and are forgiven. One of the finest of these moments appears in *Sutter's Cross*. An old lady who has lost her son, her husband, and her home, comforts a rich man, the villain of the story, when his young son is lost and presumed drowned. When Web stands during a prayer in the community church, protesting that he does not want condolences for a son who has died, but hope for his son who is missing, Miss Agnes comes forward, puts her arm around his shoulder, and comforts him. She knows what it is like to have a son missing in action—her own experience for the past 20 years. Web, a Darwinian figure who delights in his use of power, melts with this gentle gesture, kneels with her, and weeps as he accepts her forgiveness and God's grace.

In *Bad Ground*, Jeremy Prine finds himself suddenly without either father or mother. His mother's final instructions in a letter, require him to go to his uncle Aiden. As she tells him, "You have something I couldn't give him, and he has something I couldn't give you." The young man finds his uncle at a mine in the worst part of Atlanta, a badly scarred and bitter man, now known as "Snake," who has no love for his nephew and no interest in helping him. As it turns out, by joining in the cruel work that Snake and his fellow miners perform, Jeremy discovers what it is to be a man, what his own father was like, how he died, and what he himself must now believe. He finds a father in a this bitter, childless uncle.

The story is told with colorful detail and great drama, involving the reader in the intricate workings of the shaft and the tough men who labor there. It chronicles the fellowship that men develop when working together, the way that a young boy can earn their respect, and the path they find to faith and meaning in their lives. The small church that becomes a community for Jeremy and some of the others helps them to cope with the bitter lives they are forced to live. The love affair with a young girl who is watching the deterioration of her own previously wealthy family, introduces a feminine element into this primarily masculine world. By the end, Jeremy is able to function with sensitivity to a woman who loves music and manners and with toughness to men who face adversity with determination and courage. He learns to hunt and fish and to make firm decisions. But he also learns to reach out in love and understanding.

Cramer is interested in exploring the stereotypical view of men's and women's roles in the world. In *Levi's Will*, he uses the Amish community for one set of assumptions about the work of men and the work of women and the Southern tradition for a somewhat different set of assumptions about the division of labor. On one hand, we have the rough and rugged community of working men, who share the culture of hard work and sweat, who fight together in the wars, who have seen death and who risk their lives. On the other, we see the woman's concerns with the family, with love and understanding, with making her family comfortable and happy. For Will's wife, Helen, her husband's failure to tell her about his background, his family, even his real name, is a betrayal. For his daughter Katie, his failure to acknowledge her and her mother in front of the community robs him of the right to be considered her father.

In Cramer's fourth novel, *Summer of Light*, when the hero is forced to assume the role of caretaker for the children and his wife becomes the bread-winner, the characters confront this issue directly. Mick Layne is a tough guy, an iron worker on high rise buildings who loves the thrill of the danger, the lunch breaks with yarn-swapping with the fellow workers, the strong sense of masculinity. When his son is diagnosed with a developmental disorder, his wife feels she cannot leave her new, hard-won job as a legal assistant, and when Mick is hurt in a freak accident and fired, he faces the need to accept a role as homemaker. Tackling this job in a masculine way, tending to the children on his own terms, Mick finally grows comfortable with his newfound abilities. He becomes a more forgiving, more creative man, and even cures his own son through his unorthodox methods. Along the way, with the help of a neighbor, he discovers that he has talent as a photographer. Through another Christ-figure, this time the Preacher or the Man-with-No-Hands, he also discovers the world of the homeless who camp next to his last work site, and moves toward a fresh spirituality. The novel, which is based in part on Cramer's own experience, is a good family story, filled with self-deprecating laughter, newly discovered spiritual potential, and insights about family relations. It is softer, gentler than his earlier books.

Dale Cramer's novels are full of good dialogue, well-paced action, comedy, and a warm sense of good fellowship. He can choreograph a catastrophe so as to make it horrifying or hilarious. He is, in short, a good storyteller.

Critical Reception

John Mort, writing for *Booklist*, immediately spotted Cramer as a chronicler of "working-class" stiffs. He found *Sutter's Cross* a "fine first novel." *Publishers Weekly* noted that this novel revealed that the term "excellent CBA novel" is not an oxymoron. The critic, who says that "his lovely writing keeps the carefully constructed plot moving at a moderate pace," did object to the unnecessary epilogue.

Bad Ground also won good reviews. Cindy Crosby commented that Cramer's "fresh writing has a muscular toughness that's balanced by the vulnerabilities of his characters." Tamara Butler noted of *Bad Ground* that the "well-developed characters never fall into the cookie-cutter stereotype of being 'too perfect.'"

Levi's Will won even more praise and prizes. As a more complex novel, interweaving the Amish culture with Southern, it reveals new sides of both in ways that **Beverly Lewis** would never consider. Cindy Crosby notes that James Michener did a better job of "fleshing out the Amish community in *Centennial*, which included as one of its many subplots Pennsylvania Dutch boy Levi Zendt's abrupt departure from his Amish home . . . Michener took 900 pages to do it." She also notes that Cramer's prose "is beautiful." She considers the strongest part of the book to be Will's need for his father, "something that no other relationship—friendship, marriage—can replace."

Summer of Light delighted John Mort, of *Booklist,* who considered the new book "surprising" and it's "warm, believable, and often—particularly in scenes set at Disney World—hilarious." Cramer pictures the vacation at Disney World as a descent into Hell for his family, with nothing but long lines, expensive drinks, and a frightened child clinging to his leg. He much preferred a camping week at the beach, where the family found far simpler amusements in a more relaxed atmosphere.

Awards

Booklist named *Levi's Will* the Best Christian Novel of 2005; the book won the Christian Fiction Publishers' Award and the Christy Award for Contemporary Fiction. In 2005, *Bad Ground* won the Christy Award for General Fiction.

Bibliography of Novels by Author
(Published in Minneapolis, MN: Bethany House)

Sutter's Cross. 2003.
Bad Ground. 2004.
Levi's Will. 2005.
Summer of Light. 2006.

Bibliography of Works about Author

Butler, Tamara. Review of *Bad Ground. Library Journal* (June 1, 2004): 64.
Cramer, W. Dale. Homepage. http://www.dalecramer.com.
Cramer, W. Dale. Interview with Focus on Fiction. www.focusonfiction.net/dalecramer.html.
Crosby, Cindy. Review of *Sutter's Cross. Christianity Today* (March 2003): 79.
Crosby, Cindy. Review of *Levi's Will. Faithful Reader.* http://www.faithfulreader.com/reviews/07642299,58asp.
Mollet, Narelle. "W. Dale Cramer Interview." http://www.titletrakk.com/dale_cramer_interview.html.
Mort, John. Review of *Sutter's Cross. Booklist* (January 1, 2003): 845.
"W. Dale Cramer." *Contemporary Authors Online.* Detroit: Thomson Gale, 2005.

CRONIN, A. J.

Personal, Professional, and Religious Background

Archibald Joseph Cronin (1896–1981) was born in Cardross, Dumbartonshire, Scotland. He was the only son of Patrick and Jessie Montgomerie Cronin. Cronin's father was a Catholic and his mother a member of a strong Protestant family. Later memoirs suggest that Cronin's family was a subject of anti-Catholic bigotry during much of his childhood, leading him eventually to grow away from the Catholic faith. He was a precocious child, with a talent for writing that was recognized early. He won many writing competitions at Dumbarton Academy and St. Aloysius' College, earning an M.B. and Ch.B. with honors in 1919.

> (Among modern writers) there are very few giants. All the good writers are being swept away in a melancholic, oppressive, and depressive philosophy. They don't seem to have the stimulation of—I won't say the Christian ethic—but they seem to have no sort of light to guide them.
>
> —A. J. Cronin in an interview with *Newsweek*, 1961

Cronin then served in the Royal Navy as a surgeon, becoming a sub-lieutenant, after which he worked as a physician on a ship that traveled to India. Cronin took on other professional appointments before he returned to college, and then earned a scholarship to Glasgow University, where he was awarded his D.Ph. in 1923 and his M.R.C.P in 1924, his M.D. (with honors) in 1925.

In 1921, while at Glasgow Medical School, he met and married Agnes Mary Gibson, also a physician. They had three children, Vincent Archibald Patrick, Robert Francis Patrick, and Andrew James. Shortly after their marriage, Cronin and his wife moved to Tregenny, a small mining town in South Wales and then to Tredegar, another tiny Welsh community a short distance away, where they stayed three years, and where their first child was born. In 1924, Cronin moved his family to London to work for the Ministry of Mines as inspector of mines. At this time, he continued his studies, provoked by the conditions he witnessed in Wales, of pulmonary disabilities of the miners in the coal field. He also established a lucrative practice in the fashionable West End of London.

In 1930, Cronin sold his practice and took an extended holiday in Invernay, in the West Highlands of Scotland, to recuperate from gastric ulcers. At various times of his life, he worked at a Pension Hospital and became superintendent of Lightburn Isolation Hospital in Glasgow, Scotland. Much of this practice and the irrational bureaucracy that plagued him over the years became material for his fierce attacks on the medical system in England, which he came to consider an impregnable "citadel."

In 1931, A. J. Cronin finally indulged his cherished childhood dream of becoming a writer. He settled to work in his attic, where he spent three months on a 250,000-word novel, which he called *Hatter's Castle*. He was disappointed in the first draft, and discarded it. A local farmer, who discovered it when digging a ditch, returned it. Cronin was encouraged to complete the work. Gollancz, the first publisher who read it, accepted it for publication. The success of the novel allowed him to give up medicine and undertake a full-time career as a writer. This novel and the ones that quickly followed made him one of the century's most popular writers. *Hatter's Castle* tells the story of James Brodie, a hatter in a small Scottish town, who believes that his family is nobility. He wastes years in a tormented struggle to regain this lost stature. Along the way, he harms a number of others and causes one of his daughters to commit suicide, eventually destroying himself with alcohol.

Despite arguments over plagiarism, *Hatter's Castle* was made into a successful film, starring Deborah Kerr and James Mason (1941). Other novels and films

> *The Keys of the Kingdom* was made into a highly successful film, starring Gregory Peck.

quickly followed. *The Stars Look Down*, which also was a socially charged novel, described the injustices in a North England mining community. The novel earned the praise of **Graham Greene** and was made into a film starring Michael Redgrave. In 1939, Cronin and his family moved to America, where he wrote *The Keys of the Kingdom*, selling the film rights to David O. Selznick for $100,000. He first settled in Greenwich, Connecticut, then in New Canaan. He also had homes on the French Riviera and in Bermuda, and summered in Blue Hill, Maine.

By this time, Cronin had returned to his Roman Catholic faith, using it again as the central subject in *The Minstrel Boy* (1975). His concern with finding one's true calling was to become a theme in many of his stories as was his dream of tolerance. Throughout his life, he hoped for universal brotherhood and ecumenical understanding, like the relationship between the Methodist minister and the Catholic priest in *The Keys of the Kingdom*. Cronin also argued constantly for social justice. His argument, particularly for the establishment of a better health system for England in *The Citadel*, was considered a significant element in the landslide victory of the Labour Party in 1945.

A man of many talents and interests, A. J. Cronin loved travel, golfing, gardening and fishing. Everything became fodder for his novels. After the war, he traveled with his family to Europe, describing much of his own life and his travels in *Adventures in Two Worlds* (1952). He used the final two chapters of this autobiography to examine his own religious beliefs. For the last 35 years of his life, A. J. Cronin lived in Switzerland. He died of bronchitis in 1981, in Glion, Switzerland, a clinic near Montreaux. He was 84 years old.

Major Works and Themes

A. J. Cronin was a novelist, a dramatist, and a nonfiction writer. Most of his novels were written in the years between World War I and World War II, but his highly acclaimed *Keys of the Kingdom* was published in 1941, and captures something of the horrible moral dilemmas of missionaries at a time of conflict. This remarkable tribute to a Roman Catholic missionary in China is powerfully realistic about the struggles to establish a congregation in an unforgiving region with very little support from his bishop or others within the church. His best friend, an atheist doctor, comes to the aid of the mission in a time of plague, bringing medicines and expertise, giving his own life for these poor people, a man whom Francis considers a secular saint. Cronin shows tolerance of Protestants, Buddhists, and atheists. Rather than orthodox theology, he judges the upright person by kind actions and loving sacrifice. Francis, the poor priest, never achieves success in the eyes of his church, but is beloved by his congregation and those who work with him. *The Keys of the Kingdom* is full of drama—an Eden-like scene in which Francis first discovers his love for the abused and doomed Nora, his narrow escapes from disaster during his early career as a priest, his work at the disastrous mission station in China, his endurance through floods, plagues, and warfare, and his continuing love for the humble, decent folks he has come to know

A. J. Cronin used his own life as the basis for many of his stories. His early years of poverty in small towns is beautifully depicted in the hard-scrabble career of Laurence Carroll, the hero of both *A Song of Sixpence* and *A Pocketful of Rye*. In the first of these novels, the lad is an innocent, a faithful Catholic, often buffeted by the winds of fortune, but able to use his determination and brains to win a scholarship that will ensure a better future. In the second of them, he has become a non-believer, cynical about the medical profession, the women he consistently uses and discards, and the posh position he has at a clinic in Switzerland. A series of revelations brings him back to his church and to the love of his life. Although this is a melodramatic plot, it is nonetheless a moving tale of a cad who is finally trapped by the "hound of Heaven."

The Citadel traces in much greater detail the medical practice among the neglected miners Cronin treated in Wales, the miners' horrible working and living conditions, and the government officials' total lack of concern for these victims of greed and neglect. The novel reveals the difference between practicing medicine as a vocation and exploiting it as a tool for position and wealth. At the key moment in the story, the protagonist turns to God, acknowledging that crime will have its punishment and God will not be mocked. The hero's subsequent transformation comes after his powerful moment of recognition at a church.

Most of Cronin's novels tell straight-forward, action-packed stories. They usually feature a strong love interest, a commitment to principles and sometimes religion, though rarely to established institutions. Cronin despised rigid systems and those people who flourished in professions like the church and medicine, ignoring the real good they might achieve while exploiting their positions for greed and pride.

Critical Reception

Hatter's Castle, Cronin's first novel, was in some ways his most controversial. Cronin was accused of plagiarism, having been influenced by George Douglas's novel *The House with the Green Shutters*, published in 1901. Although some critics considered this a "horror story," *The Dictionary of Literary Biography* considers it a "naturalistic examination of social problems, combined with a sentimental plot."

Major critics of the time considered A. J. Cronin a "popular" writer—that is, he told his stories clearly in forceful language, using 19th-century techniques of plot and character portrayal. Some of his work smacks of Dickens, especially his interest in poor and neglected children and his disdain for hypocrisy and cruelty of wealthy people. He echoes Trollope in his criticism of churchmen and their political motivations. His moral is usually explicit, his position unequivocal—not the mark of the more modern writers who prefer more elliptical approaches to their subjects. Critics such as Jane Voiles, Fanny Butcher, G. E. Grauel, E. W. Luker, and E. J. Lineham reviewed his work, noting that he is "a man of style" and can tell a "tight little tale." Most did not praise him as a master of the novel.

Contemporary Authors On-line notes that, "Although A. J. Cronin's novels received only limited critical acclaim, his work was read by a large and international audience." By 1958, he had sold seven million copies of his books; in 1961, even Russian sales had reached three million—though he never realized a ruble of royalties from Russia. He was universally acknowledged to be a strong storyteller in the older tradition of the novel.

Awards

A. J. Cronin won the American Booksellers' Award in 1937 for *The Citadel* and was awarded a D. Litt. from Bowdoin College and Lafayette College.

Bibliography of Fiction by Author (Published by Little, Brown of Boston Unless Otherwise Indicated)

Hatter's Castle. 1931.
Three Loves. 1932.
The Grand Canary. 1933.
The Stars Look Down. 1935.
The Citadel. 1937.

The Keys of the Kingdom. 1941.
The Green Years. London: Gollancz, 1945.
Shannon's Way. New York: Grossett, 1950.
The Spanish Gardner. 1950.
Beyond this Place. 1953.
A Thing of Beauty (also known as *The Crusader's Tomb*). 1956.
The Northern Light. 1958.
The Judas Tree. 1961.
A Song of Sixpence. 1964.
A Pocketful of Rye. 1969.
The Minstrel Boy. 1975.
Desmonde. 1975.

Many of these novels were made into successful films and distributed internationally. Some became the basis for television shows as well.

A. J. Cronin's published writings, unpublished literary manuscripts, drafts, letters, school exercise books and essays, laboratory books, and his M.D. thesis are all at the National Library of Scotland.

Bibliography of Works about Author

"A. J. Cronin," *Contemporary Authors Online*, Detroit: Thomson Gale, 2002.
"A. J. Cronin," *Dictionary of Literary Biography*. http://www.bookrages.com/biography/archibald-joseph-cronin.dlb/.
"A. J. Cronin," *Wikipedia*. http://en.wikipedia.org/w/index.php?title=a-j-Cronin.
Cronin, A. J. *Adventures in Two Worlds*. New York: McGraw, 1952.
Salwak, Dale. *A.J. Cronin*. Boston: Twayne's English Author Series, 1985.

Obituaries: *Chicago Tribune*, January 10, 1981; *New York Times*, January 10, 1981; *Washington Post*, January 10, 1981; *Time*, January 19, 1981.

DEKKER, TED

Personal, Professional, and Religious Background

Ted Dekker (1961–) was born in Indonesia to missionary parents, John and Helen Dekker, whose work on a remote island has been the topic of several books. He grew up in this multicultural region, where there were headhunters and where the jungles had rich colors and a myriad of animal life. He went to high school at a multicultural school in Indonesia and then moved to California for college. In his semiautobiographical writings, including *The Slumber of Christianity*, he remembers that he had little time to spend with his parents and often felt very lonely and unhappy.

For a time during his college years, as he studied religion and philosophy, he lost his faith and dedicated himself to achieving success. He married Lisa Ann Dekker and began working for a large health care company in San Diego as a member of the marketing staff, then as its marketing director. As he climbed the ladder of success in the business world, he invested $70,000 in Comfort Care, a service for adults with incontinence problems, delivering adult diapers with privacy and discretion. Although his business thrived for four years, until Medicare ended its funding for the program, he was increasingly miserable.

When his parents moved back to the States, Dekker moved his young family to Colorado Springs to be near them. In Colorado, he began to purchase floundering businesses, working on them for a while, and selling them at a profit. During this period, he realized, while listening to a cassette on creationism, that his faith had returned. "I began to cry softly, Heaven was raining on me." Suddenly he knew that his Heavenly Father was talking to him.

> The Great Romance. We were created for intimate fellowship with our creator. In the end he will go to great extremes to woo us back into that relationship.
>
> —Ted Dekker, explaining the concept central to the "Circle" trilogy, in 2004 interview with Marcia Ford at FaithfulReader.com

For some four years, Dekker spent his evenings writing. After he had completed several novels, he sold his last business and moved to the mountains, where he began to write full-time. In 1997, Dekker's brother Danny died, leading him to write his first published novel, *Heaven's Wager*, which deals with death and the afterlife. He also wrote two sequels to this novel— *When Heaven Weeps* and *Thunder of Heaven*, less with any hope of publishing the works than the need to put his ideas on paper. Since this time, he has been a full-time writer. He and his family, his wife and four children, now live near Austin, Texas.

Major Works and Themes

Ted Dekker's first novels were direct results of his brother's death and his own experience of being "filthy rich." An author more open to pop-culture than most Christian writers, Dekker has criticized Christian booksellers for their reluctance to embrace comic books and video games. He says that Christian young people should be allowed honest choices for their entertainment, including violent stories, fantasy, and Christian speculative fiction. He himself writes horror stories, thrillers, fantasy, and romances. Many of his tales are very dark, dealing, like **Frank Peretti**'s, with demonic forces at war with angelic hosts.

From his earliest novels, Ted Dekker has tried to combine a crossover approach with a Christian message. He stays current with the culture while retaining his fascination "with all that lies beyond the skin of this world." He notes that *The Martyr's Song* reveals that "When the eyes of your heart are opened to the intoxicating bliss that awaits us, the simple pleasures of this world find their rightful place as foretastes of that bliss. They are simply samples of so much more to come. Embrace them, yes, but find first an obsession for heaven."

In his ongoing effort to reach out to people who would not otherwise read Christian fiction, he has involved himself in filming his novels and has considered transforming them into video games. Acknowledging his inspiration from **C. S. Lewis**, **Dean Koontz**, Stephen King, and others, he frequently employs the device of parallel worlds, powerful dreams, and demonic possession. He believes in the reality of Evil and accepts few limits on portraying all of the horrors of warfare and death.

Critical Reception

Some of Ted Dekker's works have been considered "too edgy" for the Christian market, with very depressing pictures of hopelessness preceding scenes of redemption. It was not until 2000 that he found a publisher for his books. By 2003, he had six novels in print. His breakthrough novel was his seventh, *Thr3e*, which won the prestigious Christy Award as well as the Gold Medallion.

The 2004 "Circle" trilogy (three interwoven stories, *Black*, *Red*, and *White*) tells of Thomas Hunter, an average man much like the author, who lives in two separate worlds, traveling between them in his dreams. These closely-linked books draw heavily on C. S. Lewis's space trilogy. Dekker's alternate world, unfallen, is much like Perelandra, and the first man there, Tanis, faces the moment in the garden much like a parallel scene in Lewis's novel, as well as the Garden of Eden. Of the three volumes, critics preferred *White*. Tamara Butler, writing for *Library Journal*, considered the book very skillfully written and Dekker himself a "master of suspense."

The most widely reviewed of his stories so far is *Thr3e*, which was also made into a film in 2007. A modern, semi-terrorist version of *The Three Faces of Eve*, this thriller was called a "page-turner" by the reviewer of *Publishers Weekly*—"an almost perfect blend of suspense, mystery, and horror." The reviewer notes that the action is built on clever twists, with plenty of suspense, comparing this crossover book to those of Dean Koontz and Frank Peretti.

Some critics believe that Dekker's recent novels have less blatant Christian content and darker themes, though they continue to affirm the power of God and the fallen nature of mankind. Christians have protested his graphic violence, tough language (oaths such as *crap*), and his fascination with evil. Douglas Kennedy calls *Obsessed* a "profoundly Manichean tract." Dekker's response is: "To minimize the darkness is to minimize the light." Like Adam in the Garden of Eden, we come to full knowledge of good by confronting its opposite—evil. Dekker often uses the Temptation in his stories, his characters tempted by the Evil One, biting down into the forbidden fruit. He sees the soul in constant struggle with evil to affirm good and find God—which he calls the "Great Romance."

The novels appear to be planned for young adults who have grown up in an age of action movies, with fast-paced plots, little depth of characterization, instant love affairs, and simplistic visions of good and evil. His blood-drinking villains in *Obsessed* are too grotesque to be believable—even as Nazis who slaughtered Jews at death camps. They seem more like vampires out of horror films. His language is also aimed at young people, full of slang and smart alec commentaries. Dekker does come back to Jesus' parable of the buried treasure, on which the story is based, but only after wild chases, near hangings, multiple stabbings, shootings, fights, near-escapes, and silly tricks. This is not the stuff of tragedy or serious drama.

Awards

Ted Dekker's novel *Thr3e* won the Christy Award, and the Gold Medallion Award from the Evangelical Christian Publishers Association.

Bibliography of Novels by Author

Haven's Wager. Nashville, TN: Word Publishing, 2000.
When Heaven Weeps. Nashville, TN: The Word Publishing, 2001.
Thunder of Haven. Nashville, TN: W Publishing Group, 2002.
The Martyr's Song (including music CD). Nashville, TN: WestBow Press, 2005.

The "Circle" trilogy (Published in Nashville: WestBow Press, 2004)

"Project Showdown" series (Published in Nashville: WestBow Press, 2006)

Other Novels, Some Coauthored

Blessed Child. (Coauthored with Bill Bright.) Nashville, TN: Word Publishing, 2001.
Blink. Nashville, TN: W Publishing Group, 2002.
A Man Called Blessed. (Coauthored with Bill Bright.) Nashville, TN: W. Publishing Group, 2002.
Thr3e. Nashville, TN: W Publishing Group, 2003.
Obsessed. Nashville, TN: WestBow Press, 2005.
The Promise: A Christian Tale. Nashville, TN: J. Countryman, 2005.
House: The Only Way Out Is In. (Coauthored with Frank Peretti.) Nashville, TN: WestBow Press, 2006.
Chosen. Nashville, TN: Thomas Nelson, 2007.

Infidel. Nashville, TN: Thomas Nelson, 2007.
Adam. Nashville, TN: Thomas Nelson, 2008.
Chaos. Nashville, TN: Thomas Nelson, 2008.
Renegade. Nashville, TN: Thomas Nelson, 2008.
A number of Ted Dekker's novels and stories have been used as the basis for films (*Thr3e, House, Blink of an Eye*).

Bibliography of Works about Author

Butler, Tamara. Review of *White: The Great Pursuit. Library Journal* (November 1, 2004).
Darlington, C.J. "Ted Dekker Interview." http://www.filetrakk.com/ted_dekker_interview.html.
Dekker, Ted. *The Slumber of Christianity: Awakening a Passion for Heaven on Earth.* Nashville, TN: T. Nelson, 2005.
"Dekker, Ted," Wikipedia. http://www.en.Wikipedia.org/wiki/Ted_Dekker.
Ford, Marcia. "Interview," October 2004. http://www.faithfulreader.com/authors/au=dekker-ted.asp.
Kennedy, Douglas. "Selling Rapture," *The Guardian*, July 9, 2005.
Mort, John. "Christian Fiction," review of *Thr3e. Booklist* (October 1, 2003): 292.
"Ted Dekker," *Contemporary Authors Online.* Detroit: Thomson Gale, 2007.
Ted Dekker Web site. http://teddekker.com.
Where the Map Ends. http://www.wherethemapends.com/Interviews/Ted_Dekker.

DEWBERRY, ELIZABETH

Personal, Professional, and Religious Background

Elizabeth Dewberry (1962–) was born and raised in Birmingham, Alabama, the setting of two of her novels. She is the daughter of James W. and Sallie Dewberry. The family was what Elizabeth Dewberry came to consider as fundamentalist. They sent her to a strict Presbyterian school. Although her life at home and church was very regimented, she was allowed to read anything she liked. This was her freedom.

Dewberry told W. Dale Brown that she had grown up believing that God would never give her more burdens than she could bear. She lost her faith in this when her grandfather molested her. She believed that her deeply religious parents knew what he was doing and did not stop him. She spent much of her maturing years coming to terms with this experience. Through her life, Dewberry has explained her areas of disagreement with her fundamentalist training—the literalism about the Bible, the emphasis on superficial rules against women wearing slacks and believers drinking wine. Then her first marriage to an abusive husband called into question the admonition "Wives submit to your husbands." Although she has lost her faith in the church, she has come to believe that words are holy, that truth is important. She acknowledges that the world of her churchgoing youth was a "rich world." "Despite all the problems of that kind of church, at the center of it was God."

> I don't know how to write in a guarded way. You have to go to what is raw in yourself.
>
> —Elizabeth Dewberry, in her interview with Dale Brown

Elizabeth Dewberry attended Vanderbilt University, earning a B.S. in 1983, and Emory University, taking a Ph.D. in English in 1989. She wrote her dissertation on Ernest Hemingway, an author on whom she has written scholarly papers, and one who has influenced her style. While studying for her doctorate, Dewberry began to draft novels, largely based on her early struggle with sexuality and faith.

She has taught at Stanford, Ohio State University, the Wesleyan Writers' Conference, the University of Southern California, the Sewanee Writers' Conference, Bread Loaf Writers' Conference, and various other places. She has also written several plays, one of which is based on her novel *Many Things Have Happened Since He Died.*

Her much-publicized marriage to the Pulitzer-Prize-winning novelist **Robert Olen Butler** in 1995 was briefly very successful, pulling her out of her long period of depression and confusion. They both spoke of being one another's best friends and helpful critics and appeared together at a number of conferences on Southern literature. The startling conclusion of that marriage in 2007 with an e-mail from Butler to the students and faculty in the English Department at Florida State University announced their impending divorce and her relationship with Ted Turner. At the time, she declined to be interviewed on the subject.

> Dewberry says that she often writes two novels at a time, and has unpublished novels at home she has never finished.

Major Works and Themes

Elizabeth Dewberry's work is highly autobiographical, intermingling her own memories, experiences, and emotions with her fictional characters, using her writing to find her way "out of fundamentalism" and to discover how to grow as a person. She chronicles her mental disorder and her feelings of failure in vivid terms. Her first novel, *Many Things Have Happened Since He Died*, shocked her family and friends, who thought that they knew her as a genteel Southern lady. This novel was published under her married name, Vaughn, and uses the central female voice she was to make her stock-in-trade. It tells of what has happened to the young woman since her father's suicide, including marriage to an abusive husband who is a Christian fundamentalist, an unwanted pregnancy and a struggle with the idea of abortion. Her husband finally dies of a drug overdose, but not before his confused young wife has lost most of her faith. The book ends with the acknowledgement that God will indeed sometimes give people more than they can bear.

Dewberry's second published novel, *Break the Heart of Me*, tells more explicitly of her grandfather's molestation. The heroine marries an older man, becomes bulimic, and dreams of becoming a country singer. She has an affair with a singer, and struggles to fit her life and her evangelical faith together. This novel was followed by an eight-year period in which Dewberry tried play-writing and sought to improve her writing skills.

Dewberry, who had been living in Louisiana for five years, moved her setting for her third novel from Alabama to Louisiana. In this Southern version of Shakespeare's *Hamlet*, a Southern politician murders his wife and marries her sister. *Sacrament of Lies*, a gender-bending version of the Shakespearean story, is based in part on Louisiana's dramatic politician Huey Long. Dewberry does not acknowledge her additional debt to Robert Penn Warren's *All the King's Men*, a masterpiece about a Southern politician whose idealism and corruption end in tragedy. Tracing the story through the daughter's psychotic anguish makes the search for truth seem cloudy at best. It is not clear why anyone would consider this governor charismatic enough to win the presidency. He is a cynical villain, willing to kill his wife, commit adultery with her sister, and destroy anyone in his path, including his beloved daughter. The neat ending, which frees the heroine from her failed marriage and her abusive father falls short of both Shakespeare and Penn Warren in power.

Dewberry's own rejection of Christian fundamentalist beliefs has led her to use the language of salvation and redemption in a way that is often ironic and mocking. Although she shows some sympathy with Catholicism in *Sacrament of Lies*, she finds this religion too full of empty rituals covering transgressions and non-belief. The ironic background of the story is Mardi Gras in New Orleans, a festival of debauchery that has little to do with Christ's passion. At least one of the characters does cross himself and show genuine pain at his transgressions, but he never confesses or makes restitution for his sins. Carter, the young husband who is the governor's assistant, never professes any faith or reveals any morality. His death in the wake of the final revelations is lamented at a proper Catholic funeral. The wife attends, as does his murderer, knowing full well that—if there is a God—this agnostic is headed for hell.

His Lovely Wife, yet another semiautobiographical book by Elizabeth Dewberry, was written when she turned from her husband to Ted Turner. The barely disguised leading character discovers the emptiness of either the physical explanation of the universe or the religious one, and finds little comfort in either and little purpose in her own life. Like most of Dewberry's novels, this is a blend of stream-of-consciousness and erratic activity. *His Lovely Wife* follows a woman who appears to be channeling Princess Diana while simultaneously reliving her own life, and searching for meaning. By the conclusion, she has arrived at no reconciliation or great breakthrough, only that she must forgive her mother. The long discourse on the sadness of being a "lovely wife" of an academic celebrity, and the pedestrian philosophizing on the nature of the universe are poor fits for this whimsical heroine, who turns to sexual experimentation and toys with suicide before returning to the status quo. This concludes the story but hardly resolves her issues.

The theme of the faithless parent appears again and again in Dewberry's work, as does the confused and self-destructive daughter, beautiful but miserable with her life. Her characters border on psychosis, have extended private conversations with themselves while carrying on different public discussions with others. Her pretty young Southern ladies, properly raised in polite society, marry well, but find no joy in marriage or sex. These childless Southern belles tend to act like willful children. They have no clear goals or great success in their careers. Past their youth, they find themselves hoping that love will somehow redeem their meaningless lives. Their dreams of instant and effortless success as singers or poets make them appear silly modern-day Cinderellas. The stories chronicle a desperate search, but without purpose other than narcissistic self-fulfillment.

Critical Reception

Elizabeth Dewberry's first novel, *Many Things Have Happened*, tells of the catastrophic events in the heroine's life after her father's suicide: the heroine marries an abusive Christian fundamentalist, becomes pregnant against her will, contemplates an abortion, and then faces her husband's death from a drug overdose. The heroine strives to maintain her faith in God and in herself as a writer through this set of experiences. Madison Smartt Bell thought the style, in which the author blends daydreams, dogmas, and psychosis, "powerfully disturbing and difficult to forget."

Dewberry's second novel, *Break the Heart of Me*, tells of her grandfather's molestation and of her own struggle with bulimia, her marriage to an older man, her dreams of being a country singer, and her affair with a country music star. She again struggles to bring together her lingering faith in Christianity with her own tortured life. The critic for *Publishers Weekly* thought the novel "carefully drawn" and her voice "perfectly pitched."

Not thoughtful enough to be an iconoclast or independent enough to be a feminist, Elizabeth Dewberry falls between the chairs. She seems to believe in the redemptive power of love, but finds little comfort in her actual relationships. None of her books has been widely reviewed outside of *Booklist*, *Publishers Weekly*, and some southern papers. The *New York Times* has published more articles on her life and loves than on her work.

Awards

Elizabeth Dewberry has won fellowships from the Sewanee Writers' Conference (1991), the Bread Loaf Fellowship in Fiction (1993), and the Wesleyan Writers' Conference (1993).

Bibliography of Novels by Author

Many Things Have Happened Since He Died and Here are the Highlights. New York: Doubleday, 1990 (published under the name Vaughn).
Break the Heart of Me. N.A. Talese, 1994 (published under the name Vaughn).
Sacrament of Lies. New York: BlueHen Books, 2002.
His Lovely Wife. New York: Harcourt, Inc., 2006.

Bibliography of Works about Author

Bell, Madison Smartt. Review of *Many Things Have Happened. Washington Post,* April 19, 1990.
Brown, W. Dale. *Of Fiction and Faith: Twelve American Writers Talk about Their Vision and Work.* Grand Rapids, MI: William B. Eerdmans Publishing Company, 1997.
"Elizabeth Dewberry," *Contemporary Authors Online.* Detroit: Thomson Gale, 2003.
Hall, Robert L. "What She Writes Is a Mystery!" (an interview with Elizabeth Dewberry) Southern Scribe. http://www.southernscribe.com/zine/authors/Dewberry_Elizabeth.htm.
Stasio, Marilyn. Review of *A Sacrament of Lies. New York Times Book Review* 107, no 9 (March 3, 2002): 21.

DICKSON, ATHOL

Personal, Professional, and Religious Background

Athol Dickson (1955–) was born in Tulsa, Oklahoma. His first name is Scottish, pronounced with a long "A" and "O," as in "hole." Athol Dickson's father was a traveling salesman and his mother a homemaker. His first bed was a drawer lined with towels. When he was three months old, his family moved to Dallas, Texas.

In his nonfiction book on his study of Judaism, *The Gospel according to Moses,* Dickson tells about the solid foundation his parents laid in his faith, encouraging him to memorize Bible verses, work on Bible "drills," and taking time to discuss with him the nature of sin, faith, and redemption, the attributes of God and humanity. Nonetheless, as he laughingly notes, "I had more questions than

> You don't have to be brave about the future. Let Jesus do that for you. Remember the Good News you once heard and believed, trust your past and future to the Lord, and act like the free person you already are!
>
> —Athol Dickson, on his blog "About Life" (www.whatatholwrote.blogspot.com)

Athol Dickson is an architect who has designed hundreds of restaurants all over the United States.

answers." As a result, he became convinced that the Bible was filled with "mistakes and half-baked truisms." He abandoned the faith of his family and descended "to a life of hedonism and destructive behavior." Over the years, he came back to a powerful faith: His experience with his Jewish study group helped him to understand that God loves an honest question. "My mind, imagination, and heart have been seized by an Other at a level I never thought possible." Throwing logic to the wind, "I accepted the gift of Jesus' sacrifice for me, the sin-addicted man I used to be dead with him, and together we rose again"

A talented artist, Dickson studied art privately and in public school and then went on to major in architecture at the university, planning to become an architect. He founded an architecture firm, designing hundreds of restaurants in the United States. He started writing in his spare time. Eventually, he became a full-time novelist. Along the way, he also worked as a taco bender, clothing salesman, boxer, carpenter, and bartender as well as a writer.

Ever since he was a child, Dickson has loved boats, often drawing pictures of them on Big Chief tablets. When he was only seven, he paddled a large piece of Styrofoam into a storm drain, emerging a quarter mile away. At one point, he sold his house and car, moved aboard a boat, planning to cruise the northern Gulf of Mexico and the Atlantic coast of the United States. He spent two years living on the boat, the *Susan A.* He notes that he can overhaul a boat's diesel engine, install a generator, repair Fiberglas, strip and varnish teak, and do any number of other essential tasks, including running "an inlet safely on the Fourth of July, navigate in fog by radar, set an anchor properly, and survive 30 degree rolls without throwing up." He enjoys taking his flat-bottom boat into the swamps, like his hero in *River Rising*. Boats appear frequently in his stories.

He has been married to "the lovely Sue from Salina" for over 20 years, a time that he characterizes as a "slice of heaven." She is a professional whose new job took them from their home in Dallas, where they loved the church, the friends, the museums and restaurants, to California, "to a different skyline and a much larger body of water." They have no children, but he considers himself a "sucker for woebegone animals like Buster, his Doberman pinscher with bad hips, and Lulu, his cat with half a tail."

He has described his richly productive life as a blend of blessings and troubles. "I have been fired unjustly from a job I worked eight years to get. People I trusted have stolen large amounts of money from me. My father and my mother both died torturous deaths." Realizing that he may one day lose his devoted wife and be all alone, "unless I am fortunate enough to die first," he considers the transitory people and things that have trickled through his fingers, and finds his peace in the knowledge that the everlasting God is in control.

The Dicksons presently live in southern California, "where he writes among the hummingbirds and palm trees, with the scent of flowers in the air."

Major Works and Themes

Athol Dickson says that his favorite book is the Bible, which he considers "a wise friend as much as a book." He thinks it important to write Christian novels, which can reach readers not otherwise open to a discussion of faith. "Encountering a well-written novel with a Christian point of view, the doubter who trusts no sermon may willingly lift the veil from his imagination and peek beyond, thereby drawing near to the indescribable joy of knowing God."

He also enjoys a number of American authors—Southerners, popular detective novelists, and philosophical writers: **Walker Percy,** Tim Gautreaux, John Irving, E.L. Doctorow, Mark Twain, Elmore Leonard, Caleb Carr, Robert Parker, Patrick O'Brian, Ross MacDonald, James Lee Burke, and "far too many others to list." He acknowledges that the books he owns say a lot about him. He loves the Talmud and has many books on Judaism and Christianity. The study of the Hebrew scriptures led to his publication in 2003 of *The Gospel according to Moses: What My Jewish Friends Taught Me about Jesus,* a nonfiction book that describes his experience as an evangelical Christian in a Reform Jewish Bible study group, or Chever Torah. Robert S. Watts reviewed the book for *Library Journal,* and noted that it is more scholarly than personal. It does reveal that the author learned to "ask questions and face difficult paradoxes" in his own faith—traits that show up clearly in his fiction.

Dickson also has a whole shelf full of books about boats and boating. In keeping with his zeal for mystery writers, he has hundreds of suspense and mystery novels, including the first five he ever read (from the Hardy Boys series). He also has the classics he read in high school and college, several dozen travel books, a section on architecture, some screenplays, and books of art—mostly the Impressionists.

His first novels were detective stories. He calls his first, *Whom Shall I Fear,* "a murder mystery with a spiritual subtheme." The hero of the story, Garrison Reed, who owns the family construction business, sounds a good bit like the author. "Garr" Reed finds himself the prime suspect in the murder of his former partner and friend. This leads to a series of trials and questioning, forcing him to rely on God. The story is classified as "Southern gothic." Like most of his murder mysteries, this book starts *in medias res.* As in actual life, the plot is complicated, with the hero moving into scenes that puzzle him, haunted by memories that seem to bring understanding—and sometimes misinterpretation—to the current circumstances. This strategy produces a difficult story-line to follow, with a steady movement towards deeper horror and violence. Dickson provides clues, like the Ellery Queen tales, and uses trains of logic that sound like Sherlock Holmes.

Garr Reed is also the central figure of *Every Hidden Thing,* another novel involving life in the South. Again, the setting reflects the author's own experience, as does some of the action and characterization. This story focuses on a demonstration of Christians at an abortion clinic. The march turns violent, resulting in the wounding of a doctor and the fatal shooting of a priest. Dickson treats abortion issues in the story in a thoughtful, balanced, and entertaining manner, not as a polemic. The scriptural theme, the "hidden things" that are known to God, even when they are kept from those we love, allows Garr to test his new-found faith and lament his years of pretending to his wife that he was a Christian. As it turns out, she has also kept things from him. Her involvement in the peculiarly New Orleans blend of abortion fanatics and voodoo cults makes for a real battle of spiritual forces. The book is haunted with memories of satanic power and a curious mingling of Christian faith with cult practices for which Dickson uses a kind of magic realism—which he was to exploit with considerably more power in *River Rising.* It is clear that Dickson does not approve of the vicious quarrels among enemies and supporters of abortion or of the violence that sometimes results.

In his third murder mystery, *They Shall See God,* Dickson draws on his interest in Judaism. The central story, which is again set in New Orleans, involves two women, Ruth Gold, now a Rabbi, and Kate Flint, an antiques dealer and lukewarm Protestant, who as young girls had served as witnesses in a murder trial and helped bring a supposed murderer to justice. They have not seen one another since that traumatic experience, largely because of the bigotry of both families. It is when Solomon Cantor, the man imprisoned for the murder of Nan Smith, an evangelical Christian, is released from prison 25 years later that strange things happen in the community. Among the events are several deaths, including one caused by the sudden release of the animals from the New Orleans zoo. As it turns out, the pattern of the murders is biblical, based on the stories in the book of Genesis. Only at the end of the book does the design come clear to the characters and the reader.

The escalating violence of the Christians who would convert all Jews centers around the temple where Ruth, the rabbi, works. Like the protesters before the abortion clinic in his previous novel, Dickson shows that these Christians are too angry to convert anyone. They belie the mild-mannered Christ they worship. Dickson disapproves of evangelical efforts to convert the Jews to Christianity, revealing the tensions caused by such clumsy, if well-intentioned, actions. Too often, neither group seeks to understand the other, resulting in greater distrust and even hatred. Here, he clearly drawing on his own experience with Judaism as chronicled in his *Gospel According to Moses*.

At the same time, he is not preaching. He uses humor, suspense, originality, and shrewd plotting to make this a highly entertaining novel. It has the same complexity of *Every Hidden Thing* and is even harder to follow, with characters appearing only briefly, explanations appearing long after events, and tangles of relationships becoming clear only at the end. Using an African American police lieutenant who had appeared briefly in *Every Hidden Thing*, Dickson links the novels, both of which deal with practical Christianity in a difficult world. Again, the title is drawn from Scripture, from the Beatitudes, and used effectively for the tombstone of the converted Jew whose memory drives much of the motivation of the rabbi in the story.

Dickson's masterpiece is *River Rising*, a work that won immediate acclaim by the critics. In it, he uses the idea of the "lost plantation," an outgrowth of the actual experience of some African Americans after the end of the Civil War, April 9, 1865. A group of slaves in Texas continued to work for their masters until June 19, "Juneteenth," the day they finally heard about their freedom. Some historians suspect that the landowners delayed providing this information in order to get one more crop out of their workers. Dickson fantasized that it might have been possible, in really remote regions of the South, by keeping them in ignorance, to keep the slaves in perpetual slavery. "All I did in *River Rising* was envision that one last harvest turned into another, and another, for 52 seasons in a profoundly isolated place."

This is different kind of detective story, with the Reverend Hale Poser searching for his own roots and for the key to puzzling disappearances of people from the small river town of Pilotville. The story is rich with the atmosphere of the Louisiana bayou, the fishing culture with flat-bottom boats that Dickson knows so intimately. The black-white relationships of the town echo the old plantation system of class structure, genial separation and the condescension of benevolent paternalism. Hale Poser, a deacon and a stranger, breaks the model of the contented servant: he is educated, inquisitive, and independent. He is also something of a saint and a prophet, able to save a child at birth, to heal by his touch. His mystical blending of two church services on a Sunday morning puzzles both congregations.

Two of Dickson's more recent novels continue his path of thrill-packed story-telling centered on a Christian message. *The Cure* ends once again with a surprise that is not altogether unrealistic, and is signaled throughout the book. *Winter Haven* also combines a mystery with a chilling thriller quality. The central story is gothic, up until the rational explanation in the final chapters, which also reveals the compelling message of God's grace in his amazing use of an autistic child who can recite verbatim the entire Bible in seven languages—and communicates no other way. Once again, Dickson tackles the problems of perverse and true faith, in this case the faith-healing minister who is father to a troubled family with mental health issues and real diseases he cannot cure and cannot understand. Only in the final moments does the heroine discover the true grace of God and find release in knowing his truth.

Dickson is interested in pointing out the wonderful gift we have in our ability "to live life in the moment." He concludes that most people worry too much about the future, feel too much guilt about the past. He insists that we reap what we have sown, that our actions have consequences. As a Christian, this means that our sins will follow us until we accept Christ's sacrifice on our behalf and realize that he has forgiven us.

Critical Reception

Most of Athol Dickson's early works were received cordially but without enthusiasm by the critics who read Christian novels. John Mort reviewed *Whom Shall I Fear?* for *Booklist*, commenting on the "charm" that lies primarily in his characters. Melissa Hudak considered it a "dark, Gothic tale of old hatreds," agreeing that it is an "engrossing novel." Hudak also reviewed *Every Hidden Thing* for *Library Journal*, calling it a "taut, fast-paced mystery," acknowledging its religious content, but noting it is "nonpreachy." The *Publishers Weekly* reviewer liked *They Shall See God*, but thought it was told from too many points of view. The plethora of Jewish terminology might also be difficult for the average reader to handle. The *New York Times* reviewer enjoyed the "moonshine, a crooked sheriff, and a redneck crucifixion" that smack of **Flannery O'Connor's** influence. *Booklist* thought his Texas accent to be "perfect."

It was *River Rising* that won the critics' praise, perhaps because of the recent events in Louisiana connected with Hurricane Katrina. *Booklist* noted that "Dickson's thriller is really an allegory, with Hale as Christ, but it's a subtle allegory with an easy mastery of Cajun ways and a nice gothic flair." *Publishers Weekly* loved the atmosphere and the "artfully constructed" characters who "glow with life." *WORLD Magazine* praised it highly.

The novels that have followed, *The Cure* and *Winter Haven*, have also won praise from *Library Journal, Romantic Times, Faithful Reader* and others, who consider them worthy successors to *River Rising*. The reviewers praise Dickson as an "intelligent" writer who knows how to tell an "absorbing story" that is both "chilling" and revealing of God's grace in a powerful way. *WORLD Magazine* notes that he combines "elements of romance, mystery, and ghost story" in his lively page-turners.

Awards

River Rising as named to the *Booklist*'s Top Ten Christian Novels for 2006 and also won the Christy Award for the Best Suspense Novel of 2006. It was also named one of the *Christian Fiction Review* Best Ten of 2006 and the *Christianity Today* Best Novel of 2006.

They Shall See God was a Christy Award Finalist in the suspense category in 2003. *Winter Haven* was the top pick by Romantic Times for 2008

Bibliography of Novels by Author

Whom Shall I Fear? Grand Rapids, MI: Zondervan Publishing, 1996.
Every Hidden Thing. Grand Rapids, MI: Zondervan Publishing, 1998.

Kate and Ruth: A Novel. Grand Rapids, MI: Zondervan Publishing, 1999.
They Shall See God. Wheaton, IL: Tyndale House Publishers, 2002.
River Rising Minneapolis, MN: Bethany House Publishers, 2006.
The Cure. Minneapolis, MN: Bethany House Publishers, 2007.
Winter Haven. Minneapolis, MN: Bethany House Publishers, 2008.

Bibliography of Works about Author

"Athol Dickson." http://www.blogger.com/profile/13946058024343277304.
"Athol Dickson," Tyndale House Publishers Web site. http://www.tyndale.com/authors/bio.asp/
code=168.
"Athol Dickson-Critically Acclaimed Novelist." Author, Inc. http://www.atholdickson.com/bio_
reviews.html.
"Dickson, Athol." *Contemporary Authors Online.* Detroit: Thomson Gale, 2006.
Dickson, Athol. "A Juneteenth Kind of Karma." *What Athol Wrote* . . . http://whatathollwrote.blogspot.
com/2007/06/juneteenth_kind_of_karma_14 htm.
Duncan, Melanie C. Review of *They Shall See God. Library Journal* (June 1, 2002): 122.
Hudak, Melissa. Review of *Whom Shall I Fear? Library Journal* (November 1, 1996).
Hudak, Melissa. Review of *Every Hidden Thing. Library Journal* (June 1, 1998): 94.
Mort, John. Review of *Whom Shall I Fear? Booklist* (November, 1996): 571.
Mort, John. *Christian Fiction: A Guide to the Genre.* Greenwood Village, CO: Libraries Unlimited,
2002.
Publishers Weekly. Review of *They Shall See God.* (April 29, 2002): 42
Today's Christian Woman. Review of *They Shall See God* and "Athol Dickson Explains Why He Takes
Time to Write 'Mere Stories,'" (May-June, 2002): 63.

DILLARD, ANNIE

Personal, Professional, and Religious Background

Annie Doak Dillard (1945–) was born in Pittsburgh, Pennsylvania, to a prosperous family. The eldest of three daughters, she was encouraged by her parents to be creative and to explore her surroundings. Her non-conformist, energetic mother and her knowledgeable father taught her everything from plumbing to economics. In *An American Childhood*, Annie Dillard tells of her early life, filled with the comforts of a country-club style life, laughter, reading and writing poetry, and exploring her small world. Here we can also trace her early love of natural science and her fascination with close study of nature.

This autobiography also reveals Dillard's distaste for the fundamentalists at summer camps she attended and her adolescent quarrels with the Presbyterian Church. Her mother and father dropped Annie and her sisters off for services, expecting them to conform to a religion that held no interest for them. While others took communion, Annie watched and judged their solemn prayer time, unmoved by any genuine conviction or passion for God. Shocked by the evil she saw in her world, she blamed God for pain and suffering. The local pastor provided her with a copy of **C. S. Lewis**'s classic *The Problem of Pain*, but she was not convinced. He then bid her farewell, assuring her that she would finally return. Later, Dillard struggled to discover a philosophy free of the Bible, but continued to find mystery

> I don't know beans about God.
>
> —Annie Dillard, from *For the Time Being*

behind all the world she studied. Throughout her life, she has puzzled over the age-old issue of a good God allowing or creating a world full of disasters and death. Yet she was always dazzled by the variety and complexity of the universe, studying God through the Book of Nature.

Annie Doak went to Hollins College, near Roanoke, Virginia, where she studied English, theology and creative writing. She married her writing teacher, Richard Dillard, who "taught her everything she knows" about writing. In 1968, she earned an M.A. in English from Hollins, having written her master's thesis on Thoreau. Annie Dillard had a near fatal attack of pneumonia in 1971, from which she recovered, but came to believe that she needed a fuller experience of life. She spent four seasons near Tinker Creek, an area in Virginia with forests, creeks, mountains, and animal life of all types. She began a journal of her observations, clearly inspired by her study of Thoreau's experience at Walden Pond. One biographer, Sandra Stahlman Elliott, notes that Dillard became so absorbed in turning her 20-plus volumes of notes into a book that she spent 15 or 16 hours a day writing, cut off all society, ignored even world news, lived on coffee and coke. "She lost 30 pounds and all her plants died." The result was her first successful book, *Pilgrim at Tinker Creek*, and her first collection of poetry, *Tickets for a Prayer Wheel*, both published in 1974.

By this time, she had become "spiritually promiscuous," drawing on ideas from a great variety of religions, feeling committed to none. She spent the years after graduation painting and writing. She was astonished that her first book received such universal praise, culminating in the Pulitzer for general nonfiction; she did not trust the fame that came with this early success. She moved to an island on Puget Sound, where she lived until 1982. This period, when she was scholar-in-residence at Western Washington University, living in a cabin with a view of the Cascades, allowed her to think deeply about her faith, which she chronicles in *Holy the Firm*. She tells of her regular attendance at the local Congregational Church, which drew Christians of all denominations. She even talked the congregation into switching from grape juice to California wine for communion services, and cheerfully took her backpack into town to pick up the wine—Christ's blood. Her combination of sacrilegious jokes and serious seeking mark her curious religious pilgrimage, which eventually ended with her conversion some years later to Roman Catholicism. When asked about her decision to become a Catholic, she told Michael Gross that she liked the anonymity of this faith. "Nobody looks at you when you go to a Catholic church. You just stand up there and worship and hang out, sort of representing the body of people on earth." She enjoys the Roman Catholic emphasis on "mere presence—of worshipers, of Christ, of the world." "I could care less" about doctrine. Dillard does not care about the details of creeds. She believes that religion is "about living the life in a relationship with God."

When her first marriage ended in divorce, she married again. The writer Gary Clevidence had children from a previous marriage. They also had a daughter, Cody Rose, who is frequently mentioned in Dillard's meditations. This marriage also ended in divorce. In 1988, she married again, this time at a Unitarian Church. Her husband, a well-respected scholar known from his biographies of William James and Henry David Thoreau, seems to have proved a compatible partner. In one of her interviews, she notes that they have been married for 20 years. She is very careful to reveal little of her private life, in spite of her open discussions of her spiritual pilgrimage. She refers to herself in one interview as a "gregarious recluse."

Her longest academic attachment has been to Wesleyan University in Middletown, Connecticut, from which she retired as professor emerita in 1999. She has traveled widely, serving as a member of the U.S. cultural delegation to China in 1982. She also speaks of trips to Antartica, Israel, and many other places. She believes that we are put on earth to be witnesses and should see as much as possible.

Major Works and Themes

Annie Dillard is most famous for her nature essays. She has written only two novels, neither of them so well-received as her other books. *Pilgrim at Tinker Creek*, her first and best nonfiction work, won her praise when she was quite young. Nothing since has equaled its impact. The passion she brought to her meditations on nature startled a public who were accustomed to seeing the natural world as background. She made it foreground.

God has no great role in Annie Dillard's stories and essays. In *Pilgrim at Tinker Creek*, the writer discovers transcendence in the lowest creatures. Her observations of the natural world are fresh and often dazzling. In *Holy the Firm*, she insists she is not a pantheist, but finds God in "the Firm." This need to reach beyond traditional orthodoxy to explain her heterodox theology reveals her to be a searcher, not a Christian in a traditional sense. She wonders whether God is really very interested in mankind. "Did Christ descend once and for all to no purpose, in a kind of divine and kenotic suicide, or ascend once and for all, pulling his cross up after him like a rope ladder home?" Dillard knows a lot of scripture, has thought about it, loves the phrasing of the Bible, but stumbles over the ideas.

Her two novels are marked by her upper-class background. They are proper, with nothing crudely sexual, no filthy language, no salacious moments. They are curiously free of theology. Her sojourn in the west inspired her first novel, *The Living*, a long chronicle of the early settlements in the Bellingham region. She uses her knowledge of the Native Americans who were there to welcome the first white settlers, the various types of people who arrived, and their efforts to establish a community. In *The Living*, we see generations come and go, living their lives in the shadows of the great cedars on the Washington coast, and dying their grotesque deaths for no apparent reasons. Geography seems to be the major force in human life, setting limits on expectations and barriers to progress. All the struggles of the generations seem to go for naught. Some individuals love one another, some hate a few of their neighbors, but God is not important to most of them, and there is no evidence that he has any plan for them or responds to their occasional prayers. The Native Americans blend their own indigenous faiths with Roman Catholicism or Methodism, finding no need for purity in practice or thought.

Years later, Dillard undertook a second work of fiction, *The Maytrees*, which was much shorter and more successful. Lou and Toby Maytree meet in the small community of Provincetown, where they are among the few year-round residents. Their lives from courtship through death play out against the backdrop of the fixed stars, demonstrating the dance of life and death. The Maytrees fall in love, marry, have a baby, love him and one another for an appointed time, then separate, lament their loss and accept their gains, grow old and needy, return to the community for comfort and prepare for death. Their lives ebb and flow like the sea, their passions are controlled by time, they leave little debris on the littoral of the world. The story is a re-telling of *Ethan Frome*, without Wharton's ironic twist. The betrayal is pictured as natural, as is the reconciliation and forgiveness. As in *The Living*, Dillard sees people less as individuals than as representatives of the millions of humans who have gone before them, each thinking he or she is important, while each is no more than a grain of sand on the shore. *The Maytrees*, as its title suggests, treats the saga of the family as a bit of natural history. They watch the stars, the sea, and the sand. Their lives blend like a modernist painting into color fields without clear edges. Their behavior is a result of their age, their circumstances, their hungers, and their geographical setting. The grace in the story is the continuing love, forgiveness, and generosity of the family members, regardless of the wayward behavior of one of its branches.

Annie Dillard may yet write the novel that is as beautiful and astonishing as her poetry and her prose meditations, but so far that novel lies dormant. Sadly, she has told interviewers, however, that *The Maytrees* is her final book. She has retiring from writing, she says.

Critical Reception

Reviewers note that Dillard ventured into new territory with her 1992 publication, *The Living*, "a sprawling historical novel set in the Pacific Northwest." Molly Gloss, in the *Washington Post Book World*, hailed the author's first novel as masterful. "Her triumph is that this panoramic evocation of a very specific landscape and people might as well have been settled upon any other time and place—for this is, above all, a novel about the reiterant, precarious, wondrous, solitary, terrifying, utterly common condition of human life." Dillard's celebrated skill with words is also much in evidence here, according to Gloss, who noted that the author "uses language gracefully, releasing at times a vivid, startling imagery."

On the other hand, the book has not won prizes or continuing praise as was the case with *Pilgrim at Tinker Creek*. While the nonfiction work brought a new sense of life and transcendence to the natural world, this novel seems too disinterested, almost stoic in tone. The abrupt style, plain narrative of horrors, and quick listings of individual anguish render it a recitation of facts, particularly horrible ones, rather than a novel. (In some of her nonfiction writing, Dillard lists the millions who have died of a disease or calamity, as if multiplication of instances can somehow relieve human distress.) The author maintains the clinical tone of a scientist studying changes in the fauna and flora of a region. The vast array of quickly sketched characters, the lack of "progress" or sense of purpose, and flat narrative make it seem more like a primitive painting of a massacre than a real story. It sounds like the book of Chronicles, with the flat recitation of facts, rather than the dramatic stories told in the books of Samuel and Kings.

Julia Reed, in the *New York Times*, called Dillard's second novel, *The Maytrees*, "a natural history of love." This reviewer thinks that the author strains to demonstrate her energetic reading and that she also reads the dictionary, cherishing the most exotic words she can discover. Reed does acknowledge that, "despite the big words and the name-dropping . . . there is also good old straight narrative and prose that is often, yes, breathtakingly illuminative." In the same paper, Michelle Green comments on the peculiar language: "Shim, scumble, saurine, skeg: It's impossible for readers who delight in such words not to be entranced by the way Annie Dillard chooses—and uses—her arsenal in 'The Maytrees.'" She sees the story as an anthropology of love. Green is especially enchanted by "Yankee the turtle," who crawls out from under the couch when a character is dying, regarding humans "with the obsidian calm of a god."

Awards

Annie Dillard won the Pulitzer Prize in general nonfiction, 1975, for *Pilgrim at Tinker Creek*; grants from National Endowment for the Arts, 1982–83, and Guggenheim Foundation, 1985–86; *Teaching a Stone to Talk* was named a Best Book of the 1980s, *Boston Globe*; Dillard was elected to the Academy Award in Literature, American Academy of Arts and Letters, 1998; and became a fellow of the, American Academy of Arts and Letters in 1999. She has held visiting professorships at various colleges and universities, received numerous honorary degrees and been selected by various states as their honoree for numerous occasions—almost always for her nonfiction.

Bibliography of Novels by Author

The Living. New York: HarperCollins, 1992.
The Maytrees. New York: HarperCollins, 2007.

Several of Dillard's writings have been adapted as plays, or as readings to accompany music and art.

Bibliography of Works about Author

"Annie Dillard." *Contemporary Authors Online*. Detroit: Gale, 2004.
Detweiler, Robert. *Breaking the Fall: Religious Readings of Contemporary Fiction*. New York: Harper, 1989.
Dillard, Annie. *Pilgrim at Tinker Creek*. New York: Harper's Magazine Press, 1974.
Dillard, Annie, *Holy the Firm*. New York: Harper, 1977.
Dillard, Annie. *The Weasel*. Claremont, CA: Rara Avis Press, 1981.
Dillard, Annie. *Living by Fiction*. New York: Harper, 1982.
Dillard, Annie. *Teaching a Stone to Talk: Expeditions and Encounters*. New York: Harper, 1982.
Dillard, Annie. *Encounters with Chinese Writers*. Middletown, CT: Wesleyan University Press, 1984.
Dillard, Annie. *An American Childhood*. New York: Harper, 1987.
Dillard, Annie. *The Writing Life*. New York: Harper, 1989.
Dillard, Annie. *Mornings Like This: Found Poems*. New York: HarperCollins, 1995.
Dillard, Annie. *For the Time Being*. New York: Knopf, 1999.
Elliott, Sandra Stahlman. "Annie Dillard, Biography." http://hubcap.clemson.edu/-sparks/dillard/bio.htm.
Green, Michelle. Review of *The Maytrees*. *New York Times*, June 25, 2007.
Gross, Michael Joseph. "Apparent Contradictions." Review of *For the Time Being*. *Boston Phoenix* (June 24–July 1, 1999). http://72.166.46.24/archive/books/99/06/24//Annie-Dillard.html.
Johnson, Sandra H. *The Space Between: Literary Epiphany in the Work of Annie Dillard*. Kent, OH: Kent State University Press, 1992.
Parrish, Nancy C. *Lee Smith, Annie Dillard, and the Hollins Group*. Baton Rouge, LA: Louisiana University Press, 1998.
Peterson, Eugene. "Annie Dillard: With her Eyes Wide Open." *Theology Today* 43 (1986): 2.
Rainwater, Catherine. *Contemporary American Woman Writers: Narrative Strategies*. Lexington, KY: University Press of Kentucky, 1985.
Reed, Julia. Review of *The Maytrees*. "A Natural History of Love." *New York Times*, July 29, 2007.
Ronda, Bruce A. "Annie Dillard and the Fire of God." http://www.religon-online.org/showarticle.asp?title=1683.
Rose, Daniel Aser. "In Conversation with Annie Dillard." *Washington Post*, January 24, 2007: BW04.
Slovic, Scott. *Seeking Awareness in American Nature Writing*. Salt Lake City, UT: University of Utah Press, 1992.
Smith, Linda. *Annie Dillard*. New York: Twayne Publishers, 1991.
Smith, Pamela A. "The Ecotheology of Annie Dillard: A Study in Ambivalence." *CrossCurrents*. http://www.crosscurrents.org/dillard/htm.

DOUGLAS, LLOYD C.

Personal, Professional, and Religious Background

Lloyd Cassel Douglas (1877–1951) was born in Columbia City, Indiana. His father, Alexander Jackson Douglas, was a country parson. His mother was Sarah Jane Cassel Douglas. He attended Wittenburg College and Seminary, in Springfield, Ohio, earning a B.A. in 1900, an M.A. in 1903, and a B.D. in 1903. Lloyd Douglas married Bessie Lo Porch in 1904. They had two daughters, Betty and Virginia. He spent his life as an ordained Lutheran minister, serving as the pastor of churches in North Manchester, Indiana; Lancaster, Indiana; and in Washington, D.C. In 1911, he became the director of religious work for the YMCA, switching from the Lutheran

> If a man has enough faith . . . he can find his way in the dark—with faith as his lamp.
>
> —Peter, in *The Big Fisherman*
> by Lloyd C. Douglas

to the Congregational church. He served Congregational churches in Ann Arbor, Michigan; Los Angeles, California; and Montreal, Canada, retiring in 1933 to become a full-time writer.

Lloyd Douglas started his writing career in 1920, first writing religious studies, then turning to fiction. He became famous for his later novels, some of which were best-sellers and were made into films. His novel *The Robe* was on the *New York Times* best-seller list for three years after its publication in 1942, and the movie version, released in 1953, was a smash hit as a Hollywood epic.

When Lloyd Douglas died in 1951, he was eulogized in most of the mainstream papers and periodicals, largely for his biblical fiction. His daughters, Betty and Virginia, collaborated on a biography of their father the year after his death.

Major Works and Themes

Although Lloyd Douglas properly belongs to the turn-of-the-century style of religious writing, some of his more famous stories did appear after World War II. Since he devoted his attention to fiction only in his later days, he brought the legacy of the old standbys—Robert Louis Stevenson or Arthur Conan Doyle—to bear on messages that worked better in fiction than in sermons. *Magnificent Obsession*, his first big success, is a romance that blends a message with a mystery discovered in an encrypted diary. The story marries moments of transcendent power with practical morality. Using the Sermon on the Mount as a set of rules for practical living and greater power, the author introduces a standard pair of romantic lovers, with a balanced pair of flawed ne'er-do-wells, keeps them carefully apart till the final pages, and then provides the expected conclusion. He begins the novel with a catastrophe and concludes it with a wedding—holding the secrets back as long as he can manage.

A far greater success with the popular reading public was *The Robe*, the fictional tale of Marcellus, a Roman guard who won the crucified Christ's robe by a toss of the dice. Haunted by the mystery of the Nazarene and the story of his garment, Marcellus felt compelled to discover the truth, retracing the path of this remarkable man, speaking to those who knew him and who witnessed his miracles and heard his message. Marcellus becomes a convert to the new religion and finally a martyr in the infamous Coliseum. In the Cinemascope version Richard Burton played Marcellus, his first important movie role.

Building on the success of this Bible fiction, Douglas used some of the same characters and setting in *The Big Fisherman*. Once again, he drew on the political world of the New Testament and stories of the disciple Peter while tracing a pair of young Arab lovers determined to avenge their family's honor. The Big Fisherman travels from the Sea of Galilee to Rome, dramatizing Peter's dramatic change from a doubter to a leader of the new faith, from cowardly denials to heroic death. The Arab lovers become Douglas's means to explain some of the complex political situation in Israel at the time of Christ. In an effort to bridge the ancient divide between the sons of Ishmael and the sons of Isaac and to avoid attacks by Rome, shrewd old

King Herod persuades the King of Arabia to allow his daughter to marry Herod's handsome but profligate son who is to become Herod Antipas. The marriage produces one child, a daughter named Fara or Esther, but soon is dissolved as the young Herod divorces her to marry his own brother's wife, Herodias. This slight to the Arabs remains unavenged for some years, until Fara feels compelled to assassinate Herod, traveling alone to Galilee, where the young Herod is now Tetrarch. She is followed by her lover, a handsome young man named Voldi, who soon makes friends with Romans and comes to understand a great deal about the political world in which his beloved Fara is entangled. Eventually, it is Voldi who serves as the avenger, not Fara. She becomes a follower of Peter and Christ, ending her days in Greece. The story's conclusion suggests that Douglas may have considered a sequel, but he never continued his story.

Critical Reception

Critics tend to applaud Lloyd Douglas for his understanding of the ancient world and for the vivid portrayal of biblical characters, not for his plots or style. He tells a good story, often waiting far too long to get to the key characters. In *The Big Fisherman*, Peter does not appear for the first hundred pages. Douglas also introduces his version of a social gospel, a very popular concept at the time, in a manner that enlivens the gospel stories. He does feel free to bring fresh ideas into the fictitious retelling of history, like his concept of the "Torchbearer," in *The Big Fisherman*, a puzzling addition to the Gospels.

Some orthodox critics note that Douglas an advocate of "sentimentalism" and "liberalism." Certainly, in *Magnificent Obsession*, he does seem to be intent on using the Sermon on the Mount without the transcendent Redeemer at the heart of the message. It is a more humanistic portrayal of how to do good, to find a scientific basis for belief, and transform the world through one's own benevolence. Mort notes dryly that this is a "sort of Dale Carnegie philosophy crossed with the Sermon on the Mount." Douglas's stories have no clear Hell, no exclusive claims for Christianity. They fit firmly into the tradition of Lew Wallace's *Ben Hur* (1880) and pave the road for later Bible epics. John Mort calls *The Robe* a "deeply moving tale," one case in which Douglas kept his melodramatic tendencies in check.

Awards

Lloyd Douglas was awarded honorary doctorates by Gettysburg College in Pennsylvania and Northeastern University in Boston.

Bibliography of Novels by Author

Magnificent Obsession. Chicago: Willet, Clark, & Colby, 1929.
Precious Jeopardy: A Christmas Story. Boston: Houghton Mifflin, 1933.
Disputed Passage. Boston: Houghton Mifflin, 1939.
The Robe. Boson: Houghton Mifflin, 1942.
The Big Fisherman. Boston: Houghton Mifflin: 1948.

Bibliography of Works about Author

Dawson, Virginia Douglas, and Betty Douglas Wilson. *The Shape of Sunday: An Intimate Biography of Lloyd C. Douglas*. Boston: Houghton Mifflin, 1952.

Douglas, Lloyd C. *A Time to Remember.* Boston: Houghton Mifflin, 1951.
"Lloyd C. Douglas," *Contemporary Authors Online.* Detroit: Thomson Gale, 2003.
Mort, John. *Christian Fiction: A Guide to the Genre.* Greenwood Village, CO: Libraries Unlimited, 2002.

Obituaries

Newsweek, February 26, 1951.
New York Times, February 14, 1951.
Publishers Weekly, February 24, 1951.
Time, February 26, 1951.

DOWNS, TIM

Personal, Professional, and Religious Background

Tim Downs is a Phi Beta Kappa graduate of Indiana University. Having spent much of his youth reading comic books and comic strips, he hatched the idea of developing his own comic strip, like the popular *Doonesbury* strip that was appearing in the Yale student newspaper. He first tried a strip in his own college paper, the *Indiana Daily Student*, and it worked. When he graduated in 1976, he sold *Downstown* to the same national syndicate that produces *Doonesbury*, Universal Press Syndicate, making that his regular work for the next 10 years.

Finding that the comic strip (carried in more than 100 daily papers) required only a portion of his time, Tim Downs also became a professional speaker, in 1979 taking a position with Campus Crusade for Christ. At one point, he realized that the common denominator between his two jobs was that both required story telling. "It suddenly dawned on me that that's what I really was—not an artist and not just a speaker, but a storyteller. That's when I began to consider other forms of storytelling—like fiction."

He is married to Joy, whom he describes as "my beautiful Joy," and currently writes books, often in collaboration with her, on conflict-resolution within families, and leads marriage seminars that he calls "A Weekend to Remember." He and his family live in North Carolina.

Major Works and Themes

Tim Downs's greatest popularity has come from the "Bug Man" Christian suspense novels, which have won him the Angel Award and the Christy. He chose the crime scene investigation approach, subsequently popular in television programs, especially *CSI: Las Vegas*, which features a forensic entomologist as the lead investigator. Downs did some serious research of his own in forensic entomology, signing up for a workshop in central Indiana designed for deputy coroners and crime scene investigators. He learned how to use the bugs that swarm over victims of violent crimes—maggots, fleas, and others—to collect and label insect evidence from the victim for a clue as to the time and means of the crime itself.

The first of his "Bug Man" novels, *Shoofly Pie*, introduced his recurring character, Nick Polchak, a forensic entomologist. The immediate success of this book

> "Inspiration is for amateurs." I think that expresses it well. If you wait to write until the words come easily, you probably won't write very much.
>
> —Tim Downs in interview with C.J. Darlington

For 10 years, Tim Downs was a successful cartoonist: *Downstown* was carried in more than 100 newspapers.

quickly led him to produce three others: *Chop Shop*, *PlagueMaker*, and *Head Game*. Each approaches a different contemporary issue—biological warfare, traffic in human organs, psychological warfare, or terrorism. Polchak is not necessarily the lead character in every novel. In *PlagueMaker*, for instance, he appears only briefly to identify fleas that spread the bubonic plague. The main character is an F.B.I. agent, Nathan Donovan.

In each case, Downs begins with a major theme. "In *PlagueMaker*, the theme was forgiveness. In *Head Game*, it was encouragement and faith." A "big fan of **C. S. Lewis**," Downs believes that blending Christian themes with good stories and humor is a winning technique. C. S. Lewis showed him how to "express profound ideas in simple terms." Thus, in *PlagueMaker*, Downs uses the idea Camus explored for very different purposes in his famous novel, *The Plague*, but shows that for most humans the real plague is the evil which becomes an infection that spreads. The antidote is forgiveness. At the climax of the story, when we expect a violent shoot-out, we instead see a gentle anointment of the villain and a pronouncement of forgiveness. The theme carries over into the lives of the two divorced people who have reunited to solve the terrorism threat: their marriage too proves to be riddled with the plague of resentment and anger. They also need forgiveness.

Critical Reception

Marcia Ford, writing for *Faithful Reader*, praises *Shoofly Pie* as a sizzler of a story that has "all of the elements that make for good fiction—among them, memorable characters, a colorful setting, a riveting plot, and believable dialogue"—all of which "come together seamlessly." Each of his thrillers is full of surprises and colorful characters. *Publishers Weekly* noted of *PlagueMaker* that "Downs evenhandedly dispenses humor, interesting technical details, and the trademark 'ick' factor that characterizes his previous books."

The *Publishers Weekly* review of *Chop Shop* notes that the novel "stands out from the pack of CSI-inspired mysteries with its quirky hero and creative handling of the Hurricane Katrina disaster." By and large, the critics agree that Downs's books are a surprise to "evangelical Christian fiction" readers.

Awards

Tim Downs has won two awards for his four novels—the Angel Award for *Shoofly Pie* and the Christy, in 2004, for *PlagueMaker*, as the Best Suspense novel of the year.

Bibliography of Novels by Author

Shoofly Pie. West Monroe, LA;: Howard Publishing, 2003.
Chop Shop. West Monroe, LA: Howard Publishing, 2004.
PlagueMaker. Nashville, TN: WestBow Press, 2006.
Head Game. Nashville, TN: WestBow Press, 2007.

Bibliography of Works about Author

Darlington, C. J. "Tim Downs Interview," www.tidletrakk.com/tim_downs/interview.html.
Ford, Marcia. Review of *Shoofly Pie*. *Faithful Reader* (September 23, 2006).

Ford, Marcia. Review of *Cope Shop. Faithful Reader* (September 23, 2006).
Ford, Marcia. Review of *PlagueMaker. Faithful Reader* (September 23, 2006).
Mort, John. Review of *PlagueMaker, Booklist* (January 1, 2006): 59.
Publishers Weekly. Review of *Chop Shop* (June 7, 2004): 30; Review of *PlagueMaker* (October 24, 2005): 36.
"Tim Downs," *Contemporary Authors Online.* Detroit: Thomson Gale, 2007.
Tim Downs Interview with *Faithful Reader*: www.faithfulreader.com, February 10, 2005.
Tim Downs' Web site: www.timdowns.net.

DUNCAN, DAVID JAMES

Personal, Professional, and Religious Background

David James Duncan (1952–) was born near Portland, Oregon. He has spent most of his life in Oregon, writing his books about this region that he loves. His father was Elwood Dean Duncan and his mother Donna Jean Rowe. As a child, he was forced to attend church with his family, who were Seventh-day Adventists. The experience alienated him from organized religion and turned him into an outspoken opponent of fundamentalists.

He attended Portland State University, earning a B.A. in 1973. His own reading reflects a lifelong love of learning, much of it in eastern mysticism. When he was 20 years old, he visited India, where he had an "intuition that my life's work would be storytelling, deciding to try to write a novel, and at 28, finally did. That book, *The River Why*, let me start eking out a living doing work I loved. I've been pretty happy ever since."

He is married to Adrian Arleo, who is a sculptor and works in her studio 50 feet away from his office. They have daughters, whom he does not name in his interviews. He is a very private person, insisting, according to *Contemporary Authors*, that "Anonymity is a midwife to my meager art."

As a child, he became fascinated with fishing, especially after he saw his first coho salmon at age six. The rivers Duncan fished as a child gradually disappeared as Portland's suburbs expanded. In addition, the coastal watersheds of western Oregon, where he had lived for 40 years, were ruined by "timber companies and the U.S. Forest Service "destroying the trees surrounding his home in less than four years." At that point, Duncan and his family moved to Montana. He also shifted to another form of writing. At the age of 40, he became a nonfiction writer, "not out of a sense of calling, but out of a sense of betrayal, out of rage over natural systems violated, out of grief for a loved world raped, and out of a craving for justice. In the following years, he began to write increasingly passionate diatribes against the Republican Party, fundamentalists, and the activities of the United States government—especially the wars in Vietnam and the Persian Gulf.

Today he is primarily an essayist and a public speaker, currently at work on a "comedy novel about reincarnation and human folly titled *Nijinsky Hosts Saturday Night Live.*" At least, that is what this straight-faced comedian told his interviewer in his talk on "My Advice on Writing Advice." The advice he gave, which apparently he also follows, is to "have fun on paper."

Major Works and Themes

David Duncan identifies himself as a "writer, conservationist, father, fly fisherman, contemplative." He has written a number of short stories and two impressive novels, but has spent

> You've got to be darned focused to make a living in the arts.
>
> —David James Duncan, in interview with *Grist*

more of his time on attacks on the "Fundamentalist Right" and those who would exploit nature. He calls himself a Druid, though his knowledge of Christian scripture is impressive and deeply felt. His main targets are the established churches, not the Christian faith itself—as he explains in *God Laughs & Plays: Churchless Sermons in Response to the Preachments of the Fundamentalist Right*.

Duncan's love of nature, especially the rivers of his native Pacific Northwest, is palpable in his stories. Like Hemingway, he relishes the details of fishing, the kind of lures or bait used, the types of fishermen, the battles with the fish. *The River Why* is especially delightful for its allusions to Isaac Walton's *The Compleat Angler*, embodied in the father figure, and explored by the son, who finally comes to terms with Walton's religion. Like St. Augustine, for whom Gus, the narrator, was named, he goes through a struggle to discover the nature of his own faith, searching through different worldviews and finally coming to a blended philosophy that satisfies him. Using such quixotic teachers as a Native American named Thomas Bigeater, a philosopher-fisherman named Titus, a thoughtful dog named Descartes, and a fellow craftsman named Nick, he comes to a Taoist "equilibrium" and a mystic experience. It is his love of Eddy (his lover) and their delight in their baby that he acknowledges his awareness of the hook that God has in his own heart. This leads him to understand in a mystic moment that "love does it, and love alone"—an insight he borrows from Meister Eckhart.

The Brothers K is also a journey into the meaning of faith. Once again the narrator must find his own path, this time using much of the symbolism of baseball. The novel also draws heavily on Dostoyevsky. The Chances are a family of strong personalities dominated by a father whose true vocation is pitching, but whose necessary path is that of a father to his children and a husband to his wife. The mother, like Duncan's own, is a Seventh-day Adventist, a faith that takes hold on only one of her sons. Ironically, it is this son who, through compassion, is forced to fight in Vietnam and who, because of his true Christian love, is considered insane. The church fails him when it is most needed and yet his faith sustains him when he is required by his commanding officer to kill a child. He keeps repeating, "Jesus loves the little children."

The love of the family, the intense relationship between the husband and the wife, the individual paths that each of these remarkable sons takes—these are the stuff of a real epic. For those readers who also love baseball, the comic/heroic struggle of the father to be faithful to his vocation and to his family makes for fascinating reading. The father's close analysis of pitching styles and tricks, his determination to return to pitching even when his thumb is mutilated, his comic decision to substitute his toe for his thumb—these make wonderful images of perseverance and commitment to one's calling.

Critical Reception

The critical response to Duncan's two novels has been positive, although the later response to his talks and nonfiction has been a reflection of the reviewer as much as the author. Mike Dodaro, who attended one of his readings, walked out when Duncan began an imagined conversation between Jesus and his mother, "Mrs Joseph Christ." He called Duncan a member of the Boomer prophets, and his ideas "cock-sure Gnosticism." Others have been more adoring and delighted with his sharp attacks and outrageous wit.

Conservationists are particularly fond of *The River Why*. The book was the first work of fiction ever published by the Sierra Club. *Book List* applauded the host of vivid characters and his "deep insight into the mysterious machination of nature." *Publishers Weekly* called the writing "energetic, excessive, sometimes merely prolix."

His second novel, *The Brothers K*, was hailed by Mitch Finley, writing for the *National Catholic Reporter*. "It's a family story the way the Book of Genesis is a family story—in your face, filled with heart-breakingly, infuriating human characters and twists and turns that could happen only in real life." Eloise Kinner, writing for *Booklist*, noted its humor as well as its intensity. She insists that it "does what a novel should do." It "teaches you something, makes you think, breaks your heart, and mends it again."

Awards

David James Duncan won a Lannan Fellowship, the 2001 Western States Book Award, and an honorary doctorate for Public Service from the University of Portland. He and Wendell Berry were cowinners of the American Library Association's 2003 Eli Oboler Award for the Preservation of Intellectual Freedom for their coauthored book *Citizen's Dissent*.

Bibliography of Novels by Author

The River Why. San Francisco: Sierra Club Books, 1983.
The Brothers K. New York: Doubleday, 1995.

Bibliography of Works about Author

Brady, Martin. Review of *The River Why*. *Booklist* (February 1, 1983): 714.

Dodaro, Mike. "David James Duncan, Reading." http://forum.imagejournal. org/showthread.php?/t=356.

Duncan, David James. "By Hook and By Book," *Grist*, April 2, 2007. http:www.grist.org/cgi-bin/print this.pl?uri=comments/interactivist/2007/04/02/duncan.

Duncan, David James. *God Laughs & Plays: Churchless Sermons in Response to the Preachments of the Fundamentalist Right*. Great Barrington, MA: Triad Institute 2006.

Duncan, David James. "My Advice on Writing Advice," Weber: *The Contemporary West*, Winter 2004, Volume 21:2. http://wwwweberstudies.weber.edu/archive/archive %20D%20Vol.%2021.2.21/Vol.%2021.

Duncan, David James. *My Story as Told by Water: Confessions, Druidic Rants, Reflections, Bird-Watchings, Fish-Stalkings, Visions, Songs and Prayers Refracting Light, from Living Rivers, in the Age of the Industrial Dark*. San Francisco, CA: Sierra Club Books, 2001.

"David James Duncan." *Contemporary Authors Online*. Detroit: Thomson Gale, 2008.

Finley, Mitch. Review of *The River Why*. *National Catholic Reporter* (October 2, 1992): 18.

Kinney, Eloise. Review of *The Brothers K*. *Booklist* (May 1, 1992): 1562.

Michaud, Charles. Review of *The Brothers K*. *Library Journal* (June 1, 1992): 172.

Sierra Club Web site: http://www.sierraclub.org.

E

ENGER, LEIF

Personal, Professional, and Religious Background

Leif Enger (1961–) was born in Osakis, Minnesota. By the third grade, he was writing poetry, demonstrating that there was no word he would not misuse, no rhythm he would not break for a rhyme. He made up ballads about cowboys, baseball players, dinosaurs, gorillas, and classmates who "seemed to have it coming." His faith appears to have been an intrinsic part of his life as long as he can remember. As he told his interviewer in Rochester, "You grow up inside the faith of your family, which is Christianity in both Reuben's and mine." (Reuben is the protagonist of *Peace Like a River*.) When you reach that time of decision about the truth of your faith, "you accept it as yours, as something to be nurtured and guarded."

Enger earned a B.A. from Minnesota State University, Moorhead, in 1983. Although he dreamed of becoming a novelist, he decided during college that he would instead become a reporter, seeing this as a more stable source of income. He became a reporter and a producer for Minnesota Public Radio in 1984, finding that the experience helped him edit his work and learn about rewriting. At the same time, he continued to write novels. He and his brother, Lin Enger, chose a joint pseudonym, L.L. Enger to write a pair of mystery novels, *Sacrifice* (1993), and *The Sinners' League: A Gun Pedersen Mystery* (2001). Leif Enger characterizes these as "crime novels about a major league baseball player turned northwoods recluse." His brother had been writing for years and taught him the elements of fiction, He says that he and Lin had "gigantic fun" with these stories. They would plot a book in one weekend, break it into chapters, and then mail the chapters back and forth. "I can't think of a better way to learn writing, or a gentler teacher than my brother."

He is married to Robin Enger and has two sons. It was after his marriage and the

> Real miracles bother people.
>
> —Leif Enger in interview with Bella Stander

experience of coping with the anguish of an asthmatic son that he began to write his master-piece, *Peace Like a River*. It took him five years to write this book, for which he felt no pressure. He read each new scene to his wife and boys: "They were awfully patient." Leif Enger and his family live in the Brainerd Lakes area of Minnesota. He told one interviewer that he now writing a novel about an aging train robber.

Major Works and Themes

Unlike most religious novelists in modern times. Enger took years to produce the single novel for which he is justly famous. *Peace like a River* describes a number of miracles from the point of view of a young boy. Enger drew on his knowledge of rural Minnesota in the 1960s to tell the story of Reuben Land, his wayward brother, David, his sister, Swede, the writer in the family, and their remarkable, miracle-working father, who is both a poet and a janitor.

Realizing that many religious classics are not masterpieces of literature, Enger acknowledges that fiction "that includes a faith element is tricky to write . . . and not getting it right can tank an otherwise good book." He says, "There are too many ways to get it wrong, too many people you might offend." He believes that faith is better illustrated than explained, being a "witness" rather than compelling belief. "All you can do is say: here is what happened."

Peace like a River is a thoroughly Christian story. Beginning and ending with miracles, punctuated with miracles throughout, filled with citations from the King James translation of the Bible, this gentle tale of a sweet man and his loving family is told from the point of view of the middle child, an 11-year-old asthmatic named Reuben. Central to the narrative is the saintly father, Jeremiah Land, a wise, knowledgeable, humble man, and a prophet. Miraculously preserved from death in a tornado, he gives up his plans for a prosperous and respected life as a physician to become a handyman and janitor at a public school. His wife eventually abandons him and the children, but Jeremiah perseveres with joy and love. He does find another woman to love, one whom he courts in a ritual out of an earlier time. In the end, he gives his life for his son in a mystical transaction powerfully described.

Jeremiah Land's love extends beyond his immediate family to include the other children at the school and the whole town, even a traveling salesman who abuses his hospitality from time to time. He belongs to a charismatic church, prays faithfully, reads his Bible with sensitivity and understanding, practices his faith with passion and humility. When he happens upon a rape scene at the school, he becomes the angel of vengeance, but then meekly accepts the damage this action causes him and his family. The oldest boy, Davy, who is clearly not a saint like his dad, refuses to turn the other cheek and accept the escalating warfare of the villains, finally killing them when they invade the Lands' home. Much of the story deals with the aftermath of this violent scene—the trial, the prison escape, the horseback chase over the frozen countryside, and the eventual solution. Like Jacob, the father wrestles with God, but makes the hard decision to help bring his beloved son to justice. When this plan backfires, and Davy returns home, his father welcomes the prodigal back into the family with love and forgiveness.

Parallel to the plot line is the "Ballad of Sunny," being written by Swede, the younger sister, whose love of poetry combines with a delight in all things Western to make the "Ballad of Sunny" a commentary on American mythology of the wild wild West. Her sensitivity and her hunger for a mother enrich the primarily masculine narrative, while her intimate knowledge of renegades in history makes their travels into the Badlands rich with meaning.

One of the themes that critics have noted in the story is loss. It is through the family's difficulties, particularly their losses, that they are tested and their true nature revealed. Using the famous hymn, "It is well with my soul," from which the title is taken, Enger reminds us that (as Horatio Stafford, the hymn composer, also found) "When peace, like a river, attendeth my way, / When sorrows like sea billows roll; / Whatever my lot, Thou has taught me to say, / It is well, it is well, with my soul." These famous words sum up much of the plot, while the river itself becomes a central image in the final scene of the Celestial City, just beyond the Garden of Eden, when Jeremiah and Reuben both journey toward death. Enger can blend **C. S. Lewis** and John Bunyan, with real landscapes from the American West to form as remarkable a scene as appears anywhere in modern novels.

Leif Enger enjoys writing stories about young boys coming of age. He indicates that he finds inspiration everywhere, especially in Robert Louis Stevenson's "deep stories cloaked as adventures for young readers," and "flawed heroes you like well and complicated villains you like better." Enger draws inspiration from sources as diverse as Jack London, Charles Dickens, **Flannery O'Connor, C. S. Lewis,** King David, Solomon, the apostle Paul and many other writers.

Enger says that, for him, word-craft is essential. "If the story and characters are compelling and the word-craft serves them without getting in the way, I'll read through to the end regardless of label or category." He believes that character is revealed through action. "The axiom counsels writers to show, not tell, which is why incident-heavy stories often feel more genuine than those driven mostly by dialogue." Enger blends the actions of the Zane Grey thrillers with the amazing events of the Old Testament prophets to produce a remarkable, ballad-like story of family love. It is one of the best novels of this new century.

Critical Reception

Peace like a River was an instant success, being chosen the Book of the Month Club main selection before publication and selling foreign rights in seven countries. Jeff Zaleski noted that it is the kind of story booksellers fall in love with. So do readers and critics, who see it as a classic in the style of Mark Twain or Harper Lee. Some compare the narrative tone to the witty homespun humor of Garrison Keillor. Karen Valby, in *Entertainment Weekly*, classifies it with other literary masterpieces such as Robert Louis Stevenson and the paperback Western greats like Zane Grey and Frank O'Rourke. Susan Salter Reynolds proclaims, "You don't see novels like this one very often." She compares it to Kent Haruf's *Plainsong* and Norman MacLean's *A River Runs Through It*. Aside from his remarkable characters and fast-paced action, Enger's language is the subject of much acclaim. Brad Hooper speaks of "his limpid sentences . . . composed with the clarity and richness for which poets strive." He also praises "Enger's profound understanding of human nature" which stands behind his compelling prose.

The writer for the *New York Times* is less delighted, especially by the miracles that are essential to the plot and theme. Katherine Diekmann protests Enger's reliance on miracles: "And when the story becomes too plain, along comes a well-timed miracle to juice it up" She admits that Enger has some storytelling skills, but insists that the ending is as "clichéd as his basic enterprise." Her major criticism is that miracles are nothing more than convenient mysticism.

Leif Enger knows that the miraculous elements of the tale are troublesome to secular readers, commenting, "Real miracles bother people."

Awards

Leif Enger's *Peace Like a River* was named the Best Book of the Year by *Amazon.com*, 2001; it was also chosen for "One Book, One Denver" reading program in 2004.

Bibliography of Novels by Author

Peace like a River. New York: Atlantic Monthly Press, 2001.

Co-authored with Lin Enger, under joint pseudonym L.L. Enger

Sacrifice. New York: Pocket Books, 1993.
The Sinners' League: A Gun Pedersen Mystery. New York: O. Penzler Books, 1994.

Bibliography of Works about Author

Changnon, Greg. Review of *Peace like a River. Atlanta Journal-Constitution* (November 25, 2001): C5.
Deckmann, Katherine. "Miracle Worker, " *New York Times Book Review* (September 9, 2001): 19.
Dederer, Claire. "Amazon.com's Best of 2001." Amazon.com, http://amazon.com/.
Ford, Marcia and Lynn Garrett. "Great Aspirations." *Publishers Weekly* (March 28, 2005): 52.
Hooper, Brad. Review of *Peace like a River. Booklist* (May 15, 2001):1 707.
"Leif Enger." *Contemporary Authors Online.* Detroit: Thomson Gale, 2004.
Maryles, Daisy. "An Indie Favorite." *Publishers Weekly* (July 16, 2001): 20.
Pearson, Michael. "A Miraculously Good Tale with a Western Twang," *Atlanta Journal-Constitution*, October 14, 2001: B5.
Reynolds, Susan Salter. Review of *Peace like a River, Los Angeles Times Book Review* (September 2, 2001): 11.
Stander, Bella. Review of *Peace like a River. People* (October 8, 2001): 59.
Valby, Karen. Review of *Peace like a River. Entertainment Weekly* (September 28, 2001): 68.
vanMeenen, Karen. "Interview with Leif Enger." *Writers and Books,* Rochester, NY. http://www.wab.org/events/allofrochester/2004/interview.shtml.
Wilkinson, Joanne. *Review of* Peace like a River. *Booklist* (June 1, 2001): 1838.
Zaleski, Jeff. Review of *Peace Like a River. Publishers Weekly* (July 16, 2001), 166.

F

FOSTER, SHARON EWELL

Personal, Professional, and Religious Background

Sharon Ewell Foster was born in Marshall, Texas, and raised in East St. Louis, Illinois. Her heritage is a blend of African American, Irish, and Native American. Of her parents' five children, she was the only daughter. Foster says of her childhood that she had a "profound sadness on the inside of me." She notes, "I was also insecure, angry, lonely, and confused. . . . I felt unloved. But as a child I learned that it was unacceptable to express my sorrow or my rage, so I hid it behind masks of perpetual joy, confidence, pride, and perfectionism."

She attended the University of Illinois at Champaign-Urbana, and the University of Maryland, where she earned her B.A. She later went to Duke University to earn her credentials in family development.

She married, divorced, and found herself the single mother of two children, Lanea and Chase, who are now adults. Going through these years of "shadows," she admits that she was one of the "broken people," who had believed that romance, the love of a man, would fix her and make her feel better. Over the years, she admits that she tried everything, including counselors, "a little alcohol, a little sex, a little bit of drugs, a lot of food, withdrawal, children, education, a career, promotions, and money." Trying to look and act perfect never really worked. The solution proved to be an intimacy with God through his Son. In this discovery, she learned to speak openly of her own fears and to rely on God.

Most of her adult life was spent working for the Department of Defense, where she served as an instructor, writer, editor, and logistician. As she notes on her Web site: "It was my great pleasure to train military and civilian students—broadcasters, journalists, graphic

> My desire is to write in a way that brings honor to my family, to my people, and most importantly to God.
>
> —Sharon Ewell Foster, in interview with African American Book Club, 2008

artists, photographers, videographers, and public affairs officers in the art of instruction." She adds, "I loved my job, and would still be there had I not felt the an urgent call to write."

Sharon Foster has been active in the church all through her life. She especially loves singing and has engaged in discipleship training. She has worked with civic leaders to bring religion into the community where she lives. Currently, this is Chicago.

Major Works and Themes

Beginning with *Passing by Samaria*, Sharon Foster has written seven novels. She has also contributed to other books and to the devotional magazine *Daily Guideposts*. Her theme is racial reconciliation. As a descendent of different races and nationalities, Foster understands the stresses faced by the various groups of people. She usually writes from the point of view of a young woman of color, attractive and intelligent, full of love for family and for God, but angry at the world which rejects her for her race. She understands the importance of historical background and of cultural setting, tying her books carefully to the place and time and specific situations that generate the drama.

For example, in *Passing by Samaria*, Foster chooses the period after World War I, when the great migration of Southern blacks shifted to the urban North. The white supremacists watched the returning African American soldiers with suspicion and fear. These men had worn the uniform of the United States rather than the overalls of the share-cropper, became officers rather than being limited to menial tasks, and experienced the freedom of life in France where no Jim Crow laws barred young black men from going into cafés or dancehalls with white women. The novel opens with a lynching, which in most of the social-protest novels of African American literary tradition would have become the theme of the story. In this case, the death of her best friend and potential husband so angers Alena that her family fears for her safety, sending her off to family members in Chicago. Foster does not turn J.C., the lynch victim, into a black Christ, but uses his death to teach Alena the poisonous fruits of hatred. When Alena discovers that the urban North has the same problems as the agrarian South, with more subtle racism which flares out into riots, she realizes that she must heed her aunt's plea to reach out to other races in forgiveness rather than adding fuel to the fire. As Christ reached out to the Samaritans, so Alena and her family reach out to white people, forgiving them even when they do not seek forgiveness.

Like most of Foster's novels, this is a romance, and in the classic romance tradition, Alena finds a new love and a new vocation. The story ends, as we would expect, with a wedding. The villain is Pearl, a porter on the train Alena takes out of the Delta, who proves a kind of "Sportin' Life" character—one who reappears in other of her novels. He is a thoroughly despicable person who responds to his own painful life experience by using and discarding others—primarily women. His egotism and slimy ways make him the classic threat to the maiden's purity, temporarily a barrier to her hopes of finding God's plan for her life.

Not all of Sharon Foster's novels fit this formula. In her series that began with *Riding through Shadows*, she uses her own tortured childhood, her insecurity and pain, to show how God can make us whole. This is a dark look at the broken homes in the African American community from the 1960s to the 1980s, with the Black Power movement, the assassination of Martin Luther King, the Civil Rights marches, and the lingering curses of racial prejudice. The young girl who endures, and prevails through all of this anguish becomes a stronger, more thoughtful, more faithful person as a result of her journey through these shadows. In *Abraham's Well*, Foster again uses her own blended racial heritage. Her story of the black Cherokees on their terrifying trail of tears across the country chronicles the African American experience within this shameful and rarely explored episode of American history.

Readers will find colorful portrayals of African American worship practices—dancing, singing, shouting, preaching—as well as the belief in faith-healing and the reality of spirit wars. Like **Frank Peretti**, Sharon Foster portrays the demonic spirits active in our midst. Although these books are full of preaching and singing, the central message is invariably that survival depends on an intimate relationship with God. Then there can be joy in the morning.

Critical Reception

Black Issues Book Review and *Ebony* have reviewed Sharon Foster's works favorably, calling her "a pioneer in African American Christian fiction." The reviews have noted that her story of Shirley Ferris, the central figure in *Riding through Shadows*, is "a tale of how faith can overcome tragedy."

John Mort has applauded each of her books in his reviews for *Booklist*. He calls *Abraham's Well* "simply told and moving." Some reviewers have occasionally found her plots confusing, but for the most part, her reviewers have been full of praises for her style and her subject matter.

Awards

Sharon Foster has won a number of prizes and awards for her fiction and has been nominated for others. Her first novel, *Passing by Samaria*, was one of the Top Ten Works of Christian Fiction in 2000 and won the 2001 Christy Award. *Ain't No River* won the Golden Pen Award from the Black Writers Alliance. *Ain't No Mountain* was named Borders Best in 2004 in the Religion and Spirituality category and *Abraham's Well* was named Reviewer's Choice Best Inspirational Novel by *Romantic Times* in 2006.

Bibliography of Novels by Author (Published in Sisters, OR: Multnomah Unless Otherwise Indicated)

Passing by Samaria. Sisters, OR: Alabaster Books, 1999.

"Ain't No River" series

Ain't No River. 2001.
Ain't No Mountain. 2004.
Ain't No Valley. 2005.

"Shadow and Light" series

Riding Through Shadows. 2001.
Passing into Light. 2002.
Abraham's Well. Minneapolis, MN: Bethany House, 2006.

Bibliography of Works about Author

Ebony, Review of *Ain't No Mountain* (November, 2004): 29.

Mort, John. Reviews of *Passing by Samaria. Booklist* (January 1, 2000): 874; (October 1, 2000): 302.

Mort, John. Review of *Ain't No River. Booklist* (January 1, 2001): 916.

Mort, John. Review of *Riding through Shadows. Booklist* (October 1, 2001): 281.

Mort, John. Review of *Abraham's Well. Booklist* (January 1, 2007): 58.

Sharon Ewell Foster Web site: www.sharonewellfoster.com.

"Sharon Ewell Foster," aalbc. www.aalbc.com/authors/sharon_ewell_foster.htm.

"Sharon Ewell Foster." *Contemporary Authors Online.* Detroit: Thomson Gale, 2008.

"Sharon Ewell Foster," *Faithful Reader.* www.faithfulreader.com/features/15_ foster_sharon_ewell. asp.

Stanley, Kathryn V. "The Ministry of Fiction: Sharon Ewell Foster Found an Eager Audience When She Finally Answered the Call to Write," *Black Issues Book Review* (January-February, 2005): 52.

GIBBONS, KAYE

Personal, Professional, and Religious Background

Bertha Kaye Batts Gibbons (1960–) was born in Wilson, North Carolina. Her father, Charles Batts, was a tobacco farmer, and an abusive alcoholic who died young, leaving young Kaye with sour memories of the father's role in the household. Her sweet, ailing mother, Alice Batts, suffered from a bipolar disorder. She committed suicide when Kaye was 10 years old, leaving the child to the mercy of "uncaring relatives and foster parents" until she landed a foster family who could love her for herself—much like her famous character Ellen Foster. For years, Kaye was also thought to be bipolar, experiencing extended periods of creativity, allowing her to write furiously for days at a time, followed by horrible periods of depression. She was hesitant to allow doctors to treat her for this problem since she felt it accounted for much of her artistic power.

Kaye Gibbons has used the rural South in which she was raised, the strong women, the hard-drinking men, and the meager circumstances as the basis for most of her fiction. Her nearest neighbors were African Americans, with whom she played until she was 13 years old. It was then that she moved to town, discovering social stratification for the first time. Early in her life, she fell in love with books, which she has called "the most important thing in my life." She told one interviewer that she used to walk three miles to a Bookmobile." She became increasingly fond of the African American poet James Weldon Johnson, who used common speech and idioms he heard from his own community in his poetry and in his prose. Her novels also reflect the influence of Eudora Welty, **Flannery O'Connor**, and William Faulkner—all of whom also gleaned their language, rhythms, plots, and characters from local folk, black and white, whose tenacity they came to admire. She has commented that even her beloved Flaubert was really a regional writer, able

> If I weren't a writer, I'd probably be a lawyer or an architect. I wouldn't want to do anything easy, and I chose to be a writer.
>
> —Kaye Gibbons in interview with Bob Summer for *Publishers Weekly*

by the magic of fiction to turn a French village into a universal scene.

After high school in Rocky Mountain, North Carolina, where she was a star student, she attended North Carolina State University and the

> Kaye Gibbons spent most of her life believing—falsely—that she was bipolar.

University of North Carolina at Chapel Hill. Kaye Gibbons began writing the story of Ellen Foster as a poem when she was a student at Chapel Hill. "I wanted to see if I could have a child use her voice to talk about life, death, art, eternity—big things from a little person."

Kaye Gibbons has been married and divorced twice, first to Michael Gibbons, by whom she had three children, Mary, Leslie, and Louise; and then to Frank Ward, an attorney whom she divorced in 1995. She says that her second divorce "was a Southern version of Rudy Giuliani's." Overwhelmed for a time with depression, she says that she thought she might make a living with her writing. She assumed that she must live in New York for that to be possible and moved there in the 1999s. She then realized that her part of North Carolina was a "breeding ground for creativity: **Reynolds Price,** Allan Gurganis, Thelonius Monk." She moved home and now lives and works in Raleigh, North Carolina.

After her success with *Ellen Foster*, she discovered that "for years and years," she had been misdiagnosed with bipolar disorder. Living that label had chewed up much of her life. She stopped taking all medications, lost about 40 pounds and found herself feeling much better. She has come to terms with her own vision of the world: "I am a little different, a little eccentric. I look at the world in an absurd way." But she does not see this as a handicap. Her fellow Southern novelist **Lee Smith** insists that "She's a genius." Her daughters are now grown; one of them still lives at home. Kaye Gibbons herself says that she mainly works. "I'm a workaholic." She is delighted and amazed that she can write for a living.

Major Works and Themes

Kaye Gibbons is not a Christian writer in any traditional sense. She mentions religion only as part of the background of her people's lives. They tend to find strength within themselves or in their families rather than in the local Pentecostal or holiness congregations and resent any intrusion into their lives. Her people build their own theology of life and death, assuming that there is a God of some sort, but show little interest in working out a clear doctrine of the afterlife. The ending of *Divining Women* is interesting as an indicator of Gibbons's theology: the pastor of the Episcopal Church is not supportive of the grieved women who are preparing to bury the stillborn child. The pastor of the African American church is not considered an appropriate part of the service, so the white women and their black friends take over and bury the child themselves, while the insufferable husband trails along protesting that this is an embarrassment. In the Epilogue, the mother says the words she has had inscribed on her child's grave: "This child has gone. She was rushed into the arms of grace. She dwells now in the heart of the Lord, which is also in the least of us, where peace and certain joy abide." The eulogist goes on to say that the child, as well as "all of us" will dwell in "the holy city above, where the mother of Lazarus weeps no longer."

Notice the assumption that there is a Heaven which welcomes the innocent and the good, where there is no further pain. It also assumes that "the heart of the Lord" dwells in the "least of us." She clearly objects to the "pride of prayer" that is too common in churches and the brimstone preaching of Southern revivalists and self-styled "prophets" who shout about Hell. She much prefers the kindly gestures of gentle people to the propriety of church-goers.

Kaye Gibbons is well-versed in Scripture, often taking her themes and ideas from the Bible. *A Virtuous Woman*, for example, begins with the description of the virtuous woman of Proverbs, "whose price is above rubies." It is no accident that the heroine is named *Ruby*. Gibbons does not hesitate to mingle biblical allusions with her own individual mythology of ghosts or souls that wander the earth after the physical death. Her characters blend magic potions and folk recipes with modern medical knowledge, finding in folk wisdom and in nature more truth than in sermons. She echoes Wordsworth's lyrical assertion, "The Tables Turned" (1798):

> One impulse from a vernal wood
> May teach you more of man,
> Of moral evil and of good,
> Than all the sages can.

Critical Reception

Kaye Gibbons has been widely reviewed and praised by critics in the *New York Times*, *Publishers Weekly*, and elsewhere. She is open to interviews and eager to talk about her work. Her novels have been republished in paperback form, made into television stories, and chosen by Oprah Winfrey for her readers. She is regularly on the best-seller lists for the *New York Times*, and has been among the "best of the year" lists as well. Because her stories are easy reads and full of humor, they delight readers.

One critic did note that she has some implausible moments in her stories, like having a folk healer who reads the *New England Journal of Medicine*. She has few sympathetic male characters, because she focuses mostly on women, their love for one another, and their ability to survive with or without men. Her love scenes are not as believable as are her scenes of abuse and cruelty. Two of her novels have spoiled sons who turn into monsters, the result of bitter and selfish mothers, who seem barely human.

Lee Smith, the author of *Fair and Tender Ladies*, likes *A Virtuous Woman* best of Kaye Gibbons's books. She sees in it Gibbons's special gift "to compress and crystallize a story in a way that lends it great urgency." Smith considers Kaye Gibbons a "major Southern writer." By and large, *Ellen Foster* has been Kay Gibbons's most successful book. It is also her most autobiographical one.

Awards

Ellen Foster won several awards for Kaye Gibbons: the Sue Kaufman Prize for First Fiction, American Academy and Institute of Arts and Letters, and a citation from the Ernest Hemingway Foundation. She also won a National Endowment for the Arts fellowship for *A Virtuous Woman*; the Nelson Algren Heartland Award for Fiction, Chicago Tribune, 1991; the PEN/Revson Foundation Fellowship for a *Cure for Dreams*; Critics Choice Award, Los Angeles Times, 1995 for *Sights Unseen*; and the Chevalier de L'Ordre des Artes et des Lettres for her contribution to French literature, 1996.

Bibliography of Novels by Author

Ellen Foster. Chapel Hill, NC: Algonquin Books, 1987.
A Virtuous Woman. Chapel Hill, NC: Algonquin Books, 1989.

A Cure for Dreams. Chapel Hill, NC: Algonquin Books, 1991.
Charms for the Easy Life. New York: Putnam, 1993.
Sights Unseen. New York: Putnam, 1995.
On the Occasion of My Last Afternoon. New York: Putnam, 1998.
Divining Women. New York: Putnam, 2004.
The Life All Around Me By Ellen Foster. Orlando, FL: Harcourt, 2005.

Some of Gibbons's novels have been made into television movies: *Ellen Foster*, 1997; *Charms for the Easy Life*, 2001; and movie rights to *A Virtuous Woman* were purchased by Oprah Winfrey's production company. *Sights Unseen* has been developed into a film script by Kaye Gibbons.

Bibliography of Works about Author

"A Conversation with Kaye Gibbons." Womankind Educational and Resource Center, Inc., 1993. http://www.womankindflp.org/newlettrer/interview/gibbons.htm.

DeMarr, Mary Jean. *Kaye Gibbons: A Critical Companion*. Westport, CT: Greenwood Press, 2003.

Hoffman, Alice. "Shopping for a New Family." *New York Times Book Review*, May 31, 1987: 13.

"Kaye Gibbons," *Contemporary Authors Online*. Detroit: Thomson Gale, 2006.

Lewis, Nancy. "Kaye Gibbons: Her Full-Time Women," *Southern Writers at Century's End*, ed. Jeffrey J. Folks and James A. Perkins. Lexington: University of Kentucky Press, 1997.

Miller, Pamela. "Kaye Gibbons's novel draws from her life," *Star Tribune*, January 15, 2006. http://www.startribune.com/entertainment/books/11381306.html.

"Oprah's Books," http://www.oprah.com/obc/pastbooks/kaye_gibbons/obe_ph_19971027.

Ryan, Laura T. "Gibbons Says Manic Depression Fuels Her Art." *The Full Story*: Syracuse On-Line. http://www.syracuse.com/entertainment/stories/19990212_fkaye_html.

Seymour, Liz. "Oh, Kaye!" *Book* (November-December, 2002): 24–26.

Souris, Stephen. "Kaye Gibbons's *A Virtuous Woman*," *Southern Studies*, summer, 1992, 99–115.

Summer, Bob. "Kaye Gibbons," *Publishers Weekly* (February 8, 1993): 60–61.

Wood, Ralph C. "Gumption and Grace in the Novels of Kaye Gibbons." *Christian Century* (September 23, 1992): 842–846.

GIST, DEEANNE

Personal, Professional, and Religious Background

Deeanne Gist is a Texan. As she notes in her epilogue to *Deep in the Heart of Trouble*, she is "the daughter of an oilman, the wife of an oilman, a Texan, and a former resident of Corsicana"—the town she features in this novel. She now lives with her family in Houston, Texas. She was raised in a Christian home, worshipped with her family, and learned about Christ early. The family had moved to the small Bible church from a large "seekers" church; Deeanne Gist finds something of value in both the practicality of the "seekers" and the close study of Scripture in the Bible church. She notes that her grandfather had a "huge" spiritual influence on her.

She attended Texas A&M University, earning a degree in Elementary Education. After marrying, Deeanne Gist taught briefly, but soon left to raise her four children. She then undertook to work from home, using her parenting and educational skills to write for a number of magazines and newspapers, including *People, Parents, Parenting,*

> Never think you have "arrived." Everybody has room for growth.
>
> —Deeanne Gist on her Web site

Family Fun, the *Houston Chronicle*, and the *Orlando Sentinel*. She also developed a line of parenting products as well as home accessories and antiques, called "I Did It!" Productions."

When looking through the romances that her own daughters were reading, Gist noticed that secular romances had sadly declining moral standards since she was a teenager addicted to romance reading. She started her fiction writing by developing a secular romance featuring a pair of Christians falling in love. Her New York agent liked the book, but could not sell it. Gist continued for five years with her line of parenting products, keeping in the back of her mind the idea that she should return to writing. This dream became possible when her line of parenting materials was licensed and she was free of the day-to-day management. At that point, she returned to her novel, rewrote it for the inspirational market, and sent it to Bethany House. At last, she had her first success.

Major Works and Themes

An avid reader of romance novels from her youth, Deeanne Gist uses their techniques for plots that are Christian in theme. *A Bride Most Begrudging*, for instance, takes two headstrong believers and drags them through a series of disasters to a recognition that they need to accept God's leadership, even when it opposes their own preferences. Like many other romance writers, Gist uses a colorful historical setting that allows her to provide her characters with a great class difference—the aristocrat and the farmer. She also sets the plot in motion by forcing a marriage between these ill-suited and reluctant young people. As expected, the sexual agenda of romance literature becomes obvious: the sparks fly between the Lady Constance Morrow and the tobacco planter, Drew O'Connor. The lady keeps revealing a bit of ankle or cleavage while admiring the handsome yeoman's rippling muscles. The attraction is so powerful that they briefly search Scripture for a justification to "rejoice in the sharing of your flesh." Gist has said that she believes that the sexual aspects of marriage should be celebrated in literature—leading some readers to consider her novels "edgy" for their display of physical desire. Before the lovers can admit their love and fall into bed, the author must construct obligatory impediments to their happiness. Aside from the class difference and the forced marriage, the barriers seem trivial: the farmer does not like red-heads or freckles; the lady is a snob.

As a historical novel, this tale of Colonial Virginia is adequate, but lacks the rich detail of the period and culture. The church elders who insist on the landowner's marriage to his "tobacco bride" have little depth or subtlety. Nor is the church an integral part of the story. The Bible in the house is used largely to explain events or justify actions, not as a source of inspiration and delight. It is clear that this began as a secular romance and was redeemed by the author for the Christian marketplace.

Later novels set in Gist's native Texas are more successful. *Deep in the Heart of Trouble*, a sequel to *Courting Trouble*, is a satire that lampoons the idea that romances may be used in solving real problems. The romance in this story soon turns into a murder mystery, and the love story turns into a serious set of complications for those who consider themselves Christians and truth-tellers. Essie Spreckelmeyer, who has been tricked by a rogue into a disastrous love affair, turns her heart to stone, determined to be a "bloomer girl," an independent woman able to shoot, ride bicycles, drive cars, and run her family's oil company. Her suitor, who hides his identity by changing his name and appearance, is encouraged in his love affair by an older woman who insists that he read popular romances to find out how to woo his love—and later how to solve the mystery. In this story as in her others, Deeanne Gist includes details of women's history, the state of education for women, their sense of daring in branching out into business, mathematics, shooting, bicycling, or other "manly" activities. Without being a feminist, Gist is clearly an advocate for opportunities for women. Gist does know a great deal about the oil industry in Texas and the life of the oil towns. This time, religion seems to be a real part of the people's lives, especially for the main love interests, Tony and Essie. Their final decision to leave their future in God's hands provides a peace that no amount of struggle can bring.

Her very popular story about 19th-century San Francisco, *The Measure of a Lady*, uses the colorful history of the larger-than-life characters who populated the city in the days of the Gold Rush. Again using class and taste differences to keep the lovers apart, Gist introduces a cultured lady from New Jersey and an uncouth man from California, where few "sunbonnet" ladies dare step off the boat into the mud and violence of everyday life. Here Gist once again takes the beauty-and-the-beast approach to feminine-masculine relations. The lovely and ladylike Rachel finds she cannot survive without the help of the cynical saloon-owner Johnnie. Unable to enforce Victorian morality and judgmentalism even with her own family, Rachel learns to forgive, to accept God's grace, and to offer a helping hand to those who want to escape the sordid life of prostitution. As Rachel moves toward understanding and tolerance, Johnnie softens toward her values, with a predictable conclusion.

In her later books, Gist has become more comfortable with the machinery of the novel. Her historical research gives the novels an additional interest, and she is able to work details of everyday life into her stories so that they are somewhat more satisfying than the traditional romances.

Critical Reception

Deeanne Gist's first novel, her revised romance, *A Bride Most Begrudging*, won a number of praises from romance critics as well as the coveted Christy Award for Romance. *Library Journal* notes that the novel will "remind readers of Johanna Lindsey's style and feisty heroines." The reviewer recommends it highly for Christian fiction and romance collections.

Awards

Deeanne Gist won the 2006 Christy Award for Romance for her first novel, *A Bride Most Begrudging*.

Bibliography of Novels by Author (Published In Minneapolis, MN: Bethany House Publishers)

A Bride Most Begrudging. 2005.
Courting Trouble. 2007.
The Measure of a Lady. 2007.
Deep in the Heart of Trouble. 2008.

Bibliography of Works about Author

Deeanne Gist Web site: http://www.deeannegist.com.
Deeanne Gist Interview with *Novel Journey*. http://www.noveljourney. blogspot.com/2006/05/author-interview-deeanne-gist.html.

Faithful Fifteen Interview. http://www.faithfulreader.com/features/15_gist_deeanne.asp.
Library Journal. Review of *A Bride Most Begrudging.* (June 1, 2005).

GODWIN, GAIL

Personal, Professional, and Religious Background

Gail Kathleen Godwin (1937–) draws on her Southern heritage and her deep love of Anglican liturgy and lore to create resonant settings for richly conceived characters who struggle with tough personal and spiritual issues. She was born in Birmingham, Alabama. Her father was Mose Winston Godwin, her mother Kathleen Krahenbuhl Godwin. Her parents divorced when Gail was a child. Gail Godwin's mother was a writer who had great influence on her daughter, encouraging her—even as a teenager—to write, polish, and submit her articles. Godwin did not meet her father until she graduated from high school. He appeared at the graduation, much to her delight, and invited her to come and live with him. Shortly after she joined him, he shot and killed himself.

Gail Godwin first attended Peace Junior College from 1955 to 1957, then moved on to earn a B.A. in journalism from the University of North Carolina in 1959. She began her writing career as a reporter for the *Miami Herald*, where she tried to avoid the stereotypical women's section assignments by becoming a general assignment reporter. After an auspicious beginning, Godwin, along with a coterie of bright young staffers, was awarded the opportunity to help start the Pompano bureau. Failing her assignment, she was called back to Miami and fired.

While she was working in Miami, she married Douglas Kennedy, a photographer for the paper, and divorced him within the year. The experience also led to the writing of *Gull Key*, the unpublished story of a young wife in Florida who is left alone all day while her husband works at a distant job. Without a job or a husband, Godwin then returned to North Carolina, where she worked for a time as a waitress at a mountain restaurant.

Eager to see the world, Gail Godwin began her European travels, eventually living for a time in England, serving as a travel consultant in the U.S. Travel Service from 1962–1965. She married an Englishman, Ian Marshall, a psychiatrist who encouraged her to begin writing seriously. After divorcing Marshall, Godwin returned to America, to become an editorial assistant at the *Saturday Evening Post* in 1966. At that time, she submitted a draft of *The Perfectionists* to the famous University of Iowa Writers' Workshop, which earned her entry to the program. She earned an M.A. from the University of Iowa, M.A. in 1968 and a Ph.D. in 1971. While there, studying with other soon-to-be famous writers like John Irving, she took classes with Kurt Vonnegut and polished her skills as a writer. *The Perfectionists*, Godwin's first published novel, was a revision of her Ph.D. thesis. She served as an instructor at the Writer's Workshop for a time, then became a fellow at the University of Illinois Center for Advanced Studies, then a freelance writer and lecturer in English and creative writing at a number of colleges, including Vassar and Columbia. In later years, she has made her home in Woodstock, New York, with her long-time companion and collaborator, the musician Robert Starer, until his death in 2001.

> A lifetime of reading and writing fiction has greatly increased my capacity for empathy, the activity of imagining from the inside out what it's like to be someone else.
>
> —Gail Godwin, to *Contemporary Authors*, 2007

Major Works and Themes

Taking Henry James's advice to be one of those on whom "nothing is lost," Gail Godwin has made a great deal out of her life, studies, and observations. She has made her reputation by writing about educated and intelligent English and Americans living lives that are in some way extraordinary. Like 19th-century novelists, she uses the rhythms of everyday life as the base for the interruptions, dramatic revelations, and new growth for her central characters. She loves small rituals like a gathering of the family for breakfast or joining friends for cocktails and talk at five. She also follows the larger rituals of the liturgical calendar, the patterns of worship prescribed in *The Book of Common Prayer*, and the meanings of prayers for each part of the day. She emphasizes the love of the lost ones, the concern for the sick, and care for the elderly. She has a shepherd's heart—a need to understand even those who infuriate her, to comfort those who mourn, to welcome the visitor. Her protagonists, usually women, seek to find their place in the world, to find God's will for their lives. These are the unremarkable subjects that form the rich body of work produced by this remarkable writer.

Gail Godwin uses her early experience at the Miami newspaper in *Queen of the Underworld*, the tale of a reporter at the *Miami Star*. Her work there reveals to her the whole underside of Miami life with madams and mobsters. The novel is redolent of the old world of the daily newspaper, with typewriters, copy paper, cigarette-smoking young women wearing high heels and trying avoid the "women's assignments" automatically handed to young female reporters.

The terrible memory of her father's suicide became part of Godwin's novel *Violet Clay*, which also explores the relationship of the artist to her art. When Violet Clay, an aspiring artist, discovers that her Uncle Ambrose, who was himself a failed writer, has shot himself, she goes to his cabin to claim his body, bury him, and try to "face the demons with her paint and brush." Godwin often deals with the arts, the creative forces within people that conflict with both family obligations and the everyday business of living

Godwin also explores her deeply felt hunger for a father-figure. In *Father Melancholy's Daughter*, Godwin draws the remarkable portrait of a young woman growing up in the American South at a time when women could begin to choose between traditional ladylike and new feminist roles. This story, which is filled with a kind of wicked humor softened with saving grace, pictures the parishioners of St. Cuthbert's church, with a blend of irony and love. Like Dorothy L. Sayers in her Episcopal novel, *The Nine Tailors*, Godwin sketches both the melancholy priest and his bumbling congregation, showing them staunchly guarding the faith against the vulgar forces of modernism. The book is organized around the liturgical calendar, filled with saints and enriched by descriptions of the actual lives and locales of these martyrs. An especially rich scene in the story recounts the reconsecration of a shattered statue of Christ, which is carried in pieces by the congregation members, a physical symbol of the broken "body of Christ."

This rambling and open-ended book, which circles back on itself, almost demanded a sequel. *Evensong*, written several years later, again draws on the image of the temporal church with the flawed parishioners, and points toward the universal, catholic church, which is the body of believers—even where two or three are gathered together. This story carries Margaret, the daughter, into marriage and her own ministry, and further challenges of the changing religious world. A old stranger, who claims he is a monk, wanders into her tidy world, fleshing out the larger history of Adrian, her husband, and his own hunger for a father. Margaret's cozy Anglican world, in this historic church on the hill, is further disrupted by Grace Munger, a flamboyant evangelist, who believes she is God's prophet, demanding a millennial birthday parade for

Jesus. The contrasting views of worship and service enlarge the meaning of the story while moving the plot toward a spectacular and melodramatic scene. The story is full of delightful meditations and insights, an interesting contrast to **Jan Karon's** world of Mitford and Father Tim, but much more explicit sexually and much less attracted to evangelical ideas and practices.

Godwin writes of Southern families, troubled marriages, absent parents and many other topics with wit, wisdom, and a sharp intellect that remind us of the 19th-century novelists who wrote big novels full of interesting characters and subtle relationships. She has an interesting mind, well-stocked and surprising. Though she knows a great deal about religion, religious practices, and religious history, she weighs her characters' different views of God with gentle irony and interest, allowing both the evangelist and the pagan to have their say, making her own preferences clear but showing understanding for other points of view.

Critical Reception

Critics writing both brief reviews and full-length studies have found Godwin a fascinating subject. Her novels are so filled with allusions and subtle ideas that they draw the reader into a discussion with the artist. Most of the major journals have praised her work. Herbert Mitgang of the *New York Times* interviewed her when she published *Mr. Bedford and the Muses*, a novella. He noted that she "has been acclaimed as an author who writes perceptively about creative women of her own generation," and that her stories "go beyond the individual and portray a whole segment of society—that of the middle-class Americans in the 1960s and 1970s."

In addition to the numerous reviews in the *New York Times, Book World, Times Literary Supplement, Christian Science Monitor*, and other journals have reviewed her frequently and favorably. Reviewers often have read a number of her books and selected their favorites, watching her progress through her career. Beverly Lowry, for example, in her review of *A Southern Family* for the *New York Times Book Review*, insists that this novel "is the best she's written." She praises her "supple intelligence working on the page."

Anita Gandolfo finds her "appearance of simplicity" to be deceiving. *Father Melancholy's Daughter*, for instance, appears to be a coming-of-age story, yet proves instead to be the story of role reversals. Rather than a "happily-ever-after" kind of romance, this is the journey of a woman who is challenged "to know her totality and live in harmony with it"—a lifetime project for both Margaret and the reader.

Awards

Gail Godwin has won numerous awards from the National Endowment for the Arts, has been nominated several times for the National Book Award, has won a Guggenheim fellowship in creative writing. She also won the Award in Literature from the American Institute and Academy of Arts and letters (1981), the Thomas Wolfe Memorial Award, and others. She has also been awarded honorary doctorates from the University of North Carolina, the University of the South–Sewanee, and the State University of New York.

Bibliography of Novels by Author

The Perfectionists. New York: Harper, 1970.
Glass People. New York: Knopf, 1972.

The Odd Woman. New York: Knopf, 1974.
Violet Clay. New York: Knopf, 1978.
A Mother and Two Daughters. New York: Viking, 1982.
The Finishing School. New York: Viking, 1985.
A Southern Family. New York: Morrow, 1987.
Father Melancholy's Daughter. New York: Morrow, 1991.
The Good Husband. New York: Ballantine, 1994.
Evensong. New York: Ballantine, 1999.
Evenings at Five. New York: Ballantine, 2003.
Queen of the Underworld. New York: Random House, 2006.

In addition to these novels, Gail Godwin has published a number of essays and short stories. She has served as the librettist of musical works by Robert Stater. Gail Godwin's archives are at the Southern Historical Collection, Wilson Library, the University of North Carolina, Chapel Hill.

Bibliography of Works about Author

Anthony, Carolyn, ed. *Family Portraits: Remembrances by Twenty Distinguished Writers.* New York: Doubleday, 1989.
"Gail Godwin." *Contemporary Authors Online.* Detroit: Thomson Gale, 2004.
Gail Godwin Web site: http://www.gailgodwin.com.
Gandolfo, Anita. *Faith and Fiction: Christian Literature in America Today.* Westport, CT: Praeger, 2007.
Godwin, Gail. *Heart: A Personal Journey through Its Myths and Meanings.* New York: Morrow, 2001.
Godwin, Gail. *The Making of a Writer: The Journals of Gail Godwin, One.* Edited by Rob Neufield. New York: Random House, 2007.
Hill, Jane. *Gail Godwin.* New York: Twayne, 1992.
Kissel, Susan S. *Moving On: The Heroines of Shirley Ann Grau, Anne Tyler, and Gail Godwin.* Bowling Green, OH: Bowling Green State University Popular Press, 1996.
Lowry, Beverly. Review of *A Southern Family. New York Times Book Review,* October 11, 1987.
Mitgang, Herbert. "Godwin Talks of Her Fiction and Her Muses," *New York Times,* October 4, 1983.
Xie, Lihong. *The Evolving Self in the Novels of Gail Godwin.* Baton Rouge: Louisiana State University Press, 1995.

GREELEY, ANDREW

Personal, Professional, and Religious Background

Andrew Moran Greeley (1928–) was born in Oak Park, Illinois. His father, Andrew T. Greeley, was a corporation executive, his mother was Grace McNichols Greeley. His family's Irish Catholic heritage has proven a central element of his life and his novels; the majority of his stories have Irish protagonists and Catholic issues. Andrew Greeley attended Catholic schools, where he was drawn to the work of Catholic poets and novelists, such as G.K. Chesterton and **Evelyn Waugh.** It struck him that fiction "was a brilliant way of passing on religion." He told the interviewer for *Contemporary*

> Stories have always been the best way to talk about religion because stories appeal to the emotions and the whole personality and not just to the mind.
>
> —Andrew Greeley in interview with *New York Times Magazine*

Greeley says that he is considered, "in the minds of many the renegade priest who wrote 'steamy' novels to make money."

Authors, "I thought it must be challenging and rewarding to write 'Catholic fiction,' even if I never expected to do it myself." Nonetheless, he was soon submitting articles and essays to Catholic magazines, at first under a pseudonym.

After his studies at Archbishop Quigley Preparatory Seminary in Chicago, Greeley went to St. Mary of the Lake Seminary in Chicago, from which he received his A.B. in 1950, a S.T.B. in 1952, and a S.T.L. in 1954, the date of his ordination as a Roman Catholic priest. After his ordination, he served as an assistant pastor at Christ the King parish in Chicago. While in this position, Greeley began studies at the University of Chicago, focusing on sociology. He received an M.A. in 1961 and a Ph.D. in 1962, writing a doctoral dissertation on the influence of religion on the career plans of 1961 college graduates.

His work in sociology and his fascination with the politics of his own church have led Dr. Greeley to vigorous and well-publicized disagreements with the church hierarchy. He advocates a great many changes within the Catholic church, including "the ordination of women, liberalized policies on birth control and divorce, and a more democratic process for selecting popes, cardinals, and bishops." On the other hand, he agrees with the church that priests are more effective if they remain celibate, and he opposes abortion. These mixed views have made him controversial with both liberals and conservatives. His insider revelations regarding the process by which Paul VI and John Paul I were chosen have angered many church leaders. He insists that, "In the early church, the Pope and all the bishops were elected by the people of their diocese. The cardinals would go into St. Peter's and pick a man and bring him out. If the faithful applauded, he was the Pope. If they booed, the cardinals went back inside and tried again."

Greeley's work at Chicago's National Opinion Research Center is not officially approved by the Catholic church and has also sparked considerable disagreement within church circles. Nevertheless, the Reverend Dr. Andrew Greeley has continued to write and speak openly and frequently on the sociology of religion, writing numerous articles and books on the subject.

His novels have also stirred up controversy because they tend to reveal an unseemly side of his church. In addition, they are often blatantly sexual. The officials in the church have determined to treat him as a "peripheral member" rather than as a priest, but he is adamant in clinging to his role as a priest—though without a parish. He acknowledges that he is a "glib smart alec who can be dangerously humorous and even pugnacious when someone tries to put him down." He is prolific, turning out two or three novels and several articles and non-fiction books each year for decades.

The funds he has received from lectures and books have allowed him to contribute a million dollar endowment to establish a Roman Catholic Studies chair at the University of Chicago and to fund an annual lecture series on "The Church in Society" at St. Mary of the Lake Seminary, where he studied in the 1950s. He also offered a million dollars from his books for the inner city Catholic schools, an offer rejected by Chicago's Cardinal Bernardin, without providing a reason. He was ostracized from the Archdiocese of Chicago, refused a parish, and treated as a "non-person" by the Catholic church. He comments that the rejection of his pledge by the church represents "the first time in history the Catholic Church has turned down money from anyone."

He is currently Professor of Sociology at the University of Arizona and a Research Associate with the National Opinion Research Center at the University of Chicago. He is also a weekly columnist, contributing regularly to the *Chicago Sun-Times*, the *New York Times*, the *National Catholic Reporter*, *America*, and *Commonwealth*. Greeley's friend Eugene Kennedy says of him that he is "obsessive, compulsive, a workaholic. . . . He's a natural resource. He should be protected under an ecological act."

Major Works and Themes

In his fast-paced novels, Andrew Greeley draws heavily on elements of his Irish background, the myths he knew growing up. The whole Irish series, which features Peg, an Irish-speaking woman, "blessed with the gift of second sight and a knack for unraveling mysteries," has its basis in this culture. Most of his priests come from Irish Catholic families—something like his own. Greeley draws heavily on Scripture and finds interesting linkages for his novels, basing many of the "Father 'Blackie' Ryan" novels on the Beatitudes, and elements of the Passover for his steamy trilogy about the career of a renegade priest. Certainly, his own experiences in the priesthood, his study of Catholic culture in America, and his arguments with his superiors form much of the background for his novels.

Among his favorite targets is the stereotype of American Catholics as anti-intellectual and different from mainstream Americans. His sociological studies convinced him that ethnicity is not so important in religious identification and that the view that religion is on the decline in America is wrong, that Americans have changed little in their religious behavior since the middle of the century. He blames the 1968 papal encyclical on birth control, *Humanae Vitae*, for much of the decline in the Catholic church membership.

He writes on many current issues, including the scandal of sexual abuse among the clergy. One of his most recent nonfiction books attacks the Iraq war as "illegal." He is most consistently outraged by the political power struggles within his church, which he frequently uses as the basis for his plots. One of his most recent novels, *The Bishop at the Lake*, shows Father Ryan checking up on a fellow priest who is jockeying for a prestigious appointment. He is a writer of ideas, filled with stories that reflect currents of modern American culture, looking at them as a sociologist as well as a novelist—and always as a man of faith. *The Los Angeles Post* has called him "one of America's most popular storytellers."

Critical Reception

A best-selling novelist, Andrew Greeley is regularly reviewed by the *New York Times*, *National Review*, *Publishers Weekly*, *Library Journal*, *Los Angeles Times*, *Booklist*, and others. Most reviewers comment on the author rather than the story, finding this priest often shocking, rarely boring. Even his many sociological treatises, filled with advice for Christians, have brought him harsh criticism. For instance, he recommended in *Sexual Intimacy* that a wife might stir up her husband's desire for greater sexual intimacy by meeting him at the door with nothing but panties and a martini—or even just a martini. Some critics said that even discussing the book "would be an occasion of sin."

His novels, which often grow from his sociological studies and his own experiences, have also been severely criticized by the church. *The Cardinal Sins*, an early novel preceding his "Passover" series, was thought to be a slanderous portrait of John Cardinal Cody, Archbishop of Chicago, a cleric with his own trail of scandals. Greeley's response was hardly conciliatory: "Patrick Donahue is a much better bishop than Cody and a much better human being." Even in his "Blackie Ryan" mysteries, Greeley takes on his church—writing *White Smoke: A Novel about the Next Papal Conclave* as a restatement of many of his assertions in the earlier *The Making of Popes*. Father Ryan, his protagonist throughout the series, confronts the politics and intrigues of his church, convincing the critic for *Publishers Weekly* that "Greeley knows his material and his opinions and sets both into delicious spins here."

Greeley enjoys the mystery genre, using it again in the "Irish" series, receiving mixed reviews for *Irish Mist* and *Irish Cream*. While some found the novels "supremely entertaining mystery-romance," others called them largely "Irish treacle," hastily written and clearly aimed at "the faithful only."

Greeley's popularity is easily explained, in spite of his being denigrated as not a great novelist: His novels help "satisfy a natural need to know about the private lives of powerful" and provide an "inside view of Catholic Church politics" with a "judicious mixture of money and clinically detailed sex." According to Webster Schott, reviewing Greeley's work in the *New York Times Book Review*, "he is never dull, he spins wondrous romances and he has an admirable ideal for what his church should become."

Awards

Andrew Greeley has received numerous awards, beginning in 1962 with the Thomas Alva Edison Award for *Catholic Hour* radio broadcasts. He also received the Catholic Press Association award for best book for young people in 1965, the C. Albert Kobb Award, the National Catholic Education Association Award, 1977; the Popular Culture Award, from the Center for the Study of Popular Culture at Bowling Green State University in 1986; the Mark Twain Award from the Society for the Study of Midwestern Literature, in 1987; the Freedom to Read Award from the Friends of the Chicago Public Library in 1989; the *U.S. Catholic* Award in 1993 for furthering the cause of women in the Church; the *America*, Campion Award in 2006; the Illinois Outstanding Citizen Award from the College of Lake County; and honorary degrees from Bowling Green State University, St. Louis University, and Northern Michigan University.

Bibliography of Novels by Author

Nora Maeve and Sebi. Paulist/Newman, 1976.
The Magic Cup: An Irish Legend. New York: McGraw, 1979.
Death in April. New York: McGraw, 1980.
The Cardinal Sins. New York: Warner Books, 1981.

"Passover Trilogy" (New York: Warner Books, 1982–1987)

All about Women. New York: Tor, 1989.
The Cardinal Virtues. New York: Warner Books, 1991.
The Search for Maggie Ward. New York: Warner Books, 1991.
An Occasion of Sin. New York: Jove, 1992.
Wages of Sin. New York: Putnam, 1992.
Fall from Grace. New York: Putnam, 1993.
Angel Light: An Old-Fashioned Love Story. New York: Forge, 1995.
A Midwinter's Tale. Tom Doherty Associates, 1998.
Younger than Springtime. New York: Forge, 1999.
A Christmas Wedding. New York: Forge, 2000.

September Song. New York: Forge, 2001.
Golden Years. New York: Forge, 2004.
The Priestly Sins. New York: Forge, 2004.
Second Spring: A Love Story. New York: Forge, 2004.
The Senator and the Priest. New York: Forge, 2006.

"Father 'Blackie' Ryan" mystery novels (New York: Warner Books, 1985–present)

Science Fiction Novels

Angels of September. Boston, MA: G.K. Hall, 1986.
God Game. New York: Warner Books, 1986.
The Final Planet. New York: Warner Books, 1987.
Angel Fire. New York: Random House, 1988.

"Nuala McGrail" novels (New York: Forge, 1994–present)

Bibliography of Works about Author

"Andrew Greeley." *Contemporary Authors Online.* Detroit: Thomson Gale, 2007.
"Andrew Greeley." *Contemporary Literary Criticism,* Volume 28. Detroit, MI: Gale, 1984.
Andrew Greeley Web site: http://www.greeley-fiction.com and http://www.agreeley.com
Harrison, Elizabeth. *Andrew M. Greeley: An Annotated Bibliography.* Metuchen, NJ: Scarecrow Press, 1994.
Kirkus Review, Review of *Irish Cream,* (December 15, 2005): 23.
New York Times Magazine, Interview with Greeley, May 6, 1984, 34.
Schafer, Ingrid, ed. *The Incarnate Imagination: Essays in Theology, the Arts, and Social Sciences in Honor of Andrew Greeley: A Festschrift.* Bowling Green University: Popular Press, 1988.
Schafer, Ingrid. *The Womanliness of God: Andrew Greeley's Romances of Renewal.* Loyola University Press, 1986.
Schafer, Ingrid. ed. *Andrew Greeley's World: A Collection of Critical Essays, 1986–1988.* New York: Warner Books, 1989.
Schott, Webster. Review of *Irish Crystal. New York Times Book Review,* December 19, 2005, p. 45.

GREENE, GRAHAM

Personal, Professional, and Religious Background

Graham Henry Greene (1904–1991) was born in Berkhamsted, Hertfordshire, England. His father, Charles Henry Greene, was the headmaster of a private school which Graham Greene attended. Robert Royal notes that this relationship set up a classic Greene conflict: "loyalty to his father versus the impossible desire to be one of the boys." He later revealed that he asked for faith while in this school, but: "I began to believe in Heaven because I believed in Hell." Apparently something significant happened to him when he was 16, causing his family to send him to live for six months

> A novel is made up of words and characters.... Are the words well chosen and do the characters live? All the rest belongs to literary gossip.
>
> —Graham Greene, "A Visit to Morin"

> During World War II, Graham Greene is thought to have been a double agent for the British and the Russians.

with a Jungian analyst, Kenneth Richmond, who turned out to be a "quack with no formal training." Biographers believe that the boy had an affair with Zoe, Richmond's wife, and fathered one of the Richmond's children—the beginning of a life-long pattern of romantic longings and illicit affairs.

Graham Greene loved danger. Even when he was at Oxford, he announced that "The only thing worth doing at the moment seems to be to go and get killed somehow in an exciting manner." He courted such a violent death much of his life, enjoying Russian roulette and dabbling in spy activities in dangerous places. As an undergraduate at Oxford, he hired himself to the British government as a spy to do espionage in Ireland and French-occupied Germany in exchange for free travel. He joined the Communist party, hoping for a free trip to Moscow; and he probably became a double agent continuing to work for British Intelligence. During World War II, Greene became involved with the mysterious spy world of his supervisor Kim Philby, who later defected to the Soviet Union. In his later years, Greene followed insurgencies, revolutions, and random violence all over the world, "not to seek material for novels, but to regain the sense of insecurity which I had enjoyed in the three blitzes of London."

Over time, Greene was sympathetic to the Soviets, the Sandinistas, Ho Chi Minh, Fidel Castro and other leftists and Communists. As late as 1987, he recommended that Roman Catholics join with Communists to fight against death squads in El Salvador, Contras in Nicaragua, and General Pinochet in Chile. He was even quoted in his Moscow speech as saying that he had a dream "that, perhaps one day before I die, I shall know that there is an Ambassador of the Soviet Union giving good advice at the Vatican."

Greene's interest in Catholicism coincided with his marriage to a Catholic, Vivienne Dayrell Browning, for whom he converted in 1926. He proved an unfaithful husband and a difficult Catholic, using both his infidelities and his quarrels with his church as the materials for his novels. His biographies and letters show him to have been an abusive lover of numerous women, including the American wife of a Labour M.P. Some critics note that Greene, like his most memorable characters, was a "burnt-out case," knowing a good deal about sin but little of joy or grace.

He loved to travel, and became a first-class travel writer, giving his attention to the people and activities of each region rather than its fauna and flora. "Nature doesn't really interest me except in so far as it may contain an ambush—that is something human," he explained. He died of a blood disease on April 3, 1991, in Vevey, Switzerland.

Toward the end of his life, when Greene became increasingly sympathetic to the Communists and dreamed of a reconciliation between Rome and Moscow, he became famous for his exaggerated views, especially regarding American anticommunists. For example, he threatened to become a Communist if Ronald Reagan were returned to office in 1984. And he told Malcolm Muggeridge that "Russia only destroyed the Church's body, while America destroyed its soul." He began to sympathize with Catholic collaborators in Communist Poland while characterizing Pope John Paul II as "unimaginative and unkind" in sexual matters. Robert Royal has lamented that "Greene's character flaws and Cold War fantasies led to the extinction of a great gift. He went from being the premier English novelist of the soul to an enabler of later and lesser lights who let their appetites and resentments rule their talents." Royal laments, "For the moment, however, he is a sad reminder of much that went awry in the second half of our century."

Major Works and Themes

Graham Greene, well read and talented, began his career with high literary aspirations, hoping to be compared favorably with such figures as Henry James and Joseph Conrad. When he wrote thrillers, or spy novels, he classified them as "entertainments," separating them from his more carefully crafted novels like *Brighton Rock* and *The Power and the Glory*. Ironically, some critics believe that the thrillers, like *The Ministry of Fear* and *A Gun for Sale* are among his better works. He had a great talent for melodrama and trickery.

Greene was a remarkably fluent writer, able to produce believable atmosphere, suspenseful plot, and telling detail. He loved a plot full of suspense, though he often refused to reconcile all the theological issues by the end of his story. His sardonic view of the world, his hunger for suffering, and his refusal to accept simple solutions to human problems make him a distinctive writer.

Brooke Allen has argued that "He was too snide and sour, for all his God-obsession, to love many of his characters. And such a lack of love keeps a novelist from being great, just as surely as any technical inadequacy can do."

Mark Bosco, in *Graham Greene's Catholic Imagination*, reveals that the writer was deeply influenced by the works of liberal theologians such as Pierre Teilhard de Chardin, Hans Kung, and Edward Schellebeeckx. As a result of his travels in South and Central America and the impact of post–Vatican II discourses, he was also a strong supporter of liberation theology. His quarrels with his church are apparent from early in his literary career. *Brighton Rock*, which he began in 1937, at first seems to be a murder mystery featuring a teenage punk, Pinkie, whose gang is responsible for the killing of a corrupt newsman. This is complicated by the gangster's depressing background, his love of a sweet Catholic girl named Rose, and his own Catholicism. By contrast, Ida, the woman who pursues him relentlessly, looking for justice, embraces all the New Age mysticism and superstition. Pinkie knows that he, like the rock candy sold in Brighton, is the same all through. Even if you bite it all the way down, the middle has the same design as the outside. The lurid story, which sounds a bit like *A Clockwork Orange*, turns out to be evidence of the age-old tension between God's sovereignty and man's free will. Pinkie seems to be doomed, yet accountable. This Catholic boy is deeply evil from the outset, yet he feels guilt and confusion for his actions. The humanistic nonbeliever seeks a kind of justice that makes no allowance for God's grace or human understanding. Critics have called it "philosophically provocative."

Perhaps the most famous of his novels to reveal his deep interest in Catholicism and politics is *The Power and the Glory*, the grim story of a "whiskey priest" in Mexico, who ironically became the last practicing priest in the region. The Communist government, represented by an idealistic lieutenant who thinks he is freeing his people from the tyranny of the Church through his crusade to eradicate all vestiges of religion, relentlessly hunts the little priest, murders innocents along the way, and finally traps, tries, and executes him. In a Christ-like gesture, the priest forgives the lieutenant and tries to help others to confess their sins and find salvation. This is a remarkable story of a pitiful little man who carries on, regardless of the odds. The vivid portrayal of human sins in the story underscores Greene's thesis that the greater the treachery and ugliness of humans, the greater the glory of Christ's death. It is also a moving portrayal of a people who retain the vestiges of their faith against persecution with full understanding of the failures of their own clergy. No matter what the sins of the priest, the wafers and wine he offers them remain the body and blood of Christ.

The Heart of the Matter and *The End of the Affair* are the other two important religious novels of Greene's middle years. Both echo his own struggles with adultery and religious belief. In *The Heart of the Matter*, Greene once again emphasizes the sinner, who is "at the very heart of Christianity." Only the sinner and the saint can really testify to the meaning of the faith. Scobie is a policeman in Sierre Leone during World War II, a Christian idealist. He is a married man who tries unsuccessfully to make his wife happy, finally promising her passage to South Africa. This impossible view leads him into a bargain with disreputable people, and finally corruption. When he becomes enmeshed in an affair with a desperate young woman, he is tormented by his obligations to his wife, his mistress, and his church. Eventually, his "honorable" decision is a disguised suicide, which Greene presents as a forgivable sin in spite of clearly contradictory Catholic teachings. In this book, Greene asks whether we are responsible for other people's happiness, and whether suicide can ever be the right choice.

The same questions appear in *The End of the Affair*, which chronicles an adulterous affair conducted during the bombing of London during World War II. The story includes both a miracle and a promise to God. The young married woman in the story prays for her lover, promising to end the affair if is he is saved. When he survives, she feels obliged to leave him without an explanation, bringing deep pain to both of them without commensurate pleasure to her husband. Echoing his own lax behavior at the time, Greene (according to some critics) seems to be saying that Christ's admonition to lovers is, "If you love me, break my commandments." He apparently decided that contrition and confession need not be followed by any change in one's behavior, that a sin could be repeated and repented again and again.

Sarah, the lover/beloved of *The End of the Affair*, is another of Greene's secular saints. Her sin and the pain she brings to other people lead her to a confrontation with God and to a conversion experience. She tries to argue that she can break her vow, that she deserves happiness, but finally admits that only God has the power to give her the only peace she can know. Her death certifies her sainthood to those who have loved her—the atheist she healed, the detective who prays to her for healing and who takes a lock of her hair as a relic; and her mother who begins to construct a hagiography, revealing Sarah was pious even as a child.

A Burnt-Out Case, one of Greene's last important theological novels, also has strong autobiographical elements. Querry, a world-weary badly damaged architect is at the end of the road in his vocation, his love life, and his faith. Abandoning everything, he seeks obscurity in the deepest reaches of a minor tributary of the Congo. Soon he finds a need to be useful, to seek out affection, and finally to act heroically. Querry is subsequently seen as a saint by a ridiculous manufacturer in the nearest town who refuses to believe his "hero" has abandoned the faith. He gives interviews to an equally ridiculous journalist, who in turn writes of this new saint, a new Schweitzer. This stirs Querry back to life. His sympathy for a young wife, whom he foolishly considers innocent, brings him to a path of further misunderstanding and finally to a violent death, which he declares as "absurd." Poor Querry, is content to be a "burnt-out case" of leprosy, one who has lost everything, including all feeling. Instead he is forced back into life and suffering. He refuses to acknowledge he is haunted in his flight from God, but he is protesting too much. He, like so many of Greene's heroes, is tracked by the "Hound of Heaven."

Critical Reception

Each of Graham Greene's books has been reviewed by all the major newspapers and journals as it appeared. Since his death, he has been carefully studied: a number of scholars have written books of analysis and criticism. His colorful life has been the subject of several studies, the latest of which by Bernard Bergorizi, *A Study in Greene*, was published in 2006. His influence on other religious writers has been impressive. Most of the Roman Catholic writers mention him in their credits, as do **P.D. James, Frederick Buechner,** and John Irving. Irwin, who was introduced to this writer by his teacher at Exeter, Buechner, says of him that, "Until his death in 1991, Graham Greene was the most accomplished living novelist in the English language; in any language, he was the most meticulous."

Mark Bosco, in his *Graham Greene's Catholic Imagination*, argues that the periods of Greene's work "represent different phases of his Catholic sensibility." The early novels were marked by their "formal originality, imaginative vitality, and strength of feeling." The mature phase "shows mastery of the medium, but combined with a certain loss of the early freshness and energy." He believes that the later novels "grow out of Greene's engagement with issues vital to Vatican II Catholicism and to the emergence of liberation theology." Greene himself acknowledged that he became "increasingly self-indulgent, reformulating the same old story—'will he won't he will he won't he save his soul?'" The so-called Greene man is a "dis-abused, cynical, often sexily jaded figure who has achieved wisdom but not grace."

Critics find most of Greene's work measures up to his own tests: "Are the words well chosen and do the characters live?" Some criticize his female characters and some believe that he is too concerned with making his characters, like those of Charles Dickens, archetypal figures rather than realistic and believable people. The women tend to be either plucky waifs or goodtime girls.

Nancy Mitford has commented on the hunger she notices among Catholic writers to save their souls. For Graham Greene, the protagonist may well go to hell at the end of his story, or be saved by God's grace, certainly not by his own pitiful, sinful behavior. Graham Greene raised so many interesting questions and disturbed so many scholars and churchmen that his legacy is one of admiration and dissent. No one denies his brilliance or his seriousness. But his bleak concept of the ongoing struggle between human love and God's love allows little joy and brings out the very worst in most of his characters. It also produces flawed but courageous saints.

Awards

In 1940, Graham Greene won the Hawthornden Prize for *The Power and the Glory*; in 1949, the James Tait Black Memorial Prize for *The Heart of the Matter*; in 1952, the Catholic Literary Award for *The End of the Affair*; in 1957, the Antoinette Perry (or "Tony") Award nomination for the best play, *The Potting Shed*; and in 1960 the Pietzak Award in Poland for his body of work. Cambridge University honored him with a doctorate in literature in 1962; Balliol College at Oxford made him an honorary fellow in 1963; the University of Edinburgh gave him a doctorate of literature in 1967. He won the Shakespeare Prize in 1968, was named chevalier, Legion d'Honneur, in France in 1969. He won the John Dos Passos Prize in 1980, the Jerusalem Prize in 1981; the Grand Cross of the Order of Vasco Nunez de Balboa by Panama in 1983, and commander, Order of Arts and Letters by France in 1984. In 1986, he was named to the British Order of Merit; in 1987, Nicaragua named him to the Order of Ruben Dario; and in 1988, he was presented with an honorary doctorate by Moscow State University.

Bibliography of Major Novels by Author (Published by New York: Viking, Unless Otherwise Indicated)

Stamboul Train. London, England: Heinemann, 1932. (Printed as *Orient Express* by Doubleday.)
A Gun for Sale. London: Heinemann, 1936. (Printed as *This Gun for Hire* by Doubleday.
Brighton Rock. 1938.
The Confidential Agent. 1939.
The Labyrinthine Ways. 1940.
The Ministry of Fear. 1943.
The Heart of the Matter. 1948.
The End of the Affair. 1951.
Loser Takes All. 1957.
Our Man in Havana. 1958.
A Burnt-out Case. 1961.
The Quiet American. 1982.
The Third Man. 1983.

Graham Greene has also produced several collections of stories, some poetry, a number of travel stories, books of essays, autobiography, films, and plays. His plays, travel books, and other works have been collected in omnibus volumes.

Among the most famous of his plays are: *Brighton Rock* (with Terence Rattigan, 1947), *The Fallen Idol* (1949), *The Third Man* (with Carol Reed, 1950), *The Living Room* (1953), *The Potting Shed* (1957), *The Complaisant Lover* (1959), *Our Man in Havana* (1960), and *The Comedians* (1967).

Bibliography of Works about Author

Allain, Marie-Françoise. *The Other Man: Conversations with Graham Greene*. London: Bodley Head, 1983.
Allen, Brooke. "A Burnt-Out Case: How Great was Graham Greene?" *The Weekly Standard*, December 4, 2006, 35–36.
Allott, Kenneth and Miriam Farris Allott. *The Art of Graham Greene*. London: Hamish Hamilton, 1951.
Bergonzi, Bernard. *A Study in Greene*. New York: Oxford University Press, 2006.
Bosco, Mark. *Graham Greene's Catholic Imagination*. New York: Oxford University Press, 2005.
Cassis. A.F. *Graham Greene: An Annotated Bibliography of Criticism*. Metuchen, NJ: Scarecrow, 1981.
DeVitis, L.A. *Graham Greene*. New York: Twayne, 1964.
Duraan, Leopoldo. Graham Greene: *An Intimate Portrait by His Closest Friend and Confidant*. San Francisco, CA: Harper, 1994.
Godman, Peter. "Graham Greene's Vatican Dossier," *Atlantic* (July-August, 2002): 84.
Gordon, Hayim. Fighting Evil: *Unsung Heroes in the Novels of Graham Greene*. Westport, CT: Greenwood Press, 1997.
"Graham (Henry) Greene." *Contemporary Authors Online*. Detroit: Thomson Gale, 2004.
Greene, Graham. *A Life in Letters*, ed. Richard Grene. New York: W.W. Norton & Company, 2008.
Hynes, Samuel, ed. *Graham Greene: A Collection of Critical Essays*. New York: Prentice-Hall, 1973.
Irving, John. *The Imaginary Girlfriend: A Memoir*. New York: Ballantine Books, 2002.
Lodge, David. *Graham Greene*. New York: Columbia University Press, 1966.
"The Religious Affiliation of British Novelist Graham Greene." (including quotes from John Irving and John Baxter). http://www.adherents.com/people/pg/Graham-Greene.html.
Renascence, Fall, 2002. (Special Greene issue.)

Royal, Robert. "The (Mis) Guided Dream of Graham Greene." *First Things*, November, 1999.
Sherry, Norman. *The Life of Graham Greene* (3 volumes). New York: Viking, 1989, 1995.
Wobbe, R.A. *Graham Greene: A Bibliography and Guide to Research*. New York: Garland, 1979.

GULLEY, PHILIP

Personal, Professional, and Religious Background

Philip Gulley grew up in a church-going household, dreaming of becoming a forest ranger. He says of school, "I was a flop, failing one subject after another, and not just barely, but spectacularly, like a spiraling plane, its engines crippled, smashing headlong into the ground." He particularly hated English, passing his composition course at Marian College by promising never to write again. As he notes of God's delight in irony: "And so God, in that whimsical way of the Divine, determined I should spend my life pastoring and writing." After college, he went to Christian Theological Seminary, from which he graduated with honors, "due to a grading error."

He married Joan (pronounced JoAnn). The family has two sons, Spencer and Sam. Speaking of himself, Gulley jokes that "before his sons were born, Philip was a pacifist and didn't believe in corporal punishment. Now he's having second thoughts."

In 1983, he took his first position was as the youth minister at Plainfield Friends Meeting in Indiana. In 1990, he became pastor of Irvington Friends Meeting in Indianapolis, which had a congregation of 12. It was then that he returned to college, to the Earlham School of Religion, studying writing under Tom Mullen. As he undertook writing his essays on God's grace and the life in his fictional town of Harmony among the congregation of Quakers, he moved to become co-pastor at Fairfield Friends Meeting near Indianapolis, the town in which he grew up. He has become a popular storyteller on radio programs and has written three nonfiction books in addition to his short stories and novels.

Major Works and Themes

Philip Gulley's fiction largely deals with the town of Harmony, which he says is impossible to find on the Rand-McNally map because it is hidden underneath the left staple. He does include a map of the town in the front of some of his novels. His stories focus on the idiosyncratic individuals who run the police station, the eateries, the funeral home, and the church in Harmony. The reader is quickly introduced to the members of the Friends Meeting House, most of whom are gentle, thoughtful, quiet people. The two exceptions are overbearing and often victorious. Gulley often speaks through the pastor, Sam Gardner, whose family has long lived in the town and attended the tiny church. The characters in the stories are types of church people—the strong women who are sometimes too strong and choose power over grace, the members who see the church as a business, the Bible-thumping troublemakers, and the quiet people who see the role of the faithful as children of God, seeking to share his love with their fellow humans.

> The Jesus I read about was really no friend of comfort. We are really called to be uncomfortable sometimes.
>
> —Philip Gulley, in interview
> November 20, 2005

Sam apparently speaks for his author in his celebration of grace and his distaste for evangelism. He has come to believe that there is no Hell, that God loves all his children, including those who are in prison, the homosexuals, and those of all races and creeds. He does not accept the notion that God saves only Christians and is not convinced of the reality of Heaven. He is a believer in good works, grace, and forgiveness.

Critical Reception

Philip Gulley's works have generally been well-received. He has written more than 13 books, most of them nonfiction. His "Harmony Novels" are especially popular and continue to flow from his pen. *Publishers Weekly*'s reviewer loves his "quirky characters," some of whom become cherished friends over time. Though Gulley acknowledges that Dale Hinshaw is a caricature, the reviewer loves this portrait of the "self-righteous and infuriating church elder." The critic also comments on his "wry humor," and likes the fact that he never succumbs to stereotype. The reviewer enjoys the "down-to-earth conversations" and applauds Gulley's "honest struggles with faith."

Sterner critics tend to agree with Ken Pierpont, who thinks that Gulley has a "kind heart and a clouded mind." Gulley is a charming man with a wonderful sense of humor, a way with words, a delight in people, and the ability to laugh at himself. He makes his point on the need for grace in our world repeatedly and gently. He laughs at the plain people among whom he lives, glad that they are not given to creeds or theological debates. Even when one of his characters leaves the Roman Catholic church to become a Quaker pastor, Gulley is silent on her struggles to reject transubstantiation, the authority of the Pontiff, or the sacraments. Krista feels God's calling and simply moves to a place where she is accepted. She finds this among the Friends, a group whose history and style of worship Gulley traces here and there in his stories. He clearly enjoys their silences and their courage.

Publishers Weekly compares Gulley's work to **Gail Godwin's** fiction, Garrison Keillor's storytelling, and Christopher Guest's filmmaking, asserting he is "in a league with **Jan Karon's** Mitford series." *Booklist* calls him "kindly, funny," and his writing "timeless inspirational reading."

Awards

In 2007, the National Academy of Television Arts and Sciences presented Philip Gulley with the Emmy Award for his PBS presentations "Porch Talk with Phil Gulley" series, presented on Channel 20, WFYI.

Bibliography of Novels by Author

"Harmony Novels" series (Published In San Francisco, CA: Harper Collins)

Christmas in Harmony. 2004.
Home to Harmony, 2004.
Life Goes On. 2004.
Signs and Wonders. 2004.
The Christmas Scrapbook. 2005.
Almost Friends. 2006.
A Change of Heart. 2006.
Just Shy of Harmony. 2006.

Bibliography of Works about Author

"An Introduction to Philip Gulley." http://pages.prodigy.net/jleonards/intropg.htm.

O'Donnell, Paul. "The Town that Grace Built." www.beliefnet.com/story/151/story_1539.html.

Philip Gulley Web site: www.philipgulleybooks.com.

"Philip Gulley: 'If Grace Is True,'" Program #4908, November 20, 2005. www_30goodminutes.org/csec/sermon/gulley_4908.htm.

Pierpont, Ken. "Philip Gulley: Good [Writing] about Bad Theology," February 14, 2008. www.kenpierpont.com/2008/oz/philip-gulley-good-[Writing]-about-bad-theology.

GUNN, ROBIN JONES

Personal, Professional, and Religious Background

Robin Jones Gunn (1955–) was born in Baraboo, Wisconsin, the second daughter of Travis Garland and Barbara Clawson Jones, both teachers. The family soon moved to California, where her father began his teaching career. Robin attended Biola University for two years and did some clerical work for various clients. In 1977, she married Ross Gunn, who is a full-time youth pastor. They have two children, Ross IV and Rachel. Robin Gunn has lived and traveled all over the world, building a stock of memories that have proven invaluable in her writing career

Robin Gunn, who always loved a good story, found she could figure out the ending well before the story concluded. She discovered her own calling as a storyteller quite early in her marriage. On a camping trip for the church youth group she and her husband were leading, she borrowed the books that her young campers were reading with such delight and was "horrified at the content." As she remembers the scene, "I told them they shouldn't be reading such books." When they challenged her to give them something else to read, she went to the local Bible bookstore and bought everything that she thought might interest them—all of which they read quickly and asked for more. At that point, she felt compelled to begin writing herself. She wrote the first chapter of a book, and took it to Sunday school to read it to her junior high school class after the lesson. She tried sending these chapters to publishers, but only Focus on the Family Publishers saw the promise of such books and asked her for a whole series. Two years later, this book began the "Christy Miller" series, which has now sold over 120,000 copies.

Major Works and Themes

Most of Robin Gunn's novels are romances designed for young women. The "Christy Miller" series (1999–1994) was followed by the "Sierra Jennies" series. At the same time, she was at work on some romances designed for adults, the "Palisades, Pure Romance" series (1995–1998). Her most recent series, "Sisterchicks," has a variety of colorful locales visited by a combination of friends. The "sisterchicks" are women in their 40s who have the leisure to plan exotic vacations, explore friendships, and allow contemplation of the loves in their lives.

Robin Gunn also writes articles for juveniles or women, appears as a radio host, and is a popular speaker at women's

> Stories are the common ground of all peoples of all nations. Stories written by Believers belong on the bookshelves of every bookstore in the world.
>
> —Robin Jones Gunn, as told to Janice DeLong and Rachel Schwedt

meetings and conferences. Her special concern is love in the Christian family. She told the editors of *Contemporary Christian Authors* that she sees her audience as "young hearts and women." Such readers will find nothing offensive or violent in her stories. Her stated goal is to "open up the gate to the garden of" her readers' hearts, "and let the Savior in. If He's already there, I want the story to compel them to surrender more of their heart's garden to Him."

Critical Reception

John Mort reviewed the "Christy Miller" series of 12 installments, followed by the "Christy and Todd" series, which tracks Christy's journey through high school and into college. He notes that this and the "Sierra Jennies" series are popular among teenage girls who enjoy the scrapes and adventures they contain. He comments that "Christy is highly emotional, and her constant talk of Jesus may be tiresome to some," in spite of her general appeal to young readers. The reviewer for *Publishers Weekly* says that Robin Jones Gunn "writes with humor and a deep understanding of the power of women's intimacy." In her review of *Sisterchicks Down Under!* for *Library Journal*, Tamara Butler indicates that the novel is a "good afternoon read."

Gardenias for Breakfast, a rare example of a stand-alone novel by Gunn, focuses on a mother-daughter team who leave Hawaii for a special visit with the grandmother and great-grandmother in Louisiana. The realistic portrayal of the pair, each seeking a relationship that accommodates their different tastes, shows the mother fixated on her own past and her need to attach her daughter to her beloved Grand Lady, while the daughter finds other women more appealing, especially her new aunt and her own grandmother. Tamara Butler thinks this one of "Gunn's best offerings to date" and considers it an "above-average mother-daughter tale." Didactic, like most of her work, the story does offer good advice about troubled relationships and false expectations. At this point, Gunn has written more than 50 books, the great majority for young people. *Gardenias for Breakfast* suggests that her future offerings may grow in depth and subtlety.

Awards

Robin Jones Gunn won first place in an article-writing contest at Biola University Writers Institute in 1988, and 1989.

Bibliography of Novels for Adults by Author

"Glenbrooke" series

Secrets. Sisters, OR: Questar Publishers, 1995.
Whispers. Unity, ME: Five Star, 1995.
Echoes. Sisters, OR: Palisades, 1996.
Clouds. Sisters, OR: Palisades, 1997.
Sunsets. Sisters, OR: Palisades, 1997.
Waterfalls. Sisters, OR: Palisades, 1998.
Woodlands. Sisters, OR: Multnomah Publishers, 2000.
Wildflowers. Sisters, OR: Multnomah Publishers, 2001.

"Sisterchick" series (Multnomah, 2003–2005)

Gardenias for Breakfast. Nashville, TN: WestBow Press, 2005.

Bibliography of Works about Author

Butler, Tamara. Review of *Sisterchicks DownUnder!*. *Library Journal* (November 8, 2004): 34.

DeLong, Janice and Rachel Schwedt. *Contemporary Christian Authors: Lives and Works*. Lanham, MD: The Scarecrow Press, 2000.

Faithful Reader interview. "Robin Jones Gunn," http://www.faithfulreader. com.author/au.gunn-robin-jones.asp.

Mort, John. *Christian Fiction: A Guide to the Genre*. Greenwood Village, CO: Libraries Unlimited, 2002.

Publishers Weekly. Review of *Gardenias for Breakfast* (November 8, 2004): 34.

"Robin Jones Gunn," *Contemporary Authors Online*. Detroit: Thomson Gale, 2006.

Robin Jones Gunn Home Page. http://www.robingunn.com.

HALL, LINDA

Personal, Professional, and Religious Background

Linda Carol Hall (1950–) spent her early years in New Jersey, where she gazed at the ocean and learned to love the water. She graduated from the Moody Bible Institute and married Rik, a Canadian who shares her love of the water. They have two grown children and live in Fredrickton, New Brunswick.

Linda Hall first worked as a journalist and a freelance writer, developing adult literacy curriculum materials. At the age of 40, she decided to try writing a mystery novel, *The Josiah Files*. As she tells the story, "I was attending a summer Christian writing institute at Prairie Bible College. I had the first three chapters of *The Josiah Files* written, and had my fifteen minute appointment with an editor there. That editor looked at me and said, 'This is good. When can I have the rest of it?' " This first effort turned out to be a success and led to a series of other novels, often set along the Canadian or Maine coastline in waterfront towns. She now teaches a mystery-writing course, sharing her secrets to success with other aspiring writers.

Major Works and Themes

Although Linda Hall writes about Christians, often about people who know one another at church, she finds in that culture a host of broken people. She told one interviewer that she felt called by God to help "hurting Christians." One of the most powerful scenes in *Black Ice*, for example, has two women who have long been at odds with one another suddenly realizing their shared experience of pain. They spontaneously hug and cry over their recognized need for fellowship.

> Non-fiction reaches our intellect, but fiction touches our emotions, those deep and private places inside of us.
>
> —Linda Hall in interview with *Focus on Fiction*

Her stories are largely mysteries, revealing secrets hidden by families, brought to light by startling events, and forcing families and friends to come to terms with their own brokenness and shame. Teenagers discover their natural parents, private investigators look for a killer and find a kidnapper. Even the local minister and his wife nurse their sad little secrets that keep them from being whole people.

Hall's female protagonists are interesting, bright, loving, suffering women who pursue the mystery at hand with vigor and intelligence. Hall introduces a wide array of characters in her stories, which have close, accurate portrayals of human emotions and the culture and geography that have formed them. Their Christian faith is integral to their lives and actions, but these flawed people are full of questions and puzzles. They use their technical equipment, know about cell phones and Internet chat rooms, and enjoy a good cup of tea with a freshly baked cinnamon bun cooked with real Vermont syrup.

Hall loves a mystery, enjoys writing interconnected stories, and relishes the process of unraveling tangled plots with reasonable solutions.

Critical Reception

Linda Hall's novels have been nominated for Christy Awards and have been complimented by such astute critics as John Mort, who finds her stories "full of thoughtful, flawed characters." The reviewer for *Publishers Weekly* found some fault with her habit of using the television technique of choppy, apparently unconnected scenes that develop a confusing narrative, but still considers *Dark Water* an "intense mystery." So far, she has not been reviewed extensively in journals other than *Booklist, Library Journal, Romantic Times,* and *Publishers Weekly.*

Awards

Linda Hall's novel *Steal Away* won the Beacon Award for best inspirational novel in 2004, the Winter Rose Award for best inspirational novel, and the Award of Excellence from Colorado Romance Writers. *Katheryn's Secret* won the award for the Best Canadian Christian Novel from Word Guild; and *August Gamble* was named a C. S. Lewis Noteworthy Book.

Bibliography of Novels by Author

The Josiah Files. Nashville, TN: T. Nelson, 1993.

"Teri Black-Addison" mystery series (Sisters, OR: Multnomah Press, 2003–2008)

"Royal Canadian Mounted Police" series (Elkhart, IN: Bethel, 1995–1997)

"Coast of Maine" series (Sisters, OR: Multnomah Press, 1998–2001)

Bibliography of Works about Author

Focus on Fiction, Interview: http://www.focusonfiction.com.
Linda Hall Home Page: http://www.writerhall.com.

Mort, John. Review of *Steal Away. Booklist* (June 1, 2003): 1740.
Mort, John. Review of *Dark Water. Booklist* (June 1, 2006): 41.

HANCOCK, KAREN

Personal, Professional, and Religious Background

Karen Hancock (1953–) was born in Pasadena, California. The family moved to Tucson, Arizona, soon afterwards, and she has lived there most of her life. She went to school in Tucson and Danville, California, graduating from the University of Arizona with a bachelor's degree in biology and wildlife biology. When she was in college, she attended a meeting about the origin of humans, expecting to be the defender of evolution. Instead, she became a convert to evangelical Christianity, completely changing her life and thoughts.

She is married to an engineer, who also has a degree in wildlife biology. They have one son, whom Karen Hancock homeschooled for eight years before she sent him off to high school. At one point, Karen complained to her husband about a popular novel, leading him to suggest that she write one herself. She began to work on *Arena*, a science-fiction allegory.

Major Works and Themes

Karen Hancock has been a reader most of her life and acknowledges that she loves to make up stories to entertain herself. In the seventh grade, she fell in love with science fiction when reading Andre Norton's *Judgment on Janus*. For a time, she read Westerns by Zane Grey and also enjoyed Edgar Rice Burroughs, **C. S. Lewis,** and many others. Her strongest influence she acknowledges to be **Dean Koontz,** whose books she has read several times. She also enjoyed a host of other science fiction films and books.

C. S. Lewis, Christian fantasy writers, and films such as *Star Wars* all inspired Karen Hancock to put her own imagination to work on an alternative world. She first wrote *Arena* and then signed a contract with Bethany House for a four-book fantasy cycle, set in the medieval world—"Legends of the Guardian King." This enormous undertaking with a host of characters, including a whole set of countries, customs, religions, and people reveals a vivid and lively imagination. The series, which has won praise from reviewers and fans, takes a handsome, sensitive young hero-prince from his original dream of the priesthood through battles for a throne he never sought and life-threatening adventures across the whole fantastic world. Hancock uses Lewis's strategy of a mirror theology with clever allusions to incidents and phrases from Scripture. She sets the stories in a time after the "Cataclysm," the "Wars of Unification," and the "Coming of the Shadow." Though this seems futuristic, the world is largely barbarian with islands of civilization that echo medieval feudalism. The god-figure, Eidon, requires that his young knight endure a series of adventures and trials to become worthy of his role as guardian-king—a bit of Platonic philosophy here. Only by turning against the false religion that has enthralled him for eight years and discovering the True Faith, does the hero finally achieve the character required of the king.

> When I am writing, it is a specialized service to God, and a time that should be regarded as sacred.
>
> —Karen Hancock, "Writing Devotions" on her Web site

Critical Reception

Reviewers were delighted with *Arena*, the first of Karen Hancock's science fiction novels. John Mort and Melanie Duncan, two of the most respected critics of Christian fiction, both found her work Christian and subtle. Duncan was especially impressed by the way the characters struggle "believably with sexual feelings and passion." *Publishers Weekly* noted that "Hancock's intense debut is an excellent . . . edgy contribution to the genre." *Christianity Today* spoke of it as a "genuinely enthralling mix of adventure, romance, and vivid imagery fused with spiritual symbolism." *Booklist* named it as one of the Top Ten Christian Novels of 2002. *Library Journal* called it "a classic in the making for the modern era."

Karen Hancock's epic series, "The Legend of the Guardian King," has proven even more successful, winning her a series of Christy awards for visionary books and fantasy. Donna W. Bowling, an educational consultant for libraries, praises the series, which she notes have echoes of **Peretti**'s "Darkness" titles. She says that *Shadow over Kiriath* "tells an exciting and complex story with characters that make mistakes, but grow and change through their experiences." Though the books are fantasy, they contain allegorical elements that illustrate important truth—such as the fact that true religion can be twisted and used by evil forces or that God's love and forgiveness, at great cost to himself, prompt fallible believers to awe and worship. The books reveal the importance of loving relationships and underscore the truth that true victory comes through submission to God.

Awards

Karen Hancock's first novel, *Arena*, was chosen by *Booklist* as one of the Top Ten Christian Novels for 2002. *Light of Eidon* won the 2004 Christy Award for fantasy, *The Shadow Within* won the 2005 Christy Award for Visionary Books, and *Shadow over Kiriath* the 2006 Christy Award for Visionary Books.

Bibliography of Novels by Author (Minneapolis, MN: Bethany House)

Arena. 2002

"Legends of the Guardian King" series

The Shadow Within. 2002.
The Light of Eden. 2003.
Shadow over Kiriath. 2005.
Return of the Guardian King. 2007

Bibliography of Works about Author

Bowling, Donna W. Review of "Legends of the Guardian King" series. http://www.christianlibraryj.org/pdf/legends.pdf.
Duncan, Melanie. Review of *The Arena. Library Journal* (April 1, 2002): 86.
"Karen Hancock." *Contemporary Authors Online.* Detroit: Thomson Gale, 2003.
Karen Hancock Interview: http:/www.swep.com/christian/oli-kh.html.

Karen Hancock Webpage: http://www.kmhancock.com.

"Karen Hancock." Wikipedia entry: http://www.en.wikipedia.org/wiki/Karen_Hancock.

Mort, John. Review of *The Arena. Booklist* (April 15, 2002): 1380.

HANSEN, RON

Personal, Professional, and Religious Background

Ronald Thomas Hansen (1947–) was born in Omaha, Nebraska, one of the twin sons of Frank L. Hansen, an electrical engineer, and Marvyl Moore Hansen, a stenographer. He attended Creighton University, earning a B.A. in 1970, then the Writers Workshop at the University of Iowa, earning an M.F.A. in 1974. He did further graduate study at Stanford, and Santa Clara, from which he earned an M.A. in 1995. Ron Hansen married Julie Vinsonhaler in 1985 and divorced her in 1993, after which he married Bo Caldwell in 1996.

He has taught at Stanford, where he was the Jones Lecturer in Creative Writing from 1978–1981, and then was affiliated with the Michigan Society of Fellows at the University of Michigan, the Writers Worship at Iowa, Cornell University, the State University of New York at Binghamton, then Santa Cruz, and finally he returned to Santa Clara, where he holds the Gerard Manley Hopkins Chair in the Arts and Humanities.

Major Works and Themes

Ron Hansen has built his reputation on his historical reconstructions. Taking a moment in history, dealing with actual people, fleshing this out with historical research and speculation, and envisioning it through the perspective of his Catholic faith, he builds a series of fascinating stories. His early works, revisionist concepts of Western tales, won him considerable praise.

Ron Hansen's later works, which are quite different in subject matter and tone, deal more specifically with spiritual issues. For example, *Mariette in Ecstasy*, tells the story of a 17-year-old girl who sought to enter a convent early in the 20th century. Her fervor for the spiritual life soon resulted in the appearance of stigmata, which appear and disappear rapidly, puzzling the members of the convent, the community, and her family—including her own doctor-father. No one seems to doubt the actuality of the blood that flows from her hands and feet, but neither is any one quite ready to declare her a saint. Eventually, she is rejected as a prospective member of the religious community, apparently because she is too disturbing and disruptive to fit into the order. In a spare, flat style, Hansen captures the facts of the case, the doubts of those who are witnesses, and the excitement of the other nuns. He leaves the question of her authenticity open at the end of the story, but appears to accept the reality of her miraculous experiences. As unadorned as the testimony at a trial, his prose reduces what could be baroque religious ecstasy to a kind of unemotional narrative.

Hansen's prosaic approach to another troubling story is parallel to this. In plain, objective language, he tells the story of Hitler's niece, a young woman whom Hitler took as a mistress before she died at 24. This time, the young Catholic girl

> I liked the idea of using a popular genre, such as the Western, as a way of expanding the appeal of my work to people who wouldn't otherwise pick it up.
>
> —Ron Hansen in letter to *Contemporary Authors*, 2003

finds herself mesmerized by the power and excitement of this uncle, 19 years her senior, who seeks her love and finally her sexual surrender. He briefly persuades her to substitute her crucifix for a swastika, bur she eventually rebels when

> Ron Hansen says that the three most important things about him are: he is from Nebraska, he is a twin, and he is a Roman Catholic.

his attentions prove nasty and controlling. Hansen draws a parallel between Hitler's hypnotism of the masses and this private seduction. He presents the case that her death was more a murder than a suicide, as were the deaths by "suicide" of Hitler's most loyal followers that followed his own death. A lapsed Catholic, Hitler turns his own understanding of the faith inside out, hating the Jews and the Jewish Messiah, trying to prove himself the messiah for the Aryan race, and producing his own "bible," *Mein Kampf,* which he expects his disciples to memorize.

Hansen is good at bringing history to life, a talent he attributes to his own reverence for life and his sense of God's guiding hand in history. Although he does not believe that God reaches out to save people from leaders like Hitler and the pain they inflict, he does believe that he offers them comfort in the midst of their confusion and suffering.

Although he is fond of such writers as **Walker Percy, Larry Woiwode,** and John Irving, he most frequently mentions Gerard Manley Hopkins and Thomas Merton as his favorite writers, men who combine a sense of poetry and faith, with attention to both the material and the spiritual world. He sees his stories as parables, "in the sense that I'm writing about ordinary people in ordinary circumstances." Only afterwards, looking back, do you discover that there was "God's influence" in the actions. Like Jesus, Hansen does not usually make the meanings of his stories explicit, leaving this activity to the creative imagination of the reader.

Critical Reception

John O'Leary notes, in his study of *Contemporary Novelists,* that Hansen's works manage to occupy "a curious half-way house between popular and high culture; between the worlds of art and entertainment." His stories of the West, especially the notorious Dalton gang, are remarkable, according to Sam Cornish, for their serious approach to their move from normal life to crime and back again to a life as part of everyday culture. His characters "pulse with life," while calling into question some of life's more interesting philosophic questions. Hansen manages to find the "moral" core of Jesse James, who became a kind of Robin Hood.

Critics praised his prose and his attention to historical detail in these early Western stories. They were surprised by his *Mariette in Ecstasy,* which had a smaller audience and a more restrained response. *Atticus,* the story that followed, is a version of the parable of the prodigal son, told as a murder mystery. At least one critic found the characterization of the difficult father-son relationship "achingly beautiful." *Hitler's Niece* received a mixed reaction, though many also found it to be insightful and beautifully written. On the other hand, at least one critic thought the scenes appeared stage-managed and voyeuristic.

For the most part, his novels receive praise for their craftsmanship and their revelations of grace. Hansen does not press his religious ideas on his audience, allowing the reader to discover them through the process of understanding, coming to see the philosophical foundation that undergirds the stories. Anita Gandolfo, however, does consider Hansen a major figure who works against the "silence, exile, and cunning" strategy embraced by many major modern writers. Hansen insists that "in a society that seems increasingly secular and post-biblical it is now writers and artists of faith who may feel exiled or silenced, who may feel that they can say the unsayable only through cunning." Gandolfo believes that Hansen's rebellion against the trivialization of religion in contemporary American culture does provide a corrective to the "dominantly secular culture with literature that expresses religious ideals and values." Rather than joining the "spiritual shoppers," Hansen embraces the mystery and majesty of traditional faith—specifically Roman Catholic Christianity.

Awards

Ron Hansen has had fellowships from the National Endowment of the Arts and the Guggenheim Foundation as well as the Lyndhurst Foundation. In addition he won an award from the American Academy of Arts and Letters in 1989.

Bibliography of Novels for Adults by Author

Desperadoes. New York: Knopf, 1979.
The Assassination of Jesse James by the Coward Robert Ford. New York: Knopf, 1983.
Mariette in Ecstasy. New York: HarperCollins, 1991.
Atticus. New York: HarperCollins, 1996.
Hitler's Niece. New York: HarperCollins, 1999.
Isn't It Romantic: An Entertainment. New York: HarperCollins, 2003.

Ron Hansen has also written stories for young people, contributed short stories to periodicals, and edited short stories. He has written screenplays, including the screenplay for *Mariette in Ecstasy.*

Bibliography of Works about Author

Cornish, Sam. Review of *The Assassination of Jesse James by the Coward Robert Ford. Christian Science Monitor,* December 28, 1983.
Gandolfo, Anita. *Faith and Fiction: Christian Literature in America Today.* Westport, CT: Praeger, 2007.
Hansen, Ron. *A Stay Against Confusion: Essays on Faith and Fiction.* New York: HarperPerennial, 2002.
McCarvey, Bill. "Busted: Authors Ron Hansen & Jim Shepard: A Catholic Conversation about Faith, Fiction and Friendship." http://www.bustedhalo.com/features/busted-authors-ron-hansen.jim-shepherd/.
O'Leary, John. "Ronald Hansen." *Contemporary Novelists,* 6th ed. Detroit, MI: St. James Press, 1996.
Prescott, Peter S. Review of *The Assassination of Jesse James by the Coward Robert Ford. Newsweek* (November 14, 1983).
"Ronald Hansen," *Contemporary Authors Online.* Gale, 2003.
Sawyer, Scott. "Puzzling Out the Graced Occasions: An Interview with Ron Hansen." http://www.leaderu, com/marshiull/mhr06/hansenl.html.
Smith, Amanda. Review of *Atticus. Publishers Weekly* (February 5, 1996).
Wright, Wendy M. "Novelist Ron Hansen Explores Faith and Fiction," Center for the Study of Religion and Society, Omaha, Nebraska, Fall 1997. Vol. 9, Number 1. http://puffin.creighton.edu/human/csrs/news/I-97–5.html.

HATCHER, ROBIN LEE

Personal, Professional, and Religious Background

Robin Lee Hatcher (1951–) was born in Payette, Idaho. Her father was Ralph E. Adams, her mother Lucille Johnson Adams. Robin completed high school, married young, had two children, divorced, and had to find work to support herself and her

> Romance fiction allows us vicariously to experience those emotions (of falling in love) once again without any of the risk or any of the pain. We can cry and rejoice with our heroines. We can cheer them on. We can mentally shout at them for not doing what we know they should do.
>
> —Robin Lee Hatcher in comments to *Contemporary Authors*

children. She was a single mother, "struggling to raise two children on a small salary and no child support from the ex." She found that the reading of romances offered her an escape from her grim life, an escape that she was later to offer to other readers. Robin Lee Hatcher began her writing career in 1981; her first novel was published by Leisure Books in 1984. In the following years, she became a best-selling author of romances.

In 1989, Hatcher turned her life around: she discovered new love, Jerry W. Neu, whom she married, and together they raised her two daughters. A second change came in 1991, with her decision to write Christian rather than secular fiction. She had been reading *Redeeming Love*, a semiautobiographical story by **Francine Rivers,** who had known considerable heartbreak and found a means to change her whole life with the grace of God. She commented, "I saw the real power of stories to change lives for the better and for eternity. It was then I also realized how many compromises I'd made in my career, seeking to please men (publishers, editors, readers) rather than God." While still writing secular romances, she came to believe that God wanted her to write for him. "Still, I had a hard time believing that my talents were good enough—or that I personally was good enough—for Him to use. But God uses who He will, even flawed, imperfect me, and His grace is sufficient."

In 1997, she had a dream that presented her with the idea for *The Forgiving Hour*. Like *Redeeming Love*, this proved to be a semiautobiographical exploration of personal pain. In this case, the pain came from the actions of an unfaithful spouse. She faced battles with her publishers and with her own conscience about this change of direction for her writing. At that point, she acknowledges that she accepted God's guidance and "sold out to him 100%."

Her daughters, Michaelyn J. Hatcher and Jennifer Lee Whit, are both now grown, with children of their own. Robin Lee Hatcher and Jerry live in Boise, Idaho, the scene of many of her books, where they enjoy a life shared with a collie dog and a cat.

Major Works and Themes

Robin Lee Hatcher's earlier experience in writing romances served as an effective apprenticeship equipping her for producing numerous Christian stories. In fact, one of her first Christian books was *Dear Lady*, a story that had previously been released as a secular romance and was rewritten to reflect a Christian worldview. It is the story of Lady Elizabeth Wellington, who flees an arranged marriage in England to become a school teacher in New Prospects, Montana. *The Library Journal* noted that readers of **Tracie Peterson's** historical novels would enjoy Robin Lee Hatcher's work. This was to be the first in her "Coming to America" series, which included *Patterns of Love, In His Arms,* and *Promised to Me*. These traditional romances were ideal for recrafting as Christian fiction.

Like many writers of Christian fiction, Robin Lee Hatcher has found that developing groups of novels in a series saves time and effort, and it also ensures a committed reading public who enjoy the characters and want to follow them into further adventures. She has also written the "Hart's Crossing" series and "The Burke Family" series, which has only two books so far.

Robin Lee Hatcher believes that romantic love is enhanced by religious love, that having God's grace in life softens the anguish that separates many families and damages relationships. Love is central to her stories, love of God, love of man, love of families, and love of friends. She presents ideal marriages that suffer terrible reversals, sometimes surviving, sometimes fractured forever.

Her plots, which are not particularly complicated, often have quick and unlikely reversals, sudden violence, and the obligatory happy endings. She chooses characters to feature all the possible angles her story requires. She likes to start in the middle of things, using flashbacks to provide background.

Not particularly fond of symbolism, Hatcher tells her story quickly and efficiently. If a character is determined to drive from Philadelphia to Boise, she stops only for meals at diners and sleep at motels. No great adventures interrupt her trip, no escaped criminals lurk in her car, she has no great problem digesting the greasy hamburgers and thick French fries. She just keeps on going until she hits Boise and then does exactly what she set out to do.

Her heroine is usually a young, beautiful woman, who is lonely and independent. She meets a man to whom she is attracted, but impediments stand in the way of a quick trip to the altar. One of the pair is a believer, the other not, and the believer is unwilling to be unequally yoked. Love seems to nurture conversion, allowing for a resolution where everyone is forgiven, the truth is miraculously exposed, the evil are left in cages or in prisons of their own making, and the good people are freed to love and to live full lives. For her heroes, money is not important, but family is everything. The happy family knows that hospitality is important, as is church attendance, usually an Evangelistic church with song and praise services, Bible reading, and prayer. Like many other Christian romances, details of food and clothing abound. The reader is exposed to no crude language or extramarital sex occurring without punishment, and sex acts are never described in detail. A Christian worldview undergirds the entire story.

A recent novel, *A Perfect Life*, takes a somewhat different tack. This time, a middle-aged woman has what she considers a perfect life: a handsome husband, a beautiful home, and two lovely, happily married, pregnant daughters. Shocking allegations about her husband send her into deep depression, cause one daughter to have a miscarriage, lead the husband to contemplate suicide, and bring the wife—Catherine—to the brink of divorce. The story is by no means a feminist rehash of Job. Except for the miscarriage, all the threats are as bogus as the original attack and can be resolved satisfactorily before the book concludes.

Hatcher is interested in women of courage and intelligence trying to survive, to carve out their places in a man's world. She stays clear of gritty scenes and real terror, keeping her tales within a comfort zone for her faithful readers.

Critical Reception

John Mort has said of romantic fiction such as that written by Robin Lee Hatcher that "in Christian romances, Christ is the love interest." Even so, there is the "tried-and-true formula of a woman being duped and exploited by Mr. Wrong, while Mr. Right, when the heroine first meets him, doesn't seem to be right. As in a mainstream romance, Mr. Wrong is revealed as less than sensitive, and Mr. Right's true, princely character establishes itself. Mr. Right, however, must be a Christian, and often the blindness of the heroine to true love is the same as her blindness to the will of God."

Hatcher has responded to such criticism of romances and of the readers of such romances: "If I may get on my soapbox for a moment, why does anyone deem it his or her right to criticize what other people choose to read? The United States ranks forty-ninth in literacy in the world." She goes on to defend her genre: "Readers of romance are in love with the written word. Isn't that the best way to keep someone reading—by providing interesting, enjoyable, satisfying stories?

Her novels, which appear at an astonishing rate, rarely win notice by the mainstream press. *Library Journal* or *Faithful Reader* may defend her, saying that she deserves her faithful following. *The Midwest Book Review* highly recommends her historical romances. But she does not achieve acclaim in the *New York Times Book Review*. Robin Lee Hatcher is a great favorite among other romance writers, who consider her a model. They speak of her "enchanting voice," her "warm, witty, sweet and heart-warming" stories. She is also a favorite among thousands of loyal readers.

Awards

Robin Lee Hatcher has served as the president of the Romance Writers of America and has won numerous awards, many of them for her romances. In 1999, she won the Christy Award for *Whispers from Yesterday* as well as the Romance Reader's Choice Award. She won the RITA awards from Romance Writers of America in 2000 for *The Shepherd's Voice* and the following year the Silver Angel Award from Excellence in Media. In 2001, she won another Romance Writers of America Award for *Patterns of Love*,

In addition to many other awards, she has been honored by having Laubach Literacy International establish the Robin Award in her honor.

Bibliography of Christian Novels by Author

Robin Lee Hatcher wrote about 30 romance novels between 1984 and 1999, published by Leisure Books, Avon, HarperPaperbacks and Silhouette before dedicating herself exclusively to Christian fiction:

Dear Lady. New York: HarperPaperbacks, 1997.
The Forgiving Hour. Colorado Springs, CO: WaterBrook Press, 1999.
Whispers from Yesterday. Colorado Springs, CO: WaterBrook Press, 1999.

"Coming to America" series (New York: HarperPaperbacks, 1998–2003)

The Shepherd's Voice. Colorado Springs, CO: WaterBrook Press, 2000.
Ribbon of Years. Wheaton, IL: Tyndale House, 2001.
The Story Jar. Portland, OR: Multnomah, 2001.
Speak to Me of Love. Wheaton, IL: Tyndale, 2003.
Catching Katie. Wheaton, IL: Tyndale, 2004.

"Hart's Crossing" series (Grand Rapids, MI: Revell, 2004-present)

Beyond the Shadows. Wheaton, IL: Tyndale, 2004.
The Victory Club. Wheaton, IL: Tyndale, 2005.

Loving Libby. Grand Rapids, MI: Grand Rapids, MI: Zondervan, 2005.
Another Chance to Love You. New York: Steeple Hill, 2006.

"The Burke Family" series (Grand Rapids, MI: Zondervan, 2006–present)

Trouble in Paradise. New York: Steeple Hill, 2007.
The Perfect Life. Nashville, TN: Thomas Nelson (Women of Faith series), 2008.
Wagered Heart. Grand Rapids, MI: Zondervan, 2008.

Bibliography of Works about Author

Duncan, Melanie C. Review of *Dear Lady*. *Library Journal* (November 1, 2000): 60.
Mort, John. Review of *The Forgiving Hour*. *Booklist* (June 1, 1999): 1792.
Mort, John. *Christian Fiction: A Guide to the Genre*. Greenwood Village, CO: Libraries Unlimited, 2002.
Reiss, Jana. Review of *Whispers from Yesterday*. *Publishers Weekly* (August 30, 1999): S15.
"Robin Lee Hatcher," *Contemporary Authors Online*. Detroit: Thomson Gale, 2002.
Robin Lee Hatcher Web site: http://www.robinleehatcher.com.

HENDERSON, DEE

Personal, Professional, and Religious Background

Dee Henderson is the daughter of a minister and has a brother who served in the Air Force. She herself worked for a time as an engineer until she found her niche as a writer. She had been writing since she was a teenager, but got serious about writing novels only when she was in her 30s. She is active in new church work in the Lake Country, near Chicago. She lives in Springfield with her parents.

Details about her life and background are not available, largely because she prefers to remain a private person who does not share personal details with her fans. It is obvious from her writing that Henderson is concerned about perils facing America in this time of terrorism, that she has friends among first responders and in security, and that she is a good student of military minutiae.

Major Works and Themes

Dee Henderson discovered the O'Malley family after trying a few early stories. Her idea for the O'Malleys turned out to be a stroke of genius. A cluster of orphans—some abandoned children, some real orphans, meet at a Chicago orphanage, develop a loving, protective relationship among themselves, decide they are one another's real family, and determine to live together after they are of legal age to leave the orphanage. They all change their last names to "O'Malley." These seven are closer than most blood families. The believers in the group are intensely concerned about their faith and care deeply about their siblings and friends who have refused to accept Christ or who have turned away from him because of family tragedies.

> Honestly, I'm hoping to give somebody three or four hours that is good, entertaining escape from what's going on in life. If I can get a good message in there somewhere too, all the better. I'm more trying not to bore somebody. That's my first objective.
>
> —Dee Henderson in interview recorded on Christianbook.com

Having overcome great difficulties themselves, the O'Malleys become first responders and helpers: Marcus is a federal marshal, Kate a hostage negotiator, Lisa a forensic pathologist, Jack a fireman, Stephen a paramedic, Rachel a psychologist who deals with children who have faced trauma. They encounter potential mates in their various adventures, discern their faith and their character as they deal with crises, introduce them to the O'Malley family, and finally determine whether they will invite them or allow them to marry into the group for life. Each novel deals with one member of the family in a frightening situation. Terrorist attacks or stalkers or accidents challenge the true grit of the characters, testing their faith. Usually, the novel will deal with one particular point of faith—the afterlife, true justice, forgiveness, mercy, or the resurrection. Henderson usually begins with a quote from Scripture, weaves the story around it, and includes some discussion about its relevance. She includes both believers and nonbelievers in her stories, but most of her believing Christians refuse to marry non-Christians.

In Henderson's second series, which derives in part from the national horror of September 11, 2001, she celebrates "Uncommon Heroes"—a Navy SEAL, a CIA officer, and others who protect the citizens in times of national peril. Each of these four stories follows the same pattern, opening with a crisis situation—a near drowning, an attempted assassination. This leads to a meeting of two attractive, mature young professionals who find themselves drawn to one another by the need to respond to the danger, the demonstrated courage of the other, and an admiration of each other's skills. In all of the stories, one of the heroes is a SEAL. One of the romantic interests is the widow of a SEAL, one a school teacher, one a CIA agent, and one a Navy pilot. The combination of professions leads to interesting situations: they are fighting terrorists, searching for weapon stashes in perilous places, hunting down paid assassins, trying to trap criminals, and seeking to avoid being shot down over enemy territory. In moments stolen from the national defense obligations, they find love, moving slowly toward an expression of passion. They carefully avoid sex, watch a lot of videos, and eat a lot of pizza and cheeseburgers. Finally, they discover a way for their tastes and backgrounds to blend: they meet and like one another's families, they share their faith, they plan a future, and they get married. Each of the novels ends with either a wedding or the plans for one.

Dee Henderson users strong characters. Her women are remarkably assertive, athletic, and self-assured. They are more interested in their cases than in clothes or dates, tend to be reluctant to accept protection, rarely cook or clean, have little interest in animals or children, and only occasionally go to church. The men, like the women, are mature, attractive, professional, and focused. None of them suggest premarital sex or talk in suggestive terms. The women, when sharing stories with one another, blush and giggle; the men hover around in protective ways, proving their interest through their vigilance and kindness.

Dee Henderson acknowledges that she writes according to a formula. She begins with a one-page definition of her voice, her target and 10 specific things she wants to do. She then develops a 50-page explosive opening scene, including dialogue between people who know each other very well. Henderson mixes humor and serious heart-to-heart talks to balance whatever is happening in the story, relying on a powerful plot that moves at a page-turning clip. She tries to keep her characters interesting. The details that she weaves into every scene are carefully researched, revealing information in small bits, not large chunks. She ends with a 30-page action-filled home run. Because powerful scenes matter so much, she concentrates on a powerful first sentence for the book, solid scene endings that open up the next scene, and a strong closing sentence.

Henderson acknowledges she is not a descriptive writer, and rarely includes elaborate details of nature, of clothing, or of food. Her characters are comfortable in jeans and sweatshirts, eating cheeseburgers, and drinking coffee heavily laced with sugar and cream. They are professionals, more concerned with their work than their appearance, keeping crazy hours, ready to move in a minute. She continues a few story lines that follow through from one novel in a series to the next (like Lisa's battle with cancer) but usually ends the narrative line quite neatly with each book.

Her first two books, published by Steeple Hill, are much more inspirational than her later ones. She reads **Francine Rivers** and **Terri Blackstock,** and professes a taste for Patricia Cornwall, John Grisham, and Tom Clancy. Their influence on her thrillers is quite clear.

Critical Reception

The prequel to the "O'Malley" series, *Danger in the Shadows*, won most of the acclaim and the awards. The sequels have all been favorably reviewed by individual authors and by critics for *Publishers Weekly* and *Booklist*. For the most part, the critics find Dee Henderson a good writer, who creates "charming minor characters" and well-conceived major ones. In one critique, the reviewer of *The Protector* for *Publishers Weekly* notes that the "behind-the-scenes approach to firefighting is truly interesting" and a couple of the theological conversations are "insightful and probing," but "Henderson's terse, choppy writing style is too heavy on dialogue and short on descriptive narration, to the point of confusing the reader. This style seems more suited to a mystery-of-the-week teleplay than a sustained, character-driven crime novel." The critic also complains that, "The early theological depth is compromised in the concluding pages by simplistic ruminations on the flames of hell that await unbelievers. Although Jack's eventual conversion has been telegraphed from the beginning, it is disappointing that it comes mostly because he wants to avoid yet another fire." Another reviewer said of *The Guardian* that "Christian readers will relish this intriguing tale."

The "Uncommon Heroes" series was hailed by the *Library Journal* for its perfect timing. Henderson's celebration of valor, courage, patriotism, honor, justice, and love hit just the right note for the times. Her treatment of Navy SEALS is so carefully done that John Mort, writing for *Booklist*, thinks readers will believe that Henderson "must have been there." *Library Journal*, *Romantic Times* and others have praised her work.

Other novels not included in these two series have also received some good reviews. *God's Gift*, a story of a weary missionary home on medical leave, has been hailed as "intriguing, insightful, and probing" as well as praised for "solid story telling" and "compelling characters."

Dee Henderson has built her own readership among both men and women, combining terror, mystery, romance, and faith. She knows how to draw her readers into her story and convince them of the dangers faced by her characters. Her underlying foundation of faith is always present in her stories, though not intrusive or preachy.

Awards

Dee Henderson's books have been a Doubleday Book Club Selection and a Crossings Book Club Selection. She has been the 2000 National Readers Choice Award Winner (for *Danger in the Shadows*), the RITA Award Winner in 2000, the Bookseller's Best Award Winner in 2000, the 2000 HOLT Medallion Finalist, the 2000 Beacon Award Winner, the 2000 WisRWA Reader's Award Winner, the *Romantic Times Magazine* Top Pick, and the Romantic Times Magazine HERO W*I*S*H AWARD winner. *True Honor* won the Christy Award in 2003 for Romance, and *The Guardian* won the same award in 2002. Dee Henderson is a member of the Writer's Guild and the Romance Writers of America.

Bibliography of Novels by Author

"The O'Malley" series (Sisters, OR: Multnomah Publishers, 2000–2003)

"Uncommon Heroes" series (Sisters, OR: Multnomah Publishers, 2000–2004)

The Marriage Wish. New York: Steeple Hill Women's Fiction, 2004.
God's Gift. New York: Steeple Hill Women's Fiction, 2008.

"Before I Wake" series (Wheaton, IL: Tyndale, 2006-present)

The Witness. Wheaton, IL: Tyndale, 2006.
Kidnapped. Wheaton, IL: Tyndale, 2008.

Bibliography of Works about Author

Authors Den. http://www.authorsden.com/visit/author.asp?AuthorD=362.
The Best Reviews. http://thebestreviews.com/review 10663.
Christian book: http://www.christianbook.com/Christian/Books/cms_content?page=356850&sp= 6214.
Dee Henderson Web site. http://www.deehenderson.com.
Faithful Reader. http://www.faithfulreader.com/reviews/0373785356.asp.
Pinkston, Tristi. Dee Henderson. http://www.authorsden.com/visit/author.asp?AuthorD=362.
Reviews are also available on individual books on the Amazon.com Web site.

HIGGS, LIZ CURTIS

Personal, Professional, and Religious Background

Liz Curtis (1956–) was raised by parents who were determined to make her into a wholesome, small-town girl. She acknowledges that she "veered off track" in her teens, when she began traveling with a fast crowd, sneaking cigarettes, cutting school, and finally smoking her "first joint" on a senior class trip to New York. For a decade, she found her pleasure in drugs and alcohol, spending four and five nights a week "on a bar stool."

She went to Bellarmine College, earning a B.A. and enjoyed working with the college radio station. After college, she became a radio personality noted for her outrageous comments and lifestyle. In her radio career, she traveled from town to town through her 20s, finding "companionship in many but comfort in none." She even did a stint at a hard rock station in Detroit, where she followed the notorious Howard Stern, who told her, "Liz, you've got to clean up your act."

The climax of this part of her life came in 1981, when she found herself in Louisville, Kentucky, playing "oldies at an AM station and playing dangerous games with marijuana, speed, cocaine, alcohol, and a promiscuous lifestyle." A husband-and-wife team extended to her a helping hand, which she describes as her "overnight delivery service." Rather than treating her as a project, these evangelists loved her "with a love so compelling that I was powerless to resist it." By

> Godly humor means not putting someone else down.
>
> —Liz Curtis Higgs in *Christian Parenting Today* Web site

Liz Curtis—later Higgs—suspected her life was out of control when the notorious shock jock Howard Stern advised her, "Liz, you've got to clean up your act."

February, 1982, she was singing in her friends' church choir. At the end of the service, she walked out of the choir loft and down to the baptistery to become a Christian. "God had delivered me from the gates of hell to the gates of heaven—absolutely, positively overnight."

In 1986, Liz Curtis married Bill Higgs. They have two children, Matthew and Lillian. The family maintains a home in Louisville. She began writing more and more as well as serving as a popular public speaker, editor of three newsletters, and regular contributor to *Today's Christian Woman* magazine.

Major Works and Themes

Much of Liz Curtis Higgs's writing began with Bible studies. Her most famous and popular Bible study book is *Bad Girls of the Bible*, a series that became Christian best-sellers. The series focuses on the fallen women of the Bible, whom Higgs calls "bad, for a reason," and "bad, but not condemned." She followed this series with individual studies of women in the Bible and a larger collection, *Slightly Bad Girls of the Bible: Flawed Women Loved by a Flawless God*, published in 2007.

She has also written Christian fiction, a parable series for children, and a series of historical novels for adults. One is the story of Jacob, his competition with his brother Esau, his trickery, and his flight to Laban and his daughters, both of whom Jacob wed. Higgs transforms this fascinating tale, with all its twists and turns, into a story of 18th-century Galloway, "The Lowlands of Scotland," with names changed to fit the circumstances. Jacob becomes Jamie, Rachael is Rose, and Leah is Leona. The delight for the reader is, in part, derived from the foreknowledge of the Bible story and the suspense of discovering how Higgs will handle such scenes as the wedding-switch for the alternate bride. Without the custom of multiple wives, she has to use the "kirk" court to replace Rose for Leona, even after a year of living together as husband and wife and a child. Each of the novels develops a portion of the Bible story: the flight from home and the marriage to wife 1; the complications of leaving the evil uncle and the switch to wife 2, and then the return to Jamie's home at Glentrool. Like Jacob fearing the confrontation with Esau, Jamie both desires and fears this reunion with his own family after years of separation.

Even after completing this trilogy, Higgs returned to the subject, following Jacob's sons and his daughter, Dinah, in the frightening tale of rape and revenge on Shechem. Fascinated by Dinah's silence, Higgs creates Davina McKie, a beautiful redhead with a talent for fiddle playing, who was rendered mute by a childhood accident caused by her twin brothers' carelessness in playing with a sword. By combining the Bible story with lore from Galloway and the Isle of Arran, Higgs weaves a tale something like the classic myth of Philomela that also draws on David's ability to charm royalty with his harp playing. Displaying a deep knowledge of 18th century Scottish music, customs, religious life, clothing, courting rituals, food, medicine, and travel difficulties, Higgs draws the reader into a romantic, melodramatic world dominated by family honor, fierce loyalties, and age-old hostilities.

She does overreach for her climactic scene of revenge, using Goatfell Mountain as a device for saving her young protectors from disaster, and she also averts the tragic ending suggested in Scripture by allowing Davina to survive and heal by the grace of God, the love of her family, and a good man. The contrast between this aftermath and the much fiercer story told by Anita Diamant in *The Red Tent* could not be more stark. *The Red Tent* retains the biblical background, hypothesizes that Dinah survives, but without hopes for a happy life. Diamant carries her story on to Egypt and a phase of Israel's history when her brother Joseph is a man of great authority. She portrays Dinah as a survivor, but not as a woman who can revive her reputation and live happily ever after.

With this string of powerful novels about the house of Jacob, Higgs may continue her work on the McKie family, drawing on the biblical parallels as the brothers betray one another and trick their aging father. Liz Curtis Higgs has invested so much effort in the study of the language, geography, culture, and mind-set of the Galloway peoples that she is likely to continue her richly conceived saga.

Critical Reception

Critics, especially of her biblical works, note frequently that Higgs has a great sense of humor and a lively manner of presentation. Her sympathy for "bad girls" is palpable, allowing her to understand them and sympathize with them in spite of their fallen nature. In her highly acclaimed "Bad Girls of the Bible" series, she looks at Jezebel, Delilah, and Lot's wife—women she sees as "Bad to the Bone," "Bad for a Moment," and "Bad for a Season, but not Forever." *Publishers Weekly* mentions her "rollicking humor and deep insight." *Mad Mary* re-tells the story of Mary Magdalene, placing her in modern Chicago, working as a prostitute.

From these fictionalized accounts of Bible characters, Higgs moved to *Mixed Signals*, a romance about a woman looking for the right man. *Bookends* takes the story of the woman looking for romance to Pennsylvania, where she is courted in an unusual way. But it is her Jacob series set in 18th-century Scotland that has elicited the most praise. *Publishers Weekly* called the first of the series an example of "fine writing" that will satisfy those who love both Scripture and historical fiction.

Most critics acknowledge that Higgs is a talented writer, with a powerful sense of the nature of sin and redemption, and a flair for transforming biblical narratives into various forms of fiction, endowing them with fresh life.

Awards

Liz Curtis Higgs has won the council of Peers Award for Excellence from the National Speakers Association, the Gold Medallion for Excellence in 1998 for her children's "Parable" series from ECPA, and the EPCA Gold Book Award in 2004 for *Bad Girls of the Bible*. She also won the 2006 Christy Award for historical Fiction for *Whence Came a Prince* and was a 2000 RITA Finalist for *Mixed Signals*.

Bibliography of Adult Novels by Author

Mixed Signals. Sisters, OR: Alabaster Books, 1999.
Bookends. Sisters, OR: Alabaster Books, 2000.

"The Lowlands of Scotland" series (Colorado Springs, CO: Waterbrook Press)

Thorn in My Heart. Colorado Springs, CO: WaterBrook Press, 2003.
Fair Is the Rose. Colorado Springs, Co: WaterBrook Press, 2004.
Whence Came a Prince. Colorado Springs, CO: WaterBrook Press, 2005.
Grace in Thine Eyes. Colorado Springs, CO: WaterBrook Press, 2007.

Bibliography of Works about Author

Butler, Tamara. Review of *Fair Is the Rose*. *Library Journal* (April 1, 2004): 80.
Hudak, Melissa. Review of *Mixed Signals*. *Library Journal* (June 1, 1999): 96.
Liz Curtis Higgs' Web site: http://www.lizcurtishiggs.com.
"Liz Curtis Higgs," *Contemporary Authors Online*. Detroit: Thomson Gale, 2005.

HUNT, ANGELA

Personal, Professional, and Religious Background

Angela Elwell Hunt (1957–) was born in Winter Haven, Florida. Her father, James Elwell, was an engineer at NASA's Kennedy Space Center; her mother, Frankie, was a telephone operator. After graduating from high school, Angela Elwell attended Brevard Community College in Florida and then Liberty University, from which she graduated magna cum laude. In the following years, she has continued her education, earning both a Master of Biblical Studies in Theology. and a Ph.D.

In 1980, Angela Elwell married Gary A. Hunt, a Baptist youth pastor. They have two children, Taryn Liu and Tyler Jordan, both now grown. To supplement her husband's salary, Angela Hunt took a number of jobs: she was an English teacher, held a full-time secretarial position, and in 1983, began working as a free-lance writer. She had been drawn to writing since she was a child. Her first writing efforts were business letters and catalog copy. A friend persuaded her to submit a manuscript to a national competition, and she won. Her first book was published in 1988. Since then, she has published over 100 books, many of them coauthored by such famous people as **Tim LaHaye** and Beverly LaHaye, John Donovan, Jay Strack, and Lori Copeland.

Angela and Gary Hunt live in Florida, where they have achieved a kind of celebrity status by raising two mastiffs, one of which was featured on *Live with Regis and Kelly* as the second-largest dog in America. Angela Hunt continues to write and to perform. She has been a member of The Re'Generation, and has 500 concerts and three recorded albums to her credit.

Major Works and Themes

The diversity and range of Angela Hunt's work is impressive. She is willing to write advice for parents, to publish picture books for children, to coauthor books on faith, to develop historical novels, romances, mysteries, or to write modern-day parables. Most of her early works were historical, one series quickly following another, targeting a young audience. As she has matured, Angela Hunt has found that she must take time to understand the locale and the people she is writing about, present them vividly, and develop her Christian theme out of the action.

Most of her first works are the young adult novels. The "Theyn Chronicles" began in 1993, followed by other historical series: "Colonial Captives," "Legacies

> I've learned that you can't borrow passion. You have to write the story that comes from the deepest place of your soul with the passion that arises with the story. . . . Someone once said that a book prepared in the mind can change people's minds; books written in the heart will change people's hearts. I think I'd like my books to do both.
>
> —Angela Hunt, as quoted in *Contemporary Authors Online*, 2008

of the Ancient Rivers," "Heirs of Cahira O'Connor," and "Keepers of the Ring." In each case, although the events have some historical basis, the characters are fictional. She chose ancient Egypt as the setting for "Legacies of the Ancient River," and medieval Ireland for "Theyne Chronicles." In "Keepers of the Ring," she uses

Angela and Gary Hunt have achieved a kind of celebrity status by raising two mastiffs, one of which was featured on *Live with Regis and Kelly* as the second-largest dog in America, earning the dogs and their owners a posh trip to New York to appear on television.

various settings in colonial America—linked by history and by a spill-over of the characters and the narrative.

She is also willing to undertake tough modern themes, like dementia or adoption. Angela Hunt also enjoys exploring modern life in terms of parables, which are sometimes disguised from the superficial reader. *The Awakening*, for example, uses the old story of Sleeping Beauty, as she signals in her use of the name "Aurora" for her heroine. She uses biblical heroines as well, writing one book on Mary Magdalene and in another story drawing on the warrior Deborah as her model. The "Heirs of Cahira O'Connor," for example, is a series about strong women, some of whom disguise themselves as men to fight for various causes, including the Union in *The Velvet Shadow* and the Normans in *The Emerald Isle*.

One of her more interesting recent books is *Uncharted*, an astonishing blend of an ancient parables about Death, including such venerable precursors as **C. S. Lewis**'s *The Great Divorce*, Sartre's *No Exit*, Tolkien's *Lord of the Rings*, and Defoe's *Robinson Crusoe*. Hunt has a vivid imagination, a real flair for drama, and skill in building suspense. Her themes emerge from the plots and characters naturally and clearly. She always hopes to leave her audience with "hope and help," but will not twist her story to force this conclusion. A good example of this talent is revealed in the scenes with Sarah, the young daughter of two of the castaways in *Uncharted*. They serve as bookends to the central story, and may seem unlikely until we agree that salvation lies entirely in God's hands.

Angela Hunt has said, "My faith influences my writing more than anything. I have an unseen writing partner, the Spirit of God, and I am constantly asking Him what to write, for ideas, for inspiration."

Critical Reception

Angela Hunt has won rave reviews from most of the Christian critics, who are the ones most likely to review her books. John Mort praises most of her books in his study on Christian fiction, and Janice DeLong finds her work delightful, insisting that the characters of *Roanoke* will "live on in the memory long after the last page is turned. Tamar Butler, who reviewed *Magdalene* for *Library Journal*, praises the writer's "attention to detail in her historical research."

Her vast readership is testimony to her popularity with readers of all ages. She has over two million books in print and remains a best-seller year after year.

Awards

Eight of Angela Hunt's novels have won Angel Awards from Excellence in Media. Two have won silver medals from *ForWord Magazine's* book of the year award (*Justice* and *The Canopy*). *By Dawn's Early Light* won her a Christy Award.

Bibliography of Novels for Adults by Author

"Theyn Chronicles" series (Wheaton, IL: Tyndale House, 1993–1995)

"Colonial Captives" series (Wheaton, IL: Tyndale House, 1996)

"Legacies of the Ancient River" series (Minneapolis, MN: Bethany House, 1996–1997)

"Heirs of Cahira O'Connor" series (Colorado Springs, CO: WaterBrook Press, 1998–1999)

"Keepers of the Ring" series (Wheaton, IL: Tyndale House, Wheaton, 1996–1998)

"Heavenly Daze" series (with Lori Copeland) (Nashville, TN: Word, 2000–2003)

The Proposal. Wheaton, IL: Tyndale House Publishers, 1996.
Gentle Touch. Minneapolis, MN: Bethany House, 1997.
The Truth Teller. Minneapolis, MN: Bethany House Publishers, 1999.
The Immortal. Nashville, TN: Word, 2000.
The Justice. Nashville, TN: Word, 2002.
The Shadow Women. New York: Warner Books, 2002.
The Pearl. Nashville, TN: Word, 2003.
The Awakening: A Novel of Discovery. Nashville, TN: WestBow Press, 2004.
The Debt. Nashville, TN: Word, 2004.
Unspoken. Nashville, TN: WestBow Press, 2005.
Magdalene. Carol Stream, IL: Tyndale House Publishers, 2006.
The Novelist. Nashville, TN: WestBow Press, 2006.
A Time to Mend. New York: Steeple Hill Books, 2006.
Uncharted. Nashville, TN: WestBow Press, 2006.
Doesn't She Look Natural? Carol Stream, IL: Tyndale House Publishers, 2007.

Many of Angela Hunt's more famous and popular works were designed for children or youth. She has also written a number of books, individually and with collaborators, that are filled with advice for parents, marriage partners and young people. Two of Angela Hunt's novels, *Uncharted* and *The Immortal,* have been optioned for film by Journey Productions and Columbia/TriStar. One, *The Note,* was used as the basis for a Hallmark film.

Bibliography of Works about Author

Angela Elwell Hunt Web site: http://www.angelaelwellhunt.com.
"Angela Hunt," *Contemporary Authors Online.* Detroit: Thomson Gale, 2008.
"Angela Hunt." Wikipedia Online. http://www.wikipedia.com.
Butler, Tamara. Review of *Magdalene. Library Journal* (April 1, 2006): 74.
DeLong, Janice and Rachel Schwedt. *Contemporary Christian Authors: Lives and Works.* Lanham, MD: The Scarecrow Press, 2000.
Faithful Reader Interview: http://www.faithfulreader.com.
Mort, John. Review of *Uncharted. Booklist* (April 15, 2006): 28.
Mort, John. *Christian Fiction: A Guide to the Genre.* Greenwood Village, CO: Libraries Unlimited, 2002.

J

JAMES, P.D.

Personal, Professional, and Religious Background

Phyllis Dorothy James, Baroness James of Holland Park, OBE, FRSA, FRSI (1920–) was born in Oxford, England, but soon moved to Ludlow. Phyllis is the eldest daughter of an Inland Revenue Official. Her father was not a demonstrative man; he was unhappy in his work, and in his marriage. On both sides, her grandfathers were teachers and churchgoers, one the Schoolmaster of Choristers for the Pilgrims' School. Both loved music, especially church music. She was consequently introduced to church music early. Her father was particularly musical, often singing in church choirs. She also learned to love the liturgy of her church from her childhood, especially *The Book of Common Prayer.* Her mother, a homemaker, was institutionalized for a few years for mental illness when the family lived in Ludlow. James describes her early years as a time when her family had little money, but the countryside was beautiful, the education was strong on fundamentals, and the church was always available.

P. D. James taught herself to read, loved history and literature, and hoped to attend high school, which was based on exams she took at the end of her first few years of schooling. She qualified for the school in Ludlow, but was excluded at the last minute because of severe admissions restrictions. Providentially, the family moved to Cambridge when she was 11, allowing her to attend the Cambridge High School for Girls. When she graduated, she took an exam that allowed her to go into the civil service. For some perverse reason, she chose a job like her father's, one in which he had been unhappy, and one that made her miserable for 18 months, at

> I still see myself as a searcher after truth rather than one confident she has found answers to the great and eternal questions of human existence, not least the problem of suffering of the innocent, and at seventy-seven I do not think I shall find all the answers now.
>
> —P. D. James, *Time to Be Earnest*, 90

> P. D. James chose to write under this name rather than calling herself "Phyllis Dorothy James," because it was shorter and would fit on the spine of a book.

which time she changed to different work for the government.

She married Ernest Conner Bantry White, a medical practitioner, on August 8, 1941. Since this was wartime in England, as soon as he graduated from Cambridge, Conner qualified as a doctor for the Royal Army Medical Corps, and was almost immediately shipped overseas, spending part of his time in India. Sadly, he returned from World War II suffering from severe mental illness, leaving him unable to work. They lived for some years with his parents, who generously helped the young mother with her children along with the care of their son. From time to time, Conner was institutionalized, coming home at irregular intervals. In spite of their difficulties, they had two daughters and proved a congenial couple. P. D. James indicates in her autobiography that she never contemplated life with anyone else but Conner.

Realizing that she was now likely to the chief support of her family, P. D. James determined to work toward a career, rather than simply hold down a job. She began evening classes at the City of London College to get the education she needed if she was to become a career hospital administrator. After Conner's father retired, the younger couple established their separate home, remaining grateful for the years of comfort and support Conner's parents had provided for all of them. Conner died in 1964. P. D. James says in her autobiography that she still thinks every day about things and people he and she would have loved to share.

In *Time to Be in Earnest*, she describes these exhausting days, living essentially as a single mother of two, holding down a job that demanded all of her energies, and visiting her husband after work. This would explain the long delay in her becoming a novelist, a dream she had nurtured since childhood. In the late 1950s, she determined that she would buckle down and write her first book. "I realized that if I didn't make the effort and settle down to begin that first book, eventually I would be saying to my grandchildren, 'Of course I really wanted to be a novelist.'" She began rising two hours earlier each morning to do some writing, continued her writing on buses and trains on the way to work, drafting her work in longhand, determined to produce her first novel, *Cover Her Face*. Over a three-year period, she completed the book, and submitted it to a publisher, Faber and Faber, who accepted it immediately. They have remained her publishers for the remainder of her career.

She decided to use her maiden name, puzzled over whether to use "Phyllis Dorothy James" "Phyllis D. James," or finally "P. D. James." She chose the last of these because it was shorter and would fit on the spine of a book. She insists she was not seeking to hide her gender, especially since women were already successfully writing crime fiction. Some of the early critics, however, thought P. D. James was a man.

Her career in the Civil Service spanned decades: she worked for the National Health Service (1949–68), then the Civil Service (until 1979), after which she became a full-time writer, writing a book approximately every three years. Because of these highly acclaimed novels, she reaped a number of honors: She served as a governor for the British Broadcasting Corporation (1988–1993). In 1991, she was awarded the OBE, and in 1991 became a life Peer, Baroness James of Holland Park. In her journal/autobiography, *Time to Be in Earnest*, she describes some of her activities, her meetings with BBC officials, her concerns about the House of Lords, her maiden speech in Parliament, and reveals herself to be a woman who (age 77 at the time) is still active on many committees, who gives talks and readings, attends celebrations, funerals, teas, and who travels widely to sign her books and talk about the craft of fiction.

At this point, she modestly describes herself as an "elderly grandmother who writes traditional English detective fiction." She retains a sharp wit, a vigorous lifestyle, and a delight in every day of her life.

Major Works and Themes

P. D. James's close working relationship with the Festival Theatre in Cambridge, her work as a Red Cross nurse during World War II, her time as a principal administrator in the police department, and other work experience have richly informed her writing. She frequently expresses her gratitude to those in Scotland Yard and elsewhere who provide her with the details of her investigation scenes. Her detailed knowledge of police work, in fact, has led her to laugh at the uninformed ideas of earlier writers (including Dorothy L. Sayers), who seem to think that investigations can be hurried, autopsies done on the kitchen table at the scene of the murder, and private amateur detectives are welcomed by local police. She takes her background very seriously and seeks to make it precise and correct—therefore convincing. At the same time, she acknowledges her debt to the "golden age" of crime novelists.

She is a devout Anglican, with a thorough knowledge of the rituals, debates, and history of her church, which she uses frequently in her stories. Part of this she attributes to her heritage. The words of the traditional prayers and the hints of the hymns provide much of the background of her novels. *The Children of Men, Original Sin*, and *Devices and Desires*, for example, take their titles from the phrases in Cranmer's great *Book of Common Prayer*. She also loves the King James translation of Scripture, adopting its phrasing and cadences in many scenes of her stories. She delights in the "flowers, brass, stones and polished wood, the whole overlaid by the occasional sweet pungency of incense." She admits that she is no fan of sermons. Her love of church buildings, their architecture, their windows, their symbolism of a faith that continues through the generations has led her to include a church or chapel in most of her novels. She also gives her characters depth of understanding of theology and ritual. Her point of view is consistently Christian, even when her characters are engaged in thoroughly un-Christian violence.

P. D. James has given so many talks and taught so many young people about writing that her ideas are well known. She insists on certain "Rules for Writers," including such sage advice as: read widely, practice writing, increase your vocabulary, and welcome experience. She takes her guidance from the example of Henry James, a writer she admires within limits. He asserted that the goal of the writer is "to help the heart of man to know itself." She says, "Certainly, for me, the intention of any novelist must surely be to make that straight avenue to the human heart."

An acknowledged follower of the classic detective story form, she has found that she can enjoy great benefits by following her detective through the entire series of her stories. Like other writers of detective fiction, she sees the advantage of keeping her hero single—in the case of Adam Dalgliesh, a widower without children. This leaves him free to write his poetry, follow his suspects, and dabble in love affairs. A tall, slender, aristocratic looking man, Adam is comfortable in any company, observant and clever. When the detective Cordelia Gray meets him in *An Unsuitable Job for a Woman*, he quickly determines her involvement in the crime, isolates her motives for becoming an accomplice to murder, and realizes that she will not be budged from her story. When she breaks down in tears, he comforts her, lends her his fresh linen handkerchief, listens to her lament about his own neglect of his subordinate and his failure to respect his death, realizing that she is employing one of his old cases and his own methods of investigation against him. Then he quietly uses this accumulated information to fill in the gaps of the case,

He is a subtle, gentle man, not so religious as his clergyman father, yet one who observes the signs and symbols of the Church of England, admires the architecture of the half-empty churches, and still measures time by the seasons of the liturgical calendar. He has various affairs, avoids succumbing to the evident love in the eyes of his subordinate, Kate Miskin, and finally, in *The Lighthouse*, acknowledges he is in love with Emma (a name undoubtedly purloined from Jane Austen) and proposes to her, bringing to an end his long flirtation with casual romance. He is a gentleman detective, but a professional, rising on his merits to the rank of Commander in Scotland Yard.

Later, James developed a female detective, Cordelia Gray, who is much younger and quite different from Commander Dalgliesh. Cordelia is the daughter of a Marxist, shuffled around to various foster homes and finally raised in a convent after the death of her mother. Although promised a scholarship to Cambridge, Cordelia is unable to attend. Ironically, she finds herself in Cambridge on her first solo case as a detective. At the young age of 22, she became a partner to a sad little private detective named Bernie Pryde, who was previously fired from the police force by Adam Dalgliesh, yet whom he insists on quoting. Bernie recognizes Cordelia's intelligence and industry, teaches her some of the techniques of investigation, and then commits suicide, leaving her to mature on her own. She has some interaction with Dalgliesh, whom she holds responsible for her deceased partner's aborted career on the police force, and sees him as a rival whenever they meet on a case.

She is pretty, cheerful, systematic, ironic, and resourceful, watching all of the action around her with a shrewd analytic mind. She is also moral. She recognizes the great evil that lies at the heart of crime, calling it by that name while smiling at the discovery of her own Christian conscience in spite of being an "incurable agnostic." She is "prone to unpredictable relapses into faith." She hesitates to swear on the Bible, for example, because she does not believe its message—a curious twist of conscience. James uses her as an example of the post-Christian culture of England, the lingering influence of the Christian faith even after the faith itself has dimmed and the churches are emptied.

P. D. James's formula for detective fiction (or, as she prefers, "crime novel") is simple: "You have a murder, which is a mystery. There is closed circle of suspects." She enjoys the spectacle of revealing the corpse, noting the reaction of each of the characters as a means of portraying deeper meanings. She likes an interesting death, a set of characters with a mixture of motives, a large number of clues that are shared with the reader, a wide-ranging suspicion, and a logical and satisfactory conclusion that conforms to the clues scattered through the story.

P. D. James has the same scholarly and imaginative approach to mystery stories that readers found in Dorothy L. Sayers. She notes that she also has considerable admiration for Jane Austen, **Graham Greene,** and **Evelyn Waugh.** She mentions a large number of writers she has read, and notes their qualities with the precision of a sharp critic. In one of her talks, which she describes in *Time to Be in Earnest*, she traces the history of detective fiction, indicating those she finds particularly useful. She admires Arthur Conan Doyle, for example, for his use of logic, but laughs at his neglect of detail in his stories. She has a fine time explaining that Jane Austen, in her own sly way, was a detective novelist, using a series of clues in *Emma* to bring about the surprising ending.

She has said that, "For me, setting, character, narrative are always interdependent." She develops an interesting, intellectual, and thoughtful investigator, sets a mystery before him or her, and describes a network of characters who would appear naturally in the given setting. She uses her own experience in the vast British bureaucracies, especially the criminal justice system, for her milieu. In *The Children of Men*, she uses the Oxford neighborhood and people she has known since childhood. In *The Lighthouse*, she creates an imaginary island off the coast of Cornwall. In *An Unsuitable Job for a Woman*, she uses her beloved Cambridge, even including her daughter's address.

Well read and intellectually adventurous, P. D. James combines bits and pieces of literary history along with details from the Church of England and its rituals. These echoes and phrases give resonance to her tales, richness to her scenes. They also provide a kind of stability against which she plays the violence and chaos created by crime. James admits that she is fascinated with death and often views a scene as a perfect place for a crime, returning to consider where the crime might be committed and where criminals might hide.

She loves the genre of the crime novel, emphasizing the sinful, criminal nature at the center of the story. She has sought to bring a new sophistication and complexity to a form that has deteriorated over the years, losing the old sense of justice that allowed the evil to be punished and the good to be rewarded. Truth is important to her plots, which often include a love story. Lust may be a motive, but is rarely described in any detail, though she does not balk at including sexual scenes. Many of her characters sleep with one another in casual alliances, often without any romantic intent. She sees much of modern sexuality as unrelated to love, marriage, or family. The consequent sterility of the scene is at the heart of her dystopian novel, *The Children of Men*.

Critical Reception

The British Council notes that "P. D. James is one of the most successful detective novelists writing in Britain today." She combines a sophisticated narrative with a popular literary genre. From the beginning, she has been well-received by critics, both in England and America. Her works have been translated into numerous languages and are often the best sellers on the Continent as well as in England. Each of her novels has been reviewed widely by the major magazines and newspapers. She reads the reviews and responds to them, usually by making adjustments in later stories.

Critics have noticed her deep moral concern, expressed in many ways through her novels. She sees a steady decline in religion and morality in her country, moving toward a "Wasteland" scenario. Although many of her characters are educated and sophisticated, they are often "consumed by jealousy, hatred, lust, sexual fears, and ambition." She also has a number of lower class figures, cooks, butlers, gardeners, and others, who are as capable of criminal intent as her high-born characters.

Her first novel, *Cover Her Face*, won immediate praise. Her 2001 novel, *Death in Holy Orders*, was cited as displaying "an insightful grasp of the inner workings of church hierarchy." Norma Siebenheller noted that Adam Dalgliesh is "a far cry from the almost comical characters who served Christie and Sayers as sleuths." Erlene Hubly considers him a "Byronic hero," unable to adjust to or accept society. Because of his fear of chaos and death, he enforces the rules of society, "convinced that they are all humanity has with which to create order . . . if he cannot stop death he can at least catch and punish those who inflict it on others."

Original Sin, which is set in an architecturally spectacular publishing house on the banks of the Thames River, was praised by the reviewer for *Tangled Web* for its "impeccable style" and for a plot that is "clever and tight as always." *Death in Holy Orders*, published the year she turned 80, is set in a High Anglican theological college. Trudy Bush noted that "James packs so much theological discussion and meaning into a suspenseful detective story, and manages sometimes to be very funny as well, [which] makes her book remarkable." She notes that this novel is "very concerned with faith and with life's ultimate questions," written by an author at the top of her powers.

Interestingly, her dystopia has also received raves. When religious leaders were asked by *WORLD Magazine* for a list of their favorite books, *The Children of Men* appeared on a number of the listings. **Walter Wangerin** compared this book to her crime novels and found her view of humankind to be "Olympian." She has also been on the *New York Times* best-seller list several times. Her many awards and honors attest to the high esteem in which she is held. Now in her 80s, she continues to win prizes for her new novels.

Her late novels have been as enthusiastically reviewed as her early ones, accompanied by promotional tours sponsored by her publishers. Her talks, book signings, and general activity in response to her faithful readers have made her the grande dame of letters.

Awards

P. D. James has been showered with honors and awards for her work and her service: The Order of the British Empire, 1983; lifetime Peerage, 1991; Fellow of the Royal Society of Literature, Fellow of the Royal Society of Arts, President of the Society of Authors, 1997; honorary doctorates from the Universities of Buckingham, Hertfordshire, Glasgow, Durham, Portsmouth, London, Essex; and honorary fellow of St. Hilda's College, Oxford, and Girton College, Cambridge.

She has won the Best Novel Award, Mystery Writers of America, for *Shroud of a Nightingale* (1971), Crime Writer's Association Macallan Silver Dagger for Fiction for the same novel the same year, the Best Novel Award, Mystery Writers of America for *An Unsuitable Job for a Woman* (1973) the CWA Macallan Silver Dagger for Fiction for *The Black Tower* (1975) and for *A Taste for Death* (1986), the Mystery Writers of America Best Novel Award for *A Taste for Death* (1986), the CWA Cartier Diamond Dagger award for lifetime achievement (1987), the Deo Gloria Award for *The Children of Men* (1992), and the Grandmaster Award by the Mystery Writers of America (1999).

Bibliography of Novels by Author

"Adam Dalgliesh" series (London: Faber & Faber, unless otherwise indicated)

Cover Her Face. Boston: G.K. Hall, 1962.
A Mind to Murder. 1963
Unnatural Causes. 1967.
Shroud for a Nightingale. 1971.
An Unsuitable Job for a Woman. 1972.
The Black Tower. Boston, G.K. Hall, 1975.
Death of an Expert Witness. 1977.
A Taste for Death. 1986.
Devices and Desires. 1989.
Original Sin. 1994.

A Certain Justice. 1997.
Death in Holy Orders. 2001.
The Murder Room. 2003.
The Lighthouse. 2005.
The Private Patient. 2008.

"Cordelia Gray" series (New York: Faber & Faber and Scribner, 1972–1982)

Innocent Blood. New York: Knopf, 1980.
The Children of Men. New York: Vintage, 1992

Co-authored with Thomas A. Critchley

The Maul and the Pear Tree: The Ratcliffe Highway Murders, 1811. London: Constable, 1971.

A large number of James's mystery novels have been used as the bases for television miniseries on the BBC in Britain and PBS in America. *The Children of Men* was a feature film in 2006, directed by Alfonso Cuarón.

Bibliography of Works about Author

Bush, Trudy. Review of *Death in Holy Orders. Christian Century* (July 4, 2001): 32.
Gidez, Richard B. *P. D. James.* Twayne's English Authors Series. New York: Twayne, 1986.
Hubly, Erlene. "The Formula Challenged: The Novels of P. D. James." *Modern Fiction Studies* (1983): 511–522.
James, P. D. *Time to Be in Earnest.* New York: Knopf, 2000.
Kresge-Cingal, Delphine. *Perversion et perversité dans les romans à énigme de P. D. James.* Lille: Presses du Septentrion, 2001.
"P. D. James," British Council Contemporary Writers. http://www.contemporary writers.com/authors/?p=auth193.
"P. D. James," Wikipedia, the free encyclopedia. http://en.wikipedia.or/wiki/p-D-James.
"Phyllis Dorothy James White," *Contemporary Authors Online.* Detroit: Thomson Gale, 2006.
Reese, Jennifer. "The Art of Murder," an interview with P. D. James. Salon.com. http://www.salon.com.
Siebenheller, Norma. *P. D. James.* New York: Ungar, 1981.
Tangled Web. http://www.twbooks.co.uk. Review of *Original Sin.*
Times Literary Supplement, October 22, 1971; December 13, 1974; March 21, 1980; October 29, 1982; June 27, 1986; September 25, 1992; October 21, 1994.
Wangerin, Walter, Jr. Review of *Children of Men. New York Times Book Review,* March 28, 1993, 23.

JENKINS, JERRY

Personal, Professional, and Religious Background

Jerry Bruce Jenkins (1949–) was born in Kalamazoo, Michigan. His father was a retired police chief and his mother a homemaker. When Jenkins was in high school, he began to write about sports events for the school paper. As he acknowledged: "I immediately realized I had found my niche."

> Fiction needs to be accurate, but the work of research needs to be blended in seamlessly.
>
> —Jerry Jenkins in interview with DeLong and Schwedt

Jerry Jenkins is the actual writer for the "Left Behind" series, though Tim LaHaye furnishes many of the ideas. Additionally, while at the Moody Institute, he published the nationally syndicated sports comic strip "Gil Thorp."

He went to the Moody Bible Institute, The Loop College, and the William Rainey Harper College in preparation for a career in journalism. For a time he was a radio news writer, a sportswriter and photographer, a sports editor, editor of *Moody Monthly*, and then director of Moody Press. He then became vice president for publishing for the Moody Bible Institute of Chicago, while continuing to edit the *Moody* magazine for some time and remaining a writer-at-large for the publication. While he has been involved with Moody, he has also continued his interest in sports, writing the nationally syndicated sports comic strip "Gil Thorp."

Jerry Jenkins gives credit to teachers and others he has known throughout his career for his long and illustrious career in writing, and he praises his wife, Dianna, as his main support and source of encouragement. He is motivated by the belief that "writing is my one gift and that I am thus obligated to exercise it to the fullest."

Major Works and Themes

Jerry Jenkins originally saw himself as a journalist, a writer of nonfiction. His first 18 books were biographies, histories, documentaries, studies of hymns, devotions, and advice on Christian living. He is especially fond of sports and enjoys writing biographies of such sports figures as Hank Aaron and Orel Hershiser. He also finds pleasure in helping such monumental figures as Luis Palau and Billy Graham with their autobiographies. At the invitation of a friend, he began a mystery novel, *Margo*, which eventually expanded to a 13-book series. The final book is *Margo's Reunion* (1983), followed by collections of *Margo Mysteries*, in two volumes (1985–1986). These were followed by the "Jennifer Grey Mystery" Series (1983–1985), again capped with a compilation. A number of these books were republished under livelier titles somewhat later by Nelson. These were aimed at younger readers and are now out of print. He found some success in other novels, a couple of them about sports figures—*Hometown Legend* and *The Rookie*.

Many of his books are coauthored. Pat and Jill Williams are two of his favorite collaborators. It was surely his talent, his ease in collaboration, his speed and facility, his ability to appeal to a popular audience that attracted **Tim LaHaye** to present him with the idea for the "Left Behind" Series—his greatest success as an author. At the end of *Tribulation Force*, as well as most of the other volumes in the series, Jerry Jenkins identifies himself as the writer of the "Left Behind" novels, crediting Tim LaHaye with the idea of fictionalizing an account of the Rapture and Tribulation.

The "Left Behind" series reveals him as a skilled writer in the thriller genre. Comfortable in the world of film and television, Jenkins leaps into the middle of the action, includes quick dialogue and interior monologues to characterize his stock figures, sets up the situation and the central mystery, fills his plot with suspense, fast action, quick reversals, surprises, violence, and even some love between the most attractive of his characters. His famous and brilliant people fly all over the world, are invited to top-level meetings with world leaders and the Antichrist, and have all the inside knowledge denied the rest of mankind. They know all about the conspiracy to make the U.N. into a global government that, in the name of peace and harmony, and will bring together all military power, all currencies, all governance, and all religions. The show of force to quell dissidents becomes a key to the more violent scenes and the need to stay alive to proselytize the unbelievers is the motivation for those who must keep their faith secret or face martyrdom. The story does not delay to meditate on the theological problems of working for the Antichrist while fighting against his evil agenda. A wise man (usually a religious figure), a rabbi, or a clergyman explains the situation with a tone of absolute certainty. A small group of true believers who are somehow more attractive, more articulate, more skilled, more religious, and more loving than normal folks, form the bond of brothers and sisters who hold the story together. The final scenes of each installment leave some threads untied, some issues unsettled, some prophesies unfulfilled, thus segueing into the sequel.

Like most thrillers, the plot lines of these stories are tied up too quickly to be believable, the action is too exaggerated, the good and evil forces too stereotyped. The important point is too obviously to flesh out the vision hinted at by Ezekiel, Daniel, and John in his Revelation. For all of his speed in composition, Jenkins is a careful writer who relies heavily on research. He insists that fiction must be accurate and based on unobtrusive research. "The ultimate goal of a writer . . . should be to be invisible." He says that he tries to keep his stories character-driven, and notes that the "theme, while overarching and undergirding, should be nearly invisible. If the reader doesn't get the point, then I have failed."

Jerry Jenkins joined with Tim LaHaye again in the two books so far published in the "Jesus Chronicles." These include *John's Story: The Last Eyewitness*, drawn primarily from the Gospel account of miracles, words, and deeds of Christ; *Mark's Story* deals with the early days of the Christian church, much of it a retelling of the book of Acts. Two more volumes are planned.

Jerry Jenkins is the author of more than 100 books, 10 of which have been listed among the *New York Times* best-sellers. He writes articles, children's books, biographies, and various other genres. A number of his books have been turned into television shows or films.

Critical Reception

Apocalyptic fiction has been popular since World War II, probably because of the increased awareness of human power for destruction and the approach of the millennium. At the same time, the evangelical movement has flourished, and the enthusiasm for evangelical fiction. **Flannery O'Connor**, who was inclined to spot apocalyptic moments herself, summarized the problems of the writers of religious fiction in her essay "Novelist and Believer." She acknowledged that bad fiction has flooded the world, especially fiction written by believers who think that they are so empowered by their faith that they feel no obligation to "penetrate concrete reality." This need to deal with reality in matters of faith becomes a special burden in stories that follow Scripture as closely as do the "Left Behind" novels. Jenkins does a masterful job of providing suspense even though his readers all know in general outline what will follow each of the scenes. He also tries to give the long explanatory discourses, probably provided by LaHaye, with some probability and liveliness. Feeling an obligation to illustrate one major conversion per volume is also a burden on his creative imagination, as is the need to make each death, catastrophe, and temptation individual and moving. Such vast numbers of miseries dull the reader's sensitivity to pain and suffering. It is hard to mourn millions of people.

The critical reception of the "Left Behind" series is predictable: mainstream papers and journals have ignored or sneered at the novels, while the religious journals have divided according to their ideology. In a number of cases, the novels have formed the basis for reading and discussion groups in churches who believe in the Rapture. Seven of the apocalyptic novels have appeared on the Christian Booksellers Association best-selling fiction list and the *Publishers Weekly* religious best-seller list. These novels were: *Left Behind, Tribulation Force, Nicolae, Soul Harvest, Apollyon, Assassins,* and *The Indwelling. Left Behind* was also nominated for the Book of the Year by the Evangelical Christian Publishers Association in 1997, 1998, and 1999. The highest praise has been the continuing popularity with the reading public, keeping these books on the *New York Times* best-seller list for weeks at a time and making them the all-time best-sellers of Christian novels.

Awards

Jerry Jenkins' *Margo* was nominated for the Novel of the Year by *Campus Life* magazine; he was awarded the Religion in Media Angel Award, for *Meaghan* and *Margo's Reunion.* He won the Biography of the Year award (*Campus Life* magazine) in 1980, for *Home Where I Belong.* He was nominated for the Evangelical Christian Publishers Association Gold Medallion for *The Night the Giant Rolled Over* and *Rekindled: How to Keep the Warmth in Marriage.*

Bibliography of Adult Novels by Author

The Operative. New York: Harper & Row, 1987.
The Rookie. Brentwood, TN: Wolgemuth & Hyatt, 1991; published as *The Youngest Hero,* 2002.
The Deacon's Woman and Other Portraits. Chicago, IL: Moody, 1992.
Though None Go with Me. Grand Rapids, MI: Zondervan, 2000.
Hometown Legend. Anderson, WV: Warner, 2001.

"Margo Mystery" series (Chicago, IL: Moody, 1979–1984)

"Jennifer Grey Mystery" series (Wheaton, IL: Victor Books, 1983–1984)

"Left Behind" series, with Tim F. LaHaye (Wheaton, IL: Tyndale House)

Left Behind: A Novel of the Earth's Last Days. 1995.
Tribulation Force: The Continuing Drama of Those Left Behind. 1996.
Nicolae: The Rise of Antichrist. 1997.
Soul Harvest: The World Takes Sides. 1998.
Apollyon: The Destroyer Is Unleashed. 1999.
Assassins: The Great Tribulation Unfolds. 1999.
The Indwelling: The Beast Takes Possession. 2000.
Desecration: Antichrist Takes the Throne. 2001.
The Mark: The Beast Rules the World. 2001.
The Remnant: On the Brink of Armageddon. 2002.
Armageddon. 2003.
Glorious Reappearing: The End of Days. 2004.
The Rapture: In the Twinkling of an Eye: Countdown to the Earth's Last Days. 2006.
Kingdom Come. Wheaton, IL: Tyndale House, 2007.

Jenkins has also been a contributor to periodicals, including *Moody Monthly, Power, Contact, Coronet, Saturday Evening Post,* and *Campus Life.*

Media Adaptations

Left Behind: A Novel of the Earth's Last Days was adapted for a feature film by Cloud Ten Pictures, 2001. Books in the *Left Behind* series have been adapted to audio cassette, interactive computer games, mugs, T-shirts, and other marketing merchandise.

Bibliography of Works about Author

Alleva, Richard. "Beam Me Up: A Repackaged Apocalypse," *Commonweal* (January 12, 2001): 17.

DeLong, Janice and Rachel Schwedt. *Contemporary Christian Authors: Lives and Works*. Lanham, MD: The Scarecrow Press, 2000.

Furnas, J.C. "Millennial Sideshow," *American Scholar* (Winter, 2000): 87.

Gross, Joseph. "The Trials of Tribulation," *Atlantic Monthly* (January, 2000): 122.

Jenkins, Jerry B. Wikipedia. http//:www.wikipedia.org/wiki/Jerry-'B-Jenkins.

Jenkins, Jerry B. *Contemporary Authors Online*. Detroit: Thompson Gale, 2004.

Jerry Jenkins Official Web site, http://www.jerryjenkins.com.

Kirkpatrick, David D. "A Best-Selling Formula in Religious Thrillers," *New York Times*, February 11, 2002, C2.

Kirkpatrick, David C. "In the Twelfth Book of Best-Selling Series, Jesus Returns," *New York Times*, March 29, 2004, A1.

Kirkpatrick, David C. "The Return of the Warrior Jesus," *New York Times*. April 4, 2004, D1.

Maudlin, Michael. Review of *Left Behind*. *Christianity Today* (September 1, 1997): 22.

Mort, John. Review of *Off the Map*. *Booklist* (February 1, 1992): 1005.

Mort John. Review of *Left Behind: A Novel of the Earth's Last Days*. *Booklist* (November 1, 1995): 455.

Mort John. Review of *Tribulation Force: The Continuing Drama of Those Left Behind*. *Booklist* (October 1, 1996): 304.

Mort John. Review of *The Rookie*. *Booklist* (March 1, 1997): 1111.

Mort John. Review of *Nicolae: The Rise of Antichrist*. *Booklist* (July, 1997): 1775.

Mort John. Review of *Though None Go with Me*. *Booklist* (January 1, 2000): 874.

Scully, Matthew. "Apocalypse Soon," *National Review* (December 21, 1998): 62.

Shepherdson, Nancy. "Waiting for Godot, the Bible Foretold It." *Los Angeles Times Magazine*, April 25, 2004, 16.

KARON, JAN

Personal, Professional, and Religious Background

Janice Meredith Wilson, or Jan Karon (1937–) grew up on a farm in Lenoir, North Carolina, with her sister, their young mother and grandparents. Her years on the farm gave her "time to muse and dream. I am endlessly grateful I was reared in the country. As a young girl, I couldn't wait to get off that farm, to go to Hollywood or New York."

By the time she was 10, she was writing her first novel. "The manuscript was written on Blue Horse notebook paper, and was, for good reason, kept hidden from my sister." Her sister found it and discovered the one curse word Jan had, "with pounding heart, included in someone's speech." Her own response was, "For Pete's sake, hadn't Rhett Butler used that very same word and gotten away with it?" However, after her grandmother sternly reproved her, she relented and has "written books without cussin' ever since." Jan Karon's novels are still free of profanity, sex, and violence—part of the reason she sells so well among Evangelical readers.

Jan dropped out of school in the eighth grade. At 16, she gave birth to a girl, Candace, and married the child's father. She was a single mother by the time she was 17 and divorced at 20. Meanwhile, she became a receptionist for an advertising firm in Raleigh, North Carolina. By demonstrating her writing abilities, she quickly rose to a successful career in advertising, eventually winning awards for TV commercials she wrote for agencies in Raleigh, New York, and San Francisco. Karon also shared honors for the prestigious Stephen Kelly Award, given by the Magazine Publishers of America for the best print campaign. She became creative vice-president at McKinney, Silver & Rockett in Raleigh.

> I just write from the heart. I've never thought of myself as a regional writer or a southern writer or a Christian writer. I am a Christian who writes.
>
> —Jan Karon, in advertisement for Washington National Cathedral talk

By the mid-1980s, Karon was a success, with a big house, a Mercedes, and plenty of awards to decorate her office walls. She knew that this was not enough. As she explained to the audience at Washington National Cathedral, "Each of us has been given a gift and when we do not use it we will be filled with despair."

Throughout her life "in the fast lane," Jan Karon retained her appetite for writing, often reading English village novels. At the age of 50, she left the security of advertising, including the good salary, insurance, and retirement, and "stepped out on faith to follow my lifelong dream of being an author." "I made real sacrifices and took big risks. But living, it seems to me, is largely about risk." She wanted to write about a way of life that is "reasonable, moral and strong."

She moved to Blowing Rock, North Carolina, to find her dream. It became the inspiration for Mitford, her fictional hamlet, though she insists that "None of the people in Mitford are actually based upon anyone in Blowing Rock." Even so, the characters are akin to those in small towns in the South and beyond. She notes that the town's quality of life is not just an accident. The various people who inhabit it all contribute in some way to the spirit of benevolence and peace. As she told Betty Carter, who interviewed her for *Christianity Today,* "If you will read a Mitford book carefully, you will see that everybody is helping Mitford happen. Mitford isn't free. You've got to reach out if you want Mitford."

In Blowing Rock, she began with some freelance advertising work while developing the first Mitford novel. For the next two years, Father Tim, his dog, his church and his community entertained North Carolinians by appearing in weekly installments in the *Blowing Rocket,* the local newspaper. Local folks enjoyed the episodes so much that the circulation of the newspaper doubled, and they began plying her with ideas and suggestions for her novels.

No major publisher was interested in her work, but a small Christian company, Lion Publishers in Elgin, Illinois, agreed to publish *At Home in Mitford* in 1994. Karon took on herself the burden of promoting the book, becoming a one-woman sales force, calling bookstores around the country, writing them letters, sending them copies of her book, writing up publicity stories and sending them out to newspapers.

The first three books did sell well in religious book stores. North Carolina booksellers found they sold well in mainstream shops as well. Liz Darhansoff became Karon's agent, and she took the book to Viking Penguin Editor, Carolyn Carlson, a Lutheran minister's daughter. Although Viking was not interested in Christian books, Carlson recognized that small-town people would love the Mitford series. She noted: "We were not buying these books as Christian books. We really responded to her wonderful writing, the characters, the humor, the small-town community feel of the book." Jan Karon became such a success that cynics referred to her as Viking's "cash cow." In addition to this series of seven books, she has written two children's books, a recipe book for those who have hunger pangs from reading about pot luck suppers at Mitford's Lord's Chapel, a book about the cat in the stories, and some Christmas stories. Most of her books are available in a variety of forms, including audio cassettes. The earliest ones have been reissued by Penguin.

Even after she became a favorite writer for millions of people, Karon never has given up on advertising. She says she likes to meet her public, but sometimes finds them overwhelming.

> You need the hurt, and you need the pain to kick your fanny and make you move into the things that are really right for you. In the end, when you're climbing into your casket, you say, "Was that really important?" What is important is that I lived my dream. I did what I was called to do.
>
> —Jan Karon in interview with Gracy Jones

They arrive by the busloads in Blowing Rock, where she used to live right on the road. They have driven her to buy and refurbish an old farmhouse further from the beaten path.

Karon worships at the local American Legion Hall with a small group of Episcopalians who use the 1928 Prayer Book. Her daughter, Candace Freeland, is a photographer, living in Asheville, where her mother also lives. Jan Karon remains proud of her decision to leave her lucrative career in advertising and follow her dream—and discover her vocation.

Major Works and Themes

From the first of the Mitford novels, *At Home in Mitford*, Jan Karon creates a little town that folks "can call their own" in the mountains of North Carolina. The main street, tree-lined and quiet, has some grand old mansions, several shops, grocery stores, and a pair of small restaurants, but no new strip malls or box stores. The well-groomed Lord's Chapel, the small and tastefully decorated Episcopal church is next door to the church office, where we find Father Tim and his bossy secretary. Generous members of the parish have provided a few valuable furnishings, which Father Tim finds more of a nuisance than a delight, including the ancient "death bell" and later a painting. The placid life of Father Tim is interrupted by a giant dog who decides the rectory is his home, a ragged urchin who comes to live with him as a foster son, and a new neighbor who sends rumbles through his chaste bachelor life. At the same time, a mystery lurks in the church attic, eventually disturbing the service and transforming some lives.

Jan Karon displays her talent for humor and for poetry in her introduction of Barnabas, the great dog who responds to Scripture and to Wordsworth. She reveals her humanitarian streak in the portrayal of the young boy, Dooley, whose alcoholic mother has abandoned him and his siblings. We come to meet the rest of his family in this and later novels and follow his life as he matures, becomes a handsome, educated young man, and falls in love. We also meet the new housekeeper and the new neighbor, Cynthia, an author of children's books, who has a cat and pretty legs. The following volumes track the courtship and marriage of Father Tim and Cynthia, their adventures as a couple, and their later challenges with bad health and retirement. The actions are never very violent or shocking, and the characters are largely quixotic or charming. Even comic figures are provided with a history that gives them poignancy. Karon does not condescend or judge people harshly. These are gentle books about—for the most part—gentle people, who display considerable grace in their interactions.

Karon does have some fun with Father Tim's shyness about women and his efforts to withstand the siege of predatory women. She clearly respects his ministry, the gracious way he deals with the old folks in the congregation, finding their romantic histories interesting, discovering their hidden talents, and planning for a nursing home with monies donated by a wealthy congregant. The stories are in the warm and fuzzy Hallmark tradition. In the central love story, it is as if Beatrix Potter fell in love with **C. S. Lewis**—a cozy read. Love but no explicit sex, crime but no blood.

Some of the books appear to have been a response to popular demand: people wanted to know more about the wedding, the life the married couple had together, the years before Mitford when Tim was but a boy in Mississippi. The novels invariably follow the revered tradition of clerical fiction dating back at least to Oliver Goldsmith's *The Vicar of Wakefield*. Many of the characters could just as easily have stepped out of *Cranford*. Karon makes clear to the reader the source of Mitford's peace and joy. Tim explains, citing Oswald Chambers: "and we never dream that all the time God is in the commonplace things and people around us." He also cites Dietrich Bonhoeffer:: "We prevent God from giving us the great spiritual gifts He has in store for us, because we do not give thanks for daily gifts. " Only he who gives thanks for little things receives the big things." Karon dwells on the ineffable holiness of small things. Her language is saturated with poetry, philosophy, and a romanticized religion. Father Tim's sermons speak of friendship, a simple love of God, the acceptance of Christ as savior—but he makes no deep theological claims. He skips the Nicene Creed in favor of an altar call, for all those who want to be anointed. He does demand repentance before forgiveness, but mostly this is a warm and comfortable faith of good friends, loving ways, and thankfulness. The Anglican tradition and the King James translation of the Bible are easy to trace throughout the series.

Good things happen in Father Tim's little town, the people continue to love him, and many of the strands of the plot come together in satisfactory ways in the final stories. Some of the later volumes trace the year that Father Tim and Cynthia spend at Meadowgate Farm, and his assignment to reopen a country chapel. The old chapel turns out to be a treasure, and the people of the congregation, abandoned for 40 years, are eager to return and worship together once again. This novel smacks of the country folk in *Christy*, charming and colorful. A still later prequel takes Father Tim back to the days of his youth in Mississippi, before he became the man he is in all the other tales. Unlike the other novels, *Home to Holly Springs* portrays Timothy as a troubled youth, at war with his father, guilty of fathering a child on a girlfriend, and ashamed of his life. By the conclusion, his later life and ministry redeem the sad mistakes of his youth and allow him to return to his home and discover his roots.

Critical Reception

All of Jan Karon's novels have been popular, especially with women. Malcolm Jones, in *Newsweek*, speaks of her as a "marketing wizard" who is both sincere and slick. Each of the novels has been reviewed, often favorably. Zachary Karabell notes that she is a writer "who reflects contemporary culture more fully than almost any other living novelist." Mary Ellen Quinn (in *Booklist*) notes her "great skill in writing novels that are cozy, comfortable, and folksy but never pious or sentimental." *Christianity Today* finds that she does not "gloss over or trivialize the sorrows of life; it's hard to carry sorrow away from them; the reader feels . . . consoled."

The *Publishers Weekly* review of the most recent of the Father Tim books, *Home to Holy Springs*, notes the importance of setting in the Mitford books. Without the town and its people, the story is less colorful. It is too hard to develop the "quirky locals in Holly Springs" and to bring the narrative to a satisfactory conclusion. The end seems, in fact, "a tad abrupt. Most frustratingly, the central drama of the novel falls flat: Father Tim discovers a long-buried family secret, but he doesn't grapple deeply enough with the emotional consequences of his discovery, nor does Karon fully explore the ways in which the secret plunges us into the Southern quagmire of race. Still, Mitford fans will enjoy this newest visit with wise, winsome, loveable Father Tim." This is a typical review of the novels: they appeal to her fans, who are comfortable with her community and her people.

Awards

At Home in Mitford was named an ABBY Honor Book by the American Booksellers Association in 1996 and won the Logos award. In 2000, Jan Karon was awarded the ECPA Gold Medallion and Christy Award for Best Fiction, for *A New Song*. For her children's story *Jeremy: The Tale of an Honest Bunny*, she won the Parent's Choice Award.

Bibliography of Novels by Author

The Mitford series (New York: Viking, unless otherwise indicated)

At Home in Mitford. New York: Penguin, 1994.
A Light in the Window. New York: Penguin, 1995.
These High, Green Hills. 1996.
A New Song. 1999.
Out to Canaan. 1999.
A Common Life: the Wedding Story. 2001.
In This Mountain. 2002.
Shepherds Abiding, 2003.
Light from Heaven, 2005.
Home to Holly Springs. 2007.

Christmas Gift Books

The Mitford Snowmen. 2001.
Esther's Gift: A Mitford Christmas Story. 2002
Violet Comes to Stay. 2006.

Bibliography of Works about Author

Bookreporter.com http://www.bookreporter.com/authors/au-karon-jan-asp.
Carter, Betty Smart. "Postmarked Mitford: Readers are Finding a Home in Jan Karon's Novels." *Christianity Today* (September 1, 1997): 18.
Crist, Renee. "Jan Karon: The Good Life in Mitford." *Publishers Weekly* (May 26, 1997): 60.
Current Biography. March 2003; http//www.hwwilson.com/currentbio/cover-bios/cover/bio/3/03 htm.
Karabell, Zachary. "Look Homeward Angel: Why The Literati Snub the Christian Fiction of Jan Karon." *Los Angeles Times Book Review* (August 22, 1999): 3–4.
Mitchell, Emily. "The Mitford Years." *People* (December 15, 1997): 31–32.
Mitford Books, official Web site: http://www.mitfordbooks.com/MeetJanKaron.asp.
Quinn, Mary Ellen. Review of *These High, Green Hills. Booklist* (July, 1996): 1802; Review of *Out to Canaan. Booklist* (April 1, 1997): 1286; Review of *A New Song. Booklist* (March 1, 1999): 1103; Review of *A Common Life: The Wedding Story. Booklist* (February 15, 2001): 1084.
Segal, Marta. Review of *Jeremy: The Tale of an Honest Bunny. Booklist* (February 15, 2001): 1542.
Titchener, Louise. Review of *These High Green Hills. Washington Post Bookworld,* November 10, 1996, 10.

KIDD, SUE MONK

Personal, Professional, and Religious Background

Sue Monk Kidd (1948–) was born in Sylvester, Georgia, a tiny town "tucked in the pinelands and red fields of South Georgia." Her family had lived there for at least 200 years, on the same plot of ground where her great-great-grandparents had settled. She describes the orderly world of her youth as "endearing, Mayberryesque." She grew to adolescence in the "cloistered, small-town world of church socials, high school football games, and private 'manners lessons' at her grandmother's." It was this patriarchal Southern Baptist background that she was to challenge in the middle of her life's journey. As a white Southern youngster, she knew a few African Americans, and became aware of the social unrest and racism by 1964, with the voter registration drives, and the "boiling racial tensions."

Although Sue Monk was a talented writer from her youth, she stopped writing by the time she was 16, and focused instead on her chosen career—nursing. She attended a local college and then graduated from Texas Christian University with a degree in nursing in 1970, after which she went on to a career in both nursing and the teaching of nurses.

> I thought I would go on writing only nonfiction the rest of my life. Ah, but never underestimate the power of a dismissed dream.
>
> —Sue Monk Kidd, in interview with Bookbrowse.com

She married Sanford (Sandy) Kidd, a counselor, and had two children, Bob and Ann. It was after her husband began to teach at a small liberal arts college that she began to take writing classes. She began writing nonfiction, and published several hundred articles for *Guideposts Magazine* as well as other magazines and newspapers.

In the meantime, Sue Kidd, dissatisfied with the faith of her childhood, was to undertake an extensive reading program, exploring the classics of Western spirituality as well as depth psychology and mythology. She became enamored of feminist theology, including the writings of Carol Christ, leading Kidd to the writing of her spiritual memoir, *The Dance of the Dissident Daughter*. The success of this memoir, which chronicles her own path from traditional Christianity to a more mythic, feminist thought, led her to continue writing spiritual memoirs.

Kidd also decided to begin studying the techniques of fiction writing, enrolling in a course at Emory University and then doing further work at Breadloaf and at Sewanee Writers Conference. Gradually, she moved from short stories to full-length fiction, completing her first novel, *The Secret Life of Bees*, in 2002 and her second three years later. She has also republished some of her earlier religious memoirs in recent years.

The Kidds, including their black lab, Lily, live "beside a salt marsh near Charleston, South Carolina."

Major Works and Themes

Sue Monk Kidd's forays into fiction writing began with short stories, including a short story she wrote in 1993 about the bees that lived inside the walls of the family guest room in her homestead in Georgia. Sometimes, her mother would find pools of honey on the floor of the room. When invited some years later to read her fiction at the National Arts Club in New York, she dug out this short story, which seemed to merit expansion. Over the next three years, Kidd studied bee legend and imagery, worked on the design of the house in which the bees lived, and contemplated the idea of the Virgin Mary as "the queen bee."

Kidd used this first novel to bring together a number of her own ideas on race relations, feminist theology, community, forgiveness, and self-knowledge. As she says, her ideas on religion are very "eclectic." She was to use the concept of the Black Madonna in her portrayal of three black Boatwright sisters who form a community of refuge for the young woman who has escaped an abusive father and a stifling, guilt-ridden life.

Her second novel, *The Mermaid Chair*, also draws on images of the Great Mother, the essential feminine power at work in the universe. This time, the Mermaid Chair, an artifact imported from a Benedictine monastery in England, plays a central role in the life of the monks and the middle-aged woman who comes seeking self-discovery and forgiveness. The imaginative use of the mermaid imagery in the death of the father and in the life of the women is poetic and powerful. This time, the escape from conformity involves a controlling husband who loves

Jessie, the protagonist, and a mad mother, who blames her daughter for the death of her father. The mother's horrifying self-mutilation, as she cuts off a finger, and the search for meaning in this act of contrition form the core of the story. The wife/daughter also seeks to find her own spiritual renewal and become a true artist, liberated sexually, religiously, and creatively. In this quest, Brother Thomas, a Benedictine monk who is in charge of the rookery, joins her—finding his own path along the way. The community of women this time, the mother, the daughter, a white friend, and a wise old African American woman, comfort and heal one another, laughing, eating, singing, dancing on the beach in a kind of sacred ceremony of feminist harmony.

Kidd's early interest in Thoreau is obvious in her close observations of nature—especially the habits of the bees and the birds. She also reveals a continuing interest in feminist writers, such as Kate Chopin, with her water imagery, and **Margaret Atwood,** with her diving deep as an image of self-discovery. The difference between Kidd and many other feminist writers is her delight in contemplative philosophers, such as Thomas Merton, and her strong sense of the sacred. She also finds a means to become reconciled to men, though rejecting their efforts to control or confine women's lives and spirits.

Critical Reception

The reviewers have loved Kidd's nonfiction and fiction both. *The New York Times*, *Publishers Weekly*, *Library Journal*, and many others have praised her beautiful metaphors, her realistic characters, and her moving scenes. She is a powerful and poetic writer, full of allusions to a vast body of myth and literature, interesting to study and to discuss. Her novels have become part of literature courses in recent years, considered classics of modern literature.

Awards

Sue Monk Kidd has won numerous fellowships and awards for both fiction and nonfiction. Among her fiction awards are: Book of the Year Award, Southeast Booksellers Association, 2003, the Literature to Life award, American Place Theatre, 2004 (for *The Secret Life of Bees*); Quill Award for general fiction, 2005, for *The Mermaid Chair.*

Bibliography of Novels by Author

The Secret Life of Bees. New York: Viking, 2002.
The Mermaid Chair. New York: Viking, 2005.
Kidd's novels have also been adapted for stage and for television.

Bibliography of Works about Author

Dyer, Lucinda. "Sue Monk Kidd: *The Secret Life of Bees*," *Publishers Weekly* (August 6, 2001): 49.
Huntley, Kristine. Review of *The Secret Life of Bees*. *Booklist* (December 1, 2001): 628.
Huntley, Kristine. Review of *The Mermaid Chair*. *Booklist* (February 15, 2005): 1036.
Kennedy, Dana. Review of *The Mermaid Chair*. *New York Times Book Review*, May 22, 2005, 24.
Kidd, Sue Monk. *The Dance of the Dissident Daughter: A Journey from the Christian Tradition to the Sacred Feminine*. San Francisco, CA: Harper San Francisco, 1996.
"Sue Monk Kidd." *Contemporary Authors Online*. Detroit: Thomson Gale, 2006.
Sue Monk Kidd Homepage. http://www.suemonkkidd.com.
Sue Monk Kidd Interview. http://www.bookbrowse.com/author_interviews/ full/indes.cfm/author_number=820.

KINGSBURY, KAREN

Personal, Professional, and Religious Background

Karen Kingsbury (1964–) was born in Fairfax, Virginia. Her father, Theodore Kingsbury, was a computer program analyst. Her mother, Anne Kingsbury, taught her to save herself for her husband. Her father encouraged her writing, telling her, "Keep writing, Karen . . . you're a wonderful, gifted writer, and one day the whole world will know about your ability to tell a story."

Determined to write fiction, but realizing that she would need to earn a living, she studied journalism at California State University, Northridge, earning a B.A. in 1986. Her first full-time newspaper job was as an intern at *Simi Valley Enterprise*, where she covered sports, religion, and news. She then took a job as a news writer for the *Los Angeles Daily News*, where she covered sports, writing stories about professional sports teams, including the Dodgers, Lakers, and Raiders. Later, she worked for the *Los Angeles Times* as a news writer. She was good at interviews and sometimes found herself interviewing naked players in locker rooms. She had to learn about sports and to learn fast to be effective. "I was never a walking encyclopedia of sports trivia, but I learned how to write about football, baseball, basketball, volleyball, and several other sports." Her favorite interview was the one she did with Magic Johnson.

She often covered crime stories as well, finding that she could describe the crime so vividly that she became a feature writer, earning a place on the front page and selling an article to *People* magazine. Her journalistic writing taught her how to organize a story, research details of background, and start strong and end strong.

Although Karen Kingsbury was raised in the Roman Catholic church, she became an evangelical in her 20s, after she met the man she was to love ever after. In 1988, she married Donald, a teacher and coach. Karen Kingsbury and her husband have six children, one girl and five boys; three of them were adopted from Haiti.

After marriage, Kingsbury knew she wanted something different, a job where she could work from home. She found that in writing novels. Using the skills and bits of the stories she had already developed, she began writing true crime stories, four of which were published by Dell between 1992 and 1995. Her first, *Missy's Murder*, is the story of a 17-year-old girl who was tortured and drowned by two of her "friends." She also began to collect stories of miracles, which were eventually published by Warner Faith Books in New York under her pseudonym, "Kelsey Tyler."

Major Works and Themes

Karen Kingsbury knows all about standard romance novels, known as "bodice rippers." She prefers bodice lacers. Her heroines are passionate but chaste. In her stories, there is no gratuitous violence or swearing. Although her characters are sorely tempted, sex usually follows marriage. When sexual passion drives people to premarital affairs, they suffer with unwanted pregnancies and a life of regret.

She has written about 30 novels, many of them on the Christian best-seller list.

With millions of books in print, she has been called the "Nora Roberts of the religious set." Because of this popularity, the Time Warner Book Group (a division of Time Inc.) signed her on to target "America's heartland" with wholesome books. She sees clearly her own ties to secular writers, acknowledging she had once dreamed of being as popular as Danielle Steele. For her, Christian fiction is "fiction plus. Mainstream writers can write a story involving the physical, intellectual, and emotional. I can do all that and also add the spiritual." The result is a much deeper story, involving the whole person.

Karen Kingsbury has used her well-honed journalistic skills to tell stories about God's work, beginning with a semiautobiographical book called *Where Yesterday Lives*. Although the manuscript won praise, her publishers were not interested in a story with a forthright Christian message that had little sex or strong language. The story tells of Ellen Barrett, a Florida reporter, whose father dies and whose husband declines to accompany her to the funeral in Michigan. Kingsbury writes in hopes of bringing change to the lives of her readers. Even when she writes for a mainstream publisher, reducing the scriptural references, as in *A Thousand Tomorrows*, she points the way toward biblical meanings. For her, the love story is a parable for non-Christians that illustrate the truths of I Corinthians 13.

Some of her stories have attracted a much wider audience, finding their way into television and film scripts written by others, like *Dandelion Dust*, which was picked up by Fox, and *Gideon's Gift*, which is planned for release in 2008. *Moment of Weakness* is being made into a Hallmark film, and *A Thousand Tomorrows* and *Even Now* are in the process of becoming films. One of her own songs, "Miracles Happen," is to be used for the soundtrack of *Gideon's Gift*.

Kingsbury writes very quickly, sometimes finishing a novel in a few weeks. She believes that the speed of her composition allows her to keep the continuity, intensity, and power of the writing. "But always I know that my story ideas come from God. As I write, I feel as if I'm reading. When I'm finished, I am in awe at the way it all comes together so quickly." She writes in a small room off her and her husband's bedroom. "It's almost entirely windows, lined with pine, and filled with a single leather loveseat. I face the windows, throw them wide open, and the stories come."

Critical Reception

John Mort, the critic for *Booklist*, thought Karen Kingsbury's first Christian novel, based on her own experience, included "some excellent newsroom scenes." *Where Yesterday Lives* describes a troubled marriage and the professional life of a young wife. In his much fuller listing of Christian novels, Mort notes another of Kingsbury's novels, *A Time to Dance*, as being especially realistic. The story again is a morality tale of a troubled marriage, this time drawing on her husband's background in sports. Abby and John Reynolds, who seem like a model couple, live in a small Illinois town where he is the school football coach. In this tale, it is the husband who is obsessed with work and the wife who feels neglected.

John Mort's critiques of *A Moment of Weakness* and *When Joy Came to Stay*, both published in 2000, are less complimentary. Both deal with sex before marriage and the problems that follow. Mort considers both of these novels evangelical melodramas.

Melanie C. Duncan, in *Library Journal*, praises *When Joy Came to Stay*, for providing insight into depression and pointing out the general intolerance for mental illness. Others also complimented Kingsbury for her courage in facing topics usually absent from Christian fiction. *A Time to Embrace*, for example, reveals the problems of high school life.

Gideon's Gift, one of her favorites, has been called a "feel-good winner." It combines a faithless, homeless man and a child who is suffering from leukemia, who offers him friendship. The miracle at the center of the story affects both of these people in a touching Christmas story.

Kingsbury's imagination, her clear knowledge of contemporary life, and her facility with words make her a strong talent, with cross-over capabilities for reaching out to a wider audience than most evangelical novelists.

Awards

Redemption was named Best Book of the Year in 2003 by Logos Retailers. In 2007, *Ever After* won the Book of the Year Award from ECPA.

Bibliography of Novels by Author

"Forever Faithful" series (Sisters, OR: Multnomah, 1999–2002)

"Women of Faith" series (Nashville, TN: WestBow Press, 2001–2002)

"Redemption" series (Wheaton, IL: Tyndale House Publishers, 2002–2004)

"Red Gloves" books (TN: FaithWords, 2002–2005)

"September 11th" series (Grand Rapids, MI: Zondervan, 2003–2005)

"Firstborn" series (Wheaton, IL: Tyndale House, 2005–2007)

"Lost Love" series (Grand Rapids, MI: Zondervan, 2005–2007)

"Cody Gunner" series (Grand Rapids, MI: Zondervan, 2005–2007)

"Sunrise" series (Wheaton, IL: Tyndale House Publishers, 2007–2008)

Where Yesterday Lives, 1998.
When Joy Came to Stay, 2000.
On Every Side, 2001.
Oceans Apart, 2004.
Divine. Wheaton: Tyndale House Publishers, 2006.
Like Dandelion Dust. New York: Center Street, 2006.
Between Sundays. Grand Rapids: Zondervan, 2007.

Bibliography of Works about Author

Darlington, C.J. Karen Kingsbury Interview. http://www.filetrakk.com/karen_kingsbury_interview.html.
Duncan, Melanie C. Review of *When Joy Came to Stay*. *Library Journal* (November 1, 2000): 60.
Faithful Reader interview. http://www.faithfulreader.com/author/au_kingsbury_karen.asp.
"Karen Kingsbury." *Contemporary Authors Online*. Detroit: Thompson Gale, 2004.
Karen Kingsbury homepage: http://www.karenkingsbury.com.
Mort, John. Review of *Where Yesterday Lives*, *Booklist* (October 1, 1998): 294.
Mort, John. *Christian Fiction: A Guide to the Genre*. Greenwood Village, CO: Libraries Unlimited, 2002.
Orecklin, Michele. "That Other Passion: The Queen of Christian Romance Tries to Cross Over," *Time Magazine*, March 14, 2005.

KINKADE, THOMAS (AND KATHERINE SPENCER)

Personal, Professional, and Religious Background

Thomas Kinkade (1958–) was born in Sacramento, California. His mother, Marianne, was a hard-working secretary who raised her three children alone. His father walked out on the family when Thomas was 5, leaving the boy filled with anger and frustration at the world. "I had a chip on my shoulder. I was in the stinky small town, and I wanted so badly to be raised in New York, where the museums were." Kinkade refers to the "darkness" in his heart during his childhood, his embarrassment at his shabby home and the absence of his father. He found most of his comfort in his youth through the humor of his brother and sister, the discovery of God's love, and in his drawing and painting.

Thomas Kinkade attended the University of California for a while, then dropped out and "bummed around the country." He also studied at the Art Center College of Design. He was a background painter for animated films for a time, then founded Lightpost Publishing, which is now part of Media Arts Group, Inc. Starting his career by peddling his paintings out of the trunk of his car, he eventually became famous as the "Painter of Light," one who produces dark, idyllic scenes of houses he dreamed of as a child, lovely stone homes that have a particular luminous glow from lamps, and bucolic scenes with other light sources, such as lighthouses, campfires, or sunsets. He has perfected a technique for mass-manufacturing these "originals" with the help of computers and a host of hired technicians who touch up the prints on canvas. The play of light in darkness is central to his style. He says that this gift of light, which distinguishes his paintings, is a gift from God. He believes that God "became my art agent. He basically gave me ideas"—including the way to produce multiple originals that did not look like posters.

He is married to his childhood sweetheart, Nanette. They have four daughters—Merritt, Chandler, Windsor, and Everett—all of whom were homeschooled. Kinkade and his wife co-authored some books, largely about joy—*A Book of Joy, Joy of Fatherhood*—and others about the blessings of the simple life. He has also illustrated a large number of books. His designs appear on everything from Bible covers and T-shirts to cookie jars. He has a string of walk-in galleries and a home-shopping network for his products. Even a 101-home "Kinkade Village" was built in Vallejo, California.

As a born-again Christian, Kinkade eagerly discusses his faith and his calling. He believes that his religion is the impetus for his art and his life. He is a garrulous person, a frequent speaker at meetings. He has a passionate following—the "cult of Kinkade," although he lives in a gated community and has no TV connection in his house.

> "Cape Light," is a place where people have the time to savor life's simple pleasures. Where they have learned to find joy in the simple—but extraordinary—blessings of everyday life.
>
> —Thomas Kinkade, quoted by Laura Miller

Major Works and Themes

Primarily an artist, enormously popular for his paintings of idyllic American scenes, Thomas Kinkade has also authored a number of books, and coauthored many others, primarily with his wife or with Elizabeth Spencer.

Inspired by the homey atmosphere of Kinkade's painting, Spencer has shaped a series of novels around "a place of refuge." Spencer, his coauthor in the "Cape Light" series of novels is an editor who had written some 20 books for children and adults. She has continued to write such novels as *Sicilian Millionaire, Bought Bride, His Child,* and *The Man from Tuscany.* Since she and Kinkade have joined forces, they have produced at least a novel a year, with Spencer providing most of the writing and Kinkade doing the cover art and introduction. Katherine Spencer lives with her husband and daughter in a small village on Long Island Sound, much like Cape Light.

Cape Light is a Massachusetts waterfront town, located an hour's drive north of Boston where "on Main Street, the storefronts and restaurants look much the same as they always have." In the town, we find Lucy Bates at the Clam Box, Digger Hegman, the old fisherman at the shore mending nets, and Pastor Ben at the local church. This small town is much like the ones we find in other Christian romances, full of friendly people, wild young folks, cranky old timers, troubled families, and good pastors. The people attend church, listen attentively to the pastor's sermon, gather for family dinners afterwards, and worry mostly about day-to-day concerns like raising children, facing sickness or death. They usually live "deep, satisfying lives" in this simple place.

The plot often has numerous flash-backs to explain the characters' peculiarities and to suggest that the problems of this generation are little different from those faced by their parents and grandparents. The good heroes and heroines are sometimes wealthy, but not snobbish; they are friendly with the blue-collar workers in the town. Many of the novels focus on the Christmas season as a time of reconciliation and camaraderie. By the end of the story, we can count on the good folks being rewarded, the predestined lovers finally coming together in marriage, and the family uniting in front of a Christmas tree or at the table full of food and fellowship—the classic ending of the comedy.

Critical Reception

Kinkade's and Spencer's little New England town is a northern version of Karon's Mitford, with a parallel set of characters, but without Karon's flashes of poetry, or the delightful whimsy of Father Tim and his Bible-loving dog. It has the marks of a Norman Rockwell painting, an acknowledged influence on Kinkade. It is a "simple" place, At least one critic, Laura Miller, thinks Kinkade has a "crutchlike overreliance on the word 'simple.'"

Readers love Thomas Kinkade/Elizabeth Spencer novels, but critics despair of their "treacle" quality, or "mechanized saccharine." *Publishers Weekly* considers the first book in the "Cape Light" series to be a "sugarcoated modern fairy tale." As the series continues with many of the same characters, the reality tends to increase, with serious problems within marriages, women juggling multiple roles as they study or work to better themselves. Misunderstandings and temptations produce stress between couples. Although some critics consider the work "simplistic" with a good deal of "Protestant proselytizing," they note that the characters are frequently engaging and well drawn.

It is no surprise that Kinkade's little world in his novels, as in his home products, bears "the Thomas Kinkade lifestyle brand." The "Cape Light" stories are predictable, but comforting: the young people with troubled backgrounds find hope, love, and peace in the friendly embrace of small-town America. Kinkade has made special use of Christmas with his novels, which often are turned into Hallmark-style feel-good films. The most commonly used word among critics is "kitsch," but the low-brow readers continue to enjoy the homey pleasure of reading a Kinkade/Spencer novel. They linger over the cover design and enjoy the predictable plot.

Awards

Most of Thomas Kinkade's awards are for his painting rather than for his writing: The National Association of Limited Edition Dealers has named him Artist of the Year (1994), Graphic Artist of the Year (1995–1998), celebrated his work for Lithograph of the Year (1996), and Print of the Year (1997–1998). He was the charter inductee for Collector Editions Award of Excellence, the Bradford International Hall of Fame, and in 1999 was inducted into the U.S. Art Hall of Fame.

Bibliography of Novels by Author

"Cape Light" series (with Katherine Spencer, published by Bantam Books).

Cape Light. 2002.
Home Song. 2002.
The Gathering Place. 2003.
A Christmas Promise. 2004.
A New Leaf. 2004.
The Christmas Angel. 2005.
A Christmas to Remember. 2006.
A Christmas Star. 2008.
A Christmas Visitor. 2008.

Bibliography of Works about Author

Cray, Dan. "Art of Selling Kitsch," *Time,* August 20, 1999, 62.
Della, Cava, Marco R. "Thomas Kinkade: Profit of Light," *USA Today.* http://www.usatoday.com/life/2002/2002-03-112-kinkade.htm.
Doherty, M. Stephen. "Thomas Kinkade Shares His Light," *American Artist* (October, 2001): 20.
"Katherine Spencer," *Contemporary Authors Online.* Detroit: Thomson Gale, 2008.
Miller, Laura. "The Writer of Dreck," *Salon.com.* http://dir.salon.com/story/books/feature/2002/03/18/light.
Persaud, Babita. "A Light for All to See," *St. Petersburg Times,* March 8, 2001, 36W.
Review of *Cape Light. Publishers Weekly* (February 25, 2002): 41.
Teller, Jean. "World of Cape Light a Delight to Visit," *Grit* (December, 2004): 6.
"Thomas Kinkade," *Contemporary Authors Online.* Detroit: Thomson Gale, 2002.

KOONTZ, DEAN

Personal, Professional, and Religious Background

Dean Ray Koontz (1945–) was born in Everett, Pennsylvania. His mother was Florence Koontz and his father, Ray Koontz, was an abusive alcoholic. He grew up in a poor family—a background that has led him to great sympathy with children in such families and with working-class people. While attending Shippensburg State College, Dean Koontz converted to Roman Catholicism. After graduation, Koontz worked as a teacher-counselor with the

Appalachian Poverty Program and then as a high school English teacher in Mechanicsburg, Pennsylvania, where during his spare time he began writing *Star Quest*, which he published in 1968. Since 1969, he has been a full-time writer.

Dean Koontz married Gerda Ann Cera in 1966. They live in Newport Beach, California, where most of his novels are set. The pictures of the handsome young writer have varied over the years, for a time revealing a balding man with a beard, then a younger looking fellow with a full head of hair, without a beard. He told those who questioned him about his hair transplant that he was tired of looking like G. Gordon Liddy. In many of his biographical summaries, his golden retriever Trixie is mentioned as a third member of the household. With her death, he immortalized her with the story *The Darkest Evening of the Year*, in which a golden retriever becomes the hero—an angel in canine disguise.

> I am no Pollyanna, by any means, but I think we live in a time of marvels, not a time of disaster, and I believe we can solve every problem that confronts us if we keep our perspective and our freedom. Very little if any great and long-lasting fiction has been misanthropic.
>
> —Dean Koontz, quoted in *Contemporary Authors Online*

Major Works and Themes

Dean Koontz has written many of his novels under various pen names, largely because editors advised him that his shifts among different genres created "negative crossover" reactions among his audiences. Among his known pseudonyms are: Deanna Dwyer, K. R. Dwyer, Aaron Wolfe, David Axton, Brian Coffey, John Hill, Leigh Nichols, Owen West, Richard Paige, Leonard Chris, and Anthony North. Koontz was to use a parallel name-change technique in his novels, allowing his characters to hide their identity and shift their lifestyles by a change in their names.

Dean Koontz is a remarkable writer who can bring religion into his stories by nuance or by rich exploration of theological questions. He writes romances, thrillers, fantasy, science fiction, and horror stories with imagination and style. Koontz began as a science fiction writer, branching out into suspense novels, and then found he could write interesting blends of genres. *Brother Odd*, for example, is a futuristic gothic tale using science fiction monsters in a curious blend of *Frankenstein*, *Dr. Jekyll and Mr. Hyde*, and *The Name of the Rose*. He has read widely, alluding in his novels to Odysseus, Dante, and Superman in a crazy-quilt blend of ideas. In the "Odd Thomas" stories, the spirit of Elvis Presley and a ghost dog accompany the hero on his adventures, providing both guidance and comic relief.

Trixie Koontz, the golden retriever in the household, is credited with coauthorship of two of his novels and becomes the heroine of the third. She was a service dog in her earlier career, coming to the Koontz family at age 3, changing "careers" because of an elbow problem that forced her "retirement" from Canine Companions for Independence. Trixie Koontz's writing career began in 2004 with *Life Is Good: Lessons in Joyful Living*, followed by *Christmas Is Good*—both books published by Yorkville Press, with all the royalties donated to the charitable organization for guide dogs.

> Dean Koontz was so fond of his dog, Trixie, that he made her immortal by writing a novel in which a golden retriever is an angel in disguise. Trixie Koontz is also credited as coauthor of two of his novels.

Koontz's central characters are usually working-class people—bakers, builders, gardeners, or even clowns. The villains are more likely to be highly educated, materialistic, and evil. They know how to manipulate data on the Internet, wire bombs, and eavesdrop on their targets. They torture their children (*The Darkest Evening*) or raise them without love (*The Husband*), and they have ice cubes where humans might have hearts or conscience. The good guys are classics of bright, decent folks with damaged childhoods or broken marriages that they have overcome through good works and perseverance. The bad guys and gals often come from the same background—as the sinister brother in *The Husband*—but choose to use their experience for evil. Koontz uses psychology as well as parapsychology in his characterizations, considering the abuses of Skinner-type child-raising practices or the Ayn Rand objectivist view of self-fulfillment as well as the possibilities of psychic magnetism, reading of entrails, correspondence with the near-dead, and miraculous abilities of various sorts. As a result, his stories often turn quickly, reversing the apparently realistic plot line with a miraculous intervention, even the resurrection of the dead. In his mysteries, characters can sometimes intuit the evil nature of the real villain or his location. His villains are so obviously evil as to become comic-strip characters in some cases, but are always colorful and invariably annihilated by the protagonist.

His setting, usually California and contemporary, is a reinforcement of his themes: evil people tend to prefer wastelands (deserts), live in sterile quarters, move frequently, and enjoy luxurious surroundings. His decent folk are happy in cottages with gardens and dogs, and enjoy snacks in the kitchen with family and friends. They love to walk in the park, run along the sea shore, and plant flowers to provide color for the neighborhood.

Dean Koontz brings his Catholic worldview to his novels as well as to many of his characters. He sets *Brother Odd* in a monastery, with nicely characterized nuns and priests central to the narrative. The gentle heroine of *The Darkest Evening of the Year*, which features the angel golden retriever, was raised by loving nuns, providing her with a core of beliefs in spite of her fractured life. Koontz's conservative critiques include his deeply felt respect for human life—as well as all of God's creation. He has a heart for abused children, especially those who are mentally challenged. Unlike many of the evangelical writers, he rarely includes prayer, Bible-reading, or church attendance in his stories, allowing the religious themes to emerge through a bit of Scripture or a discovery of truth.

Although most of his dialogue is modern and popular, using imagery from films, he sometimes creates beautiful lyrical passages to emphasize the transcendent message of his tales. At times, he echoes Dante, at others Kurt Vonnegut. His overreliance on imagery from contemporary films may date his novels for future readers, but allusions to classics of world literature will ensure that most conservative audiences will continue to enjoy them for years to come.

Critical Reception

Dean Koontz is one of America's foremost, most prolific, and most popular modern writers, the master of a variety of genres, appearing regularly on the *New York Times* best-seller list. His first success was *Whispers*, a horror story praised by Michael A. Morrison but not by a *Publishers Weekly's* reviewer, who thought readers would need strong stomachs to handle the novel. Morrison judged his monster-character "one of the most original psychological aberrations in horror fiction," while more traditional critics worried about the "overheated scenes of rape and mayhem." Rex E. Klett also worried about Koontz's theology, noting that he was "dangerously close to ruinous occultism."

The more elite press, particularly the *New York Times* and *Salon*, while acknowledging his skill, complained about his audience and his approach. Janet Maslin noted that his heroes are "humble four-square" guys, "clean-cut, virginal" young fellows "who resemble a California surfer from the Eisenhower years;" and his heroines are too "cute," by far. His books "are devout, inspirational and warmly celebratory of the family." While he avoids "profanity and gently satirizes the debased state of popular culture," she notes, he "is definitely a red state kind of guy." She compares him to "treaclemeister **Thomas Kinkade,**" while noting that he is a skilful storyteller who is good at domestic scenes. She complains that he plays tricks on the reader, pretending to present an event that he later clarifies and reverses, jolting his audience with exaggerations and false alarms. Her major complaint is that he peppers his thrillers with sermons against cloning, genetic engineering, puppy-mills, child abuse, stem cell research, Harry Potter, and artists like Christo, while "cashing in on the very sinfulness he decries." His stories are lurid studies in abnormal psychology, with villains eager for mayhem—arson, murder, mutilation, castration, and rape. The atmosphere he creates is that "of an endless video game" where every twist or turn leads to another chase or confrontation, the door to a fresh nightmare.

These were to prove continuing charges and counter-charges by the critics: On the one hand, Koontz has proven himself to be a master of plot, style, and suspense, with characters who are individualized and interesting, often chilling in their revelations. On the other hand, the people in his stories (Brother Odd, for example) do have psychic powers. Although they often use them for good purposes, their dealings with the dead and their faith in their own psychic magnetism and other powers create a problem for some Christian readers. The graphic violence is also disturbing to many accustomed to more gentle reads.

Awards

Dean Koontz won the *Atlantic Monthly* college creative writing award in 1966 for his story "The Kittens." He has been nominated for various other awards, including the World Science Fiction Convention award in 1971 and the Bram Stoker Award. In 1989, his alma mater, Shippensburg State College awarded him an honorary doctorate.

Bibliography of Novels by Author

Star Quest. New York: Ace Books, 1968.
The Fall of the Dream Machine. New York: Ace Books, 1969.
Fear That Man. New York: Ace Books, 1969.
Anti-Man. New York: Paperback Library, 1970.
Beastchild. New York: Lancer Books, 1970.
Dark of the Woods. New York: Ace Books, 1970.
The Dark Symphony. New York: Lancer Books, 1970.
Hell's Gate. New York: Lancer Books, 1970.
The Crimson Witch. New York: Curtis Books, 1971.
A Darkness in My Soul. New York: DAW Books, 1972.
The Flesh in the Furnace. New York: Bantam, 1972.
Starblood. New York: Lancer Books, 1972.
Time Thieves. New York: Ace Books, 1972.
Warlock. New York: Lancer Books, 1972.
Demon Seed. New York: Bantam, 1973

Hanging On. New York.: M. Evans, 1973.
The Haunted Earth. New York: Lancer Books, 1973.
A Werewolf among Us. New York: Ballantine, 1973.
After the Last Race. New York: Athenaeum, 1974.
Nightmare Journey. New York: Putnam, 1975.
Night Chills. New York: Athenaeum, 1976.
The Vision. New York: Putnam, 1977.
Whispers. New York: Putnam, 1980.
Phantoms. New York: Putnam, 1983.
Darkfall. New York: Berkley, 1984 (also published as *Darkness Comes*).
Twilight Eyes. Westland, MI: Land of Enchantment, 1985.
Strangers. New York: Putnam, 1986.
Watchers. New York: Putnam, 1987.
Lightning. New York: Putnam, 1988.
Midnight. New York: Putnam, 1989.
The Bad Place. New York: Putnam, 1990.
Dragon Tears. New York: Berkley, 1992.
Hideaway. New York: Putnam, 1992.
Mr. Murder. New York: Putnam, 1993.
Winter Moon. New York: Ballantine, 1993.
Dark Rivers of the Heart. New York: Knopf, 1994.
Intensity. New York: Knopf, 1995.
Strange Highways. New York: Warner Books, 1995.
TickTock. New York: Ballantine, 1996.
Santa's Twin. New York: HarperPrism, 1996.
Sole Survivor: A Novel. New York: Ballantine, 1997.
Fear Nothing. New York: Bantam, 1998.
Seize the Night. New York: Bantam Doubleday Dell, 1999.
False Memory. New York: Bantam, 2000.
From the Corner of His Eye. New York: Bantam, 2000.
One Door Away from Heaven. New York: Bantam, 2002.
By the Light of the Moon. New York: Bantam, 2003.
The Face. New York: Bantam, 2003.
Odd Thomas. New York: Bantam, 2004.
Robot Santa: The Further Adventures of Santa's Twin. New York HarperCollins, 2004.
The Taking. New York: Bantam, 2004.
Forever Odd. New York: Bantam, 2005.
Velocity. New York: Bantam Books, 2005.
Brother Odd. New York: Bantam Books, 2006.
The Husband. New York: Bantam Books, 2006.
The Darkest Evening of the Year. New York: Bantam Books, 2007.
The Good Guy. New York: Bantam Books, 2007.

Dean Koontz has also coauthored books, including some with his wife, written an e-book, and written under numerous pseudonyms, including Brian Coffey, Deanna Dwyer, K. R. Dwyer, Leigh Nichols, and Owen West. In addition Dean Koontz has edited a number of works, contributed to books edited by others, and had several of his works filmed—including *Demon Seed, Shattered, Watchers, Hideaway,* and *Mr. Murder.*

Bibliography of Works about Author

"Dean Koontz," *Contemporary Authors Online.* Detroit: Thomson Gale, 2008.
"Dean Koontz," Wikipedia. http://en.wikipedia.org/wiki/Dean_Koontz.

Klett, Rex E. Review of *Whispers*. *Library Journal* (May 15, 1980): 1187.

Kotker, Joan G. *Dean Koontz: A Critical Companion*. Westport, CT: Greenwood Press, 1996.

Lemke, Steve W. "Supernatural Evil and Good in the Novels of Dean Koontz: Toward a Theology of Hope," Art, Literature, and Religion Section of the Southwest Regional Meeting of the American Academy of Religion. http://www.nobts.edu/Faculty/ItoR/LemkeSW/Personal/Koontz.html.

Maslin, Janet. "One Man's 5 Dates with Fate, Scheduled at Birth." Review of *Life Expectancy, New York Times*, December 6, 2004); "Receiving Moral Instruction, Courtesy of a Serial Killer," Review of *Velocity, New York Times*, May 23, 2005; "Odd Again, on Armageddon's Highway," Review of *Forever Odd. New York Times*, December 12, 2005; "Not Just Man's Best Friend but God's Best Ally," Review of *The Darkest Evening of the* Year, *New York Times*, November 22, 2007.

Morrison, Michael A. Essay in *Sudden Fear: The Horror and Dark Suspense Fiction of Dean R. Koontz*, Bill Munster, ed. Mercer Island, WA: Starmont House, 1988.

Publishers Weekly, Review of *Whispers* (April 4, 1980): 61.

Ramsland, Katherine M. *Dean Koontz: A Writer's Biography*. New York: HarperPrism, 1997.

L

LAHAYE, TIM

Personal, Professional, and Religious Background

Tim LaHaye (1926–) was born in Detroit, Michigan, the son of Francis T. LaHaye and Margaret Palmer LaHaye. His father was an electrician and his mother a fellowship director. From 1944–1947, during the final years of World War II and afterwards, Tim LaHaye was in the U.S. Army Air Force, attaining the rank of sergeant. In 1947, he married Beverly Jean Ratcliffe, a writer and lecturer, with whom he was to coauthor a number of books and provide a radio and television ministry. They have four children and nine grandchildren.

Tim LaHaye attended Bob Jones University, earning his B.A. in 1950, and then Western Conservative Baptist Seminary, where he earned a Doctorate in Ministry in 1977. At the same time he was taking classes, he served as pastor of Baptist churches in Pickens, South Carolina, (1948–1950) and in Minneapolis, Minnesota, (1950–56). He became the senior pastor of the Scott Memorial Baptist Church, El Cajon, California, in 1956 and remained there for 25 years. During that time, the church grew exponentially, to three locations in the San Diego region. LaHaye became an active writer on biblical themes, Christian living, and social issues about which he was growing increasingly concerned. The LaHayes hosted a television program, "La-Hayes on Family Life," and wrote a number of books counseling Christian couples on their marriages They have also lectured for Family Life Seminars since 1972. Tim LaHaye is the founder and president of FamilyLife Seminars.

> The "Left Behind" books by Tim LaHaye and Jerry Jenkins are the best-selling Christian series in history.

Tim LaHaye was an evangelical pastor from the beginning and became aware of the transformed worldview so eloquently described by Francis Schaeffer in his books. The LaHayes attacked humanism as an anti-Christian force undermining traditional family values, in such best-sellers as *Spirit-Controlled Temperament*. Realizing the importance of education, Tim LaHaye worked to establish a private school system that reflected his faith, resulting in the establishment of two accredited Christian high schools, a Christian school system of 10 schools, and Christian Heritage College. He has written over 40 books, with over 11 million copies in print in 32 languages.

LaHaye was also alarmed at the worldwide organizations such as the United Nations and the World Council of Churches, which he saw as structures that would eventually be used for evil purposes. During the 1980s, both LaHayes became part of the Moral Majority, along with Jerry Falwell and others. Beverly LaHaye also became politically active, joining with **Terri Blackstock** and other women to form the Concerned Christian Women of America to fight the rising tide of feminism, abortion, and promiscuity. These two women collaborated on a series of popular novels that gave life to their ideas, the "Seasons Under Heaven" novels (beginning in 1999) and the "Seasons of Blessing" stories (2002).

As a dispensational premillenialist, one who believes in a literal interpretation of the biblical prophesies of the Last Days, Tim LaHaye writes books on prophesy and has founded a prophesy institute, The PreTrib Research Center. He speaks at major Bible prophesy conferences in the U.S. and Canada, seeking to send an alarm to his fellow believers about the times he sees ahead. He finally approached the accomplished writer **Jerry Jenkins,** presenting him the set of his ideas developed in his search of the apocalyptic books of Scripture. The two authors are collaborating in developing a dozen books known as the "Left Behind" series, as well as simplified versions of these books for children.

The LaHayes live in southern California, where they continue their ministry of writing and speaking.

Major Works and Themes

The major fictional works of Tim LaHaye and Jerry Jenkins are the dozen "Left Behind" books—the best-selling Christian series in history. (These are listed and discussed under the Jenkins entry.) These apocalyptic thrillers are based on LaHaye's premillennial dispensational faith—the belief in a Rapture event separate from and prior to the Second Coming of Christ. This belief is held by a number of evangelicals and derives from the teachings of John Nelson Darby (1800–1882) that were later systematized in our country by C. I. Scofield (1843–1921) and Lewis Sperry Chafer (1871–1952). In 1970, Hal Lindsey published the best-selling *The Late Great Planet Earth*, which interpreted this dispensationalism in terms of current events and made it popular in American culture. It is a view that has been argued at length by modern theologians, rejected by the Roman Catholic Church, the Eastern Orthodox churches, and a number of the major Protestant denominations.

At the same time this series was appearing, LaHaye joined with other collaborators to produce the "Babylon Rising" series, featuring as the hero Michael Murphy—"cool, brainy, sexy, and valiant." Murphy undertakes to discover one lost treasure of Scripture after another, beginning with the writing on the wall of Babylon, moving on to Noah's ark and the lost temple of Dagon. Like Indiana Jones, this heroic scholar confronts the forces of darkness as he undertakes breathtaking adventures. His collaborators to date include Bob Phillips and Greg Dinallo. Once again, with this series LaHaye has provided the ideas for books that have hit the *New York Times* best-seller list.

In another new series, the "Jesus Chronicles," Tim LaHaye has rejoined his favorite collaborator, Jerry Jenkins, to tell the gospels stories in more detail. The first two, *John's Story: The Last Eyewitness* and *Mark's Story* have been published by Bantam Books. Two more volumes are planned. *John's Story* does follow most of the events chronicled in the Gospel of John, but *Mark's Story* leads off into the early days of the Christian church, telling of the conflicts faced by the early believers.

Critical Reception

Critical reception to the "Left Behind" series has depended on the theology of the reviewer. Many of the early critics were Christians who agreed with the apocalyptic vision of LaHaye and Jenkins and were delighted to have "sizzle" added to the discussion in these pop-fiction versions of the prophesies. John D. Spalding classified the books as Christian thrillers and warned readers that *Left Behind* is "full of diatribes and unflattering portrayals of women, liberals, Jews, Californians and the media." It is also anti-Catholic and Fundamentalist in tone, with the authors preferring the small evangelical churches to the large liberal denominations. Spalding caught some of the basic difficulty of apocalyptic pop-fiction: "How better to prepare the masses for the end than to mask the message as a fun beach read?"

Those who, like Michael Standaert, find LaHaye's political views distasteful criticize the series as propaganda for the Radical Right. This author also attacks Hal Lindsey, Arno Froese, Ed Hudson, Mark Hitchcock, John Walvoord, John Van Impe and all the rest of the evangelicals who write books with wooden characters to promote the ideas of dispensational premillenialism and to castigate contemporary American culture. On the one hand, liberals suspect LaHaye and his allies of being part of a "Right Wing Conspiracy" rendering them unable to judge his novels without prejudice. On the other hand, those who agree with him politically about the potential threats in the United Nations, the World Council of Churches, and other "universal" organizations find the books ideal. They see the need to confront the perils of our times well worth the sacrifice of aesthetic value.

Anita Gandolfo traces the long tradition of apocalyptic novels that led up to the "Left Behind" series, making a strong case that other writers, including **Paul Maier,** who wrote *The Third Millennium* about the Second Coming of Christ, had already presented the End Times dramatically. Gandolfo suspects that LaHaye knew the work of Maier, but thought by joining with Jerry Jenkins, an experienced writer, he could develop an extended series to sell his own theories masked as faithful accounts of the book of Revelation. The anti-Catholicism of the series is especially offensive to her, as is his "Manichean" perspective.

John Mort, who reviewed the books for *Booklist,* noted in his encyclopedia of Christian fiction that although the "Left Behind" books are the most successful fiction series ever and have caught the imagination of the general reading public, appearing week after week on the *New York Times* bestseller lists, they are nonetheless inferior as fiction to the trilogies of Bill Myers and **James BeauSeigneur.** Both of these authors have a stronger background in science and are not constrained like LaHaye and Jenkins by the literal words of Scripture. Mort notes that, "Unlike BeauSeigneur's 'Antichrist, Jenkins and LaHaye's creation seems crimped by verses in Revelation and is without nuance. He's about as scary as Lex Luther in Superman comic books, and as predictable." Mort does acknowledge that the writers are occasionally funny and that they are successful in their appeal to millions of readers, many of them secular. Others prefer the more limited approach to the End Times that **C. S. Lewis** uses in *That Hideous Strength.*

Steve Rabey, who has reviewed the series for *Christianity Today*, summarized his views in "Apocalyptic Sales Out of this World": "With its fast-paced plots and high-velocity sales, the *Left Behind* fiction series has popularized pretribulational premillennialism much as **Frank Peretti's** *This Present Darkness* interested readers in spiritual warfare in the 1980s." He also notes the extensive spin-offs: the "Left Behind"–themed youth novels, audiotapes, videotapes, clothing, and a popular Web site (www.leftbehind.com), which generates more than 50,000 hits a day. Rabey quotes the marketing director for Tyndale, who insists that the publishers are not engineering this—"It's God really using it in a mighty way."

Awards

Tim LaHaye has been awarded a D.D. from Bob Jones University and a D. Lit. from Liberty University.

Bibliography of Novels by Author

"Left Behind" series (with Jerry Jenkins; Wheaton, IL: Tyndale House listed under Jerry Jenkins's entry)

"Babylon Rising" series (with Bob Phillips and Greg Dinallo; New York: Random House)

Babylon Rising. 2003.
The Secret on Ararat. 2004.
The Europa Conspiracy. 2005.
The Edge of Darkness. 2006.

"The Jesus Chronicles" series (with Jerry Jenkins; New York: Bantam Books)

John's Story: The Last Eyewitness. 2006.
Mark's Story: The Gospel According to Peter. 2007.

A series for young people is also available, as well as three films produced by Sony Pictures. Tim LaHaye has written over fifty books, most of them non-fiction. Recently, he has been at work on prequels to the "Left Behind" series:

Bibliography of Works about Author

Frykholm, Amy J. *Rapture Culture: Left Behind in Evangelical America.* New York: Oxford University Press, 2004.
Gandolfo, Anita. *Faith and Fiction: Christian Literature in America Today.* Westport, CT: Praeger, 2007.
Goodstein, Laurie. "Fast-selling Thrillers Depict Prophetic View of Final Days." *New York Times,* October 4, 1998, 1.
Kirkpatrick, David D. "A Best-Selling Formula in Religious Thrillers," *New York Times,* February 11, 2002.
Menconi, Jan, ed. *The Battle for the Mind Study Guide.* Old Tappan, NJ: Revell, 1983.
Mort, John. *Christian Fiction: A Guide to the Genre.* Greenwood Village, CO: Libraries Unlimited, 2002.

Olson, Carl F. "The 12th Coming of Less-Than-Glorious Fiction." http://www.nationalreview.com.

Rabey, Steve. "Apocalyptic Sales Out of this World." *Christianity Today* (March 1, 1999): 19.

Scully, Matthew. Reviews of *Tribulation Force, Soul Harvest, Nicolae,* and *Left Behind. National Review* (December 21, 1998): 62.

Spalding, John D. Review of *Left Behind. Christian Century* (May 22, 1996): 587.

Standaert, Michael. *Skipping toward Armageddon.* Brooklyn, NY: Soft Skull Press, 2006.

Tim LaHaye official Web site: www.timlahaye.com.

"Tim LaHaye." *Contemporary Authors Online.* Detroit: Thompson Gale, 2007.

"Tim LaHaye." Wikopedia online: http://www.wikopedia.com.

Walvoord, John, ed. *The Rapture Question.* Grand Rapids: Zondervan, 1979.

LEWIS, BEVERLY

Personal, Professional, and Religious Background

Beverly Jones Lewis (1949–) was born in Lancaster, Pennsylvania—the center of the Pennsylvania Dutch country. As she acknowledges in her dedication in *The Shunning,* her grandmother Ada Ranck Buchwalter (1886–1954), left the Plain community and married the man who would become Beverly's grandfather. This heritage has colored Lewis's whole literary life. Her father, Herbert L. Jones, was a minister. Lewis told *Faithful Reader* in an interview that her mother remembered her daughter's earliest "leanings toward the Lord," which came when she was only three years of age. At age six, she "walked the sinner's aisle and opened my heart to Jesus in Reading, Pa. at a revival meeting" Some of this fervent love of Jesus probably came from her "godly heritage" that she drew from her pastor-father and his faithful wife. It certainly determined her hunger for writing. As she explains it: "To think that God is using me to help spread the Good News of the Gospel—that Jesus Christ came to this world to save humanity—via storytelling (one of the tools Christ Himself used) is a daily blessing and privilege."

From her earliest years, Beverly Lewis was also in love with books. "Reading, writing, and music were an immense part of my life." Her first project was a song-poem written at age four; she then became a pen-pal in the fourth grade, when she began corresponding with a Canadian girl. In the sixth grade, she wrote a 77-page novel, "a bittersweet, semi-autobiographical tale of a young girl whose parents couldn't afford music lessons. I read it to my cousin under a tree in her backyard. She couldn't wait for the last chapter."

Beverly Lewis went to Cowley County Junior College, where she earned an associate of arts degree in 1969, then to Evangel College, for a Bachelor of Music Education in 1972, and then the University of Colorado at Colorado Springs from 1973–74. She loves music and has been an instructor of voice, piano, and composition in Colorado Springs since 1973. This musical interest is clearly reflected in such books as *The Sunroom,* where the child's love of piano playing becomes her sacrificial offering before the throne of God—a sad misunderstanding of the proper use of God's gifts. The story is autobiographical, a remembrance of her own mother's brush with death.

> I grew up with the notion that books were much more than bound pages.
>
> —Beverly Lewis, quoted in *Contemporary Authors Online*

In 1987, she married Dave Lewis, a biographer and musician, and had three children: Julie, Janie, and Jonathan. She frequently cites her husband as her best editor and sometimes as her coauthor. They now live in Colorado, in the foothills of the Rocky Mountains, "enjoying their three grown children and one grandchild." Mrs. Lewis notes she is "content to settle into the church pew while focusing on writing inspirational fiction, as well as speaking at local Christian women's groups and writer's conferences, along with cheering my husband on in his music ministry."

Major Works and Themes

Beverly Lewis has never forgotten her early days among the Amish and has continued to study and write about these amazing people, producing a host of books for young people over the years. Her admiration for the simple style of Amish life combines with an implicit criticism of the sometimes cruel custom of shunning. The lives and loves of adolescent girls in the Amish community are the main subjects of Beverly Lewis's books. The stories are usually simple, often constructed as multiple volumes of a single narrative over an extended period of time. They are aimed at an audience of teenage girls who will resonate to the concerns of her characters—friendship, love, marriage, and faith. Lewis is particularly interested in and critical of the Old Order Amish of Lancaster County, one of the strictest faith communities in America. She follows whole families, showing their daily habits, their clothing, their food, their festivities, their religious functions, their frustrations and sorrows. Full of details of food, courting customs, concerns for new babies, quilting parties, and conversations, her stories have the slow pace of the community's life, the rhythm of the seasons and of the lives of the characters. She rarely speaks of the men's work, the barn-raisings, the labor in the fields, the leathercraft, woodworking, and animal husbandry.

In some of her stories, the outsiders—the journalist in *The Postcard* and *The Crossing*, the guest in *Sanctuary*, or the aunt in *The Redemption of Sarah Cain*—become the justification for revealing the curious habits and theology of the Amish. Lewis finds a number of the Old Order Amish practices un-Christian. She believes the code of unwritten rules, the ordnung, which she considers largely the prejudice of the current bishop, to be frustrating for more imaginative members of the community, pushing them toward rebellion. In *The Crossing*, she describes the white witchcraft practiced by powwow doctors, condoned by the bishop. In *Abram's Daughters*, she shows the control over profession, location, and religious practices, even the limits on prayer and Bible reading.

Beverly Lewis is particularly appalled by the custom of shunning wayward members of the community, revealing the resulting pain caused to the sinner and to the whole family. This arbitrary power of the local bishop also strikes her as totalitarian and un-Christian. In the Old Order group, this authority restricts members from reading the Scripture, from seeking comfort in spontaneous prayer, or from claiming the promises of Heaven. She much prefers the gentler, more evangelical pattern of the New Order or Amish Mennonites, and the Baptists.

Certain women who find themselves uncomfortable with the restrictions of education and lifestyle, such as Mary Ellen in *Abram's Daughters*, who hunger to go to high school and college, to teach school, and to find a more open life, win a sympathetic treatment by Lewis. Other characters, such as Leah, in the same series, are content in their work and life. At least one woman, Sarah Cain's sister Ivy, converts to the Plain life. "The Legacy of Lancaster County" series deals directly with this theme, based on Lewis's own grandmother's decision to leave the Amish community and to marry outside it. The hidden-birth story, the discovery that Katie is really Katherine, to a manor born, is a bit more like the romance novels than the typical Lewis story, but Katie does return to a modest life after giving away most of her inheritance. It is obvious that Lewis admires the Plain people for their dedication to their faith, their families, for their moral seriousness, and for their simple lives.

Critical Reception

Because Beverly Lewis writes primarily for an adolescent audience, she has not been the subject of intense critical scrutiny. Zsolia Anna Toth reviewed two of her books, *The Covenant* and *The Betrayed*, and found herself disappointed, judging Lewis's "super idyllic depiction of the Plain life" less than authentic. She considers the plots too much like soap operas and the characters so flat that not even a "road roller could have been able to make them flatter." Her harshest criticism is that the books appear to present the Plain life as "lifeless."

The evangelical critics, such as Violet Nesdoly, are gentler in their commentary, accepting the religious motivation behind the stories and the goal to reach younger readers with stories of romance and Christian faith. In her review of *The Brethren*, the final book in the "Annie's People" series, Nesdoly notes that Beverly Lewis "continues to give her readers what they have found irresistible in her previous best-selling books."

Even this commentator admits that it is hard to read just one of her books. The narratives and characters are so intertwined from volume to volume that they really should be read in order and in full to be understood. A series like "Abram's Daughters," for example, begins with a betrayal and ends—four volumes later—with a reconciliation. Whole volumes pass without any real change in the situation of the central characters.

Some of her books do stand alone. *The Redemption of Sarah Cain*, which has recently been made into a film, does have a free-standing plot. In the novel, a successful young real-estate saleswoman in Portland, Oregon, is jarred by the death of her only sister, Ivy, who had recently been widowed. Ivy and her husband had chosen a path diametrically opposite Sarah's: they joined the Amish community, embraced the Plain life, settled on a farm in Lancaster County, and raised five children. Ivy leaves these children to the tender mercies of their Aunt Sarah, who wants neither the Plain life nor children. The film changes this story of the simple transformation of the agnostic city slicker into a Christian farm wife, making Sarah a journalist who takes the children back to the city with her, thereby emphasizing the contrasting life styles much more dramatically. The love interest with the college boy friend is used in both. Michael Landon, Jr. who has worked on a number of religion-friendly films, is the director.

When Lewis tries for too complex a plot, as in *Sanctuary*, a bit like the film *The Witness*, she is at her worst. She fails in her effort to sound knowledgeable about the Russian Mafia, insider trading, the workings of FBI investigations, and the use of tracking devices—all of which have a jarring tone in this bucolic setting. She is a far better writer when she stays with the lives of the women in her beloved Amish community.

For those not interested in the Amish or their language, Lewis's books do present a problem. Colloquial Pennsylvania Dutch speech and specific German terminology abound in these stories of people seeking to remain separate and free from the world's temptations. Ironically, the Amish themselves eschew novels as lies, unworthy of the Lord's people and a misuse of their time. Only an outsider could write these stories.

Awards

Beverly Lewis is a member of the Society of Children's Book Writers and Illustrators, the Colorado Christian Communicators, the National League of American Pen Women, and is listed on the C. S. Lewis Noteworthy List of Books. She won the 2001 Silver Angel Award and the Quill Award for *The Postcard*.

Bibliography of Novels for Adults by Author (Bloomington, MN: Bethany House Publishers)

"The Heritage of Lancaster County" series (1997–1998)

"Abram's Daughters" series (2002–2005)

The Sunroom. 1998.
The Crossroad. 1999.
The Postcard. 1999.
The Redemption of Sarah Cain. 2000.
October Song. 2001.
Sanctuary (with David Lewis). 2001.

A film was made of *The Redemption of Sarah Cain*. Beverly Lewis has also written a number of novels for young people, beginning with the "Holly's Heart" series, published by Zondervan, Augsburg Fortress, Star Song, and others, beginning in 1993.

Bibliography of Works about Author

"Beverly Lewis." *Contemporary Authors Online*. Detroit: Thomson Gale, 2002.
FaithfulReader. "Beverly Lewis" http://www.faithrfulreader.com/features/15-lewis-beverly.asp.
Nesdoly, Violet. "Book Review: *The Brethren* by Beverly Lewis. Blogcritics online. http://www.blogcritics.org/archives/2006/11/28/202544.php.
Toth, Zsolia Anna. Reviews of *The Covenant* and *The Betrayed* http://www.Womenwriters.net/summer05/book reviews/The Covenant.

LEWIS, C.S.

Personal, Professional, and Religious Background

Clive Staples Lewis (also known as C.S. Lewis, N. W. Clerk, and Clive Hamilton) (1898–1963) was born in Belfast, Ireland. He was the son of Albert James Lewis, a solicitor, whose father, Richard, had come to Ireland from Wales. His mother was Florence (Flora) Augusta Lewis née Hamilton, the daughter of a Church of Ireland (Anglican) priest. C.S. Lewis had one older brother, Warren Hamilton Lewis ("Warnie"). At the age of four, shortly after his dog Jacksie was hit by a car, Clive announced that his name was now "Jacksie." At first he would answer to no other name, but later accepted "Jacks," which eventually became "Jack," the name by which he was known to friends and family for the rest of his life. When Jack was six, his family moved into "Little Lea," the house the elder Mr. Lewis built for Mrs. Lewis in the Strandtown area of East Belfast.

> A man who was merely a man and said the sort of things Jesus said would not be a great moral teacher. He would either be a lunatic—on a level with the man who says he is a poached egg—or else he would be the Devil of Hell. You must make your choice. Either this man was, and is, the son of God; or else a madman or something worse. You can shut Him up for a fool, you can spit at Him and kill Him as a demon, or you can fall at His feet and call Him Lord and God.
>
> —C.S. Lewis, *Mere Christianity*, p. 56

Jack and his brother read many of the books in their father's extensive library, especially enjoying the works of Beatrix Potter and the anthropomorphic animals she included in her works. They invented their own world, run by animals, which they called "Boxen." Jack Lewis wrote and illustrated his own animal stories.

Lewis was initially schooled by private tutors before being sent (in 1908) to the Wynyard School in Watford, Hertfordshire, where his brother was already enrolled. In *Surprised by Joy,* Lewis called the school "Belsea." About this time, his mother died of cancer. The school was closed not long afterwards due to a lack of pupils, and the headmaster, Robert "Oldie" Capron, was committed to an insane asylum. Although it is not clear what happened to Lewis at Wynyard, some believe that the combination of the death of his mother and the atmosphere of the school traumatized Lewis, making him the subject of "mildly sadomasochistic fantasies." After Wynyard closed, Lewis attended Campbell College in the east of Belfast, about a mile from his home, but he left after a few months due to respiratory problems. As a result of his illness, Lewis was sent to the health-resort town of Malvern, Worcestershire, where he attended the preparatory school Cherbourg House, which he called "Chartres" in his autobiography.

It was at Malvern College, where Lewis enrolled in 1913, that he abandoned his Christian faith and announced that he was an atheist. He thought that the Roman poet Lucretius had the most effective argument and philosophy for a materialistic creation of the universe. For some years, Lewis studied the occult and mythology, having already been steeped in Irish myths as a child. He also witnessed a number of homosexual relationships, which he understood and rejected. After Malvern, he studied privately with his father's old tutor, William T. Kirkpatrick. This former headmaster of Lurgan College. Kirkpatrick, whom Lewis dubbed "The Great Knock," led the boy into a study of Greek literature and helped him develop his reasoning and debating skills. By his teenage years, Lewis was also in love with the songs and legends of Scandinavia and Iceland, and was trying his hand at epics and opera to capture his love of Norse mythology.

In 1916, C. S. Lewis won a scholarship to University College, Oxford, where he attended only one year before World War I began and he enlisted in the British Army. He became a commissioned officer in the 3rd Battalion, Somerset Light Infantry. He arrived in France on his 19th birthday and was immediately introduced to the horrors of trench warfare. The following year, he was wounded at the Battle of Arras. After his recovery a few months later, he was assigned to duty in England, where he remained until his discharge the following December, 1918, having achieved the rank of second lieutenant.

It was during this time of loneliness and depression that he became deeply involved with Jane Moore, the mother of a fellow soldier who was killed in combat. Paddy Moore and he had made a pact to take care of both families if anything should happen to either of them during the war. Jane Moore, left without her son after his death, became Lewis's friend and surrogate mother in the following years. Some even speculated on a romantic relationship between the 18-year-old Lewis and the 45-year-old Moore.

Lewis returned to Oxford after his discharge, taking a First in Honour Moderations (Greek and Latin Literature) in 1920, a First in Greats (Philosophy and Ancient History), in 1922, and a First in English in 1923. Subsequently, Lewis became a tutor at the college, later rising to become a lecturer. In 1930, Lewis moved into "The Kilns," a house on the outskirts of Oxford, where he was joined by Mrs. Moore and her daughter Maureen. Later, Lewis's brother Warren joined them there. Mrs. Moore suffered from dementia in her later years and finally had to be moved into a nursing home, where Lewis visited her every day until she died there in 1951.

Most of Lewis's career was spent at Oxford, where he became a fellow and tutor in English literature at Magdalen College in 1925, and served in that post until 1954, when, having been denied further advancement at Oxford, he became professor of Medieval and Renaissance English at Cambridge, remaining there until his death. During his long and productive academic career, Lewis also served as a lecturer for short periods at the University of Wales, the University of Durham, and other places. He was a dramatic and immensely popular speaker and debater, and was often invited to universities, churches, public events, and appeared on BBC Radio.

Lewis and Warnie, along with a cluster of Jack's friends, began to meet frequently at their house for a cup of tea or a glass or sherry, talking about shared intellectual interests. Charles Williams, editor at the Oxford University Press; J.R.R. Tolkien, author of *The Lord of the Rings*; and others in this convival group called themselves the "Inklings." This small band of brothers in the faith became the forerunners of much of modern Christian creative writing. C.S. Lewis acknowledged that Tolkien was instrumental in his conversion, though Tolkien himself was a Roman Catholic, and was never quite happy with Lewis's embracing of the Anglican Church. As Lewis recalled the experience in *Surprised by Joy*, at the age of 30, he became "a very ordinary layman of the Church of England." This conversion experience changed the course of his writing, turning him from a highly respected scholar of English literature into an apologist of Christianity. He became known as the "Apostle to the Skeptics."

Late in his life, he met and married Joy Davidman Gresham, who was an American, a poet, a novelist, a former Communist, a divorcée, and a Jewish convert to Christianity—largely through her reading of Lewis. She died of cancer in 1960 at the age of 45, four years after their marriage, leaving him with two stepsons, David and Douglas Gresham.

Much of his life, his conversion experience, and his delight and surprise in his late marriage is told in *Surprised by Joy*, his spiritual autobiography. *Shadowlands* is a dramatized account of this experience of love and death. His own anguish is powerfully described in *A Grief Observed*. Lewis's openness and frankness about his own spiritual journey have given comfort to many others. He died the same day as John F. Kennedy, whose assassination overshadowed Lewis's quiet passing. His home for many years, the "Kilns," has been restored and is visited by many scholars and fans who enjoy seeing Oxford and discussing the life, works, and ideas of C.S. Lewis.

Major Works and Themes

Because C.S. Lewis was both a literary scholar and a Christian, he found rich opportunities to speak to an educated audience about the profound truth that he had discovered through his own experience. Lewis followed the standard academic path through much of his life, commenting on medieval and renaissance literature, building a solid reputation as a scholar. His study of the medieval tradition of love soon became a classic; his works on Milton, Shakespeare, Spenser, and others were published by Cambridge University Press. His attraction to ancient and medieval myths led him to a larger exploration of the essential truth that lies behind much of mythology. His own Irish background, with a love of fairy tales and whimsy, set him to creating his own works of imagination, often drawn from academic sources. *Till We Have Faces: A Myth Retold*, which was published in 1957, is a remarkable retelling of the story of Psyche and Cupid. In this, as in many of his other imaginative works, C.S. Lewis makes a rich story out of a simple tale, turning figures into philosophical positions, discovering truth behind fiction.

Lewis found especial delight in writing for children, in spite of being an old bachelor, living with his bachelor brother in a community of bachelors for most of his life. The "Narnia" chronicles, beginning with *The Lion, the Witch, and the Wardrobe* in 1950, became popular all over the world. This delightful tale of children who enter the wardrobe in Lewis's own attic, and discover a whole world of witches and lions and romance, was finally expanded to seven volumes, entitled *The Chronicles of Narnia*. More recently, these stories have been the basis for films of enormous popularity. Some of his fellow scholars at Oxford thought those popular creations were beneath the dignity of an Oxford don and blocked his opportunities for honors there, forcing his move to Cambridge.

Using the name "Clive Hamilton," Lewis also wrote three collections of poetry, beginning in 1919, and continuing till his death. These have been collected and edited by his friend and editor, Walter Hooper.

C. S. Lewis's adult fiction, which is often as imaginative as his stories for children, as scholarly as his academic works, and as lyrical as his poetry, has also achieved a wide audience. The first of these "novels," *The Pilgrim's Regress*, an allegory based on Bunyan's famous book, is subtitled an "apology for Christianity, Reason, and Romanticism."

His great series, the space odyssey of Dr. Ransom, began in 1943 with *Out of the Silent Planet*. His hero in the series, whom he said he based on his philologist friend Tolkien, shares Lewis's love of long walks in the English countryside and his enthusiasm for folklore. On one such walk, Dr. Ransom finds himself taken prisoner and forced into a journey to Mars. Here, his understanding of language allows him gradually to discover the meaning of the speech of the curious creatures who live lives altogether different from those on Earth—a planet they call the "silent planet." Ransom discovers deeper meanings to the creation and guidance of the universe, the truths that lie behind some of our deepest myths, including a lively spirit world that humans cannot see.

The following books in this series continue Ransom's adventures—*Perelandra* describes Ransom's more willing adventure to the planet Venus, which presents an alternative Garden of Eden, with Adam and Eve in an unfallen condition. Ransom's arch rival Weston reveals himself as the snake in this garden, whom Ransom must battle for the sake of the whole planet. This allows the reader to discover more of the possible truth in the original Temptation and in Eve's original sin.

The third of the series deals more forcefully with earth itself. *That Hideous Strength: A Modern Fairy-Tale for Grownups*, was published in 1945, reflecting (as does *Perelandra*) the impact of World War II on Lewis and on English culture. This story is a fitting conclusion to the trilogy, bringing the story back to planet Earth and to the academic community, which has its own temptations and spiritual darkness. The young couple at the center of this story are like the figures Lewis describes in *Abolition of Man*—barren, superficial, egocentric, and hollow—"men without chests." Until their world is threatened by spiritual forces that result in a final catastrophe, they cannot see the natural path of love or the true joy of faith. Lewis ends the story with a glorious epithalamion, where animals and humans join in a joyous paeon of God's good world. Ransom, whose work is finally completed on Earth, returns to Venus, the place of love, where his wound will finally be healed.

Lewis did begin yet another science fiction novel, which was never finished. *The Dark Tower*. The incomplete story was published in 1977 but has never been fully accepted as his work or of the same calibre as the other novels in the trilogy.

Lewis's influences are as far-reaching and eclectic as his amazing mind: Greek, Norse, and Irish mythology, W. B. Yeats, William Wordsworth, mystical poetry of the medieval and Renaissance periods, Aristotle, Arthur Balfour, Beatrix Potter, the Bible, Chaucer, Dante, George MacDonald, G. K. Chesterton, H. G. Wells, H. Rider Haggard, John Milton, J.R.R. Tolkien, Plato, William Blake, W. T. Kirkpatrick, and many others. He was widely read and deeply learned, yet his talent for making complex ideas simple and colorful has endeared him to audiences of children, common folk, creative artists, and scholars for over half a century. His influence on modern Christian literature is incalculable.

Critical Reception

Lewis's first novel, *The Pilgrim's Regress*, was never particularly popular. His various works on Heaven and Hell, including *The Great Divorce*, also won few words of praise, probably because modern readers were not comfortable with his use of medieval forms of allegory and dream vision.

His rewriting of the ancient myth of Cupid and Psyche, *Till We Have Faces*, did win more readers and more praise than his other studies of love and the medieval vision of the types of love. This fascinating, though puzzling, work set in the pre-Christian world takes the point of view of the ugly sister of Psyche, Orual, who loves and envies her beautiful sibling. The character of Fox, the tutor, underscores the choice between his dry reason and Psyche's romanticism. The work has been called Lewis's "most mature and masterful work of fiction," though it was never a popular success. It was his own favorite work.

Lewis's stridently satirical tone, most obvious when dealing with academic politics as in *That Hideous Strength*, takes away from the "willing suspension of disbelief" required for the novel. Using some of the same tone we find in *The Screwtape Letters* and some of the same temptations of modern man, Lewis creates in this novel a world of petty sins that can lead the unwitting to damnation. The young hero, Mark, and his wife, Jane, never win the reader's full sympathy. The loving and decent characters tend to be types or allegorical figures, and the evil ones are so purely evil as to be caricatures. Nonetheless, this series of science fiction novels anticipated the apocalyptic sci-fi novels written 50 years later. John Mort is particularly fond of the final novel in the trilogy: "In his most vivid scenes Lewis revives the wizard Merlin, a magnificent primitive, but a crafty soul who takes on godlike qualities and who crowds out Ransom as the novel's hero."

One of the greatest tributes to Lewis's popularity is that his works have been translated into more than 30 languages and have sold more than one million copies per year. Of course, *The Chronicles of Narnia* remain the most popular of his stories, and has sold more than 100 million copies, but other of his books, particularly his *Mere Christianity*, have also remained enormously popular. In addition, films have been made of the "Narnia" books and of his final poignant years with the doomed Joy Gresham.

Awards

C. S. Lewis won many awards during his lifetime: the Hawthornden Prize in 1936, the Gollancz Memorial Prize for Literature in 1937 (for *The Allegory of Love*); the Carnegie Medal Commendation from the British Library Association in 1955 for *The Horse and His Boy*; the Library Association Carnegie Medal in 1957 for *The Last Battle*; the Lewis Carroll Shelf Award in 1962 for *The Lion, the Witch, and the Wardrobe*. He also was awarded honorary doctorates by the University of St. Andrews, Laval University, the University of Manchester, the University of Dijon, and the University of Lyon. He was a member of the British Academy, the Royal Society of Literature, the Sir Walter Scott Society (where he served as president in 1956), the Oxford Socratic Club (of which he was the founding member and president from 1941–1954), and the Athenaeum Club. His most famous membership was in the informal literary group that often met in his cottage—the Inklings.

Bibliography of Novels for Adults by Author

The Pilgrim's Regress: An Allegorical Apology for Christianity, Reason, and Romanticism. London: Dent, 1933.
Out of the Silent Planet. London: John Lane, 1938.
The Screwtape Letters. London: G. Bles, 1942.
Perelandra. London: John Lane, 1943.
That Hideous Strength: A Modern Fairy-Tale for Grownups. London: John Lane, 1945.
The Great Divorce: A Dream. London: G. Bles, 1945.
Till We Have Faces: A Myth Retold. London: G. Bles, 1956.
The Dark Tower and Other Stories (including two unfinished novels), ed., Walter Hooper. New York: Harcourt Brace Jovanovich, 1977

C. S. Lewis also wrote *Chronicles of Narnia*, fiction for children, poetry (under the name Clive Hamilton), literary criticism, and nonfiction, much of it apologetics for Christianity. *Mere Christianity* and *The Screwtape Letters* are his most popular defenses of Christianity. His letters have been collected in a dozen volumes, as have been many of his essays.

Bibliography of Works about Author

"C. S. Lewis." *Contemporary Authors Online.* Detroit: Thomson Gale, 2004.
"C. S. Lewis." Wikipedia.com.
Carpenter, Humphrey. *The Inklings: C. S. Lewis, J.R.R. Tolkien, Charles Williams and Their Friends.* London: Allen & Unwin, 1978.
Christopher, Joe R.C.S. and Joan K. Ostling. *C. S. Lewis: An Annotated Checklist of Writings about Him and His Works.* Kent, OH: Kent State University Press, 1974.
Como, James T., ed. *"C. S. Lewis at the Breakfast Table" and other Reminiscences.* New York: Macmillan, 1979.
Hooper, Walter. *Past Watchful Dragons: The Narnian Chronicles of C. S. Lewis.* New York: Macmillan, 1974.
Hooper, Walter. *C. S. Lewis: A Companion and Guide.* San Francisco: HarperSanFrancisco, 1996.
Howard, Thomas. *C. S. Lewis, Man of Letters: A Reading of the Fiction.* Worthing, England: Churchman, 1987.
Lewis, C. S. *Surprised by Joy: The Shape of My Early Life.* New York: Harcourt, 1956.
Lewis, C. S. *A Grief Observed.*(under the pseudonym N.W. Clerk) London: Faber & Faber, 1961.
Lindskoog, Kathryn. *Light in the Shadowlands: Protecting the Real C. S. Lewis.* Sisters, OR: Multnomah Publishers, 1994.
Mort, John. *Christian Fiction: A Guide to the Genre.* Greenwood Village, CO: Libraries Unlimited, 2002.
Walsh, Chad. *The Literary Legacy of C. S. Lewis.* New York: Harcourt, 1979.
Wilson, A.N. *C. S. Lewis: A Biography.* New York: Norton, 1990.

C. S. Lewis has been the subject of several biographies, a few of which were written by some of his close friends. There has been considerable argument about the authenticity of some of the claims by biographers and "friends." In 1985 William Nicholson dramatized Lewis's complex relationship with Joy Gresham in a screenplay *Shadowlands*. In 1989, the story was staged as a theater play, and in 1993 *Shadowlands* became a feature film. His life was also used for a one hour made-for-TV movie entitled *C. S. Lewis: Beyond Narnia*.

Lewis's papers are collected in several places: The Marion E. Wade Center at Wheaton College contains the world's largest collection of Lewis's papers and works about him. It also has his desk and holds many papers of the others in the Inklings group; The Taylor University, Upland, Indiana, has the world's largest private collection of C. S. Lewis first editions, letters, manuscripts, and ephemera (the Edwin W. Brown Collection); and the Arend Smilde's CSL site. has several unique or hard-to-find texts and resources.

LUCADO, MAX

Personal, Professional, and Religious Background

Max Lee Lucado (1955–) was born in San Angelo, Texas, to Terrell and Thelma Esther Kincaide Lucado. The youngest of four children in a faithful family that moved to Andrews, Texas, and the oil fields, Max proved a rebellious youth. When he started college, he planned to be a lawyer. He also planned to continue to do a lot of drinking. Then he took a required Bible course in his second year of college, and had a "Damascus Road type experience." He had assumed he was too great a sinner to be forgiven. He recognized his alcohol addiction and praised God for giving him a second chance.

Max Lucado studied for a B.A. at Abilene Christian University, majoring in mass communications; he also has an M.A. in biblical and related studies from Abilene Christian University—a school that later named him their outstanding young alumnus in 1991.

He married Denalyn Preston in 1981. They have three daughters—Jenna, Andrea, and Sara—all of whom have become known to his readers through anecdotes he includes in sermons and books.

Lucado served as associate minister for a church in Miami from 1980–1983 before going to Rio de Janeiro, Brazil as a church-planting missionary. Since 1988, he has served as the senior minister at the Oak Hills Church of Christ in San Antonio. Because he realizes his talents lie in writing and speaking rather than in administration and counseling members of his large church, he has staff who serve the congregation in these areas. He takes no salary for his ministry, choosing to support himself and his family through his writing. In the early spring of 2007, he shocked his church by announcing that, after 20 years at the church, and seven months after having been diagnosed with atrial fibrillation, he was leaving the ministry: "My health concerns are not so severe that I feel I'm in any danger, just severe enough that I think a change needs to be made." He insists he will still regularly preach at the church, which is no longer affiliated with the Church of Christ, and he will continue his writing. He is usually working on two books at a time. He says, "I compare what is happening to going from being president of a college to joining the faculty."

> Books go where I could never go.
>
> —Max Lucado

Major Works and Themes

Max Lucado's books grow out of his own experiences and his sermons. Most of them sound like sermons—well-told tales with a biblical basis that provide encouragement to believers and help for those struggling through difficult times. Most of his fiction is aimed at children, but a handful of his books are designed for adults. Even those in the "Tell Me" series, combining short chapters with beautiful illustrations by Ron DiCianni, are designed for families. These are stories that parents can read to their children, showing them the pictures, explaining the ideas. *Tell Me the Story*, for example, has a series of short stories with illustrations that present messages of creation, the fall, redemption, forgiveness, and spiritual warfare. *Tell Me the Secrets: Treasures for Eternity* describes a magical journey to discover the eternal treasure in God's word. This book centers on a retired missionary sharing his memories with three children as the means to help the children discover the treasures.

Always a teacher and preacher, always thoughtful and evangelical in his approach, Max Lucado has written numerous allegories, using the format of the short story, to draw families to God. He is willing to talk about the archangel Gabriel or the boy next door. His themes are usually God's free-flowing and unmerited grace, forgiveness, and unconditional love. Lucado's ability to put himself in the place of his reader or listener gives his books the quality of an old friend talking straight to the heart.

Critical Reception

Critics who regularly review evangelical books have praised Max Lucado for his presentation of an "authentic spiritual life," for "his graceful style and his thorough exposition of biblical texts." Janice DeLong and Rachel Schwedt note, of *Just in Case You Ever Wonder*, that Lucado writes in first-person style "simply with expressions that could have come straight from the hearts of his daughters. In language both childlike and profound, he reassures the little listener or young reader that both the loving parent and God will always be there, even into eternity, and will always love them—just in case they ever wonder."

Awards

Max Lucado has a long list of awards, most of them for nonfiction works or for his own leadership. He has won Gold Medallion Awards for *The Applause of Heaven* (1991), *Six Hours One Friday* (1991), *In the Eye of the Storm* (1992), *Tell Me the Story* and *Just in Case You Ever Wonder* (1993), *Tell Me the Secrets* (1994), and *The Crippled Lamb* (1995). He has also won the Campus Life Award (1993) and the Evangelical Christian Publishers Association/Christian Booksellers Association Christian Book of the Year Award for *When God Whispers Your Name* (1995) and *In the Grip of Grace* (1996). *Christianity Today* named him "America's Pastor" in 2005, and *Readers Digest* has named him the "Best Preacher in America."

Bibliography of Novels for Adults by Author

Tell Me the Secrets: Treasures for Eternity. Wheaton, IL: Crossway, 1993.
Tell Me the Story. Wheaton, IL: Crossway, 1993.

When God Whispers Your Name. Nashville, TN: Word, 1994.
Cosmic Christmas. Nashville, TN: Word, 1998.
The Christmas Cross: A Story about Finding Your Way Home for the Holidays. Nashville, TN: Word, 1998.

Max Lucado is also a prolific columnist, essayist, and writer of books for children and adults on Christian topics.

Bibliography of Works about Author

Booklist (July, 1005): 1834; (July, 1997): 1772.
DeLong, Janice and Rachel Schwedt. *Contemporary Christian Authors: Lives and Works.* Lanham, MD: The Scarecrow Press, 2000.
Max Lucado Home Page: http://www.maxlucado.com.
Max Lucado Books: http://maxlucadobooks.com.
"Max Lucado." *Contemporary Authors Online.* Detroit: Thomson Gale, 2002.

MAIER, PAUL

Personal, Professional, and Religious Background

Paul Luther Maier (1930–) was born in St. Louis. His father, Walter Arthur Maier, was a famous professor and radio preacher, the founding speaker of "The Lutheran Hour" radio broadcast.

Paul Maier earned his M.A. from Harvard University in 1954, his B.D. from Concordia Seminary in 1955, and won a Fulbright scholarship for postgraduate studies at the University of Heidelberg in Germany, where he studied from 1955–1956. The following year, he spent at the University of Basel in Switzerland, where he studied under Karl Barth and Oscar Cullman. He earned his Ph.D. from the University of Basel, summa cum laude, in 1957. In 1958, he took a position as chaplain for Lutheran students at Western Michigan University, where he became professor of history in 1960.

Dr. Maier married Joan M. Ludtke in 1967; they have two daughters, Laura Ann and Julie Joan. Dr. Maier is an active preacher as well as a teacher. In his novels, his numerous books of commentary, and in his talks, he serves as an apologists for conservative Christian doctrine. He is frequently invited to speak and participate in discussions in this country and in Canada. He was one of the panelists who criticized Dan Brown's 2003 best-selling novel *The Da Vinci Code* for its historical flaws and untruths. He also coauthored *The Da Vinci Code: Fact or Fiction?* with Christian apologist Hank Hanegraaf.

> I also hope to demonstrate the historical reliability and credibility of the Christian faith.
>
> —Paul Maier, in DeLong and Schwedt

Dr. Paul L. Maier, Ph.D., is the Russell H. Seibert Professor of Ancient History at Western Michigan University. He has also served as the Second Vice President of the Lutheran Church—Missouri Synod.

Major Works and Themes

Some of Paul Maier's first work as a writer was a tribute to his father. In 1963, he published a biography of this remarkable communicator: *A Man Spoke, A World Listened: The Story of Walter A. Maier*. Later, he collected some of his father's more famous sermons in *The Best of Walter A. Maier*, which was published by Concordia in 1980.

Paul L. Maier has also become known as a theological historian. His first work in this area was published in 1959: *Caspar Schwenckfeld on the Person and Work of Christ*. He is best known for his scholarship on Eusebius, the first historian of the Christian church. He served as editor and translator of the "essential writings" Josephus, the Jewish historian who was a contemporary of Christ, and provided the commentary on Josephus in William Whiston's *The New Complete Works of Josephus* in 1998. Dr. Maier enjoys his studies and teaching about the ancient Near East, ancient Greece, ancient Rome, Christianity and the Roman Empire, and the Reformation.

His more popular works include a number of books on Easter and Christmas, tracing these holy days back to their original meanings. He has also written on the first Christians in his 1976 book on the Pentecost as well as several children's books, such as *The Very First Christmas*.

His adult historical novels grow out of his scholarship, beginning with *Pontius Pilate*, which has been reprinted in numerous editions and translations. He came to believe that the background discoveries related to the New Testament accounts of the trial of Christ have been unknown by the majority of the laity, such as the politics behind Pontius Pilate's decisions on Good Friday. Through his "documentary novel," in which he builds character and plot on known data, he created a lively story of the events leading to Good Friday.

Pontius Pilate was followed by *The Flames of Rome*, another tale that uses New Testament documents along with contemporary accounts. Maier uses few fictitious characters, as he demonstrates in his voluminous notes at the end of the book. By drawing on his own deep and rich understanding of the world of the Roman Empire, he sets the background in the days of Claudius and Nero for the execution of both Peter and Paul. He assumes that Paul did indeed go to Spain and that Peter asked to be executed upside down, but that the Romans probably refused to honor his request. He explains and defends these decisions in very lively notes.

A Skeleton in God's Closet is more fictional than the earlier books, a thriller based on something of Maier's own personality and background. The central character, Dr. Jonathan Weber, a professor at Harvard, uses his sabbatical leave to work with his old Oxford professor, Austin Balfour Jennings, at a dig in Ramah, in Israel. The discovery of a large set of ruins that appear to be the home of Joseph of Arimathea, and the further uncovering of a tomb and sarcophagus with bones and a scroll in three languages set the team on a trail of investigations, verifications, and discussions about the resurrection of Jesus. If the bones belong to Jesus, then this would suggest that the resurrection narrative is a hoax, a message that quickly leaks out to the press and discourages much of the Christian world. Jon, the protagonist, who is the son of a Lutheran pastor (Missouri Synod), finds himself torn between good scholarship and good theology.

The central problem opens up interesting discussions of the importance of Christ's physical resurrection from the dead, with different religious leaders handling it according to their theology and politics. Some are happy to abandon the historical reality, some blame the archaeologists as anti-Christs, and some are horrified at this attack on the truth of Scripture. For Jonathan's father, a gentle pastor in Hannibal, Missouri, the home of Mark Twain, the discouragement to his flock is devastating, yet he continues to love his son and respect his search for truth. The final reconciliation of God's truth and man's comes only after a long series of adventures (including Jonathan's swimming across the Dead Sea and flying out of England disguised by a beard and carrying a fake passport). It also involves a love affair, a problem of friendship and fidelity, and an understanding of good motives that result in bad actions. It is an exciting and carefully crafted novel, filled with interesting insights into modern theology, archaeology, and religious ideas.

A second novel on archaeology, again using Jonathan Weber in a dig in Israel, raises new questions about the Messiah. A young man, Joshua Ben-Yosef, has begun to captivate the world with his charismatic personality, vast learning, and band of followers. He does appear to be Christ in his Second Coming. Once again, in *More Than a Skeleton*, Jon is disturbed by this revisionist Messiah: "Where are His miracles? Where is His death and resurrection?" Although Shannon, now his wife, falls under the spell of Ben-Joseph, Jon once again uses his vast knowledge and research to find the truth behind the appearance.

Dr. Maier describes his writing process as first "identifying an important problem or gap in our knowledge—about Jesus and the origins of Christianity, for example—and then trying to fill that gap by 'beating the bushes' of the ancient world for additional data." His novels are a refreshing blend of good writing and good scholarship.

Critical Reception

Critics were enthusiastic about *Pontius Pilate*. *Moody Magazine* commended the book as "an exciting supplement to the New Testament itself." *The Atlanta Constitution-Journal* called it "a book to be read with eagerness and talked about with enthusiasm." The *Boston Sunday Globe* praised it as "a serious historical study treated so well that it is difficult to drop the volume once begun." *Christianity Today* considered it "tremendously rewarding reading," and the *Chicago Daily News* said it was "unique in biblical novels . . . [*Pontius Pilate*] raises the genre of the historical novel to a plateau it has rarely reached."

DeLong and Schwedt note that *A Skeleton in God's Closet* addresses foundational beliefs of the Christian faith and notes, "Maier packages his message in an extensively researched thriller format." Bethanne Kelly Patrick does warn that the plot of the sequel, *More Than a Skeleton*, "has its problems" with some unbelievable activities and relationships. She also warns that "his academic execution of pacing, dialogue and setting mean that some readers will drop off before the going gets interesting." She thinks Jon Weber speaks "stiffly" and that Shannon is "slightly-too-perfect." She describes Maier as "a specialist in ancient Rome" who "is a personally conservative but intellectually liberal academic." She also believes that he has modeled his protagonist on himself. Actually, the character has a bit more of Indiana Jones in his daring-do adventures.

Awards

Dr. Maier has received a Fulbright scholarship, and the Alumni Award for Teaching Excellence at Western Michigan University (1974). He was named Outstanding Educator of America (1974–1975), Professor of the Year at Western Michigan (1981), and Professor of the Year by the Committee for the Advancement and Support of Education, Washington D.C. (1984). He was given the Academy Award by the Michigan Academy of Science (1985). He won the

Gold Medallion Award for *Josephus: The Essential Writings* (1989), and he was presented with a doctor of letters degree by Concordia Seminary (1995).

Bibliography of Novels by Author

Pontius Pilate. New York: Doubleday, 1968.
The Flames of Rome. New York: Doubleday, 1981.
A Skeleton in God's Closet. Nashville, TN: Thomas Nelson, 1994.
More Than a Skeleton. Nashville, TN: Thomas Nelson, 2008.

Bibliography of Works about Author

DeLong, Janice and Rachel Schwedt. *Contemporary Christian Authors: Lives and Works.* Lanham, MD: The Scarecrow Press, 2000.
Patrick, Bethanne Kelly. Review of *More than a Skeleton. Faithful Reader.* faithfulreader.com/reviews/0765262385.
"Paul L(uther) Maier," *Contemporary Authors Online.* Detroit: Thomson Gale, 2002.
"Paul Maier," in Wikipedia. http://www.wilipedia.org.

MARSHALL, CATHERINE

Personal, Professional, and Religious Background

Sarah Catherine Wood Marshall (1914–1983) was born in Johnson City, Tennessee. Her father, John Ambrose Wood, was a minister and her mother, Leonara Whitaker Wood a homemaker. The family lived in Canton, Mississippi, until Catherine was nine, and then moved to Keyser, West Virginia, where John Wood became the pastor of the Presbyterian Church. Catherine went to schools in Keyser, enjoying piano, debate, scouting and church activities. She finished high school in 1932.

She attended Agnes Scott College, in Decatur, Georgia, majoring in history, and earning a B.A. in 1936. Her plans at the time were to write books and to teach in West Virginia. Instead, she met Peter Marshall. He was an immigrant from Scotland, 12 years her senior, whose dramatic story of commitment to God and recipient of his blessings had led him to America, to Georgia, to Columbia Theological Seminary, and in 1933, to the Westminster Presbyterian Church in Atlanta, where he served as pastor.

That same year that she graduated from Agnes Scott, she married this handsome, charming, and charismatic Scotsman who was to become a popular minister, serving for 12 years at the New York Avenue Presbyterian Church in Washington, D.C., a few blocks from the White House, and for two years as the chaplain of the United States Senate. His eloquent sermons drew overflow crowds to the church Sunday after Sunday. The Marshalls had one son, Peter John Marshall, who was to become an ordained Presbyterian clergyman with a national speaking ministry.

In March, 1943, Catherine Marshall came down with tuberculosis, a life-threatening disease

> Literature, if it is accurately to reflect life, must at times reach past the reader's intellect to the emotional level. In order to achieve that, the writer has to *feel* something as he writes.
>
> —Catherine Marshall in interview with *McCalls*

at the time. The next two years she spent in bed, fighting to regain her health and struggling with her faith. In 1947, as she gradually recovered both her health and her faith, her husband had his first heart attack. His second, fatal, attack came two years later.

After Peter Marshall died unexpectedly in 1949, at age 46, Catherine Marshall taught at the National Cathedral School for Girls for a year and then determined she must dedicate her energies to collecting his papers, publishing some of his best sermons and meditations. Her memories of their marriage, which she chronicles in *A Man Called Peter: The Story of Peter Marshall*, were published in 1951, making her a famous writer on her own. This beautiful book, which describes the painful experience of her husband's death, became a bestseller in 10 days and remained on the bestseller list for more than 3 years. It was turned into an Oscar-winning film in 1955. Other of her works, such as *To Live Again, Beyond Our Selves, Something More, The Helper, Meeting God at Every Turn*, and several collections of sermons and prayers by Peter Marshall, which she edited, were also immediate best-sellers, selling over 16 million copies.

In 1959, Catherine Marshall married Leonard LeSourd, a divorced father of three children, the editor of *Guidepost Magazine*. LeSourd says Marshall had been working on *Christy* for less than a year when she married the second time. "She was a courageous woman to become, at 44, a mother to my 3 young children, ages 3, 6 and 10. *Christy* was put aside for a time as we established a new home together." The LeSourds formed an editorial team, producing a number of nonfiction books. In 1974, they joined John and Elizabeth Sherill to form the Chosen Books Publishing Company in Lincoln, Virginia.

In 1982, Catherine Marshall again found herself critically ill, spending the entire summer in the hospital, working on a new manuscript—*Julie*. Her husband says that they spent visiting hours talking about the book's characters and Catherine Marshall's research into the background. *Julie* was to be published posthumously. Marshall died as she was writing this, her 20th book. The LeSourds had been married for 28 years. In January, 1984, Leonard LeSourd paid tribute to his late wife in a foreword to *Julie*:

"Though the void she leaves in my life can never be filled, I am sustained by memories—of our adventures in faith, of our tumultuously creative family life and of our fulfilling editorial partnership."

She was buried beside Peter Marshall in the Ft. Lincoln Cemetery, in Bladensburg, Maryland.

Major Works and Themes

Christy, Catherine Marshall's justly famous first novel, was a tribute to her mother, who had spent time at a mission station in the Cumberland Mountains in 1912 when she was only a teenager. Her mother took Catherine back to the small community where she had served as a schoolteacher and described to her the people and circumstances she had discovered there. Two world wars later, the two women looked back at the lost culture of the Scots who had inhabited the small cabins in the Appalachian Great Smoky Mountains. In 1936, President Franklin Roosevelt had incorporated this region into the Cherokee National Forest; in 1940, he dedicated 460,000 acres as the Great Smoky Mountains National Park. Most of the families had sold their small holdings to the Government and moved away. This lost culture seemed worth remembering, so Catherine Marshall spent 10 years collecting her mother's stories of individuals, doing research on the people and their history, and drafting a narrative that would be fiction rather than biography.

The resulting novel, *Christy*, is beautifully written. At the center is a young girl who has dedicated her life to Christ and is determined to follow a call to serve as a schoolteacher and missionary. Naive, energetic, boundlessly optimistic, pretty, and emotional, Christy finds herself faced with one surprise after another. No one meets her train; the path to her home station proves difficult, a tragic accident forces her to see the true grit of the community; the people she discovers are suspicious of her motives and sullen about her ideas. Her school is a single room that also serves as the church on Sundays. It becomes the center for educating 67 children, some of whom are bigger than she, all of them barefoot—even in mid-winter. She comes to love them, to help and comfort these proud and independent folk, and to recognize her own pride and intolerance. In the meantime, she finds a mentor in Miss Alice, the Quaker woman who established this interdenominational mission. She also discovers love—for David, the young pastor who is the product of fuzzy liberal theology, and then for Dr. MacNeill, the dour Scot who loves her for the pilgrim soul in her.

In preparation for writing *Julie*, Catherine Marshall again did her homework. Just as she had prepared for *Christy* by studying the mountain culture, the medical details for treating diseases at the turn of the century, the problems of schooling, and the details of clothing, food preparation, herbal knowledge, and many other things, so with *Julie*, she did her research in order to portray another part of the Alleghenies, where she herself had lived. Although she moved the story from West Virginia to Pennsylvania, she kept the landscape and the issues she remembered. She needed to know more about dam construction, about iron furnaces, about the living condition of the workers, about the floods in the Johnstown region, and about the newspaper business.

Drawing on this rich store of factual knowledge and her own lived experience as a teenager in the mountain country, she pictures another young girl, much like Christy (and probably like Catherine), who is ready to step out into life, love, and adventure. She faces the poverty of her environment, explores the depressing conditions of those workers who live in company houses in the Lowlands, and faces her own need to learn how to write for newspapers. The setting is urban this time, the threats are economic and natural. The story is set in the middle of the Depression, and at the time of the great Johnstown flood. She makes the period come to life with vivid strokes and carefully chosen characters from each part of the culture.

Again the lovely young heroine is in love with love, finding one man after another attractive until she finally realizes that it is the older, wiser Englishman who has won her heart. The young minister who woos her has some of the same limitations of David in Christy's story: he is eager to do good but has little understanding of how to explain his faith to the average person. Marshall clearly endorses muscular Christianity that is applied to the circumstances of life, but she decries the inability of pastors to serve as spiritual comforters for their people. She blames the seminaries for their zeal for new doctrines, but not for old verities.

In *Christy*, Marshall made good use of her own experience with illness to give realism to the scenes with diphtheria. She also drew on her life with Peter Marshall to comment on the problems of the grim Calvinism of the Scots and the vague liberalism of the American theological seminaries. Her heroes here and in *Julie* reveal her romantic memories of the love of the older, more educated man from across the seas, whose experience and wisdom can enrich the young woman's life. Both Christy and Julie are young women at the beginning of their adulthood. Both have good minds, social consciences, and an eagerness to step out in faith. Both need to learn self-restraint, to seek advice, and to understand the larger picture of those they are quick to judge.

Critical Reception

John Mort considers both *Christy* and *Julie*, perennial bestsellers, to be young adult classics. Other critics agree: Elizabeth Thalman notes that Catherine Marshall "gives a clear expression of the proud Scotch-Irish mountaineers and their harsh, lonely lives." In the *New York Times Book Review*, Adele Silver points out that *Christy* reveals the "same mixture of family, faith, and fortitude" found in the rest of Marshall's writing. The readers have flocked to this book, making it an all-time favorite with readers.

Julie, coming late in her career, won fewer comments and fewer readers. It has a ragged conclusion, partially because it was not completely edited prior to Marshall's death. The last section suggests that she may have planned a series of stories related to the various loves in Julie's life, taking her into old age. Mort notes that the description of the flood is "magnificent," and the ensuing crisis "draws out the best in Julie, who in turn draws out the best in everyone around her."

The finest critical tribute to Catherine Marshall is the institution of the "Christy" awards, given annually for novels in several categories that express the spirit of her famous first novel.

Awards

Catherine Marshall received numerous awards: she was named "Woman of the Year" in the field of literature by the Women's National Press Club in 1953, awarded a D.Litt. by Cedar Crest College in 1954 and Westminster College in 1979; the Paperback of the Year Award by *Bestsellers* magazine in 1969 for *Christy*; and a L.H.D. from Taylor University in 1973.

Christy has proven to be such an immediate and continuing success that it became the model for hundreds of novels to follow. **Janette Oke**, like many others, readily acknowledges her debt to Catherine Marshall, and evangelical writers still believe themselves honored by receiving the Christy Awards, established in 2000 and given annually for various categories of writing, including General Fiction, Futuristic Fiction, International Historical Fiction, North American Historical Fiction, Romance Fiction, Suspense, and First Novel. Winners are chosen by industry insiders, including editors, reviewers, bookstore owners, and book buyers. They have included **Jan Karon, Francine Rivers,** Janette Oke, **Davis Bunn,** and **Sharon Ewell Foster.**

Bibliography of Novels by Author

Christy. New York: McGraw Hill, 1967.
Julie. New York: McGraw Hill, 1984.

Catherine Marshall wrote 20 books, but only 2 could be considered novels. *Christy* was also made into a successful television series in an adaptation by Michael Ray Rhodes and a film. Word Publishing has also launched the Christy Juvenile Fiction Series, adapted by C. Archer for younger readers—an extended series of books.

Bibliography of Works about Author

Boyer, Paul. "Minister's Wife, Widow, Reluctant Feminist: Catherine Marshall in the 1950s." *American Quarterly* 30 (winter 1978): 703–721.
"Catherine Marshall," *Contemporary Authors Online.* Detroit: Thomson Gale, 2003.
Chase, Elise. "Peter and Catherine Marshall." *Twentieth-century Shapers of American Popular Religion.* Westport, CT: Greenwood Press, 1989, 283–292.
"Interview with Catherine Marshall," *McCalls,* August, 1953.

Koob, Kathryn. "Catherine Marshall," Bright Legacy. Servant Books, 1983, 45–63.

Mort, John. *Christian Fiction: A Guide to the Genre.* Greenwood Village, CO: Libraries Unlimited, 2002.

Silver, Adele. *New York Times Book Review* (November 22, 1967): 70.

Thalman, Elizabeth. *Library Journal* (October 1, 1967): 92.

MORRIS, GILBERT

Personal, Professional, and Religious Background

Gilbert Leslie Morris (1929–) was born in Forrest City, Arkansas. He is the son of Jewell Morris and Irene Gilbert Morris. He attended Arkansas State University, earning his B.A. in 1948. That same year, he also married Johnnie Yvonne Fegert and began to work on a M.S.E. degree, which he earned in 1962. He was to combine a busy life of a growing family (two daughters) and education along with service as a Baptist minister for 10 years. He then became a professor of English at Ouachita Baptist University in Arkansas while continuing his studies, earning a Ph.D. at the University of Arkansas. During the summers of 1984 and 1985, he did postgraduate work at the University of London. His first published novel appeared in 1983.

Eventually, Dr. Morris was to leave teaching to dedicate himself full-time to writing. In addition to over a 100 novels (and more scheduled for the new year), he has published a host of scholarly articles and poems. Along the way, he found pleasure in joining forces with other talented people who have collaborated with him on his novels. His daughter Lynn is one of his favorite coauthors.

For a time he and his wife lived in the Rocky Mountains of Colorado, but more recently they have settled on the Gulf Coast, in Gulf Shores, Alabama.

Major Works and Themes

Gilbert Morris is one of the most enduring, prolific, and endearing of all the Christian novelists. His books are good, clean reads. They are filled with adventure, interesting background materials rich in historical insights, and lively characters. With over 150 titles to his credit, he has written in many genres—poetry and prose, science fiction, fantasy, historical fiction, Westerns, detective novels, and children's stories. A craftsman, with little concern for elegance or complexity, he has summarized his strategy in his book on the secrets of fiction writing—*How to Write (and Sell) a Christian Novel: Proven and Practical Advice from a Best-Selling Author.* The one abiding theme in all of his stories is the Christian faith. His heroes are, or become, Christians. His villains are punished, and often transformed by a conversion experience. He believes firmly in the providence of God and the power of prayer.

> I have fought the fight against producing a Sunday school lesson under the facade of a novel. It is a grubby world we live in, with snares laid for all who serve God. I would like for one stream of American fiction to give the truth about the Christian element. I believe the truth is that there are those like Elmer Gantry—pious hypocrites. There are also, however, those like Corrie ten Boom—strong, attractive Christians who struggle heroically to maintain their faith in a bent world.
>
> —Gilbert Morris, quoted in *Contemporary Authors Online*

Some of his earliest stories were written for young people. In the "Seven Sleepers" series, a collection of ten novels, he portrays teenagers in the mystic land of NuWorld, much of it underwater. Drawing on the mythology of lost Atlantis, he portrays the Dark Lord, a power lusting for world domination. The good god, "Goel," helps the young people even in their final battle.

Some of Morris's more popular stories, especially those targeting young people, feature pioneers, country folk, or animals. His "Ozark Adventure" novels draw on his intimate knowledge of life in the Arkansas mountain country and the people who dwell there. He is careful to avoid stereotypes of rednecks and hicks, instead showing the wisdom often found in people close to nature, as well as their interest in the details of the landscape and their comic view of city people. He draws on this same love of the folk, akin to that which we find in Faulkner's country people, in many of his other novels. His Western novels, like those in his "Reno Western Saga" series, feature active, down-to-earth people. Like Zane Grey and others, he tells a lively story, starring mysterious loners, setting out on adventures, welcoming the challenges of the rugged frontier.

His great success has been his "The House of Winslow" series, his epic study of American history, focusing on a single family that begins in England, comes over on the Mayflower, and goes through the joys and sorrows of life throughout the sweep of the great American adventure. This series has sold in the millions, with many fans buying all 40 of the novels, which have issued forth regularly since 1986. Morris's love of America and his pride in a kind of sturdy independence, characterized by lonely frontiersmen and strong, moral women, the simple folk who have proven the sturdy stock of American history, are palpable in many of his novels.

Gilbert Morris enjoys collaborating with other writers in his novels. His daughter, Lynn Morris, helped him with historical background for the "Cheney Duvall, M.D." series, and Alan Morris joined with him for the "Katy Steele Adventures." Aaron McCarver, who at the time was Dean of Students at Wesley College in Florence, Mississippi, worked with Morris in "The Spirit of Appalachia" series. For "The Price of Liberty" series, he collaborated with Bobby Funderburk, and J. Landon Ferguson helped write "The Chronicles of the Golden Frontier" series. Dan Meeks was coauthor of "The Daystar Voyages" series. Morris has clearly found that the process of collaboration has enlarged his spectrum of writing, encouraged other writers, and provided valuable assistance. A conversation between a couple of friends can become the inspiration for a series in which they collaborate. Gilbert Morris is generous in his own expressions of appreciation for the help of others.

Morris displays his preaching background in most of his novels. One series covers the background of Jesus of Nazareth. In another, the titles are taken from the book of Ecclesiastes. In fact, numerous titles are biblical quotations. He often involves his character with a minister, includes bits of a sermon, and manages to preach about repentance, salvation, and other theological ideas in the course of his novels. Like most of the other writers for the Christian market, he disapproves of Christians choosing to be "unequally yoked"—marrying outside of their faith. As a result, he manipulates the plot so that the toughest of the characters is a convert by the end of the story, and therefore suitable as a mate for the other leading character.

Morris loves to quote Scripture, particularly the New Testament and the Psalms, and uses colorful examples from Bible history relevant to individual characters and situations. He also loves to quote hymns and poetry. His use of Gerard Manley Hopkins's "The Windhover" (in *All that Glitters*) is nicely integrated into the story. That same novel is replete with poetic reference, from "Sweet Afton" Burns, the heroine, to John Dunne, the hawklike hero.

At the same time, Morris is tolerant of other religions and aware that they bring meaning to lives of suffering humanity. His respect for the faith of the Native Americans and others is always touched by a sense that they have less than the full revelation of God's glory and his redeeming grace. Morris does not force this religion on his readers, but the sense of it lingers always in the background—as does a judgment on sinful behavior. His characters preach at one another only when invited and only when conditions seem right for a conversion experience.

Gilbert Morris knows a great deal about many things—falconry, furniture, log cabins, logging, wars, Indians, seamanship, herding oxen, clothing customs over the ages, and ever so many others. It is fun to read his books for the incidental knowledge that the reader can pick up regarding hunting, or movie-making, or doctoring practices in the 19th century. He works hard to avoid anachronisms, leaning on the expertise of others to keep his novels correct. Sometimes he is a bit too detailed on clothing or rigging, but that is a small price to pay for the information that flows from every page.

Critical Reception

The "Seven Sleepers" series, designed for young adults, written from 1994–1997, published by Moody Press, is like the children of Narnia series, according to John Mort, who notes that the "dialogue is wooden, the characterization thin, but Morris does devise excellent otherworldly creatures" that will bring delight to young readers.

"The Ozark Adventures" series, published by Tyndale House in the 1980s, is also designed for young folk, with titles like *The Bucks of Goober Hollow*. Neither this group nor the "Reno Western Saga" series of Westerns is usually listed as explicitly Christian fiction. In these novels, featuring the drifter Jim Reno, the stereotypical Western hero "fights corrupt cattle barons, cleans up mining camps, rescues white boys raised as Indians, and generally befriends the friendless" in what Mort calls a "sturdy series."

It was "The House of Winslow" series that won Morris his reputation among adults, especially those in love with American history. At last count, 40 books have been published in this epic of American history published by Bethany House. The novels trace several generations of an American family, from their arrival on the Mayflower, immigrating from England, taking them through 18th-century life, the Alaskan gold rush, missionary work in Africa, the sinking of the Titanic, and more. Melissa Hudak complimented *The White Hunter*, noting that "Morris has his formula just right."

The "American Odyssey" series follows much the same pattern, this time following generations of the Stuart family in the major eras of the 20th century. "The Appomattox Saga" series, following the post-Civil War events, has a parallel formula. Even the "Cheney Duvall, M.D." books, which describe a woman doctor, who goes West by ship, traversing the Panamanian Peninsula before the building of the canal, takes the historical background of 19th century medicine, women immigrating westward, and the consequences of the Civil War for widowed women into account, beginning a series about life in the West at the time of the Gold Rush.

Gilbert Morris's output is so prodigious that it is impossible to give proper appreciation to all of his stories. Shelley Townsend-Hudson of *Booklist* enjoyed the story of Chip, a white-food mouse who is recruited to be leader of the white-foot mice, only to be attacked by the brown rats—a story she describes as "poignant." The very diversity of Morris's production suggests that he, like his favorite poet, Hopkins, loves the freckled, speckled variety apparent in God's great creation.

Awards

In 2001, *Edge of Honor* tied for the North American Historical Christy Award.

Bibliography of Novels by Author

"House of Winslow" series (Minneapolis, MN: Bethany House, 1986–2007)

"The Appomattox Saga" series (Wheaton, IL: Tyndale House, republished beginning in 2000 by Living Books, 1992–1998)

"The Price of Liberty" series, with Bobby Funderburk (Dallas, TX: Word Publishing Group)

"Far Fields" series, coauthored with Bobby Funderburk (Lancaster, PA: Starburst Publishing Company, 1993–1997)

"American Century" series (originally named "American Odyssey" series). (Grand Rapids, MI: Revell, 1994–2008)

"Wakefield Dynasty" series (Wheaton, IL: Tyndale House, 1994–1998)

"Cheney Duvall, M.D." series, coauthored with Lynn Morris (Minneapolis, MN: Bethany House, 1994–2000).

"The Liberty Bell" series (Minneapolis, MN: Bethany House, 1995–2000).

"Katy Steele Adventures" series with Alan Morris (Wheaton, IL: Tyndale House, 1996–1997).

"The Spirit Of Appalachia" series, coauthored with Aaron McCarver (Minneapolis, MN: Bethany House, 1996–2002)

"The Chronicles Of The Golden Frontier" series, with J. Landon Ferguson (Wheaton, IL: Crossway Books, 1998–2000)

"Omega Trilogy" coauthored with Lynn Morris and Alan Morris (Nashville, TN: Thomas Nelson, Co., 1999–2000)

"Dani Ross Mysteries," also known as the "Danielle Ross" series (Wheaton, IL: F.H. Revell, some republished by Crossway Books, 1991–)

"Cheney and Shiloh: The Inheritance" series, coauthored with Lynn Morris (Minneapolis, MN: Bethany House, 2001–2005)

"Lions of Judah" Series (Minneapolis, MN: Bethany House, 2002–2006)

"Lonestar Legacy" series (Nashville, TN: Integrity Publishers, a division of Thomas Nelson, 2003–2005)

"The Creole" series, co-written with Lynn Morris (Nashville, TN: Thomas Nelson, 2003–2005)

"Singing River" series (Wheaton, IL: Zondervan Publishers, 2005–2007).

Delaney. Wheaton, IL: Tyndale House, 1984.
All That Glitters. Wheaton, IL: Crossway Books, 1999.

Through A Glass Darkly. Minneapolis, MN: Bethany House, 1999.
Jacob's Way. Grand Rapids, MI: Zondervan, 2000.
Edge Of Honor. Grand Rapids, MI: Zondervan, 2001.
Jordan's Star. Grand Rapids, MI: Zondervan, 2002.
The Spider Catcher. Grand Rapids, MI: Zondervan, 2003.
God's Handmaiden. Grand Rapids, MI: Zondervan, 2004.
The Angel Of Bastogne. Nashville, TN: Broadman Holman (B&H Books), 2005.
Charade. Grand Rapids, MI: Zondervan, 2005.
Heaven Sent Husband. New York: Steeple Hill Books, 2005.
Santa Fe Woman. Nashville, TN: Broadman Holman (B&H Books), 2006.
A Man for Temperance. Nashville, TN: Broadman Holman (B&H Books), 2007.
The Mermaid in the Basement: Lady Trent Mystery. Nashville, TN: Thomas Nelson, 2007.

Bibliography of Works about Author

"Gilbert (Leslie) Morris". *Contemporary Authors Online.* Detroit: Thomson Gale, 2006.
Hudak, Melissa. Review of *Over the Misty Mountains. Library Journal* (February 1, 1997): 66.
Hudak, Melissa. Review of *The White Hunter. Library Journal* (June 1, 1999): 96.
Mort, John. *Christian Fiction: A Guide to the Genre.* Greenwood Village, CO: Libraries Unlimited, 2002.
Townsend-Hudson, Shelley. Review of *Journey to Freedom. Booklist* (December 15, 2000): 820.

MORRISON, TONI

Personal, Professional, and Religious Background

Chloe Anthony Wofford (1931–) was born in Lorain, Ohio, a small industrial town near Lake Erie. Morrison was later to note that this community was "close enough to the Ohio River for the people who lived [there] to feel the torpor of the South, the nostalgia for its folkways, to sense the old Underground Railroad underfoot like a hidden stream." She is the daughter of George and Ramah Willis Wofford. In the early years, when she was in school, she found she could earn money by cleaning houses for white people—an activity that made her aware of her own race and the vast differences between her life and the lives of those with "blue eyes," people who had the power to be generous or terrible to those in their employ.

After graduating with honors from high school, she attended Howard University, where she changed her name from Chloe Anthony to "Toni." After earning a B.A. in 1953, she went to Cornell University, earning an M.A. in 1955. That year, she began teaching English at Texas Southern University in Houston, Texas, and then moved to Howard University, where she first began to write fiction.

When she was at Cornell, Toni Morrison met and married Harold Morrison, an architect, whose name she assumed. After the birth of two sons, Harold Ford and Slade Kevin, Toni Morrison and her husband divorced. A single mother needing to earn a good living, Morrison moved her family to New York, where she joined Random House, serving as senior editor from 1965 to 1985. During this time as an editor, Toni Morrison sought to encourage young black authors.

> Fiction should be beautiful, and powerful, but it should also work. It should have something in it that enlightens, something in it that opens the door and points the way.
>
> —Toni Morrison in *Black Women Writers (1950–1980)*

> Toni Morrison is America's only living winner of the Nobel Prize for Literature.

Having had some success with her own fiction, Morrison left Random House to teach at the State University of New York, Purchase, and then at Albany, where she was the Schweitzer Professor of Humanities from 1984–1989. She now teaches creative writing at Princeton University, where she is the Robert F. Goheen Professor of Humanities. She has also served as visiting lecturer at Yale, Bard, Cambridge, and Harvard.

Toni Morrison is considered by many to be our greatest living writer—a powerful representative of the ideas of African Americans and feminists, with an independence of spirit and thought that makes her a difficult writer to classify.

Major Works and Themes

From the beginning, with her novel *The Bluest Eye*, a fictionalized account of life in her Ohio hometown, Toni Morrison has dealt forthrightly about the painful condition of blacks in racist white America. The Christian church has been a consistent target in that critique, with Morrison's accusation that white Christians condoned slavery and fought to keep black people in subservience even after the Civil War. She tracks the black self-hatred to the internalization of white ideals in the African American community—including the accepted standards for beauty, morality, and religion. Like many feminists, Morrison attacks the patriarchal nature of the dominant culture, the persistence of power that determines what is right and what is wrong in human conduct.

Although she is no systematic theologian, Toni Morrison makes liberal and colorful use of Christian terms, names, and symbols. The cross, for example, is discussed at length in *Paradise*. Morrison sprinkles biblical quotations and theological debates through her novels, manipulating the history of religion for her own purposes. Thus, the Convent in this novel, which was originally the mansion of a lavishly sensual wealthy man, becomes the school for Arapaho children and a haven for nuns, then the last resort for a group of misfits—women who seem to form a coven rather than a convent. It is in this final configuration that the town of Ruby—and primarily the men of the town—see the Convent as a threat, and the women housed there as a source of the curse that seems to have descended on the town. The novel, based on the dream of a man-made paradise on earth, never returns to the Christian vision of God's eternal kingdom, but chronicles the failure of the kingdom of woman on Earth. The community of women owes more to Alice Walker's version of "Womanism" than to the actual history of nuns in America or to the Gospel accounts of the kingdom Christians pray will come.

One of Morrison's dominant themes is the superiority of African religions, with their full use of physical expression through dance, song, and shouts. She believes that Western religion has unfortunately preached a dichotomy between flesh and spirit in direct contrast to the more fleshly African culture. This artificial division has created a sterile, rationalistic faith that focuses too much on the life to come and too little on the delights of life here and now. While much of the Christian community finds its hope in transcendence, Morrison is more interested in immanence. Thus, her "Paradise" is a community of people who live together and love one another without rules and without theology—a "Convent" unlike any known in traditional Western religion. Rather than relying on a male minister educated in a seminary, she prefers "unchurched" leaders, much like the African elders, who lead in the "ring shout," chanting, dancing, and clapping with the whole community of worshippers, who are physically engrossed in their worship experience. She has a continuing interest in and preference for the long-lost African religious culture, much of which has been submerged in the Christian worship practices of the black community.

The revival of African mythology is central to Toni Morrison's thought. For example, underlying *Song of Solomon* is the myth of the flying African. Morrison uses the song about "Sugarman" (or "Solomon") that is a corruption of the original myth as an introduction to the novel. Later, the whole community in Virginia proves to be the home of the "flying" slaves, led by Solomon. This discovery provides Milkman, the protagonist, insight into his own hungers for an alternative "truth" to modern American materialism, so firmly embraced by his twisted father, Macon Dead. Choosing the Eve figure, curiously named *Pilate*, as his true mother rather than Ruth, the Mary figure, who castrates him by her cloying love, this new hero "flies" off Solomon's Leap to his freedom—and death.

Morrison dwells primarily on the anguish of modern racism, the absence of community, the violence even among the blacks, and their tragic sense of alienation. She does find some relief in human love, in reaching out to one another physically, in delight in the flesh and in compassion and joy. She searches for a sense of community, and finds herself drawn to the belief that white people are what Elijah Mohammed considered "white devils." She feels at one with the Black Consciousness movement which developed in the1960s, a reversal of the old vision of white values, culminating in the "black is beautiful" theme. In *Song of Solomon*, *Paradise*, and elsewhere, she especially targets the perverse race snobbery within the black community, where the blacks themselves prefer lighter skin to the point of obsession—a mark of self-loathing.

Toni Morrison's people are motivated by their sense of impassioned search—for self-understanding, for family, and for community. While her heroines are usually black, female, and poor, they are also named in such a way as to sound allegorical and mystic. Morrison introduces ghosts, chants, myths, and mystical moments, leading the reader to believe that her own effort to move more deeply into the heart of her own people is driving her toward a transcendent principle.

No one has accused Toni Morrison of writing Christian fiction, in spite of the reappearance of the peacock symbol in *Song of Solomon*, along with the possible mysticism of the traditional interpretation of the Song of Songs. She knows the language and imagery of Scripture, but seems to have missed the sense of God's grace or the transcendent power of the Incarnation. Her focus is more on life here and now, on the tragedy of the human condition that knows alleviation only in human love and physical bliss. Although one of her characters, who sacrifices all for love, is named *First Corinthians*, she nonetheless keeps her focus on earthly love, primarily Eros, missing the delights of heavenly love also promised in that wonderful portion of Scripture. The grotesque murderous Madonna in *Beloved* is surely Morrison's most horrific character—a woman so determined to be free that she kills her own baby rather than seeing her taken back into slavery. The novel has a perverse message of fearsome power that turns the biblical message of love and the cherishing of children upside down. It is full of ghosts and haunting, centering on a love that destroys.

The richness of Morrison's prose and the complexity of her narrative style tantalize the reader, promising more than the author can provide, concluding in more questions than answers to the quandaries of the human condition. She is one of our most provocative modern writers.

Critical Reception

An articulate and forceful advocate for her ideas, Toni Morrison has had enormous success in her career as teacher, lecturer, novelist, and commentator on society. Each of her novels has been widely reviewed by critics from the *New York Times*, the *Wall Street Journal*, the *Washington Post*, to a host of magazines and papers in this country and abroad.

Most of the critics praise her for her lyrical style, her powerful vignettes, her insightful glimpses of African American life. Some criticize her obsession with the black experience in America, especially the anguish of racism, but she responds that she is writing for a community who understands this and needs a spokesperson. Other writers are available for other themes. The violence in her stories, especially the infanticide in *Beloved*, has shocked some readers, but it too has been justified as historical. Slave women did kill their children rather than see them return to slavery. Most critics have come to accept that her stories are not recipes for solving problems but poignant portrayals of those problems and discoveries that we must learn "to live this life intensely and well."

Awards

Toni Morrison is a winner of the Nobel Prize in Literature (1993) as well as the recipient of numerous honorary doctorates in letters. In addition, she won the Ohioana Book Award, for *Sula* in 1975; the National Book Critics Circle Award and American Academy and the Institute of Arts and Letters Award, both in 1977, both for *Song of Solomon*; the Pulitzer Prize for Fiction, Robert F. Kennedy Award, and American Book Award, Before Columbus Foundation, in 1988, all for *Beloved*; and the Elizabeth Cady Stanton Award, from the National Organization of Women. She was honored in 1996 for her Distinguished Contribution to American Letters by the National Book Foundation; and won the National Humanities Medal in 2001.

Bibliography of Novels by Author (Published in New York: Knopf, Unless Otherwise Indicated)

The Bluest Eye. New York: Holt, 1969.
Sula. 1973.
Song of Solomon. 1977.
Tar Baby. 1981.
Beloved. 1987.
Jazz. 1992.
Paradise. 1998.
Love. 2003.

Toni Morrison has also written a play, *Dreaming Emmet*, and a number of children's books (coauthored with her son, Slade Morrison). She has also written lyrics for a number of musical works, coauthored with André Previn and Richard Danielpour, has edited a number of collections, published some of her speeches, and seen some of her novels adapted for film and television.

Bibliography of Works about Author

Bjork, Patrick Bryce. *The Novels of Toni Morrison: The Search for Self and Place within the Community*. New York: Peter Lang, 1992.

Bloom, Harold, ed. *Toni Morrison*. Philadelphia, PA: Chelsea House, 1990.

Bruccoli, Matthew J., ed. *Toni Morrison's Fiction*. Columbia, SC: University of South Carolina Press, 1996.

Century, Douglas. *Toni Morrison*. Philadelphia, PA: Chelsea House, 1994.

Christian, Barbara. *Black Women Novelists: The Development of a Tradition, 1892–1976*. Westport, CT: Greenwood Press, 198

Furman, Jan. *Toni Morrison's Fiction*. Columbia, SC: University of South Carolina Press, 1996.

Gates, Henry Louis, Jr., and R.A. Appiah, eds. *Toni Morrison: Critical Perspectives Past and Present*. New York: Amistad, 1993.

Harding, Wendy, and Jacky Martin. *A World of Difference: An Inter-Cultural Study of Toni Morrison's Novels*. Westport, CT: Greenwood Press, 1994.

Harris, Trudier. *Fiction and Folklore: The Novels of Toni Morrison*. Knoxville: University of Tennessee Press, 1991.

Heinze, Denise. *The Dilemma of "Double-Consciousness": Toni Morrison's Novels*. Athens: University of Georgia Press, 1993.

Jones, Bessie W. and Audrey L. Vinson, eds. *The World of Toni Morrison: Explorations in Literary Criticism*. Dubuque, IA: Rendall/Hunt, 1985.

McKay, Nellie, ed. *Critical Essays on Toni Morrison*. Boston, MA: G.K. Hall, 1988.

Mekkawi, Mod. *Toni Morrison: A Bibliography*. Washington, D.C.: Howard University Library, 1986.

Morey, Ann-Janine. "Toni Morrison and the Color of Life." http://www.religon-online.org/showarticle. asp/title = 966.

Peach, Linden. *Toni Morrison*. New York: St. Martin's Press, 1995.

Samuels, Winfred D. and Clenora Hudson-Weems. *Toni Morrison*. Boston, MA: Twayne, 1990.

Taylor-Guthrie, Danille, ed. *Conversations with Toni Morrison*. Jackson: University Press of Mississippi, 1994.

"Toni Morrison," *Contemporary Authors Online*. Detroit: Thomson Gale, 2006.

Woollams, Alice. "Religion in Morrison's Paradise: The Values of Two Communities, Ruby and the Convent." Suite101.com, June 17, 2008. http://african-american-fiction.suite101.com/article.cfm/ religon_in_morrisons_paradise.

O'BRIEN, MICHAEL D.

Personal, Professional, and Religious Background

Michael D. O'Brien (1948–) was born in Ottawa, the eldest of four children. His father, who was not a believer, was an air force pilot and later a bush pilot in the Arctic. His mother was a devoted Catholic from a strong Catholic family. The O'Briens lived in numerous places, following the father's work. When Michael was in his teens, they lived in a small Inuit village for four years. At another time, they lived in Los Angeles for a year.

Michael O'Brien's artistic gift was inherited from his father, who was a Saturday-afternoon painter. When Michael was 12, his father gave him his first set of oil paints, which he dabbled with briefly and then set aside. During his late teens, he lost his faith, drifted away from the church, and "never thought about God." Then, when he was 21, he had a "St. Paul type" of conversion. "It was total, instantaneous, a stunning surprise, and it was really the hand of God taking over my life at a very dark period." Soon after this experience, he picked up a pencil and went out into the woods and drew a tree. "Then I drew another, and couldn't stop—didn't want to stop. An amazing torrent of creativity came pouring out which I had hardly given a thought to since I was a child. I began to draw everything." Within two years, he had an exhibit at a major Canadian gallery and sold almost all of his paintings.

Following this exhilarating experience, he took a long journey in British Columbia, using the proceeds of his sales. Along the way he met a priest who was inviting "young people to work in a lay apostolate among the rural poor." O'Brien stayed, put his art on the shelf, worked in that ministry for several years, and met his "wonderful wife, Sheila," also a devout Catholic. They were married in the village in the Rockies where they both worked.

> I never work without praying.
>
> —Michael D. O'Brien, interview with Joy Wamboke

Soon after they had married, his wife convinced him that he was an artist. She believed that God wanted him to give at least a year of his life to Christian art. After Mass on May 1, 1975, he quit his job and "put my brushes under the altar and consecrated all my talents to the Lord and for the Church."

> Michael D. O'Brien is an acclaimed artist who specializes in painting icons, using some of his designs as covers for his books.

He worked in a "studio," a small shack, where he waited for God's guidance. He felt led to paint Byzantine icons. He and his wife, who was expecting their first child, sold their house to finance his education in icons. They moved to eastern Canada and lived in a religious community, where he hoped to learn the basics in icon-painting. "With my Western eyes, I had a lot to learn." After seven years of painting icons, O'Brien found that most of his commissions were post-Renaissance, Western style. These years of "radical trust" in God's guidance were years of poverty for the growing family. Nonetheless, the O'Briens learned in these hard times they shared that divine providence provided for the basic needs of a family with six children: "we learned that the Lord is always dependable—it's a path of total trust, continually expanding our capacity for confidence in God."

His fiction, like his painting, comes from what he considers the "baptized imagination." It is the fruit of prayer. He draws on his own wide experience of different peoples and cultures. Michael O'Brien is a self-described "Catholic writer," who notes that Catholic fiction, which is created through the same process as painting, is somewhat different. "Every novelist writes from his own experiences, his own struggles, and those of his friends, and observations of human nature—not observation in the clinical sense, but rather in the sense of pondering things in the heart while invoking grace." This is a process that Catholic theologians call "co-creation. It is similar to a married couple bringing a child into the world."

For a time, Michael O'Brien was editor of the Catholic family magazine, *Nazareth Journal*. In the late 1970s, he felt inspired to write *Strangers and Sojourners* and *A Cry of Stone*, both novels "which just kept fountaining up in my imagination." Neither found publishers in Canada because of their strong Catholic vision. O'Brien did not even consider publishing in the United States. He simply tucked his novels away in a box, "chalking it up to experience, an exercise in writing, and no more." Almost 20 years later, he says he found himself praying in his local parish church, "deeply grieving over the devastated condition that my particular Church—the Church in Canada—and for all the associated troubles of raising a large family in an anti-life society, moreover as a Christian painter, which is a difficult calling at any time in history." Weeping and crying out to God, he suddenly felt "an extraordinary supernatural peace." He suddenly knew that God was bringing good out of all the desolation. He felt a conviction that he must write down what he was seeing—"like a film." For the next eight months, he spent every spare moment writing, going each morning to ask for that day's grace for writing and "for an angel of inspiration." The result was *Father Elijah*, which immediately became a best-seller. Ignatius Press has since published the whole series of his novels, which have found many faithful readers.

He has continued writing essays on religion and culture, his essays appearing in several international journals and anthologies. He has also continued to work as a professional artist, having his first one-man show in a major gallery in Ottawa in 1970. Since that time, he has had more than 40 exhibits, continuing to work in a Byzantine style with contemporary interpretation. He now sells paintings for "upwards of $10,000." He has designed the covers for all of his books with his own art work. Since 1978, he has dedicated his painting exclusively to religious imagery, including liturgical commissions "to work reflecting on the meaning of the human person, transcendence and immanence." His paintings hang in churches, monasteries, universities, community collections and private collections in the U.S.A., Canada, England, Australia, and Africa.

Michael O'Brien, his wife, and their six children still live near Combermere, Ontario, where O'Brien continues to paint and write.

Major Works and Themes

Michael O'Brien attributes much of his imagination to the Holy Spirit and much to his Irish heritage. He writes from a strong and open Catholic worldview, one he has found is repellent to the majority of publishers in Canada. He accepts the structure and sacraments of the church with zeal and defends them vigorously. His nonfictional essays and books on abortion, tyranny, flawed fiction, and other topics have raised much controversy. In his *A Landscape with Dragons: The Battle for Your Child's Mind* (Ignatius Press, 1994), he argues that much contemporary children's literature and culture has strayed from Christian to pagan ideology, including in his critique **C. S. Lewis**'s *The Chronicles of Narnia* and J.R.R. Tolkien's *The Lord of the Rings*. He insists that dragons are forces of evil, for Satan, not sympathetic characters to be enjoyed. Later, he makes similar arguments from orthodoxy regarding the Harry Potter books, which he sternly rejects. He laments the fuzzy lines between good and evil in modern children's literature.

Michael O'Brien is best known for his apocalyptic novels, *Children of the Last Days*, which were published near the turn of the 21st century, joining the host of Last Days books being published at the time. He is concerned with the loss of faith in the world, the steady march toward totalitarianism, the brutality of man to man, and the hunger for personal freedom and love. His ideal tends to be the small community of like-minded people who live simple lives, much like the world he knew as a child in the Alaskan wilderness—before he moved to the cities.

The books are loosely related, though the characters and settings differ. Nor were they written in chronological order, thus making *Sophia's House* a prequel to *Father Elijah*. *Sophia's House* is set in Warsaw during the Nazi occupation. In this novel, Pawel Tanowski, a bookseller, rescues the Jewish child David, who is to become the hero of *Father Elijah*. Pawel hides the boy in an attic of his book shop during the winter of 1942 to 1943, talking with him about "good and evil, sin and redemption, literature and philosophy, and their respective religious views of reality." Decades later, after Pawel's murder by the Nazis and David's escape to Israel, David he becomes a revolutionary and finally a convert to Catholicism.

This background is covered in part in *Father Elijah*, which tracks the man, now a Carmelite monk, as he helps the Pope to confront the powers of the anti-Christ and his totalitarian powers. We learn about Father Elijah's conversion experience, his marriage and his loss of both wife and unborn child, his rejection of violence and of dreams of a human utopia. It is clear in this story that O'Brien considers Satan a real force, prayer a real help, and the church the last bastion against the forces that would bring the world to an end. Although he is a great believer in the power of love, he seldom allows sexual scenes in his stories, and he characterizes Father Elijah as a celibate priest, even though he falls in love. The novel is rich in its spiritual insights and powerful writing. The vision of a world hurtling toward darkness is compelling.

Strangers and Sojourners tells of Anna Ashton, a nurse, who falls in love with Stephen Delaney, an Irish expatriate. Anna's horrible experience in World War I with wounded soldiers has troubled her so that she immigrates to the backcountry of Canada "to reinvent her life" and run an experimental school. She and Stephen marry, have children, but the marriage remains rocky largely because of their religious differences.

Eclipse of the Sun follows this story, chronicling how Canada suddenly becomes a police state. A hippie colony in British Columbia, a microcosm of the larger culture, also "devolves into a petty dictatorship." An old priest rescues a child from the colony, hoping to liberate him. For O'Brien, the stripping of civil liberties by his government is the latest manifestation of the Nazi mindset.

The Plague Journal is the final of the Canadian novels in the "Children of the Last Days" series. Nathaniel Delaney, who is the editor of a small-town newspaper, speaks out against the authoritarian government described in the previous novel.

In *Island of the World*, O'Brien returns to his story of Europe in the wake of Nazi tyranny. This dramatic story of a child born in 1933, in Croatia, traces his life from the slaughter of his family and the partisans' burning of his tiny mountain village, the bleak times in Belgrade with his aunt and her brutal husband, the halcyon days of love and creativity in a seaside town, to the hideous island prison, the swim to freedom, the time in an insane asylum in Italy, and finally his long stay as a janitor in New York City. At times, the book sounds like *The Painted Bird*, at others like the *Gulag Archipelago*. The violence goes beyond most American literature, the fear of totalitarianism is real and justified.

Josip, the young boy at the center of *Island of the World*, learns to swallow his grief, to stifle any arguments against Communism and Tito, to turn to the pure science of mathematics as an escape from the philosophy and politics of his community. At college, he is lured back into individualism, poetry, and love. He becomes a professor, marries, and looks forward to the birth of his first child, only to find himself stripped of everything by a totalitarian government which cannot tolerate his small corner of individual freedom. Even in a prison, Josip finds a way to communicate with fellow dissidents, to escape through flights of fancy, and finally to use his skill as a swimmer. The degradation of his life after this gradually turns to faith, to peace, and to hope. He becomes a man who uses his sorrow and pain to help others and bring joy to a troubled black child and an autistic teenager. He reaches out in love and friendship to those around him, making lasting friendships that finally replace the family he held so dear. His self-denial at the end of the story reveals him to be a saint. He also becomes a poet, his mathematical skills long since lost. By the conclusion, he is a famous man, loved by many, living the life of the ascetic.

Michael O'Brien takes evil very seriously. He has seen it at work in Europe and fears its creeping powers in America. He also believes in the power of prayer, the plan of an Almighty God, and the necessity of a communion of believers—the church. His novels are mammoth, often fragmented, but powerful.

Critical Reception

Peter Kreeft, a storyteller of note himself, says of Michael D. O'Brien that he is a "superior spiritual storyteller worthy to join the ranks of C. S. Lewis, **Flannery O'Connor, Graham Greene,** and **Evelyn Waugh.**" Others who have praised him include Thomas Howard, David Lyle Jeffrey, Michael Coren, Joseph Pearce, James V. Schall, S.J., and Dr. Edoardo Risti.

Some of his themes appear in other writings, including Robert Hugh Benson's *Lord of the World*, a Catholic apocalyptic novel written in 1907. It is easy, especially in his European stories, to see the influence of Dostoyevsky and Solzhenitsyn. His visions and characters sometimes overlap with the American writer **Frank Peretti** as well. *Plague Journal*, for example, bears a resemblance to Peretti's *This Present Darkness*.

John Mort has described his "Children of the Last Days" as "an interesting alternative to the Left Behind series." He does describe them as occasionally "shrill and punishing" while noting that "each of these novels is compelling." Mort acknowledges that his love stories are often sweet.

Bibliography of Novels by Author
(Published in Ft. Collins, CO: Ignatius Press)

Father Elijah: An Apocalypse. 1998.

"Children of the Last Days" series

Eclipse of the Sun. 1998.
Strangers and Sojourners. 2002.
Plague Journal. 2003.
Sophia House. 2005.
A Cry of Stone. 2003.
Island of the World. 2007.

Bibliography of Works about Author

Kreaft, Peter. Review of *Island of the World*. http://www.hopeforabetterworld.wordpress.com.
Mort, John. *Christian Fiction: A Guide to the Genre*. Greenwood Village, CO: Libraries Unlimited, 2002.
"Novelist of the Last Days: An Interview with Michael O'Brien, April 30, 2005." http://ignatiusinsight_com/features2005/print2005/mobrien_intvw_apr05.html.
O'Brien, Michael D. Web site: http://www.studiobrien.com.
Wamboke, Joy. "Hunger for God and the Passion for Art: Interview with the *National Catholic Register*, June 5, 2005." http://studiobrien.com/site/index.php?option=com_content&task=view&id-112&Itemid=74.

O'CONNOR, FLANNERY

Personal, Professional, and Religious Background

Mary Flannery O'Connor (1925–1964) was born in Savannah, Georgia. Both of her parents were members of old Georgia Catholic families, leading their daughter to become a devoted Roman Catholic—a rare creature in the modern South. Flannery attended parochial schools until 1938, when the family moved to Milledgeville, a lovely old, historic Georgia town, where she was schooled at the

> The sharper the light of faith, the more glaring are apt to be the distortions the writer sees in the life around him.
>
> —Flannery O'Connor in a *Life* magazine editorial

Peabody Laboratory School, associated with the Georgia State College for Women. When Flannery was 15, she lost her father to systemic lupus erythematatosis, a disease that was to take her life at the age of 39. Because of the blow this death dealt the family, Flannery O'Connor chose to attend college locally, at the Georgia College for Women, later to become Georgia College and State University. She took her bachelor's degree in an accelerated three-year program, while living at home.

> Everywhere I go I'm asked if I think the universities stifle writers. My opinion is that they don't stifle enough of them. There's many a best-seller that could have been prevented by a good teacher.
>
> —Flannery O'Connor in *Mystery and Manners*

When Flannery O'Connor was in college, she edited the school's literary magazine, the *Corinthian,* contributing fiction and cartoons for the magazine. She was a social science major, but soon recognized her talent lay in writing, especially satire and comedy. In 1945, she won a scholarship in journalism from the State University of Iowa, later named the University of Iowa, where she decided that she was less interested in journalism than in creative writing. A shy young woman, O'Connor is remembered by other students and faculty in the Iowa Writers' Workshop from the time she first appeared, speaking in a thick Georgia dialect that was impossible for her teacher to understand. Her instructor found that it was preferable for him to read her compositions aloud, even though they often included portions of Southern speech, so that the rest of the class could follow the narrative. This workshop is world-famous. O'Connor is now named among the more impressive graduates, whose teachers have included Robert Penn Warren, John Crowe Ransom, Austin Warren, and Andrew Lytle.

Flannery O'Connor began publishing some of her short stories while still in college. Her master's thesis was a collection of short stories, entitled *The Geranium.* After she completed her M.F.A. in 1947, she won the Rinehart Iowa Fiction Award for a first novel, based on her amazing tale of Southern fundamentalist preachers and apostates, *Wise Blood.* She was accepted at Yaddo, the artists' retreat at Saratoga Springs, New York, where artists congregated to work on major projects and enjoy the community of fellow writers and painters. While there, she became friends with the poet Robert Lowell. She also became friends with Sally and Robert Fitzgerald, who invited her to live in their garage apartment in Ridgefield, Connecticut. In this enduring friendship with fellow Catholics, she found generous people who could share her ideas and encourage her talent. This blissful time of community and solitude was interrupted in 1950, when she discovered that she had lupus, the incurable disease that had struck down her father. Although she survived the first life-threatening attack, she had to return to Milledgeville permanently. From there, she wrote regularly to the Fitzgeralds.

Flannery O'Connor's mother moved to Andalusia, the beautiful family farm outside Milledgeville, where the writer could live out her days on a single floor, cared for by her mother and others, surrounded by her beloved peacocks. Many of her letters describe these "peachickens" and their interesting habits. At one point, she had 40 of these beautiful birds on her farm, delighting in the peacocks' display of glory. In one of her essays, she calls the peacock "the king of birds." She and her mother invited school children to come to see her "fowl," enjoying their fresh reactions to this remarkable natural beauty.

> Flannery O'Connor raised "peafowl," peacocks which roamed all over her yard, displaying their gorgeous tall feathers and screaming at one another.

The letters to Sally Fitzgerald were collected after O'Connor's death in a prize-winning volume titled *The Habit of Being*. In these fresh and lively letters, we come to understand Flannery O'Connor's day-by-day life, her beliefs, and her brave humor in the face of disease and impending death. These letters chronicle her determination, regardless of the pain and weakness, to work at her typewriter hours every day. O'Connor saw literary talent as a gift from God, requiring that she work every morning, knowing that the weakness would soon force her to stop. Even during her final, pain-wracked years, walking with the help of crutches, she managed to take some trips to speak and to read from her works. She gave a number of talks about the craft of writing, some of which are included in *Mystery and Manners*. It was through letters that she came to know many important writers, critics, and theologians of her time—Catherine Gordon, **Walker Percy,** and others. The comments she makes in them, her responses to the letters of friends, indicate her lively mind and rock-solid faith.

A period of remission from the dread disease ended in 1964 with surgery for a fibroid tumor. In the following months, Flannery O'Connor's health deteriorated rapidly. After several days in a coma, she died on August 3, 1964, and was buried in Milledgeville, beside her father.

Major Works and Themes

For Flannery O'Connor, fiction was an incarnational art. Although her whole point of view was Christian, the ideas for the stories had to become flesh in order to live. A preacher can tell his congregation about the truth in abstract terms, but the artist is bound by the rules of her art. Neither propaganda nor pornography can properly be considered art, a form that exists for its own sake, not to move others to action nor to convert them. As she told audiences in talks collected in *Mystery and Manners*, the best writing springs organically from the writer's own surroundings. She wrote about the South, particularly small-town and rural Georgia, because that was the region she knew best. She wrote from the point of view of a devout Catholic, because that was who she was. From her experience of the world, she came to believe that these people in her stories represent universal qualities, that their situations are hardly unique.

She talked about the use of "manners," that is the details of speech and behavior that mark a people of a certain region in a certain time. Behind these manners, she senses the "mystery," God's glory shining forth. At the heart of her stories usually lies a moment of revelation, a point of surprise, which no logic can explain. This moment of mystery, when an old woman realizes that an outlaw is just like her own children, or when a young prophet cannot resist baptizing a child, is the moment that flashes of God's grace show forth.

Flannery O'Connor was a painstaking and disciplined writer. She revised her stories conscientiously, polishing, deepening, sharpening them over time. The short story proved her natural form—short scenes that reveal truth in astonishing actions and grotesque ways. She gave the same attention to names that a reader finds in much of Scripture. Hazel Motes has a "mote" in his eye that keeps him from seeing the truth while he spends his time fighting. Francis Tarwater refuses to be "Frank" in simple American dialect or behave like St. Francis, but insists on being "Tarwater"—a folk remedy that has the nasty quality of turpentine. Like his old grand-uncle, he drives persistently for a cure to modern ills that repels the "intellectuals." Often O'Connor's characters are provided with ironic names: the dimwit named "Bishop" or the clumsy girl named "Mary Grace."

The situations and conversations are inevitably startling, and usually packed with biblical allusions. People in Flannery O'Connor's stories, often poor whites or African Americans, appear to be driven by forces beyond contemporary sociology and psychology. They hear the voice of God leading them, and they have revelations of his will—regardless of their own preferences in the matter. Often the actions are exaggerated, forcing the reader to look behind the plot twists for the deeper meanings. For example, in *Wise Blood*, Haze cannot avoid his mission to preach his "truth," that there is no God. He uses his rat-colored car as a pulpit to speak to the people coming out of movie houses, trying to form his Church Without Christ. Comically, he asserts that, if a man has a car like his Essex, he doesn't need salvation. His "church" soon gathers its own apostates, one of whom turns it into a money-making production of "The Holy Church of Christ Without Christ" and the other his lackey, who has his own black hat and rat-colored car. When he sees another "saint," a fake blind man on his own mission of perverted faith, he follows him and emulates him, blinding himself. This self-mutilation demands the reader think about the blindness of Paul and the blind man in Scripture healed by Christ. An anti-Christ, Haze brings confusion rather than light to this congregation of materialists searching for a new "jesus." Using bits of Christian history, Southern fundamentalist preaching style, and moments out of Scripture, Flannery O'Connor constructs a fantastic world that sounds strangely familiar, punctuated with highway signs demanding we repent.

The shrunken "jesus," the mummy from the museum, is a shocking symbol that forces the reader into deeper contemplation of images of Jesus in modern theology. O'Connor recognizes the human hunger for faith and the contemporary distortions of the great story of God's great love for fallen mankind. She sees the modern world as grotesque, and the modern "jesus" as perverse because she remembers the beauty of the original sacrifice on the cross, the true story of God's redemptive love. As she says, Southerners tend to use grotesque exaggeration because they know what is normal. They live in a world that is not so much Christian as "Christ-haunted."

This twisting of faith is apparent again in *The Violent Bear It Away*. Old Tarwater, living a solitary life as a bootlegger in the Georgia countryside, schools his grandnephew in his own faith, demanding that he follow in the same calling. As eccentric as the old man, young Tarwater has no desire to serve as a modern day prophet, the Elisha to his grand-uncle's Elijah. Yet when the time comes to act in defiance of his calling, he performs his first baptism. He knows that he, like Jonah, is now doomed to preach to the city, the modern day Nineveh. He wants to rest under his own gourdvine, or in the shelter of his fields and forests, but he has incinerated this earthly paradise, forcing him to undertake his pilgrimage and preach to the unredeemed.

This novel, like many of O'Connor's short stories, includes "intellectuals" who try to make sense of religious fanaticism without understanding it. Rayber, the uncle of young Tarwater, is a logical materialist, convinced that sociology and psychology have the solutions to modern problems, rendering faith obsolete. He believes that he can rescue "Frank" by providing him normal clothing to replace the black hat and overalls, and by sending him to a public school and integrating him into modern city life. As it turns out, he is himself deaf (as his hearing aid symbolizes) to the Gospel message and blind (his glasses) to the reality of the human condition. He proves impotent, unable even to save his own son or to destroy him. Nor can he understand the blinding love he sometimes feels for this miniature parody of himself.

Flannery O'Connor did not want her readers to be looking constantly for symbols. She insisted that she wanted readers to enjoy her books and stories, to read them for pleasure, not as puzzles to be solved. Yet they are so troubling that the reader is invited into the mystery that lies behind the surface manners. The deeper understanding is always worth the effort. The reader is rewarded with a shocking epiphany.

Critical Reception

Critics love Flannery O'Connor's short stories, as her distinguished list of awards and prizes indicates. They were less dazzled by her novels. Perhaps her sharp wit, her distance from her characters, and her bizarre plots are more difficult to enjoy over an extended work of art than in brief tales. Actually, a large number of her short stories eventually became chapters in her novels, with only slight changes in phrasing and in names.

Flannery O'Connor's first novel, *Wise Blood*, received mixed reviews. Critics appeared to be at a loss as to how to describe this unique novel. They decided to call it "Southern Gothic," but this hardly captures the intense religious meaning of the characters, setting, and action. She bears very little resemblance to the other Southern writers with whom they tried to class her—Edgar Allan Poe, William Faulkner, and Erskine Caldwell. Her editor at Rinehart had warned her that this was not a "conventional novel." Later, when the same critics had seen her short stories, they began to understand how she used her outrageous comedy to make deep, philosophical points. Later critics have come to acknowledge her resemblance to Walker Percy and T. S. Eliot rather than to other modern American writers.

Undoubtedly, O'Connor's heavy use of Southern dialect alienated a number of the urbane critics, who bristled at her frequent use of "nigger" and had trouble enjoying the deliberate misspellings of words like "bidness" for "business." She saw the humor in expressions by country folk that often hide a kind of wisdom or laughter at the outlanders.

As it turned out, *Wise Blood* proved too fascinating to ignore. Critics and fans have continued to study it, gradually coming to consider it a classic. Her own comments on her writing, which are filled with wit and wisdom, have forced others to reread her stories. One critic-writer, who grew up "minutes" away from Flannery O'Connor in Georgia, and who shares nothing of her Catholic faith, nonetheless finds her "white folks without magnolias" refreshing and surprising. **Alice Walker** took time to visit Milledgeville and show her mother the places where O'Connor had lived and worked, describe her life and talent to her, and consider her remarkable, though brief career. She was delighted with a Christian writer who "wrote no religious tracts, nothing haloed softly in celestial light, not even happy endings." She applauded this fellow Georgian for her insights and fidelity to truth and her freedom from the nostalgia for antebellum culture that lingers in so much of Southern literature.

O'Connor's second and last novel, *The Violent Bear It Away*, was also largely misunderstood by critics, most of whom were not Christians and did not recognize the allusions. They did acknowledge O'Connor's remarkable talent by this point, and most of the major reviewers of American literature undertook to write essays—many of which have been collected by Douglas Robellard, Jr. in his book *The Critical Response to Flannery O'Connor*. By and large, no critics have proven as powerful in understanding the characters, the setting, and the action of her novels as Flannery O'Connor herself.

Awards

Flannery O'Connor won a number of prestigious awards and grants in her brief career: the *Kenyon Review* fellowship in fiction, 1953; the National Institute of Arts and Letters grant in literature, 1957; first prize in the O. Henry Memorial Awards, in 1957 for "Greenleaf", in 1963 for "Everything That Rises Must Converge", and in 1965 for "Revelation"; the Ford Foundation grant in 1959; she received a Litt.D. from St. Mary's College, 1962, doctorate of letters from Smith College, 1963; the Henry H. Bellaman Foundation special award, 1964; the National Book Award (posthumously, in 1972) for *The Complete Short Stories*; the Board Award, National Book Critics Circle, 1980, for *The Habit of Being*; and the "Notable Book" citation from the *Library Journal*, in 1980 for *The Habit of Being*.

Bibliography of Novels by Author

Wise Blood. New York: Farrar, Straus & Giroux, 1949.
A Good Man Is Hard to Find (short stories). New York: Harcourt, 1955.
The Violent Bear It Away. New York: Farrar, Straus & Giroux, 1955.
Everything That Rises Must Converge (short stories). New York: Farrar, Straus & Giroux, 1965.

O'Connor's papers are collected at the Georgia College Library.

Her works have been translated into French, Italian, Portuguese, Spanish, Greek, Danish, and Japanese. Cecil Dawkins used "The Displaced Person" for a two act play that was produced in New York, 1966. John Huston directed a movie version of *Wise Blood*, which was released in 2004. Bill T. Jones adapted "The Artificial Nigger" as the basis of a dance in 2004.

Bibliography of Works about Author

Baumgaertner, Jill P. *Flannery O'Connor: A Proper Scaring*. Chicago, IL: Cornerstone Press, 1998.
Bloom, Harold, ed. *Flannery O'Connor*. New York: Chelsea House Publishers, 1998.
Brinkmeyer, Robert. *The Art and Vision of Flannery O'Connor*. Baton Rouge: Louisiana State University Press, 1989.
Browning, Preston M., Jr. *Flannery O'Connor*. Southern Illinois Press, 1974.
Coles, Robert. *Flannery O'Connor's South*. Athens: The University of Georgia Press, 1993.
Driskell, Leon V., and Joan T. Brittain. *The Eternal Crossroads: The Art of Flannery O'Connor*. Lexington: University of Kentucky Press, 1971.
"Flannery O'Connor." *Contemporary Authors Online*. Detroit: Thomson Gale, 2004.
The Flannery O'Connor Bulletin. Milledgeville: Georgia College and State University, 1972-present.
Friedman, Melvin J. and Beverly Lynn Clark, eds. *Critical Essays on Flannery O'Connor*. Boston: Hall, 1985.
Hyman, Stanley Edgar. *Flannery O'Connor*. Minneapolis: University of Minnesota Press, 1966.
Kreyling, Michael. *New Essays on Wise Blood*. New York: Cambridge University Press, 1995.
McMullen, Jeanne Holleran and Jon Parrish Peede, eds. *Inside the Church of Flannery O'Connor: Sacrament, Sacramental, and the Sacred in Her Fiction*. Macon, GA: Mercer University press, 2007.
O'Connor, Flannery. *Mystery and Manners: Occasional Prose*. (essays) Ed. by Sally Fitzgerald and Robert Fitzgerald. New York: Farrar, Straus, 1969.
O'Connor, Flannery. *The Complete Short Stories*. New York: Farrar, Straus & Giroux, 1971.
O'Connor, Flannery. *The Habit of Being* (letters). Edited by Sally Fitzgerald. New York: Farrar, Straus & Giroux, 1979.
Robelland, Douglas, Jr. *The Critical Response to Flannery O'Connor*. Westport, CT: Praeger Publishers, 2004.
Walker, Alice. *In Search of Our Mothers' Gardens*. New York: Harcourt Brace Jovanovich. 1983.
Wrestling, Louise. *Sacred Groves and Ravaged Gardens: The Fiction of Eudora Welty, Carson McCullers, and Flannery O'Connor*. Athens: The University of Georgia Press, 1985.

OKE, JANETTE

Personal, Professional, and Religious Background

Janette Steeves Oke (1935–) was born in Champion, Alberta, Canada, but is a United States citizen. Her father, Fred Steeves, was a farmer and her mother, Amy Ruggles Steeves, a farm wife. The farm on which Janette was raised taught her the values of hard work, perseverance, and productivity—qualities she was to demonstrate throughout her life.

She attended Mountain View Bible College, from which she received a diploma in 1957. That same year she married Edward L. Oke, a professor, who was to become the academic dean of Rocky Mountain College in Calgary, Alberta. They have four children: Terry, Lavon, Lorne, and Laurel—all born within a five-year period. They now have a host of grandchildren.

Over the years, Janette Oke worked at a number of jobs: as a teller and ledger-keeper at the Canadian Bank of Commerce and later at the South Bend, Indiana National Bank and Trust Company. She was also a proofreader and bookkeeper. For one year after her graduation from college and marriage, she acted as a mail clerk. She has also served as treasurer of Mountain View Bible College, an office worker at Reimer Industries, and a loan officer at the Royal Bank of Canada. Since 1959, she has considered herself a full-time writer. She finds that she can write her best work by retreating to her mountain condo, where she outlines her novels, then returning home to complete the writing and editing of her manuscripts.

As a young person, Janette Oke loved the works of Louisa May Alcott, I. M. Montgomery, and **Catherine Marshall.** *Christy* proved to be her favorite book, the model for much of her work. She also loved the prairie novels of Laura Ingalls Wilder, "The Little House on the Prairie" series designed for children, which celebrated the strong family values and stubborn love among pioneers in the American West. She is a member of the Missionary Church.

Major Works and Themes

Having grown up on the prairie of Alberta and having lived there for most of her life, Janette Oke tends to present her characters against this prairie landscape. Drawing on her own experiences and on the many stories she heard as she was growing up, as well as on extensive research in libraries, she develops stories in which she uses teenage girls and young women for her heroines. For example, her most famous series, "Love Comes Softly," is set on the Iowa prairie. It opens with a scene of joy and sorrow: Marty and her husband have come west as homesteaders, thrilled with the prospects of a new life together. In a surprise attack, he is killed before they reach their destination, leaving her pregnant and homeless in a strange land. At his funeral, Clark Davis, a widower she has just met, proposes that she marry him and stay with him and his motherless daughter, Missy, for the winter, planning to return East in the spring. Gradually, this awkward situation becomes more comfortable and her grief turns to happiness as she has her baby, wins Missy's love, and finds Clark to be a mature God-fearing man whom she can accept fully as a husband. The following books continue the saga, showing Missy growing up, marrying, moving still further west, and the other children also finding their paths in life. In each volume, the young woman is seeking for the right path through life, the right partner, and discovering God's enduring blessings.

> Society is searching for a deeper, more committed type of lasting love.
>
> —Janette Oke in an interview with *Contemporary Authors*

Over the years, Janette Oke has gathered a vast library of research materials on which she can draw to provide historical accuracy for her novels. Thus, in her series about the Canadian West, she can comfortably discuss life on the frontier in the 1890s. Oke insists that her plots are character-driven. She follows Catherine Marshall in her development of interesting, sensitive women and God-fearing men, set in difficult circumstances. Her characters move beyond the experience of courtship into the hardships and rewards of marriage, childbearing, farm labor, hostile threats, harsh weather, illness, and death. Although she presents much of the family love of the "Little House on the Prairie" series, she is much more open and uncompromising in her religious message than Wilder. Oke's characters endure terrible accidents, long separations, tragic losses, and yet maintain their faith. They help build churches, worship in their own makeshift "sanctuaries" and insist that God is in charge of their lives.

> Janette Oke's prairie novels, patterned on a blend of Catherine Marshall's *Christy* and Laura Ingalls Wilder's "The Little House on the Prairie" series, set the tone for Christian fiction aimed at the evangelical audience—particularly young women—for the final decades of the 20th century.

Critical Reception

John Mort notes that Janette Oke "is the gold standard for prairie romances, and indeed for all of Christian fiction." Taking her lead from Catherine Marshall, whose *Christy* had already won acclaim, Oke wrote more of the same simple fiction celebrating the values of the American past, romantic love, and God's blessings. Mort grants that Oke owes a debt to Laura Ingalls Wilder and perhaps even more to Beth Streeter Aldrich, but she can nonetheless be said to "have invented the prairie romance—a genre romance celebrating old-fashioned, pioneer virtues." She is also the one who saw the potential for the sequel to maximize profits, retain the readership, and flesh out the story by carrying it to later periods and subsequent generations. Although sequels tend to draw on the devoted fans rather than luring in new readers, increasingly narrowing the audience to the converted, they do sell well. Because secular critics tend to ignore sequels, they become marginalized, selling primarily in Christian bookstores. Mort insists that her books will be read for many years to come and recommends all of her titles for young adults, especially for young girls.

Martha Duffy, writing about Oke in *Time*, indicates that her popular romance and historical novels combine fast-moving plots with a strong Christian faith. She notes that this combination has proven successful in *A Gown of Spanish Lace*, an adventure set in the old West, featuring a God-fearing young woman named Ariana. This novel sold over 250,000 copies, "more than the latest novels by Jackie Collins, John Irving or James Michener."

When Oke teamed up with another Christian writer, **T. Davis Bunn,** in 1996, some critics thought that the two writers were too different in their approaches to work successfully together. Marty Sanchez remarked that "Oke is noted for strong emotional connections to readers through the ordinary details of her characters' lives, while Bunn builds his stories with more attention to description and intricate plots." To the delight of both authors, they found that they are a good team, writing a number of novels in the following years. Most of these are designed for a young adult audience.

Though not praised by most critics, Oke is beloved by readers. Her books, which have proven best-sellers, capture a simple period of American pioneer experience that resonates with many evangelical readers, and several of her stories have been turned into television dramas.

Awards

Janette Oke won the Gold Medallion Award presented by the Evangelical Christian Publication Association, in 1983, for *Love's Long Journey*. She also won the Award of Merit for Fiction for *Love's Unending Legacy* in 1985; was a finalist for several awards, won the President's award in 1992; won Angel Awards for *A Woman Called Demaris* in 1992, *They Called Her Mrs. Doc* in 1993, *A Bride for Donnigan* in 1994, *Reflections on the Christmas Story* in 1995, and *The Red Geranium* in 1996. She was presented with the Honorary Alumnus Award for Personal Achievement by Bethel College in 1993.

Selected Bibliography of Novels by Author

"Love Comes Softly" series (Minneapolis, MN: Bethany House, 1979–1989)

"Seasons of the Heart" series (Minneapolis, MN: Bethany House, 1981–1989)

"Canadian West" series (Minneapolis, MN: Bethany, 1983–1986)

"Prairie Legacy" series (Minneapolis, MN: Bethany, 1987–2000)

"Women of the West" series (Minneapolis, MN: Bethany, 1990–1996)

Other novels by Janette Oke

The Red Geranium. Minneapolis: Bethany, 1995.
Nana's Gift. Minneapolis: Bethany, 1996.

"Song of Acadia" series (with T. Davis Bunn; Minneapolis, MN: Bethany, 1999–2002)

Other Novels co-authored with T. Davis Bunn (Minneapolis, MN: Bethany).

Return to Harmony. 1996.
Another Homecoming. 1997.
Tomorrow's Dream. 1998.

Janette Oke has written many other books on special occasions or for young people. The "Love Comes Softly" series has been turned into a successful television series.

Bibliography of Works about Author

DeLong, Janice and Rachel Schwedt. *Contemporary Christian Authors: Lives and Works.* Lanham, MD: The Scarecrow Press.
Duffy, Martha. Review *of A Gown of Spanish Lace Time* (November 13, 1995).
Logan, Laurel. *Janette Oke: A Heart for the Prairie.* Bethany House, 1993.
Mort, John. *Booklist.* September 1, 1996.
Mort, John. *Christian Fiction: A Guide to the Genre.* Greenwood Village, Colorado: Libraries Unlimited, 2002.
"Oke, Janette." *Contemporary Authors Online.* Detroit: Thomson Gale, 2002.

PALMER, CATHERINE

Personal, Professional, and Religious Background

Catherine Leilani Cummings Palmer (1956–) is the daughter of Harold and Betty Cummings, missionaries who moved to East Pakistan (now Bangladesh) when Catherine was three years old. When she was seven, they moved to Kenya, where she lived until she was ready for college. Catherine Palmer told the interviewer for "The Faithful Fifteen Feature" that she surrendered her life to Jesus when the family lived in Kenya: "I was about eight years old when—during a worship service—I came to realize my sinful state. I was baptized during another service shortly after that." Through all the years that have followed, she has tried to "learn more about Jesus, yet I know I now can only see through a glass darkly. I look forward to seeing Him face to face."

Catherine Palmer attended Southwest Baptist University for her bachelor's degree and Baylor University for her master's in English. She married Tim Palmer and, at almost the same time, began her writing career. She wrote a long medieval saga about a woman's life in England. No one was interested in the manuscript, so she put it away and would have forgotten it except for her mother-in-law, who told her about a romance convention coming up in Albuquerque, near where they lived. She suggested that Catherine send in "that medieval thing you wrote." Palmer added a romance hero to fit the rules of the contest and sent it in—only to win the contest and her first contract. Later, Steeple Hill Press published this revised and expanded tale, which she called *The Briton*. It is a swash-buckling story of a beautiful young woman and her faithful knight, a handsome Norman, whom she scorns for his race and his religion.

The Palmers have two sons, Geoffrey and Andrei. They now live in Missouri.

> I don't believe I have any power to help or change people. That is God's work, and I'm just His servant.
>
> —Catherine Palmer in interview with
> "The Faithful Fifteen Feature"

Catherine Palmer's first novel, which she wrote while working on her master's degree, was a medieval epic—which she submitted as an entry into a romance-writing contest. She won the contest and got her first contract with a publisher.

Major Works and Themes

As her favorite books, Catherine Palmer cites first the Bible. "Because I grew up in Africa, we didn't have all that many books. The Bible, of course, is my primary influence." She also had access to stacks of *Reader's Digest* "Condensed Books." She later came to enjoy J.R.R. Tolkien, **C. S. Lewis,** Jane Austen, Shakespeare, Chaucer, Anne Tyler, **Francine Rivers, Jan Karon,** Alexander McCall Smith, Fannie Flagg, and many others.

She believes that fiction has a powerful effect on readers, encouraging them to step into another person's shoes and to walk with them through experiences. Because of her own religious background, even when writing secular romances, she refuses to allow her characters to have premarital sexual relationships. She tries to convey the idea that a "truly successful marriage must be founded on Jesus Christ"—as has been the case in her own enduring marriage. Her early editors struck most of this message out of her books, and were uncomfortable with her point of view. She was finally able to convince a Christian press—Tyndale—to consider a line of Christian romances. Since that time in the 1990s, all of her fiction has been published by Tyndale. The first of her books to be produced primarily for the Christian market was *The Treasure of Timbuktu,* reprinted as *A Kiss of Adventure* in 2000.

Palmer draws heavily on her background and research for realistic settings for her novels, which are wildly varied. She has written not only medieval romance, but 19th and 20th-century stories, dealing with topics as diverse as dolphin intelligence, the Nantucket whaling trade, white scalpers of Indians, or the archaeology of Western graveyards. Palmer has no hesitation about letting her characters roam over much of the world. In *Fatal Harvest*, for example, two teenagers run from thugs hired by a mega corporation dealing in agricultural products, seeking someone who can publish the information they have found in company records, racing to Texas, Mexico, Paris, and the Sudan as they track the network of distributors of charity intended for starving peoples. The descriptions of Africa are particularly vivid in this cyber-thriller.

In *The Happy Room*, Palmer considers the difficult lives of missionaries' children, living apart from their families in boarding schools much of their youth—neither as a part of their own family nor with any vital connection with the indigenous peoples. On the advice of Francine Rivers and with the permission of her own parents, Catherine Palmer talks openly and sensitively about the struggles of children of missionaries in Africa, where they rarely see their parents after they hit the age they can attend boarding schools. In some cases, the children, feeling abandoned, grow angry, feel lost, and try too hard to please these beloved parents, who themselves feel justified in their neglect of their children because they are "doing God's will." It is only with the tragedy of their youngest daughter, who starves herself to death, that these loving parents come to realize that they need to see their own children as part of their ministry. (This story, unlike the much more vitriolic Barbara Kingsolver bestseller about Congo missionaries, *The Poisonwood Bible*, is sympathetic to both the missionaries and the children, and does not denigrate the work of the missionaries who have sacrificed their family for their calling.)

Only with *A Dangerous Silence* does Catherine Palmer depart from the romance genre to write about a family mystery that comes between a dutiful daughter and a father whom she comes to despise. Most of Palmer's stories contain an element of family alienation, loss, or stress. She investigates damaged relationships between parents and children, husbands and wives, brothers and sisters, suggesting strongly that the solution lies in a shared faith in Christ and in his admonition to love one another. She repeatedly explains that loving and forgiving those nearest to us must precede our efforts to do good in the larger world.

Critical Reception

After a string of successful secular romance novels that follow the Harlequin model, though without premarital sex, Catherine Palmer turned to Christian romances. At last count, she had written about 50 novels, some coauthored with Gary Chapman. Most of her stories have the standard furnishings of romances—the handsome hero ready to come to the defense of the feisty and beautiful heroine, the immediate attraction of the pair, the stumbling blocks put in their way by society, family, or their own misunderstandings, the central role of Christian faith in their union, and the final joining in wedlock.

John Mort has praised a number of her novels, which he notes are "popular" with audiences, and recommends that readers try others as well. Her long listing of titles has been reviewed also by *Booklist, Christian Reader, Library Journal, Publishers Weekly* and other standard reviewers of Christian romances. Melissa Hudak, Melanie Duncan, Penny Kaganoff, and Jessica Lewis Watson have all written favorably about her novels.

Awards

Catherine Palmer's awards fall into two categories, those won for romances from *Romantic Times,* and those won for Christian writing. *A Touch of Betrayal* won the 2001 Christy Award for Inspirational Romance.

Bibliography of Christian Novels by Author (Wheaton, IL: Tyndale House)

Sometimes Forever. 1996.
Lone Star. 1998.
Touch of Betrayal. 2001.
English Ivy. 2002.
The Happy Room. 2002

"Finders Keepers" series (1999–2001)

"Treasures of the Heart" series (2000)

"A Town Called Hope" series (1997–1999)

"Fatal Harvest" series (2003–2004)

"Miss Pickworth" series (2006)

"Four Seasons" series (with Gary Chapman)

Catherine Palmer has also contributed to numerous collections and joined with other authors in various publications.

Bibliography of Works about Author

"Catherine Leilani Cummings Palmer," *Contemporary Authors Online*. Detroit: Thomson Gale, 2002.

Catherine Palmer Interview with *The Faithful Reader*, "The Faithful Fifteen Feature." http://www.faithfulreader.com/FEATURES/15_palmer_cathrine.asp.

Catherine Palmer Interview with *Focus on Fiction*. http://www.focusonfiction.net/catherinepalmer.html.

Catherine Palmer Web site: www.catherinepalmer.com.

Mort, John. *Christian Fiction: A Guide to the Genre*. Greenwood Village, CO: Libraries Unlimited, 2002.

PELLA, JUDITH

Personal, Professional, and Religious Background

Judith Pella's parents, a truck driver and a factory worker, found that their child loved history and all kinds of stories. By the time Judith was 11, she was creating her own Civil War epic. Assuming that reading and writing were avocations, not vocations, she went to California State University at Humboldt, where she earned a B.A. in social sciences. She then went to St. Francis Memorial Hospital in San Francisco to study for a nursing degree. She used this education to become a nurse and a teacher. At times in her life, she has also been a pickle packer, a sales clerk, a church secretary, and a Tupperware saleslady. Through all of this activity, including a marriage and children, she has continued to love history and experiment with writing.

In her spare time, Pella would take up a pen or sit down at a typewriter and craft a few pages. It was one such page that her old friend **Michael Phillips,** an evangelical writer and bookstore owner, spotted when he was visiting for a Bible study. When he asked whether she had written the selection, she minimized her efforts, asserting she was "just fooling around." Phillips at the time was very busy with his work, his family, and his writing. He had an idea for a series about Scotland, and asked Judith Pella if she would be interested in collaborating with him. Her love of history blended with his need for rich historical background. The resulting books, most of which were coauthored with Phillips were "The Stonewycke Trilogy" and "The Stonewycke Legacy." Other series followed, the "Journals of Corrie Belle Hollister" series, "The Highland Collection," and "The Russian" series. Although the idea for this last series also came from Phillips and the two writers began working in tandem, Pella concluded the work by herself. This began her career as a full-time novelist.

Judith Pella begins a book by reading the general literature of a period or place so as to gain an overview. As she writes, on her word processor, she continues her research into details that become relevant to her narrative. She works out of her home office, taking advantage of time when her children are in school. She considers herself a "night person" who comes into her own in the late afternoon and evening. Pella indicates on her Web site that she does most of her writing in her home in Oregon. She lives there with her family, filling her free time with "quilting, collecting things for her doll house, and reading." She also enjoys sailing with her husband on the Columbia River.

> There is simply no place in Christ for all the petty rules and legalism that unfortunately crop up in the Church.

Major Works and Themes

Having discovered in her work with Michael Phillips that she enjoyed working as a collaborator, she joined with another friend, **Tracie Peterson,** to create two series: "Ribbons of Steel" and "Ribbons West," novels dealing with the construction of the intercontinental railroad. Pella also discovered in this work that she could develop her own narratives and produce stories single-handedly. The "Lone Star Legacy" series is her own work, revealing her strengths and weaknesses as a writer.

> Judith Pella began her novel writing when Michael Phillips came by for a Bible study, noticed a bit of writing in her typewriter, and asked her about it. He was so impressed that he suggested she work with him on a series.

Judith Pella continues to count both Phillips and Peterson as friends and acknowledges their influence on her own growth as a writer. Of Phillips, she says, "He has been the most influential to me as a writer and as a person. He was instrumental in instilling confidence in me with his praise and his gentle criticism. I doubt that I would have finished those first books without his nudging, and I know that I wouldn't have had the nerve to actually send them to a publisher." Undoubtedly, Michael Phillips's influence with Bethany House, where he served as an editor for the George MacDonald series, provided Pella with an important entré into the evangelical fiction field.

Judith Pella, like so many contemporary evangelical writers, grew up with films and television as constant influences in their lives. This has led to a pattern of brief scenes with rapid action, high adventure, melodramatic reversals of fortune, and exaggerated characterization. Pella does distinguish herself from her fellow writers by her abiding interest in historical context. She links her stories to specific periods and geographic areas, using the great national or international events in her narratives. The setting reflects the Civil War, the Russian Revolution, or the building of the railroads. Often famous figures appear in her stories. Buffalo Bill shows up in *Warrior's Song*, and Cornelius Vanderbilt in *Westward the Dream*. She uses the tragedies of the Native Americans as both context and motivation in *Warrior's Song*, and also shows in this tale her abiding concern for tolerance. Several of her novels touch on the irrational suspicion of people of other races, nationalities, classes.

Like those she admires, Judith Pella does make the Christian faith central to her stories, often the key to relationships and the solution to difficulties. Her characters are often brought low so that God may raise them up. Pella is not particularly doctrinaire, more generally evangelical, believing that God will redeem those whom he has chosen. She rarely mentions the specific church to which a person belongs, but does note the old time hymns that they sing, most of which are part of the evangelical tradition.

Since she views her audience as primarily female, she tailors her stories to meet their predictable concerns: "self-identity, spousal abuse, dealing with the death of a spouse, and the importance of family and heritage." She is a fearless writer, willing to take on medieval history, the 19th-century West, the struggles of Russian people in the last years of the Czar, or the beginning years of World War II. She is dauntless in her approach to narratives set in Russia, Scotland, California, Texas, Russia, or Oregon. Her love of history and her interest in ideas drive her stories.

Critical Reception

Most of the critics who follow Christian romances are fond of Judith Pella's work. Her varied historical settings, her fast-faced action, and her melodramatic plots make for good reading.

Because she leaves so many plot lines incomplete at the conclusion of each volume, she lures her readers into the sequels to her novels. Although many of her novels could stand alone, they are far richer if we have the insights afforded by reading the full series.

Since so much of Pella's work is hopelessly entangled with her coauthors', most criticism avoids attributing specific description to her efforts, noting only that her work is fast-paced and exciting. She insists that her novels are "for the most part action and character driven." At least one critic has complained that she makes little effort to maintain a consistent point of view. She is also such a speedy writer that she tends to be colloquial rather than precise in her word choice. Her characters are inclined to speak like modern Americans with a sprinkling of the idioms of their peculiar period or nation, sometimes choosing quite unlikely words to express themselves. She makes liberal use of stereotypes to characterize foreign correspondents, drunken Indians, rich railroad men, or innocent young maidens. As a writer who produces at least a volume a year, Pella does not pause for poetry or grope for the precise word. She is content to tell her story in simple language, recognizing that her readers are more interested in the romantic adventure than in carefully crafted narratives.

Awards

Member of the Romance Writers of America.

Bibliography of Novels by Author (Minneapolis, MN: Bethany House)

Blind Faith. 1996.
Beloved Stranger. 1998.
Texas Angel. 1999.

"Lone Star Legacy" series (1993–1996)

Heaven's Road. 2000.

"Daughters of Fortune" series (2002–2005)

"Patchwork circle" series

Mark of the Cross. 2006.
Co-authored with Michael Phillips.

"The Stonewycke Trilogy" (1985–)

"The Highland Collection" (1987)

"The Stonewyke Legacy" (1987–1988)

"Journals of Corrie Belle Hollister" series (1990–1991)

"The Russians" series (1991–1998)

Some of these were written by Judith Pella alone, some by Michael Phillips:

Co-authored with Tracie Peterson.

"Ribbons of Steel" series (1996–1998)

"Ribbons West" series (1999)

Bibliography of Works about Author

Carrigan, Henry, Jr. "Christian Fiction—*Warrior's Song* by Judith Pella. *Library Journal* (February 1, 1996, Vol. 121, Iss. 2): 66.

DeLong, Janice and Rachel Schwedt. "Judith Pella," in *Contemporary Christian Authors: Lives and Works*. Lanham, MD: The Scarecrow Press, 2000.

Duncan, Melanie. "*Separate Roads*" and "*Texas Angel*." *Library Journal* (November 1, 1999, Vol. 124, Iss. 18): 68.

Harrison, Nick. "Christian Publishing Booms Despite 'Embarrassments.'" *San Francisco Chronicle Sunday Edition*, July 26, 1981, 2.

Hesdoly, Violet. "Book Review: *Mark of the Cross* by Judith Pella. BC Books. http://blogcritics.org/archives/2006/28/134924.php.

Judith Pella Official Web site. http://www.judithpella.com.

"Judith Pella." http://ww.stevelaube.com/authors/judithpella.htm.

Ramsdell, Kristin. "*Westward the Dream*." *Library Journal* (November 15, 1998, Vol. 123, Iss. 19): 56.

Tracy's Book Nook. http://www.tracysbooknook.com/authors/judith_pella.html.

Zaleski, Jeff. "Written on the Wind." *Publishers Weekly* (October 22, 2001, Vol. 248, Iss. 43): 42.

PERCY, WALKER

Personal, Professional, and Religious Background

Walker Percy (1916–1990) was born in Birmingham, Alabama—in a suburb next to a golf course. His father, Leroy Pratt Percy, was part of a very old distinguished Southern family. This urban setting is far distant in tone and culture from the region which his family had earlier settled, St. Francisville, "Feliciana Parish." He described this portion of Louisiana is a "strip of pleasant pineland running from the Mississippi River to the Perdido, a curious region of a curious state." The Percy family traces its history back to Harry Hotspur, who was made famous by Shakespeare in his historical drama *Henry IV, I.*

Walker Percy lived in Athens, Georgia, until he was13, when his father committed suicide, an incomprehensible action that left a permanent mark on the teenager. For a time, the family lived with the grandmother in Athens, Georgia. Then his father's famous cousin, William Alexander Percy, invited the widow and her three sons to move to Greenville, Mississippi, to live with him in the old family home. Walker Percy came to see his charming, cultured, wealthy, 45-year-old bachelor cousin, whom he called "Uncle Will," as his surrogate father and literary tutor. Two years after this move, his mother, Martha Phinizy Percy, was killed in an automobile accident. This double trauma was to have significant effect on his thinking and writing, leaving him with a deep awareness of human tragedy.

> The Christian novelist nowadays is like a man who has found a treasure hidden in the attic of an old house, but he is writing for people who have moved out to the suburbs and who are bloody sick of the old house and everything in it.
>
> —Walker Percy, from "A Novel About the End of the World," in *The Message in the Bottle*

Walker Percy believed in God's covenant with the Jews, famously asking how else we could explain the Jews in modern America. After all, where are the Hittites? Only God's grace could explain the perseverance of this remnant of Jews throughout history and the incarnation of Christ as our Savior.

Life at the Percy home in Greenville opened up to the teenager a whole community of intellectuals and poets who enjoyed Uncle Will's hospitality. In an essay titled "Life in the South," Percy noted that "it did not seem in the least extraordinary to find oneself orphaned at 15 and adopted by a bachelor-poet-lawyer-planter and living in an all-male household visited regularly by other poets, politicians, psychiatrists, sociologists, black preachers, folk singers, itinerant harmonica players." It was here he became friends with Shelby Foote and learned to enjoy Shakespeare and opera and romantic novels. Uncle Will paid a price for taking on this burden. After the family descended on him, he wrote little poetry—and he died relatively young. On the other hand, Percy Walker said, "I know what I gained: a vocation and in a real sense a second self; that is, the work and the self which, for better or worse, would not have been open to me." He lived in Uncle Will Percy's house from age 14 to age 26.

In 1934, Percy left for the University of North Carolina, where he studied chemistry in preparation for medical school, completing this work at the Columbia College of Physicians and Surgeons. While in New York, he stayed at the famous West Side Y.M.C.A., a setting he later used in *The Last Gentleman*. After Percy completed his work at Columbia in 1941, he began his residency at the Bellevue Hospital in New York. His work in pathology required him to perform autopsies on homeless alcoholics, who had often died of tuberculosis—a disease which Percy himself contracted. He was forced to spend the next three years in a sanatorium in upstate New York, the Trudeau Sanatorium at Saranac Lake, where he passed the days reading French and Russian literature, psychology and philosophy. Percy was to describe this sojourn in his second, unpublished novel, *The Gramercy Winner*. By 1944, Percy was well enough to go back to Columbia and teach pathology, but then suffered a relapse. At this point, he decided to leave medicine.

It was at about this time that he found himself reading Kierkegaard and feeling drawn to Roman Catholicism. Given the confusing theologies available to modern humans and the genuine need for an answer beyond scientific materialism, he was convinced that Christianity is the only true solution for human alienation. He enthusiastically believed in his new-found faith, corresponded with other Roman Catholics (like Allen Tate and **Flannery O'Connor**) about his beliefs, and used it as the basis for his aesthetic.

In 1946, he married Mary Bernice Townsend. The Percys have two daughters, Ann Boyd and Mary Pratt. One of their children was born deaf, leading Percy to the study of semiotics, the study of symbols and human communication. A number of the essays in his nonfiction books deal with his theories of language and with his faith.

After his marriage, he and his wife moved their family to Covington, Louisiana, a place to which they were attracted by its very isolation as well as its propinquity to New Orleans with all of its rich culture. As his biographer Father Samway noted: "Percy could sniff clean air in Covington, eat crawfish étouffée, drink an occasional Jack Daniels, enjoy his family life, visit friends, feel about as good as one may on this green earth and write fiction while looking out his study window." When questioned by a neighbor as to what he did, he first responded that he wrote books. When that proved unsatisfactory for his neighbor, he admitted he did "nothing." That seemed to be more satisfying. Because of an inheritance, the Percys were able to live comfortably without any requirement that he return to medicine.

Walker Percy was generous in his attention to other writers and open to discussions of his works, his faith, and his life. When he died in 1990, he was widely praised and genuinely mourned. His wide reading, deep thought, and innate gentility made him one of the more beloved modern Christian writers.

Major Works and Themes

Like Matthew Arnold, in "Dover Beach," Walker Percy believed that: the Sea of Faith is retreating and that the world lying before us "hath really neither joy, nor love, nor light, / Nor certitude, nor peace, nor help for pain, / And we are here as on a darkling plain, / Swept with confused alarms of struggle and flight, / Where ignorant armies clash by night." For both Arnold and Percy, living in this middle state, between the old world of religious certitude and the new world of scientific arrogance, the postmodern, post-Christian world of radical individuality, we reach out for human love.

Walker Percy's conversion to Roman Catholicism, after his long study of science and humanism, gave him a powerful theological framework. When asked by skeptics why he was a Catholic, he simply stated, "Because it's true." This is a breathtaking assertion in an age he considered "radically incoherent," where all truth is relative. From his perspective, most writers are advocating flawed ideas—Marxism, millennialism, romanticism, scientism, and so on. Serious fiction, he believed, was diagnostic, not designed to instruct, edify, or titillate. He did not consider pornography or polemics art. He saw the novelist, like God, creating something new, singing a "new song." In his essay "Science, Language, Literature," Walker Percy explained that it is important in this "incarnational" form (the novel) to place the human (like Robinson Crusoe) in a specific place in a specific time and have him or her discover something, do something, reveal something. The emotions of the novelist should be those of Crusoe, "wonder and curiosity."

Walker Percy saw himself as a Southerner, but not the brand of Southerner who would defend sharecropping as his Uncle Will had done or yearn for the antebellum South. He was a skeptic who mocked the New South, the Sunbelt, a triumphant part of modern American commercialism, pollution, and violence, while oddly remaining a "Christ-haunted" land, full of true believers and religious hucksters. A man of principle, he had no respect for bigots or hustlers, and could laugh at friends as well as foes. Although he was involved in the Civil Rights movement of the 1960s, he was able to satirize pompous African American characters as quickly as he did country club white supremacists.

Walker Percy loaded his novels with historical and literary allusions, to the delight of educated readers. Calling his characters Lancelot Andrews or Thomas More, he brought English history into stark contrast with modern Southern glad-handing churchmen who have trouble answering the simple question: "Do you believe in God?" He played with the double meaning of *Lancelot*, the knight guilty of adultery yet committed to the quest for the Holy Grail, and More, the divine who translated portions of the King James Version of the Bible. He loved Yeats's poetry and his image of the "Second Coming," played with that poet's idea of history as a gyre, drew on Robert Browning's and Edwin Arlington Robinson's techniques for dramatic monologues, and satirized the sexual fantasies of Southern writers like Faulkner and Tennessee Williams. His playful use of other writers gives a special resonance to his novels.

All of Walker Percy's novels have certain common characteristics, many of them drawn from his own sense of alienation. The hero, or mock-hero, is usually an orphaned, penniless

Southern gentleman, with education, taste, gentility, and family connections. Sometimes a lawyer or a doctor, he is a pilgrim searching for the meaning of life. Like Alice in her Wonderland, his protagonists find that things seem to happen to them; random events lead to adventure or love or disaster. Haunted by the suicide of the father, these secular saints seem to be drifting, in an alien world, strangers even in their own families. Like Isaac, threatened by his own father, the protagonist often senses impending doom, a coming apocalypse. The countervailing force is love—sexual love and *agape* love—that they seek and that can redeem them. God hovers over his universe seemingly in despair of the grotesque distortions of real faith by the actual religious left on earth. Ministers and priests rarely offer living water to thirsting pilgrims.

One scholar, Patrick H. Samway, has noted that all of Percy's novels "represent from one perspective, an unconscious quest to locate his family roots and to explore those locales that were significant in his personal development." Thus, he uses Birmingham, his birthplace; Athens, the place of his father's suicide; New York City, where he studied and worked; and Covington, where he spent most of his creative life. The place of the Percys' honeymoon became the setting of his first novel, *The Charterhouse*. In this novel, he portrayed a vacation home he and his brothers knew from their youth, called "Brinkwood" in Sewanee. This lovely spot became Percy's temporary home during his honeymoon, and appears again as the setting in *Lancelot*, a much later novel.

Covington was to figure in his first published novel, *The Moviegoer*. This novel uses bits and pieces of Percy's own life and experience in a brilliant commentary on the post-Christian era. The antihero of the novel, a 30-year-old stockbroker in New Orleans, Binx Bolling, has all of the comforts modern America has to offer. but lacks ambition. Binx's Catholic family, a blend of Garden District snobs and Faulknerian country folk, dream of his eventually making something of himself, perhaps going to medical school and devoting himself to research. His father, a surgeon, is dead and his mother has remarried, thereby reinventing herself as a middleclass housewife. Binx comes to define himself as a "sincere Laodicean." Finding his greatest delight in sex and movies, Binx. laments living in a world with neither the sensual delights of the pagan nor the torments of Christian orthodoxy. He discovers *merde* rather than mystery, settling for a kind of weary half-life with a cousin he loves and pities. In the background, New Orleans is a scene of raucous Mardi Gras celebrations, but Binx and Kate miss this madness, returning only for Ash Wednesday. The lost pair of lovers stand outside the church, watching worshippers and penitents come out marked with ashes on their foreheads.

In *The Last Gentleman*, Will Barrett, another genteel Southerner, is adrift in the North. A victim of periodic amnesia, Will tries to make sense of the random bits and pieces of the world he observes. He happens on to a bourgeois Southern family who adopt him, providing him work, love, friendship, and purpose. They ask him to accompany Jamie, the dying son, on his final journey—in a Trav-L-Aire camper, provided with instant grits and other supplies. Percy again sees his characters as accidental pilgrims, "in transit, in journey."

Deeply philosophical, yet witty and satiric, Walker Percy refrains from sermonizing. When a child or a friend dies, neither the author nor his protagonist makes any effort to explain this as part of God's plan. He uses Jamie's death to satirize the Baptist family into which Jamie was born that denied the efficacy of infant baptism, the Episcopal church, which never inquired whether he had been baptized, and the Catholic nun who insists on baptizing the dying boy, though no one believes he is a Christian. Like most of Percy's stories, the plot stops without ending. He rejects Aristotle's pat structures that suggest a neat narrative line, with beginning, middle, and end. This is no match for our random adventures in this world.

Love in the Ruins is a mock-apocalyptic tale. The country has undergone a revolution, roles are reversed and civilization is in rubble. The subtitle of the novel is *The Adventures of a Bad Catholic at a Time Near the End of the World*. Using the landmarks of the modern South, Percy follows the adventures of a Christ-forgetting, Christ-haunted doctor, who knows only that "something is about to happen." This ironic Tom More, no saint and no hero, fights his way through this landscape of nightmare, searching for no Utopia, but only for a way to survive and respect himself and his work. He is satisfied finally that he is a good doctor, who ends up with a Presbyterian mate, a rowdy bunch of little children, and a thrill from once again receiving the Sacraments: "I eat Christ, drink his blood." This happy celebration of Christmas actually concludes the novel, making it atypically cheerful.

In this story the "lapsometer" which Tom More invents is Walker Percy's clearest reference to human depravity in a fallen world. This comic device allows him to measure all manner of illnesses, most of which are spiritual rather than physical. Like most of his other mechanical references—the telescope in *The Last Gentleman* or the camera in *The Moviegoer*—the mechanical wonder represents some lingering spiritual hunger in people, some need to see, to fix, to understand.

Lancelot is a mock romance, with the antihero questing for "unholy Grail." He believes that the evil of sexual sin may turn out to be the heart of evil, but finds the Sodom he destroys is really an empty shell. Lance, the protagonist of this extended dramatic monologue (or confession to a priest/jailer/friend), is a kind of Miniver Cheevy who longs for the olden days when the difference between whores and ladies was clear. Like Candide or Thoreau, he finally settles for a solution of everyday simplicity—cultivating his garden.

The Second Coming returns to Percy's obsession with the coming apocalypse. The hero, again Will Barrett, is convinced that the Jews have disappeared from America and are congregating in Israel for the Battle of Armageddon. By now, this "engineer" has grown weary of "engineering." He rebels against his bossy daughter who wants to plan his final days and decide how his fortune is to be used. He falls down a rabbit hole of sorts and meets Allison, the daughter of his old lover, who is as mentally unstable as he and as frightened of being forced into the neat grooves of modern culture. Percy manages to cast a satiric eye on almost all religions and faux religions in this comic quest of an ageing romantic. A once-born man in a world of twice-born Christians, Will finds both the evangelicals and the atheists equally distasteful and misguided. He returns to basic questions: "Is there a God?" "Do you believe in God?" These queries embarrass the clergymen and confuse his friends. He undertakes a kind of challenge to God, a gamble like Pascal's, in which he enters a cave to see whether he will live or die. As it happens, through a funny set of events, he almost dies before he comes alive, like Lazarus (or the man emerging from Plato's cave), seeing the whole world fresh.

Walker Percy's final novel, *The Thanatos Syndrome*, once again uses Feliciana, the locus of his family's roots. This time, he pictures it as a kind of modern Eden, harboring "all manner of fractious folk, including Texans and recent refugees from unlikely places like Korea and Michigan." They enjoy L.S.U football and reruns of M*A*S*H, drink Dixie beer, and refuse to worry about the pollution of the Mississippi. The hero again is Dr. Tom More, who has just returned to find his former patients are behaving strangely. His discovers that the local water supply is being laced with heavy sodium from the coolant of a nearby nuclear power plant, uncovering the plot by a pair of local doctors to salvage the "American social fabric" by chemical means. As in *The Second Coming*, Percy ponders the current American fixation with "happiness" and "normalcy" even at the expense of creativity and fierce emotions. Tranquilizers can make people more content, but less than totally human. Like his hero, he prefers anguish to contentment, freedom to planning.

Combining his critique of the ghosts of the old South, the hucksters of the New South. and the general looniness of the new Gnostics of the North, Percy recognizes he is as "mean as a yard dog." As a scientist, he has studied the modern wasteland, diagnosing the devaluation of human life. Walker Percy laughs at humans who think they can live without faith or fidelity. On the other hand, he is not comfortable with most contemporary Christian writers: he complains that most Christian novels are a "turn off," full of clumsy and repetitive religious language. He insists that the writers often sell out their art for a "pot of message." He prefers a more subtle discovery that underscores the sacramental value of ordinary things. He does believe that the novel is the ideal form for talking about faith. Like Christianity itself, it is "incarnational," revealing God's hand in everyday life. The novelist, he often said, is like the canary in the coalmine, reacting to the dangers before average men realize their peril.

Critical Reception

The Moviegoer, Walker Percy's first novel, was at first ignored by the critics, but finally celebrated for its profundity and wit, winning the National Book Award. From this point forward, Percy was recognized as a major talent, invited to speak at numerous conferences and to teach briefly at nearby colleges, showered with awards, and generally lionized by the intellectual community. Numerous scholars have studied his works and written on his ideas.

The critics have praised Walker Percy's novels, finding them challenging and fresh. Jac Tharpe, who has written extensively on Walker Percy, is one of numerous academic scholars who consider him a major talent. He has been the subject of a vast number of academic studies.

Alfred Kazin notes that Walker Percy is "atypical" of both Southerners and Roman Catholics, providing a kind of religious humanism, picturing the "existential theme of life as shipwreck." His themes are more akin to French existentialists than to those of American writers, particularly his sense of alienation and inauthenticity, the failure of human communication, the awareness of shallowness of contemporary life, and the malaise that grips so much of the intellectual community. He is clearly an artist of ideas. As he said of himself, "I lived a hundred miles from William Faulkner but he meant less to me than Albert Camus." He found his fictive example in Camus, choosing to write about characters who were the embodiment of certain pathologies in the twentieth century. He told an interviewer for the *New York Times* that he preferred the French approach to fiction: "The French see nothing wrong with writing novels that address what they consider the deepest philosophical issues." He never changed his theme or approach, always grappling with the same theme, malaise, a disease of "depression and despair, intensified by the awareness of a moral and metaphysical wasteland in which intellectuals claim to have outgrown the rituals and beliefs of organized religion."

Walker Percy has been reviewed widely in the usual places: the *New York Review of Books*, the *New Republic*, the *New Yorker*, the *New York Times*, as well as in *Commonweal*, *Mississippi Quarterly*, *Modern Age*, *Sewanee Review*, *Southern Literary Journal*, and many other journals. Most of the critics have found each novel and nonfiction work entertaining and puzzling. He invites discussion in response to his deep and challenging philosophy.

Those who would seek to understand Walker Percy better can find rich resources in his own nonfiction works. His essays, speeches, and random thoughts have been collected in two volumes of fascinating reading. In *The Message in the Bottle* and *Signposts in a Strange Land* (which was selected and edited after his death), we find fuller descriptions of his own life, his memories of "Uncle Will," his view of science in opposition to the novel, his judgment on many modern novels and novelists, his comments on various places and his own Louisiana, his commitment to the Roman Catholic Church, and many explanations of symbols and symbolism—the whole science of semiotics. His is indeed a lively mind.

Many evangelical readers will find his novels troubling. He, like Dante, considers a thorough investigation of sin, especially lust, to be a vital part in his path to God. His central characters are modern-day seekers, not comfortable in their faith. He treats his priests and pastors with the same satiric disdain he showers on his Buick dealers and land speculators. Nor will Southern aficionados find him a comfortable companion: he laughs at the reduction of the old South to a series of garden-and-home-tours for midwesterners who want to believe in the myths of antebellum culture popularized in *Gone with the Wind*. He also sneers at the crudeness of the new South with its highway systems, motels, and golf courses. He even makes fun of planned, gated, boring retirement communities full of carefully organized activity. Walker Percy's novels include something to offend almost every segment of society—but also to amuse and delight most of his readers.

Awards

Walker Percy's awards, prizes, and memberships are too numerous to list. The most impressive include: the National Book Award for Fiction, 1962, for *The Moviegoer*; the National Institute of Arts and Letters grant, 1967; the National Catholic Book Award, 1971, for *Love in the Ruins*; *Los Angeles Times* Book Prize, 1980, National Book Critics Circle citation, 1980, Notable Book citation from American Library Association, 1981 for *The Second Coming*; *Los Angeles Times* Book Prize for current interest, 1983, for *Lost in the Cosmos: The Last Self-Help Book*; St. Louis Literary Award, 1986; and the Ingersoll Prize from Ingersoll Foundation, 1988.

Bibliography of Novels by Author

The Moviegoer. New York: Knopf, 1961, reprinted, Avon, 1980.

The Last Gentleman. New York: Farrar, Straus & Giroux, 1966, reprinted, Avon, 1978.

Love in the Ruins: The Adventures of a Bad Catholic at a Time Near the End of the World. New York: Farrar, Straus & Giroux, 1971, reprinted, Avon, 1978.

Lancelot. New York: Farrar, Straus & Giroux, 1977.

The Second Coming. New York: Farrar, Straus & Giroux, 1980.

The Thanatos Syndrome (Book-of-the-Month Club selection), New York: Farrar, Straus & Giroux, 1987.

Bibliography of Works about Author

Allen, William Rodney. *Walker Percy: A Southern Wayfarer.* Oxford: University Press of Mississippi, 1986.

Bloom, Harold, ed. *Modern Critical Views: Walker Percy.* New York: Chelsea House, 1986.

Coles, Robert. *Walker Percy: An American Search.* Boston: Little, Brown, 1978.

Crowley, J. Donald, and Sue Mitchell Crowley, eds. *Walker Percy: Critical Essays.* Boston: G. K. Hall, 1989.

Desmond, John F. *At the Crossroads: Ethical and Religious Themes in the Writings of Walker Percy.* Troy, NY: Whitson Publishing Company, 1997.

Dupuy, Edward J. *Autobiography in Walker Percy: Repetition, Recovery, and Redemption.* Baton Rouge: Louisiana State University Press, 1996.

Gray, Paul. "Implications of Apocalypse: THE THANATOS SYNDROME by Walker Percy." *Time,* March 30, 1987. http://www.time.com/time/printout/0.8816.963883.00.

Hardy, John Edward. *The Fiction of Walker Percy.* Champagne/Urbana: University of Illinois Press, 1987.

Hobson, Linda Whitney. *Walker Percy: A Comprehensive Descriptive Bibliography.* New Orleans: Faust, 1988.

Hobson, Linda Watney. *Understanding Walker Percy.* Columbia: University of South Carolina Press, 1988.

Kazin, Alfred. *Bright Book of Life.* Boston: Little, Brown and Co., 1975.

Lauder, Robert E. *Walker Percy: Prophetic, Existentialist, Catholic Storyteller.* New York: P. Lang, 1997.

Lawson, Lewis A., and Victor A. Kramer, eds., *Conversations with Walker Percy.* Oxford: University Press of Mississippi, 1985.

Lawson, Lewis A., ed. *Following Percy: Essays on Walker Percy's Work.* Troy, NY: Whitson, 1987.

Lawson, Lewis A. *Still Following Percy.* Oxford: University Press of Mississippi, 1996.

Luschei, Martin. *The Sovereign Wayfarer: Walker Percy's Diagnosis of the Malaise.* Baton Rouge: Louisiana State University Press, 1972.

Mills, Henry, ed. "The Walker Percy Project." http:www.ibiblio.org/wpercy/.

Percy, Walker. *The Message in the Bottle: How Queer Man Is, How Queer Language Is, and What One Has to Do with the Other.* New York: Farrar, Straus & Giroux, 1975.

Percy, Walker. *Lost in the Cosmos: The Last Self-Help Book.* New York: Farrar, Straus & Giroux, 1983.

Percy, Walker. *Novel-Writing in an Apocalyptic Time* (limited edition). New Orleans: Faust Publishing Company, 1986.

Percy, Walker. *State of the Novel: Dying Art or New Science.* New Orleans: Faust Publishing Company, 1988.

Poteat, Patricia Lewis. *Percy and the Old Modern Age.* Baton Rouge: Louisiana State University Press, 1985.

Quinlan, Kieran. *Walker Percy: The Last Catholic Novelist.* Baton Rouge: Louisiana State University Press, 1996.

Samway, Patrick H., S. J. *Walker Percy: A Life.* New York: Farrar, Straus & Giroux, 1997.

Samway, Patrick H., S. J. "Walker Percy's Homeward Journey." The Walker Percy Project. http://www.ibiblio.org/wpercy/samway.html.

Tharpe, Jac, ed. *Walker Percy: Art and Ethics.* Oxford: University Press of Mississippi, 1980.

Tharpe. Jac. *Walker Percy.* New York: Twayne, 1983.

Tolson, Jay. *Pilgrim in the Ruins: A Life of Walker Percy.* Chapel Hill: University of North Carolina, 1994.

Tolson, Jay. *Walker Percy: The Making of an American Moralist.* New York: Simon & Schuster, 1990.

Wright, Stuart. *Walker Percy: A Bibliography: 1930–1984.* Westport, CT: Meckler, 1986.

Wyatt-Brown, Bertram. *The House of Percy: Honor, Melancholy, and Imagination in a Southern Family.* New York: Oxford University Press, 1994.

PERETTI, FRANK

Personal, Professional, and Religious Background

Frank E. Peretti (1951–) was born in Lethbridge, Alberta, Canada. His father, Gene E. Peretti, was a minister and his mother, Joyce E. Schneider Peretti, a homemaker. Jeremy Lott indicates that Peretti's childhood was "hellish." He had a glandular birth defect, cystic hygroma, which led to infected and swollen lymph nodes in his neck. This caused a baseball-sized lump on his throat, for which he had seven operations. When the cyst was finally removed, his tongue was affected, swelling and elongating, turning black and oozing blood. After still more operations on his tongue, he continued to live with a protruding tongue, which made speech difficult. Peretti's family, who had moved to Seattle, Washington, by this time, took him to the faith healer Oral Roberts, who could do nothing for these grotesque symptoms.

> When you're writing Christian thrillers, you have to be very mindful of your readership. . . . I never put any swearing in my books.
>
> —Frank Peretti in interview with Gustav Niebuhr, *New York Times*

His family proved loving and supportive through this time of trial, but the young boy was embarrassed at school by his tongue and his diminutive size. Considering himself a "small, frail freak," he felt safe at home with loving parents and siblings, enjoying his room filled with comics, trading cards, and books. Frank Peretti began creating stories about movie monsters and writing monster stories. In his memoir, *The Wounded Spirit*, he recalled that he and his brother created their own monsters, called "Xenarthex."

Eventually, Peretti's physical condition improved with the help of a speech therapist, who taught him, at age 12, to talk with his tongue inside his mouth. His own life as a "monster" led him to understand the student massacre at Columbine, which supposedly began with bullying and developed into antisocial behavior, finally exploding in violence. As Peretti said, "I think part of me wanted to be one, at least a monster who wins. I wouldn't have minded being Frankenstein." With his family's love and his doctor's assistance, he turned his anguish into creative shapes, storytelling and music. By the time he was in high school, he found that he could attract the neighborhood children with his storytelling skills. Then, after school, Peretti began playing banjo in a local bluegrass group. He also served as an assistant to his father, who was pastoring a small Assembly of God church on Vashon Island, Washington.

After he married Barbara Jean Ammon in 1972, Frank Peretti left the bluegrass group and started his own Christian music ministry,. From 1976 to 1978, he studied English and film at the University of California, Los Angeles. In addition to serving as the associate pastor of a community church in Washington state from 1978 to 1984, he worked in a ski factory as a ski maker from 1985–88, and began writing short stories and his first adult novel, *This Present Darkness*. Since Peretti could not find a publisher who would accept his idiosyncratic style of story-telling, he was obliged to self-publish both this and his second novel, *Piercing the Darkness*. Since 1986, he has been a full-time writer and a public speaker. He also continues to be a musician and a storyteller.

Etta Wilson notes that Frank Peretti "is a quiet man who wears his fame well. He lives a simple life that includes carpentry, sculpturing, bicycling, hiking, and banjo making." He and his wife, who had settled in a trailer near Seattle until he became a success, now live in a lovely log home deep in the woods of northern Idaho. His books, which have sold in the millions, have been translated into many languages, including Icelandic and Korean. He looks at this success and notes that he has changed Christian fiction. It used to be "very nonconfrontatitive—you know, the young woman struggling against the rigors of prairie life meets a fine young Christian minister." Now, he notes, he has opened up the Christian market for a new kind of book, the Christian thriller.

Major Works and Themes

Frank Peretti has made his reputation with stories of spiritual warfare. Early in his life, he became fascinated with storytelling, then dabbled in short story writing and comic strips.

Most of his early works were designed for children. The "Cooper Kids Adventures" series appeared every few years from 1986 to 1997. He then began his adult novels, starting with *This Present Darkness*, a novel that describes the spirit warfare in a small town. Like novels by the Inklings, the novel portrays the spiritual wars between angels and demons in literal terms, describing them with great detail and ferocity. Peretti chooses an evangelical minister as his hero and a fearless publisher with his faithful sidekick. Peretti's villains are mysterious strangers, unscrupulous tyrants, and liars. The local college allows the seeds of evil to germinate in the New Age teachings of a psychology professor. The greedy trustees and president allow financial mismanagement to fund the college's own downfall. Gradually, Omni Corporation, an international conspiracy supported by demonic forces, takes over the real estate and power in the small town of Ashton.

Peretti's second adult novel, *Piercing the Darkness*, is a sequel, with some of the same characters and motives. This time, the Omni group has targeted the larger education system, seeking to eliminate Christian schools and to infiltrate the public schools, with Eastern mysticism and meditation replacing academic subjects. Again the giant conspiracy reaches like a system of mole hills all through the country, apparent only to the shrewd investigator. The local police station, the post office, the schools, even the church find spies or plants who are seeking to undermine traditional values.

Unlike many other modern Christian novelists, Peretti makes his spirits quite vivid, providing names and personalities. Like Milton in *Paradise Lost*, he describes the battle of the angels in graphic and violent terms. Strongman and Destroyer sound, in fact, much like the superheroes and monsters in comic books, with "Zoom!" "Crash!" or Wham!" reminding us of Flash Gordon and Spiderman. The short scenes, quick speeches, and rapid changes of scene also seem to derive from comics. It is rare to see a prolonged or meditative statement other than a quoted letter. Curiously, the lesser spirits often have names taken out of medieval morality plays—Despair, Lust, and Pride.

Frank Peretti uses language that is obscene, and he does not shy away from murder, rape, torture, or mutilation. However, he does not dwell on the violent details as do most other writers of thrillers. In his stories, the reader can be assured that good will finally triumph over evil and that those who have died in Christ will be rewarded in Heaven. He loves to bring the chief sinners to repentance and redemption, to see the evil forces crumble, and to rejoice in the chaos and blame-sharing of the defeated diabolical creatures.

He places his epic dramas in small towns with average American people leading humdrum lives. The community churches, evangelical, Pentecostal, and Bible-centered, become the locus of hope and truth. The network of saints who pray fervently establish a hedge about the beleaguered characters. Peretti shows the blessings that come from suffering—the gold burned clean of its dross by the refiner's fire. This is particularly true of the central figure in *Piercing the Darkness*, a tortured woman named Sally Roe, who survives and finds redemption after a near fatal time in thrall to the forces of darkness.

Peretti also uses his own experience liberally to reveal truths he has discovered. The minister and the false messiah in *The Visitation* both share characteristics with Peretti. The firm belief in demons as well as angels, in demonic possession and the constant warfare for the Christian is central to his novels. His monsters are colorful and interesting; his people know real threats and face humiliation and death, the novels have real suspense and tension, but good finally triumphs in the end. God's people cannot be vanquished unless they give in to the powers of the world, the flesh, and the devil.

Critical Reception

Frank Peretti's novels have sold in the millions. His publishers acclaim him as the successor to **C. S. Lewis.** Others consider him an evangelical Stephen King and a writer who "out-Grishams Grisham." Nonetheless, until recently his works have been "virtually unknown outside the Christian community." Critics for *Time* and *Newsweek* have reluctantly recognized him after decades of success as the creator of crossover Christian thrillers. Even the *New York Times* has acknowledged he paved the way for novels by Chuck Colson and Pat Robertson.

His early work was ignored by critics for years until the Christian singer Amy Grant praised his books. By 1988, *This Present Darkness* had become a best-seller, prompting Peretti to undertake the sequel, *The Piercing Darkness.* Both owe debts to the *Star Wars* films that had enthralled audiences. His children's books in the "Cooper" series took advantage of the delight in adventures, with heroes slaying dragons and undertaking exotic adventures. These novels, like the *Raiders of the Lost Ark* films, star an archaeologist hero, Dr. Jake Cooper, who is accompanied by children in his search for treasure and his battles with satanic forces.

Some of this same fantasy is central to his 1995 novel, *The Oath,* a book labeled a "Christian thriller" by Gustav Niebuhr of the *New York Times.* The novel was referred to by *Christianity Today's* critic as "Saint John Wayne and the Dragon." The good guys are still clearly distinct from the bad guys, as is clear in their names and behavior. As this critic notes, "Our team is made up of tall, strong, courageous guys and a few gals, usually housewives, who are prayer warriors with skirts. The bad guys are creepy, greedy, and sleazy. And they get their butts kicked in the end—by Jesus, of course." The story deals with a landscape photographer in the remote Pacific Northwest, where he and a local woman have an affair that echoes *Bridges of Madison County.* But the sin is soon punished by a monster that has been killing people for a 100 years. This dragon attacks only the sinners, not the saved citizens of the region. At least one critic thought the dragon was the best character in the story—"clever, subtle, surprising."

It was *The Wounded Spirit,* his painful revelation of his own hellish experience that came out at the time of the shootings at Columbine, which won him a following among those concerned with youth violence. He was to use much of his own life story again in *The Visitation,* a novel about a fake messiah, a less fantastic story about a young, burnt-out minister. His criticism of the church "stuff" that gets in the way of true faith struck many as revealing a new maturity in his approach. Etta Wilson noted that the book had the same theme of the never-ending conflict between good and evil, that it includes his "vintage trademarks of fast action and multiple scene changes," but nonetheless is more subtle than earlier novels. Peretti himself acknowledged, in his interview with her for *BookPage,* "I'm not writing about spiritual warfare here. This book is more the story of a crisis of faith. It deals with the deeper unspoken things that most Christians face at one time or another and points back to the heart of the reader, rather than being a battle out there somewhere."

Anita Gandolfo traces Peretti's rise to fame in part to the taste already cultivated by Stephen King, whose secular blockbusters included *Salem's Lot* (1975), a similar tale of spiritual warfare. These novels demonstrated "that there was an audience for such intimations of the supernatural," though Christian readers were reluctant to read King's stories. By Christianizing this demonic warfare, Peretti appealed to the horror-loving members of his own culture. Though *This*

Present Darkness, which ushered in much of the vogue for Christian fiction, "took Christian readers by storm," Gandolfo insists "the novel reflects the work of the amateur writer." It is "filled with turgid prose, stereotypical characters, and plodding narration interspersed with scenes of violent battles." The narrative is "awkwardly constructed," the novel a "classic horror" story.

Theologians are more mixed in their assessment of his worldview. Pierre Gilbert worries about his influence on Mennonites and other Pentecostals. He notes that the "Third Wave" movement, including C. Peter Wagner of Fuller Theological Seminary's School of World Mission, Tom White, founder of Mantle of Praise Ministries, John Dawson, Southwest U.S. Director of Youth with a Mission, and Peretti have developed a growing interest in the demonic that he considers unbiblical. He attributes this to a belief in the ancient Mesopotamian creation myths as opposed to Genesis. For Peretti and others, creation is born out of violence and war; the universe is populated by a great number of evil entities in a hierarchy under a supreme ruler, and human life is characterized by war and uncertainty. Dr. Gilbert argues that the New Testament portrays spiritual warfare as "simply one of many metaphors Scripture uses to characterize different aspects of the Christian life." For Peretti, it is the central, even the exclusive image.

Awards

Frank Peretti won the Gold Medallion Award from the Evangelical Christian Publishers Association and the Readers' and Editors' Choice awards, *Christianity Today*, for *Piercing the Darkness*.

Bibliography of Novels for Adults by Author

This Present Darkness. Westchester, IL: Crossway, 1986.
Tilly. Westchester, IL: Crossway, 1988.
Piercing the Darkness. Westchester, IL: Crossway Books, 1989.
Prophet. Westchester, IL: Crossway Books, 1992.
The Oath. Nashville, TN: Word Publications, 1995.
The Visitation. Nashville, TN: Word Publications, 1999.

Frank Peretti is the author of the radio drama *Tilly*. The *Wild & Wacky Totally True Bible Stories* series has been produced on videocassette and DVD, has a number of "retellings" of Bible stories. Peretti is a regular contributor to Christian periodicals.

Bibliography of Works about Author

Blodgett, Jan. *Protestant Evangelical Literary Culture and Contemporary Society*. Westport, CT: Greenwood Press, 1997.
Duffy, Martha. Review of *The Oath*. *Time* (November 13, 1995): 105.
"Frank Peretti," *Contemporary Authors Online*. Detroit: Thomson Gale, 2003.
Frank Peretti Home Page. http://thewoundedspirit.com/.
"Frank E. Peretti." Wikipedia. http://en.wikipedia.org/wiki/Frank_Peretti.
Gandolfo, Anita. *Faith and Fiction: Christian Literature in America Today*. Westport, CT: Praeger, 2007.
Gilbert, Pierre. "Spiritual Warfare and the Third Wave Movement: A Critique." http://www.mbseminary.edu/main/articles/gilbert2.htm.
Howard, Jay R. "Vilifying the Enemy: The Christian Right and the Novels of Frank Peretti," *Journal of Popular Culture* (Winter, 1994): 193–206.
Lott, Jeremy. "Peretti's Past Darkness." Review of *The Wounded Spirit*. *Christianity Today* (March 5, 2001).
Mort, John. Review of *The Oath*. *Booklist* (September 1, 1995): 6.

Mort, John. Review of *The Visitation*. *Booklist* (June 1999): 1743.

Niebuhr, Gustav. "The Newest Christian Fiction Injects a Thrill into Theology." Review of *The Oath* and other thrillers. *New York Times*, October 30, 1995.

Peretti, Frank. *The Wounded Spirit* (a memoir), Nashville, TN: Word Publications, 2000.

"Saint John Wayne and the Dragon." Review of *The Oath*. *Christianity Today* (April 29, 1996).

Wilson, Etta. "Maturity Marks Frank Peretti's *The Visitation*." Interview for BookPage, July, 1999. http://www.bookpage.com/9907bp/frank_peretti.html.

PETERSON, TRACIE

Personal, Professional, and Religious Background

Tracie Peterson (1959–) grew up in a Christian household where she read the Bible daily, following the example of her parents. She always loved stories. Even as a child she loved to entertain her friends by telling them stories. In high school, however, she was denied entrance into a creative writing class because she supposedly lacked imagination or talent. With the encouragement of her mother and grandmother, she continued to read widely among a range of 19th- and 20th-century authors and to write her own secular romances.

Peterson began her career as a magazine writer and editor, but found her taste for historical romances demanded more space than the short story would allow. Her first novel appeared in 1993. Since then, she has sold millions of novels, some coauthored, some in extended series. With her great success in romance writing, she has formed her own company, Peterson Ink, Inc., which has been outsourced by Barbour Publishing for Heartsong Presents Inspirational Romance line of books. She has three employees. In addition to these activities, she likes to give advice to other writers, and is a frequent contributor to conferences on Christian fiction.

She was married to Jim Peterson, an editor, in 1981 and is the mother of three children. She currently lives in Belgrade, Montana with her husband and their youngest son, having moved there from Kansas. She takes her Christian commitment very seriously, using it as the basis of her work. She was converted at six years of age and now worships with her husband at a nondenominational church, believing that details of doctrine tend to interfere with Christian harmony.

Major Works and Ideas

Tracie Peterson writes within the evangelical tradition, chronicling universal hardships and struggles, offering encouragement and guidance. She sees herself as a "Titus 2" woman, encouraging younger women. Her goal in her writing is to include the plan of salvation in each book, weaving together stories that interest the reader, providing challenging concerns, and incorporating biblical applications in response to these life experiences.

The central characters in her novels tend to be intelligent, beautiful young women and strong, handsome young men, clearly destined for one another. They face barriers to their love and temporary reversals in their lives. Unwilling to see her characters "unequally yoked," the author structures the plots with sufficient moments of enlightenment to allow a conversion prior to marriage. The women see marriage and family as central to their lives, their Christian mission. They worry constantly about perils of health and travel faced by their loved ones. In the background are colorful historical

> Tracie Peterson, the author of over seventy books, was told that she did not qualify for a creative writing class in high school because she did not have the imagination or talent for writing.

events, crimes, natural catastrophes, and the usual sad and happy events of human existence. The frequently expressed prayers of the Christian protagonists are usually answered by either a favorable outcome or deeper understanding because of the disappointment. Peterson also interrupts her narrative with biblical applications which the characters discuss at length, usually with the mature Christian teaching the new convert.

Tracie Peterson clearly loves history, enjoys doing her homework on details of life in the different eras and places she chronicles, and consequently provides easy-to-read and informative historical novels. She weaves the background into the narrative, including interesting details of everyday life of the old West or the Yukon. Her Western novels, some coauthored with **Judith Pella,** are justly famous.

Tracie Peterson has a voracious appetite for fiction, showing the influence of 19th-century English and American writers as well as modern best-sellers. As a young person, she was an avid reader of Jane Austen, Louisa May Alcott, and others, noting, "I read a lot of classics as a child. I enjoy the historical detail and plotting from writers like Kathleen Woodiwiss and Jude Deveraux, and Rosamunde Pilcher, as well as **Liz Curtis Higgs,** Judith Pella, Judith Miller and others." She indicates she has read Charles Dickens, Oswald Chambers, **Max Lucado** and numerous contemporary best-sellers, including authors like Herman Wouk and Tom Clancy.

Critical Response

Peterson tells a lively story, while avoiding bad language, graphic sex, and violence. Her strengths lie in her well-constructed plots, readable style, and her use of richly researched background, with details of architecture, furnishings, food, and clothing. Conforming to the guidelines of her publisher, she is usually ignored by the critics of major papers and journals and her works are only described rather than criticized by critics like Mort, Hudak, Duncan, and DeLong, who deal with the evangelical press products.

Her audience is clearly Christian women with a taste for lively adventure in "gentle reads." Because she writes so fast, she is not a polished stylist, but is an imaginative tale teller, with plenty of foreshadowing and a delight in adventure and suspense. Though Peterson deals frankly with the evils of the world, including abandonment and rape, the reader can be assured of her favorite characters being duly rewarded and a happy ending to all the trials and tribulations.

Awards

Tracie Peterson was voted favorite author for 1995, 1996 and 1997 by the Heartsong Presents readership, and awarded Affaire de Coeur's Inspirational Romance of the Year 1994, for *Iditarod Dream*, American Christian Romance Writers' (ACRW) Book of the Year in Inspirational Long Historical Romance for 2002 and other awards.

Bibliography of Novels by Author
(Minneapolis, MN: Bethany, Unless Otherwise Indicated)

"Heartsong Presents" (Uhrichsville, OH: Heartsong Presents, 1992–1999)

"Westward Chronicles" (1998–2000)

"Yukon Quest" series (2001–2002)

Entangled. 1997.
Controlling Interests. 1998.
Framed. 1998.
A Slender Thread. 2000.
The Long-Awaited Child. 2001.
Julotta. Promise Press, 2002.

"Desert Roses" series (2002–2003)

"Bells of Lowell" series (Coauthored with Judith Miller, 2003)

Silent Star. 2003.
Castles. Uhrichsville, OH: Barbour Publishing, 2004.
"Lights of Lowell" series. (Coauthored with Judith Miller, 2004–2005).

"Heirs of Montana" series (2004–2005)

"Alaska Quest" series (2006)

"Ribbons of Steel" series (Coauthored with Judith Pella, 1996–1998)

"Ribbons West" series (Coauthored with Judith Pella, 1999–2000)

"Shannon Saga" series (Coauthored with James Scott Bell, 2001–2002)

A number of Tracie Peterson's works have been republished as anthologies and collections, largely by Barbour.

Bibliography of Works about Author

Faithful Readers Connection. http://www.faithfulreader.com/features /15_peterson_tracie.asp.
Mort, John. *Christian Fiction: A Guide to the Genre.* Greenwood Village, CO: Libraries Unlimited, 2002.
Mort, John. Reviews of *Treasures of the North* and *City of Angels. Booklist* (March 1, 2001): 1228.
The Romance Reader's Connection. Review of *Rivers of Gold.* http://www.theromancereadersconnection.
    com/aotm/authorofthemonthpetersonmillerjan05.html.
Tracie Peterson's Web site: http://www.traciepeterson.com/meettracie.shtml. http://profile.myspace.
    com/index.cfm?fuseaction=user.viewprofile&friendid=50218762.
"Tracie Peterson," *Contemporary Authors Online.* Detroit: Thomson Gale, 2002.

PHILLIPS, MICHAEL

Personal, Professional, and Religious Background

Michael Phillips (1946–) was born in Arcata, California. His father, Denver C. Phillips, was a businessman; his mother, Eloise Clark Phillips, was a bookkeeper. His family traces its descent in a direct line back to Scotland's King Malcolm and Queen Margaret—a heritage that appears to have inspired some of his work on Scots history. His father was a major influence on his life, as he indicates in the foreword to *A Rift in Time.* Up until the time of his death, Denver Phillips proofread all of his son's books.

In 1984, Michael Phillips went to Lincoln University and then completed his B.S. (magna cum laude) in 1969 from Humboldt State University, part of the California system. The influence of Humboldt University and of the region in which it is situated have proven

> He has given me the job of helping people learn to grow in their faith.
>
> —Michael Phillips, in interview with Janice DeLong and Rachel Schwedt

significant in Phillips's life and work. He settled permanently in Humboldt County, which is located in northern California on Humboldt Bay—the region of the coastal redwoods and an important port for the California Gold Rush days.

While still a student at Humboldt University, Phillips became interested in *A Testament of Devotion*, a book by Thomas Kelly. He began giving copies away, finally deciding that the easiest way to obtain books at a discount and to make them available to others was to own a bookstore. He and his future wife, Judy, set up a "store" in the corner of a room where he lived, an enterprise which expanded over time into the One Way BookShop, eventually growing into the largest Christian bookstore in Northern California and expanding to become a chain of five stores in California and Oregon. He still serves as manager, president, and owner of One Way BookShops. The stores, which he likes to mention in novels like *Hidden in Time*, carry Christian titles. Phillips encourages his staff to be generous in giving away books. For Phillips, this is part of his plan to make "the ministry of literature" an integral part of the Humboldt County Christian Community. An additional part of that ministry is his active involvement in church and Bible study, reaching out to other Christians and to nonbelievers.

At the same time, Michael Phillips began writing his own books, first offering advice to Christian families, and then writing about other topics important to his faith. He writes to a large number of correspondents and has proven instrumental in encouraging fledgling writers to undertake Christian novels, sometimes inviting them to collaborate with him, sometimes introducing them to his publishers. **Judith Pella** and **Tracie Peterson** both cite him as a major influence in their work. As his writing career has taken shape, Michael Phillips has gradually divested himself of all branches of the store except the one in Eureka—the town in which he lives.

In 1971, Phillips married Judy Margaret Carter, a teacher, who became his life's partner. They have three boys, twin sons, Robin and Patrick, and Gregory. The Phillips family homeschooled their children, thereby learning a great deal about young boys' interests and effective teaching techniques, some of which have impacted his writing—especially such stories at *Grayfox*. Michael Phillips's first published book was about his wife's pregnancy and the birth of their twins.

He has said of his career that he finds writing novels an additional means for communicating the basic truths in which he believes. "My desire as a writer and editor is to convey truth from a Christian perspective." He refuses to "propagate any form of narrow religious dogma," but instead prefers "to reflect the broad scope of right, truth, and integrity which is so lacking in much of what is being published today."

He says that he loves to write, "to make sense of complex issues and ideas, and to communicate those notions in an enjoyable format. I would write whether I was a Christian or not." He insists that he is "not on a divine mission to the world." His motivation is "to entertain and give pleasure," yet he acknowledges that his worldview is "necessarily Christian" and does come through in his stories. His intention is to continue writing novels, both historical and contemporary, with an occasional biography now and then.

Major Works and Themes

A number of Michael Phillips's novels are aimed at youthful readers, particularly boys. His family often travels together to those places where he is doing research for his writing. Because of his own experience, in his novels he consistently emphasizes the importance of family and God's plan working through generations of families.

Over the years, Michael Phillips has found his work enriched by coauthoring stories—especially those in series—with his friend and fellow Christian, Judith Pella, who enjoys doing the research for the background and details of everyday life for his books about Russia, the American West, and Scotland. He has undertaken a vast body of work, in both fiction and nonfiction. Phillips is renowned as a writer of Western adventure tales, Russian romances, and modern thrillers. His goal as a writer is to "change the way people think." He insists that the task God has given him is to "tell of the Father," not to become an evangelist. He hopes that readers, when reading his books, "might look up and behold the face of their Father."

In the early 1970s, Phillips discovered the work of George MacDonald, a Victorian author and minister, who told lively stories filled with spiritual wisdom. MacDonald's novels are filled with Scottish dialect, making them too difficult for most contemporary young readers. Michael Phillips undertook the work of his life, to write a biography of MacDonald and to edit his works so that moderns would come to love this remarkable writer. He began with *Malcolm.* After five years and 30 rejections, he finally interested Bethany Publishers in his project. The 28 redacted volumes to date have sold over two million copies.

In the following 20 years, Phillips produced about 50 other books and studies about MacDonald (with sales of over five million), and began a periodical, *Leben.* In his eagerness to reveal the vision of this remarkable man, he undertook to write novels in the same style, using many of the same devices. He was particularly interested in the combination of compelling, well-written stories with penetrating spiritual conceptions. He blends the techniques and ideas of **C. S. Lewis** with some of the devices found in Mark Twain and James Fenimore Cooper to provide lively tales for both children and adults. An alert reader will find echoes of numerous writers in Phillips's works.

The historical series, "Secrets of Heathersleigh Hall," which includes *Wild Grows the Heather in Devon* (1998), *Heathersleigh Homecoming* (1999), *Wayward Winds* (1999), and *A New Dawn Over Devon* (2001), is, according to John Mort, a "frank imitation of his literary hero George MacDonald." In this series, Phillips captures the intellectual turmoil of Victorian England at the beginning of the 20th century—a time when basic components of the Christian world-view were under attack. The series reveals both the strengths and weaknesses of Phillips's fiction—a love of historical context, and an over-reliance on the plot devices of 19th-century melodrama.

Since so many of his novels are coauthored, his own peculiar views are difficult to isolate. The series that he has written with Judith Pella do include some of the same ideas and characteristics of the "Heathersleigh Hall" novels: the ancestral home as a symbol of values central to the characters' lives, the tracking of generations of God's people, the gradual unveiling of God's plan for them, the need for his help to make life full and meaningful, and the importance of ideas in a community or nation. Like Francis Schaeffer and C. S. Lewis, he believes that ideas have consequences, that we live in a post-Christian world, that the culture has been twisted so as to produce men without chests and women without hearts. Among the major enemies he identifies are Darwin, Freud, and Marx. The attacks on the infallibility of Scripture, producing a vague, eclectic liberalism, have produced a sense of embarrassment among those who hold to the old creeds and old fidelities.

The "Caledonia" novels, including *Legend of the Celtic Stone* (1999) and *An Ancient Strife* (2000), focus more tightly on Scottish history. Once again, Phillips asserts that an understanding of the past is essential to dealing with the present. In this case, Andrew

Trentham, a member of Parliament, who is a rich bachelor in search of the proper mate, learns about early Scotland and his own ancestry, thereby finding the path to becoming a better legislator and a better person in his world.

The series of novels coauthored with Judith Pella, "The Russians," reveals again Phillips's concept of the sweep of history and the plan God has for his people. The attention to royalty, large estates, and handsome, aristocratic heroes follows the pattern that recurs in most of Phillips's works.

The" Journals of Corrie Belle Hollister" breaks from these European and Scottish novels, using instead Phillips's California connection. This is a more popular, sentimental set of stories, recounting the adventures of a family who have come West to find their father. The children, having lost their mother on the westward trail, end up in the Gold Rush region of California, finally locating the runaway father. It is a series designed primarily for young readers who will enjoy the firsthand account by a spunky young girl who tries to care for her younger siblings.

The companion novel, designed for young boys, is *Grayfox*. It tells about a young brother of Corrie who is in rebellion against his father. He runs away and joins the Pony Express, is chased by Indians, saved by a mountain man, and becomes a hero by saving an Indian princess. He learns the wisdom of God's good earth in his time away from home, returns as a prodigal son ready to love and respect his father. Unlike Mark Twain's stories for boys, which often challenge traditional values, this one teaches a Christian worldview in a natural manner.

A pair of more recent novels, written apparently to mark the millennium, are Phillips's own work and may signify his vision better than the collaborative efforts. *Rift in Time* (1997) and *Hidden in Time* (2000), reveal his wide reading and interest in modern technology. Both novels feature Adam, a hero whose name proves important in his research. He is an archaeologist, an agnostic who becomes entangled with biblical artifacts. His research into Noah's Ark, the Garden of Eden, Mt. Sinai, and the Ark of the Covenant force him to a belief in the literal truth of Scripture. As he searches and studies the Bible, he becomes convinced that he is chosen to reveal the mysteries that will usher in the Last Days. His discoveries and the consequent worldwide renewal of faith stir up the forces of evil—the Council of Twelve, who have the otherworldly feel of C. S. Lewis's N.I.C.E. in *That Hideous Strength*. John Mort classifies these novels as part of the "Alternative Universe" grouping, much akin the cluster of recent apocalyptic novels.

Like other of his novels, these stories show little subtlety in characterization. People are good or bad, Christian or pagan. Family background is important, often determining the whole path of a life. The interest in secret societies, in this case, the Knights Templar and the Illuminati, is much like that used in the very different novels by **Dan Brown**. Brown also likes the bright, handsome young scholar at the center of his stories, accompanied by a beautiful young helper. The intrigue, wild chases, and echoes of the old Grail legend make these theological versions of spy thrillers. Michael Phillips, of course, uses his stories to convert the world, while Brown uses his to challenge the Catholic Church.

Critical Reception

Although Michael Phillips is properly credited with reviving interest in George MacDonald, some purists argue that his editions of the novels go too far. John Mort notes that Phillips "went to great lengths to dust off MacDonald's romances, re-titling them (sometimes pointlessly), condensing them (by as much as half), and modernizing their language for impatient modern readers. No writer could be comfortable with such treatment, but Phillips would have been the first to recommend the originals over his modernization."

Michael Phillips's novels are best-sellers in Christian bookstores across the country, have been offered through book clubs, and translated into foreign languages. They have been published in over 120 editions, with sales of over three million. He is one of the Christian booksellers' most prolific and versatile authors.

Although Michael Phillips rarely wins prizes, he is often nominated for the top prizes. Undoubtedly, his obvious haste producing such a prolific output stands in the way of the kind of loving attention that creates masterpieces. He loves a good story with a useful moral and is not concerned with subtlety or elegance. Critics insist Phillips sometimes fails to digest the ideas he introduces, draws too heavily on the hackneyed devices of thrillers and romances, and brings in too many extraneous elements. He is often too didactic and diffuse, and includes characters and scenes that bear little intrinsic relationship to his story. His fertile imagination and his lively interest in ideas keep him constantly creating, relishing the process of communication.

Phillips has an enthusiastic following. Many of his books are aimed at adolescent readers and seekers who are considering the possibility of becoming Christians. Melissa Hudak has noted in the *Library Journal* that aficionados of historical fiction with find considerable delight in most of his tales.

Bibliography of Novels by Author

"The Journals of Corrie Belle Hollister" series (1990–1997)

"The Maxwell Chronicles" (1991–1992)

"The Secret of the Rose" (1993–1995)

"Mercy and Eagleflight" (1996–1997)

"The Livingston Chronicles" (1997–2000)

"The Secrets of Heathersleigh Hall" (1998–2001)

"Caledonia" (1999–2000)

"Shenandoah" (2002–2004).

"Carolina Cousins" (2003–present)

"American Dreams" coauthored with Judith Pella, (2005-present; published by Bethany House unless otherwise indicated)

"Stonewycke" series (1985–1990).

"The Russians" series (1991–1992)

(Many of these one co-authored with Judith Pella.)

Bibliography of Works about Author

Christian Reader. Review of *Rift in Time* (September, 2000): 6.

DeLong, Janice and Rachel Schwedt. "Michael Phillips." *Contemporary Christian Authors: Lives and Works.* Lanham, MD: The Scarecrow Press, 2000.

Hudak, Melissa. Review of *A Dangerous Love. Library Journal* (April 1, 1997): 80.

Hudak, Melissa. Review of *A Rift in Time. Library Journal* (June 1, 1998): 72.

Hudak, Melissa. Review of *Wild Grows the Heather in Devon. Library Journal* (September 1, 1998): 96.

Hudak, Melissa. Review of *The Garden at the Edge of Beyond. Library Journal* (April 1, 1999): 164.

"Michael Phillips." *Contemporary Authors Online.* Detroit: Thomson Gale, 2006.

"Michael Phillips." Tyndale Authors. http://www.tyndale.com/authors/bio.asp/?code+519.

Michael R. Phillips Home Page, http://www.macdonaldphillips.com.

Mort, John. Review of *The Garden at the Edge of Beyond. Booklist* (October 1, 1998): 294.

Mort, John. *Christian Fiction: A Guide to the Genre.* Greenwood Village, Colorado: Libraries Unlimited, 2002.

Person, James E., Jr. Review of *George MacDonald: Scotland's Beloved Storyteller. National Review* (February 24, 1989): 59.

Publishers Weekly. Review of *Angels Watching over Me* (January 13, 2003): 41.

"The Writings, Spiritual Vision, and Legacy of George MacDonald & Michael Phillips." http://www.macdonaldphillips.com/future.html.

PRICE, REYNOLDS

Personal, Professional, and Religious Background

Reynolds Price (1933–) was born in Macon, North Carolina, a town he often uses in his stories. His father, William Solomon Price, was a traveling salesman, and his mother, Elizabeth Rodwell Price, was considered an "eccentric rogue." Some of his more independent female characters are attributed to her. In *Clear Pictures: First Loves, First Guides*, Price talks about the first 21 years of his life and the small towns that "formed the backdrop of his youth: Macon, Asheboro, and Warrenton." He was raised in the Methodist church, but soon found the racial segregation a problem in his full participation in worship. As a teenager in Raleigh, he attended Broughton High School.

From an early age, he showed writing talents, winning a scholarship to Duke University as the Angier Duke scholar. He graduated with an A.B. summa cum laude, and then won a Rhodes Scholarship to Merton College for three years, earning a B.Litt. from Oxford in 1958. He returned to teach at Duke University, rising from instructor to professor and was finally granted the James B. Duke Professor chair of English. Along the way, he taught such remarkable students as **Anne Tyler** and Josephine Humphries. He has also served as writer-in-residence at the University of North Carolina at Chapel Hill, the University of Kansas, and the University of North Carolina at Greensboro. He has also been the Glasgow Professor at Washington and Lee University, and a member of the Salzburg Seminar in Austria.

Perhaps the most traumatic experience of Reynolds Price's life was his bout with cancer of the spinal cord in 1984. It was a time of great pain and a remarkable vision, in which he saw himself with Christ near the Sea of Galilee. Christ told him his sins were forgiven, and touched the scar for his cancer surgery, telling him he was healed. Although the cancer was cured, the medical treatment left Price permanently paralyzed from the waist down. This event transformed his life, leading to one of the most "fertile periods of his career."

> I don't write with a conscious sense of the hangman at my door, of my own mortality. But I am a tremendously driven person, and I have gotten more so since sitting down. Words just come out of me the way my beard comes out. Who could stop it?
>
> —Reynolds Price interview in the *Washington Post*

He continues to live in North Carolina, in a house near his students, which is "filled with memorabilia he affectionately refers to as 'a *lotta* stuff.'"

Major Works and Themes

Reynolds Price calls himself an "outlaw Christian." He is not a regular churchgoer, but he does pray regularly and has become a scholar of Scripture, writing commentaries on the Gospels and a number of meditations on the meaning of pain. In *A Whole New Life*, he talks about his recovery from cancer and the lessons this experience has taught him. Through his own pain he came to believe that wisdom comes only through suffering; cancer made him a "different kind of communicant and a different kind of communicator with the human race." Another of Price's nonfiction works, *Letter to a Godchild*, reveals his critiques of religion, his hopes, his doubts, and his times of loneliness. He cites two "visions" in his life, one of nature that convinced him that God is the creator of the universe, the other of Jesus at Capernaum. Yet he does not consider himself a mystic, only a person with an enduring faith in God.

Although most of his fiction is set in North Carolina, Reynolds Price does not label himself a Southern writer. He admits that he has been much influenced by Eudora Welty, he has also been influenced by Dante, T. S. Eliot, John Milton, and many others—including the Gospel writers. His works also reflect a rich understanding of both the Old and New Testaments and of the whole tradition of English poetry.

In spite of his strong emphasis on religious thought, including Buddhist and Hindu scripture, Price rarely offers solutions to the perennial problem of evil. He sees God as "deeply loving" but non-interfering. Humans, he believes, are left as pilgrims in a lonely world, discerning little pattern in their lives. His disagreements with institutional religions leaves characters like Kate Vaiden fingering a rosary, but never joining a church. She kneels in the Methodist church when no one else is present, but discovers no miraculous answer to her search for meaning, accepting finally that she is nothing but an orphan without roots in a world where, by her own choice, she has few permanent attachments. Kate, like Moll Flanders, has little sexual morality, no thoughts about those she has left behind on her own quest for identity. People love her, but she offers little love in return.

Another novel, written years later, again has a solitary protagonist, Mabry Kincaid, who finds little comfort in family, the institutional churches, or any plan of God's. Like many of Price's characters, Mabry faces the onslaught of disease (multiple sclerosis) with questions about God's use of pain. Mabry has problems with family ties, with commitment to those who love him, and with the death of a loved one. He admits his infidelity, but has little anguish over this character flaw. He is sorry that it has ruined his marriage, but continues to carry his lust beyond his own abilities to perform. The hunger for another person appears to be more psychological and spiritual than physical in Price's characters. Even Mabry's father—the "good priest"—admits his own infidelity with a parishioner. It mirrors his failure to remain faithful to the church he has served for a lifetime, rejecting it in his final days.

Several of Reynolds Price's novels trace the path of the Mayfield family of east North Carolina. The blended family, with black and white members, follows the pattern of modern history from the Civil War to the present. The colorful characters with their love of the land,

In 1984, Reynolds Price was diagnosed with cancer of the spinal cord. At the time of his pain, he had a vision of himself with Christ near the Sea of Galilee, and of Christ telling him that his sins were forgiven and that he was healed. The cancer was cured, but the treatment left Price paralyzed from the waist down.

their education and talents, their refusal to succumb to conservative Southern traditions, have their sexual adventures, elope, experiment with "giving and taking pleasure" with both sexes and with both races, and end in suicide, separation, disease, and disappointment. Price adopts for his protagonist Hutch Mayfield, who, like Price, is an English professor at Duke. Mayfield complains that Faulkner's epics are too narrow, but Price does seem to steal pages from Faulkner's books for his own sometimes more philosophic purposes. He is more inclined to preach against Southern conservatives than is Faulkner, who also despised the Baptists. Hutch says, in what sounds like Price's voice, "I never found a church that didn't turn my stomach."

Disease, understandably, haunts Price's novels. *The Promise of Rest* takes on the horrors of AIDS, the effects on the family and friends, the caregivers, the different stages of the disease itself. The book chronicles the death of a talented and handsome son of a professor and his wife, who try to understand without judging the young man. This is the final of the "Mayfield" novels. Price consistently shows sympathy with homosexuals and refuses to consider their love or their sexual behavior to be sinful. He is harsh with those "Baptist deacons with literal faith in Jonah and the whale and stoning women who lie with donkeys," who are quick to relegate to Hell those who have found love in different places. He seems to applaud Straw, the character with whom Hutch has been half in love for most of his adult life, as a "sexual mystic," one who sees sex as a means of knowledge.

Price is most famous for his sensitive portrayal of women. Roxanna Slade is especially interesting—a strong woman who lives a normal middle-class life, sees her first love die, marries his brother, loves and fights with her mother-in-law, nurses her own mother near the end, has children who grow up and either leave or complicate her life with their own transgressions, relies on family and supports those, black and white, who are part of the web of relationships that make up her world. She never writes a great novel, stars in a film, sings beautifully, or even goes regularly to church. But she is an admirable, moral, thoughtful human being.

Reynolds Price writes beautifully. He builds lively and believable characters, who have their own quirks and who surprise us at every turn. Many have biblical counterparts and some have mystical moments. Though they often seem like picaresque heroes, they have more sustained concern for meaning, more meditative responses to events. Most circle about a small region and a tiny group of friends and relations, trying to make sense of the events that face them— sickness, surviving, and death. His laughter at the human comedy lightens his stories, which have little violence, though violent scenes are hinted at by a scar, a wound, or an absence. He is especially effective in his portrayal of African Americans, women, and gays—never as stereotypes, always as individuals.

Critical Reception

Reynolds Price has been widely reviewed and praised by most of the journals and papers as each of his volumes has appeared. Everyone from *National Review* to the *New York Times* has found him talented and thoughtful, well worth discussing and profiling. From his first novel, *A Long and Happy Life*, he has been praised for his style and themes. Critics especially enjoyed *Kate Vaiden* because of the "unforgettable female protagonist." The "Mayfield" novels, including *The Surface of Earth* and *The Source of Light*, which tell the colorful stories of Eva Kendal and Forrest Mayfield, reveal the tensions between individuals and their families.

Awards

In addition to his scholarships, including his three years as a Rhodes scholar, Reynolds Price won the William Faulkner Foundation award for the most notable first novel and the Sir Walter Raleigh Award in 1962 for *A Long and Happy Life*. He has been a Guggenheim fellow, has won the National Association of Independent Schools Award, has been a fellow of the National Endowment for the Arts, and has won the National Institute of Arts and Letters Award. In 1986, *Kate Vaiden* won the National Book Critics Circle Award for Fiction.

Bibliography of Novels by Author

A Long and Happy Life. New York: Athenaeum, 1962.
A Generous Man. New York: Athenaeum, 1966.
Love and Work. New York: Athenaeum, 1968.
The Surface of Earth. New York: Athenaeum, 1975.
The Source of Light. New York: Athenaeum, 1981.
Mustian: Two Novels and a Story. New York: Athenaeum, 1983.
Kate Vaiden. New York: Athenaeum, 1986.
Good Hearts. New York: Athenaeum, 1988.
The Tongues of Angels. New York: Athenaeum, 1990.
Blue Calhoun. New York: Athenaeum, 1992.
Michael Egerton. Mankato, MN: Creative Education, 1993.
The Promise of Rest. New York: Scribner, 1995.
Roxanna Slade. New York: Scribner, 1998.
A Singular Family. New York: Scribner, 1999.
Noble Norleet. New York: Scribner, 2002.
The Good Priest's Son. New York: Scribner, 2005.

Bibliography of Works about Author

Freitas, Donna. "Reynolds Price: Letter to a Godchild," *Publishers Weekly* (April 19, 2006). (http:/;/donnafreitasinterviews.blogspot.com/2006/07/reynolds-price-letter-to-godchild.html.

Humphries, Jefferson, ed. *Conversations with Reynolds Price.* Jackson: University Press of Mississippi, 1991.

Kimball, Sue Leslie, and Lynn Veach Sadler, eds. *Reynolds Price: From "A Long and Happy Life" to "Good Hearts."* Fayetteville, NC: Methodist College Press, 1989.

Price, Reynolds. *Clear Pictures: First Loves, First Guides.* New York: Athenaeum, 1989.

Price, Reynolds. *A Whole New Life: An Illness and a Healing.* New York: Athenaeum, 1994.

Price, Reynolds. *Letter to a Godchild.* New York: Athenaeum, 2006.

Price, Reynolds. *Letter to a Man in the Fire: Does God Exist and Does He Care?* New York: Scribner, 1999.

Ray, William. *Conversations: Reynolds Price and William Ray.* Memphis, TN: Memphis State University, 1976.

"Reynolds Price." *Contemporary Authors Online.* Detroit: Thomson Gale, 2007.

"Reynolds Price: Profile," *Religion & Ethics News Weekly* (July 17, 1998). (http:www.pbs.org/wnet/religionandethics/week146/profile.html.

Schiff, James A. *Understanding Reynolds Price.* Columbia: University of South Carolina Press, 1996.

Schiff, James A., ed. *Critical Essays on Reynolds Price.* Boston: G.K. Hall, 1998.

Smith, Rick. "The Gospel and Reynolds Price: North Carolina's Literary Lion Looks to the Future with Optimism," www.metronc.com/article/index.aspx?id=483.

R

RICE, ANNE

Personal, Professional, and Religious Background

Anne Rice (1941–) also known as Anne Rampling, A. N. Roquelaure, and Howard Allen, was named Howard Allen O'Brien, after her father. She was born in New Orleans, Louisiana, to Howard O'Brien, a postal worker, novelist and sculptor, and Katherine Allen O'Brien, an alcoholic who died when Anne was only 14. The O'Briens, who lived on the edges of New Orleans' famous Garden District, were faithful Catholics who regularly attended daily Mass and sent their daughter to the Catholic school, where boys and girls were segregated and studied Bible, catechism, and church history—as well as the usual subjects. On her first day at school, the young girl told the nuns her name was Anne—the name she was to use for the rest of her life.

She attended Texas Woman's University from 1959–1960. At the age of 18, when she was at San Francisco State University, she stopped believing that the Catholic church was "the one true church established by Christ to give grace." She also stopped believing in God. In 1962, Anne O'Brien married her childhood sweetheart, Stan Rice, a poet and painter and a committed atheist, in a civil ceremony in Denton, Texas. She has called her husband "one of the most honorable and conscience-driven people I ever knew." The couple had two children, Michele, who died in 1972 of leukemia at age six, and Christopher, who was born six years later.

Anne Rice continued her education at San Francisco State College, earning a B.A. in 1964, an M.A. in 1971. She did further graduate study at the University of California at Berkeley from 1969–70. Over the years, she worked at a number of jobs in addition to her writing: she has been a waitress, cook, theatre usherette,

> In 1976, I felt that the vampire was the perfect metaphor for the outcast in all of us, the alienated one in all of us, the one who feels lost in a world seemingly without God.
>
> —Anne Rice, on her Web site

and insurance claims examiner. By 1976, Anne Rice had begun her writing about vampires.

In 1996, Anne Rice appeared in the television series *Ellen*.

In the early 1990s, Anne Rice and her husband returned to New Orleans, where she continued to write a couple of novels every year. They were affluent enough to buy a large, beautiful home, one of the historic treasures of the Garden District. By 1998, she began "to be more and more concerned with my relationship with God in my books. I wanted to be in the company of God, in the company of the drama . . . what we can know, what we don't know, what we believe." She talked with her priest about some of her quarrels with the church, including her liberal views of homosexuality and other issues. He assured her that there was room for her in the faith, allowed her to attend Mass and to participate in the sacraments. In 2000, in spite of his own atheism, her husband agreed to remarry her in the church.

Her beloved husband died in 2002, only four months after showing symptoms of brain cancer, leading Anne Rice to further soul-searching. She subsequently announced that "In 2002, I consecrated my work to Jesus Christ." She asserted that this did not involve a denunciation of works she had previously written that reflected her life's journey. "It was rather a statement that from then on I would write directly for Jesus Christ. I would write works about salvation, as opposed to alienation. I would write books about reconciliation in Christ, rather than books about the struggle for answers in a post World War II seemingly atheistic world."

Although Anne Rice announced that she was through with vampires and wanted to move away from witches, to write something completely different, she has recently indicated that she may write one more novel about her ever-popular vampires, one that would complete the series and bring the light of God into the story.

In the meantime, she has dedicated her energies largely to the writing of a series of books on the life of Christ, called *Christ the Lord.* Starting with his childhood in Egypt and Nazareth, she brings the story to the point of his recognition of his divinity. In a second volume, she continues, taking him through his adolescence to the beginning of his ministry at Cana.

Her husband's death led her to sell her New Orleans home and move to California, where she lives closer to her son, who is now a writer himself. Her grand Mediterranean-style villa overlooks the Pacific. It is in this idyllic place that she continues her studies and her writing. She told her interviewer from *WORLD Magazine* that she has "never been this happy in my life before. I never expected things to come together like this, to be so completely unified in purpose and intent."

Major Works and Themes

Anne Rice is known chiefly for her "dark fiction"—novels she traces back to Dante's dark work, where Hell is described in "considerable detail." She traces this thread of literature through John Milton's "Paradise Lost" and Mary Shelley's *Frankenstein*, which she calls "a dark classic" that "is a highly moral indictment of the mad doctor for his meddling with life and death and abandoning the monster, his wretched offspring." The Brontë sisters, Charles Dickens, Nathaniel Hawthorne, Herman Melville, and **Flannery O'Connor** have also contributed to this particular line of literature. She believes that such dark stories are "transformative," inviting readers on a journey that can help them experience catharsis. They require fear and suffering as the "price of eventual affirmation."

For that reason, her vampire novels, the "Mayfair Family" trilogy, *Servant of the Bones*, *Violin*, *Cry to Heaven*, and *Feast of all Saints* are all novels she considers "transformative stories" with a "strong moral compass." She does not glorify evil in these books, but portrays the continuing battle against evil in the search for good.

Her first great success was *Interview with a Vampire*, the story of an alienated being who, like Frankenstein's monster, searches the world for meaning. Critics applauded her sympathetic and complex hero in Louis, an eloquent and introspective vampire who was seduced by Lestat—the master-vampire and Rice's favorite villain. She shows the young vampire as a tangle of desire, grief, and moral struggle. Other vampires, or "blood drinkers," tell their complex tales in other stories, often struggling against gods of various pagan cultures who prove to be quite lively characters in the vampire sagas. They span history, with the vampire Marius, for example, having been a senator in imperial Rome and subsequently a part of various cultures from Renaissance Italy to Dresden and England.

His vampire nature is clearly a metaphor for human consciousness or moral awareness. His distress comes from his inability to find redemption, his recognition that he is a part of evil. Rice contends that "This book reflects for me a protest against the post World War II nihilism to which I was exposed in college from 1960 through 1972. It is an expression of grief for a lost religious heritage that seemed at the time beyond recovery."

Two themes that Anne Rice identifies in her early work are moral and spiritual hunger, and the quest of the outcast for a context of meaning. Whether her stories are set in 18th-century Italy or in antebellum New Orleans, they face the same issues. She insists that her works are not immoral or Satanic or demonic—an unfair and uninformed characterization of the books that causes her deep personal pain. She is no advocate of "Goth" culture and has no personal belief in vampires.

Anne Rice's highly publicized reconciliation with her church and her dedication of her talents to Christ brought a major change in her writing. The "Christ the Lord" series began with *Out of Egypt*, a first-person narrative of the young Jesus, beginning in Egypt, where his family has been hiding since Herod's slaughter of the innocents. Rice carries the story through the voyage to Palestine and the resettling of the family in Nazareth, where Mary is still under a cloud for her pregnancy prior to her marriage to Joseph. Using a great deal of archaeology, social history, and the Gnostic gospels, Anne Rice builds the story of a very real community. She assumes that Joseph would have become more skilled in building fine furniture while in Egypt, making him a welcome part of the local Roman community. She accepts the stories of Jesus's precocious miracles, allowing the child to discover his own nature gradually. Mary is a major actor in this narrative, revealing to her son as much of his birth story as she believes he can understand.

In *The Road to Cana*, Jesus takes center stage. He finds himself a laughingstock in Nazareth for being "sinless" and unmarried at 30 years of age. The pressure to marry the young woman he loves and to settle down into normal life is difficult for even the Son of God to resist—just as Kazantzakis had noted in *The Last Temptation of Christ*. Rice carries Jesus through his baptism, the temptation in the wilderness, to the beginning of his ministry at Cana, where his beloved marries another man. The story is told primarily from Jesus's point of view, with emphasis on his human nature. The romantic elements distinguish this from most tellings of the Gospel story. She even introduces a bit of action and intrigue by a near-rape, which is blamed on Jesus. Rice's decision to have Jesus donate the gifts of the Magi as wedding presents is interesting, endowing his supposed true love an importance for which there is no Scriptural basis.

The third volume in the trilogy will necessarily deal with the ministry, passion, and crucifixion of Christ.

Critical Reception

Ironically, the vampires of Anne Rice's early novels brought her both success and pain. Most reviewers did not understand her metaphoric use of vampires and either praised them for the wrong reason or refused to read her books because they assumed them to be defenses of evil. Her books have been widely read, assigned to students in high schools and in college, and reviewed in many papers and journals.

The reviews of *Christ The Lord: Out of Egypt* were mixed. About half of them assume that her new work on a new subject is a continuation of her old novels. *Kirkus Reviews* called it "A riveting, reverent imagining of the hidden years of the child Jesus." Tamara Butler, writing in *Library Journal*, credits "Rice's superb storytelling skills" that "enable her to succeed where many other writers have failed." On the other hand, Julie Wittes Schlack, writing for the *Boston Globe*, is not pleased by the childlike prose required by the first-person narrative of the prepubescent Jesus. She notes that Rice relies on "simple, declarative sentences and repetition to create a sense of innocence, but the effect is merely tedious." She then adds, "despite that, the story she's chosen to tell is almost engaging enough to appeal as much to fans of vampire stories as to those of Bible tales. As literary feats go, that's a near-miracle." Old fans of Rice found this a brave and wonderful new novel, which they admired for its simplicity and its use of scholarship.

On the other hand, Mark Harris, writing for *Entertainment Weekly*, found it was not so entertaining: "*Christ* reads like a bland young adult novel, written in language that's supposed to be unadorned and poignantly simple but is instead as flat and leeched of poetry as the Good News Bible." Reviewers for the *Chicago Tribune* and the *Washington Post* did not like the novel a bit; Alan Cheuse calling it "ill-conceived, ill-wrought and, worst sin of all, quite boring." Jules Bukiet summed it up by asserting that, "Rice has sucked the life out of the greatest story ever told."

Such rewrites of the Gospel stories inevitably bring criticism from those who believe in the infallibility of God's Word. *WORLD Magazine* worries about Rice's decision to give Satan the same physical features as Jesus. Rice responded that she could not claim to know Satan's appearance, but she thinks that "Satan would want to present Jesus with a lavish image of Himself in fine clothes, and the regalia of power." The Temptation is usually pictured as far too easy. She prefers a more subtle approach, while emphasizing that Satan does not really understand that Jesus is God, only that Jesus believes himself to be God. Obviously, some would argue this point.

Bibliography of Novels by Author

"Vampire Chronicles" series (New York: Knopf, 1976–2003)

"Witching Hour" trilogy (New York: Knopf, 1990–1994)

The Feast of All Saints. New York: Simon & Schuster, 1980.
Cry to Heaven. New York: Knopf, 1982.
The Mummy: or, Ramses the Damned. New York: Ballantine, 1989.
Servant of the Bones. New York: Knopf, 1996.
Violin. New York: Knopf, 1997.

"Christ the Lord" series

Out of Egypt. New York: Knopf, 2005.
The Road to Cana. New York: Knopf, 2008.

Anne Rice wrote a few erotic novels under the pseudonym A.N. Roquelaure (1983–91). She also wrote two novels under the pseudonym Anne Rampling (1985–86).

Works adapted for film include: *Exit to Eden* (1994); *Queen of the Damned* (2001); *The Vampire Lestat* was adapted as a graphic novel (1991), and has also been adapted as a stage musical.

Bibliography of Works about Author

Anne Rice Web site: http://www.annerice.com.

Bukiet, Jules. Review of *Out of Egypt*. *Washington Post* (November 13, 2005).

Butler, Tamara. Review of *Out of Egypt*. *Library Journal* (November 1, 2005): 70.

Cheuse, Alan. Review of *Out of Egypt*. *Chicago Tribune* (November 13, 2005).

Harris, Mark. Review of *Out of Egypt*. *Entertainment Weekly* (November 1, 2005).

Metacritics (summary of criticisms of *Out of Egypt*) http://www.metacritics.com/books/authors/rice.

"On the Road with Jesus." *WORLD Magazine* (February 23/March 1, 2008). (Pre-publication review of *The Road to Cana*.)

Review of *Out of Egypt*. *Los Angeles Times* (October 31, 2005).

Schlack, Julie Wittes. "The Vampire Queen Gives Voice to Jesus," Review of *Out of Egypt*. *Boston Globe* (January 3, 2006).

Vincent, Lynn. "Into the Light." *WORLD Magazine* (December 3, 2005).

RIVERS, FRANCINE

Personal, Professional, and Religious Background

Francine Sandra Melbourne Rivers (1947–) was born in Berkeley, California, the daughter of a coroner and a nurse. She attended the University of Nevada in Reno, graduating with a B.A. in English and journalism. She acknowledges a period prior to her marriage when she was sexually active, culminating in the heartbreaking experience of an unwanted pregnancy, an abortion, and a long aftermath of guilt that led to writer's block. In 1969, she married Richard (Rick) Rivers, a business executive. She and her husband have three children, Trevor William, Shannon Moriah, and Travis Richard.

Francine Rivers studied at the California State University, Hayward, earning teaching certification in 1974. Rather than settling down to teach or to any of the many other jobs she tried briefly (reporter, playground director, airline stewardess, secretary, lifeguard, waitress, and so forth), in 1977 she chose to became a full-time writer. A successful career from then until 1985 in secular writing for the general market followed, with Rivers pro-

> Are you going to be a "Christian writer" or a Christian who writes?
> What's the difference? A Christian who writes may weave Christian principles into the story, but the work can stand when those elements are removed. A Christian writer is called to present a story that is all about Jesus. The Lord is the foundation, the structure, and Scripture has everything to do with the creation and development of the characters in the story. Jesus is central to the theme. If you remove Jesus and Biblical principles from the novel, it collapses.
>
> —Francine Rivers

ducing romance novels at a prodigious rate, including such titles as *Pagan Heart, Outlaw's Embrace, A Fire in the Heart, Rebel in His Arms*. She sold over 13 million books, becoming one of the most successful romance writers in America, winning the Western Romance Award (*Romance Times*), and the Bronze Porgie Award (*West Coast Review of Books*) in 1964 for *Sarina*.

Although Rivers had been raised in a Christian family and came to a "saving knowledge of Jesus" when she was 12 years old, she did not decide to make Christ "LORD" of her life until she was in her late30s. As she recounts the experience in her preface to the "Mark of the Lion" series: "When I became a born-again Christian in 1986, I wanted to share my faith with others. However, I didn't want to offend anyone and risk 'losing' old friends and family members who didn't share my belief in Jesus as Lord and Savior. " She found herself hesitating and keeping silent. "Ashamed of my cowardice and frustrated by it, I went on a quest, seeking the faith of a martyr. *A Voice in the Wind* [volume 1 of the series] was the result."

After her conversion experience, which she describes in the author's note at the conclusion of *Redeeming Love*, she and her husband made massive changes in their lives. They sold their house, gave away half of their furnishings, and moved to Sonoma County to start a new business. They joined a church that changed their lives from the inside out. They were baptized by immersion, and Francine Rivers became a different kind of writer. Since then, she has been a prolific creator of Christian books, primarily with Tyndale House Publishers.

Rivers insists that there is a difference between "a Christian who writes and a Christian writer. I am a Christian writer. Therefore, everything I write must glorify Jesus Christ." For Francine Rivers, writing is a form of worship. In her many novels, she constantly uses Scripture and the central dogmas of the Christian faith as an intrinsic part of her narrative, motivating her characters, giving them healing, peace, and hope. She includes some miracles, occasional angelic apparitions, but generally uses natural means for accomplishing her goal, the conversion of her characters and her readers.

Major Works and Themes

Francine Rivers chronicles her own experience of redemption in her disguised autobiographical story, *Redeeming Love*, a retelling of the story of the Old Testament prophet Hosea, who married a harlot. The prophet found through this earthly love both holy love and love for fellow humans. This discovery came through reliance on God's guidance "between the sheets as well as between the pews," according to Lauren Sandler. The novel, set in the 19th century, describes the deep wounds in Sarah, alias Angel, who is sold into prostitution as a child, becomes a career prostitute in her teens, travels to California, and is redeemed and married by a farmer, Michael Hosea. For a long time, the painful memories of her life as a "soiled dove" and her forced abortions keep her from accepting Michael's gift of love, tempting her (like the biblical Gomer) to run back to her life as a prostitute.

Rivers is far more realistic in her sexual scenes than most evangelical writers, and allows her characters to fall into deep periods of depression. Again in *The Atonement Child*, she uses her own experience of sin and sorrow to serve as the basis of her study of abortion and its effects. Frequently, her novels contain critiques of feminism and the of belief that one's primary loyalty is to self and to one's own pleasure and independence.

When listing influences on her life and writing, Francine Rivers usually cites people she has known rather than writers or philosophers—her mother and father, her husband, her Sunday School teachers, and her friends.

The "Mark of the Lion" series, which chronicles the early Christian Church's turbulent experiences, has sold over a million copies. This trilogy reveals her ability to weave historical research into a melodramatic narrative line, producing epic tales in the mode of *The Robe* or *Ben Hur*. She relishes pairing manly men—warriors with magnificent physiques—with beautiful doe-eyed Christian maidens who gentle the rough-hewn men while retaining their own faith and virtue. Her wicked women tend to be feminists conjuring with dark forces, hungry for power, committed to evil. They manage to destroy marriages and lives, provoke murders, but eventually face death and judgment—usually alone.

Scripture itself is clearly her major literary influence and inspiration. In her carefully crafted novels, especially in her historical ones, she also relies on vast reading. "The Mark of the Lion," for instance, has scenes drawn from Josephus, Tacitus, Seneca, Juvenal, and others. She has read about the Essenes, the early scribes working on manuscripts of the Gospels and the epistles, and knows about the excavations at Pompeii. She displays detailed knowledge of customs of the first-century Mediterranean world—the clothing, food, architecture, transportation; the lives of slaves, of gladiators in the arena, of early Christians and pagans in Ephesus and Rome, of the barbarians in the forests of Germania, and many others. She has done her homework in order to produce a realistic portrayal of life in a different period.

Rivers says she reads at least 35 books a year "that are not related to what I'm writing. It's important to me to know what is going on in the world and how other people think." She reads both current and classic novels, largely from 20th-century writers. This eclectic taste is reflected in her novels. In addition, she listens to contemporary music, to the news, to her friends and tries to discover what her readers are struggling with in their lives. She turns these issues into stories, with vivid characters and carefully crafted dialogue, encouraging the readers to work through to answers with the characters. In *Leota's Garden*, for example, she traces the heartbreaking anger in a family to core experiences and misunderstandings.

Typically, Rivers holds back certain facts of the family's history, revealing them as the story progresses. Gradually, the different people come to understand the challenges faced by an immigrant German family during World War II. The son joins the army, only to discover the guilt of his own extended family in the horrors of the concentration camps. His mother never understands either his anguish or her husband's humiliation at not being able to support the family because of prejudice.

The largest challenge faced by the characters is dealing with age and death. The granddaughter, Anne, discovers her grandmother, a lonely old woman on the verge of death. The young woman joins with the old one in the revival of her beloved garden to bring her back into life, into family, into her community, and into church. In the novel, Rivers carefully reveals the cruelty of sterile and practical "solutions" to old age—akin to Hitler's "ultimate solution" to the Jewish question. Although these novels have young heroines as the center of consciousness, they appeal to a much larger—though largely female—audience. As Rivers notes, "I always start from a place of pain or question and use writing as a tool to go before the Lord and find out what to learn—like the atonement I had to do with my abortion."

In another of her novels she considers the problems created in an aging church by the calling of a vigorous new pastor, more intent on his own agenda and career than ministering to his congregation. Paul Hudson, the son of a successful pastor of a mega-church, wants to build buildings for his own ego rather than to build a fellowship for the greater glory of God. John Mort, in his review of *And the Shofar Blew*, in *Booklist*, notes that this story of an ambitious young minister reflects a growing tendency in Rivers to become "more moralistic with each book but as usual turns in a strong narrative, posing issues that ring loud and clear if only within church circles."

Francine Rivers is a remarkable writer, willing to undertake a great variety of subjects and periods in her novels. She says that she seeks to give word pictures to readers. Much of her acclaim and her sales records have come from her historical novels. Other of her novels, often in series, deal with figures in the Bible—the "Sons of Encouragement" series, which includes a priest, a prince, and a prophet, or the "Lineage of Grace" series, which includes the highly imaginative stories of five women. At the end of the books, which hold fairly close to the biblical narrative, Rivers includes study guides, obviously designing these books as support for Bible study groups. These carefully constructed narratives are too brief to allow the power and scope of her "The Mark of the Lion" books. Tamara Butler judges these books "action packed with appeal for both male and female readers."

Francine Rivers writes well and is popular with evangelical readers. Even her historical novels stay close to ordinary life, move quickly, introduce suspense, conflict, and surprises. Her dialogue is realistic, revealing character and conflict. Her setting is meticulously described to enrich understanding of character. Her Christian message is clear, blended into the characterization, story line, and dialogue. Although she deals with such edgy topics as sexuality, witchcraft, homosexuality, euthanasia, and abortion, Rivers handles them with taste, avoiding either foul language or explicit scenes of violence or lust. Her emphasis on miraculous events and the power of prayer is especially appealing to evangelicals, but she identifies with no particular denomination in her works. In her novel *And the Shofar Blew*, she does imply that small, Bible-centered fellowships are more effective for deepening the faith than megachurches and televangelism.

Critical Reception

Francine Rivers's most discussed and reviewed story is *The Last Sin Eater*, which was made into a film. Cal Thomas, reviewing this film along with another Christian film that was released about the same time, noted that it "tells the story of 10-year-old Cadi Forbes. While attending her grandmother's funeral in the Appalachian Mountains of the 1850s, she witnesses a mysterious man 'absolve' her grandmother of her sins by eating bread and wine at her gravesite. Cadi decides she wants the same redemption from a deep and dark secret and she seeks out the man in order to be forgiven while she is still alive." Thomas notes that the story is based on a Welsh myth, and gives it high praise.

Most evangelical critics, like those who write for *Faithful Reader* and *Today's Christian*, find her a good, if somewhat predictable writer. Chattaway, for example, compares her film *The Last Sin Eater* with similar films made by Michael Landon, Jr. of works by **Janette Oke** and Laura Ingalls. He does think it was unnecessary to make the sins so extreme that ordinary people would fail to identify with them. No need to have Indian massacres and murders, when sin can be much more humdrum for most folks.

Secular critics, such as those in the *New York Times, The Village Voice*, or *Variety* think her works are far too preachy, designed not as art but as propaganda for Christianity. Matt Zoller Seitz, writing for the *New York Time*, after noting a few good qualities in the film, concludes that it's "a blunt and rather prosaic Christian allegory . . . a big-screen Sunday school story with sumptuous scenery, graceful crane shots and Rembrandt lighting—designed mainly to impart and then repeat wisdom about guilt, sin and redemption."

Individual books have been reviewed favorably for "all libraries where inspirational fiction is popular" by *Publishers Weekly*, *Library Journal*, and *Romantic Times*. Rivers's books have sold millions of copies and are a staple in most public libraries. The novels are enormously popular, with the novels selling upwards of 80,000 copies. Many of her books are available in paperback and on cassette, and many have been translated into other languages.

Awards

Francine Rivers won the Western Romance Award, *Romance Times*, and the Bronze Porgie Award, *West Coast Review of Books*, in 1984, for *Sarina*. Her first statement of faith in fictional form, *Redeeming Love*, was voted the favorite novel of 1991 by *Affaire de Coeur* readers and was a finalist for the Romance Writers of America Choice Award. Her "The Mark of the Lion" trilogy, which included *A Voice in the Wind*, won a Campus Life Book of the Year award. The second of the series was an Evangelical Christian Publishers Association (ECPA) Gold Medallion finalist and won the Romance Writers of America (RWA) RITA Award, as did the third in the series. *The Scarlet Thread* was voted the best inspirational romance in 1997. A careful and talented writer, Francine Rivers has won a host of awards, including the ECPA Gold Medallion for *The Last Sin Eater*, and the Romance Writers of America's RITA award for three of her novels, culminating in being named to the Romance Writers of America Hall of Fame in 1997. She has also won the Christy Award.

Bibliography of Christian Novels by Author

Redeeming Love. New York: Bantam Books, 1991.
The Scarlet Thread. Wheaton, IL: Tyndale House Publishing, 1996.
Leota's Garden. Wheaton, IL: Tyndale House Publishing, 1999.
The Atonement Child. Wheaton, IL: Tyndale House Publishers, 2002.
And the Shofar Blew. Wheaton, IL: Tyndale House Publishers, 2003.
The Last Sin Eater. Wheaton, IL: Tyndale House Publishers, 2007.

"The Mark of the Lion" series (Wheaton, IL: Tyndale House Publishers, 1993–1995)

The "Sons of Encouragement" series (Wheaton, IL: Tyndale House, 2005–2006)

"A Lineage of Grace" series (Grand Rapids, MI: Zondervan Press, 2006–2007)

Rivers has also coauthored books and edited collections, and she wrote a number of secular romances, prior to conversion, published by Berkley, from 1981–1987. *The Last Sin-Eaters* was produced as a film in 2007.

Bibliography of Works about Author

Butler, Tamara. Review of *The Warrior*. *Library Journal* (February 1, 2005): 62
Chattaway, Peter T. "The Last Sin Eater." *Christianity Today*, 2/9/07. http://www.christianitytoday.com/movies/features/newonvideo.html.
Christian Reader Review of *Unveiled*. (September 2000): 6. Review of *Unashamed*. (March 2001): 6.

Davis, Nina. "Unspoken." *Booklist* (September 15, 2001, v. 98 I2): 206.

Faithful Reader Interview with Author, May 2004. http://www.faithfulreader.com/authors/au-rivers-francine.asp.

"Fiction First; What's Hot in the Fiction Aisle." *Today's Christian Woman* (March-April 2005, Vol. 27 I2): 20.

"Francine Rivers," *Contemporary Authors Online.* Thomson Gale, 2007.

Galbreath, Edward. "Redeeming Vision," in *Today's Christian* (March/April 2007). http://www.christianitytoday.com/tc/2007/002/7.14.html.

Knapp, Mary. "A Voice in the Wind." *Library Journal* (2/1/2005, vol. 130, I4): 124.

Mort, John. Review of *An Echo in the Darkness. Booklist* (October 15, 1994): 401.

Mort, John. "Christian Fiction." Review of *And the Shofar Blew. Booklist* (June 1, 2002): 1740.

Rivers, Francine. Official Web site: http://www.francinerivers.com/.

Sandler, Lauren. "Throbbing Hearts and Thumping Bibles." http//archive.salom.com/books/feature/2001/07/12/christian-romance/print.html.

Seitz, Matt Zoller. "Sins Devoured, Hope Restored." *New York Times,* February 9, 2007.

Thomas, Cal. Review of the film *The Last Sin Eater. Jewish World Review* (Jan. 22, 2007/3 Shevat: 5767.

Today's Christian Woman. Review of *Unspoken* (September, 2001): S4.

ROBINSON, MARILYNNE

Personal, Professional, and Religious Background

Marilynne Summers Robinson (1943–) was born in Sandpoint, a town on the shores of Pend Oreille Lake in northern Idaho. It was the switching yard for the three great railroads that served the Northwest and northern tier of the United States. She was to use this locale, including details of the house in which she and her older brother grew up, in her first novel, *Housekeeping.* Her father is John J. Summers, and her mother Ellen Summers. Her great-grandparents had settled in Idaho, a region she still sees as a wilderness. Both her parents' families had settled and "established themselves in the northern mountains, where there is a special sweetness in the light and grace in the vegetation, and as well a particular tenderness in the contact of light and vegetation." She loves to search for strawberries in the meadows and discover the tiny flowers hidden in the grass. Her novels capture something of this love of the land, with descriptions of watching the sun on one side of her world and the moon on the other, of fields and forests, mountains and lakes. She is clearly in love with this countryside. She even uses the sleeping porch where she and her brother lay listening to the sounds of the trees.

Marilynne Robinson's family moved around to other small Northwestern towns such as Sagle and Coolin, which had no colleges, but did have some dedicated teachers, including one Latin teacher who introduced the young woman to Horace, Virgil, and Cicero and instilled in her a respect for reading primary sources.

In one of her essays ("Psalm Eight") in her insightful collection *The Death of Adam,* she describes herself as a pious child. She recalls going with her grandfather to hear an Easter sermon at a small Presbyterian Church in northern Idaho, listening intently as the minister read the story of the Resurrection from the King James version of the Scripture, and then described the discrepancies among the gospel accounts, leaving the congregation with "beautiful questions" to settle in their own minds. In later years, she left the Presbyterian

> Everything always bears looking into.
>
> —Marilynne Robinson in *The Death of Adam*

> I miss civilization, and I want it back.
>
> —Marilynne Robinson in *The Death of Adam*

church and moved to the Congregational, acknowledging that she began and ended as a pagan—"though only in the sense that I have never felt secure in the possession of the ideas and loyalties that are dearest to me." She is essentially a mystic who loves good sermons, attends worship regularly, and is a Calvinist to the core. Readers are often confused, finding in her characters a liberal spirit of inquiry combined with a conservative respect for the literal meaning of Scripture.

After graduating from Coeur d'Alene High School, she went to Pembroke College, formerly the women's college at Brown University, earning a B.A. in 1966. Her brother was a senior at Brown when she entered and began her studies in religion and creative writing. She then taught for a year at the Université d'Haute Bretagne, in Rennes, France, before returning to America and completing her studies at the University of Washington, earning her M.A. and Ph.D. in 1977. Her dissertation was on Shakespeare's *Henry VI*.

During graduate school, she married and had two sons, James and Joseph. Following the publication of her first book of essays, *Mother Country*, a book which won her even more fame than her first novel, she was sued for libel by Greenpeace. (Robinson believes that all environmental organizations tend to be useless. In this book, she attacked the Sellafield Nuclear Processing Plant in England, providing in the book exhaustive documentation against both Greenpeace and the British government.) At the same time she was facing this libel charge, she and her husband separated. She was left to raise the boys as a single mother. Teaching became her livelihood from this point forward.

She taught at the New York State Writers Program at Skidmore for several years (1989–91). She has also been writer-in-residence or visiting professor at numerous universities: the University of Kent, Amherst, and the University of Massachusetts, before joining the faculty of the highly acclaimed Iowa Writers' Workshop. She lives and works in Iowa City, the home of the University of Iowa. Her love of the people of this region and her research into their "archaeology of radicalism" have provided the stuff of her latest two novels, *Gilead* and *Home*.

Major Works and Themes

A thoughtful, careful, and imaginative writer, Marilynne Robinson explores her Christian faith and life, family relationships, and the world around her with delight and power. She has written only three novels: *Housekeeping*, *Gilead*, and *Home*. The first two appeared 24 years apart, and all have been highly praised. The stories are interesting contrasts, the first told from a young woman's point of view, the second from an old man's. The third is a sequel to the second, with the focus moved to a younger generation of townspeople. In addition to standard narrative techniques, Robinson uses interior monologues in her construction, though *Gilead* is ostensibly a letter to the old pastor's young son. *Housekeeping* describes two lonely girls in a hostile town that forces them to conform or escape. *Gilead* pictures, by contrast, a loving town, full of gracious people, who allow for frailty and eagerly share casseroles and love. *Home*, which follows the path of a minor, fascinating dark character from *Gilead*, is the painful story of a prodigal who finds little comfort in his earthly home and little hope for an eternal one.

Every phrase, scene, and image is carefully wrought, the ideas sparkle like lines in poetry. Robinson has a sacramental view of life, integrating her faith with her world, seeing all water from the biblical perspective of baptism and the living water of the well, the rain that replenishes life, the Flood that cleansed the earth. She deserves and rewards a thoughtful reader who takes time to savor her ideas, turning them over in her own mind as she reads.

Marilynne Robinson is difficult to classify, having the delight in each individual moment we see in Virginia Woolf, the wise comic vision of Dorothy L. Sayers, the thrill of nature we relish in Wordsworth. In a gesture—like a lover pulling down the limb of a tree to create an artificial shower to tease his beloved—she can convince us of the joys of life here on earth. At the same time, she insists on life's transience, showing an old man studying the painful movements of his good friend, remembering the young man that he once knew. Robinson deals frankly with death—from accidents, suicide, old age or sickness. She allows her characters to wonder about the dead, who they really were, where they are now, whether they will see them and recognize them in the afterlife.

Her first novel, *Housekeeping*, tells the peculiar story of a family whose grandfather came West to see mountains, settling in the small town of Fingerbone, a desolate little place on the shores of a glacial lake. The grandfather works for the railway, builds his own home on the hillside, plants an orchard, marries and fathers three daughters. One evening, the train hurtles off the tracks when crossing the bridge over the lake, taking the grandfather and numerous others with him, entering the dark water "like an otter." The all-female family struggles on, fixated on keeping their home together, but in the way of nature, the daughters leave and go their separate ways. One ends in Seattle, where she marries, is abandoned with two little girls, and finally borrows a car, returns to town, leaves the children on the porch, and drives the car into the same lake that killed her father. The story focuses on the lives of these two girls, Lucille and Ruth. It is told from the point of view of Ruth. Eventually their grandmother dies, leaving them in the care of two maiden aunts who are puzzled and troubled by children. They eventually turn them over to their aunt Sylvie, a free spirit who has no settled home.

The family never fits into the life of the town, but Lucille finally determines she will try, leaving to live with her home economics teacher. It is Ruth who wants to stay with her mad aunt, going where she goes like her biblical namesake, though this eventually means a life of drifting. Sylvie, a pagan spirit, is at ease with the floods in the springtime, the gradual decay of the house, the leaves that gather in the corners, and the dying trees in the orchard. The housekeeping imagery is rich and often funny—as when Sylvie decides to collect tin cans, cleaning and stacking them neatly in a house that is disintegrating. The couch, sodden from the flood, never dries out. Only when frightened by the authorities, who threaten to separate them, do they undertake serious housekeeping.

The summary at the end is revealing of the theme: "Fact explains nothing." The story line is not the explanation of the family, the relations, the meaning of life or nature or transience. The pair of misfits walking along the road in their billowing raincoats leave one house and live in others, haunted by the absence of those who are dead, who have left them, whom they have left. The final conflagration of the house, the town's belief that this pair of eternal wanderers are dead, frees them from the expectations of society. They cross the dangerous bridge, jump on to a train, and take up their exploration of the world, knowing only the love of one another. God intended families.

As Robinson explains, "families will not be broken. Curse and expel them, send their children wandering, drown them in flood and fires, and old women will make songs out of all their sorrows and sit in the porches and sing them on mild evenings." Songs are the children of sorrows, all the result of the Fall. Cain, she insists, troubled the waters in the image of God, becoming a creator of pain—the human condition. She sees human history as a search for the first family before Cain's "second creation," a dream of hugging the First Mother and never knowing death. When Ruth's mother left her children and killed herself, she broke the family and released the sorrow—"and we saw its wings and saw it fly a thousand ways into the hills." Surely the sins of the fathers and mothers are borne by the children, whose teeth are set on edge by the bitter grapes their ancestors have eaten.

The housekeeping imagery is perfect for this story of confused women. Sylvie's preference for wind, water, and leaves makes no sense to her priggish neighbors in this stern little town. If the children are not being raised properly by their lights, attending school regularly, properly dressed, then they should be taken away from the surrogate mother, who enjoys their irregularities, their singularity, their individual needs. The well-meaning town would stifle these free spirits, who must conform or escape. Sylvie and Ruth do not keep house nor are they kept by their house. They are ancient mariners on their own quest, sharing their love for one another and their delight in each day, each experience.

Gilead is a much more settled, traditional story, the tale of an old man looking back over his life, his ancestors, and his pastorate. The preacher of many sermons, the good friend of at least one man (the local Presbyterian minister), the husband of two women (the first of whom died in childbirth in her 20s), the father of a young boy (born to his second wife when he was 70 years old), John Ames is a man worth knowing. His mind is as well-stocked as his creator's. He is as interested in theology, history, literature, hymnody, and human nature as is Robinson herself, and has the same delight in little known details of history. He loves so many things in his life that it will be hard for him to leave this earth. His visions of Heaven are expansions of life here and now—with the wife he married late and the son he fathered even later.

The Ames men have been Congregational ministers in this Midwestern town for three generations. The first was a fierce abolitionist who lost an eye in the war. The comic characterization of this old zealot is masterful. He came back from the war determined to follow the Scripture literally, giving all he had to the poor. His family was stripped of all their possessions in the process, and the Presbyterian church found their offering missing during one fit of benevolence. The second Ames, probably in reaction to his father's excess, was really a Quaker. Out of respect for his mother he eventually returned to his father's church. The third Ames preacher, the epistle writer, is a thoughtful man, full of grace. He has contemplated fiery sermons in the vein of Jonathan Edwards but has torn them up to preach loving homilies to his aging parishioners. He recognizes that the church council will change everything, even tearing down the building he loves, when he dies, but he loves them for waiting.

He and his friend Boughton, the Scottish pastor of the Presbyterian church, have shared a lifetime of conversations and fellowship. They also share their worries over John Ames's godson and namesake, John Ames Boughton, or "Jack." The young man has proven a wastrel, tough, talented and charming. His reckless sexual indulgence, involving an "unsuitable" young woman near his college, resulted in an illegitimate child, which he never supported. He has been a haunted wanderer (like Cain) for most of his life, finally settling into another relationship that the world finds "unsuitable," a common-law marriage with an educated and devoted black woman. Jack's concern that he is damned leads him to inquire about the doctrine of Predestination and forces Ames to seek for the words he needs to bring the beloved prodigal back to the healing balm of faith.

At the same time, the old pastor is nervous at the sympathy Jack engenders in his wife and the admiration he encourages from his son. Old John Ames senses danger and tries to warn these innocents against this aging delinquent. The 7-year-old boy born of the late marriage has proven a blessing Ames never anticipated. His wife, a young woman with a past he only hints at, is uneducated but devoted. She gives him such joy, yet he knows he is leaving her and their child to face poverty and hard times. Like his grandfather, he has given all he has to clothe the poor, never anticipating the needs of his own family.

The setting of the story, a small prairie town modeled after Tabor, the home of Oberlin College, is named "Gilead" for good reason. It is a healing place for its people, a community that welcomed all races from its beginnings during the turbulent years leading up to the Civil War, was a center for abolitionists, a stop on the Underground Railroad for runaway slaves, a place where the people built churches and colleges. In preparation for writing the novel, Robinson did considerable research into the history of the Middle West in the 1830s and 1840s. The colleges in the region that they created "were already racially integrated, gender integrated." The colleges were open to all classes, encouraging students to work for their keep to avoid economic barriers. As a person who had come from the University of Massachusetts to Iowa, Robinson was interested in the 19th-century New Englanders who settled on the frontier of Iowa. The stories she tells about the tunnel in the sand and the sunken horse are drawn from the actual history and landscape. She also knew stories—like those told of Grandfather Ames—of abolitionist ministers with muskets in their cellars. Ironically, in *Home*, Robinson pictures a modern Gilead filled with latent racism, where Jack could not comfortably marry his African American mate and raise their mulatto child. No black or blended families live in this town.

Gilead also reveals Marilynne Robinson's love of good sermons. She enters the old pastor's mind as he snatches various ideas that might build into sermons, thinking of rich illustrations, Bible passages that would work with the ideas, phrasing of admonitions he might use. His love of language certainly matches her own. Robinson loves the tone of voice, the insights from conversation, the look in the speaker's eye or the twist of his mouth—all a rich part of our communication. Each person is a whole civilization, she believes, and each is reaching out, using all of the clumsy tools we have at hand. She acknowledges that she discovers things as she writes: "You create the occasion for your imagination, then all kinds of things come into play and surprise you. The best part of writing."

Home, a companion novel to *Gilead*, tracks the Rev. Robert Boughton's family at about the same time that the earlier novel covers, focusing this time on Mercy, the youngest daughter, and Jack, the prodigal son and eternal misfit. Both have returned home in anticipation of their father's death. This painful novel traces the family's love of Jack, his inevitable alienation and isolation. He does those things he meant not to do, those things which he knows he ought not to do, mourns his transgressions and the pain he inflicts on those who love him, and yet never reforms. He wants to believe in the Christian religion, but honestly cannot—no matter how much he reads and thinks and hopes. Robinson quietly uncovers the terrible sadness of the sinner and his entire family, his own sense of damnation, and their efforts to convince him of God's mercy and their love. The litany of apologies and new delinquencies exhaust everyone, but never diminishes the unconditional love of his family.

Only in the ending, which is signaled by the background provided in *Gilead* and by hints throughout *Home*, do we see that Jack is not the only sinner and not the only member of his family in need of repentance. Ironically, he proves too gentle and kind to insist on their facing their racism and complacency. Robinson refuses to provide a happy ending: it would be dishonest.

Again, Robinson makes brilliant use of music, of literary allusions, of Bible imagery, and of the everyday things of life. The hymns, which reinforce the conversations; the meals, which become sacred rituals; and the final communion, which brings a fitting conclusion to the shared experience of the two old preachers, are all richly developed in this sensitive, delicately nuanced tale of love and disappointment. Readers who enjoyed *Gilead* will find this second book much more painful, but nonetheless thoughtful.

Critical Reception

Critics have loved Marilynne Robinson's novels from the moment they were published. They have delighted readers, won prizes, and been the subject of discussions across the country. The reviewer of *Housekeeping* for *New Republic*, Marc Granetz, insisted that "every sentence of *Housekeeping* is well written." Anatole Broyard, writing for the *New York Times*, also praised the writing: "a first novel that sounds as if the author has been treasuring it up all her life, waiting for it to form itself." Deeper studies appeared in the *Times Literary Supplement* and the *Los Angeles Times*, with full discussions of the characters and the imagery. Critics were so thrilled with this long prose poem of a novel that she won numerous awards and was nominated for the Pulitzer.

Her books of essays that followed also found reviewers, most of whom were enthusiastic about many of her ideas and interested in others. Some did find her defenses of Calvinism and her harsh views of environmental degradation at odds with their own thinking.

Gilead won even more praise. James Wood reviewed it for the *New York Times Book Review*, commenting that "To bloom only every 20 years would make, you would think, for anxious or vainglorious flowerings." He goes on to note that the delay is a result of "moving at her own speed," thereby producing a "fiercely calm" and beautiful work. Thomas Meaney's review in *Commentary* was equally full of praise, noting that she "achieves moments of near Melvillean grandeur and dazzling lucidity, where her meandering syntax reaches for metaphors that are not only vessels of her religious faith but also an invitation to engage it." The book won both the National Book Critics Circle Award and the Pulitzer Prize for Fiction.

Home, as David Propson notes, has characters who "talk less about their emotions than they do about biblical exegesis of early 20th-century philosophy." Bob Thompson observes that this "unusual new book "manages to be both intertwined with its predecessor and a work that stands alone." He finds the book interesting, but not from the "common spring." Marilynne Robinson draws her ideas from her very own idiosyncratic experience and mind.

Awards

With her first novel, *Housekeeping*, Marilynne Robinson won the Ernest Hemingway Foundation award for Best First Novel from PEN American Center, the Richard and Hinda Rosenthal Award from the American Academy and Institute of Arts and Letters. She was also nominated for the PEN/Faulkner fiction award and the Pulitzer Prize. *Gilead* won her even more praise—the National Book Critics Circle Award for fiction and the Pulitzer Prize for fiction in 2005.

Bibliography of Novels by Author

Housekeeping. New York: Farrar, Straus, 1981.
Gilead. New York: Farrar Straus & Giroux, 2004.
Home. New York: Farrar, Strauss & Giroux, 2008.

Marilynne Robinson is also the author of stories and articles in various periodicals, including the *New York Times Book Review* and *Harper's*.

Housekeeping was adapted by Bill Forsyth into a film and released by Columbia in 1987.

Bibliography of Works about Author

Broyard, Anatole. Review of *Housekeeping*. *New York Times*, January 7, 1981.

Granetz, Marc. Review of *Housekeeping*. *New Republic* (February 21, 1981).

Hart, Jeffrey. "Now, a Masterpiece." Review of *Gilead*. (http://www.nationalreview.com/books/hart_200505200838.asp).

Kavanaugh, Julie. Review of *Housekeeping*. *Times Literary Supplement* (April 3, 1981).

Kimball, Roger. "John Calvin Got a Bad Rap." Review of *The Death of Adam*. *New York Times Book Review*, November 28, 2004.

"Marilynne Robinson." *Contemporary Authors Online*. Detroit: Thomson Gale, 2007.

Meaney, Thomas. "In God's Creation," Review of *Gilead*. *Commentary* (August 16, 2005): 81.

Propson, David. "Weaving Humanity into History," *Wall Street Journal*, September 30, 2008.

Robinson. Marilynne. *The Death of Adam: Essays on Modern Thought*. Boston: MA: Houghton, 1998.

Robinson, Marilynne. *Mother Country: Britain, the Nuclear State, and Nuclear Pollution*. New York: Farrar, Straus, 1989.

Robinson, Marilynne. *Puritans and Prigs*. New York: Holt, 1999.

Robinson, Marilynne. Interview. *Religion and Ethics* (March 18, 2005): Episode No. 829. http://www.pbs.org/wnet/religionandethic/week829/p-interview.html.

Schaub, Thomas. "An Interview with Marilynne Robinson." *Contemporary Literature* 35, no. 2 (Summer, 1994): 231–251.

Seidenbaum, Art. Review of *Housekeeping*. *Los Angeles Times*, January 14, 1981.

Thompson, Bob. "At 'Home' with the Past," *Washington Post*, October 20, 2008, C01.

Wood, James. "Acts of Devotion." Review of *Gilead*. *New York Times Book Review*, November 28, 2004.

S

SAMSON, LISA

Personal, Professional, and Religious Background

Lisa Ebauer Samson (1964–) was born in Baltimore, Maryland. Her father, William Ebauer, was an optometrist and her mother, Joy Snider Ebauer, was a pro-life activist, who encouraged her daughter to fight against torture and other issues. Lisa attended Liberty University, earning a degree in telecommunications, though her first interest was art.

Lisa Ebauer married William "Will" Samson in 1988. He maintains his own blog (www. will2head.typepad.com), in which he describes his concerns with religious, social, and political issues. He is concerned with living an "intentional" life, having left his job to attend seminary and begin his work on a Ph.D. degree. Will Samson teaches sociology and social politics at Georgetown in Kentucky, and is working on a dissertation on the role of religion in the social work movement toward environmental sustainability. The couple have three children, Elizabeth Tyler, Jacob Patrick, and Gwynneth McLeod.

The Samsons lived in Maryland until 2006, when they moved to Lexington, Kentucky. Samson notes that she and her husband deliberately chose to live downtown Lexington, not only because she enjoys being near the University of Kentucky, but also because they feel it is important to minister to the poor and needy—and it is easier when "they're right in front of you." She echoes something of this hunger for service in her novel *Quaker Summer*.

Lisa Samson does have a rustic cabin where she can escape the city and the pressures of family to write her stories. A Presbyterian, she and her husband have become public speakers and leaders of "Serenity Retreats," writing weekends that feature "good food, quiet setting, gathering together to talk about writing, to brainstorm and then, to actually write!"

> We live intentionally. That means we try and make whatever we do intentionally count for the kingdom.
>
> —Lisa Samson in interview with *Faithful Reader*, November 10, 2006

She acknowledges that her diagnosis of Wolff-Parkinson-White Syndrome, a disease that speeds up the heart and creates "weird rhythms," has revealed to her that life is very short and precarious. This insight paved the way for her to accept her life "in intentional Christian community." Her constant prayer to Christ is, "Show me! Please show me what it means to be a harvester, to be a laborer."

Major Works and Themes

Lisa Samson's earliest novels, written in the 1990s, are historical romances in the 19th-century pattern. They trace characters through grand adventures in Scotland, England, France, and elsewhere, aiming largely to delight a young audience. After a time, Samson turned to contemporary stories, using her own region and people she knows to portray families—and particularly women—in crisis. She acknowledges that another Maryland writer, **Anne Tyler,** provided some guidance in the path she followed. She also credits Larry McMurtry, Chaim Potok, **C. S. Lewis,** Madelaine L'Engle, and **Annie Dillard**—and even Jack Kerouac. Her dream is to find her own voice, just as W. Somerset Maugham, her "all time favorite writer," did.

Unlike many contemporary Christian women writers, Lisa Samson brings a more disturbing point of view to stories about families in contemporary America. She insists that her multi-ethnic characters are like the people whom one would find sitting in adjacent pews on a Sunday morning. The frenetic women who form the center of consciousness in her stories are deeply disturbed about their lives, haunted by a sense of sin, obsessed with the need to change their values. They are also non-stop talkers. They race from place to place, from person to person, finding little peace in churches or friendships or family. They do sometimes come to a place of peace in service and to a Quaker-like stillness.

Her themes reflect her own battles with depression, conflicts in marriage and motherhood, issues involving faith and social justice. Her central character in *Church Ladies* has an affair, laments her infidelity, and works through her guilt. In *Songbird*, the mother is a schizophrenic, the central character tends to clinical depression. In her tough stories, some young people die in the flower of their youth and innocent people are unfairly tarred by the sins of others. And yet, Samson approaches her subjects with a surprising sense of humor, a real flair for words, and a deep passion. She captures the voice of Southern middleclass people, their lifestyle, their taste for Christian music, their evenings at Suds 'n' Strikes Forever (a combination bowling alley and "washateria"), and their love of rich desserts—including "dump" cakes. She sees life filled with blessings and temptations, with God's grace undergirding all of human existence.

In *Quaker Summer*, Lisa Samson reveals her central theme of the need to reject consumer-driven modern life in the suburbs, step outside the cozy Christian community of evangelicals, and try to relate to the poorest of the poor. The shopaholic heroine and her overworked surgeon husband decide to leave their elegant home and swimming pool, turning to mission work in the inner city. Two ancient Quaker ladies show Heather the way to peace and forgiveness. The novel, like many of her other more recent works, mirrors her own life.

Critical Reception

John Mort describes Lisa Samson's early historical series, "The Highlanders," as "a highly romantic series somewhat in the manner of George MacDonald." "Shades of Eternity" he also describes as "melodramatic." This is a series dealing with the fortunes of Earl John Youngblood that are set in France, England, and Scotland in the 1860s, featuring appearances by Queen Victoria and a few of the early feminists.

Lisa Samson's 1998 novel, *The Moment I Saw You,* is quite different, moving to modern America, where Natalie St. John, a woman of affluence, purchases an inn in the Blue Ridge Mountains. The central romance with an attractive professor who stays at the inn forces Natalie to confront her own distrust of men. In her review for *Library Journal,* Melissa Hudak called it a "standout contemporary romance."

When Samson broke from this historical melodramatic pattern of writing, she transformed some of her earlier interest in feminism into more contemporary issues. She continued to use a woman's point of view and to talk about women bonding and searching for a Christian path of service in male-dominated churches. She reveals a kind of creative discontent that allows her women to grow into stronger Christians, more fashioned for service in today's society.

Awards

Lisa Samson won the 2004 Christy Award for Contemporary Christian Fiction with her novel *Songbird. Quaker Summer* was selected by Women of Faith as the 2007 Novel of the Year.

Bibliography of Novels by Author

"Highlanders" series (Eugene, OR: Harvest House, 1994–1996)

"Abbey" series (Eugene OR: Harvest House, 1996–1997)

The Moment I Saw You. Eugene, OR: Harvest House, 1998.
Indigo Waters. Grand Rapids, MI: Zondervan, 1999.
Fields of Gold. Grand Rapids, MI: Zondervan, 2000.
The Church Ladies. Sisters, OR: Multnomah Publishers, 2001.
Women's Intuition. Colorado Springs, CO: WaterBrook Press, 2002.
The Living End. Colorado Springs, CO: WaterBrook Press, 2003.
Songbird. New York: Warner Faith, 2003.
Tiger Lillie. Colorado Springs, CO: WaterBrook Press, 2004.
Club Sandwich. Colorado Springs, CO: WaterBrook Press, 2005.
Apples of Gold. Colorado Springs, CO: WaterBrook Press, 2006.

"Hollywood Nobody" series (Colorado Springs, CO: NavPress, 2008)

Straight Up. 2006.
Quaker Summer. 2007.
Embrace Me. 2008.

Bibliography of Works about Author

Cosby, Cindy. "Lisa Samson Interview." *Author Talk,* November 10, 2006. http://www.faithfulreader.com/authors/au=samson-lisa.asp.
Hudak, Melissa. Review of *The Moment I Saw You. Library Journal* (April 1, 1998): 78.
"Lisa Samson," *Contemporary Authors Online.* Detroit: Thomson Gale, 2006.

Mort, John. *Christian Fiction: A Guide to the Genre*. Greenwood Village, CO: Libraries Unlimited, 2002.
Random House Web site: http://www.randomhouse.com.
Samson, Lisa. Homepage: http://www.lisasamson.com.

SINGER, RANDY

Personal, Professional, and Religious Background

Randy Darrell Singer (1956–) grew up admiring Atticus Finch, the hero of Harper Lee's *To Kill a Mockingbird*. He told an interviewer that he always knew he would become a lawyer because he was a member of the Singer family—"you grew up arguing." In high school, he was on the basketball team and was kicked off for what he calls "teenage troubles." This shock brought him to a recognition of his own inadequacy and the need for Christ in his life. Singer remembers himself as a rebellious teenager, who was impressed by an evangelist who spoke at his church and led him, gradually, to change his life, to live in the spirit and not in the flesh.

He went to Houghton College, a religious college, from which he graduated in 1978. The following year, he married Rhonda Pursifull, a teacher. Randy Singer was accepted to Cornell Law School and was on his way to New York State when he felt that God was calling him to teach at the small Christian school before training for his career in law. He taught and coached for five years at the Alliance Christian School in Portsmouth, Virginia, before entering William and Mary Law School. He graduated second in his class in 1986, after which he took a position with Wilcox and Savage, moving from trial lawyer to head of the firm. In 1997, Randy Singer left the law firm to become executive vice-president and general counsel of the North American Mission Board of the Southern Baptist Convention in Atlanta. He then became president of FamilyNet television, a family-friendly, faith-based cable country.

In 2007, he returned to Virginia Beach to become a partner in his old law firm. He said he missed the area and the courtroom. Since his return to the Hampton Roads/Virginia Beach region, he has become the teaching pastor for Trinity Church at the Oceanfront in addition to his law practice. In 2002, he started writing a novel a year, beginning with the award-winning *Directed Verdict*.

His wife teaches at Norfolk Christian schools. They have two children, Rosalyn and Joshua, both planning careers in the law.

Major Works and Themes

Randy Singer uses his legal background, his Christian convictions, and his knowledge of the Virginia Beach region for his legal thrillers. He builds characters who are colorful and complex, like people we might meet on the street. His interest in personal injury cases and his fascination with complicated issues in the law make each of the novels an interesting study in a specific area: international law, abortion, internet security, malfeasance on the part of officers of the state in this country and elsewhere, abusive parents, bioethical issues, and many others. He sets forth the law, explains the complications, presses toward a "just" solution, and reveals the limitations of human courts.

> I still mess up all the time, but now I sense a power that comes through Christ. Randy is not in charge anymore.
>
> —Randy Singer, in interview with Philip Walzer, 2008

When Randy Singer won a Christy award for his first novel, he stepped forward to make a brief speech—and thanked the wrong publisher.

His novels are lively, fast-moving, vivid, and full of suspense. He knows how to tell a story, and how to tease the spiritual meaning out of a complex issue. His novels grow out of his Christian worldview without being specifically Christian in message. They deal with topical issues that he has confronted in the courtroom and leave no participant untouched by the outcome. He also introduces humor, romance, and faith along the way. The stories are not full of biblical quotations, nor does he indulge in heavy-handed preaching, but they do press gently toward a Gospel message.

Singer has indicated that he plans in the future to work on a book dedicated to the experience of Paul, particularly his challenges to the Roman system of justice.

Critical Reception

The reviewers have been delighted with the legal thrillers published each year by Randy Singer. *Publishers Weekly* even called him "the Christian John Grisham." He shares Grisham's love of a good story that moves at a fast pace with plenty of twists and turns, leaving the reader in suspense until the final scene. *Directed Verdict* is a story of a missionary who was brutally beaten by Saudi law enforcement, her husband killed, and both injected with cocaine—and then accused of being major drug dealers. The widow, now back in Virginia, finds that even her American insurance company will not agree to pay her husband's death benefits to support her and her two children. The issues of "sovereign immunity," the obvious violation of international agreements to allow freedom of religion and eschew violence, and the very real human interest story make the case one that screams out for justice to be served. Ironically, this must occur in a courtroom where only legal niceties are really served

In another of his stories, *False Witness*, Singer again addresses his concerns for the persecuted church. Singer takes on the Chinese abuse of Christians, who seek to survive in spite of "Triads" operating in America. These foreign agents attack those who testify against them in spite of the witness protection program offered by the U.S. government. In this case, an algorithm that can untangle the most sophisticated codes on the Internet has been discovered by a Chinese Christian. The relentless attempts by both the Chinese and the Americans to gain the secret to discovering prime numbers quickly makes both into opponents to the central characters—who are not innocents themselves. In the meantime, the Chinese house-church has been destroyed while the governments play their game.

Other novels by Randy Singer attack other contemporary issues with intellect and sensitivity. The critics for *Library Journal, Christianity Today, Kirkus Review,* and *Publishers Weekly* all praise this talented writer.

Awards

Directed Verdict won the Christy Award for best Christian suspense novel in 2003.

Bibliography of Novels by Author (Colorado Springs, CO: WaterBrook Press, Unless Otherwise Indicated)

Directed Verdict. 2002.
Irreparable Harm. 2003.
Dying Declaration. 2004.

The Judge Who Stole Christmas. 2005.
Self Incrimination. 2005.
The Cross Examination of Jesus Christ. 2006.
The Cross Examination of Oliver Finney. 2006.
False Witness. 2007.
By Reason of Insanity. Wheaton, IL: Tyndale House, 2008.

Bibliography of Works about Author

Butler, Tamara. Review of *Dying Declaration. Library Journal* (June 1, 2004): 116.
Crosby, Cindy. "Courtroom Thriller," *Christianity Today* (September 2004): 91.
Darlington, C.J. "Randy Singer Interview." http://www.titletrakk.com/author/interview/randy-singer-interview.htm.
Publishers Weekly. Review of *False Witness* (March 5, 2007): 38.
"Randy Singer," *Contemporary Authors Online.* Detroit: Thomson Gale, 2008.
Randy Singer Web site: http://www.randysinger.net.
Walzer, Philip. "Region, faith play key roles in Norfolk lawyer's novels," *The Virginian-Pilot*, May 27, 2008.

SMITH, LEE

Personal, Professional, and Religious Background

Lee Smith (1944–) was born in Grundy, Virginia, a small coal-mining town in the Blue Ridge Mountains, near the Kentucky border. It is a region that was to feed her imagination and anchor her writing to a strong sense of place, with the various classes of people, from country-club socialites to coal miners and farmers. Her father, Ernest Lee Smith, was a native of the area. He operated a dime store, where Lee Smith learned much about the different shoppers, listening to their dialects, observing their clothing from a peephole in the ceiling of the store. Her mother, Virginia Marshall Smith, was a college graduate who had come to Grundy to teach school. Lee Smith credits her mother with much of her story-telling ability: "My mother could make a story out of anything; she'd go to the grocery store and come home with a story." Her heroines often echo this taste she developed so early, begging people to tell them stories.

Smith has described herself as a strange child, an insatiable reader. As she notes, when she was 9 or 10, she tried writing her first story, "about Adlai Stevenson and Jane Russell heading out west together to become Mormons." Smith notes that this precocious bit of writing foreshadowed her preferred themes, "religion and flight, staying in one place or not staying, containment or flight—and religion."

Lee Smith approached religion, even as a teenager, more as a student than a seeker, except perhaps for a recorded personal experience that did reflect some emotional involvement: One summer at camp, she heard the voice of God speaking directly to her. When she told the others about her experience, they put her in the infirmary and called her parents. Perhaps as a result of this, she became interested in some of the extreme forms of spiritual expres-

> God wants us to express His love in our lives through using our creative gifts to the fullest. He wants us to *use* this life which He has given us to be artists for Him.
>
> —Katie Croker in *The Devil's Dream*, 298

> Lee Smith's first story was "about Adlai Stevenson and Jane Russell heading out west together to become Mormons."

sion, traveling to Jolo, West Virginia, and Big Rock, Virginia, where members of the congregation sometimes took up serpents as a prelude to their religious ecstasy. Later, she returned to this group, trying to envision the life of a minister's child in such a congregation, the story she told in *Saving Grace*. Though she admits she went to "gape and gawk," she sensed that the experience of the believers was "powerful."

Her final two years of high school were spent at St. Catherine's in Richmond, Virginia. From there, she enrolled in Hollins College in Roanoke, where she was a classmate of **Annie Dillard.** The newfound freedom of college and the encouragement of professors in the excellent creative writing program made this a "kind of breakout period" for her. Smith describes the small, select women's college experience in *The Last Girls*, where she found close friendships and liberation. She indicates that she and Dillard became go-go dancers for an all-girl rock band, the "Virginia Woolfs." A group of the girls also took the same trip down the Mississippi that she described years later in her novel—an imitation of Mark Twain's travels and also an echo of the trip that Annie Dillard's father began but did not finish.

It was at Hollins that Smith's writing first achieved some recognition. Her coming-of-age novel, *The Last Day the Dog Bushes Bloomed*, won the Book-of-the-Month Club contest, one of twelve scholarships awarded in 1967, and was published two years later. The book describes the life of a "deeply weird" young girl in a small town, drawing heavily on her own background and on her reading of Southern fiction—especially Welty, Faulkner, and McCullers. Smith later attended the Sorbonne, University of Paris—an experience that rarely is mentioned in her fiction. Her stories are solidly American in venue and tone.

After her graduation from college, Lee Smith married James Seay, who is a poet and a teacher, born into a distinguished southern family. He has taught at numerous universities in Virginia, Alabama, Tennessee, and North Carolina. For the next few years, Lee Smith spent most of her time traveling from campus to campus while her husband taught creative writing and she raised their two little boys, Josh and Page. She found little time for her own fiction, but did work for various newspapers. By 1971, she had completed her second novel, *Something in the Wind*, which received favorable reviews. Her next novel, *Fancy Strut*, published in 1973, won wider praise as a "comic masterpiece."

By 1974, the family had moved to Chapel Hill, where Smith taught high school and continued her writing. She produced a much darker novel, *Black Mountain Breakdown* (1981), in which she is thought to have found her voice—the dialect of her native Appalachian region, full of lively imagery and vivid phrasing. During this period, she had also been writing some short stories, largely for women's magazines, which she collected in *Cakewalk*.

At this time, her first marriage broke up and she moved from Chapel Hill to Raleigh, North Carolina, to accept a position at North Carolina State University, where she taught for the next 19 years. She has continued to write novels and short stories and some poetry, to edit materials, and to speak at conferences. She is a very popular speaker.

She married a second time. Her husband, Hal Crowther, is a journalist, who has been called "the best essayist working in journalism today," as well as an editor, and a regular contributor to *The Atlanta Journal-Constitution* and a political columnist for *The Progressive Populist* of Austin, Texas. Lee Smith and Hal Crowther make their home in Hillsborough, North Carolina.

Major Works and Themes

Lee Smith tends to write two kinds of stories—contemporary women's stories and mid-20th-century Appalachian folk tales. She captures the speech, the habits, the history, and the longings of the old hill folk with their ballads and superstitions, their hardscrabble lives in tiny log cabins perched on hillsides. They are natural storytellers, as is she. Smith echoes Eudora Welty in her attention to the cruel lives many of these women live, marrying young, producing many children, and dying young. She delves into different histories, showing a romantic town girl racing off on horseback with a dashing farm boy, a beautiful young girl singing haunting melodies as she wanders in the woodlands, a witch enchanted by a lover who finally abandons her. Some of the youngsters have bright minds and dim futures. Most of her people are limited by inbreeding, poverty and ignorance. The schools are pitiful, the missionary activities occasionally helpful, and only a few children are blessed by an opportunity for education and success.

Some of the husbands are nasty and vicious, some kind and loving. They work at backbreaking labor in the fields and mines and forests. They live on the edge of poverty and wear out young. Her scenes on front porches are touching, with the weary couples sitting and talking, the men whittling or singing and smoking, the old companions rocking and watching the sun disappear over the mountains.

For entertainment, nothing beats a church revival or a dance. Visitors are important interruptions to the lives of these people, music and sex their joy, and children their greatest treasures. Smith contrasts this farm life with the gritty mining villages and the lumber camps, obviously preferring the simple life before electrification and progress. Like Faulkner, she puts her trust in the common folk, not in the tacky middle class, nor in the rare upper-class "aristocrats" with their traditions and snobbery.

Many of these hill people, especially the men, are Christ-haunted, but not quite to the extent we see in **Flannery O'Connor's** stories. Smith sounds more like **Doris Betts,** who shares her religious doubts and her prejudices against the fundamentalists. The hard-shelled Baptists cannot abide the fiddle playing of the Devil's children (in *The Devil's Dream*). Requiring a call to the ministry, a young man may search for a lifetime for God's will, praying at the top of his voice, neglecting his family, while never feeling quite certain he is God's elect. On the other hand, Smith pictures Miss Elizabeth, the iron-clad lady of *Family Linen*, changing from the Methodist to the Episcopal Church because she prefers the beauty of the language and the elegance of the ritual. The simpler and deeper folk seek love and freedom, worry about loss and death.

Neither group is consumed with issues of faith or deep philosophical issues. Her more educated pastors, contrasted with those who preach as soon as they have the "call," are students of comparative religion, cynical about the reality of religious experience, and hardly paragons of virtue. In the older days of the itinerant preachers, the circuit riders who served vast areas of the region, the locals would flock to the meetings where the clergyman would perform the rituals saved up for their visits—the funerals, baptisms, and marriages. In the meantime, the people would have cohabited for months, borne children out of wedlock, and buried their dead without the blessings of the church.

Smith has a particular animus for the more fiery and charismatic evangelical preachers who land in town for a few nights, conduct revival services, seduce the girls and fleece the guys, and then blow out of town, leaving barely a footprint. Gracie's charismatic itinerant serpent-handling father in *Saving Grace* is a good example of this figure. Nor has Smith much praise for the northern missionaries, some of whom are ministers, some teachers. These outsiders believe themselves superior to the locals, distribute books and culture, but have less real humanity or faith than the local lay leaders with their wild sermons and altar calls. Smith knows a lot about hard-shelled Baptists with their double predestination, the differences between Primitive Baptists and Missionary Baptists. She laughs at those who expect God to explain the world's pain or to find God's plan for their lives. Deep down, she seems to believe that most people are fated to follow either fiddlers or preachers, to dance their lives away or to race to church the minute the front door is cracked.

Her most sympathetic characters are inclined to folk superstitions rather than Christian orthodoxy. Ivy, in *Fair and Tender Ladies*, for example, acknowledges she is "ruint" and damned, but has too much integrity to pretend she is saved. She is a pagan, "suckled in a creed outworn," happier cavorting on the mountaintop with the bee man than sitting on a bench in church. When she does read the Bible, she finds her tastes lie with Ecclesiastes; she thinks Proverbs is too sour and the Song of Solomon just plain dirty. Lee Smith's comments are original and informed, though rarely sympathetic when she deals with organized religion

Smith reveals a more serious view of religion in *The Devil's Dream*, when she finally allows a sympathetic character, Katie Crocker, to find her authentic self through God's love. The Ministry of Care, Hallelujah Congregation provides for her "Yes! Yes!" to creative energy and self realization in contrast with the dreary "No! No!" of the old Chicken Rise theology. Through her checkered career, Katie tries a number of cultures, including the laid-back California Buddhists, but finds comfort in a simple expression of God's love.

Saving Grace is Smith's most thoroughly religious novel. In it, she explores the mystery of the snake handlers, the burdens of the family of the minister of this faith, and the culture of the believers. The combination of authentic dialogue with shocking scenes of religious fanaticism makes this a remarkable book, but not so well received as some of her earlier stories.

In other stories, Lee Smith is a chronicler of the New South, with its shopping malls, cheap motels, tacky homes, and miniature golf courses. Her people, who range from waitresses to grand dames, speak in very individual dialects. The shallower ones worry about their clothes and homes, their appliances and social status. She laughs at the brick bungalow subdivision culture, the love of big cars and glitsy clothes. In these sketches, Smith shows that love and family are the real keys to happiness.

Lee Smith is best known for family histories, stories of women seeking to find happiness, to escape claustrophobic marriages, to discover some meaning in their lives. Her women try divorces or affairs with other men. Rarely do they find answers to their problems in religion. Her approach to religion continues to be that of an interested and precise observer. As a feminist, she remarks on the religious men who abuse their wives and children or who use their authority and charisma for sexual indulgence. Her characters' passion for a blend of religion and superstition contrasts powerfully with the sedate, cultured, dying mainline churches. She never tries to articulate her own faith clearly, perhaps a response to her proper parents' discouragement of her teenage encounter with God and her humiliating moment of enthusiasm.

In these stories—such as *Oral History* or *Fair and Tender Ladies*, Lee Smith draws on a host of interviews, folklore studies, personal experiences, and wide reading. She loves to include the music culture as a symbol of the people, moving from the old-time Gospel music, the folk ballads, to the contemporary rockabilly country singers She knows the region, enjoys using colorful names like Frog Level, Cripple Creek, Pig Branch, Cana, and Pisgah—the incongruous jumble she has known since childhood. She can make a region like Scrabble Creek seem fresh and alive to the reader, at the same time making it the background for her character's spiritual pilgrimage.

Critical Reception

Critics have been kind but not generous in their praise of Lee Smith's work. The first of her stories to receive major critical praise was *Fancy Strut*, which the *New York Times Book Review* notes is a "genuinely funny book that is satiric without being mean." The *Virginia Quarterly* also noted the "deftness" of the writer. It was *Black Mountain Breakdown* that established Smith's capacity for presenting the doomed hope for escape from the web of fate. Using the pattern of country music or the themes of the old Appalachian ballads, Smith found a voice and a theme in this tale of a "girl of 12 who catches fireflies by a river to a woman of 32 who lies catatonic in her childhood home." Not all of the critics relish her cornpone characters, whom they characterize as "hickish" and insist that she patronizes them. Most do acknowledge her powerful use of the particulars of life in the hollers and hills of Virginia. Most critics also recognize her debt to Carson McCullers, Flannery O'Connor, and Eudora Welty.

Lee Smith's subsequent novels have won her a readership, but it is *Fair and Tender Ladies* that established her as a popular teller of wonderful stories. Like many of her other stories, this novel is filled with religion and religious people, but it is the unrepentant pagan who wins the reader's affection.

Awards

Lee Smith began her career with the Book-of-the-Month Club fellowship in 1967, for *The Last Day the Dogbushes Bloomed*. She has also won the O. Henry Award from Doubleday, 1979, for "Mrs. Darcy Meets the Blue-Eyed Stranger at the Beach," and 1981, for "Between the Lines." She won the Sir Walter Raleigh Award in 1984; the North Carolina Award for Literature in 1985; the Weatherford Award for Appalachian Fiction in 1988; the Lyndhurst grant for 1990–92; the Robert Penn Warren Prize for Fiction in 1991; the Lila Wallace/*Reader's Digest* Award, 1995–97; and the Academy Award in Literature,. She became a member of the American Academy of Arts and Letters in 1999.

Bibliography of Novels by Author

The Last Day the Dogbushes Bloomed. New York: Harper, 1968.
Something in the Wind. New York: Harper, 1971.
Fancy Strut. New York: Harper, 1973.
Black Mountain Breakdown. New York: Putnam, 1980.
Cakewalk (short stories). New York: Putnam, 1980.
Oral History. New York: Putnam, 1983.
Family Linen. New York: Putnam, 1985.
Fair and Tender Ladies. New York: Putnam, 1988.
Me and My Baby View the Eclipse: Stories. New York: Putnam, 1990.
The Devil's Dream. New York: Putnam, 1992.
We Don't Love with Our Teeth. Portland, OR: Chinook Press, 1994.
Saving Grace. New York: Putnam, 1995.
The Christmas Letters: A Novella. Chapel Hill, NC: Algonquin Books, 1996.
News of the Spirit. New York: Putnam, 1997.

The Last Girls. Chapel Hill, NC: Algonquin Books, 2002.
On Agate Hill. 2006. Chapel Hill, NC: Shannon Ravenel Books, 2006.

Lee Smith has collected and edited an oral history of Grundy, Virginia, which she calls *Sitting on the Courthouse Bench,* and is also a contributor to periodicals, including *Redbook, Mc-Call's, Mademoiselle,* and *Writer.*

Bibliography of Works about Author

American Spectator. Review of *Saving Grace* (December, 1995): 38.

American Women Writers. Detroit, MI: St. James Press, 1999.

Collins, Jennifer Renee. *The Detrimental Effects of Organized Religion in Lee Smith's Fiction.* (thesis). East Tennessee State University, 2002. http://etd-submit.etsu.edu/etd/thesis/available/etd0107102-135940/unrestricted/Collins/011502.

Dickinson, Charles. Review of *Family Linen. Detroit News,* October 6, 1985.

Hill, Dorothy Combs. *Lee Smith.* New York: Twayne Publishers, 1992.

Hooper, Brad. Review of *The Last Girls. Booklist* (May 15, 2002): 1555.

"Lee Smith." *Contemporary Authors Online.* Detroit: Thomson Gale, 2004.

"Lee Smith." *Contemporary Literary Criticism,* Volume 25. Detroit, MI: Gale, 1983.

"Lee Smith." *Contemporary Novelists.* Detroit, MI: St. James Press, 2001.

"Lee Smith." *Contemporary Southern Writers.* Detroit, MI: St. James Press, 1999.

Lee Smith Web Site, http://www.leesmith.com/.

Lehmann-Haupt, Christopher. Review of *Black Mountain Breakdown. New York Times,* July 29, 1983.

Oswalt, Conrad. "Witches and Jesus: Lee Smith's Appalachian Religion." *Southern Literary Journal* (September 22, 1998).

Parrish, Nancy C. *Lee Smith, Annie Dillard, and the Hollins Group: A Genesis of Writers.* Baton Rouge: Louisiana State University Press, 1998.

Publishers Weekly, Review of *Saving Grace* (March 27, 1995): 74.

Publishers Weekly, Review of *The Last Girls* (July 1, 2002): 44.

Religious Studies Review. Review of *Saving Grace* (October, 1996): 34.

Scura, Dorothy. Review of *Saving Grace. Southern Review* (Autumn, 1997): 859.

Smith, Lee. *Conversations with Lee Smith,* Linda Tate, ed. Jackson: University Press of Mississippi, 2001.

Thompson, Caroline. Review of *Black Mountain Breakdown. Los Angeles Times,* February 16, 1981.

T

TATLOCK, ANN

Personal, Professional, and Religious Background

Ann Tatlock (1959–) was born in Parkersburg, West Virginia. Her father, Edward L. Shurts, is a retired chemical engineer, and her mother, Jane Tatlock Shurts, was a registered nurse.

> And yes, Virginia, in an age of relativism, there is an Absolute. His name is Jesus.
>
> —Ann Tatlock on her Web site, which contains an elaborate critique of postmodernism

Ann Tatlock attended Oral Roberts University, earning a B.A. in 1981, before entering Wheaton Graduate School, from which she graduated with a M.A. in communications in 1987. In her mid-20s, she suffered the painful loss of her mother to cancer. After her mother's death, Ann took her mother's maiden name as her writing name to honor her memory. Tatlock had been doing editorial work for *Decision* magazine when this grief led her into the writing of fiction. Over the next few years, in her spare time, she wrote seven novels—none of which were published. She found in the writing a new way to deal with her grief.

In 1992, she married Robert Blank. When her husband discovered her cache of unpublished fiction, he encouraged her to find an agent and a publisher. Within six months, she had an agent and an editor at Bethany House who helped her to bring out her first novel, *A Room of My Own*.

Ann Tatlock and her husband have one daughter, Laura Jane. Tatlock now tries to write a book every 18 months while she leads a private and peaceful life with her family. She and her husband lived for a time in Minneapolis "in a house overlooking one of the 10,000 lakes." They now live in North Carolina.

Major Works and Themes

Ann Tatlock finds her ideas through inspiration, bolstered by research and thought. Her first successful novel, *A Room of My Own*, reveals the pattern of her work. She tells the story from the point of view of a young girl, just on the brink of becoming an adult. Ginny still lives with romantic dreams, surrounded by the love and care of her family and friends. Though her family is living in the midst of the Great Depression, they are barely affected by the harsh economic times. The father, a doctor, is a gentle, Christ-like man much on the order of Atticus Finch. His wise words and medical skills make him much in demand. Yet he finds time to go down to the collection of vagrants in "Soo City," a makeshift community of unemployed wanderers near the railroad tracks. He begins to take Ginny along—to teach her something about real life. She enjoys the role as his assistant, undertakes a blanket drive to keep the people warm through the winter months, and learns to listen to their stories and love the people as individuals. When they suffer, she suffers along with them, finding common cause with them and creating within her the heart of a missionary. It is a gentle, loving tale of a girl's coming of age, beautifully told and full of forgiveness and joy.

A later, much praised novel, *I'll Watch the Moon*, picks up on the education of a young girl, Tag, at a somewhat later period—just after World War II. This time, Tatlock uses the horrors of the Nazi violence in Poland, the prison camps, and the polio epidemic that struck America to reveal the broken world in which the child must learn to live. Divorce, betrayal, abuse, and disease have embittered Catherine, Tag's mother, so that the distressed woman is ready to do as Job's wife suggested, "Curse God and die." After moving to work with her sister at her boarding house, she becomes a friend and confidant of Josef, a survivor of the Holocaust who has lost his own family and yet has learned to forgive and to hope for a time when he will understand God's sovereign will. The moving tale of his suffering blends with the poignant story of Catherine's discovery that she is like the living dead, the *muselmann*, of the prison camps. His Christ-like life and death redeem Catherine and her family, bringing them back to God and a new hope. This is a powerful story of making good out of evil, filled with rich imagery and parables, pulled together with a power that moves the reader to tears. The pain is touched with joy and with understanding in a remarkable way. The language is lyrical and yet perfect for the characters and the period.

Things We Once Held Dear is a gentle story of a homecoming. Like Willa Cather's displaced artists, Neil Sadler can not survive in the Midwest among his farming relatives. He escapes to New York, where he learns his craft, finds good work, marries a woman he loves, and establishes an independent life. The horrors of September 11, the later death of his young wife, and the sense of isolation and confusion lead him back to Mason, his home town, and the old house he always admired—the "Gothic Horror." His cousin Grace, who is transforming the family home into a bed-and-breakfast, seeks his help. The summer among relatives allows Neil to rediscover individual truths about crimes of the past, relationships, personalities, and the Truth itself. His saintly Uncle Bernie, a retired Episcopal priest, leads him back into the belief that only God is unchanging Truth in a confusing world and into the comfort that we will know the "rest of the story" in the fullness of time. Like other Tatlock novels, the story combines shocking tragedies, real crimes, and a strong sense of grace. The love story that traces its way through the pages is resolved in a gentle and faithful manner. The imagery and the subtle symbolism of the house, the room at the top, the fields full of corn where children lose their way when they wander too far from the path—all are marks of Tatlock's consummate mastery of the novel form.

Critical Reception

Critics have loved Tatlock's work. *Publishers Weekly*, in awarding the prize for *Things We Once Held Dear*, said, "Like an artist working with small chips of colored glass, Christy Award–winning novelist Tatlock takes multiple characters and fragments of their stories and pieces them together into a tranquil mosaic of commitment, faith, love and homecoming." The critic calls Tatlock "one of Christian fiction's better wordsmiths and her lovely prose reminds readers why it is a joy to savor her stories." *WORLD Magazine* praised *The Returning*, noting that it is a "well-written family story" about a broken family, a husband returning home from prison to alienated children, and the damage that has been caused by sin. It also chronicles the difficulties in reconciliation, though the "tone is always hopeful."

Booklist called Tatlock's first novel, *A Room of My Own*, "Perhaps the best Christian novel of the year." Each novel in turn has won praise for Tatlock's careful use of context, her deep understanding of character, and her rich sense of grace.

Awards

Most of Ann Tatlock's novels have won awards. *A Room of My Own* was the winner of the Silver Angel Award, Excellence in Media, 1999; *A Place Called Morning* was on *Booklist*'s "Top Ten" novels for 1999; *All the Way Home* was on *Booklist*'s "Top 10 Christian Novels" in 2002 in addition to being named the Adult Fiction Winner by the Midwest Independent Publishers Association (2003) and winning the prestigious Christy Award for Contemporary Fiction. *I'll Watch the Moon* was also a winner of the General Fiction category by the Midwest Independent Publishers Association in 2003 and was named the Best of the Genre, Christian Fiction, the same year by *Library Journal*.

Bibliography of Novels by Author
(Published in Minneapolis, MN: Bethany House)

A Room of My Own. 1998.
A Place Called Morning. 1998.
All the Way Home. 2002.
I'll Watch the Moon. 2003
Things We Once Held Dear. 2005.
Every Secret Thing. 2008.
The Returning. 2009.

Bibliography of Works about Author

"Ann Tatlock," *Contemporary Authors Online*. Detroit: Thomson Gale, 2004.
Ann Tatlock Web site: http:www.annhatlock.com.
Interview with the Author: http:www.noveljourney.blogspot.com/2006/author-ann-tatlock.html.
Mort, John. Review of *A Room of My Own*. *Booklist* (October 1, 1998): 290.
WORLD Magazine. Review of *The Returning* (February 14, 2009).

THOENE, BODIE AND BROCK

Personal, Professional, and Religious Background

Bodie Thoene (1951–) and Brock Thoene (1952–) (pronounced *Tay-nee*) have lived lives so inextricably entwined that it is impossible to describe one of them without the other. They both began school in Bakersfield, California. Brock was one year behind Bodie, but caught up with her in the second grade. Bodie's difficulties in learning, which her third grade teacher attributed to laziness, turned out to be dyslexia. She had to work so hard to read the words that were "unattainable to me" that she "developed a fascination with them and an ear for storytelling."

Brock loved history and learned easily, making straight As while Bodie labored to survive. It was only in their senior year of high school that Bodie noticed at choir how handsome Brock was and invited him to the Christmas formal. This first date turned out to be memorable because of their excitement about shared ideas. "We almost didn't dance, but we insisted on one dance and then went to dinner and kept talking."

The young couple, though attracted to one another, found profound differences in their faith. Bodie was not a Christian, and Brock was a legalistic one. They broke up and attended different colleges. In their first nine months apart, both of them changed. Attending a conference sponsored by the Campus Crusade for Christ, at which Hal Lindsay was teaching about modern day prophesy, Bodie accepted Christ. When they both returned to Bakersfield for the summer, they resumed their dating and were married two days after Christmas. The Thoenes moved to Waco, Texas, where Bodie began writing Westerns using cowboy stories, while Brock continued his college studies. Both of them eventually finished their college programs: Bodie Thoene has degrees in journalism and communications. Brock Thoene did his work in history and education.

Bodie, who had begun her writing career as a teenage journalist for her local newspaper, found her work appearing in *U.S. News and World Report*, *The American West*, and *The Saturday Evening Post*. The Thoenes went to Hollywood after graduation, where they worked as screenwriters and researchers for Batjac Productions, writing for John Wayne's films, including *The Fall Guy*. Described as "a writer with talent that captures the people and the times," Bodie was also a writer and researcher for ABC Circle Films.

In the mid-1970s, Bodie Thoene's writing career had hit such a relentless pace that she felt driven to reevaluate her career. "I didn't think I could write again," she admitted. At the same time, she and Brock were becoming more interested in Israel. She told John Wayne about her dream of writing about the events surrounding Israel's statehood. "That's one you ought to do," Wayne replied. "It's the Jewish Alamo!" A producer encouraged her to write a script concerning the day in 1948 when Jerusalem's mayor received the key to the Old City from the British. Her subsequent visit to Jerusalem, the people she met there who remembered the events of Israel's birth out of the ashes of history, and Brock's vast knowledge of the archaeology, history, and politics of the Jerusalem led the pair into three series of novels about Israel.

Together they found their calling, blending his research and story line with her skills as a storyteller. In some of their

> No little elves come out of my closet to write 650 manuscript pages. Some mornings I don't feel like writing, but I do it out of obedience to God.
>
> —Bodie Thoene in interview
> with W. Terry Whalin

early works of collaboration, Bodie acknowledged Brock for his role in research. On some occasions, he worked on novels independent of her. His continuation of the story of Mark Twain's Jim in *The Legend of Storey County*, for example, was well received by the critics. But it is as a couple they have flourished and won their prizes and fame.

> Bodie Thoene wrote scripts for Westerns in Hollywood in the mid-1970s, including some films for John Wayne. When Mrs. Thoene mentioned her interest in Israel's fight for statehood, Wayne encouraged her to pursue this obsession, noting, "It's the Jewish Alamo!"

In an interview with Terry Whalin, the Thoenes described their typical writing day. They work together on every aspect of the story, using their particular talents in tandem. In an early morning conference, they talk over the day's writing program. Brock may provide Bodie with the research material related to their project at this point. He brings her newspaper clippings on microfilm to make certain that every detail is historically correct. Then Bodie goes to her computer, where she pecks away with two fingers, sometimes until 10:00 at night. For each day, they set a goal of a certain number of pages. As she told her interviewer, "No little elves come out of my closet to write 650 manuscript pages. Some mornings I don't feel like writing, but I do it out of obedience to God."

They find the first 20 or so pages of each novel, the opening scenes, the hardest. After that, the pace can pick up so that she can write as many as 20 pages a day. Brock reads these pages aloud to Bodie, and they talk about the rough spots. If she has to rewrite a portion, she does it on the spot, and never looks at the pages again. Using this methodology, they have kept up their remarkable pace, with imagination and precision, producing over 45 novels, many of them of epic length and power.

The Thoenes have four grown children—Rachel, Jake, Luke, and Ellie. They also have number of grandchildren. Their sons Luke and Jake also are writers, and Luke produces the Thoene audiobooks. The Thoenes now divide their time between homes in London and Nevada.

Major Works and Themes

Bodie and Brock Thoene have written over 45 works of historical fiction, which have sold more than 10 million copies. Their early works reflect their period in the film industry, telling the story of the American West. Brock Thoene wrote *The Legend of Storey County*, an interesting portrait of an ex-slave who settled in the American West. He also wrote *Hope Valley War*, a tale that is more filled with adventure than religion, set in Utah in the 1850s. Then, using Brock's research and Bodie's film-writing experience, the Thoenes produced a Christian Western series, "Saga of the Sierras." The first of the novels in this collection, *The Man from Shadow Ridge*, is the story of a group of ranchers who are terrorized by Confederate smugglers.

Next, they undertook a detailed and expansive study of yet another war—World War II. In this series of epic tales, they show the early rumblings of war, the horrors of the Nazi onslaught, and the later battles. In these, they reveal their sympathy with both the combatants and the civilians, especially the Jews, who were arrested or dislocated, threatened, or killed. They capture the tenor of normal life in cities like Vienna or Paris and show the panic that results in the migration of millions from their homes and farms, fleeing before the Nazi war machine. Typically, they include both European nobility and military leaders to provide a larger perspective on the war scenes, some victims to point to the moral consequences of the actions of the planners, and some women and children who scramble for their lives. They love to include a few newspaper reporters, largely to involve American voices. The authors use available documents to show the actual events, the actual words and plans of the various leaders, characterizing such people as Hitler or Churchill clearly. Maps help clarify the action and allow readers to trace the paths of the action.

At the same time the Thoenes were at work on this series and on the Zion chronicles, they undertook a very different group of quarrelling peoples in a different period—the Irish in the 19th century. The "Galway Chronicles," again follows a host of people through difficult times. In this case, the Irish troubles, which precipitated the great Irish immigration to America, reveal a combination of battles with the English and with nature. The potato famine comes on top of the cruel English laws, heartless managers, and the constant battles between the Catholics and the Protestants, forcing an impoverished and depressed people to rebel or emigrate.

By selecting a handful of "typical" people in their novels, some of whom become the love interests, some the comical eccentrics, some the fearless prophetic voices, the Thoenes allow for multiple points of view and a sense of epic sweep. By choosing a single year or season, such as the fall of 1931 for *Shiloh Autumn*, they are able to encapsulate a much wider picture of a dramatic time in history—in this case, the Great Depression. This novel, which echoes the biblical story of the Hebrews' flight from Egypt, its slavery and plagues, ends the travels of the migrants in the Thoenes hometown, Bakersfield, California. *Shiloh Autumn* shows an Arkansas farm family bravely confronting one wave of anguish after another, some human, some environmental. The family manage to endure through their intrepid spirit, their love for one another, and their abiding faith.

The Thoenes' novels usually focus on a small area, such as the village of Ballymockanore in "The Galway Chronicles" or the École de Cavalerie in *The Twilight of Courage*. By bringing in an outsider, often a newspaper correspondent or an American visitor, the writers balance the subjective experiences of the characters with an objective commentator. Their cast of characters includes small children (usually young boys with more curiosity than common sense), old people who bring perspective to the events, young lovers, married couples with their family concerns, and outsiders who threaten the peace and stability of the community—Romans, Nazis, industrialists, and others.

They also make imaginative use of music and literature as thematic patterns in their stories. For the Nazis' rise to power, they use the Faust legend and Milton's Satan from *Paradise Lost*. The musician in *Vienna Prelude* finds consolation in musical themes, particularly from Bach, who proclaims the power and goodness of God.

The Thoenes were to continue using these techniques as they moved through their three series of Jerusalem novels, which are set largely on the Temple Mount. The geography of Jerusalem is integral to the action of each of the stories, and the types of people whom one would expect to meet on this historic site include old rabbis, young hooligans, militant Muslims, secular Jews, Arab Christians, foreign tourists, news reporters, terrorists, scholars, and archaeologists. The Thoenes' range of work is breathtaking. Their Christian historical novels follow the path provided by secular writers such as James Michener and John Jakes. As Mort notes, that they blend readability and plausible history. Their three Zion series that recreate the history of Israel "dominate the field, and rightfully so."

The "Zion Covenant" series ends with the *Warsaw Requiem*. The "Zion Chronicles," which they were writing even before their work on the rise of Nazi Germany, tells of the waves of refugees who poured into Israel after World War II. The "Zion Legacy" series, which begins with *Jerusalem Vigil*, is a "Michener-like tale of Israel in its first five days of nationhood." They blend the discovery of the Dead Sea Scrolls with the U.N. declaration of Israel's founding of a new state for the first time in almost 2,000 years, the battles involved in the pull-out of British troops and the Arab attempt to take the Holy City. Characters from the "Zion Covenant" reappear here, to provide historical and creative continuity. These stories are fast-paced, action-packed, and violent. They have moments of tenderness, with love stories and family reunions. For the most part, they are powerful for their revelation of the political intrigues and military strategies rather than for their religious content.

In the "A.D." series, which begins with *First Light*, the stories follow tangentially the last days of Christ on earth. The authors make imaginative use of scrolls, purportedly discovered beneath the Temple Mount. These chronicle life in a leper colony, reveal the desperation of a blind child waiting by the Pool of Shilom, and show the brutality of the Roman rulers. The books blend the Old and New Testaments with details of history to provide a richly imagined texture of contemporary life in Jesus's day. The Thoenes' deep faith in the words and meaning of Scripture, their creative use of visions and miracles, and their passionate sense of the power of God make these books remarkable indeed.

The Thoenes' novels reveal a masterful technique for displaying lived Christianity. There is little preaching in the stories. Rather, the characters who have a strong faith demonstrate grace under pressure. They are the ones who show the courage to face torture and death, to persist in pursuit of a goal, and yet who are quick to forgive. Although they rarely are the ones who make the major decisions, change the course of history, they do help in redeeming one soul at a time—a child, a beggar, a prisoner, or even an enemy. They take seriously, as do their creators, that reaching out unto "the least of these my children" is the act of mercy that can transform lives. The Christians in their stories do not avoid pain or depression. They simply have the strength to endure, acknowledging that somehow God will bring blessings out of the most horrific circumstances.

Critical Reception

Readers and critics have loved the works of the Thoenes. The various series are seen as the standard for historical novels in the Christian writing community, held up to new writers as examples of careful research, strong plotting, and effective character development. John Mort has praised most of them in his reviews. Reviewers for *Publishers Weekly* tend to note the strong characterization, especially of the women. In a few cases, such as *First Light* (the first of the "A.D. Chronicle" series) critics have noted that the authors take too much time to rehash the past and that the book lacks the "narrative punch" of earlier Zion books. This suggests that the writers have established such a high standard of historical writing that readers will demand of them that they produce only the best.

Awards

The Thoenes have won eight ECPA Gold Medallion Awards. The American Library Association and Zionist libraries around the world consider several of their works, including the "Zion Chronicles" series, to be classic historical novels. They are also used to teach history in college classrooms.

Bibliography of Christian Novels by Authors

All Rivers to the Sea. Nashville: Thomas Nelson Publishers, 2000.

"The Zion Legacy" series (New York: Viking, 200–2003)

"A.D. Chronicles" series (Wheaton, IL: Tyndale House, 2004–2008)

"Zion Covenant" series (Wheaton, IL: Tyndale House, 2005–2006)

"Zion Chronicles" series (Minneapolis, MN: 1998)

"Shiloh Legacy" series (Minneapolis, MN: Bethany House, 1992–1996)

"Saga of the Sierras" series (Minneapolis, MN: Bethany House, 1990–1993)

"Galway Chronicles" (Nashville, TN: Thomas Nelson Publishers, 1998–1999)

"Wayward Wind" series (Nashville, TN: 1997–1998)

Brock Thoene, writing under the name William Brock Thoene, also wrote some Westerns in the 1999s and a book on income protection and management. A number of the Christian novels were published under one name at first, with acknowledgement of research by the other, and then republished under the coauthorship of both Thoenes. The four "Zion" series have been reprinted by Tyndale House as *The Gates of Zion, A Daughter of Zion, A Return to Zion,* and *The Key to Zion.*

Bibliography of Works about Authors

Bodie & Brock Thoene Home Page, http://www.thoenebooks.com.

"Bodie Thoene" and "Brock Thoene." *Contemporary Authors Online.* Detroit: Thomson Gale 2002.

Duncan, Melanie C. Review of *Jerusalem Vigil. Library Journal* (April 1, 2000): 86; Review of *Thunder from Jerusalem.* (September 1, 2000): 188; Review of *Jerusalem's Heart.* (April 1, 2001): 88; Review of *The Jerusalem Scrolls.* (September 1, 2002): 158; Review of *Stones of Jerusalem.* (February 1, 2002): 82.

Hudak, Melissa. Review of *Only the River Runs Free. Library Journal* (November 1, 1997): 66; Reviews of *Of Men and Angels. Library Journal,* (November 1, 1998): 66, (March 1, 1999): 127.

Mort, John. *Christian Fiction: A Guide to the Genre.* Greenwood Village, DO: Libraries Unlimited, 2002.

Mort, John. Review of *The Twilight of Courage. Booklist* (September 15, 1994): 84; Review of *Shiloh Autumn. Booklist* (November 15, 1996): 571; Review of *Of Men and of Angels. Booklist* (October 1, 1998): 276; Review of *Thunder from Jerusalem. Booklist* (September 15, 2000): ; Review of *Jerusalem Vigil. Booklist* (October 1, 2000): 302; Review of *Jerusalem's Heart. Booklist* (February 15, 2001): 1086; Review of *The Jerusalem Scrolls. Booklist* (October 1, 2001): 282, 335; Review of *Stones of Jerusalem. Booklist* (January 1, 2002): 777; Review of *Jerusalem's Hope. Booklist* (September 1, 2002): 8; Review of *First Light. Booklist* (June 1, 2003): 1711.

Publishers Weekly. Review of *Jerusalem Vigil.* (January 31, 2000): 82; Review of *Thunder from Jerusalem.* (August 14, 2000): 324; Review of *Jerusalem's Heart.* (March 12, 2001): 63; Review of *The Jerusalem Scrolls.* (August 27, 2001): 48; Review of *Stones of Jerusalem.* (February 4, 2002): 52; Review of *First Light.* (July 7, 2003): 51.

Thorup, Shawna Saavedra. Review of *Jerusalem's Hope. Library Journal* (November 1, 2002): 74.

Tickle, Phyllis. "Nelson Signs Couple to Big 11-Book Deal." *Publishers Weekly* (August 23, 1993): 9.

Today's Christian Woman. Review of *Second Touch* (March-April, 2004): 8.

Whalin, W. Terry. "A Determined Couple: Bodie and Brock Thoene." www.right-righting.com.

Wilson, Etta. "Birth of a Nation: Thoenes focus on Israel's First Days." www.bookpage.com.

TURNER, JAMIE LANGSTON

Personal, Professional, and Religious Background

> I like to show my notebooks of rejected manuscripts to audiences, when I speak about writing, as well as my box of rejection slips. "These were my education in writing," I tell them.
>
> —Jamie Turner, on her Web site, "Frequently Asked Questions"

Jamie Langston Turner (1949–) was born in Greenville, Mississippi. Her father, James Tyndall Langston and her mother Carolyn Thomas Langston were Christians who raised their daughter to believe in God's grace. They had met at Bob Jones University in 1967, which was then located in Cleveland, Tennessee. In an interview with *Faithful Reader*, Jamie Langston Turner said, "I grew up in a Christian home with parents who sincerely loved God and served him faithfully. I attended a small independent church called the Church of the Open Door in Greenville, Mississippi, where I heard the gospel preached regularly." Jamie became a committed Christian herself when she was only five years old. She notes that at that tender age, "I understood that . . . I was born in sin and needed a Savior to cover my sins with the sacrifice of his blood. One night, kneeling with my mother beside her bed, I asked Jesus into my heart."

Like her parents, Jamie Langston went to Bob Jones, which was by then a university and located in Greenville, South Carolina. Having been strongly influenced by a teacher in the fifth grade, she was intent on becoming a teacher, majoring in education while taking many courses in literature. After graduation from college, she "spent 10 very happy years in the elementary classroom" in Champaign-Urbana and began teaching English courses at Bob Jones University.

In 1971, she married Daniel Lynn Turner, who is a music professor at Bob Jones. He is now the chairman of the Music Education Department and has written two books on the history of Bob Jones University. He also conducts the University Symphonic Wind Band and teachers a variety of music courses. They have one son, Jess Langston, who is also a talented musician, and who was named the national winner of the Music Teachers Association Composition Contest for a sonata for trumpet and piano. He plans to works toward a doctorate in music. The Turners are members of Heritage Bible Church, where Jamie Langston Turner sings in the choir and her husband helps with the music program.

After her marriage and the birth of her son, Jamie Turner earned her master's degree from the University of Illinois. For years, she had been writing short pieces, often stories that were printed in *Moody Monthly*. She was surprised in 1992, when a man she had never met called her and recommended that she consider writing a novel. Turner describes the strong sense of calling she felt at that moment: "that was how God led me into writing novels."

Jamie Langston Turner describes her life as a novelist, creative writing teacher, and homemaker, living in the Smoky Mountains: "The older I get, the more I find that the simple joys of life are the most satisfying—a ride in the North Carolina mountains, a walk through the neighborhood, an evening with friends, a game of badminton in the backyard, a good book."

Major Works and Themes

Jamie Langston Turner's novels are loosely conceived as a series of stand-alone stories, with shared settings, characters and elements of plot. They are set in three tiny fictitious towns in South Carolina, Derby, Berea, and Filbert—all in the neighborhood of Greenville. The characters may be featured in one book and show up in "cameo appearances" in other novels.

The events may also overlap slightly. As Turner notes, however, it is not necessary that they be read in order.

Jamie Langston Turner finds it useful to approach the Christian life from the outside, not using the Christian character as the voice of the narrator, but often as the object of her attention. In *Some Wildflower in My Heart,* for example, Margaret, a 50-year-old woman whose life was soured by the abuse of the "upright" "Christian" grandfather, is puzzled and moved by the life lived by the gentle Birdie, who comes briefly into her life and leads her to an awakening. The style is clear, rich with allusions, frequently funny, moving, and firmly rooted in reality. Margaret Tuttle, the central character and narrator, manages to provide a wry vision of the world, filled with parallels to the imaginary world of literature in which she has buried her feelings. Like **Walker Percy**'s Moviegoer, Margaret has difficulty understanding life apart from art, trying to picture her situation as a piece of literature she has read. Her "Jubilee Year" proves the time of her opening up to love, faith, and the full blooming of the wildflowers that lie in her heart.

Turner draws her characters from acquaintances, family members, and reading, naming them from phone books, obituary write-ups, or "even shower-heads." She builds her plots on her characters, but feels no need to produce great adventures for her place-bound people. They usually stay within a few miles of their origin, rarely rising above the status into which they were born. Their journeys are largely internal—into the spirit, the mind, and the heart.

In her richly conceived books, the tiny world she has observed and identified for her fiction comes alive with very real people, filled with spiritual hunger, deep sorrows, and lived experience. She weaves her Christian themes into the stories in a gentle and natural manner, allowing the reader to discover the truths along with the characters.

Critical Reception

Critics have acclaimed Jamie Langston Turner as "one of the best writers in the Christian market, noting that *Winter Birds* is "beautiful writing, full of wisdom, literary allusions and stylistic elegance" and comparing the work to **Marilynne Robinson**'s *Gilead.* Phyllis Tickle, writing for *Publishers Weekly,* praises the book: "Steady, soft-spoken, elegantly plain, Turner takes us by the hand of our mutual imaginations and with the pure, sweet voice of the accomplished writer, she sings us down into the kingdom of the believing heart." She concludes with, "I love her books." All the reviewers note her well-crafted characters and genuine humor.

Awards

Two of Jamie Langston Turner's novels have won Christy Awards: *A Garden to Keep* won the award for Contemporary Fiction in 2002; and *Winter Birds* won the same award in 2007.

Bibliography of Works by Author

The Suncatchers. Nashville, TN: Thomas Nelson Publishing, 1995.
Some Wildflower in My Heart. Bloomington, MN: Bethany House Publishers, 1998.
By the Light of a Thousand Stars. Bloomington, MN: Bethany House Publishers, 1999.
A Garden to Keep. Bloomington, MN: Bethany House Publishers, 2001.
No Dark Valley. Bloomington, MN: Bethany House Publishers, 2004.
Winter Birds. Bloomington, MN: Bethany House Publishers, 2006.

Bibliography of Works about Author

Duncan, Melanie C. Review of *The Suncatchers. Library Journal* (September 1, 2000): 190.

"Jamie Langston Turner," *Contemporary Authors Online*. Detroit: Thomson Gale, 2003.

"Jamie Langston Turner: Faithful Fifteen," in *FaithfulReader.* http://www.faithfulreader.com/features/15_turner_jamie_langston.asp.

Jamie Langston Turner Web site. http://www.jamielangstonturner.com/ ME2/Sites//dirmod.asp.

Publishers Weekly. Review of *The Suncatchers* (August 14, 1995): 71; Review of *A Garden to Keep* (August 13, 2001): 287.

TYLER, ANNE

Personal, Professional, and Religious Background

Anne Tyler (1941–) was born in a commune in Minneapolis, Minnesota. Her father, Lloyd Parry, was an industrial chemist; and her mother, Phyllis Tyler, was a social worker and a "sometime journalist." Both parents were members of the Society of Friends. The family, which also included three younger brothers, lived in a series of Quaker communities throughout the Midwest and North Carolina while Anne was growing up. The children were homeschooled with supplemental materials from the Calvert School Correspondence System. Anne Tyler considered this childhood spent in communes a "setting-apart" that left her uncomfortable in the outside world when she emerged at 11. At that point, she had never used a telephone. At 16, Tyler completed the public high school in Raleigh, Broughton High School, where **Reynolds Price** had earlier been a student.

Although Tyler was a Russian major at Duke University, she also enrolled in the first writing course taught by Reynolds Price. He immediately recognized her talent and encouraged her to write and submit short stories for publication. Price even introduced her to his agent, Diarmuid Russell, who was also the literary agent for Eudora Welty. After earning a B.A. from Duke in three years with a Phi Beta Kappa Key, she enrolled in graduate studies at Columbia University from 1961–1962. Then Tyler became a Russian bibliographer for Duke University Library from 1962–1963, before moving to Montreal, where she was the assistant to the librarian at the McGill University Law Library from 1964–1965.

In 1963, Anne Tyler married a psychiatrist and writer, Taghi Modaressi, an immigrant from Iran. His visa expired in 1964, forcing the young couple to move to Canada, where Modaressi continued his medical studies at McGill University. At the time, they planned to move back to Iran, but discovered fewer opportunities for their careers there than in America. They decided instead to settle in Baltimore, moving there in 1965. In Baltimore, the family established Modaressi's medical practice, and both husband and wife wrote novels and raised their children. The couple have two children, Tezh and Mitra. Mitra is an artist, and has illustrated her two books for juveniles. Dr. Modaressi died in 1997.

Baltimore is still Anne Tyler's home as well as the subject of many of her novels. She lives a quiet life, rejecting opportunities for appearances and interviews, preferring to view life "through windows."

> You set out to tell an untrue story and you try to make it believable, even to yourself, which calls for details; any good lie does.
>
> —Anne Tyler in interview with Patricia Rowe Willrich, 1992

Major Works and Themes

The influence of Reynolds Price and of Eudora Welty is clear in much of Tyler's

Anne Tyler, who was raised in a series of Quaker communities, had not used a telephone until she was 11 years old.

writing. She told Marguerite Michaels that, "Reading Eudora Welty when I was growing up showed me that very small things are often really larger than the large things." Her talent is the build up of a series of small incidents, which may or may not add up to a linear plot. She cherishes the randomness of life, the strange obsessions of ordinary people, the remarkable endurance of families in spite of their quarrels and disappointments.

For example, in *Dinner at Homesick Restaurant*, Ezra, the good son of the family, is determined to gather the family for a celebratory meal. Over and over he plans the menu, invites the various members, and sometimes even gets them together for a minute, only to see the scene disrupted by a fit of anger or an unfortunate word that scatters the group. His continuing hunger for community, even if it is only the community of his kitchen and dinner table, drives Ezra to persevere. Without any church involvement, except for funerals or weddings, the family has only the dream communion of sharing a dinner at Ezra's table.

Tyler is interested in families, even as families disperse over the countryside, losing track of members as letters stop, telephone calls become replacement rituals for holiday observance, and only funerals draw families back together. Anne Tyler's story of the Beck family, *Searching for Caleb*, traces the efforts of a 90-year-old retired judge, Daniel Peck, to find his brother, Caleb, who left home at the turn of the century. The granddaughter's delight in joining in the quest brings them together for a time on a grand adventure. Justine and Duncan, both grandchildren of Daniel as well as husband and wife, are themselves gypsies. Though their conformist daughter, Meg, marries an assistant minister, they are happy pagans. Justine tells fortunes, though she is not clear that the future is predetermined or that anything other than character determines the progress of human life.

Tyler loves her little ironies, noting that the church fairs often feature fortune-telling booths, and that fortune tellers consult the paper for weather forecasts and rely in part on astrology. She enjoys seeing people struggle for something that will finally prove disappointing, twisting plots into pretzels. The search for Caleb is successful in some ways, but a failure in others. The ending leaves the family ready to set out on another adventure with the same merry heart that led them into marriage and into one small town after another. They are vagabonds at heart, seeking to escape the trap of the established family and claustrophobic life of the proper Baltimore Pecks.

Anne Tyler considers thoughtfully ideas of time, of predestination, and the quest for meaning in apparently meaningless human life. She does not seem to believe life is ordered by any God of history who reaches down to turn the accidents of life into turning points on the journey. Most of her events are random, and only occasionally rise to the level of changing a life. In one scene in *Homesick Restaurant*, the diary of the mother reveals a series of "events" that have no follow-up, beaux who never returned, gifts that led to nothing more.

On the other hand, one of her more famous stories, *Saint Maybe*, begins with a disastrous set of events and choices that change the whole life of the protagonist. Ian Bedloe, a young student, watches his brother, Danny, fall in love and marry Lucy, a brassy young divorcée with two children. The couple have another child and seem happy, though Ian grows suspicious of Lucy, who leaves Ian to baby-sit while she disappears for unexplained, prolonged periods, only to return home with expensive new clothes and trinkets. Ian blurts out his suspicions to Danny, apparently destroying their marriage and causing both Danny and Lucy to kill themselves, only to discover his suspicions were misguided. In his grief and shame, Ian begins a transformation in his own life, accepting responsibility for the orphaned children, dropping out of school, and joining the Church of the Second Chance—becoming "Saint Maybe." Each of the children has a different view of what he is doing with his life, why he is doing it, and how the world is structured: Agatha, a cynic, is agnostic and scientific in her explanation. Thomas, a happy, superficial lad, accepts whatever life has to offer. Phoebe, a believer, is a rebel who goes off on independent searches for the truth.

In this beautiful story and in others, Anne Tyler treats each of the various attitudes toward life with respect, even providing a comic scene of her own heritage in a Quaker meeting in *Searching for Caleb*. Tyler is especially interested in revealing a post-Christian view of the world, where the minister barely knows the family of the person he is burying, where the families rarely mention Scripture or draw their morality from any source deeper than family customs. They try to avoid family gatherings. When forced to see relatives, they exchange meaningless comments and then write polite "thank-you" notes that follow a prescribed format. Without shared communities, the scattered family members are lost, remembered only by the dusty old photos in albums. They rarely live in one another's memories.

Even more curious is Tyler's sense of static characters, who like Melville's Bartleby, tend to settle into a path and refuse to deviate. Jeremy, in his top floor studio, constructing odd works of art, unable to leave even for his own wedding, becomes a symbol of the isolated modern man artist. Jeremy acknowledges that he admires the cavemen who stayed home from the hunt, painting the walls of the cave while the others had their grand adventures. Jeremy is not even willing to venture forth to his own one-man show.

The circumscribed life, the accidental adventure, the random events, and the brevity of time—these are among Anne Tyler's themes. Her quirky characters with their funny hats, their dirty shirts, and their dilapidated cars are simultaneously funny and pitiful. Their homes are reflections of their characters: some love their winged chairs for the sense of being encased by blinders, and others delight in scattering their possessions as they go on fresh journeys.

Having come from a family deeply immersed in the Quaker experience, Anne Tyler finds herself uncomfortable with preachers and their sermons. She told Caren J. Town, who interviewed her for the *Dictionary of Literary Biography*, that: "It's not that I have anything against ministers. . . . I'm particularly concerned with how much right anyone has to change someone, and ministers are people who feel they have that right." This reluctance to provide advice (which is central to *Saint Maybe* and *Searching for Caleb*) leaves the people in Tyler's world with scant guidance. Burdened with guilt, these pilgrims have no guideposts identifying the path to either sin or redemption, leaving them to wander according to their own dim lights in a confusing world of random trails. Even their fellow pilgrims, their families, provide little useful advice. Her protagonists find friends are more likely to give the comfort and love for which they hunger. No one expects a gracious God to reach down and reveal his grace to him or her.

Anne Tyler's characters are small, scattered, comic, confused common folk, who somehow manage to persevere. They are not beautiful or heroic; their strengths and their flaws are modest; their problems reveal no grand design and lead to no great theological insights or any clear view of an afterlife. They simply plod on, following their individual path, often with a kind of courage and delight in each passing day.

Critical Reception

Except for her first few novels, which were neglected by the major reviewers, Anne Tyler's novels have been widely reviewed. **Gail Godwin** discovered her remarkable talent in *Celestial Navigation*; and then **John Updike** recommended *Searching for Caleb*. Updike also reviewed *Dinner at the Homesick Restaurant*, insisting that the book achieves "a new level of power and gives us a lucid and delightful yet complex and somber improvisation on her favorite theme, family life." Larry McMurtry and Benjamin DeMott also considered the both book funny and deep. *Saint Maybe* won reviews in the *New York Review of Books* and the *Christian Science Monitor*, which note that the novel is realistic and sophisticated, and precipitating some interesting discussions of the role of families in the life of individuals.

By now, Anne Tyler has written so many books that reviewers are inclined to generalize about her work, noting her rejection of plot for delightful prose style and for observations about middle class life in America. Critics tend to agree that few contemporary writers have captured the "clamor" of family better than Anne Tyler.

Awards

Anne Tyler has won a number of awards, beginning with a prize for her short stories at Duke, and then the *Mademoiselle* award for writing (1966). Later she won the Award for Literature from the American Academy and Institute of Arts and Letters (1977), the Janet Heidinger Kafka prize (1981); and the Pulitzer Prize for *Breathing Lessons* in 1989. She also was nominated for a number of other awards.

Bibliography of Novels by Author
(New York: Knopf)

If Morning Ever Comes. 1964.
The Tin Can Tree. 1965.
A Slipping-Down Life. 1970.
The Clock Winder. 1972.
Celestial Navigation. 1974.
Searching for Caleb. 1976.
Earthly Possessions. 1977.
Morgan's Passing. 1996.
Dinner at the Homesick Restaurant. 1982.
The Accidental Tourist. 1985.
Breathing Lessons. 1988.
Saint Maybe. 1991.
Ladder of Years. 1995.
A Patchwork Planet. 1998.
Back When We were Grownups. 2001.
The Amateur Marriage. 2004.

Most of Anne Tyler's novels have been reprinted, some by Ballantine, others by Fawcett Columbine, and some in collections by Avenel Books, Wing Books, Bright Sky Press, and Ballantine. In addition to three collections of stories she edited, Anne Tyler has written two books for juveniles, a screenplay for *Breathing Lessons*, and contributed short stories, articles, and poetry to a number of periodicals. Her novel *The Accidental Tourist* was adapted as a film by Warner Brothers in 1988, and *Back When We Were Grownups* was made into a film for Hallmark Hall of Fame in 2004.

Bibliography of Works about Author

"Anne Tyler," *Contemporary Authors Online.* Detroit: Thomson Gale, 2008.

Bail, Paul. *Anne Tyler: A Critical Companion.* Westport, CT: Greenwood Press, 1998.

Gardner, Marilyn. Review of *Saint Maybe. Christian Science Monitor,* September 25, 1991, 13.

Godwin, Gail. Review of *Celestial Navigation. New York Times Book Review,* April 28, 1974, 34.

Lehmann-Haupt, Christopher. Review of *Dinner at the Homesick Restaurant. New York Times,* March 22, 1982, 21.

McMurtry, Larry. Review of *Dinner at the Homesick Restaurant. Chicago Tribune Book World,* March 21, 1982.

Updike, John. Review of *Morgan's Passing. New Yorker* (June 23, 1980): 95; Review of *Dinner at the Homesick Restaurant. New Yorker* (April 5, 1982): 193.

Willrich, Patricia Rowe. "Watching Through Windows: A Perspective on Anne Tyler," *The Virginia Quarterly Review,* Summer, 1992. http://www.vqponline.org/articles/1992/summer/willrich-watching-windows/.

U

UPDIKE, JOHN

Personal, Professional, and Religious Background

John Hoyer Updike (1932–2009) was born in Reading, Pennsylvania, the town that is portrayed in his stories as Brewer. His mother, Linda Grace Hoyer Updike, was herself an aspiring author, who encouraged her son to write, bought him a subscription to *The New Yorker* magazine, and even published one of his novels under her own name. His father, Wesley Russell Updike, was a "beleaguered, though beloved" high school teacher, who taught junior and senior high school mathematics, the inspiration of a number for Updike's schoolteacher heroes. John Updike's paternal grandfather, Hartley Updike, was a Presbyterian minister. The family moved to a farm outside Shillington, Pennsylvania, where Updike spent 13 years, graduating from the high school there as president and co-valedictorian of his senior class. Shillington is portrayed in his stories as Olinger. A comic version of the father-son relationship appears in Updike's 1963 prize-winning novel *The Centaur*.

With his mother's strong encouragement, Updike applied to Harvard University and won a tuition scholarship. At Harvard, he began drawing and writing for the humor magazine, the Harvard *Lampoon*, thinking this would be good preparation for becoming a cartoonist for *The New Yorker*. In 1953, he married Mary E. Pennington, a fine arts major at Radcliffe. She was the daughter of a Unitarian pastor in Hyde Park and was two years older than he. During his senior year, Updike demonstrated a life-long fascination with 17th-century English poetry by choosing Robert Herrick as his topic for a senior essay.

> My subject is the American Protestant small town middle-class. I like middles. It is in middles that extremes clash, where ambiguity restlessly rules.
>
> —John Updike in interview with Jane Howard, *Life* magazine

He graduated from Harvard in 1954 summa cum laude and from 1954 to 1955 he attended the Ruskin School of Drawing and Fine Art in Oxford. The first of the couple's four children was born in 1955.

While in England, Updike met E. B. and Katherine White

> John Updike is our time's greatest man of letters, as brilliant a literary critic and essayist as he was a novelist and short story writer. He is and always will be no less a national treasure than his 19th century precursor, Nathaniel Hawthorne.
>
> —Philip Roth, in the obituary for John Updike, *New York Times*, January 28, 2009

and was offered a staff position with *The New Yorker*, where he worked for two years, writing more than a hundred essays, articles, poems, and short stories, and bits for "The Talk of the Town" section. He left his full-time position with the magazine to concentrate on his own creative writing, moving his family to Ipswich, Massachusetts, where he and his wife had spent their honeymoon (the model for Tarbox in *Couples*). By 1958, he had published his first book, *The Carpentered Hen and Other Tame Creatures*, and was fully engaged with writing *The Poorhouse Fair*. From the time he moved his allegiance to Knopf and published his first novel with them, he was enormously productive, turning out a book almost every year while continuing to contribute articles to *The New Yorker*. In 1959, he won a Guggenheim Fellowship to work on his idea for *Rabbit, Run* and began reading Soren Kirkegaard, Karl Barth, and other theologians. These writers were to have significant influence on his own ideas and are reflected in many of his stories, essays, and novels. In the years that followed, he won numerous prizes and fellowships, traveled with different groups to represent America all over the world, and was awarded several honorary degrees.

In 1976, the Updikes divorced. The following year, John Updike married Martha Ruggles Bernhard. She had three sons who lived with them at their home in Georgetown, Massachusetts. In 1982, he moved to Beverly Farms, Massachusetts, and joined St. John's Episcopal Church.

He continued to write, to travel, to comment on contemporary events, and to be crowned with awards. As to his lifelong "tour of Protestantism," he noted that his first girlfriend was the daughter of a Methodist chaplain. He was the grandson of a Presbyterian minister, but his family raised him as a Presbyterian in Pennsylvania. After marriage to the daughter of a Unitarian minister, he and his wife joined the Congregational church. After marrying his second wife, he has worshipped in the Episcopal church. He noted that he preferred Luke's gospel, but trusted Mark's as "the earliest and least prone to wishful thinking." Regular worship was important to him, not just for the "words and sacraments. It's the company of other people, who show up and pledge themselves to an invisible entity" (as quoted in a talk he gave at St. Bartholomew's Church in New York City). "When on Sunday morning," says one of his characters, "make no mistake. There is nothing but Christ for us. All the rest, all this decency and busyness, is nothing. It is the Devil's work."

John Updike died in Danvers, Massachusetts, at 76. He died of lung cancer at a hospice on the North Shore. Obituaries appeared in all the major papers, calling him "a lyrical writer of the middle-class man" and a "literary high priest."

Major Works and Themes

From the time he was 23 years old, Updike supported himself and his family by writing. He began with a collection of poetry, then published a novel about the residents of an old people's home—*The Poorhouse Fair*. This was followed by his tender story of a father and son that echoes some of his own experience as a teenager in Pennsylvania. *The Centaur* is a curious piece of work, using the structure of Greek mythology to tell about a high school teacher who is a minister's son, searching futilely for the truth, loving and hating his work.

This theme of the minister's son—in this case five generations of ministers—reappears in other of Updike's novels, most notably his epic of American Protestantism *In the Beauty of the Lilies*. John Updike's lifelong study of and meditation on theology, particularly the ideas of Kierkegaard and Barth, inform his critique of American cultural history. *In the Beauty of the Lilies* is particularly interesting as an overview of American Calvinism in the twentieth century, from the liberalism of the turn-of-the-century Presbyterian minister, through the defrocked son who lost his sense of calling, through to his own son who was angry with God and refused to attend church, though he lived his life as a gentle, kindly, and Christlike man. The final generation in the book rediscovers faith, but the false faith of the fake messiah in a western commune. His humanistic decision, to save the disciples rather than to join in the apocalyptic conclusion of the movement, marks this last as the strongest and most heroic of the "ministers" of this doomed family.

Most religious readers are confused and disturbed by Updike's insistence on blending sexuality with religion. His randy pastor in *A Month of Sundays* can barely counsel a needy woman without bedding her. The minister sees himself as the answer to all of the hungers that surround him; and he assumes that all needs must be met. This particular predilection to include vivid sexual scenes in most of his books led David Foster Wallace to call him a "Champion Literary Phallocrat"—one of the last of the "Great Male Narcissists." Updike has noted in various places that we make a mistake in believing that we are in charge of our lives, leaving God out of consideration. He once said, "It is consoling to think that if not every detail is the will of God, there is a kind of will bigger than your own. You can't change everything. You have to accept the world as it is." In *A Month of Sundays*, the delinquent pastor spends a month in the desert, recovering under the watchful eye of Miss Prynne (of *Scarlet Letter* derivation). Rather than changing his will to couple, the therapy only convinces him of the need to seduce Miss Prynne. At the end, we discover that his real intent is to seduce his readers into following his spiritual struggles through his obsession with his groin.

S is a parallel novel, this time from the woman's point-of-view. Again the novel is epistolary, again using the modern faux-messiah and flirtations with Eastern mysticism, but this time partially explained. Repeatedly, Updike mentions John Donne and the Metaphysical poets of the 17th century, who used religious and sexual imagery interchangeably with startling results. For Updike, as for Donne, the religious ecstasy is parallel to the sexual ecstasy. For the true believer, the mystic moment is as real as our bodies and as intense as an orgasm. Updike assumes the hunger for this connection, an empty "god space" in all humans, must be filled—if not by faith in God, then by intense human relationships or fake messiahs. His reality-based faith is grounded in Barth's thinking, which accepts the miracles and the great mystical moments of Scripture as actual.

Updike also wrote a great variety of other stories, one about the ex-dictator of a fictitious African state (*The Coup*), one a prequel to Hamlet (*Gertrude and Claudius*), one about a woman who was mistress to a number of the great painters of our century, each of whom saw her through his peculiar artistic lens, which is also based on *The Scarlet Letter* (*Seek My Face*), and one about a devout Muslim teenager, hungry to die for his faith (*Terrorist*).

His most famous series by far is the group of "Rabbit" stories, beginning with *Rabbit, Run* in 1960. Rabbit is Harry Angstrom, a talented high school athlete whom we first meet as a young man. He is a blue-eyed Swede, sexually magnetic, purportedly Christian, but not particularly insightful. His career in a small town in Pennsylvania takes him through middle age (*Rabbit Redux*) with the trauma of his wife's infidelity and his economic success (*Rabbit Is Rich*) to his old age in *Rabbit at Rest*. The series tracks much of American pop culture at the conclusion of the 20th century, with an ironic commentary on the decay that its author deplored.

Most of Updike's novels, like the much maligned *Couples*, deal with sex, art and religion—which the author calls "the three great secret things" in human experience. James Yerkes has collected the essays on Updike's religious vision, commenting in his introduction that Updike's religious consciousness "may be best be characterized as our sense of an unavoidable, unbearable, and unbelievable Sacred Presence."

Critical Reception

The books, essays, and articles that have appeared on the work of John Updike demand a whole study unto themselves. His awards testify to the serious respect that his works have received. Philip Roth has even claimed for him the same genius found in Hawthorne. Updike's own commentary on his work and thought is more insightful than is most of the critics'. He demands sensitive study to follow his train of thought, but most critics are content to see him as the sociologist who mapped the American middle class at the end of the 20th century. They acknowledge that he has captured 20th-century America in a vivid, almost cinematic way: "Man, wife, home, children, job—these . . . concerns have rested at the heart of his art since he published his first book . . . and they have continued to help him dissect, lovingly and clearly, the daily routine of middle America in small town and suburb" (according to Donald J. Greiner).

Joseph Kanon, writing for *Saturday Review*, noted that most people have strong opinions about Updike's work—some admire him for his brilliant language, others lament that he "writes beautifully about nothing very much." Many have greeted one novel after another as a work of art, lyrical, brilliant, and subtle. They praise his mastery of language, but find that his narrative gifts are not equal to his style, nor are his characters "dynamic or colorful or deeply meaningful" (according to John W. Aldridge). He was particularly criticized for his female characters, who rarely are more than housewives and who have little of the richness of his men. Robert Detweiler finds it difficult to judge the books or the artistry because of the furor over his explicit depiction of sexual amorality. Richard Brookhiser, in his obituary commentary, noted that the "only sacrament" of Updike's Christianity "seemed to be adultery." But, he added, "we don't go to novelists for theology." His depictions of Satan in *Roger's Version* and *The Witches of Eastwick* add little to our understanding of the fallen angel.

Nonetheless, each of the books has been an almost immediate success with the reading public, many have been reissued, and the critics have awarded him numerous prizes to attest to their importance in cultural circles. At his death, Michiko Kakutani said, in the *New York Times*, that he "was arguably this country's one true all-around man of letters. He moved fluently from fiction to criticism, from light verse to short stories to the long-distance form of the novel: a literary decathlete in our age of electronic distraction." Richard Brookhiser summed up his great skill as a writer: he had respect for "the tools of the trade." He was a man, "Victorian in his industriousness and almost blogger-like in his determination to turn every scrap of knowledge and experience into words."

Awards

John Updike was a member of the American Academy and Institute of Arts and Letters, the American Academy of Arts and Sciences, and won a number of awards and fellowships: the Guggenheim fellowship in poetry (1959), the American Academy and National Institute of Arts and Letters Richard and Hilda Rosenthal Foundation Award in 1960 for *The Poorhouse Fair*; the National Book Award in fiction (1964) and the Prix Medicis Estranger award (1966) for *The Centaur*; the O. Henry Award for fiction (1966); a Fulbright fellowship in Africa (1972); the Edward MacDowell Medal for Literature, MacDowell Colony (1981); the Pulitzer Prize for fiction (1981) and the National Book award for fiction (1982) for *Rabbit Is Rich*; the National Book Critics Circle award for criticism (1984); the Medal of Honor for Literature, National Arts Club (1984), and many others. He has also been awarded honorary doctorates by Ursinus College, Moravian College, Lafayette College, Albright College, and Harvard University.

Bibliography of Novels by Author

The Poorhouse Fair. New York: Knopf, 1959.
Rabbit, Run. New York: Knopf, 1960.
The Centaur. New York: Knopf, 1963.
Of the Farm. New York: Knopf, 1965.
Couples. New York: Knopf, 1968.
The Indian. Marvin, SD: Blue Cloud Abbey, 1971.
Rabbit Redux. New York: Knopf, 1971.
A Month of Sundays. New York: Knopf, 1975.
Marry Me: A Romance. New York: Knopf, 1976.
The Coup. New York: Knopf, 1978.
Rabbit Is Rich. New York: Knopf, 1981.
The Witches of Eastwick. New York: Knopf, 1984.
Roger's Version. New York: Knopf, 1986.
S. New York: Knopf, 1988.
Rabbit at Rest. New York: Knopf, 1990.
Brazil. New York: Knopf, 1994.
In the Beauty of the Lilies. New York: Knopf, 1996.
Toward the End of Time. New York: Knopf, 1997.
Gertrude and Claudius. New York: Knopf, 2000.
Seek My Face. New York: Knopf, 2002.
Villages. New York: Knopf, 2004.
Terrorist. New York: Knopf, 2006.

John Updike also wrote a number of short stories, plays, poems, and essays. He was a prolific writer, who contributed introductions to collections of stories and wrote essays explaining much of his own background and thought. Some of his stories and novels have been purchased for production as television plays or films, including *Couples, Bech: A Book, Too Far to Go*, and *The Witches of Eastwick*. His work also inspired *S: An Opera in Two Acts Based on the Novel by John Updike*.

Bibliography of Works about Author

Aldridge, John W. *Time to Murder and Create: The Contemporary Novel in Crisis.* New York: McKay, 1956.

DeBellis, Jack. *John Updike: A Bibliography, 1967–1993.* Westport, CT: Greenwood Press, 1994.

Detweiler, Robert. *John Updike.* Boston, MA: Twayne, 1972.

Greiner, Donald J. *John Updike's Novels.* Athens: Ohio University Press, 1984.

Howard, Jane. *Life.* November 4, 1966. (Interview with John Updike.)

"John Updike." *Contemporary Authors Online.* Detroit: Thomson Gale, 2007.

Karon, Joseph. *Saturday Review,* September 30, 1972.

"Life and Times: John Updike." *New York Times* Online. http://www.nytimes.com.

The Literary Encyclopedia. http//www.litencyc.com/php/people.php?rec=true&UID=4502.

New York Times Books: http://www.nytimes.com/books/97/04/06.

Newman, Judie. *John Updike.* New York: St. Martin's Press, 1988.

Plath, James, ed. *Conversations with John Updike.* Jackson: University Press of Mississippi, 1994.

Schiff, James A. *Updike's Version: Rewriting the Scarlet Letter.* Columbia: University of Missouri Press, 1992.

Tallent, Elizabeth. *Married Men and Magic Tricks: John Updike's Erotic Heroes.* Berkeley, CA: Creative Arts, 1981.

Thornburn, David, and Howard Eiland, eds. *John Updike: A Collection of Critical Essays.* Boston: G.K. Hall, 1982.

Updike, John. *Self-Consciousness: Memoirs.* New York: Knopf, 1989.

Updike, John. Speech at St. Bartholomew's Church in New York City, Thursday, November 18, 2004. http://www.pbs.org/wnet/religionandethics/week812/p-exclusive.html.

Updike Web site: http://www.userpages.prexar.com/joyerkes/-36k.

Uphaus, Suzanne Henning. *John Updike.* New York: Ungar, 1980.

Yerkes, James, ed. *John Updike and Religion: The Sense of the Sacred and the Motions of Grace.* Grand Rapids, MI: Eerdmans, 1999.

Obituaries

Allen, Brooke. "John Updike, Literary High Priest of Sex and Suburbia, Is Dead at 76," *Wall Street Journal,* January 28, 2009, D1.

Brookhiser, Richard. "Rabbit's Great Run," *National Review* (February 23, 2009): 43.

Kakutani, Michiko. "A Relentless Updike Mapped America's Mysteries," *New York Times,* January 28, 2009.

Lehmann-Haupt, Christopher. "John Updike, a Lyrical Writer of the Middle-Class Man, Dies at 76," *New York Times,* January 28, 2009.

Updike, John. "From Our Pages," *The New Yorker,* February 9 and 16, 2009, 64–79.

WALKER, ALICE

Personal, Professional, and Religious Background

Alice Malsenior Walker (1944–) was born in Eatonton, Georgia. Her father was Willie Lee Walker, her mother Minnie Tallulah Grant Walker. Her home town, where her family had lived for generations, was a relic of the postbellum South in which most of the African Americans had tenant farms. It was here she learned the black vernacular that was to mark much of her writing and the sense of oppression that was to make a stamp on her sensibility. Her brother accidentally shot Alice in the eye with a BB gun when she was eight. Because her parents were too poor to own a car, they could not take her to a doctor for several days, costing her vision in her right eye. Ironically, this loss of vision led to her isolation from other children and to the cultivation of rich insights into human relationships—and turned her into a poet.

Alice Walker proved to be an excellent student, winning a scholarship to Spelman College, which she attended from 1961–1963 and then earning a B.A. from Sarah Lawrence College in 1965. In her last year of college, she took her first trip to Africa and also got pregnant. Knowing that her mother would be horrified at her condition and yet disapproving of abortions, the young woman contemplated suicide. With the support of a friend, she finally decided to abort the baby. The following days were intensely creative ones for her, as she poured out poems, which she shoved under Muriel Rukeyser's door. This favorite teacher, who was a renowned poet herself, took the poems to her publisher and arranged for their publication two years later.

Walker had been raised in the Methodist church, but came during her college years to identify

> Dear God. Dear stars. Dear trees, dear sky, dear peoples. Dear Everything. Dear God.
>
> —Final letter Celie writes to God in *The Color Purple*

the church with racism and male dominance. She said she came to understand "Christianity as an imperialist tool used against Africa." She turned to social activism as an alternative to religious faith, creating her own concept of "womanism," which differs from feminism in its outreach to women of all colors.

> One of Alice Walker's brothers shot her in the eye with his BB gun when she was eight years old. Because it was not treated properly, Walker has been blind in the right eye for most of her life.

Alice Walker began her career in civil rights as a voter registration worker in Georgia. She then worked with a Head Start program in Mississippi and joined the staff of the New York City welfare department. In much of this, she was supported by her husband, Melvyn Rosenman Leventhal, a Jewish civil rights lawyer, whom she married in 1967. They lived for a while in Jackson, Mississippi at a time of racial change and turmoil. They were the only interracial married couple in the region, where they were in violation of the laws against miscegenation. They had one daughter, Rebecca, about whom Walker frequently writes. They were divorced in 1976.

After her divorce, Alice Walker began a more active career in writing and teaching. She became writer–in–residence and teacher of Black Studies at Jackson State College from 1968–69, then moved to Tougaloo College from 1970–71. The following year she was a lecturer in literature at Wellesley College and the University of Massachusetts. Hers were some of the first courses in the country that focused on black women writers. After a decade of full-time writing, she became Distinguished Writer in African American Studies at the University of California, Berkeley (1982), then the Fannie Hurst Professor of Literature at Brandeis for a semester. For a while she was involved with the Wild Trees Press in Navarro, California, of which she was cofounder and publisher (1984–88). She was also a regular contributor to *MS.* magazine.

Alice Walker's continued production of novels, poetry and essays has kept her in the public eye for decades. She remains one of the most admired, debated, and controversial of the modern African American authors. Like most of her heroines, she is a "womanist," a Buddhist, and a Vegan. Her deep interest in the ancient Mother Goddess permeates most of her work.

Major Works and Themes

Alice Walker's signature character is the strong, black, independent woman. *Meridian*, one of her early novels, portrays the maturation of this young woman from a witless child, used by black men as well as white, finally realizing her own worth. Meridian proves to be a kind of secular saint—the female version of the familiar Black Christ stereotype. She is willing to suffer for her fellow blacks, but she is not ready to die for them. Her solution is to live, to create protest literature, and to bring awareness to the community whom she serves. In this novel, the Christian church, which is at first a stumbling block for civil rights activists, finally becomes a source of strength for them, with the pale white crucified Christ replaced by a triumphant black hero.

In some cases, Walker's heroine is "Woman," a spirit of fecundity and power that transcends time and place, a human expression of the ancient Goddess worshipped in much of the Mediterranean region prior to Christianity. Walker portrays the Christian Church as the enemy of this womanist spirituality, exploiting the earth, women, and animals. The particular victims of this white man's faith are the dark peoples, which white Christians have sought to subjugate and whose culture and faith they have tried to obliterate. Using the standard black history of the 1960s and 1970s, Walker rediscovers a kind of Peaceable Kingdom in precolonial Africa. *The Temple of My Familiar* is a particularly colorful summary of the author's ecofeminist spirituality, including transmigration of souls, Goddess worship, and her very own sense of bonding with the animal kingdom—a fellowship supposedly lost through masculine aggression. A still later novel, *Possessing the Secret of Joy*, continues the story of one of the characters we have previously met—Tashi, a tribal African woman. Conforming to the customs of her people, she submits to the genital mutilation expected of her. The story involves her gradual comprehension of this horror and the history of such violations of women over the centuries.

The eternally feminine character of Shug, whom Walker had introduced as Celie's Savior in *The Color Purple*, reappears elsewhere, preaching her own gospel of inner strength, generosity, inclusiveness, laughter, and love of strangers, of the earth, and of the body. She joins this with the language of "lamentation, outcry, and blues." Alice Walker's delight in the songs, secular and religious, and the person of Bessie Smith provide some insight into her sense of joy, pain, and independence. Her women feel free to love one another openly, to kiss and caress, to act without concern for society and traditional morality. Marriages are seen as prisons, though divorced couples may enjoy a kind of freedom of love that has no artificial barriers.

Her characters are often sketched quickly and overlap so as to provide confusing plot lines. The marriages, divorces, love affairs, and friendships become a kind of exotic dance with much partner-switching and little moral judgment. Rather than relying on the classic designs of narration, Alice Walker provides long sections of polemic—sometimes in the form of letters, poems, or memoirs. Her wise old people prove fonts of wisdom, who have discovered truth through their time on earth—including the generations before this present manifestation. Love, lust, touching, massaging, healing, hugging, raping, hitting, and killing provide most of the action, primarily derived from the old protest novels of the 30s.

Readers interested in Alice Walker's views on women, race, religion, the environment, and politics may find her nonfiction helpful. For those who want to know more about her view of "womanism," which she says, compared to feminism, is the difference between lavender and purple, the best source is *In Search of Our Mothers' Gardens: Womanist Prose*. In this colorful book, she also tells about her great-great-great-grandmother walking to Georgia with a baby on each hip, about her own response to the traumatic accident that blinded her in one eye, and to her father's encouragement of her brothers to live with sexual abandon while denying the sisters any information on their sexuality and calling them "sluts" for showing interest in young men. She also describes the South of her youth as a region that an ambitious young black person had to escape. The book does help the reader to understand many of Walker's judgments on society.

Critical Reception

The Color Purple, Alice Walker's third novel, was an instant success and has remained a classic used repeatedly as a text in African American studies programs and in feminist studies classes. The combination of race and gender, the gripping story, the pathetic central figure, and the grim realism of the setting combine to make a powerful statement about the plight of the black woman in the modern South. Alice Walker has been reviewed by all the mainline press, provided with grants by Rockefeller, Guggenheim, and others. Her fluency and vivid expressions have brought lavish praise for her works. *The Color Purple* won both the Pulitzer Prize and the American Book Award. Peter S. Prescott, reviewing the novel for *Newsweek*, noted that "*The Color Purple* is an American novel of permanent importance."

The remainder of her many works have not been greeted with the same level of praise, although *Meridian*, her novel reflecting some of her own experiences, was called by Gloria Steinem "the best novel of the civil rights movement." *The Temple of My Familiar*, which revives some of the characters from *The Color Purple*, was met with a barrage of criticism. Paul Grey, writing for *Time*, said that "Walker's relentless adherence to her own sociopolitical agenda makes for frequently striking propaganda," but not necessarily for good fiction.

Many of her novels are drawn from her own experience or her perceptions of current events. One of her later novels, *Now Is the Time to Open Your Heart*, for instance, takes an African American novelist named Kate, who is approaching 60, on a voyage of self-discovery. Ellen Flexman, who reviewed the book for *Library Journal*, complained that the few interesting insights on "the power of stories and the nature of spirit" are "buried among improbable situations and characters who have read too many bad books on spirituality." Debby Waldman was even less generous, calling it "New Age hooey." Some reviewers enjoy both the spiritual insights and the dreamlike atmosphere of the later novels, but more conservative critics tend to wish Walker had adhered less faithfully to her trinity of eros, activism, and pantheism.

Awards

In addition to invitations to numerous writers' conferences and fellowships that Alice Walker has received, she has won the Richard and Hinda Rosenthal Foundation Award, the American Academy and Institute of Arts and Letters, in 1974, for *In Love and Trouble: Stories of Black Women*; the Pulitzer Prize and American Book Award in 1983 for *The Color Purple*, Best Books for Young Adults citation, American Library Association, in 1984, for *In Search of Our Mother's Gardens: Womanist Prose*; as well as a D.H.L. from the University of Massachusetts, Freedom to Write Award, PEN West, in 1990, the California Governor's Arts Award, 1994, and the Literary Ambassador Award, the University of Oklahoma Center for Poets and Writers, 1998—as well as many other honors and awards.

Bibliography of Fiction by Author

The Third Life of Grange Copeland. San Diego, CA: Harcourt, 1970.
In Love and Trouble: Stories of Black Women. San Diego, CA: Harcourt, 1973.
Meridian. San Diego, CA: Harcourt, 1976.
You Can't Keep a Good Woman Down (short stories). San Diego, CA: Harcourt, 1981.
The Color Purple. San Diego, CA: Harcourt, 1982.
The Temple of My Familiar. San Diego, CA: Harcourt, 1989.
Possessing the Secret of Joy. San Diego, CA: Harcourt, 1992.
By the Light of My Father's Smile. New York: Random House, 1998.
The Way Forward Is with a Broken Heart. New York: Random House, 2000.
Now Is the Time to Open Your Heart. New York: Random House, 2004.

Alice Walker has also written three books for children, a number of poems, nonfiction collections, and has contributed to numerous anthologies and periodicals. *The Color Purple* was made into a feature film by Warner Bros. in 1985 and adapted as a Broadway musical in 2005.

Bibliography of Works about Author

"Alice Walker," *Contemporary Authors Online*. Detroit: Thomson Gale, 2007.

Grey, Paul. Review of *The Temple of My Familiar*. *Time* (May 1, 1989): 69.

Kramer, Barbara. *Alice Walker: Author of "The Color Purple."* Berkeley Heights, NJ: Enslow, 1995.

O'Brien, John. *Interviews with Black Writers*. New York: Liveright, 1973.

Prenshaw, Peggy., ed. *Women Writers of the Contemporary South*. Jackson: University Press of Mississippi, 1984.

Smith, Pamela A. "Green Lap, Brown Embrace, Blue Body: The Ecospirituality of Alice Walker," *Cross-Currents*. http://www.crosscurrents.org/smith2.htm.

Steinem, Gloria. "Do You Know This Woman? She Knows You," *Ms.* (June, 1982): 35.

Waldeman, Debby. Review of *Now Is the Time to Open Your Heart*. *People* (May 3, 2004): 45.

Walker, Alice. *In Search of our Mothers' Gardens*. New York: Harcourt Brace Jovanovich, 1983.

Walker, Alice. *The Same River Twice: Honoring the Difficult: A Meditation of Life, Spirit, Art, and the Making of the film "The Color Purple," Ten Years Later*. New York: Scribner, 1996.

WANGERIN, WALTER

Personal, Professional, and Religious Background

Walter Wangerin, Jr. (1944–) was born in Portland, Oregon, the oldest of seven children. His father, Walter M. Wangerin, was a nomadic Lutheran pastor, noted for his dramatic sermons. Wangerin comments that "he speaks with some energy. But I outdo him." His mother, Virginia Stork Wangerin, an intensely religious Christian, was a businesswoman, also a person "who lived at a dramatic level. . . . She was able to translate her feelings into an intense language. She speaks in poetic language, in metaphor, in hyperbole, by nature. And I think that's part of why I do."

Walter Wangerin describes much of his early religious life in *The Orphean Passages* and *Little Lamb, Who Made Thee?* Both of these meditative memoirs are semiautobiographical, revealing a child desperate for a close relationship with Christ. When his mother goes forward to receive communion, the boy asks her what he smells on her breath. She replies that it is the blood of Christ. He also chronicles his first communion, his excitement about becoming a full member of the community of believers, laughing at his fear that his cowlick would become an object of derision by the congregation. His own sensitivity as a child has led Walter Wangerin to write with great feeling of the spiritual hunger of young children.

The family lived in various parts of the country as Walter was growing up: Shelton, Washington; Chicago, Illinois; Grand Forks, North Dakota; and Edmonton, Alberta, Canada. He attended Concordia Senior College (which is now called Concordia Theological Seminary) in Fort Wayne, Indiana, receiving his B.A. in 1966. His M.A., in 1968, was from Miami University in Oxford, Ohio.

In 1968, he married Ruthanne Bohlmann, whom he calls "Thanne." Their marriage and their four children—Joseph Andrew, Matthew Aaron, Mary Elisabeth, and Talitha Michal—have provided interesting materials for a number of his self-help books and for many thoughtful studies. He even acknowledges that the characters in *The Book of the Dun Cow* echo his children. He

> I do think that writing is a request of the deity. The writer names things that have gone unnamed since creation.
>
> —Interview with W. Dale Brown, 260

includes his adopted daughter, Talitha, by name and describes her dark beauty in *Mourning into Dancing*, which starts with her plans for a party in their home.

> Walter Wangerin sometimes finds critics sneer at his writing because of his profession, admitting that one of his novels is a "pretty good book for a minister."

Over his early years, Wangerin worked at a variety of jobs. Among other things, he was a migrant pea picker, a lifeguard, and a ghetto youth worker. In 1969, he became a producer and announcer for KFUO-Radio in St. Louis, Missouri, then an instructor in English literature at the University of Evansville, in Evansville, Indiana (1970–74). He studied at Christ Seminary, Seminex, earning his master's in divinity in 1976. Beginning in 1974, he served as the assistant pastor of Grace Lutheran Church in Evansville, then senior pastor from 1977–85. Considered to be a part of the "Jesus Revolution" in the 1970s, he found work in the bustling inner city exciting. He describes something of this ministry, its strains and disappointments in *The Orphean Passages: The Drama of Faith*. After 1991, he served as the Jochum Professor in English and Theology at Valparaiso University. He is now a full-time writer.

He and his wife, Thanne, live on their farm in Valparaiso, Indiana, where he continues his busy schedule of writing and speaking. He revealed in a 2006 interview that he now has metastatic lung cancer and seeks prayers for peace.

Major Works and Themes

Much of Walter Wangerin's work has grown out of his life and ministry. When he had become the pastor of a small Lutheran church in Evanston, he started work on his first book, *The Book of the Dun Cow*, a strange fantasy that astonished and delighted the critics and won him immediate attention and devoted readers. Using Chaucer's Chauntecleer and Pertelote, as well as his wily fox, Wangerin weaves a tale that echoes Orwell's *Animal Farm* as well as *Beowulf*, portraying the animals with distinctive and human characteristics. The story shows a world almost like Eden or Isaiah's Peaceable Kingdom, ruled over by its benevolent monarch, the rooster. In this case an evil kingdom lies on the other side of the mountain, ruled by the malevolent Cockatrice. Under it all is Wyrm, a destructive force that encircles the world, but can be defeated or at least held in abeyance by the Keepers of the Earth. The epic battles sound a bit like those in *The Lord of the Rings*, with sinister basilisks slithering out of the river. Wangerin mingles medieval bestiary figures with modern language, biblical events with contemporary concerns, weaving a dramatic and powerful tale of good and evil on a grand scale.

The popularity of this book led his publishers to request a trilogy. Wangerin soon found the demands of his everyday life too cumbersome to allow him to complete such a grand project, but did write *The Book of Sorrows*, continuing some of the story line with Chauntecleer and his fellow animals in their on-going fight against Wyrm.

Walter Wangerin is famous for his children's books and for his theological ruminations. He frequently blends fact and fiction, myth and theology, mystery and reality in his thoroughly individual tales. In the midst of telling a story, he feels free to step back and discuss the theological or psychological problems presented by the scene he has just described. He is not afraid to describe all of the horrors and perils of modern life, yet makes this presentation a part of the larger battle between good and evil in the universe.

In 1985, Wangerin relinquished his pastoral duties, becoming a full-time writer. He found that both ministry and writing proved full-time activities, requiring integrity and affection.

His position as a professor of English and theology proved less challenging, allowing him to schedule evening classes and spend his days writing at his desk. He also enjoys an active life as a public speaker and is especially popular at religious meetings.

For him, Scripture is the central story that defines all of life. His retelling of *The Bible as a Novel*, beginning with Abraham and ending with Christ and the new covenant, is a colorful paraphrase, focusing on one character and event after another. He continues this device in his novel about Paul, which traces the events of Paul's conversion and ministry, providing Roman background with the voice of Seneca and Jewish resistance to his ministry through the use of James' point of view. He also allows minor figures to speak their responses to this amazing man, trying to understand what Priscilla or Timothy or Titus must have felt.

Critical Reception

Eugene Peterson has called Wangerin "one of the master storytellers of our generation." Calvin Miller adds that he is perhaps "Christianity's most important writer." *Christianity Today* adds that "Wangerin's intelligence is so rich he could become a lasting voice in American letters." Numerous critics have given Wangerin high praise for his children's books and for his creative use of mythology. Virginia Stem Owens, for example, notes that, "His mythic universe also shapes for children a world latent with meaning. It persuades them that they are capable of more than coping, that 'they themselves bear strength and goodness into the world,' that they are a necessary part of the sacred hoop, of the meaning of the universe."

The *Book of the Dun Cow* has proven to be the novel most praised of all his work. The sequel, *The Book of Sorrows*, which continues the story of Chauntecleer's struggles in the fight against Wyrm has a sudden and sad ending, that John Mendelsohn noted "breaks the reader's heart." At the same time, Wangerin involves his readers with his allegorized characters, evoking in his readers tender emotions. The *New York Times*, which ran reviews of both books and the musical that followed, considered *The Book of the Dun Cow* the best children's book of the year.

The Crying for a Vision, another of his stories designed for young adults, is based on his deep interest in the Lakota Indians. In this novel, Wangerin tracks Waskn Mani, a young boy without earthly parents who is gifted with special powers. He finds himself forced to battle against a vicious warlord who seeks to drag his people into warfare with their neighbors. John Wilson noted that reading the book can help us to understand "what it might be like to hear the gospel for the first time . . . a message at once strange and hauntingly familiar." Anne O'Malley considers *The Crying for a Vision* to be "a particularly strong addition to historical fiction and Native American fiction and legend collections."

Walter Wangerin is a natural storyteller, who brings Bible stories to life in his dramatic retelling of them He is especially talented in his combining of his own experience with Norse and Greek mythology. He has discovered in the pages of Scripture a wealth of short stories, full of rich characterization, plot twists, and universal meaning. In his grand undertaking, *The Book of God: The Bible as a Novel*, he tracks a series of characters whose relationships with God have transformed history. Abraham and Jacob, Joseph and David interest him far more than the prophets, though he has clearly read and studied the prophetic books as well. *Publishers Weekly* commented that this is a good book for readers who are "intimidated by the size and bulk of the Bible."

In *Paul: A Novel*, he continues this pattern of filling in the gaps left by Luke in his narrative of the early Church, seeking to flesh out Paul's motives for travels and epistles, speculating on the personalities of minor figures like Silas or Timothy, and blending these into a dramatic story of a remarkable man. He uses the same strategy in *Jesus: A Novel*, which begins with Mary's experiences with the infant Jesus and traces the life of Christ through the gospel of John, using multiple points of view. John Mort has observed that Wangerin "eschews melodrama, favoring instead an approach that is conservative, quiet, lyrical, and scholarly."

Both of these novels invite comparison with others who have undertaken the same task, such as Dorothy L. Sayers, who wrote the highly acclaimed *The Man Born to Be King*, a radio drama with stage directions that brilliantly characterize the situations and the people in the Gospel story, and Sholem Asch, the amazing Jewish writer who wrote prize-winning novels focused on Mary, Jesus, and Paul, stories full of rich detail of history and theology. Wangerin's novels are simpler, closer to the text, easier to follow than Asch's—more in the tradition of Sayers. They adhere more closely to Scripture than the highly advertised *Out of Egypt: Christ the Savior*, written by **Anne Rice.** Previously noted for a very different style of novel, Rice tells a dramatic story in lively terms, using modern archaeological discoveries and choosing some of the episodes attributed to Christ in the various Gnostic Gospels. She is especially interested in The Gospel of Mary Magdalene, which Wangerin finds unnecessary to include.

Walter Wangerin does follow through beyond the crucifixion and the resurrection with the final days of Jesus's mother, Mary, showing John serving as a true son in her old age. He tracks the paths of the various disciples as they go into all the world. The conclusion of Wangerin's book is very powerful, winding around to the opening chapter of the Gospel of John: "In the beginning."

Walter Wangerin believes that his ministry has dulled the critical response to his work, with critics for the *New York Times Review* saying "I'd written a pretty good book for a minister." He insists that he just writes stories. "I resist the labels: religious writer, fantasy writer, children's author, theologian, memoirist." He rejects contemporary Christian romances, thrillers, and other popular fiction which he insists are not art.

Awards

In 1978, Wangerin was awarded the prize for Best Children's Book of the Year by the *School Library Journal* and the *New York Times*. In 1980, he won the National Religious Book Award (children/youth category), the National Book Award for paperback science fiction, and the American Library Association Notable Book citation, all for *The Book of the Dun Cow*. In 1983, *Thistle* was named the Best Book of the year by the *School Library Journal*. In 1986, he won the ECPA Gold Medallion for *The Book of Sorrows* and in 1996, for *The Book of God*. He has also won numerous other awards for his meditative literature.

Bibliography of Novels for Adults by Author

The Orphean Passages: The Drama of Faith. New York: Harper, 1986.
Miz Lil and the Chronicles of Grace. New York: Harper, 1988.
The Manger Is Empty. New York: Harper, 1989.
The Crying for a Vision. New York: Simon & Schuster, 1994.
The Book of God: The Bible as a Novel. Grand Rapids, MI: Zondervan, 1996.
Paul: A Novel. Grand Rapids, MI: Zondervan, 2000.
Jesus: A Novel. Grand Rapids, MI: Zondervan, 2005.

Walter Wangerin is also the author of some books for children and young adults, the most famous of which is the fantasy, *The Book of the Dun Cow*. He has also published a collection of short stories and writes a weekly column in the *Evansville Press* (Evansville, IN), is a regular columnist for *The Lutheran*, and a contributor to *Christianity Today*, *Leadership*, and the *Evansville Courier*.

Miz Lil and the Chronicles of Grace has been optioned for a motion picture by Wind Dancer Productions. *The Book of the Dun Cow* was transformed into a musical by Mark St. Germain and Randy Courts and played briefly in February 2006 off, off Broadway.

Bibliography of Works about Author

Brown, W. Dale. "Walter Wangerin," in *Of Fiction and Faith*. Grand Rapids: William B. Eerdmans Publishing Company, 1997.

Malone, Michael. "The Cosmos and the Farmyard." *New York Times*, May 2, 2009.

Mendelsohn, John. Review of *The Book of the Dun Cow*. *Los Angeles Times Book Review*, September 29, 1985.

Morphew, Clark. "Walter Wangerin Combines Thoughtful Theology, Storytelling." *Knight-Ridder/Tribune News Service*, September 20, 2000, K2160.

Mort, John. Review of *Paul Booklist* (June 1, 200): 1799.

O'Malley, Anne. Review of *The Crying for a Vision*. *Booklist* (December 15, 1994): 747.

Owens, Virginia Stem. "Walter Wangerin and the Cosmic Explosion." *Christianity Today* (December 14, 1994): 1190.

Peterson, Eugene. "Walter Wangerin." http://www.christianbook.com/htmll/authors/1465.

Publishers Weekly. Review of *The Book of God: The Bible as a Novel* (February 12, 1996): 70.

"Walter Wangerin" http://www.novelreviews.blogspot.com/2006/02.

"Walter Wangerin" http://www.noveljourney.blogspot.com/2006/03/walterwangerin.

Wilson, John. Review of *The Book of God: The Bible as a Novel*. *Christianity Today* (April 8, 1996): 75.

WAUGH, EVELYN

Personal, Professional, and Religious Background

Evelyn Arthur St. John Waugh (1903–1966) was born in Hampstead, London. He was the son of Catherine Charlotte Raban Waugh and Arthur Waugh, who was an editor and publisher at Chapman & Hall. His brother Alec Waugh was also a writer.

Evelyn Waugh, though he demonstrated obvious verbal fluency from his early years, at first thought he would make his name in the decorative arts. He attended Hertford College, Oxford, from 1921–24, leaving because of poor grades. He subsequently attended art school and took a series of jobs as a schoolmaster, leaving three positions in two years. Clearly a failure as a teacher, he became a writer, beginning with *Decline and Fall*, a satiric novel based on his own Oxford experience. The success of this novel set the pattern for future stories, most of which fictionalized his own life or described his travels. This first novel was followed by a sequel of sorts, *Vile Bodies*, again a comic chronicle of his age, written in the superficial, chattering style of the period.

> I know I am awful. But how much more awful should I be without the Faith.
>
> —Letter from Evelyn Waugh to Edith Sitwell on the occasion of her conversion

Waugh's marriage in 1928 to Evelyn Gardner and his divorce the following year because of her adultery and her decision to marry one of his friends left the

> Evelyn Waugh hated the changes in the Mass, and providentially died before he was forced to hear it in a language other than Latin.

young man bitter and shocked. From this time on, adultery was thematic in his stories, with marriage described as a constant struggle. In 1930, Waugh converted to Roman Catholicism, having earlier requested that a friend recommend a "Jesuit to instruct me." The experience transformed his fiction and his life.

After falling in love with Laura Herbert, another Catholic convert and a young woman from an aristocratic family, he arranged for the annulment of his first marriage and married again. His second marriage proved far happier. The couple had seven children, one of whom was stillborn. They established a home at Piers Court, near Durlsey, Gloucester, and lived together for the rest of Waugh's life.

He continued to write travel stories and comic novels for some time, gradually growing more serious. *Brideshead Revisited* was his great success, followed by *The Loved One*, a satire based on his visit to America.

During World War II, in spite of his age, Evelyn Waugh volunteered for a commission in the Royal Marines, served as company commander, and then joined the Brigadier staff in 1944, serving for a time in Yugoslavia. His trilogy about World War II, which concluded with *Unconditional Surrender*, is considered by some critics as his most powerful work. It also proved to be his last. He died soon after completing the work.

Though considered by many to be a snob in love with a vanishing aristocracy, as well as a racist, an elitist, and a remarkably rude man, Evelyn Waugh became more humble late in his life. He acknowledged his sinful nature, confessed his own failures. He had a deep sense of vocation, accepted the reality of Original Sin, and retained an unwavering faith that the Catholic Church provided for him the Truth. Evelyn Waugh hated the changes in the Mass, and providentially died before he was forced to hear the Mass in a language other than Latin.

Major Works and Themes

Evelyn Waugh's early comic novels, *Decline and Fall* and *Vile Bodies*, memoirs of Oxford and of the superficial culture of the 1920s, are witty portrayals of the bright young things of the period, full of drink and frivolity, obsessed with parties, content with superficial relationships and meaningless sexuality—both homosexual and heterosexual. These "beautiful" people have the satiric quality of Noel Coward's caricatures. Deeply moralistic in spite of his peers, Waugh reveals through his laughter the absurdity and shallowness of his society and their taste.

After his first marriage ended in infidelity and divorce, his tone darkened. The publication of *A Handful of Dust*, a bitter commentary on loveless marriage, adultery, and divorce reveals a sterile society obsessed with parties, food, drink, and gossip. The title, taken from T.S. Eliot's *The Wasteland*, reflects Waugh's pervasive theme—a critique of the cheap, materialistic culture, the meaningless sexuality, and the failure of love—both sacred and profane in his society. Waugh provides his readers with alternative endings for the story, one a reasonable and satisfying satiric reversal of roles, and the other a wild travel to the promised Utopia in the Amazon that turns into a dystopia, which is ruled over by a crazy old man who enslaves his visitor, forcing him to read and reread the works of Charles Dickens for the rest of his life. These are what **C. S. Lewis** called "men without chests," educated, wealthy, idle, and useless.

After his conversion, Waugh wrote a number of Catholic novels, in which his religious sensibility became more prominent: a hagiography of Helena, the mother of the Emperor Constantine; a reverent account of Thomas Campion, and also novels of contemporary social criticism. The most famous of these is *Brideshead Revisited*, a remarkable achievement that has enchanted those who read it for its religious insights and those who see only its vivid portrayal of the decline of the old aristocratic order in England. The protagonist is Charles Ryder, a painter and finally a Catholic convert, much like the author. Brideshead, the beautiful building in which much of the action takes place, enchants the narrator, who loves it for its splendor and its history. It appears to represent the Roman Catholic faith itself—originally an organic part of the family and their life, then gradually restricted to a chapel with a quaint old priest saying Mass for the faithful matriarch and serving the Last Rites to family members. Finally, during time of war, it is overrun by the unthinking, unbelieving soldiers who throw covers over the art and eat their hasty meals in its cavernous rooms. Each of the characters in the Marchmain family represents a response to this demanding faith: the mother is the guardian of the family faith, the father tries his best to abandon it, one son lives by the letter of the law, another rejects the laws yet holds true to the spirit, and the daughter fights for independence but finally succumbs to the implacable demands of her old beliefs. The death scene of Lord Marchmain, on which Waugh indicates he originally built the entire narrative, is a powerful moment of grace. As a BBC production and as a film, the story has continued to win fans.

For many, "Sword of Honour," the trilogy of war stories that Waugh wrote after his curious days in the military, is his crowning achievement. He traces the experience of an English officer, using polished prose, sympathy, insight, and humor. Based on some of his own deeds and misdeeds, the final book in the series, *Unconditional Surrender*, contains a bit of a confession of his own striving to be a saint and failing badly in the effort.

One of the best summaries of Waugh's basic fictional theme was expressed by his friend Ann Fleming, who was married to the creator of James Bond: "He liked things to go wrong."

Critical Reception

Evelyn Waugh has been the topic of criticism since his earliest stories appeared when he was 25 years old. The commentators of the period, who loved his satiric attacks on the Bright Young Things of the 1920s, praised him as "the finest comic writer of the modern age." Alec Waugh considered him "the funniest man of his generation." The later stories, especially those that reflect his conversion experience, have elicited a different kind of reaction—a more interesting theological investigation that links his life and his often autobiographical fiction.

Brideshead Revisited, partially because of its popularity as a film and a television production, has produced thoughtful criticism by such impressive theologians as George Weigel. Several have analyzed the difference between the theology of the original work and the interpretations restricted to the implied homosexuality of the hero. Others have been concerned at the revelation of God's grace that allows for the conversion of an old roué and the designation of Sebastian (who is named for a homosexual saint) as a "holy" man in spite of his degraded life. Lady Marchmain, who is a near-saint in the original, is portrayed in the film as a witch who devours her children. This is a clear case where the medium is the message.

Ironically, *The Loved One*, the attack on the American way of death, has been exceedingly popular in America, where critics and readers are delighted with the attacks on the sentimental excesses of Forest Lawn cemetery and the grotesque funeral services for animals. This work combines Waugh's fabled comic sense with his moral outrage at the exaggerated mourning and extravagant burials that seem to elevate animals to the level of humans, with the distressed owners even endowing their dear-departed loved ones with an afterlife. Waugh's traditional faith acknowledges no "doggie heaven."

Waugh's final great work, the "Sword of Honour" trilogy, has been particularly interesting to British readers, who were personally involved with the whole horror of World War II. Critics have proclaimed this his finest work. Writing a review for the *New Republic*, Patrick O'Donovan called it "the one genuine masterpiece to come out of the war."

Awards

Evelyn Waugh won the Hawthornden Prize in 1936 for his biography of Edmund Campion, and the James Tait Black Memorial Prize for Best Novel from the University of Edinburgh in 1952 for *Men at Arms*; he was named a fellow of the Royal Society of Literature and "companion of literature" in 1963; and he was awarded an honorary degree from Loyola College. He refused to accept the Commander of the British Empire honor. In 2003, *Brideshead Revisited* was voted "one of the 100 best-loved novels" by the British public.

Bibliography of Novels by Author

Decline and Fall. London: Chapman & Hall, 1928.
Vile Bodies. New York: J. Cape & H. Smith, 1930.
Black Mischief. New York: Farrar & Rinehart, 1932.
A Handful of Dust. New York: Farrar & Rinehart, 1934.
Scoop. Boston: Little, Brown, 1938.
Put Out More Flags. Boston: Little, Brown, 1942.
Brideshead Revisited. Boston: Little, Brown, 1945.
Scott-King's Modern Europe. London: Chapman & Hall, 1947.
The Loved One: An Anglo-American Tragedy. Boston: Little, Brown, 1948.
Helena. Boston: Little, Brown, 1950.

"Sword of Honour" trilogy

Love Among the Ruins: A Romance of the Near Future. London: Chapman & Hall, 1953.
The Ordeal of Gilbert Pinfold: A Conversation Piece. Boston: Little, Brown, 1957.
Basil Seal Rides Again; or, The Rake's Regress. Boston: Little, Brown, 1963.

Bibliography of Works about Author

Basham, Megan. "Grace Withheld," *WORLD* (August 23, 30, 2008).
Bradbury, Malcolm. Evelyn *Waugh*. Oliver & Boyd, 1964.
Carpenter, Humphrey. *The Brideshead Generation: Evelyn Waugh and His Friends*. Boston: Houghton Mifflin Company, 1990.
Douthat, Ross. "Tales of Waugh", *National Review* (September 1, 2008).
"Evelyn Waugh." *Contemporary Authors Online*. Detroit: Thomson Gale, 2004.

Morriss, Margaret and D.J. Dooley. *Evelyn Waugh: A Reference Guide*. Boston: G.K. Hall, 1984.

New Republic (July 11, 1955). Phillips, Gene D. *Evelyn Waugh's Officers, Gentlemen and Rogues: The Fact Behind His Fiction*. Chicago: Nelson-Hall, 1975.

O'Donovan, Patrick. Review of first novel in the "Sword of Honour" trilogy.

Stannard, Martin. *Evelyn Waugh: The Early Years, 1903–1939*. New York: Norton, 1987.

Stannard, Martin. *Evelyn Waugh: The Later Years, 1939–1966*. New York: Norton, 1992.

Waugh, Alec. *My Brother Evelyn and Other Profiles*. New York: Farrar, Straus, Giroux, 1967.

Waugh, Evelyn: *A Little Learning: An Autobiography, The Early Years*. Boston: Little, Brown and Company, 1964.

Waugh, Evelyn. *The Diaries of Evelyn Waugh*, ed. Michael Davie. Boston: Little Brown, 1977.

Waugh, Evelyn. *The Essays, Articles and Reviews of Evelyn Waugh*, ed. by Donat Gallagher. Boston: Little, Brown, 1984.

Waugh, Evelyn. *The Letters of Evelyn Waugh*, ed. Mark Amory. Boston: Ticknor & Fields, 1980.

Weigel, George. "St. Evelyn Waugh," *First Things* (May, 1993).

Wykes, David. *Evelyn Waugh: A Literary Life*. New York: St. Martin's Press, 1999.

WEST, JESSAMYN

Personal, Professional, and Religious Background

Mary Jessamyn West (1902–1984) was born in Jennings County, Indiana. Her mother was Grace Anna Milhous West, and her father, Eldo Ray, was a citrus farmer. She was related to Richard Nixon through her mother's family and became one of his lifelong friends. When Jessamyn West was a young girl, her father moved to California to an undeveloped wilderness near Yorba Linda. She and her brother and sister had considerable freedom to explore the countryside and she developed her pleasure in solitude and quiet observation. Jessamyn West was a great reader, early discovering the work of Thoreau and other classics.

Hoping to become a school teacher, Jessamyn West attended Whittier College, from which she earned a B.A. degree in 1923. Shortly after graduation, she married Harry Maxwell McPherson, who was a school superintendent. Later, they adopted Ann Cash, their only daughter. For a time, she taught in a one-room school, but soon grew hungry for further education, attending a summer session at Oxford University in 1929, and then enrolling at the University of California at Berkeley. Her studies were interrupted just before she took her doctoral orals: she suffered a lung hemorrhage, which was diagnosed as an advanced case of tuberculosis.

The following two years were spent in a sanatorium in Los Angeles, where the doctors gave her little hope of survival. Seriously ill and still young, in her 20s, Jessamyn West contemplated suicide. Her mother refused to accept the doctors' diagnosis of an early death and brought her daughter some of her favorite foods and kept her entertained with stories of her own childhood and the heritage of the Quakers. Jessamyn West gradually recovered from her exhausted and gloomy condition with her mother's reconstructing of her Quaker heritage. "Grace gave me southern Indiana," she said of the year and a half her mother told her stories "about courtship and farming, blizzards and Quaker meetings." The ailing daughter was slowly "wooed back to life" as she accepted her mother's gift of the Quaker reverence for life.

With encouragement from her loving husband, the young

> Writing fiction is an almost certain way of making a fool of yourself.
>
> —Jessamyn West, quoted by Julian Muller in introduction to her *Collected Stories*

invalid began writing sketches of her mother's memorable tales, building them into a book about an Indiana Quaker couple who were raising a family on a farm during the days before the Civil War. The short stories that she wrote, which her husband sug-

> Jessamyn West was in her 20s when she contracted tuberculosis and learned that she was likely to die after a painful and lingering illness. Though considering suicide, she was nursed back to health by her mother's good food and the stories of her Quaker girlhood—stories that became the basis for much of West's later work.

gested she submit to magazines, were finally collected into her most famous book, *The Friendly Persuasion*. The enthusiastic response from readers of the *Atlantic Monthly*, the *Ladies' Home Journal*, and other journals who printed her stories helped her back to health. The publication of the whole collection in 1945 made her famous. Jessamyn West, began writing in 1935 and continued writing until her death, often telling of the Society of Friends, or Quakers.

As it turned out, Jessamyn West did earn her Ph.D. and was eventually awarded nine honorary doctorates in humane letters and literature. She was a popular lecturer at colleges and universities, and was persuaded to take a few short-term posts as a teacher of creative writing and a writer-in-residence. She taught at writers' conferences at the prestigious Breadloaf, at Indiana University, the University of Notre Dame, the University of Colorado, Squaw Valley, the University of Utah, the University of Washington, Stanford University, the University of Montana, Portland University, the University of Kentucky, and Loyola Marymount University as well as serving as a visiting professor at Wellesley College, the University of California at Irvine, Mills College, and Whittier College, among others.

She died suddenly of a massive stroke in 1984, the same year that her final novel was published. Her editor and friend, Julian Muller, praised "her fortitude, generosity, and gentleness; her loveliness and femininity; her fierce devotion to truth as she perceives it; her delight in kindly laughter; her sense of beauty; her startling ability to pierce the light and dark veils of human conduct; her deep affinity with nature; and her abiding humanity."

Major Works and Themes

Jessamyn West's gentle tales of her Quaker heritage, told with humor and charm, have been cherished for decades. *The Friendly Persuasion* was published first in magazines as a series of short stories which were collected as a novel and finally turned into a film which starred Gary Cooper, Dorothy McGuire, and Anthony Perkins. Like *The Little House on the Prairie* books or **Janette Oke's** stories, *The Friendly Persuasion* is the loving portrait of a farm family. The Birdwells are Quakers, living in Indiana in the years just before the Civil War. They are pictured as peaceful folk, with their friendly family home, the mother a Quaker preacher, the father a nurseryman who buys, grows, and sells trees and plants for a wide area of their state. Jess, the father, is sensitive to his wife, his children, and his neighbors. He does have a few un-Quaker longings—like his love of proscribed music, the desire for an organ in his house, and his dream of a horse fast enough to beat the Reverend Goodley to church. The family's response to their eldest son's decision to fight Confederate marauders is one of the most poignant portions in the novel. Josh Birdwell discovers a number of the same truths about warfare that Henry did in *The Red Badge of Courage*.

Jessamyn West's own Quaker heritage informs the stories, as do her memories of tales told by her family. She includes many realistic touches—the cold bed at night and the cold floor on a winter morning, the hard work on the farm, the rare flower brought inside to wilt in a vase on the table. Children die as do some parents, not all romances work out well, a man may have a wen on his neck for much of his life and simply learn to live with it. The gentle, natural, loving response of the Friends in the story reflects the uplifting pattern of faith West found among her own relatives and friends.

Cress Delahanty, a series of short stories, is Jessamyn West's own chronicle of adolescence in rural California. The young heroine, who is pictured from ages 12–16, is in love with romantic literature, with elegant language, with exaggerated passion. With her characteristic gentle irony, West remembers her own hunger for romantic love, for music and poetry and grand gestures. Her comic efforts to look like a Pre-Raphaelite lady in her grand hat and high heels end with a slapstick event where her hat falls into a fish tank, poisoning the fish and drawing a delighted crowd, including the young man she is seeking to attract.

More controversial are her accounts of her struggle with her sister's incurable battle with cancer. In the novel *A Matter of Time* and the memoir *The Woman Said Yes: Encounters with Death and Life*, West acknowledges that she cooperated with her sister, who was faced with inevitable pain and death, to cut the suffering short and commit suicide. West considered these two books more a chronicle of individual choice rather than a general recommendation, but her endorsement of euthanasia nonetheless aroused sharp debate.

In 1975, West undertook a new genre, the historical novel. *The Massacre at Fall Creek* is based on the first American trial of white men for killing Indians. She published her final novel, *The State of Stony Lonesome*, the same year that she died—1984.

Jessamyn West's great talent lies in her short stories. Sometimes they follow naturally from one another to shape an episodic novel, but they are also capable of standing alone. A number of her stories are aimed at young adults, but are entertaining for mature readers as well. West is witty without being cruel, sensitive without growing sentimental. She was a remarkably versatile writer, turning out novels, memoirs, poetry, essays, screenplays, and even an opera. Her works are included in more than a hundred anthologies. She told *Contemporary Authors* that the four cornerstones of her life were "family, words on paper (this means books and writing), the world of nature (weeds, wind, buzzards, clouds), and privacy."

Critical Reception

Jessamyn West's most dependable reception came from happy readers. She was a popular contributor to a number of magazines; her books were often best-sellers, and they frequently were book club selections. Even today, many of her stories and books are available in fresh editions and she herself has become the subject of biographers and critics.

John Mort describes *The Friendly Persuasion* as "warm, funny short stories of Jess and Eliza Birdwell" that have "something in common with **Jan Karon's** work, though their milieu is much different: the Civil War." The critics almost universally praised this book for its natural use of local color and for its author's resistance of the moralizing impulse. Nathan L. Rothman, writing for *Saturday Review*, noted that the readers get "an intimate knowledge of their [the Quakers'] inner life . . . the lovely, gentle, ethical essence." The mood he describes as, "nostalgic, primitive, like a dream of vanished innocence." Critics were delighted that Jessamyn West was able to remain fairly objective in spite of her loving sympathy with these pioneers.

Most of the critics also praised the Cress Delahanty stories for their appeal to both teens and adults. Frances Gaither, writing for the *New York Times*, called it a "warm-blooded morsel of humanity."

The nonfiction books received mixed reviews, usually tied to the mindset of the critic. The historical novels that came later, such as *The Massacre at Fall Creek*, were less warmly received and less widely reviewed.

Robert Kirsch reviewed *The Life I Really Lived* in 1979, looked back over the whole of her work, and announced that it was time for us to recognize Jessamyn West as "one of the treasures of this nation's literature."

Awards

Cress Delahanty was a Book-of-the-Month Club selection. *The Massacre at Fall Creek* was a Literary Guild main selection. Jessamyn West won the Indiana Author's Day Award in 1956 for *Love, Death, and the Ladies' Drill Team*; the Thermod Monsen Award in 1958 for *To See the Dream*; the California Commonwealth Club award in 1970 and the California Literature Medal in 1971, both for *Crimson Ramblers of the World, Farewell*; the Janet Kafke prize for fiction in 1976; the Indiana Arts Commission Award for Literature in 1977; and honorary doctorates from Whittier College, Mills College, Swarthmore College, Indiana University, University of Indiana—Terre Haute, Western College for Women, Wheaton College, Juniata College, and Wilmington College.

Bibliography of Novels by Author

The Friendly Persuasion. New York: Harcourt, 1945.
The Witch Diggers. New York: Harcourt, 1951.
Cress Delahanty. New York: Harcourt, 1953.
Little Men. New York: Ballantine, 1954. (Reprinted as *The Chile Kings*).
South of the Angels. New York: Harcourt, 1960.
A Matter of Time. New York: Harcourt, 1966.
Leafy Rivers. New York: Harcourt, 1967.
Except for Me and Thee: A Companion to *The Friendly Persuasion* (short stories). New York: Harcourt, 1960.
Crimson Ramblers of the World, Farewell (short stories). New York: Harcourt, 1970.
The Massacre at Fall Creek New York: Harcourt, 1975.
The Life I really Lived. New York: Harcourt, 1979.
The State of Stony Lonesome. New York: Harcourt, 1984.
The Collected Stories of Jessamyn West. New York: Harcourt, 1986.

Jessamyn West also wrote plays, nonfiction, and many short stories and articles which are found in collections such as *O. Henry Memorial Award Prize Stories of 1946* and *The Living Novel*, 1957. Her stories have been published in *Town and Country, Mademoiselle, Collier's, Ladies' Home Journal, New Mexico Quarterly, Yale Review, Kenyon Review*, the *New Yorker*, and other magazines. She wrote film scripts for *The Friendly Persuasion, The Big Country*, and *Stolen Hours*, as well as the libretto for an opera—*A Mirror for the Sky*.

Her papers have been stored at Whittier College.

Bibliography of Works about Author

Farmer, Ann Dahlstrom. *Jessamyn West: A Descriptive and Annotated Bibliography*. Lanham, MD: Scarecrow Press, 1998.
Gaither, Frances. Review of *Cress Delahanty*. *New York Times Book Review*, January 14, 1954.

Gleasner, Diana. *Breakthrough: Women in Writing.* New York: Dodd, 1959.

Kirsch, Robert. Review of *The Life I Really Lived. Los Angeles Times*, November 18, 1979.

"Mary Jessamyn West." *Contemporary Authors Online.* Detroit: Thomson Gale, 2003.

Mort, John. *Christian Fiction: A Guide to the Genre.* Greenwood Village, CO: Libraries Unlimited, 2002.

Muir, Jane. *Famous Modern Women Writers.* New York: Dodd, 1959.

Rothman, Nathan L. Review of *The Friendly Persuasion. Saturday Review* (November 17, 1945).

Shivers, Alfred S. *Jessamyn West.* New York: Twayne, 1972.

West, Jessamyn. *To See the Dream.* New York: Harcourt, 1957.

West, Jessamyn. *Hide and Seek: A Continuing Journey.* New York: Harcourt, 1973.

West, Jessamyn. *The Woman Said Yes: Encounters with Death and Life.* New York: Harcourt, 1976.

West, Jessamyn. *Double Discovery: A Journey.* New York: Harcourt, 1980.

Wigan, Angela. *Time* (May 24, 1976).

Obituaries: *Newsweek*, March 5, 1984; *New York Times*, February 24, 1984; *Publishers Weekly*, March 9, 1984; *Time*, March 5, 1984; *Variety*, February 29, 1984.

WICK, LORI

Personal, Professional, and Religious Background

Lori Hays Wick (1958–) was born in Santa Rosa, California, and spent her childhood there. Her father was Harland Hays, her mother Pearl Hays. "Even as a child," Wicks indicates, she had a vivid imagination. "I had to embellish everything." After high school, she attended a Bible college for three semesters. It was there that she met and married Bob Wick. Her husband works for a large manufactured-housing firm owned and operated by his family, and in addition, he is her agent. The Wicks have three children, Timothy, Matthew, and Abigail, and make their home in Wisconsin.

Lori Wick does her writing alone in her office in the center of the home. She began her writing in March of 1998. She thought she had a good idea for a story, drafted it on paper, showed it to her husband and then to a publisher, and finally submitted the manuscript to Harvest House Publishers. At first rejected and then revised, the novel finally satisfied the publishing firm. Since then, she has written about two books a year.

Major Works and Themes

Lori Wick started writing novels in 1990 with *A Place Called Home.* Over 30 novels have followed, usually in clusters around a family and a locale. She is fond of the American West and likes to draw a family portrait that takes the generations along from the 19th to the 20th century. She has perfected a formula for her novels: centering her the series on families of several brothers or sisters who have very different life experiences. She insists that her novels are character-driven, though her love of a good story dominates every thing except her need to spread her faith.

> I love romance and a happy ending, but unless there is more—a personal relationship with Christ—something will always be missing.
>
> —Lori Wick, interview in Janice DeLong's
> *Contemporary Christian Authors*

Lori Wick sees her audience as mostly adult women, but realizes that men and teens also read her novels. She likes to begin with a mystery or puzzle that must be solved. "My goal is romance, but not only romance; it's also to show that characters are whole in and of themselves. I include the gospel message . . . in every book." She attributes her creativity to her faith. "Jesus Christ is the basis for all, and without Him nothing can have full meaning."

Wick clearly draws on a combination of both English and American fiction, primarily by women writers, though she pays homage to *The Red Badge of Courage* by Stephen Crane. The clearest tradition in her work is the one set in motion by Louisa May Alcott with *Little Women*, amplified by Laura Ingalls Wilder with the *Little House on the Prairie* books, and modified for modern Evangelical readers by **Janette Oke**. Like Wilder and Oke, Wick follows through with characters that reappear in the clustered stories. The reader can also make out the influence of 19th-century British writers like Jane Austen and the Brontë sisters. Her plots often show strong older men confronted by naïve young women who stand up to them and thereby attract their attention. One of her heroines, like Jane Eyre, works in an orphanage to become a nanny to the small son of the widower. The lively young woman shows this stern and lonely older man how to enjoy love and spontaneity, and finally marries him. In some ways, this is also a pious version of Samuel Richardson's risqué tales of lovely and vulnerable servants who fall in love with their masters and either convert them or are ruined by them. The gentle reader can anticipate that a Wick heroine will meet the happy fate of a Pamela, whose virtue is rewarded, rather than the sad fate of Clarissa, who dies a tragic death after having been "ruined."

Like Jane Austen, Lori Wick believes that certain people are clearly ordained for one another, held apart only by pride or prejudice. Her stories reveal the weaknesses of her heroines and heroes, provides them with opportunities to reform, and then consummate the marriage. Usually her stories conclude with a wedding and an epilogue in which the unsanctified characters become converts and the married couple produce children. In *Promise Me Tomorrow*, part of the "Rocky Mountain Memories" series, the couple are blessed in the epilogue with eight children. She clearly believes that marriage is the ideal condition and that the family is not complete without children.

On occasion, the barrier to a happy courtship turns out to be the young woman's independence. Some of her perky young beauties are in "masculine" professions. One is a deputy sheriff, one an undercover agent for the Treasury Department. The contemplation of wedded bliss converts such independent lasses to different roles, allowing the men to assume the leadership in the family and to provide the protection and security that Wick seems to believe both men and women need in order be happy.

In her more recent series—"The English Garden"—Lori Wick locates her standard plot in a 19th-century English village. The story is partly *Emma*, partly *The Vicar of Wakefield*, without the real dangers and social horrors lurking in the background of these much more realistic, if sentimental, novels. The modest maiden is never really threatened, even after marriage. Everyone is comfortably settled in proper friendships and love affairs with other Christians. The village could be in Texas except for the tea that is faithfully presented and the butler who replaces the housekeeper. Wick is much more comfortable in Texas, Montana, or California, where her characters are more natural and the conversations less stilted.

Lori Wick specializes in a modern novel of manners, recommending through the action the proper respect for adults by children, the kind gestures of gratitude to any who have supplied meals, and careful control of conversation so that no uncouth or vulgar expressions interrupt the flow of the discourse. Her people spend an inordinate amount of time saying "Thank you" and apologizing to one another. She pays especial attention to the appropriate stages in a courtship, displaying great distress when a man kisses a woman to whom he has not already proposed or tries to take advantage of their engagement. Having once planned marriage, the couple must live in separate homes in order to avoid the appearance of impropriety. The suitor, who must be a wage earner, capable of supporting a family, should ask the father's permission to court the daughter, introduce her to his family and meet her family to assure he is making a wise choice of a bride. Above all, both the bride and groom must be Christians. This means they must be able to point to a time when they were born-again. They must pray regularly, attend church, and say blessings before all meals. The courtship ritual and the unchanging set of assumptions in her lively novels have allowed this writer to turn into a dependable production machine, with novels appearing at frequent intervals to the great delight of her many fans.

Critical Reception

Most critics of evangelical fiction mention Lori Wick with other writers in the Janette Oke tradition, but make little comment on her stories. If anything, the critics tend to summarize the plot and list the characters. Wick's loyal readers, who buy each book as it appears and send her sales numbers into the millions, are enthusiastic in their praise of her stories. She provides an easy read, focusing on housewifely activities, dedicating most of her pages to personal relations, and providing the recipe for happy families.

Although she draws her plots and characterization from such classics as *Wuthering Heights*, *Jane Eyre*, or *Pride and Prejudice*, Lori Wick is no Brontë sister or Jane Austen. Rather than sharpening the ironic phrases or capturing the passionate hunger for experience and meaning that we see in these masterpieces, Wick over-explains her characters' not-very-complicated relationships, leaving little to the imagination. While the original Jane Eyre considers the mission field or looks out over the landscape with longing, Wick provides no hint of a larger world, even in her Civil War scenes. She does move her sets from place to place, but the same people reappear and face much of the same dilemmas.

Even when she places her stories in London, she is more focused on the limited gardens of her title than on the vast, chaotic world that Dickens knew in the 19th century in that same city. Lori Wick's is a safe, enclosed space. Furthermore, the gardens have no reality. She names few of the herbs or flowers that they contain, ignores their layout and colors, refuses to explore the rich symbolism in their history. When she tries to transfer her novels to other times and other climes, as in the "Kensington Chronicles," she reveals her ignorance. She knows too little about ships and shipping to handle this material well. Nor is she wise to undertake a study of life in Henry VIII's turbulent lifetime. She succeeds better in her return to Token Creek, Montana or to Tucker Mills, Massachusetts, where she can discuss indentured servants or the life of average folk. Wick, having studied catalogues and newspapers of the 19th century, does have a good sense of the life and times of America around the Civil War.

John Mort has noted that Wick has also tried her hand at novels of a different style—either setting them in a region of England adjacent to Queen Victoria's Kensington, or undertaking the "fat romance" style of Nora Roberts or Janet Dailey. He thinks that *Pretense* is "really a fairy tale"—the story of two sisters who dabble in "tastefully rendered sin as young women" before they meet with "dazzling literary, marital, and spiritual success." With *Sophie's Heart*, she follows her usual formula, using an immigrant from Czechoslovakia who goes from rags to riches, winning the love of the lonely widower who employs her. *The Princess* repeats the formula, this time with a contemporary woman marrying the prince of a small kingdom. Although this unlikely arrangement is based on necessity rather than love, the heroine's faith and character predictably win over the prince and eventually produce a solid marriage.

Lori Wick's books are didactic, full of Scripture, descriptions of the Christian walk, prayers for children, and sermons about Christian behavior. She acknowledges that, "You don't come to Lori Wick for a history lesson. My books focus on interpersonal relationships, and since there are billions of people in the world, the ideas are legion." She indicated in one interview she still has more than fifteen books left on her story board, plenty of material to keep her producing her novels for years to come.

Awards

Lori Wick has been a finalist several times for the ECPA Gold Medallion, the Evangelical Christian Publishers Association for *A Place Called Home, Sophie's Heart, Where the Wild Rose Blooms,* and *Whispers of Moonlight.* Her goal is to win the award.

Bibliography of Works by Author
(Eugene, Oregon: Harvest Home Publishers)

"A Place Called Home" series (1990–1991)

"The Californians" series (1992–1994)

"Kensington Chronicles" series (1993–1995)

"Rocky Mountain Memories" series (1996–1997)

"The Yellow Rose Trilogy" (1999–2001)

Sophie's Heart. 1995.
Beyond the Picket Fence. 1998.
Pretense. 1998.
The Princess. 1999.

"English Garden" series (2002–2003)

"Tucker Mills" series (2005–2006)

"Big Sky Dreams" series (2007)

Bibliography of Works about Author

DeLong, Janice and Rachel Schwedt. *Contemporary Christian Authors: Lives and Works.* Lanham, MD: The Scarecrow Press, 2000.
Mort, John. *Christian Fiction: A Guide to the Genre.* Greenwood Village, CO: Libraries Unlimited, 2002.

WOIWODE, LARRY

Personal, Professional, and Religious Background

Larry Alfred Woiwode (1941–) (whose name is pronounced to sound like "why woody") was born in Carrington, North Dakota, one of four children. His family had lived for generations in North Dakota, where they had settled into this tiny German Catholic town. His mother, Carole Ann Peterson Woiwode, had been a school teacher, and his father, Everett Carl Woiwode,

> Most poets are rooted in the natural world, spokespersons for the inarticulate in nature, as well as the wordless desires of the common person—or poets should be searching for words for those sides of the world.
>
> —Larry Woiwode, Poet Laureate, North Dakota

was also a teacher, and then principal, and finally superintendent of schools in the town. Woiwode's mother died when Larry was 8 years old, leaving him saddened for life and ignorant of the "geography" of women. He and his father became friends for life, his father serving as a steady force when the young writer was discouraged, broke, or exhausted. Everett Woiwode's quiet Catholic faith and his constant prayers for this son became a constant in a confusing life until he died in 1978—a story gently told in *A Step from Death*. The family moved to Illinois after the death of the mother, the father taking a position as teacher and administrator. In *What I Think I Did*, Woiwode describes his father as a fine orator, a talented teacher of Shakespeare and other classics. His ability to act out roles in the plays he taught influenced his son's interest in theater and in poetry.

Larry Woiwode went to the University of Illinois in Urbana for five years, acted in plays, took most of the creative writing and literature courses available, tried to rewrite *Macbeth*, and met the love of his life, Care, whom he later married. While at the University of Illinois, he became a lapsed Catholic and a heavy drinker, falling into the promiscuous sexual activities of the time.

With encouragement from one of his professors and a friend at the *New Yorker* magazine, William Maxwell, Woiwode left to live in New York, trying at first to make a living with his writing. Maxwell became a literary father to him, encouraging and editing his work, lending him money, worrying about his health, feeding him occasional lunches, and demanding that he continue his writing. The young man finally wrote a number of stories for that prestigious magazine and became one of their contract writers.

The new salary allowed him to marry Care and create a home with her in New York, where their first child was born some time later. They thought that Newlyn would be their only child. The couple's discussion of baptism led Woiwode back to a consideration of his faith, which culminated with a conversation with a friend, James Wright, which began with the question, "So tell me, do you think Jesus is God?"

Seeking to find a way to provide for a growing family, Woiwode took a number of teaching positions, serving as a professor at SUNY/Binghamton and also chairing the creative writing program there. Soon, Woiwode found his life falling into a pattern of temporary appointments at various colleges and universities, including Wisconsin, Wheaton, and many others.

At one point, Woiwode became so frenetic with his half-finished writings and his drinking and teaching that his discouraged wife took their daughter and left him for a year, living with her parents in Chicago. Woiwode, distressed by this experience, took time for spiritual revival and for psychological counseling. He acknowledged that God was important to their marriage and to his life, and eventually reconciled with his family. He converted to a conservative branch of Presbyterianism at the time. The couple eventually had three more children, all of them now grown with children of their own. His latest book is addressed to his only son, Joseph, who is a helicopter pilot in Iraq.

In 1978, the Woiwode family returned to North Dakota, choosing to buy a farm near one

> Larry Woiwode started his writing career as a regular contributor to the *New Yorker* magazine.

of the churches in his Calvinist denomination, the Presbyterian Church of America. In 2004, he was appointed distinguished visiting professor at the University of North Dakota. He was also named Poet Laureate of North Dakota. At present, he is a visiting professor at Jamestown College, a tiny college in Jamestown, North Dakota, where he teaches poetry, writing, Shakespeare, and "Spiritual Encounters in Contemporary Fiction." Larry Woiwode prefers a small, collegiate school, where faculty can join for lunchtime conversations about literature and where students are not bound by the "Cyclopean" or uni-vision so common in most universities. He feels free to talk about his faith in his classes.

Larry Woiwode lives near Mott on a 160-acre farm with his wife and raises registered quarterhorses as well as enough silage to keep them fed for the winter. He clearly loves the farm life, the pleasure of fixing things himself, the smell of the soil, and the feel of the seasons. William Maxwell, his mentor, once said of Larry Woiwode that he is "the only writer I know who's gone off and lived his convictions, not just put them in writing."

Major Works and Themes

Larry Woiwode writes primarily about his own life, his memories, his family, and his faith. He prefers the material world, with all its storms and cruelty, to the fantasy world he sees in much Christian fiction. Although he frequently quotes the Bible, especially in his later works, he only occasionally bases his stories on an explicitly Christian theme. His first novel, *What I'm Going to Do, I Think*, traces a pair of honeymooners, whose sterile marriage is doomed from the start.

His early stories are often realistic sketches of people he has known, especially his own family in their North Dakota milieu. He tracks their German Catholic heritage, particularly important in *Behind the Bedroom Wall*, his epic of the Neumiller family. In this long, meandering narrative, Woiwode introduces four generations of the family, beginning with Charles, who is returning to his own father's home, faced with the task of building the coffin, washing and dressing the body, and digging the grave for the man who has become an outcast in the community. His neighbors blame him for their own losses in these grim Depression times. The story ends with another funeral, this time of Charles himself, and the survival of his own son and grandson. The faith that underlies this story is centered more in marriage and family than in God.

At the time he was writing this grand sprawling narrative, Larry Woiwode was increasingly captivated by studies of the Bible, which were to lead him to a conversion to the Reformed faith. The novel that followed this transformation, *Poppa John*, proved quite different. It is explicitly evangelical, the story of an aging star of a soap opera, in which he is a wise old Bible-spouting figure on television. When the writers kill off the character, the old actor experiences his own kind of death—facing "the bitter truths of aging, unemployment, and uselessness." Using his own experience in acting, failure, and alcoholism, Woiwode pictures Poppa John's descent into despair. The combination of a loving wife and a haunting memory of Scripture bring him to a conversion and a deeper understanding of himself.

Woiwode's next novel, *Born Brothers*, returns to the Neumillers, his literary version of his own family. The two brothers, Charles and Jerome, are much like Larry and his own brother, who were in college together before going quite different ways. Charles, the "bad" brother, is the writer, actor, drunkard, who measures himself by the "good" brother, Jerome, the straight arrow who becomes a doctor. Charles sinks deep into degradation before rising through the power of Christ to be saved and return to North Dakota, where he tries to build a conventional family life close to the land.

At this point, having already written a great deal about his own life, Woiwode began describing his Christian beliefs in detail, using nonfiction as his mode of expression. All of his stories and commentaries are at least faintly autobiographical. His evocative, meditative tone gives a lyricism to these memories, but he has no qualms about explicit sexuality or crude language. Where his characters commit incest, he acknowledges this, and when his boisterous old men are profane or vulgar, Woiwode provides the reader with all the gruesome details. He is not a typical evangelical writer. Gene Veith, who wrote a thoughtful essay on him for *WORLD Magazine*, sums up Woiwode's challenges as an evangelical writer, noting his "hard-edged realism, soul-baring honesty, and tough-minded complexity," which Veith considers "a refreshing change from typical contemporary Christian fare. And his materiality is an important counter to a hyper-spiritual rejection of the physical realm, such Gnosticism (an ancient heresy) now influences much of American religion. Mr. Woiwode has not yet written the great evangelical novel, but if anyone can do it, he can."

Critical Reception

Largely because he was already well known for his short stories in the *New Yorker*, Larry Woiwode's first novels were widely reviewed in major papers and journals. His first novel, *What I'm Going to Do, I Think*, the story of a doomed marriage of two young people, was favorably reviewed and won an award from the William Faulkner Foundation. *Beyond the Bedroom Wall* is generally considered his major work, a summing up of a number of his short stories and a massive statement about family. Chilton Williamson, Jr. reviewing the book in *National Review*, thought it a powerful evocation of the "world hewn from the North Dakota sod, decorated with frame houses and peopled with carpenters, high-school superintendents, and Catholics." The book was favorably reviewed in the *New York Times*, the *New Republic*, and the *Village Voice* by such luminaries as John Gardner and **Anne Tyler.** Clearly the critics assumed they were witnessing the beginning of a major career.

Joyce Carol Oates was given the task of reviewing *Poppa John* for the *New York Times*. The novel is much briefer and much changed in tone from the sprawling narrative of the Neumillers. This poor Falstaff of a hero is an aged man who "seems to have outlived himself." He actually "died" on screen before he faced his own mortality. Jonathan Yardley applauded Woiwode's bold effort "in a cynical age" to make the unfashionable effort "to convey the emotional struggles and doubts attendant to a discovery of religious faith." He does complain that Woiwode simply "does not pull it off; the crucial moment that he intends to be an epiphany fails to rise above the level of a soap opera." An ironic tone unfortunately clouds the conclusion.

After this, Woiwode's critics became increasingly disturbed by his work. The next of Woiwode's novels was *Born Brothers*, which traces two Neumiller brothers' lives, one a potential suicide. Sven Birkerts, calling the book one of "the saddest—most heartbreaking—of all American novels," nonetheless considers *Born Brothers* "a grand failure." When Woiwode, in *Indian Affairs*, returned to his young married couple and their struggle to make a life together a year after the honeymoon he had earlier described, Woiwode won faint praise. Ron Hansen, reviewing it for the *New York Times Book Review*, thought it "too imaginary, grotesque and adventitious"—weaker than Woiwode's previous works, including this novel's prequel.

As the mainstream press began to cool toward Woiwode's more faith-oriented novels, the Christian critics warmed to his works—especially his nonfiction. John Mort notes that, although "Woiwode was among the brightest lights on the literary scene in the 1970s, the winner of many prizes, and a regular contributor to the *New Yorker*," he did not receive the same level of attention since his conversion to Presbyterianism. "Though they are always respectfully reviewed, his subsequent novels, memoirs, and religious explorations (*Acts* 1993) have lost him much of his literary following." Mort muses that, ironically, "he hasn't, on the other hand, caught on among evangelicals, partly because of his high style, more because he does not shy away from profanity and the depiction of explicit sex when he feels his story requires it." The critic soberly notes, "Besides Christianity, his other religion is realism."

John Mort lists three Woiwode novels that are explicitly Christian: *Born Brothers* (1998), *Indian Affairs* (1992), and *Poppa John* (1991).

Awards

Larry Woiwode has won two awards from the American Academy and the Institute of Arts and Letters, has been awarded a Guggenheim Foundation Fellowship, and the John Dos Passos Prize. He has also been the recipient of numerous other awards: he was given the Rough Rider Award; named the Poet Laureate of North Dakota; won the William Faulkner Foundation Award. In 1970, he won the Notable Book Award from the American Library Association for *What I'm Going to Do, I Think*; he won the award in fiction from Friends of American Writers in 1976 for *Beyond the Bedroom Wall*. Larry Woiwode has also been named Doctor of Letters at North Dakota State University and Doctor of Literature by Geneva College.

Bibliography of Novels by Author

What I'm Going to Do, I Think. New York: Farrar, Straus, Giroux, 1969.
Beyond the Bedroom Wall. New York: Farrar, Straus, Giroux, 1975.
Poppa John. New York: Farrar, Straus, Giroux, 1981.
Born Brothers. New York: Farrar, Straus, Giroux, 1988.
Neumiller Stories. New York: Farrar, Straus, Giroux, 1989.
Indian Affairs. New York: Atheneum, 1992.
Silent Passengers: Stories. New York: Atheneum, 1993.

Bibliography of Works about Author

Birkerts, Sven. Review of *Born Brothers*. *New Republic* (September 12, 1988): 47.
Cheang, J.B. *Taming Memory: The Fiction of Larry Woiwode*. New York: World and I, 2002.
Hansen, Ron. Review *of Indian Affairs*. *New York Times Book Review*, July 26, 1992, 15.
Kauffman, Bill. "Memoirist of a Companionable Prairie Home." Review of *A Step from Death*. *Wall Street Journal*, March 8, 2008.
"Larry Woiwode." *Contemporary Authors Online*. Detroit: Thomson Gale, 2004.
"Larry Woiwode." Wikipedia. http://en.wikipedia.org/wiki/Larry_Woiwode.
Mort, John. *Christian Fiction: A Guide to the Genre*. Greenwood Village, CO: Libraries Unlimited, 2002.
Oates, Joyce Carol. "A Man Who Became his own Grandfather." Review of *Beyond the Bedroom Wall*. *New York Times*, November 15, 1981.
Rothstein, Mervyn. "Larry Woiwode's Life and Work in Words." Review of *Born Brothers*. *New York Times*, September 5, 1988.

Sullivan, Robert. "A Landscape of Words." *New York Times*, December 3, 2006.

Veith, Gene Edward. "Getting too Real?" *WORLD Magazine* (July 4, 1998).

Vernon, John. "Little House on the Prairie." Review of *Season of Survival in Two Acts*. *New York Times*, June 11, 2000.

Williamson, Childton, Jr. Review of *Beyond the Bedroom Wall*. *National Review*, January 23, 1976.

Woiwode, Larry. *What I Think I Did: A Season of Survival in Two Acts*. New York: Basic Books, 2000.

Woiwode, Larry. *A Step from Death: A Memoir*. Berkeley: Counterpoint, 2008.

WRIGHT, VINITA HAMPTON

Personal, Professional, and Religious Background

Vinita Hampton Wright (1958–) is a product of Kansas, where some of her relatives were coal miners. Her ancestors, having emigrated from England in the late 1800s, ended up first in McCune, Kansas, and finally in Cherokee. In her note on "The Story of the Story" at the conclusion of *Dwelling Places,* Wright tells about part of southeast Kansas where she grew up as one of the "town kids whose father worked in a factory of the neighboring community." She remembers the "wheat, silo, corn, and soybeans" on the farms around the town and the sorrows of the small farmers as they were forced off the land with the changes in agriculture.

Vinita Hampton began writing in grammar school. The small towns she knew as a child, Cherokee and Pittsburg, were to become the basis of her imaginary community of Bender Springs—a small farming community in southeast Kansas. As she notes in her "Foreword" to *Grace at Bender Springs,* this is a "town that no longer has its own grocery" though it once had "multiple retail businesses, a newspaper, banks, and hotels." The history of the place lives only in the memory of the older citizens. When her "grandmas mention old friends, they are often evoking the names of families that founded the town." She "grew up surrounded by religion, touched by Pentecostal, Baptist, and Methodist theologies."

She majored in music education at Pittsburg State University in Pittsburg, Kansas, graduating in 1982. Like most of the other young people in her community, she then left for greener pastures. For a while, she worked as a teacher in Jordan and in the Missouri public school system. She then earned her master's degree in communications from Wheaton College and worked as an assistant editor for Harold Shaw Publishers. From there, she moved to Tyndale House as editor and finally took a position with Loyola Press. Vinita Wright wrote her first two novels while working as an editor, then reduced her editing schedule so that she could dedicate more of her time and energy to her own writing. She also directs and participates in writing workshops.

In 1991, Vinita Hampton married Jim Wright, a photographer and graphic designer whom she met at an artists' retreat. They moved to Hyde Park, a neighborhood near the University of Chicago, where they lived until 2005, then moved to a small bungalow on the south side of Chicago.

> I think Christians who are writers have been given a freedom in the last few decades to learn more about what it means to be a true artist. . . . When you are a true artist, you aren't so concerned about controlling the material. Today, more and more writers are discovering the freedom to trust the Holy Spirit to speak truth.
>
> —Vinita Hampton Wright in interview with Lauren F. Winner, June 25, 2008

Major Works and Themes

Vinita Hampton Wright wrote her first novel, *Grace at Bender Springs*, when she was seeking a degree in communications at Wheaton College. It was

> Vinita Hampton Wright began her career as an editor, turning later to writing novels about the small town she had left to go off to college, and finding success in writing about her memories.

her way of "getting out of taking comprehensive exams." The requirements were that the novel had to deal with some creative theme in a creative manner. This ambitious novel chronicles the life of a Kansas community from the drought of 1873 to the present, captures the spirit of Midwestern life in much the same way that Willa Cather or William Inge did—the patterns of speech, of meals, of church revivals, old women's card parties, and many other daily rituals.

The dark side of the town is also exposed, with "water witches," satanic-worshipping young people, the drunken brother of the Pentecostal preacher, the New Age visitor, the teenage waitress with an abusive home life and a dying mother. Even the pastors and their wives have their problems—the small tragedies of a typical community with bits of grace, like the surprising colors in a new paint job at Mamie's house or the ruined garden that springs to life in Dave Seaton's yard. The novel weaves back and forth, tracing several plot lines, bringing them all together from time to time, and smoothing them out in a beautifully lyrical ending. Although the novel is full of religious people, some thoughtlessly following the rituals, some deeply committed, the theological message is muted. Only at the end of the novel do the readers see the recurrent pattern of water imagery with springs and wells brought together. Then the readers remember the many times that the people in this dusty land have paused for a drink with friends and neighbors—whether it is a glass of lemonade at Mamie's or a cold beer at Perky's Tap. Gradually, these begin to remind us of communion. The miracle of the spring that brackets the narrative reminds the reader of the woman at the well, the mystery of the "living water."

Wright's later novels continue this same pattern of exploring the humdrum, the painful, and the richly varied lives of small town Midwestern people. She has thought deeply about the changes in the economy and the religion of the people in her native region. In *Dwelling Places*, she uses the images of abandoned homes and farms as gentle reminders of what has been lost in the past century. She shows the older citizens trying to survive on farms and in small towns abandoned by young people for the big cities. We witness the small charities that make up their days, the effects on the men who face one family tragedy after another, sometimes committing suicide, sometimes going into clinical depression. Teenagers play with Goth clothing and music, meditate far too much on the dead, or they turn to apocalyptic religious cults. Wright sees the dark side of small town life, along with the graces that redeem these people, allowing them to weep together and to reach out in faith, finding solace in abiding rituals and loving gestures.

Vinita Wright has the delightful ability of transforming small details into rich symbols. A chicken-rice-mushroom soup casserole, a nameless dog finally being named, a husband joining his wife on midnight walks, a policeman patrolling the streets when the town is asleep all point to paths of grace in a weary land. Her novels deal with ordinary people—a cook and janitor, a handyman, a waitress, a widow, or a farmer. Such people know the same depth of sorrow, the same torments of loss and the same need for redemption as any tragic hero or heroine. She understands family relationships, sometimes revealing children as the true believers, filled with the spirit of the Gospel.

In *Dwelling Places*, Wright uses the technique that we also find in **Marilynne Robinson's** work—using the places as symbols of the life lived within. Beulah, Iowa has elements in common with Robinson's *Gilead*, and her homes, many of them historic, remind us of the crumbling abode in *Housekeeping*. Wright is excellent in her portrayal of older women, allowing Velma to tell the story of Leeway, Kansas, and Rita to tell about Beulah. Echoing some techniques typical of Eudora Welty, Wright makes food the language of love by such scenes as Rita's feeding the whole community of forgotten old folks by preparing soup out of leftovers she collects at the grocery store. The continuing mundane concerns of women, the clothes they wear, the decorations for their homes, the day-to-day care of their children, reveal character and point to more lasting concerns. As John Mort notes in his review of *Grace at Bender Springs*, "Pain—and—grace—await them all."

Critical Reception

Vinita Wright's first novel, *Grace at Bender Springs*, got a mixed review from *Christianity Today*, but was praised by other critics. Lauren Winner notes that the novel was "devoured by readers" and that "her second novel garnered more attention, earning Wright, 43, a two-page spread in *Publishers Weekly*." Although the Bender Springs story was criticized for its "rather heavy-handed metaphor of a drought to depict a community's spiritual dryness," it still reveals a talented new writer at work. Winner compares the loosely connected episodes to Sherwood Anderson's *Winesburg, Ohio*, "only Christian." The critic believes that she may prove to be "the industry's fastest rising star."

The response to Wright's novels, though sparse, has been mainly good. In a starred review, *Publishers Weekly* noted that *Dwelling Places* "eschews hackneyed pietism." The reviewer called the book "An authentic portrait of people who do not completely regret their mistakes and are still learning how to accept God's consolation." The *Romantic Times* Book Club described the book as "captivating, heartwarming."

John Mort includes *Grace at Bender Springs* and *Velma Still Cooks in Leeway* in his listing of books on "The Christian Life." He describes Wright's characters as familiar, "but sharply drawn," including the "lonely pastor's wife, longing for a more cultural place in life and afflicted with impure thoughts." The story of Velma is a blend of "characters [who] cross and crisscross, resulting in a novel composed of small sorrows, celebrating faith as a matter of course, quietly triumphant."

Award

Dwelling Places was named a *Publishers Weekly* top book of the year.

Bibliography of Works by Author

Grace at Bender Springs. Nashville, TN: Broadman & Holman, 1999.
Velma Still Cooks in Leeway. Nashville, TN: Broadman & Holman, 2000.
The Winter Seeking. Colorado Springs, CO: Winterbrook, 2003.
Dwelling Places. San Francisco, CA: HarperSanFrancisco, 2006.

Bibliography of Works about Author

Author Interview: InterVarsity Press. http://www.ivpress.com/spotlight/3231.php.

Chicago Public Radio. Interview, June, 2006.

Christianity Today (April 23, 2001).

"A Life of Quiet Grace," *Publishers Weekly* (September 18, 2000). http:www.publishersweekly.com/article/ CA689214.html.

Mort, John. *Christian Fiction: A Guide to the Genre.* Greenwood Village, CO: Libraries Unlimited, 2002.

Prism. Interview. (September/October, 2005).

Vinita Wright Web site: http://www.vinitahamptonwright.com.

Winner, Lauren F. "The Wright Stuff: With *Velma Still Cooks in Leeway,* Vinita Hampton Wright leads a quiet transformation of Christian fiction." *Christianity Today* (June 25, 2008). http://www.christianitytoday.com/ct/article_print.html?id=6561.

YOUNG, WILLIAM PAUL

Personal, Professional, and Religious Background

William Paul Young (1955–) was born in Grand Prairie, Alberta, Canada. He notes that most of his first decade "was lived with my missionary parents in the highlands of Netherlands New Guinea (West Papua), among the Dani, a technologically stone-age tribal people." These became his family. He was the first white child and the first outsider who ever spoke their language. "I was granted unusual access into their culture and community. Although at times a fierce warring people, steeped in the worship of spirits and even occasionally practicing ritualistic cannibalism, they also provided a deep sense of identity that remains an indelible element of my character and person." He says that, by the age of six, when he flew away to a boarding school, he was "in most respects a white Dani."

Shortly afterwards, in the middle of a school year, Young's parents returned to Western Canada, where his father served as pastor for a number of small churches, taking Paul through 13 schools by the time he graduated from high school. After high school, Paul Young worked his way through Bible college, taking jobs as a radio disc jockey and a lifeguard; he even did a stint in the oil fields of northern Alberta. Young spent one summer in the Philippines and another as a member of a drama troupe touring the region. He also worked in Washington, D.C. at Fellowship House, an international guest house. He completed his degree in religion in 1978, earning a bachelor's degree from Warner Pacific.

The following year, he met and married Kim Warren, worked for a while as a staff member at a large suburban church and attended seminary. The Youngs now have six children, two daughters-in-law, and two grandchildren at last count. The couple did survive a bad time, when Young had an

> If anything matters . . . everything matters.
>
> —William Paul Young, on his posting on MySpace, and expressed by Sarayu in *The Shack*

extramarital affair, followed by a decade in therapy, when he sought to earn back his wife's and his family's trust.

Over the years, William Young has worked at a variety of businesses, from "insurance to construction, venture capital companies to telecom, contract work to food processing: whatever was needed to help feed and house" his growing family. He insists he has always been a writer, "whether songs, poetry, short stories or newsletters," but always for friends and family rather than public consumption.

The great change in his life came when he had the inspiration for a novel he called *The Shack*. When he had written it, he shared it with a couple of his former pastors, who were so excited about it that they helped him raise the $300 he needed to self-publish it. The first run was 1,000 copies, which he stored in his garage, but the instant attention and popularity encouraged Windblown Media to take over the marketing, followed by a partnership with Hachette Book Group USA, which became the publisher and distributor.

Major Work and Themes

The work for which Young has become suddenly famous is *The Shack*, the remarkable story of a man who sounds much like the author. Drawing from literary antecedents like George MacDonald, **C. S. Lewis,** Kahlil Gibran, Soren Kierkegaard—including **Marilynne Robinson** and Maya Angelou, and many others—Young wrote of a father who faced the tragic death of his youngest child. The father, Mackenzie Allen Phillips, took several of his children on a family vacation in a wilderness area, where they all enjoyed the day together. As they were packing to leave, he suddenly realized that one of his children was missing. After a frantic search for Missy, which ended in a shack where the police discovered her bloody dress, Phillips returned home to enter into a period which he called his "Great Sadness."

This period comes to a sudden end when he finds a curious note in his mailbox, inviting him to come to the "shack." It is signed "Daddy." Since his own father had been abusive and no model of a loving parent, Mack has refused to consider God as a father figure. His wife, Nan, on the other hand, does like to call God "Daddy." Puzzled, Mack borrows a friend's Jeep and sets off for this mysterious meeting. As he is nearing the shack, he finds his world as transformed as C. S. Lewis's fictional children did when they climbed into the magic wardrobe. Suddenly, the world is changed from winter to spring and the shack has become a charming log cabin. "Daddy" turns out to be a jolly black woman, who invites him to meet the other members of the Trinity, Jesus (a carpenter of distinctly Semitic appearance), and the Holy Ghost (Sarayu, a wispy Asian woman). In their company for the weekend, Mack learns about relationships, the nature of sin, the importance of free will, and much about his own lingering hatred for his father and his fury at Missy's abductor. Only when he is able to forgive the "Lady Bug killer," the serial murderer who took Missy and several others, is Mack allowed to discover her body and become a mourner at her gentle funeral in the magical garden.

The book is full of conversations, insights, pronouncements, and visions. Young insists that the novel is based on a personal experience of spending some time in his own 'shack' when he was 38 and dealing with painful memories of abuse in his own childhood.

Critical Reception

Almost immediately *The Shack* became what the *New York Times* called "a surprise bestseller," resulting in a number of related projects that deal with William Young's favorite ideas.

Since he is critical of institutional religion and decidedly iconoclastic in his portrayal of the Trinity, the critics have divided between praising and condemning him. The novel quickly rose to number 1 on the *New York Times* trade paperback fiction best-seller list and remained there for some time. It has developed a cult following, with readers buying stacks of copies to share with friends.

Many Christian readers find the book "too edgy," especially the characterization of the Trinity. At least one critic noted the "serious flaws" in his extended discussion of the relationships among the persons of the Trinity. Some pastors call it blasphemy and heresy. The Rev. R. Albert Mohler Jr., who is president of the Southern Baptist Theological Seminary, called it "deeply troubling" and insisted that it undermines orthodox Christianity.

Bibliography of Work by Author

The Shack. Los Angeles, CA: Windblown Media, 2007.

Bibliography of Works about Author

Rich, Motoko. "Christian Novel Is Surprise Best Seller," The *New York Times*, June 24, 2008.
"William P. Young's Rejected Novel, The Shack." http://entertainment.timesonline.co.up/toll/arts_and_entertainment/books/article=434024.
William P. Young's Web site: http://theshack.book.com/willie.html.

SELECTED BIBLIOGRAPHY

Barrett, Rebecca Kaye. "Higher Love: What Women Gain from Christian Romance Novels." *Journal of Religion and Popular Culture*, IV, Summer 2003. (http//www.usaskk.ca/resls/jrpc/art4-romance nov-print.hmtl.

Blodgett, Jan. *Protestant Evangelical Literary Culture and Contemporary Society*. Westport, CT: Greenwood Press, 1997.

Brown, W. Dale, ed. *Of Fiction and Faith: Twelve American Writers Talk about their Vision and Works*. Grand Rapids, MI: William B. Eerdmans Publishing Company, 1997.

Buechner, Frederick. *The Clown in the Belfry: Writings on Faith and Fiction*. San Francisco, CA: Harper-SanFrancisco, 1992.

DeLong, Janice, Rachel Schwedt. *Contemporary Christian Authors: Lives and Works*. Lanham, MD: The Scarecrow Press, 2000.

Gandolfo, Anita. *Faith and Fiction: Christian Literature in America Today*. Westport, CT: Praeger, 2007.

Gandolfo, Anita. *Testing the Faith: The New Catholic Fiction in America*. Westport, CT: Greenwood Press, 1992.

Hansen, Ron. *A Stay Against Confusion: Essays on Faith and Fiction*. New York: Harper-Perennial, 2002.

Mort, John. *Christian Fiction: A Guide to the Genre*. Greenwood Village, CO: Libraries Unlimited, 2002

Neal, Lynn S. *Romancing God: Evangelical Women and Inspirational Fiction*. Chapel Hill: The University of North Carolina Press, 2006.

Noll, Mark A. *A History of Christianity in the United States and Canada*. Grand Rapids, MI: William B. Eerdmans Publishing Company, 1982.

Oehlschlaeger, Fritz. *Love and Good Reasons: Postliberal Approaches to Christian Ethics and Literature*. Durham: Duke University Press, 2003.

Radway, Janice. *Reading the Romance: Women, Patriarchy, and Popular Literature*. Chapel Hill, NC: University of North Carolina Press, 1991.

Sayers, Dorothy L. *The Mind of the Maker*. Westport, CT: Greenwood Press, 1941.

Veith, Gene Edward, Jr. *Reading Between the Lines: A Christian Guide to Literature*. Wheaton, IL: Crossway Books, 1990.

Wadell, Paul J. *The Moral of the Story: Learning from Literature about Human and Divine Love*. New York: The Crossroad Publishing Company, 2002.

Wright, Robert Glenn. *The Social Christian Novel*. Westport, CT: Greenwood Press, 1989.

Wuthnow, Robert. *The Restructuring of American Religion: Society and Faith Since World War II*. Princeton, NJ: Princeton University Press, 1988.

Wuthnow, Robert. *The Struggle for America's Soul.* Grand Rapids, MI: William B. Eerdmans Publishing Company, 1989.

Zinsser, William, ed. *Going on Faith: Writing as a Spiritual Quest.* New York: Marlowe & Company, 1999.

Zinsser, William. *Spiritual Quests: The Art and Craft of Religious Writing.* Boston: Houghton Mifflin Company, 1988.

INDEX

Note: Page numbers that refer to an encyclopedia main entry appear in **bold.**

About the Author

NANCY M. TISCHLER is Professor Emerita of English and Humanities from Pennsylvania State University. She has written three books on Tennessee Williams and coedited the first two volumes of his letters. In addition, she has written on Dorothy L. Sayers, Southern fiction, and most recently has produced a series of Bible studies for Greenwood Press—*Men and Women in the Bible*, *All Things in the Bible*, and *Thematic Guide to Biblical Literature*. Dr. Tischler has been married for more than 50 years to Merle Tischler and has two grown sons, three grandchildren, and one great grandchild. She lives in Boalsburg, Pennsylvania, enjoying her retirement with her family, her church, her books, her dogs, and her garden.